Readings in
Child Psychology

Readings in
Child Psychology

BRIAN SUTTON-SMITH

APPLETON-CENTURY-CROFTS, *New York*

Educational Division, MEREDITH CORPORATION

Library of Congress Card Number 73-3399

73 74 75 76 77 / 10 9 8 7 6 5 4 3 2

390-81872-0

Contributors

MARY D. SALTER AINSWORTH
Johns Hopkins University

ALBERT ANTHONY

PHILIPPE ARIES

DONALD M. BAER
University of Kansas

CHARLES T. BAKER
Vancouver General Hospital,
University of British Columbia

SILVIA M. BELL
Johns Hopkins University

URSULA BELLUGI
Salk Institute

MARION BLANK
Albert Einstein College of Medicine,
Yeshiva University

LOIS BLOOM
Teachers College, Columbia University

JEANNE BROOKS-GUNN
Educational Testing Service

ROGER BROWN
Harvard University

JEROME S. BRUNER
Harvard University

MICHAEL COLE
Rockefeller University

JAMES COLEMAN
University of California, Los Angeles

PEGGY E. EMERSON
University of Strathclyde

WALTER EMMERICH
Educational Testing Service

DANIEL G. FREEDMAN
Committee on Human Development,
University of Chicago

ROBERT M. GAGNÉ
Florida State University

HOWARD GARDNER
Harvard University

JUDITH GARDNER

HARRY F. HARLOW
Primate Laboratory, University of Wisconsin

CORINNE HUTT
University of Reading

JOSEPH J. JANOWSKI
National Institute of Child Health and
Human Development

JEROME KAGAN
Harvard University

RICHARD KLUCKHOHN

LAWRENCE KOHLBERG
Harvard University

PATRICIA LANDER
Institute of Latin American Studies

GILBERT LAZIER
Florida State University

ERIC H. LENNEBERG
Cornell University

MICHAEL LEWIS
Educational Testing Service

ELEANOR E. MACCOBY
Stanford University

MICHAEL MACCOBY
Fels Institute for Policy Studies, Washington

WALTER MISCHEL
Stanford University

NANCY MODIANO
New York University

FRANK B. MURRAY
College of Education, University of Delaware

VIRGINIA L. NELSON
The Fels Research Institute, Antioch College

B. L. NEUGARTEN
University of Chicago

FRANK A. PEDERSEN
National Institute of Child Health and Human Development

JEAN PIAGET
International Institute of Genetic Epistomology, Geneva

GEORGE RAND
University of California, Los Angeles

B. G. ROSENBERG
Bowling Green State University

MARY K. ROTHBART
Stanford University

JUDITH L. RUBENSTEIN
National Institute of Child Health and Human Development

ALICE JUDSON RYERSON
Cambridge Friends' School

H. R. SCHAFFER
University of Strathclyde

JEROME L. SINGER
City College, City University of New York

FRANCES SOLOMON
Albert Einstein College of Medicine, Yeshiva University

LESTER W. SONTAG
The Fels Research Institute, Antioch College

STEPHEN J. SUOMI
Primate Laboratory, University of Wisconsin

BRIAN SUTTON-SMITH
Teachers College, Columbia University

SEYMOUR WAPNER
Clark University

HEINZ WERNER
MARTIN WHITEMAN
Columbia University School of Social Work

JOHN W. M. WHITING
Harvard University

PETER H. WOLFF
Harvard Medical School

LEON J. YARROW
National Institute of Child Health and Human Development

DOUGLAS ZAHN
Florida State University

Contents

Preface

The following is a collection of readings designed to supplement Sutton-Smith's *Child Psychology*. The articles are arranged by general topic area into ten sections, each preceded by an introduction which briefly summarizes the significance of the articles. Each introduction defines the controversial issues in that particular area, and discusses where the viewpoints taken in the articles fall within the larger context of psychological thought—both current and historical—on that subject.

Because child psychology is essentially a research-oriented field, the body of knowledge in the text is largely research-based. Thus, the readings in this volume are particularly important, because they expand upon the descriptions of theories and research findings presented in the text, and because they give the student some firsthand contact with the research that makes up the field. By reading original studies the student acquaints himself with the nature of formal psychological papers. He becomes familiar with their tone, language, and approach. He will also become acquainted with several methods of organizing research data in an understandable and effective manner. The reading of original work helps the student to get the most accurate impression possible of the scientists' theories, research methods, and conclusions. After reading the primary sources included here, the student will have a better understanding of the current scientific controversies and the theoretical nature of the field. He will be better able to bring an objective viewpoint to other psychological papers he may read.

The papers reprinted here cover a wide range of topics, representing the major areas of research in the field of child psychology. One area discussed is the two major sets of alternatives that have characterized our ideas about the child—as demonic or innocent, as active or passive—and how these varying concepts of children have affected the theory and practice of child rearing. Biology's role in determining the infant's psychology, from the very beginning of his life, is another basic topic covered. The influence of the family on the child's psychological development is discussed, as well as how children affect their parents' behavior. Theories about the development of language and of cognition are presented, as are opinions about the development of the child's imagination, as expressed through his art work; of his intelligence, as influenced by his school experience; and of his social and moral senses. Other articles deal with the issue of predictability in an individual's behavior, and document research efforts to find both the specific influences of certain cultural factors on personality, as well as the so-called universals in personality, which are immune to such influences.

Because of the limited space available in a Reader of this kind, only research papers of major importance have been included. Although reports of significant *recent* research findings are emphasized, certain classic works whose impact on the field is still being felt today are also included. In addition, wherever possible, the authorities speak for themselves. For example, in the section on Cognition, the summary of Piaget's all-important work in the field is presented in a paper written by Piaget himself.

The readings also represent a wide range of significant opinions on each topic covered, rather than emphasizing any single point of view. In this way, as the student is exposed to a variety of scientific approaches and theoretical viewpoints, he will be better able both to develop a framework for approaching other types of writing scientifically, and to pick out additional reading matter in those schools of thought or by those authors which particularly interest him.

Since the ability to present such a well-rounded selection of primary sources depends to a large extent on the cooperation of a great many other people, much appreciation and thanks are extended to all the authors and publishers who have allowed their articles to be reprinted in this Reader.

B. S.-S.

Part 1

Introduction

We tend to think we agree on what a child is: a child is small, immature, and a nuisance. Beyond this very limited descriptive level, however, our intellectual ideas of what a child is may be quite varied; they certainly would be at odds with the ideas of a few generations ago. In a sense, we each "construct" the child. What we think of as a child today is very much an invention of our own culture, our own class, and even our personal histories. The child of the Middle Ages, for example, was considered simply a miniature adult—a being quite different from the sheltered child of the eighteenth century or the meticulously studied child of the twentieth century.

The articles by Ryerson and Aries in this section of readings illustrate these changes in the concept of the child. As these authors show, there has been a gradual process of distinguishing and separating the child from the adult, on both sociological and cognitive grounds.

During the past 400 years, two major sets of alternatives have characterized our ideas about the child. On the one hand, the child has been seen as either demonic or innocent, and on the other hand as either passive or active. The view of the child as demonic has found expression in such early behavioristic infant-care practices as rigid feeding schedules and attempts to eliminate thumb-sucking. The opposite view—that the child is innocent and may be taken as a model for society—is reflected in the child-training practices advocated by Gesell and Spock.

The alternative approach to the concept of the child—seeing him as either passive or active—has resulted in a somewhat parallel treatment of the child. If considered as malleable and perfectible, he is subject to behavioristic training. If he is believed to be an active being with an intelligent mind of his own, rather different and more democratic relationships with the child necessarily follow. Werner and Baer, in their attempts to describe and understand the underlying process of human development, illustrate these two classically different approaches. Werner focuses on the character of organisms wherever they may develop, while Baer calls attention to the controlling importance of the environment.

Medical Advice on Child Rearing, 1550-1900

Alice Judson Ryerson

In a large society every child knows many kinds of people. If personality could be selected from a rack like a suit of clothes he would have an almost infinite variety from which to choose. Usually, however, his adult personality lies safely within the boundaries defined by his culture. What, then, is the mechanism which makes an adult American react differently from a Japanese? To what extent do adults from different cultures share common reactions? What basic necessities does a particular child share with other children everywhere, and how does his particular society deal with these inevitable needs in order to re-create itself in every generation?

During the first part of the twentieth century, psychology offered the most relevant answers, simply because psychology is deeply concerned with the development of personality. Following Freud many psychologists framed their studies of personality with reference to three basic bio-logically conditioned drives characteristic of all human beings: the oral, anal and sexual. Be-

havioral psychologists identified secondary drives such as dependency and aggression, which they believe to be equally characteristic of the human condition. All societies are forced to deal with these areas of behavior, since all children must eat, excrete, and learn their sexual roles. All babies are dependent, and frustration generates some aggression in all societies. Psychologists suggested that the way a society permits these drives to be expressed, and the way the individual learns to relate himself to them are the principal determinants of personality.

But for a long time psychologists worked within the framework of Western European culture, and it gradually became clear that they could not draw conclusions about human reactions to environmental conditioning unless they could examine these reactions in a wide variety of environments. They were, in effect, trapped by the limitations of their own culture. So it seemed logical to turn to anthropology for further information.

Unfortunately, anthropological data were often

Alice Judson Ryerson, "Medical Advice on Child Rearing, 1550–1900," *Harvard Educational Review, 31,* Summer 1961, pp. 302–323. Copyright © 1961 by President and Fellows of Harvard College.

unrelated to psychological problems and frequently proved to be of little use to the psychologist, but because it was important to examine these new problems, the emphasis of anthropological field work began to change. The field worker began to spend less time measuring skulls and more time watching babies, and, as a result, field reports about the five basic drives began to accumulate for many different cultures. The data were of two kinds. First there were observations about adult personality in a particular society. The field worker noted the values, beliefs and techniques of society as indices of adult personality patterns. But at the same time he had become interested in recording the ways that a society handled the basic drives when they first appeared in the individual, and so he studied the child-rearing patterns of the society. New techniques of field work began to develop and finally the Human Relations Area Files were evolved in order to summarize and codify material from many cultures. In these files child rearing variables and certain measures of adult personality are recorded from approximately one hundred societies. These files are available at several universities and are being constantly expanded as new material accumulates. This enormously simplifies the work of the psychologist who wishes to use cross-cultural material in testing his hypotheses.

The present study is closely related to other cross-cultural studies of personality, but with the significant difference that it is concerned with the past instead of the present. Most of the societies described in the Human Relations Area Files still exist. A few are societies which have recently been modified beyond recognition, but all of them are described at a particular time without reference to their past development. The present study makes use of the techniques and assumptions discussed above but emphasizes the dimension of time. If child rearing practices determine the development of personality, it is immensely interesting to discover the antecedents of our American child rearing patterns because these cast a new light on the sort of ancestors we had. But there is another reason for making such an historical study. Child-rearing patterns have changed markedly in Anglo-American society during the past three centuries. Because of this

some light can be thrown on the reasons for change in the area of child rearing.

This is not history as the historian knows it. An attempt is made to document only one aspect of the past. There are probably no societies in the world where past adult behavior has been more carefully studied than our own, but child-rearing patterns, as conceived by the cultural anthropologist, have been almost entirely neglected and historians have never concerned themselves with toilet training in Cromwellian England, or weaning at the time of George the Third. This study attempts to fill the gap.

In a sense this is a developmental ethnography. Most ethnographers study both children and adults in a culture at a given moment in its history, but this study takes a longitudinal slice of a culture and examines only child rearing recommendations in successive periods.

The anthropologist in the field talks to people who live in the culture he is studying. The reports of these people and the anthropologist's own observations form the basis for his judgments about the society. Since this study is concerned with the past, interviews and direct observation were obviously impossible, and it was necessary for books to serve as informants, and libraries to take the place of village squares. Many kinds of books about children were sampled and those authors who seemed best able to tell what was needed were finally selected. These proved to be the doctors and medical men who were particularly interested in the physical care of young children and who described their beliefs and techniques for the benefit of parents and other lay readers. These were the most comparable sources available through the entire period. (See list of sources at end of article.) It is in the books by these men that one can find the richest source of material about the kinds of child rearing practices under investigation.

It should be made very clear that this study is concerned with *advice* on the subject of child rearing. The sources used do not provide the basis for definite conclusions about the actual practices of the various periods although there is some reason to believe that they do give evidence of what the actual practices were. Sometimes an author comments on "current practices" or phrases his advice in terms of "the mistakes most parents make." The actual existence of such objects as cradles and nursing bottles is sufficient evidence that they were used, and other studies based on other kinds of sources have indicated the existence of many of the practices discussed. It is usually true that the advice of experts gradually becomes general practice in the literate upper middle class and that this group sets the patterns which are taken over by other segments of a society. Many of the books used as sources were published over long periods of time and this fact increases the likelihood of their having had real influence on the lives of real children. Finally, it is important to remember that the character of the advice itself throws light on many of the problems and prejudices of a society, quite apart from any relationship it may have to the way children are actually reared. Analysis of the changes in expert opinion is also of value to cultural anthropology.

The selection of sources for this study was determined by the primary interest in American child-rearing patterns and their antecedents. The period considered is from 1550 to 1900. All the books used, except one, were either originally written in English or translated into English. No books by doctors, about children, for laymen, originated in America until nearly 1800 and so English sources were used until that time. After 1800 only sources published in America were used, although these too were sometimes reprints of books by European authors.

In selecting areas of child rearing for investigation this article employs the oral, anal, sexual, dependence and aggression categories which have become standard tools in the field of cross-cultural anthropology. In order to determine which specific areas to examine in detail, reference was made to *A Field Manual for the Cross-Cultural Study of Child Rearing.*[1]

In order to make statistical treatment of this material possible, the time span covered by the study has been divided into eleven periods. The first, from 1550 to 1650, is long because sources in this period are scarce; only four are available. After 1650 the time is divided into intervals of twenty-five years. All the books known to have existed over an extended time are included in

[1] J. W. M. Whiting *et al., A Field Manual for the Cross-Cultural Study of Child Rearing* (New York: Social Science Research Council, 1953).

each of the periods during which they were published. The number of sources in each period ranges from four to eleven and the total number of books considered is thirty-nine. In this way it has been possible to compare the opinions current in one period with those of another.

Using these methods, this study presents new material on child rearing in the Anglo-American tradition. See Figures 1-12.

The material presented in the following charts makes it clear that there was a dramatic change in the character of the advice given about child rearing, a change which took place rather abruptly in the middle of the eighteenth century. The first step will be to describe that change in terms of the five behavior systems outlined above. For purposes of this discussion, the time from 1550 to 1750 is listed as the "first period" and the time from 1750 to 1900 as the "second period."

In the first period all the sources believed that mothers should nurse their own babies if possible, but that, should the mother be unable to nurse, a wet nurse should be employed. The nursing period was to last for approximately two years, and weaning was to be a gradual process. Babies were to be fed when they were hungry. These represent permissive attitudes towards oral training. Thumbsucking and pacifiers are never mentioned in this period which suggests that at least there was no strong taboo on these forms of oral gratification.

On the repressive side, we find the authors of the earlier period showing considerable concern about overeating, and suggesting various mechanical devices to discourage the child from nursing when the time came to wean him. Nursing bottles had not yet been introduced, so in case breast-feeding failed, no alternative form of sucking was available. The custom of binding the child's arms for several months after birth precluded the possibility of thumbsucking during that time.

In the second period of this study we still find overwhelming approval of breast-feeding by the mother. If, however, the mother could not nurse the child, nursing bottles were recommended as the preferred alternative. Weaning was still to be a gradual process. These are relatively permissive attitudes. On the other hand, we find in the second period that feeding schedules were introduced, the age for weaning was reduced to approximately

Figure 1

% of those reporting on this subject who believed in giving the newborn a *purge* as a matter of course.

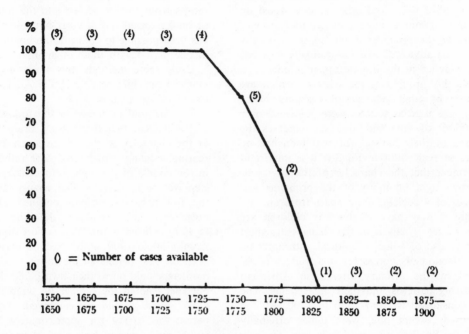

Figure 2

% of doctors reporting on this subject who limit times of feeding by *schedules*

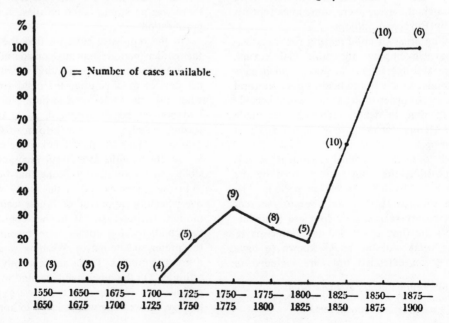

Figure 3

% of sources reporting on this who favor wet-nurses as alternative to mother's milk.

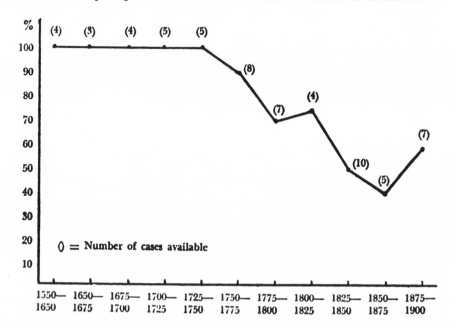

Figure 4
Age of Weaning

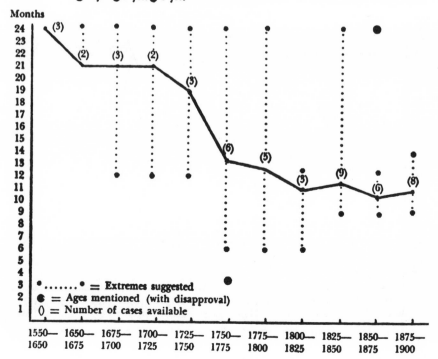

Figure 5

% of those who mention the subject who approve of *cradles*.

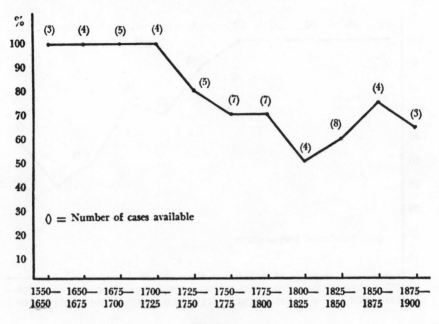

0 = Number of cases available

Figure 6

% of doctors (who mention) who consider *teething a dangerous disease* ————
% of doctors (who mention) who suggest *magical cures* for teething · - · - · - · -

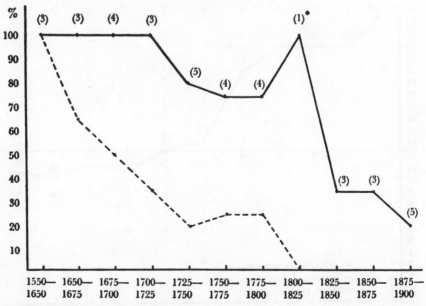

* The fact there is only one case here doubtless gives a false impression of the curve at this point.

Figure 7

% of those reporting on this subject who favored *cold baths* after infancy ———————
% of those reporting on this subject who favored baths to "harden" the child · · · · · ·

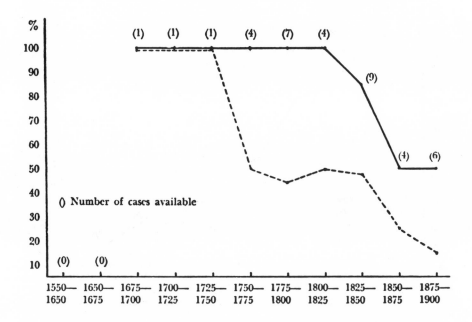

Figure 8

% of doctors reporting on this subject who favored *swaddling*

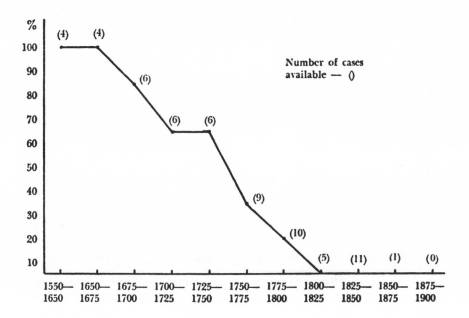

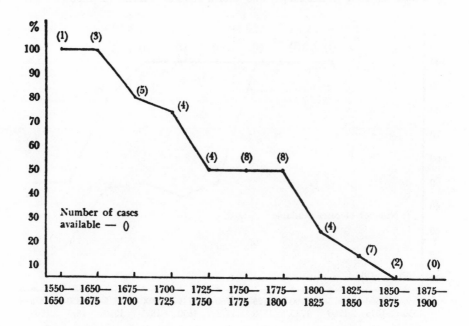

Figure 9

% of those who discussed *temperature* who stressed keeping the infant warm.

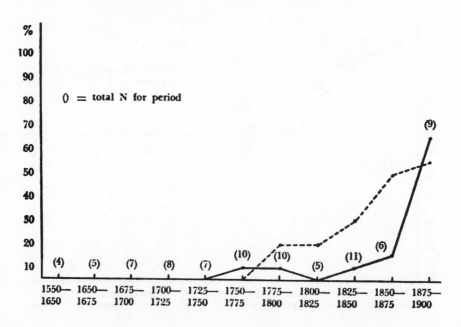

Figure 10

% of total N in period who mention *sex-play* among children (all oppose) ————
% of total N in period who mention *masturbation* (all oppose) · · · · · ·

Figure 11

% of total N who show *eagerness for child to become independent.*

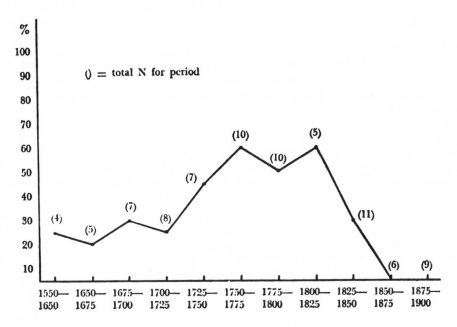

Figure 12

——— = % of doctors expressing any view on this subject who conceive of the child
as *born evil.*[*]

· · · · · = % of doctors expressing any view on this subject who conceive of the child
as *born good.*[*]

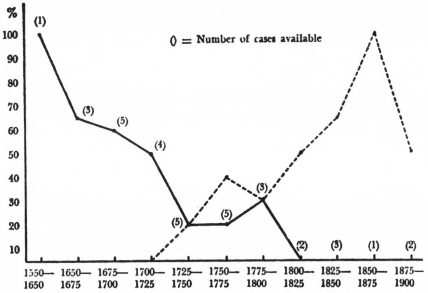

[*] Because there are so few cases available this graph only suggests the trend.

nine months, the use of wet nurses was discouraged, bitter substances on the breast were still used to hasten the weaning process, pacifiers and thumbsucking were explicitly forbidden, and the fear of overeating began to be superseded by an insistence that a child eat whatever he was offered. The second period thus shows a considerable decrease in the amount of oral gratification permitted to the child.

Turning to anal training, for the period before 1750, the inference can be made that toilet training began at approximately one year. The child was not expected to be consistently dry at night until he was five, punishment for lapses in training was discouraged, and general cleanliness was lightly stressed. While these attitudes represent considerable indulgence of the child's anal drives, two repressive measures are suggested; that suppositories be used for bowel training and that certain mechanical devices, doubtless punitive in effect, be used to prevent bed-wetting after age five.

In the period after 1750, all advice about anal training is clearly repressive. Toilet training was to begin at between three weeks and six months, the child was expected to be reliably dry at night by the age of three, punishments were sometimes recommended for failures in cleanliness, suppositories were still suggested for bowel training, and punitive measures for the bed-wetter. Furthermore, attitudes towards bathing and general cleanliness had changed markedly. Cleanliness was on its way to becoming an obsession, an obsession which strongly influenced attitudes about the child's anal drive.

In the case of sexual training, conclusions about this behavior system are based largely on negative evidence. In the first period of the study no prohibitions are found against masturbation, nudity, or sex-play among children, or against the sexual stimulation of children by adults. After 1750 one finds all these aspects of sexual behavior emphatically forbidden. In both periods the belief is held that adult conversation should be appropriately edited for the ears of children, but also that children's questions should always be honestly answered. Although neither period explicitly forbade intercourse to the new mother, the earlier period does prohibit intercourse to the wet nurse and one suspects that these two customs have

some relationship to each other. Whiting and Child [2] suggest that a post partum sex taboo is a measure of cultural anxiety about sex. If the significance of this taboo can be extended to include the wet nurse, we have one measure of sex anxiety in the earlier period which does not exist in the later one. Because this is a doubtful measure it seems wiser not to emphasize it, and since there were four sexual activities which were specifically prohibited in the second period but not in the first, it is judged that the second period was more repressive than the first in the area of sex training.

Before 1750 the child's dependency was given considerable encouragement. The swaddled baby needed constant attention and care; he could not even brush a fly off his own nose. Rocking and singing were the approved methods for putting the child to sleep, and handling and dandling by the adults in his household was freely permitted, along with a quick and nurturant response to the infant's crying. Although the child may not have been put to sleep in his mother's bed until several months after birth, he was allowed to remain there until he was weaned at the age of two, and when he did finally move out of his parents' room he was expected to move into a bed with his siblings or a servant. In the second period these attitudes were very nearly reversed. The practice of swaddling was emphatically disapproved of by medical writers after 1750, as were rocking and singing, handling and cuddling, and the immediate indulgent response of adults to the baby's cry. Although the child was to sleep with his mother as a newborn baby, he was to be removed from her room to an unshared bed before he was a year old. These changes represent a clear trend toward disapproval of dependent behavior.

In addition, in the second period positive encouragement was given to the child's desire for free motor activity. He was to be permitted to kick freely as an infant, to crawl and walk when he pleased, and he was to exercise energetically as an older child, an admonition which applied even to girls. Such freedom of movement was never advised in the earlier period; it represents, therefore, a new tendency to encourage autonomy

[2] J. W. M. Whiting and Irvin L. Child, *Child Training and Personality: A Cross-Cultural Study* (New Haven: Yale University Press, 1953).

and self-initiated activity in the child—the opposite of dependence.

The sources used in this study provide little information about the training of aggression. Although authors of both periods put a high premium on obedience, little is said at any time about such measures of aggression as fighting, verbal attacks on other people, or destruction of property. Temper tantrums are mentioned in the second period but not in the first: this may mean that the second period was more tolerant of children's aggression, or perhaps only that children were more aggressive at a time when repression and adult control were characteristic of training in the oral, anal and sexual spheres.

Although information about direct aggression is sparse, there are several beliefs, common before 1750, that are of interest in connection with aggression. First, milk was believed to be white blood. Could this imply a conception of the child as a vampire which destroys what it feeds on? Secondly, character was supposed to be literally transmitted through the milk. This again suggests an almost cannibalistic ingestion of the mother by the child. The third significant belief was that teething was mortally dangerous to the child. Since teeth are manifestly aggressive weapons, it is possible that this belief camouflaged a deeper conviction that the child must be punished for aggression. Finally, we find in the earlier period, the theologically based belief that the child is "born evil." Society expected the child to show signs of his depravity and one of these signs may well have been aggression.

In the second period all of these beliefs have vanished and a new one, of equal interest, has taken their place. After 1750, we begin to find doctors warning every mother against the danger of nursing the child immediately after she has experienced any strong emotion. If she were to nurse him after a fit of anger it might even prove fatal to the infant. Is this perhaps a veiled allusion to the hostility which the mother may feel towards the child, a taboo which protects her from her own phantasies of destroying him in anger? If this interpretation is valid, it suggests that fear of the child's aggression against adults is characteristic of the first period, whereas fear of adult aggression against children is more typical of the second.

In considering the five basic behavior systems one finds that there was a decrease of permissiveness in oral, anal, sexual and dependence training, and an increase of permissiveness in regard to aggression training. Figure 13 illustrates the relative degrees of permissiveness in the early and late periods of this study. It also indicates the relative standing, on a scale of permissiveness, of extended families and nuclear families over the world. More will be said on this subject later but there are other cross-cultural relationships which need to be examined first.

Basing the information on the study of seventy-five primitive societies by Whiting and Child,[3] one finds that in all five behavior systems the period from 1550 to 1750 closely approaches the cross-cultural average in respect to permissiveness. On the other hand, the advice given in the period from 1750-1900 is considerably more severe than the cross-cultural average in the oral, anal, sexual and dependence categories, and less severe in aggression training. The advice of the later period is also considerably more severe, in everything but aggression training, than the twentieth century advice of Spock[4] or than the practices described by Sears, Maccoby and Levin[5] in their study of 379 mid-twentieth century New England families. These comparisons make it clear that the advice of 1750-1900 was not merely more severe than that of the periods preceding and following it, but more severe in most respects than advice and practices in the majority of societies in the world.

This leads to one of the most tantalizing questions posed by the findings of this study: namely, *why* did these dramatic changes in child-rearing patterns occur in the middle of the eighteenth century?

One of the reasons for the change may well have been an ideological one. McClelland[6] has suggested that the strong Methodist movement led by John Wesley in the first half of the

---

[3] *Ibid.*

[4] Benjamin Spock, *The Common Sense Book of Baby and Child Care* (New York: Duell, Sloan and Pearce, 1945).

[5] Robert R. Sears, Eleanor E. Maccoby and Harry Levin, *Patterns of Child Rearing* (Evanston: Row, Peterson and Co., 1957).

[6] David C. McClelland, *The Achieving Society* (Princeton: Van Nostrand, 1960).

Figure 13

RELATIVE PERMISSIVENESS OF TRAINING:

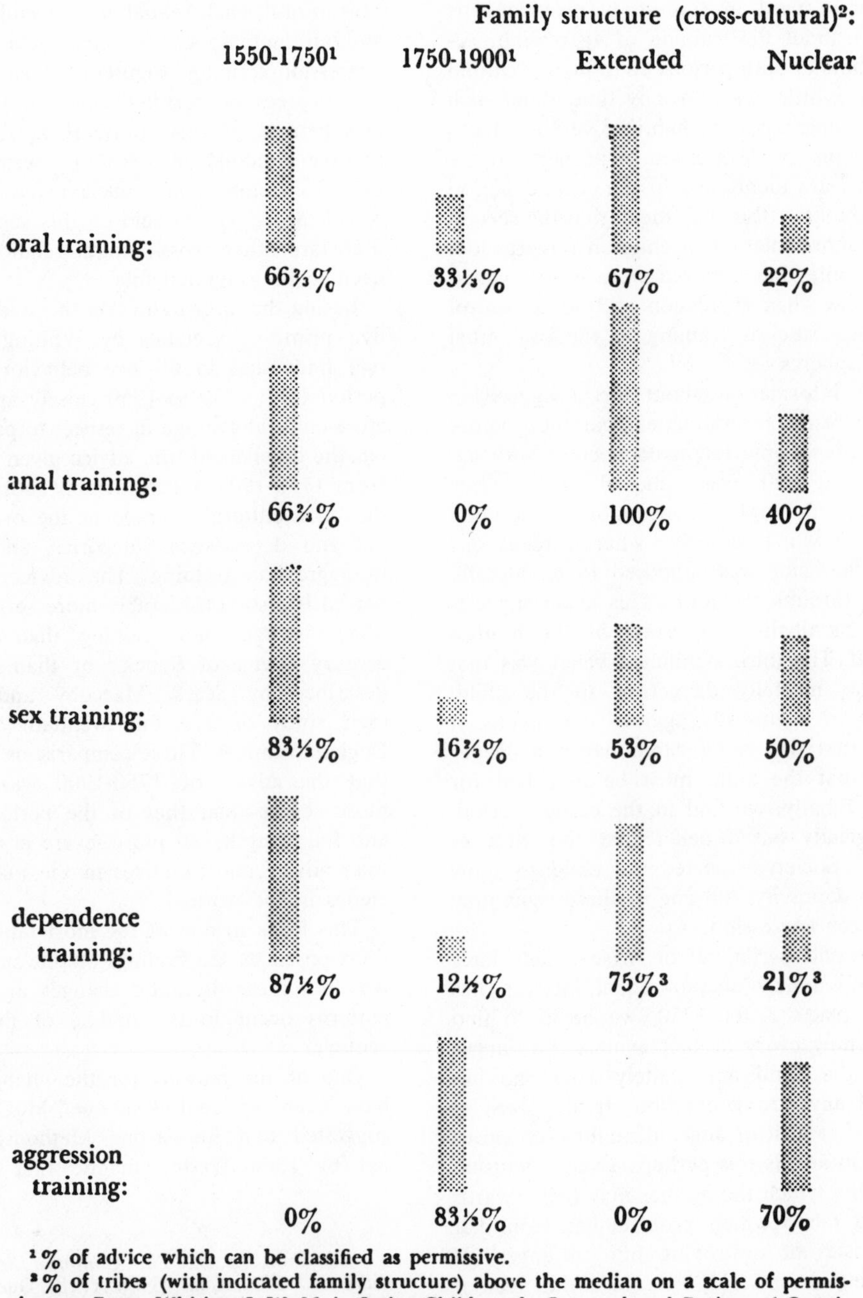

	1550-1750[1]	1750-1900[1]	Family structure (cross-cultural)[2]:	
			Extended	Nuclear
oral training:	66⅔%	33⅓%	67%	22%
anal training:	66⅔%	0%	100%	40%
sex training:	83⅓%	16⅔%	53%	50%
dependence training:	87½%	12½%	75%[3]	21%[3]
aggression training:	0%	83⅓%	0%	70%

[1] % of advice which can be classified as permissive.

[2] % of tribes (with indicated family structure) above the median on a scale of permissiveness. From: Whiting, J. W. M. in Irving Child, et al., *Cross-cultural Ratings of Certain Socialization Practices* (unpublished manuscript).

[3] Based on transition anxiety score of Child et al. *Ibid.*

eighteenth century may have had repercussions on personality development. He points out that Methodism stressed the importance of personal communion with God and of the Christian perfection of the individual. Both of these virtues depended on self-reliance, a quality best taught by early independence training. In other words, it is suggested here that the demands of Methodist theology forced a pattern of early independence training on Protestants of this sect. McClelland goes on to point out that, although Methodism was the strongest of these non-conformist sects in the first part of the eighteenth century, there were others with similar points of view about the responsibility of the individual, and he feels that the strength of the non-conformist movement was sufficient to cause general changes in child-rearing patterns.

Another innovation which may have had considerable influence on child rearing was the change from one family pattern to another.[7] In the mid-eighteenth century the traditional patriarchal family, living in a household with many relatives and ramifications, began to be replaced by the nuclear family in which parents and children live alone together. In other societies it has been found that the existence of the nuclear family accentuates certain kinds of parent-child relationships, which, in turn, affect the patterns of child rearing in those societies. The nuclear family is apt to come into being in a social context where the child has great economic importance to the family or where he is important in enhancing or detracting from the status of the parents. In a large household children are likely to be pushed into the background. They may be mildly productive in an economic sense, but they are not the focal points of adult attention; apprentices, maiden aunts, grandparents and servants occupy the parents' minds. On the other hand, these other members of the family may also give the child attention: there is always somebody at hand if he wants help. In the nuclear family, independence becomes a virtue in the child for the very practical reason that the mother has less help with her household

tasks and therefore has less time to tend the child herself and no one to whom she can delegate his care. The more the child can do for himself the better pleased his mother is likely to be. This means that in the extended family the child is both more dependent on adults and less specifically oriented toward his mother. In the nuclear family his mother may be the center of his world but it is a centrifugal world constantly urging him outwards.

Living in a nuclear family doubtless has other effects on the life of the child. The Whitings [8] have pointed out that there is less aggression allowed in the extended family because, in a situation crowded with many adult personalities, expressed aggression threatens and irritates too many people and must be suppressed for the sake of peace in the household. In the nuclear family it is likely that the parents can tolerate and ignore a certain amount of aggression because it does not bring them into conflict with other members of the household. This reasoning helps to explain why aggression training should have been less severe after 1750.

One also finds cross-cultural evidence which suggests that sexual training is earlier in the nuclear family. In the nuclear family the child competes more directly with the parent of the same sex for the attention of the other parent. Direct sexual expression is forbidden the child because it constitutes a threat to his parents. This applies to a certain extent even in the extended family, but in the small nuclear family greater intimacy between parents and children increases the underlying fear of incest, and therefore the child's sexual expressions are dealt with more strictly.

Finally, oral training in the nuclear family, cross-culturally speaking, is likely to be earlier and more repressive. The reasons for this are similar: the mother is busy and great demands are made on her physical stamina; her husband cannot turn to other members of the household for the companionship which he fails to get from his wife. In order to relieve the resulting tensions she weans the baby early. When the child eats solid foods he can wait longer between feedings, and when

---

[7] For an interesting discussion of a related topic see Bernard Bailyn, *Education in the Forming of American Society, Needs and Oportunities for Study* (Chapel Hill: University of North Carolina Press, 1960).

[8] J. W. M. Whiting and Beatrice B. Whiting, "Contributions of Anthropology to the Methods of Studying Child Rearing," *Method of Studying Child Rearing,* ed. Paul Mussen (New York: John Wiley, 1960).

he is weaned there is one less demand made on her physical strength. The introduction of schedules for infant feeding also simplifies the demands made on the mother's time.

Both cross-cultural evidence and the intrinsic logic of the situation suggest that the growth of the nuclear family may well have influenced the changes in oral, sexual, dependence, and aggression training. There is no cross-cultural evidence suggesting that the nuclear family pattern produces earlier anal training but similar logic suggests a similar conclusion in this area also. [See Figure 13.]

The increase in scientific knowledge during the eighteenth century also had an obvious effect on child rearing advice, and it is not surprising to find that doctors' advice reflects the scientific and medical renaissance of the period. Although the germ theory of disease was a much later scientific development, by the end of the eighteenth century much of the knowledge which led up to the germ theory lay ready at hand. Bacteria had been discovered, and the connection between dirt and disease was becoming constantly clearer. The eighteenth century doctors did not yet know that microbes could make people sick, but they did know that certain illnesses were mysteriously associated with dirt. Once this connection was made, it was reasonable that cleanliness should have assumed a new and crucial significance.

The science of nutrition was also beginning to make its first faltering steps at this time. This was the period when it was discovered that lime juice prevented scurvy in sailors and the implications of this discovery were not long in affecting advice about children's diet. Although no one had any idea that fruits and vegetables contained vitamins and minerals, their nutritional value had been pragmatically determined and they began to be recommended, for the first time, as important elements in a child's diet. The same was true of milk. Milk had long been thought of as a menace to the child's health, but as the obsessive interest in cleanliness was extended to food preparation, clean milk was found to be a valuable addition to the child's diet. Along with these nutritional discoveries, a change is seen in the attitude toward children's eating. The preoccupation with overeating begins to disappear and in its place we find an insistence that the child must eat what is "good

for him." Food had ceased to be a simple pacifier of hunger and had become a medical prescription.

There were a number of other changes in child rearing advice which were unquestionably influenced by the new empirical approach to medicine. Advice about feeding the newborn infant was certainly affected. Advice in the area of anal training was influenced by the new emphasis on general cleanliness. Observations on anatomy and growth affected recommendations about swaddling and walking, and the new permissiveness towards freedom of movement influenced deeper attitudes about autonomy and dependence.

Certain changes in the areas of oral, anal and dependence training can thus be attributed directly to the scientific and medical advances of the late eighteenth century.

Three kinds of influence which may well have accounted for the mid-eighteenth century change in child rearing patterns have been identified. The resurgence of enthusiasm for an individualistic Protestantism may have helped to produce a more rigorous pattern of independence training. The increasing prevalence of the nuclear family household may have encouraged earlier oral, anal, sexual and independence training, and there is reason to suspect that this same family pattern allowed more permissive aggression training. Finally, scientific developments undoubtedly helped to increase the severity of oral, anal and independence training.

Up to this point this paper has considered child-rearing patterns as a product of other factors. A shift of focus leads to exploration of the effects which the child rearing patterns themselves may have had on personality development.

Cross-cultural evidence is available to show that early weaning, sex training, and independence training are crucial in producing strong guilt reactions in the individual. Since early training in these areas was characteristic of the second period in this study but not of the first, we would expect guilt to be more typical of the second period.

Whiting and Child [9] have used attitudes toward illness as a measure of guilt: does the patient himself assume responsibility for getting sick, a reaction of self-blame (guilt), or does he project that responsibility onto some external agent? If one applies this measure of guilt to the two periods

9 Whiting and Child, *op. cit.*

of this study one finds a preponderance of self-blame reactions in the second period. Before 1750, many magical remedies were used, which, by their very nature, suggests that some supernatural force must be propitiated in order to cure the disease. This is essentially a projection of blame. After 1750, these magical cures were no longer recommended, and illness was generally attributed to something the patient himself had done or failed to do. He was sick because he had eaten green apples, or gotten his feet wet, or gone out without a hat. These are reactions of self-blame.

Philanthropy is another convincing index of guilt in Western European culture. Using this measure one finds overwhelming evidence that strong super-egos flourished during the greater part of the second period of this study. The nineteenth century was the great era of humanitarian movements and philanthropic enterprises originating in the middle class. Usually this is attributed to the fact that the Industrial Revolution intensified the misery and suffering of the working classes, but this does not really explain why the middle class reacted to this situation with an effort to help. It is reasonable to assume that an increase in conscience, the faculty of guilt, may have been responsible. Before the Industrial Revolution, poverty had been accepted with extraordinary equanimity by the middle class as a whole.

It is also possible to consider the degree of responsibility assumed by the parents for the development of the child as another measure of guilt. If the parent feels that the child's fate is predetermined and that nothing the parent can do will ensure his salvation, he is projecting all responsibility onto a divine agent. If, however, parents feel that the child is perfectible and can be made into a successful adult by proper parental pressures, then those parents are assuming the burden of guilt in case the child fails to come up to expectation. Certainly the first point of view is typical of the early Puritan period, just as the second is characteristic of the later period.

Finally, reference is made to a piece of advice given by three authors after 1750. They say that the child should not be allowed to strike the floor in anger if he falls on it. He should not be encouraged, in other words, to project the blame for his fall onto an external agent, but instead should be forced to take full responsibility for his

own carelessness. This piece of advice neatly illustrates the need that adults felt to encourage a sense of self-blame in children.

This short analysis of reaction to illness, philanthropy, and parental responsibility, leaves one with a strong presumption that guilt reactions were actually stronger in the period after 1750. It has not, of course, been proved that this increase in guilt resulted from earlier sex training, independence training, and weaning. This paper merely records the observation that increase in guilt reactions coincides with increased severity in these aspects of child rearing, and it is pointed out that this coincidence exists in the majority of those cultures for which these variables have been recorded.

McClelland's studies of achievement [10] add another dimension to the interpretations suggested by the study. He has said that early independence training produces in the child a high need for achievement. He suggests that this need for achievement is shown in the Industrial Revolution itself, and he offers evidence to show that early independence training produces a kind of adult personality which is immensely effective in creating an industrial society.

Historians, because they are familiar with adult patterns of behavior, will be able to contribute much additional insight into the causes and results of the child-rearing patterns here identified, and new cross-cultural and psychological insights should make possible more extensive use of the material presented here.[11]

Appendix

SOURCES USED FOR THE STUDY AND COMMENTS ON THE AUTHORS

The majority of the sources used can be located at the Boston Medical Library. The remainder are at either the Yale Medical Library or the New York Academy of Medicine Library.

---

[10] McClelland, *op. cit.*
[11] Alice Ryerson, "Medical Advice on Child Rearing, 1550-1900" (unpublished Ed.D. dissertation, Graduate School of Education, Harvard University, 1959).

ALCOTT, WILLIAM A. *The Young Mother or the Management of Children in Regard to Health.* Boston: Strong and Brodhead, 1849. (Alcott was a New Englander, a graduate of the Yale Medical School and a doctor notable for his distrust of drugs and medicines.)

ARMSTRONG, GEORGE, M.D. *An Account of the Diseases most incident to Children to which is added an Essay on Nursing with a Particular View to Infants Brought up by Hand.* London: T. Cadell and W. Davies, 1808. (Founded and paid for the first public dispensary for children in England, in spite of the fact that he was very conservative in his medical views.)

Art of Nursing or the Method of Bringing up Young Children according to the Rules of Physick for the Preservation of Health, and Prolonging Life. London: J. Brotherton and L. Gulliver, 1733.

BAYNARD, DR. EDWARD. *History of Cold Bathing, both ancient and modern.* Part II. London: William and John Innys, 1722.

BLACKWELL, DR. ELIZABETH. *Counsel to Parents on the Moral Education of their Children.* New York: Brentano's, 1880. (The first woman to graduate from a medical school in America, she was much interested in public health.)

BUCHAN, WILLIAM. *Family Medical Library.* Cincinnati: J. A. James, 1843. (Over twenty editions of this book were published in England. Many editions appeared in America as well, and its popularity lasted for well over seventy-five years.)

BULL, THOMAS, M.D. *The Maternal Management of Children in Health and Disease.* Philadelphia: Lindsay and Blakiston, 1849.

CADOGAN, WILLIAM. *An Essay upon Nursing and the Management of Children from their Birth to Three Years of Age.* London: J. Roberts, 1752. (The author was one of the strongest mid-eighteenth century advocates of change in the area of child-rearing.)

CHAVASSE, PYE HENRY. *Advice to a Mother on the Management of her Children.* Philadelphia: Lippincott, 1883. (An English doctor popular on both sides of the Atlantic, he had a sentimental approach to children characteristic of his period.)

CHEYNE, GEORGE, M.D. *An Essay of Health and Long Life.* London: George Strahan, 1724.

COMBE, ANDREW, M.D. *A Treatise on the Physiological and Moral Management of Infancy.* Edinburgh: Maclachlan, Stewart and Co., 1846. (A Scottish Calvinist with a caustic style and a hard headed rationalistic approach to the subect of children.)

CULPEPER, NICHOLAS. *A Directory for Midwives or, a Guide for Women in their Conception, Bearing,* *and Suckling their Children.* London: T. Norris, 1724. (An early writer on obstetrics and child rearing.)

DARWIN, ERASMUS. *A Plan for the Conduct of Female Education.* Philadelphia: John Ormrod, 1798. (Grandfather of Charles Darwin and a distinguished eighteenth century scientist and poet.)

DE VALLAMBERT, M. SIMON. *De la Maniere de nourir et Gouverner les Enfans des leur naissance.* Poitiers: Marnesz et Bouchetz, freres, 1565. (A French doctor whose work on obstetrics and infant care was written in the vernacular of a period when Latin was still the respectable language for scholars.)

DEWEES, WILLIAM P., M.D. *A Treatise on the Physical and Medical Treatment of Children.* Philadelphia: Carey, Lea and Carey, 1829. (A popular nineteenth century American.)

DIX, TANDY L. *The Healthy Infant.* Cincinnati: P. G. Thomson, 1880.

EBERLE, JOHN, M.D. *A Treatise on the Diseases and Physical Education of Children.* Philadelphia: Grigg and Elliot, 1837.

GRIFFITH, J. P. CROZER, M.D. *The Care of the Baby, A Manual for Mothers and Nurses.* Philadelphia: W. B. Saunders & Company, 1903. (The most moderate of the late nineteenth century Americans.)

GUILLEMEAU, JAMES (JACQUES). *Childbirth or the Happy Delivery of Women, containing a Treatise for the Nursing of Children.* London: Norton and R. Whitaker, 1635. (A French court surgeon whose works on obstetrics and infant care were quickly translated into English.)

HARRIS, WALTER, M.D. *A Treatise of the Acute Diseases of Infants to which are added Medical Observations on several grievous Diseases.* London: G. & J. Innys, 1742. (An English doctor, inordinately proud of his aristocratic clientele, he developed an "acid theory" of disease, widespread in popularity but of doubtful utility.)

HOLT, L. EMMETT, M.D. *The Care and Feeding of Children.* New York: D. Appleton & Co., 1905. (The most famous of all American pediatricians at the end of the nineteenth century. His book, revised by his son, is still in print.)

JACOBI, A., M.D. *Infant Diet.* New York: G. P. Putnam's Sons, 1876. (The first American to think of himself as a pediatrician.)

LOCKE, JOHN, ESQ. *Some Thoughts on Education.* London: J. Hatchard and Son, 1836.

MAURICEAU, FRANÇOIS. *Traité des Maladies des Femmes Grosses.* Paris: N. Gosselin, 1673.

NELSON, JAMES. *An Essay on the Government of Children under three General Heads: viz. Health, Manners, and Education.* London: n.p., 1753. (A very articulate apothecary who provides useful and amusing insights into mid-eighteenth century practices and prejudices.)

PECHEY, JOHN. *A General Treatise of the Diseases of Infants and Children collected from the best Practical Authors.* London: n.p., 1697. (An editor more than an original writer, Pechey assembled the works of previous medical writers on childhood.)

PEMEL, ROBERT. *De Morbis Puerorum or a Treatise of the Diseases of Children; with their Causes, Signs, Prognosticks, and Cures, etc.* London: P. Stephens, 1653. (The second doctor who discussed the problems of childhood, chiefly the medical problems, in English.)

PHAIRE, THOMAS. *The Boke of Children.* Edinburgh and London: E. & S. Livingstone Ltd., 1955. Reprinted from 1545 edition. (The first doctor to write on medical treatment of children in English. Full of picturesque and sometimes horrifying medical prescriptions.)

QUILLET, CLAUDE. *Advice to New-Married Persons or the Art of having Beautiful Children.* London: A. Goodby and W. Owen, n.d.

ROUSSEAU, JEAN JACQUES. *Emile.* Trans. by Barbara Foxley, M.A. New York: E. P. Dutton, 1911.

Rules for the Management of Infants and Children. Boston: Board of Health of the City of Boston, 1876.

SAINTE MARTHE, SCÉVOLE DE. *The Art of Bringing Up Children.* London: R. Goodby and W. Owen, n.d.

SMITH, HUGH, M.D. *The Female Monitor. Letters to Married Women on Nursing and the Management of Children.* Wilmington: P. Brynberg, 1801. (Inventor of the first infant feeding bottle used in England. One of the first doctors' books to be concerned only with the management of the healthy child.)

STARR, LOUIS, M.D. *Hygiene of the Nursery.* Philadelphia: P. Blakiston's Sons & Co., 1888.

STRUVE, CHRISTIAN AUGUSTUS, M.D. *A Familiar Treatise on the Physical Education of Children.* Trans. by A. F. M. Willich, M.D. London: Murray and Highley, 1801. (A very rigid and interesting German doctor, translated into English in 1801.)

THEOBALD, JOHN, M.D. *The Young Wife's Guide to the Management of her Children.* London: W. Griffin, R. Withy, and G. Kearsly, 1764.

UFFELMAN, JULIUS, M.D. *Manual of the Domestic Hygiene of the Child,* ed. Mary Putnam Jacobi, M.D. New York: Putnam, 1891. (The violently repressive point of view of this German doctor was apparently accepted by his translator, Mary Putnam Jacobi, the eminent wife of Jacobi, the pediatrician.)

UNDERWOOD, MICHAEL, M.D. *A Treatise on the Diseases of Children With General Directions for the Management of Infants from the Birth.* Philadelphia: T. Dobson, 1793. (The author of the most complete and up-to-date work on diseases and management of children. His book went through many editions both in England and America.)

VERDI, TULLIO SUZZARS, A.M., M.D. *Maternity: A Popular Treatise for Young Wives and Mothers.* New York: J. B. Ford and Company, 1870.

From Immodesty to Innocence

Philippe Aries

One of the unwritten laws of contemporary morality, the strictest and best respected of all, requires adults to avoid any reference, above all any humorous reference, to sexual matters in the presence of children. This notion was entirely foreign to the society of old. The modern reader of the diary in which Henri IV's physician, Heroard, recorded the details of the young Louis XIII's life is astonished by the liberties which people took with children, by the coarseness of the jokes they made, and by the indecency of gestures made in public which shocked nobody and which were regarded as perfectly natural. No other document can give us a better idea of the non-existence of the modern idea of childhood at the beginning of the seventeenth century.

Louis XIII was not yet one year old: 'He laughed uproariously when his nanny waggled his cock with her fingers.' An amusing trick which the child soon copied. Calling a page, 'he shouted "Hey, there!" and pulled up his robe, showing him his cock.'

He was one year old: 'In high spirits,' notes Heroard, 'he made everybody kiss his cock.' This amused them all. Similarly everyone considered his behavior towards two visitors, a certain de Bonières and his daughter, highly amusing: 'He laughed at him, lifted up his robe and showed him his cock, but even more so to his daughter, for then, holding it and giving his little laugh, he shook the whole of his body up and down.' They thought this so funny that the child took care to repeat a gesture which had been such a success; in the presence of a 'little lady', 'he lifted up his coat, and showed her his cock with such fervour that he was quite beside himself. He lay on his back to show it to her.'

When he was just over a year old he was engaged to the Infanta of Spain; his attendants explained to him what this meant, and he understood them fairly well. 'They asked him: "Where is the Infanta's darling?" He put his hand on his cock.'

During his first three years nobody showed any

reluctance or saw any harm in jokingly touching the child's sexual parts. 'The Marquise [de Verneuil] often put her hand under his coat; he got his nanny to lay him on her bed where she played with him, putting her hand under his coat.' 'Mme de Verneuil wanted to play with him and took hold of his nipples; he pushed her away, saying: "Let go, let go, go away." He would not allow the Marquise to touch his nipples, because his nanny had told him: "Monsieur, never let anybody touch your nipples, or your cock, or they will cut it off." He remembered this.' Again: 'When he got up, he would not take his shirt and said: "Not my shirt, I want to give you all some milk from my cock." We held out our hands, and he pretended to give us all some milk, saying: "Pss, pss," and only then agreeing to take his shirt.'

It was a common joke, repeated time and again, to say to him: 'Monsieur, you haven't got a cock.' Then 'he replied: "Hey, here it is!"—laughing and lifting it up with one finger.' These jokes were not limited to the servants, or to brainless youths, or to women of easy virtue such as the King's mistress. The Queen, his mother, made the same sort of joke: 'The Queen, touching his cock, said: "Son, I am holding your spout." ' Even more astonishing is this passage: 'He was undressed and Madame too [his sister], and they were placed naked in bed with the King, where they kissed and twittered and gave great amusement to the King. The King asked him: "Son, where is the Infanta's bundle?" He showed it to him, saying: "There is no bone in it, Papa." Then, as it was slightly distended, he added: "There is now, there is sometimes." '

The Court was amused, in fact, to see his first erections: 'Waking up at eight o'clock, he called Mlle Bethouzay and said to her: "Zezai, my cock is like a drawbridge; see how it goes up and down." And he raised it and lowered it.'

By the age of four, 'he was taken to the Queen's apartments, where Mme de Guise showed him the Queen's bed and said to him: "Monsieur, this is where you were made." He replied: "With Mamma?" ' 'He asked his nanny's husband: "What is that?" "That," came the reply, "is one of my silk stockings." "And those?" [after the manner of parlour-game questions] "Those are my breeches." "What are they made of?" "Velvet."

"And that?" "That is a cod-piece." "What is inside?" "I don't know, Monsieur." "Why, a cock. Who is it for?" "I don't know, Monsieur." "Why, for Madame Doundoun [his nanny]."

'He stood between the legs of Mme de Montglat [his governess, a very dignified, highly respectable woman, who however did not seem to be put out—any more than Heroard was—by all these jokes which we would consider insufferable today]. The King said: "Look at Madame de Montglat's son: she has just given birth." He went straight away and stood between the Queen's legs.'

When he was between five and six, people stopped talking about his sexual parts, while he started talking more about other people's. Mlle Mercier, one of his chambermaids who had stayed up late the night before, was still in bed one morning, next to his bed (his servants, who were sometimes married, slept in his bedroom and do not appear to have allowed his presence to embarrass them). 'He played with her, toyed with her toes and the upper part of her legs, and told his nanny to go and get some birch twigs so that he could beat her, which he did . . . His nanny asked him: "What have you seen of Mercier's?" He replied calmly: "I have seen her arse." "What else have you seen?" He replied calmly and without laughing that he had seen her private.' On another occasion, 'after playing with Mlle Mercier, he called me [Heroard] and told me that Mercier had a private as big as that (showing me his two fists) and that there was water inside.'

After 1608 this kind of joke disappeared: he had become a little man—attaining the fateful age of seven—and at this age he had to be taught decency in laguage and behaviour. When he was asked how children were born, he would reply, like Molière's Agnès, 'through the ear'. Mme de Montglat scolded him when he 'showed his cock to the little Ventelet girl'. And if, when he awoke in the morning, he was still put in Mme de Montglat's bed between her and her husband, Heroard waxed indignant and noted in the margin of his diary: *insignis impudentia*. The boy of ten was forced to behave with a modesty which nobody had thought of expecting of the boy of five. Education scarcely began before the age of seven; moreover, these tardy scruples of decency are to be attributed to the beginnings of a reformation of manners, a sign of the religious and moral restoration which took place in the seventeenth century. It was as if education was held to be of no value before the approach of manhood.

By the time he was fourteen, however, Louis XIII had nothing more to learn, for it was at the age of fourteen years two months that he was put almost by force into his wife's bed. After the ceremony he 'retired and had supper in bed at a quarter to seven. M. de Gramont and a few young lords told him some broad stories to encourage him. He asked for his slippers and put on his robe and went to the Queen's bedchamber at eight o'clock, where he was put to bed beside the Queen his wife, in the presence of the Queen his mother; at a quarter past ten he returned after sleeping for about an hour and performing twice, according to what he told us; he arrived with his cock all red.'

The marriage of a boy of fourteen was perhaps becoming something of a rare occurrence. The marriage of a girl of thirteen was still very common.

There is no reason to believe that the moral climate was any different in other families, whether of nobles or commoners; the practice of associating children with the sexual ribaldries of adults formed part of contemporary manners. In Pascal's family, Jacqueline Pascal at the age of twelve was writing a poem about the Queen's pregnancy.

Thomas Platter, in his memoirs of life as a medical student at the end of the sixteenth century, writes: 'I once met a child who played this trick [knotting a girl's aiguillette when she married, so that her husband became impotent] on his parents' maidservant. She begged him to break the spell by undoing the aiguillette. He agreed and the bridegroom, recovering his potency, was immediately cured.' Père de Dainville, the historian of the Society of Jesus and of humanist pedagogics, also writes: 'The respect due to children was then [in the sixteenth century] completely unknown. Everything was permitted in their presence: coarse language, scabrous actions and situations; they had heard everything and seen everything.'

This lack of reserve with regard to children surprises us: we raise our eyebrows at the outspoken talk but even more at the bold gestures, the physical contacts, about which it is easy to imagine what a modern psycho-analyst would say. The psycho-analyst would be wrong. The attitude to sex, and doubtless sex itself, varies according to environment, and consequently according to period and mentality. Nowadays the physical contacts described by Heroard would strike us as bordering on sexual perversion and nobody would dare to indulge in them publicly. This was not the case at the beginning of the seventeenth century. There is an engraving of 1511 depicting a holy family: St. Anne's behaviour strikes us as extremely odd—she is pushing the child's thighs apart as if she wanted to get at its privy parts and tickle them. It would be a mistake to see this as a piece of ribaldry.

The Concept of Development
from a Comparative and Organismic Point of View

Heinz Werner

The field of developmental psychology, as it is conceived here, transcends the boundaries within which the concept of development is frequently applied: development is here apprehended as a concept not merely applicable to delimited areas such as child growth or comparative behavior of animals, but as a concept that proposes a certain manner of viewing behavior in its manifold manifestations. Such a developmental approach to behavior rests on one basic assumption, namely, that wherever there is life there is growth and development, that is, formation in terms of systematic, orderly sequence. This basic assumption, then, entails the view that developmental conceptualization is applicable to the various areas of life science, and is potentially useful in interrelating the many fields of psychology.

The developmental approach has, of course, been clearly of tremendous heuristic value in systematizing certain aspects of biological phenomena in various fields of life science such as compara-

tive anatomy, neurophysiology, and embryology. Analogously, developmental psychology aims at viewing the behavior of all organisms in terms of similar genetic principles. However, this aim of developmental psychology is perhaps even farther reaching than that of developmental biology. Developmental psychology does not restrict itself either to ontogenesis or phylogenesis, but seeks to coordinate within a single framework forms of behavior observed in comparative animal psychology, in child psychology, in psychopathology, in ethnopsychology, and in the general and differential psychology of man in our own culture. Eventually, in linking these variegated observations, it attempts to formulate and systematically examine experimentally testable hypotheses.

In order to clarify and evolve its conceptual framework, developmental psychology has to search for characteristics common to any kind of mental activity in the process of progression or regression. In this comparative venture one has

Heinz Werner, "The Concept of Development from a Comparative and Organismic Point of View," from *The Concept of Development: An Issue in the Study of Human Behavior,* edited by Dale B. Harris. University of Minnesota Press, Minneapolis © 1957, University of Minnesota.

to be wary of the error made by early evolutionists such as Haeckel and G. Stanley Hall, who sought to treat as materially identical various developmental sequences when the data warranted only the assertion of similarity or parallelism. The statement, for instance, that the individual recapitulates in his development the genesis of the species, and the attempt to identify childlike and abnormal forms of behavior, have, in their extreme formulation, aroused just criticism, but criticism which has spread more and more toward undermining comparative developmental psychology as a discipline.

Between the extremes, on the one hand, of viewing as identical various developmental sequences, and on the other, of denying completely any comparability among them, some beginnings toward a theory of development have been made. These beginnings take into account the formal similarities in these various developmental sequences as well as material and formal differences distinguishing each developmental sequence from another.

The Orthogenetic Principle of Development

Developmental psychology postulates one regulative principle of development; it is an orthogenetic principle which states that wherever development occurs it proceeds from a state of relative globality and lack of differentiation to a state of increasing differentiation, articulation, and hierarchic integration.* This principle has the status of an heuristic definition. Though itself not subject to empirical test, it is valuable to developmental psychologists in leading to a determination of the actual range of applicability of developmental concepts to the behavior of organisms.†

We may offer several illustrations of how this orthogenetic principle is applied in the interpretation and ordering of psychological phenomena.

According to this principle, a state involving a relative lack of differentiation between subject and object is developmentally prior to one in which there is a polarity of subject and object. Thus the young child's acceptance of dreams as external to himself, the lack of differentiation between what one dreams and what one sees, as is found in psychosis, or in some nonliterate societies, the breakdown of boundaries of the self in mescaline intoxication and in states of depersonalization—all of these betoken a relative condition of genetic primordiality compared to the polarity between subject and object found in reflective thinking. This increasing subject-object differentiation involves the corollary that the organism becomes increasingly less dominated by the immediate concrete situation; the person is less stimulus-bound and less impelled by his own affective states. A consequence of this freedom is the clearer understanding of goals, the possibility of employing substitutive means and alternative ends. There is hence a greater capacity for delay and planned action. The person is better able to exercise choice and willfully rearrange a situation. In short, he can manipulate the environment rather than passively respond to the environment. This freedom from the domination of the immediate situation also permits a more accurate assessment of others. The adult is more able than the child to distinguish between the motivational dynamics and the overt behavior of personalities. At developmentally higher levels, therefore, there is less of a tendency for the world to be interpreted solely in terms of one's own needs and an increasing appreciation of the needs of others and of group goals.

Turning to another illustration, one pertaining to concept formation, we find that modes of classification that involve a relative lack of differentiation between concept and perceptual context are genetically prior to modes of classification of properties relatively independent of specific objects. Thus, a color classification that employs color terms such as "gall-like" for a combination of green and blue, or "young leaves" for a combination of yellow and green, is genetically prior to a conceptual color system independent of objects such as gall or young leaves.

It may be opportune to use this last example as an illustration of the comparative character of the

---

* This, of course, implies "directiveness." It seems to us, therefore, that one must on logical grounds agree with E. S. Russell (33) that organic development cannot be defined without the construct of "directiveness."

† In regard to the following discussion, see item 47 in the References.

developmental approach. That the color classification attached to specific objects involves a mode of cognition genetically prior to a classification independent of specific objects is, of course, consistent with the main theoretical principle of development. In regard to the comparative character of our discipline, however, it does not suffice for us merely to find this type of classification more typical of the man of lower civilization than of the man of higher. The anthropological data point up the necessity of determining whether there is a greater prevalence of such primitive color conceptualization in areas where cognition can be readily observed in terms of lower developmental levels, e.g., in the early phases of ontogenesis. Experimental studies on young children have demonstrated the greater prevalence of concrete (context-bound) conceptualization with regard not only to color but to many other phenomena as well. Again, to take organic neuropathology as an example, in brain-injured persons we find, as Goldstein, Head, and others have stressed, a concretization of color conceptualization symptomatic of their psychopathology; similar observations have been made on schizophrenics.

At this point we should like to state that a comprehensive comparative psychology of development cannot be achieved without the aid of a general experimental psychology broadened through the inclusion of developmental methodology and developmental constructs. There have appeared on the scene of general psychology beginnings of an extremely significant trend toward the studying of perception, learning, and thinking, not as final products but as developing processes, as temporal events divisible into successive stages. Such "event psychology," as one may call it, introduces the dimension of time as an intrinsic property into all experimental data. It stands thus in contrast to approaches, like that of classical psychophysics, in which the treating of successive trials as repetitive responses eliminates as far as possible sequential effects. European psychologists, particularly in Germany and Austria, have turned to the direct study of emergent and developing mental phenomena (34, 42, 46). For instance, using a tachistoscope, we may study the developmental changes in perception which occur when the time of exposure is increased from trial to

trial. In studies of this sort, such developmental changes, or "microgenesis," of percepts are predictable from a developmental theory of the ontogenesis of perception. Some of the ensuing parallels between microgenesis and ontogenesis might be summarized as follows (5): In both microgenesis and ontogenesis the formation of percepts seems, in general, to go through an orderly sequence of stages. Perception is first global; whole-qualities are dominant. The next stage might be called analytic; perception is selectively directed toward parts. The final stage might be called synthetic; parts become integrated with respect to the whole. Initially perception is predominantly "physiognomic." * The physiognomic quality of an object is experienced prior to any details. At this level, feeling and perceiving are little differentiated. Again, in the early stages of development imaging and perceiving are not definitely separated.

There is another important technique of studying the emergence and formation of perception. This method was originally utilized in Stratton's well-known experiments in which a person wearing lenses had to adjust to a world visually perceived as upside down. More recently, Ivo Kohler of the Innsbruck Laboratory has utilized this method in extremely significant long-range experiments. He studies stages of perceptual adaptation to a world visually distorted in various ways by prisms or lenses (16, 17, 49). Again, these perceptual formation stages are found to conform to ontogenetic patterns. Ontogenetic studies have made it reasonably certain that the experience of space and spatial objects grows through stages which can be grossly defined. There appears to be an early sensorimotor stage of spatial orientation, succeeded by one in which objects emerge in terms of "things-of-action" (44), where perceptual qualities of things are determined by the specific way these things are handled. For instance, a chair is that object which has a "sitting tone" (Uexküll). A later stage is that of highly objectified or visualized space where the spatial phenomena are perceived in their rather "pure" visual form and form relations.

Keeping these ontogenetic states in mind, it is

* In regard to this term, see item 44 (p. 69) and item 45 (p. 11) of the References.

most enlightening to follow the reports of the subjects used in the Innsbruck Laboratory as they move from level to level in developmental order, adjusting themselves to a disarrayed world. First, they learn to master space on a sensorimotor level; that is, they are able to move about without error. But, though they may be able to ride a bicycle quite skillfully, the visual world as such may, at this stage, still be extremely confused, upside down, or crooked. The further development toward visual adaptation shows some remarkable features: the objects seem to fall into two classes, things-of-action and purely visual things. The observer conquers first the things-of-action and only later purely visual things. For instance, observers wearing prisms which invert left and right can see an object already in correct position if it is part of their own actions, but incorrectly—that is, reversed—when purely visually grasped. In a fencing situation, a subject sees his own sword correctly pointing toward the opponent, but at a moment of rest it becomes visually inverted, pointing toward himself. By the same token, a little later in development any object-of-action, such as a chair or a screwdriver, whether it is actually handled or not, is correctly transformed, whereas purely visual objects, such as pictures or printed words, remain reversed. Only at a last stage the differences disappear, and complete transformation of the visual world is achieved.

Another area of general psychology where genetic methodology has been fruitfully applied is that of problem-solving behavior. Whereas Wertheimer's contribution to productive thinking, outstanding as it was, remains essentially agenetic, the signal importance of Duncker's work (7) lies in its genetic methodology. Duncker studied the problem-solving process in terms of genetic stages which follow each other according to developmental laws well established for ontogenesis.*

---

* Duncker has also clearly seen one aspect of creative thought processes, hitherto little recognized, namely, the fact that successful problem-solving depends not only on the ability to progress along new ways, but also on the ability to regress back to a point from which new development can take place. In other words, he has observed a most important genetic principle, that of oscillatory activity in terms of progression and regression. (See the last section of this paper.)

Uniformity versus Multiformity of Development

The orthogenetic law, being a formal regulative principle, is not designed to predict developmental courses in their specificity. To illustrate, it cannot decide the well-known controversy between Coghill's and Windle's conceptions (6, 50) concerning ontogenesis of motor behavior. According to Coghill, who studied the larval salamander, behavior develops through the progressive expansion of a perfectly integrated total pattern, and the individuation within of partial patterns that acquire varying degrees of dicreteness. Windle's conception, derived from the study of placental mammals, is that the first responses of the embryo are circumscribed, stereotyped reflexes subsequently combined into complex patterns. It may be possible to reconcile, under the general developmental law, both viewpoints as follows: The development of motor behavior may, depending on the species or on the type of activity, involve either the differentiation of partial patterns from a global whole and their integration within a developing locomotor activity (Coghill) or the integration of originally juxtaposed, relatively isolated global units which now become differentiated parts of a newly formed locomotor pattern (Windle). In both cases there are differentiation and hierarchic integration, although the specific manifestations differ.*

Now, it is precisely this polarity between the uniformity of a general regulative principle and the multiformity of specific developmental changes that makes the study of development necessarily a comparative discipline. If we were merely to seek the ordering of changes of behavior in terms of a universal developmental principle, developmental theory might still be of interest to the philosophy of science and theoretical psychology, but it would be of far lesser value to empirical psychology.

In order to get a clearer picture of what is involved here, it might be advantageous to refer to one of our studies, namely, that of the develop-

---

* Cf. the excellent discussion by Barron, presented at the Chicago Conference on Genetic Neurology (2).

ment of the acquisition of meaning, by the use of a word-context test (48).

In this experiment eight to thirteen-year-old children had the task of finding the meaning of an artificial word which was embedded successively in six verbal contexts. For instance, one such artificial word was "corplum." After each of these six sentences the child was interrogated concerning the meaning of the artificial word.

The six sentences in which "corplum" (correct translation: "stick" or "piece of wood") appears, are as follows: (1) A corplum may be used for support. (2) Corplums may be used to close off an open place. (3) A corplum may be long or short, thick or thin, strong or weak. (4) A wet corplum does not burn. (5) You can make a corplum smooth with sandpaper. (6) The painter used a corplum to mix his paints.

Now, the task confronting the subjects in the word-context test is essentially the synthesis of the cues from a set of six contexts for the purpose of forming a general meaning of the word, that is, a meaning applicable to all six sentences. The success of such an operation is reflected in two kinds of results. The first shows a steady and continuous increase in the achievement of a correct solution with increasing age. The second reflects changes in the underlying patterns of operation. As to the first point, there is a developmental increase in achievement which signifies the increasing capacity for hierarchization, that is, for integrating the various cues within a common name. However, the finding concerning a steady rise in achievement of correctness was, for us, not the most important result. Our main aim was to study the processes underlying such achievement. We were far more concerned with detecting the fact that conceptual synthesis is not achieved by a unitary pattern of operations, but that there are various sorts of processes of synthesis which differ from each other developmentally. The lower forms were found to emerge, to increase, and then to decrease during intellectual growth, yielding finally to more advanced forms of generalization (48, p. 97).

Studies of this sort inform us that the workings of the orthogenetic law as a uniform, regulative principle have to be specified through the ordering and interpretation of the multiform operations.

Such a view implies the rejection of a tacit assumption made by many child psychologists that the measured achievement always reflects unequivocally the underlying operations, or that overt achievement is necessarily a true gauge of the developmental stage. This assumption is untenable; the same achievement may be reached by operations genetically quite different (41). An analysis of types of operations rather than measurement merely in terms of accuracy of performance often reveals the truer developmental picture.* In fact, a greater accuracy in certain circumstances may even signify a lower developmental level, as in the case of a decorticate frog who shows greater accuracy in catching flies than the normal frog. Gottschaldt (10) presented normal and mentally deficient eight-year-old children with the task of constructing squares or rectangles from the irregular pieces into which these figures had been cut. The normal children had difficulties with the test because they tried to relate the figuratively unrelated pieces to the end form. Operating on a purely mechanical level, the mentally deficient children matched the edges of the same length and thus performed quicker and with fewer errors. Again, a thinker oriented toward and capable of highly abstract thought may be at a disadvantage in certain concrete tasks of concept formation, compared with a concretely thinking person.

---

* It is not accidental that out of the immense field of potentially great significance for developmental psychology, the two main areas emphasized by psychologists in this country were the area of intelligence and the area of learning. They were chosen because they were clearly amenable to rigid quantification on a continuum in terms of more or less. The successes of workers in these fields obtained by statistical treatment of overt behavior and the successes in practical application have reinforced the conviction that outside the rather trivial notion of continuous increase in achievement with increase of age, developmental theory is not needed. In regard to intelligence the evaluation of G. Stanley Hall, the father of comparative genetic psychology, still seems to hold: Intelligence tests and measurements, he stated, have done a great work in applying psychology to life and industry but have added scarcely a scintilla to our knowledge of human development (11, p. 450). As to the situation in the area of learning, it seems significant that a man as deeply informed as Hilgard, in a well-balanced evaluation of this field of research, comes to the conclusion that undue stress on quantification may lead to a collapse when underlying processes are not understood (13, p. 328).

Continuity versus Discontinuity of Development

The orthogenetic principle of increase in differentiation and hierarchic integration is not meant to imply continuous progress as the exclusive characteristic of developmental change. A good deal of the controversy centering in the continuity-discontinuity problem appears to be due to a lack in clarification of these terms. In particular, there has been considerable confusion about two different aspects of change. One is the quantitative aspect of change. Here the problem of continuity versus discontinuity is related to the measurement —in terms of gradual or abrupt increase with time —of magnitude, of efficiency, of frequency of occurrence of a newly acquired operation in an individual or in a group. The other aspect concerns the qualitative nature of changes. Here the problem of continuity versus discontinuity centers in the question of the reducibility of later to earlier forms—emergence—and the transition between later and earlier forms—intermediacy.

It seems that discontinuity in terms of qualitative changes can be best defined by two characteristics: "emergence," i.e., the irreducibility of a later stage to an earlier; and "gappiness," i.e., the lack of intermediate stages between earlier and later forms. Quantitative discontinuity * on the other hand, appears to be sufficiently defined by the second characteristic.

Now it seems that in many discussions, particularly among psychologists, the quantitative and qualitative forms of continuity and discontinuity have not been clearly kept apart. Thus, a change may be discontinuous in terms of quality but may

become distinguishable (e.g., measurable) only gradually; i.e., there may be a continuous quantitative increase, such as in frequency of occurrence or in magnitude. For instance, the attempt of the young child to walk on two legs is discontinuous with four-limb locomotion, though the successive actual attempts may show gradual progress toward precision and success.* In accordance with our definition given above, two-legged locomotion cannot be reduced to four-limbed locomotion, and, furthermore, there is limitation in regard to intermediate steps.

Another related mistake is that of accepting smallness of change, whether qualitative or quantitative, as an indicator of continuity. For instance, the genetic changes termed "mutation" may be very slight, but there has to be "discontinuity inasmuch as there are no intermediate forms between the unchanged and the changed." † This significant fact in mutation, namely, discontinuity, says Schroedinger, "reminds a physicist of quantum theory: no intermediate energies occurring between two neighboring energy levels. He would be inclined to call de Vries's mutation theory . . . the quantum theory of biology." Because of the smallness of change, in developmental psychology as well as in developmental biology, one often will find it possible to argue for discontinuity only on the basis of extensive data accumulated in extensive temporal sequences; discontinuity in change may then be concluded after a trait has become sufficiently distinct in terms of frequency, permanency, and magnitude.

Other factors that are often not clearly recognized for their importance in determining sequences as either continuous or discontinuous are

---

* To facilitate distinction and alleviate confusion, I would suggest substituting "abruptness" for quantitative discontinuity, reserving the term "discontinuity" only for the qualitative aspect of change. It also appears feasible to distinguish between two types of emergence: (a) emergence of a single operation, e.g., abstract function, (b) emergence of a novel pattern of operation. A novel pattern may emerge as a consequence of new operations that enter the pattern, or it may also emerge through a reorganization of the existing characters within a certain pattern, through a changing dominance between these existing characters, etc. One may note here some analogies between psychological emergence and biogenetic emergence coming about (a) through mutant genes, and (b) through changes in local constellations of genes.

* Such paradoxical coexistence of qualitative discontinuity and gradualness of appearance (progression) seems to pertain to developmental changes of various kinds. For instance, regenerative development of transplanted tissue is either determined according to the domicile within which the transplant is embedded (place-wise) or according to the original extraction of the transplant (origin-wise). This determination is an all-or-none phenomenon; however, visible differentiation is not instantaneously evident but progressive (26, pp. 70f).

† Schroedinger, p. 34 (37). Schroedinger points out that Darwin was mistaken in regarding the small, continuous chance variations within a species as the basis of evolution by natural selection. These variations (e.g., length of awn in a pure-bred crop) cannot be formants of a new species because they are not inheritable.

(a) the handling of the data and (b) the nature of the universe of discourse.

Concerning the first factor, it should be realized that discontinuous process changes typical in individual development may be obscured by averaging developmental achievement scores of individuals to secure a composite curve for a group which then suggests continuous growth.*

Another fallacy in deriving continuity of behavioral development from group scores has been most recently discussed by Lashley (21) in regard to a particular feature of the usual mental tests, namely, the heterogeneity (discontinuity) of the items which the test patterns comprise. Lashley's criticism implies that discontinuity of processes may be obscured by interpreting developmental data on the assumption that variations in achievement can be based only on variations in a single underlying process. As noted before, the achievement of correctness on our word-context test shows a steady increase with age, whereas underlying processes give a picture of the rise and decline of more or less primitive operations and the abrupt rise of an adult type of generalization around ten or eleven years of age. Reference should be made here to the important study by Nancy Bayley (3) concerning mental development during the first three years. She could show that in terms of accumulated scores there was a steady increase with age; however, a further analysis of the test items in terms of underlying operations revealed a shift from one type of function ("sensorimotor") to a qualitatively different type ("adaptive") occurring at approximately nine months of age.

Secondly, it should be recognized that it is the universe of discourse, the interpretational frame within which the material is grasped, that often determines the ordering in terms of continuity or discontinuity. To illustrate by an analogy, one may represent the relation between color hues in physical terms, i.e., wave length, that change continuously within the range of visibility. Within the psychological frame of reference, however, there is discontinuity. The gradual variation from blue to green is discontinuous with the gradual variation from green to yellow, which, in turn, is discontinuous with the gradual variation from yellow to red.

There is no logical necessity for a concordance in terms of continuity between the quantitative and qualitative aspects of any developmental series. A discontinuous (epigenetic) qualitative change may become distinct gradually; that is, it does not need to be "saltatory" in a quantitative sense, if by that word is meant that a new form or function becomes suddenly overt. Nor does unevenness—spurt versus depression—of any growth curve necessarily point to novel process formation. However, though we have to beware of confusing quantitative discontinuity-continuity with qualitative discontinuity-continuity, quantitative unevenness may, possibly more often than not, point to qualitative discontinuity or emergent evolution. We may illustrate this from Paul Weiss's discussion (40) on embryonic growth: "An obstacle to simple mathematical treatment of growth is its lack of continuity; for embryonic growth advances unevenly, in spurts and jumps, with intermittent depressions. These depressions correspond to phases of intensive histological differentiation" (p. 44). Furthermore, if embryonic growth curves in terms of weight are compared with progress in terms of differentiation and morphogenesis, one finds that both kinds of progressions advance unevenly, but, that "maxima of differentiation coincide with minima of growth." From this, Weiss concludes that "acceleration of differentiating activity is attended by retardation of growth activity, or in other words, that there is some antagonism between differentiation and growth" (p. 134).*

Weiss's observations point to an important instance where the saltations and depressions of "accumulating" activity (growth in terms of quantitave discontinuity) appear to be vicariously related to morphogenetic processes directed toward the production of "discrete discontinuous . . . cell types which are not connected by intergradation"—development in terms of qualitative discontinuity (p. 98).

Quite possibly there are analogies to this vicari-

---

* Lecomte DuNoüy (8) in his remarkable book, *Biological Time,* takes the extreme view that continuity always is "manufactured" by our treatment of the data: "one of the roles of consciousness is to manufacture continuity from discontinuity."

* One may note the possibility of discriminating between "growth" as a process of accumulation versus "development" defined by differentiation.

ous correspondence between quantitative growth and qualitative development on the level of psychological behavior. To illustrate, one such analogy might be found in a frequent observation concerning certain phases of speech development. There appears to occur between the stage of babbling and that of naming, a period during which vocalizing is depressed (22, p. 82). It seems plausible to interpret this period as one during which the awareness of sound patterns as verbal symbols emerges. Once this novel operation has emerged, the child bursts forth with naming, increasing its vocabulary at a swiftly accelerating rate.

In conclusion, it seems to me that development cannot be comprehended without the polar conceptualization of continuity and discontinuity. Within the "universe of discourse" in which the orthogenetic law is conceived, development, insofar as it is defined as increase in differentiation and hierarchization is, ideally, continuous. Underlying the increase in differentiation and integration are the forms and processes which undergo two main kinds of changes: (a) quantitative changes which are either gradual or abrupt, and (b) qualitative changes which, by their very nature, are discontinuous.*

Unilinearity versus Multilinearity of Development

The orthogenetic law, by its very nature, is an expression of unilinearity of development. But, as is true of the other polarities discussed here, the ideal unilinear sequence signified by the universal developmental law does not conflict with the multiplicity of actual developmental forms. As implied in the conclusion of the preceding section, coexistence of unilinearity and multiplicity of individual developments must be recognized for psychological just as it is for biological evolution. In regard to human behavior in particular, this polarity opens the way for a developmental study of behavior not only in terms of universal se-

* For further discussion of the continuity-discontinuity problem, see Bertalanffy, ch. 12 (4); DuNoüy (8); Huxley, ch. 5 (14); Lillie (23); Novikoff (27); Simpson, ch. 14 (39); Schneirla (35, 36).

quence, but also in terms of individual variations, that is, in terms of growth viewed as a branching-out process of specialization or aberration.

To illustrate, "physiognomic" perception appears to be a developmentally early form of viewing the world, based on the relative lack of distinction between properties of persons and properties of inanimate things (44, pp. 67f). But the fact that in our culture physiognomic perception, developmentally, is superseded by logical, realistic, and technical conceptualization, poses some paradoxical problems, such as, What genetic standing has adult aesthetic experience? Is it to be considered a "primitive" experience left behind in a continuous process of advancing logification, and allowed to emerge only in sporadic hours of regressive relaxation? Such an inference seems unsound; it probably errs in conceiving human growth in terms of a simple developmental series rather than as a diversity of individual formations, all conforming to the abstract and general developmental conceptualization. Though physiognomic experience is a primordial manner of perceiving, it grows, in certain individuals such as artists, to a level not below but on a par with that of "geometric-technical" perception and logical discourse.

Fixity versus Mobility of Developmental Level of Operation

The assumption that all organisms normally operate upon a relatively fixed and rather sharply circumscribed developmental level appears to be tacitly accepted by many psychologists. A contrary view is that all higher organisms manifest a certain range of genetically different operations. This means, for instance, that a child of a certain age or an adult, depending on the task or on inner circumstances, may, qua normal, perform at genetically different levels. Furthermore, there is, so to speak, not only "horizontal" differentiation but also "vertical" differentiation; that is, the more mature compared with the less mature individual has at his disposal a greater number of developmentally different operations.

It should be recognized that these views are not

necessarily antagonistic; i.e., fixity as well as mobility of levels of operation coexist as polar principles of development. The principle of fixity is implied in, or can be inferred from, the intrinsic trend of any evolution toward an end stage of maximum stability. Such maximum stability, as the end stage of a developmental sequence, implies the ceasing of growth; that is, implies the permanency, for instance, of specialized reaction patterns, or automatization of response. But the principle of fixity would finally lead to rigidity of behavior if not counterbalanced by the polar principle of mobility. As most generally conceived, mobility implies "becoming" in contrast to "being"; it implies that an organism, having attained highly stabilized structures and operations may or may not progress further, but if it does, this will be accomplished through partial return to a genetically earlier, less stable level. One has to regress in order to progress. The intimate relation of regression to progression appears succinctly expressed in the statement of one of the early evolutionists, Richard Owen (32). On interpreting the resemblance of the embryo to the phylogenetic ancestry, Owen said: "We perceive a return to the archetype in the early embryological phases of development of the highest existing species, or ought rather to say that development starts from the old point" (p. 108).

An impressive illustration of the relation between renewed development and regression on the biological level can be found in the processes of regeneration. Such regeneration, as extensively studied at the amphibian level, consists of two phases, regressive as well as progressive. The progressive phase—analogous to normal embryonic development—starts with the formation of the "blastema" or regenerative bud. But prior to progression there is regression. The regressive phase involves de-differentiation of already specialized cells (26, p. 3). Another probable source for blastema formation is reserve cells, that is, cells that have remained at a low state of differentiation (40, p. 466). It is noteworthy that power of regeneration, being associated with capacity to de-differentiate is, in general, inversely correlated with the organism's ontogenetic or phylogenetic status of differentiatedness (26, p. 62).

In speculating by analogy from biological events of this sort to human behavior one might argue that in creative reorganization, psychological regression involves two kinds of operations: one is the de-differentiation (dissolution) of existing, schematized or automatized behavior patterns; the other consists in the activation of primitive levels of behavior from which undifferentiated (little-formulated) phenomena emerge.

The polar conceptualization of normal levels of operation in terms of fixity-mobility appears thus closely linked to another polar distinction, namely, that involved in the relation between lower and higher levels of operation. In regard to this relation, one particular problem among many has aroused considerable interest. It concerns the degree of fixity or mobility of an operation emerging at a certain level, in relation to developmentally later forms of operation.

As mentioned before, development, whether it concerns single functions, complex performances, or the totality of personality, tends toward stabilization. Once a certain stable level of integration is reached, the possibility of further development must depend on whether or not the behavioral patterns have become so automatized that they cannot take part in reorganization. We may refer here to Rapaport's concept of "apparatus" (31, p. 76) or to Piaget's concept of "schema" (30). The individual, for instance, builds up sensorimotor schemata, such as grasping, opening a box, and linguistic patterns; these are the goal of early learning at first, but later on become instruments or apparatuses for handling the environment. Since no two situations in which an organism finds itself are alike, the usefulness of these schemata in adaptive behavior will depend on their stability as well as on their pliability (a paradoxical "stable flexibility").

Furthermore, if one assumes that the emergence of higher levels of operations involves hierarchic integration, it follows that lower-level operations will have to be reorganized in terms of their functional nature so that they become subservient to higher functioning. A clear example of this is the change of the functional nature of imagery from a stage where images serve only memory, fantasy, and concrete conceptualization, to a stage where images have been transformed to schematic symbols of abstract concepts and thought.

Differential versus General Developmental Psychology: Individuality As a Problem of Developmental Psychology

At Clark University we are becoming increasingly impressed with the fruitfulness of the developmental frame of reference for the study of group and individual differences. We may illustrate this approach to the many problems which are in need of investigation by referring to a few studies on cognitive organization.

One problem concerns the over-all maturity status of the individual, that is, his cognitive level of operation under optimal conditions, and the stability of this level under varying internal and external conditions. Friedman, Phillips, and their co-workers at Worcester State Hospital and at Clark University have constructed a genetic scoring system of the Rorschach test founded on developmental theory, and standardized through an ontogenetic study of children. The scoring system is based essentially on the occurrence and frequency of "genetically low" and "genetically high" scores. Restricting ourselves here mainly to the various whole and detail responses, genetically low responses are those which indicate amorphous, diffuse, or confabulatory percepts where little attention is given to part relations and to perception of contours. The genetically high percepts are reflected in the responses whereby the percept is that of a precisely formed unit with integrated parts, where the whole is composed of relatively independent sub-wholes brought together in an integrated fashion. Applying this developmental scoring analysis to the responses of 160 children of from three to eleven years of age, Hemmendinger found the basic principle of development confirmed. That is, with age there is a decrease of the undifferentiated diffuse whole and detail responses along with an increase of the highly articulated, well-integrated whole and detail responses. There is further an interesting shift from the early whole responses toward small detail responses between the ages of about six and eight; later on there is a decline in favor of the integrated whole responses (12).

This genetic scoring method has been utilized for the gauging of developmental levels of cognitive organization in normal and deviant persons in studies carried out at Worcester State Hospital, Clark University, and Boston University.* According to the theory, the most severely impaired groups should here show the genetically lowest responses, and there should be a decrease of these responses and an increase in the genetically high responses with less impaired or unimpaired groups. The evidence is in good agreement with this expectation (see Figures 1 to 4). It was found that the genetic scores of the hebephrenic-catatonic schizophrenics resembled those of children three to five years of age. The paranoids were similar to children six to ten years of age; the psychoneurotics were intermediate between the ten-year-olds and normal adults (9, 28, 38).

We may add at this point that for the study of individual differences in their developmental aspects, experimental methods other than those based on ontogenesis have become available. Among these, probably the most promising method is that of "microgenesis." This method, already mentioned above, is based on the assumption that activity patterns, percepts, thoughts, are not merely products but processes that, whether they take seconds, or hours, or days, unfold in terms of developmental sequence.

To study microgenesis of perception, Framo presented the Rorschach cards to 80 normals. Twenty subjects in each of four groups viewed the cards at exposures of 0.01 second, 0.1 second, 1 second, and 10 seconds, respectively. A comparison of the responses in this study with the ontogenetic data obtained by Hemmendinger show striking agreements (29).**

The over-all conclusion is that the responses of the clinical groups represent various, more or less immature levels of perceptual development as compared to those of normals.

This evidence is supplemented by a study which E. Freed carried out under the direction of Leslie Phillips (29). Freed hypothesized that hebephrenic and catatonic schizophrenics would fail

---

* The illustrations given here refer to perceptual organization. From some of our pertinent studies on language behavior, see items 1, 9, 15, 24, 45, and 47 of the References.

** Figures 1 to 4 show the W. D. and Dd responses and the genetically high responses (Mature W%, Mature D%) for (a) microgenetic changes and (b) ontogenetic changes, and (c) the responses of hebephrenic-catatonic schizophrenics, paranoids, and normals under the usual Rorschach test conditions.

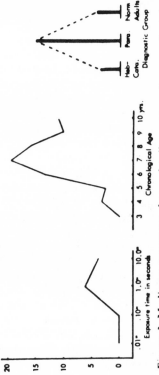

Figure 1. Median percentage of whole responses in normal adults at tachistoscopic exposures, and in children and diagnostic groups at full exposure, of the Rorschach.

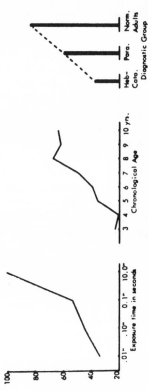

Figure 3. Median percentage of rare detail responses in normal adults at tachistoscopic exposures, and in children and diagnostic groups at full exposure, of the Rorschach.

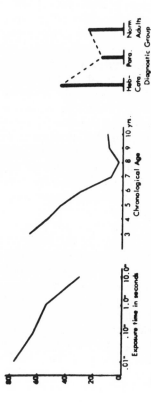

Figure 2. Median percentage of usual detail responses in normal adults at tachistoscopic exposures, and in children and diagnostic groups at full exposure, of the Rorschach.

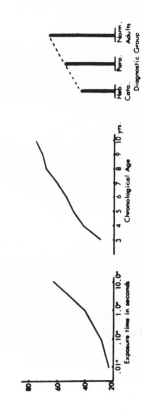

Figure 4. Percentage of developmentally-mature whole responses of all whole responses in normal adults at tachistoscopic exposures, and in children and diagnostic groups at full exposure, of the Rorschach.

to show increased differentiation with time. Using the same design as Framo, he exposed the Rorschach to a group of 60 hebephrenic-catatonic schizophrenics, 15 at each of four exposure times. At the shortest exposure time their performance was not grossly different from that of the normal adults, but as exposure time was increased these schizophrenics increasingly lagged behind in the development toward perceptually mature responses (see Figure 5). It can be concluded, therefore, that unlike the normal subjects, these schizophrenic groups did not utilize the increases in exposure time to improve their perceptual adequacy and integration.*

If we combine the notions and the evidence in terms of ontogenesis, microgenesis, and regression, we may conclude that perceptual processes develop and come to a halt at different levels. At what level the processes stop depends on such conditions as age, experience, and complexity of stimuli, and on the normal or pathologic maturity status of a person. Thus, it might be said that by evaluating the Rorschach responses of a person through genetic scores, one tests the level of perceptual formation to which such a person under

* Another area of abnormal behavior to which the microgenetic methodology has been applied is that of speech pathology. Experiments on apprehension of tachistoscopically presented words by normal subjects suggest that paraphrasic naming is related to microgenetically early stages of name formation (46).

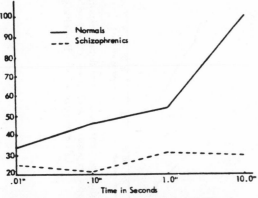

Figure 5. Median percentage of developmentally mature whole responses for normals and schizophrenics at four exposure times.

optimal time conditions progresses.

Not only has degree of psychiatric intactness been found to correspond to levels of development, but preliminary work at Worcester suggests that forms of symptom expression can also be ordered to the developmental sequence, as indicated by the genetic Rorschach scores. Thus, a number of studies have shown that persons whose symptoms are characterized by immediacy of overt reaction function at developmentally lower levels than those whose symptomatology represents displacement to more mediated forms of behavior. This has been shown by Misch, who found that a directly assaultive group is developmentally lower than a group of individuals who only threaten to assault (25). Similar findings have been obtained by Kruger (19) for subjects who demonstrate overt sexual perversion in contrast to those who only fear that they may act in a sexually perverse fashion. In addition, Kruger found that those patients who make a serious suicidal attempt were developmentally lower than those who only threatened to commit suicide.

Another developmental aspect of individuality that is in need of experimental and clinical study concerns what one might call the genetic stratification or the developmental heterogeneity of a person. Developmental stratification means that a person is structured into spheres of operations which differ in regard to developmental level. Still another aspect concerns the flexibility of a person to operate at different levels depending on the requirements of a situation.

In a particular way, it seems to us, this aspect of flexibility is connected with a further problem of individuality, namely, that of creativity. Now creativity, in its most general meaning, is an essential feature of emergent evolution, and this, in turn, implies progression through reorganization. Since we assume that such progress through reorganization cannot be achieved without "starting anew," that is, without regression, it follows that a person's capacity for creativity presupposes mobility in terms of regression and progression. The hypothesis would then be that the more creative the person, the wider his range of operations in terms of developmental level, or in other words, the greater his capacity to utilize primitive as well as advanced operations. This hypothesis is currently being tested at Worcester State Hospital and Clark University by means of the genetic Rorschach scores of relatively creative versus relatively noncreative adults.*

It might also be possible to study persons at the other extreme end of mobility, that is, those who, because of their excessive yearning for security, are coping with the environment in terms of rigidly formalized behavior. In this regard the work by the Swedish psychologist Ulf Krogh (18) seems very suggestive. He studied the microgenesis of complex pictures with various groups of people. Among other results he found that persons

* The study, well advanced, is being carried out by C. Hersch.

such as the compulsion-neurotics, whose reaction patterns to the environment are inordinately formalized, are lacking in microgenetic mobility, that is, they are lacking the intermediate steps that are normally present during the unfolding of percepts.

We should like, then, to conclude with this observation: The original aim of developmental theory, directed toward the study of universal genetic changes, is still one of its main concerns; but side by side with this concern, the conviction has been growing in recent years that developmental conceptualization, in order to reaffirm its truly organismic character, has to expand its orbit of interest to include as a central problem the study of individuality.

1. BAKER, R. W. "The Acquisition of Verbal Concepts in Schizophrenia: A Developmental Approach to the Study of Disturbed Language Behavior." Unpublished Ph.D. thesis, Clark University, 1953.

2. BARRON, D. H. "Genetic Neurology and the Behavior Problem," in P. Weiss, ed., *Genetic Neurology,* pp. 223–31. Chicago: University of Chicago Press, 1950.

3. BAYLEY, N. "Mental Growth during the First Three Years," *Genet. Psychol. Monogr.,* Vol. 14 (1933), No. 1, p. 92.

4. BERTALANFFY, L. *Modern Theories of Development.* London: Oxford University Press, 1933.

5. BRUELL, J. "Experimental Studies of Temporally Extended Perceptual Processes and the Concept of 'Aktualgenese,'" in symposium on *The Developmental Viewpoint in Perception,* A. P. A. Meetings, Washington, D. C., 1952. Mimeogr. copy, Clark University.

6. COGHILL, G. E. *Anatomy and the Problem of Behavior.* New York: Macmillan, 1929.

7. DUNCKER, K. "On Problem-solving," *Psychol. Monogr.,* Vol. 58 (1945), No. 5, pp. ix + 113.

8. DUNOÜY, P. LECOMTE. *Biological Time.* New York: Macmillan, 1937.

9. FRIEDMAN, H. "Perceptual Regression in Schizophrenia: An Hypothesis Suggested by the Use of the Rorschach Test," *J. Genet. Psychol.,* Vol. 81 (1952), pp. 63–98.

10. GOTTSCHALDT, K. "Aufbau des Kindlichen Handelns," *Schrift. Entwickl. Psychol.,* Vol. 1 (1954), p. 220. Leipzig: Barth.

11. HALL, G. S. *Life and Confessions of a Psychologist.* New York: Appleton, 1923.

12. HEMMENDINGER, L. "A Genetic Study of Structural Aspects of Perception as Reflected in Rorschach Responses." Unpublished Ph.D. thesis, Clark University, 1951.

13. HILGARD, E. R. *Theories of Learning.* New York: Appleton, 1948.

14. HUXLEY, J. *Evolution.* London: Allen & Unwin, 1944.

15. KAPLAN, B. "A Comparative Study of Acquisition of Meanings in Low-Educated and High-Educated Adults." Unpublished M.A. thesis, Clark University, 1950.

16. KOHLER, I. *Über Aufbau und Wandlungen der Wahrnehmungswelt.* Wien: Rudolph M. Rohrer, 1951.

17. ———. "Umgewöhnung im Wahrnehmungsbereich," *Die Pyramide,* Vol. 5 (1953), pp. 92–95, Vol. 6 (1953), pp. 109–13.

18. KROGH, U. "The Actual-Genetic Model of Perception-Personality," *Stud. Psychol. Paedag.,* Series altera, Vol. 7 (1955), p. 394. Lund: Gleerup.

19. KRUGER, A. "Direct and Substitute Modes of Tension-Reduction in terms of Developmental Level: An Experimental Analysis by means of the Rorschach Test." Unpublished Ph.D. thesis, Clark University, 1955.

20. LANE, J. E. "Social Effectiveness and Developmental Level," *J. Personal.,* Vol. 23 (1955), pp. 274–84.

21. LASHLEY, K. S. "Persistent Problems in the Evolution of Mind," *Quart. Rev. Biol.,* Vol. 24 (1949), pp. 28–42.

22. LEWIS, M. M. *Infant Speech.* New York: Harcourt, 1936.

23. LILLIE, R. S. "Biology and Unitary Principle," *Philos. Sci.,* Vol. 18 (1951), pp. 193–207.

24. MIRIN, B. "A Study of the Formal Aspects of Schizophrenic Verbal Communication," *Genet.*

Psychol. Monogr., Vol. 52 (1955), No. 2, pp. 149–90.

25. MISCH, R. "The Relationship of Motoric Inhibition to Developmental Level and Ideational Functioning: An Analysis by means of the Rorschach Test." Unpublished Ph.D. thesis, Clark University, 1953.

26. NEEDHAM, A. E. *Regeneration and Wound Healing.* New York: Wiley, 1952.

27. NOVIKOFF, A. B. "The Concept of Integrative Levels and Biology," *Science,* Vol. 101 (1945), pp. 209–15.

28. PEÑA, C. "A Genetic Evaluation of Perceptual Structurization in Cerebral Pathology," *J. Proj. Tech.,* Vol. 17 (1953), pp. 186–99.

29. PHILLIPS, L., and J. FRAMO. "Developmental Theory Applied to Normal and Psychopathological Perception," *J. Personal.,* Vol. 22 (1954), pp. 464–74.

30. PIAGET, J. *Play, Dreams, and Imitation in Childhood.* New York: Norton, 1951.

31. RAPAPORT, D. "The Conceptual Model of Psychoanalysis," *J. Personal.,* Vol. 20 (1951), pp. 56–81.

32. RUSSELL, E. S. *Form and Function.* London: Murray, 1916.

33. ————. *The Directiveness of Organic Activities.* Cambridge: Cambridge University Press, 1945.

34. SANDER, F. "Experimentelle Ergebenisse der Gestalt Psychologie," *Bar. ü.d. Kongr. f. Exper. Psychol.,* Vol. 10 (1928), pp. 23–87.

35. SCHNEIRLA, T. C. "A Consideration of some Conceptual Trends in Comparative Psychology." *Psychol. Bull.,* Vol. 6 (1952), pp. 559–97.

36. ————. "Problems in the Biopsychology of Social Organization," *J. Abn. and Soc. Psychol.,* Vol. 41 (1946), pp. 385–402.

37. SCHROEDINGER, E. *What is Life?* Cambridge: Cambridge University Press, 1951.

38. SIEGEL, E. L. "Genetic Parallels of Perceptual Structurization in Paranoid Schizophrenia." Unpublished Ph.D. thesis, Clark University, 1950.

39. SIMPSON, G. G. *The Meaning of Evolution.* New Haven: Yale University Press, 1950.

40. WEISS, P. *Principles of Development.* New York: Holt, 1939.

41. WERNER, H. "Process and Achievement," *Harvard Educ. Rev.,* Vol. 7 (1937), pp. 353–68.

42. ————. "Musical Microscales and Micromelodies," *J. Psychol.,* Vol. 10 (1940), pp. 149–56.

43. ————. "Experimental Genetic Psychology," in P. Harriman, ed., *Encyclopedia of Psychology,* pp. 219–35. New York: Philosophical Library, 1944.

44. ————. *Comparative Psychology of Mental Development,* rev. ed. Chicago: Follet, 1948.

45. ————, ed. *On Expressive Language.* Worcester: Clark University Press, 1955.

46. ————. "Microgenesis in Aphasia," *J. Abn. and Soc. Psychol.,* Vol. 52 (1956), pp. 347–53.

47. ————, and B. KAPLAN. "The Developmental Approach to Cognition: Its Relevance to the Psychological Interpretation of Anthropological and Ethnolinguistic Data." Mimeogr. paper, Clark University, 1955.

48. ————. "The Acquisition of Word Meanings: A Developmental Study," *Monogr. Soc. Res. Child Developm.,* Vol. 15 (1952), No. 1, p. 120.

49. ————, and S. WAPNER. "The Innsbruck Studies on Distorted Visual Fields in Relation to an Organismic Theory of Perception," *Psychol. Rev.,* Vol. 62 (1955), pp. 130–38.

50. WINDLE, W. F., and J. E. FITZGERALD. "Development of the Spinal Reflex Mechanism in Human Embryos," *J. Comp. Neurol.,* Vol. 67 (1937), pp. 493–509.

An Age-Irrelevant Concept of Development

Donald M. Baer

It seems clear that the great majority of developmental psychologists study children. Many of this majority study children almost exclusively. Thus one meaning of developmental psychology may be, quite simply, *child psychology:* the behavioral characteristics of children, the processes responsible for these characteristics, and their future consequences. Of course, most psychologists characterize themselves and their journals by the processes they study, rather than their usual experimental subject. Thus we have physiological, sensory, perceptual, and clinical psychology, rather than monkey, rat, pigeon, or ambulatory-schizophrenic psychology. However, this need not be an important objection to the concept of child psychology.

The equation of developmental psychology with child psychology has other problems. The most striking of these is the heterogeneity of children, such that a child psychology derived from the study of infants will be quite different in many ways than that derived from ten-year-olds. One solution to the possibly unmanageable diversity of child psychology is to concentrate on a particular sub-child psychology, on the grounds, perhaps, of the intrinsic fascination of this type, or more prosaically, its availability.

There is another way to respond to the apparently unmanageable diversity of child psychology. Any diversity can be managed if it can be cataloged in a systematic manner, and if the cataloging system itself is not too diverse. Child psychologists have noted that the age of the child is exactly such a cataloging device. It is a simple linear dimension, based exclusively upon time. Time is an operationally definable concept. A technology has been aimed at its precise definition for some centuries. However, child psychology has rarely required this sort of accuracy. It has found it more than sufficient simply to note the daily sunsets and mediate their succession with a calendar, to produce a useful concept of age.

The basic virtue of age, however, is that it really does manage the diversity of child behavior.

Donald M. Baer, "An Age-Irrelevant Concept of Development," *Merrill-Palmer Quarterly of Behavior and Development, 16,* 1970, pp. 238–245.

It organizes the differences between infants and ten-year-olds by laying them out ten points away from one another on a scale of years. More important than that, it makes the ten-year-old look like he belongs in the same textbook with the infant, simply by presenting the behavior of one-year-olds, two-year-olds, three-year-olds, and all other children of intermediate age, *in order*. An ordering by age, it appears, is at the same time an ordering on many other dimensions of behavior: elaboration, precision, complexity, strength, amount, variety, and internal organization.

Consequently, a new psychology emerges: *age psychology* replaces, or subsumes, child psychology. The age-cataloging psychologist does not restrict himself to the study of a single sub-type of child so as to avoid diversity. His essential technique is the ordering of that diversity, and the more diversity, the better his chance to note its orderliness. He studies children only because they represent a condition of the organism in which a great deal of behavior does in fact vary in an orderly way. Typically, as age increases beyond childhood, behavior change becomes less thoroughly ordered by it, and the interest of the age psychologist wanes correspondingly. Late in life, age change may again take on a powerful function in correlating with behavior change; thus a developmental psychology, concerning this time of senescence, again is possible. Furthermore, the target of the age psychologist is that period in *any* organism when age change orders behavior change. Thus he may study young monkeys rather than young children, and still speak to a warmly receptive Society for Research in Child Development.

The research design of the age psychologist consequently has a single distinctive feature: the age of his subjects is an organizing variable in his studies. What worries me is that my own studies do not include age as an independent variable. Even so, I feel strongly that they are developmental studies. They use environmental variation, they achieve a certain control over behavior, and they are aimed *exactly* at developmental change —but they do not include age as a variable.

Let me begin to defend the developmental character of my own studies by pointing to someone else's instead. In 1958, Wendell Jeffrey pub-

lished a report which greatly clarified my own partially formulated ideas about development. (However, let it be clear that Jeffrey cannot be blamed for any errors I commit in response to his design.) His study (1958) was concerned with mediational processes in children. As a case in point, he had examined the ability of four-year-old children to discriminate left from right. The left-right discrimination was embodied in two stimulus cards, each a picture of a stick figure pointing either to its left or to its right. The child was asked to learn that the figure pointing off to the left was called "Jack"; the one pointing off to the right, "Jill." The left-right difference was the only stimulus dimension distinguishing the cards. The children were shown these cards in a random order and were reinforced for correct naming. It seems clear that older *S*s, say seven-year-olds, could have learned this task quite readily. Jeffrey's four-year-olds, however, did not; as a group, they largely remained at chance levels of guessing, even after 80 trials. Thus, it begins to qualify as developmental research: an age difference could organize a major difference in the response of children to a given teaching technique. All that is missing is the actual testing of some seven-year-olds.

Jeffrey, however, continued with the four-year-olds who did not learn to discriminate left from right—Jack from Jill. He presented them with a slightly different problem to learn. Showing them the same cards while they were seated at a table, he asked them not to name the cards, but instead to make a distinctive motor response to each figure. In response to the card pointing off to their left, the children were to reach out to their left and touch a pushbutton mounted on the left side of the table-top. In response to the card pointing off to their right, the children were to reach out to their right and touch a pushbutton mounted on the right side of the table-top. The four-year-olds who had failed to make different *verbal* responses to the figures now quickly learned to make different *reaching* responses to them.

I think it worthwhile to point out that this phase of the study was not developmental research according to the criterion of age. The children were still four years old. All that had been shown was that with these techniques, these four-year-olds could discriminate particular motor responses to certain stimuli but could not discriminate particular verbal responses to them.

After the children had learned the correct reaching response to each of the stick figures, they were once again returned to the original naming problem. But now most of the children learned the discrimination quite readily.

Let me assume that control groups of four-year-olds who were given some innocuous activity during a break between two sessions with the Jack and Jill problem would still have failed to learn the discrimination during the second session. Let me also assume that a certain self-selection by Jeffrey's subjects did not alter the outcome of the study in any significant way. Those are not the kinds of design characteristics which I want to discuss. What I want to emphasize is that by the end of the study, the four-year-olds apparently had *developed*. They were not older than at the beginning, but their Jack and Jill learning behavior had become functionally like that of seven-year-olds. Jeffrey may well have shown us an effective developmental mechanism. The first part of his study had suggested that if a four-year-old who cannot solve the left-right problem is simply allowed to grow three years older, he will probably be able to solve it then. What is it that happens during those years? Obviously, various processes of development go on; but the demonstration of an age difference is not thereby the demonstration of one or more of these developmental processes. On the other hand, the second and third parts of Jeffrey's study point to exactly an environmental process which *can* produce that delightful ability of a seven-year-old to tell his Jack from his Jill.

It may be asked: is that what happens during the three years? Do four-year-olds begin to discriminate motor responses to stimuli differing on various left-right dimensions, such that about three years later the Jack and Jill problem will be one they can easily mediate with some already existing part of their repertoire? I don't know, of course. What Jeffrey's study tells us is that such a mechanism is a demonstrated possibility. It is not merely logical; it is feasible.

In my opinion, Jeffrey's design is the essence of developmental research: it describes a *possible process* of development. In my opinion, it is the process of development, not merely the *outcome* of development, which should be our subject matter.

Consequently, I have one more suggestion to make about Jeffrey's design. The "missing" part of it should not be considered essential to its status as developmental research. That missing part was the demonstration that seven-year-olds could learn the left-right discrimination quite readily. With this study, restricted entirely to four-year-olds, it seems to me that we know exactly as much about a developmental process relevant to left-right discrimination as we could learn from a larger design including seven-year-olds. The age difference is irrelevant to the developmental process displayed in the study. The only children in whom we know that this process operated are the four-year-olds of the study. Seven-year-olds are an essentially mysterious group; we do not know what process gives them their ability to make left-right discriminations. Hence the developmental aspects of the study, as I see them, are restricted to the actual study, in which age was *not* a variable.

Let me move to a different study, which also combines developmental and non-developmental aspects. In this case, I am referring to an unpublished study by Jill McCleave, conducted at the University of Washington a few years ago as her senior honors thesis. I advised her, and did so on the assumption that development is largely an age-irrelevant concept.

Jill studied a single child. He was enrolled in the University's Laboratory Preschool, and was a much-studied boy. During most of his early years, he had suffered from cataracts. In addition to a good deal of visual deprivation, he had developed tantrum and self-destructive behaviors which were so severe that they effectively overcame all efforts of his parents to control and teach him. Montrose Wolf, Todd Risley, and Haydon Mees undertook the extinction of his tantrum and other destructive behaviors; shaped the behavior of wearing glasses; elaborated his verbal repertoire; set up the rudiments of ordinary social control; returned the child permanently to his home from the institution in which he had been confined; and trained his parents in certain techniques of maintaining and extending these repertoires (1965). The child was then enrolled in preschool, largely to build and elaborate a repertoire of social interaction with other children—a class of behaviors which, initially, he lacked almost completely. While he was there, it seemed reasonable to do something about the effects of his early visual deprivation, so that he might be able to learn to read when he entered the public school's special education system the next year. Jill McCleave took on that project. Essentially, she meant to develop discriminations of small, complex visual stimuli, eventually culminating in letter recognition. She used a variety of reinforcers, ranging from social to ice cream, choosing whatever worked well at the time.

Much of this training went along quite smoothly. Some of it went so well that I would not insist on calling it developmental research. If it needs a systematic label, it could be called the discrimination of differentiated verbal operants to visual stimuli by differential reinforcement, or, in simpler terms, calling an "A" an "A" and not a "V," calling a "Y" a "Y" and not an "X," and the like. When I was a boy, we called that learning. Subsequently, I have found that reinforcement, punishment, extinction, discrimination, and differentiation are better defined terms. However, one may use "learning" as an inclusive term to refer to any combination of the previously mentioned processes which produce behavior change.

Jill McCleave found that most of the letters were quickly learned by the boy. That is, she set up reinforcement and extinction contingencies for the verbal responses he might make to various letters. For the most part, these contingencies produced their usual effects, and the correct verbal response soon was attached only to the corresponding letter. That could be called development. But it is also called the discrimination of differentiated verbal operants to visual stimuli through differential reinforcement, or learning; and still another label seems the last thing that anyone would need.

However, in a few instances, the reinforcement and extinction contingencies did *not* produce the expected effect. The letter "C," for example, could be chosen from a group of letters when asked for, but was as likely to be put down backward as forward. The boy did not discriminate a forward C from a backward C,

even when differentially reinforced for doing so. Similarly, he had trouble with a few letters, and the classic confusion between lower case "b" and "d," and "p" and "q," seemed very likely in his future reading. To avoid this, Jill resorted to techniques other than the standard learning procedures she had used so far, and the outcome appeals to me as another example of clearly developmental research.

First, she began showing the boy displays of five letters at a time. Four of the letters were forward C's, and the fifth was a backward C. He was asked to choose the letter that was different. The position of the backward C among the four ordinary C's varied randomly from trial to trial, of course. Under these conditions, despite differential reinforcement, the boy repeatedly failed to discriminate forward C's from backward C's. He showed a similar failure to discriminate a few other letters in their forward and backward orientations. Yet, at the same time, he was quickly mastering all other letters of the alphabet in this type of problem, and so his specific failures could not be attributed to a general ineffectiveness of the learning techniques being used. Consequently, Jill had to try something else.

She introduced displays in which the backward C was appreciably larger than the forward C's. The boy immediately achieved perfect discrimination. Therefore, on successive presentations, randomly varying the position of the backward C, Jill had its size shrink until it was the same size as the ordinary C's. The boy continued to discriminate perfectly until the last stage, when all C's were the same size; he then reverted to his usual chance level. Jill had to try something else again.

She introduced displays containing four ordinary C's and an "O." A "C," of course, is simply an "O" with a gap in its perimeter on the right side. However, the boy could discriminate C's from O's, and immediately reached perfect performance. Now, Jill began to degrade the O in the direction of a backward C: she presented displays in which a very small gap was opened on the left side of the O. That made it a backward C, but one which was very like an O. The boy continued to discriminate perfectly. As the presentations proceeded, the gap in the O-like backward C gradually opened and became the standard backward C. Nevertheless, the boy's discrimination remained perfect. Thus, at the end of one session of these trials, he was performing a problem at which he had consistently failed for many previous sessions. Now Jill examined him again on the other letters which previously he had failed to discriminate in their forward or backward orientations. All of them were immediately discriminated, without any special techniques of training being applied to them. Perhaps some pattern of visual inspection of small forms was developed in the "C" exercise which generalized to the other problems. At any rate, this is another example of what I am calling developmental research.

Now, I can better generalize this age-irrelevant concept of development, and perhaps I can contrast it to learning at the same time. I argued previously that the mere demonstration of a behavior change over time was unsatisfyingly mysterious to me. I wanted to know the process which produced the change, not just its outcome or its typical calendar schedule. Learning procedures, in their considerable variety, are exactly behavior-changing processes. But they need not be called developmental processes for two reasons. One is that they already have names which are considerably more precise than "learning" and tremendously more precise than "development." The other is that a particular learning procedure may not produce its expected effect in an organism, *unless it occurs at the right time.* Jeffrey's study and McCleave's study both showed just that. But both studies also showed that the "right time" was not an age, but a point in a sequence of experiences. Both studies also used nothing but learning procedures: patterns of reinforcement, punishment, extinction, differentiation, and discrimination, in general. Such procedures take time to produce their effects, *but they do not take much time.* Consequently, even sequences of these procedures will not take much time. In my opinion, they rarely will take enough time to require calendar-sized units for their application. At least, they will not require much time if they are applied promptly, one after another, in the effective sequence. Consequently, age has no relevance to development; sequence, or *program,* has.

The natural environment should not be ex-

pected to apply a correct sequence of learning procedures to the typical organism in the quickest possible order. The natural environment very likely exposes an organism to a great variety of learning procedures, almost constantly. Within its pattern of presentation, many correct sequences no doubt are imbedded—as are many *more* incorrect sequences. Natural sequencing thus is often inefficient sequencing. Jeffrey's four-year-olds required only about half an hour to become functionally similar to seven-year-olds in a particular left-right problem, when their instructor knew what he was about. It is illuminating that natural sequencing takes something approaching three years. If such findings are general, it would indicate that the age-based concept of development reflects two things: very poor programming by nature, and a thorough ignorance of how to do better in the age-cataloging psychologist. That ignorance, I think, is not likely to be improved by institutionalizing nature's bad programming into an age-based concept of development. If I am right, a great deal of that aging is a thorough waste of time.

This age-irrelevant concept of development hence is simply a sequence-relevant, or sequence-dependent, concept of learning. Both Freud and Piaget make heavy use of the same idea, but in two tremendously different ways. Both seem to rely upon sequential processes which are unrealistically slow, in my opinion. Those lazy successions of their stages simply do not remind me of the changes that are seen in organisms whose environments press them toward development. This is especially true when the organism's environment is under constant experimental analysis by an investigator who *knows* that it need not take this long. Freud and Piaget also do not seem to envision any reasonable *variety* of effective environmental sequences. It seems to me implicit in modern behavioral technology that there must be quite some number of environmental programs, or sequences, which will bring an organism to any specified developmental outcome. This is a very happy characteristic, I suggest, if it is a correct one. It allows for alternative programs of instruction when a particular one is not possible; thus it suggests that behaviorally, it is rarely too late—or too early—for a good outcome.

Looking back over this argument, it must be apparent that it derives from the typically quick effects produced by learning procedures, such that even programs or sequences of them will not require enough time to justify measurement in terms of age. I am sure it is clear that I rely upon learning mechanisms because they are the ones that I know something about. If there are other important and unavoidable mechanisms of behavior change which intrinsically require much more time to produce their effects, then my argument fails to that extent. Learning technology, as I know it, is comprehensive, powerful, flexible, and readily amenable to experimental study and to practical application. Consequently, it seems thoroughly reasonable to build a concept of development squarely upon that technology. The concept that results—to summarize it for the final time—is that to produce certain behavioral changes, the procedures of learning technology, which ordinarily work in isolation, in this case may be effective only if applied in a correct sequence to a well-chosen series of behaviors. There must be many such sequences for any specified behavioral outcome; and the sequences are not intrinsically lengthy in time. Thus, development is behavior change which requires programming; and programming requires time, but not enough of it to call it age. That, I think, is exactly what Sidney Bijou and I had in mind when, in our first volume of a book called *Child Development* (1961), we defined development as "progressive changes in the way an organism's behavior interacts with the environment" (p. 1). Development in this argument is based upon learning, but is slightly super-ordinate to learning, as a concept. If anyone feels that the programming of learning procedures is so slightly super-ordinate to the learning procedures themselves that it does not deserve the status of a separate concept, that will not distress me at all. And if anyone should suggest that programming is, in fact, *sub*ordinate to the concept of learning, again I shall not be disturbed. Perhaps that is why the program for this symposium suggests that I will present a *learning* concept, in contrast to Eugene Gollin's presentation of a *developmental* concept.

REFERENCES

BIJOU, S. W. & BAER, D. M. *Child development.* Vol. I. New York: Appleton-Century-Crofts, 1961.

JEFFREY, W. E. Variables in early discrimination learning: I. Motor responses in the training of left-right discrimination. *Child Develpm,* 1958, 29, 269-275.

KESSEN, W. Research design in the study of developmental problems. Chapter 2 in P. H. Mussen (Ed.), *Handbook of research methods in child development.* New York: Wiley, 1960.

WOLF, M. M., RISLEY, T. R., & MEES, H. Application of operant conditioning procedures to the behavior problems of an autistic child. *Behav. Res. Ther.,* 1964, 1, 305-312.

Part 2

Early Development

In discussing human development, we tend to look more closely at biological factors (the role of heredity, the structure of the organism) in the early stages than in the later stages of life. This tendency stems in part from the fact that human beings appear to be biologically much more similar at birth than later in life. But this appearance can be deceptive, since it is based on limited information about psychological conditions prior to birth. Moreover, we largely ignore the impact of genetic factors on later stages of life, while stressing these factors in studies of infancy.

The articles in this section are meant to achieve two objectives. First, they emphasize the importance and intricacy of biological controls, and, second, they indicate the ways in which these influences enter into the extremely autonomous psychological life of the infant from the very beginning. The nature of the child's emotional development, and even the role played by his earliest schema of self, are touched by subtle biological influences. Biological differences in infants' responses are explored in the first two papers: Hutt's article reviews behavioral differences between boys and girls; the second, by Schaffer and Emerson, explores differences in infants' reactions to physical contact. Following these is a recent article by Lewis and Brooks-Gunn which suggests a radical shift in the way we have been conceptualizing the infant's attachment relationships and its stranger anxieties. It had been assumed that these were mainly a matter of the child's relationship to the mother. Now we see that the child's own perception of himself must be reckoned as a key element as well. In the last paper, Wolff examines the basic concepts in Piaget's sensorimotor theory of intelligence and raises serious questions about their adequacy in accounting for the affective life.

Sex Differences in Human Development

Corinne Hutt

During the past two decades there has been a regrettable silence on the subject of sex differences in human development in the psychological literature. What reports there were, clearly influenced by the 'Psychosexual-neutrality-at-birth' theory [Diamond, 1965], dealt mainly with questions of sex-role identification, sex-role adoption, learning of appropriate sex-role behaviours, and so on.

Two timely rebukes were administered recently by Garai and Scheinfeld [1968] and Carlson and Carlson [1960]. Each pair of authors was lamenting the lack of attention paid to sex differences in their own field—the former in developmental psychology and the latter in social psychology. They noted that in each area a large number of studies failed to look for sex differences; others used single-sex samples, and some were even unaware of the sex of their subjects.

Based, in part, on a paper read to the Annual Conference of the British Psychological Society, Exeter, 1971, in a symposium on 'The biological bases of psychological sex differences' convened by the author.

Since these two areas account for a substantial proportion of psychological research undertaken, the neglect of sex differences seems to have been particularly regrettable.

A turning-point in this trend was the publication in 1966 of the book 'The development of sex differences' edited by Eleanor Maccoby. Although still reflecting a predominantly 'psychosexual-neutrality-at-birth' orientation, it nevertheless brought to light a large amount of incriminating evidence. Then followed the third edition of 'The psychology of human differences' [Tyler, 1965] which contained a cogent review of cognitive sex differences, and more recently, the impressive monograph by Garai and Scheinfeld [1968]. Since then, and given an ironic fillip by the Women's Liberation Movement no doubt, many reports acknowledging the presence of sex differences have once again appeared in the literature. It is notable that, since its inception two years ago, the journal 'Developmental Psychology' has contained one or more reports on sex differences in nearly every issue.

Corinne Hutt: Sex Differences in Human Development. *Human Development, 15:* 153–170 (1972).

In many ways, however, psychological sex differences are the tip of the iceberg. By the time differences in behaviour and performance manifest themselves, so much differentiation has already taken place. As contributors to the symposium on 'The biological bases of psychological sex differences' made only too clear, many of these differences are determined from the moment an ovum is fertilised by a sperm carrying an X or a Y chromosome. Possession of a Y chromosome, for example, confers a particular flavour on the development of the male zygote and embryo—an effect more pervasive than would result from simply the determination of masculinity [Ounsted and Taylor, 1972]. Subsequently, the gonadal hormones exert their organisational influence on reproductive structures and, more significantly, on the central nervous system [Harris, 1964, 1970; Levine, 1966; Whalen, 1968; Hutt, 1972a; Michael, 1971].

In this paper, therefore, I would like to discuss some empirical results of behavioural and intellectual sex differences in early human development in the context of what is known about the biological determination of such differences.

Embryological Development

As Garai and Scheinfeld [1968] point out, from the moment of conception males and females exhibit radically different patterns of development. The neuroendocrinological processes and their influence on early development are essentially the same in all placental mammals and these have been adequately described elsewhere [Harris, 1964, 1970; Gorski and Wagner, 1965; Whalen, 1968; Hutt, 1972a].

The most notable feature of mammalian development is that there is no *neuter* sex. In the presence of a Y chromosome, the male gonad differentiates and then produces the androgenic evocator substance which exerts its action upon hypothalamic centres to produce the acyclic pattern of gonadotrophic hormone release characteristic of the male. In the absence of a Y chromosome, or more specifically, early androgenic influence, the natural propensity of mammalian creatures is to differentiate as *females*. This is so even in the case of a genetic male in

whom, due to early castration or some disorder, the testicular hormone is absent or ineffective. Such an instance occurs in humans in the syndrome of testicular feminisation, where, due to a recessive disorder, the testes of the genetic male often develop in an inguinal hernia and the gonadal hormone, if produced at all, is without effect [Federman, 1967]. This individual differentiates as a female. Conversely, in the presence of androgens during the critical period, even the genetic female will differentiate as a male, as happens in the case of the adrenogenital syndrome [Wilkins, 1962; Bongiovanni and Root, 1963; Federman, 1967]. Curiously, in the absence of *any* gonadal hormone, the development might be described as excessively 'feminine': this happens in the case of Turner's syndrome, where one sex chromosome is lacking, the karyotype being XO, and there is gonadal dysgenesis. The comparison of behavioural and psychological features in androgenised females and in cases of Turner's syndrome made by Money and Erhardt [1968] is most instructive.

The particular interest of the processes and determinants of sexual differentiation to psychologists lies in the fact that it is not merely the reproductive structures which are organised in a typically male or female pattern, but higher neural centres as well. Characteristic differences appear, therefore, in patterns of sexual behaviour as well as in non-sexual behaviour. The behavioural differences are particularly striking in the higher mammals, namely, the primates [see Hamburg and Lunde, 1966; Goy, 1966, 1968, for informative reviews].

Physical Growth, Maturation and Susceptibility

From very early in uterine life males show their characteristic vulnerability: on average 120 males are conceived for every 100 females and by term this ratio has decreased to 110:100 [Glenister, 1956]. The majority of spontaneous abortions (miscarriages), therefore, are of male foetuses [Stevenson and McClarin, 1957]. In terms of live births the ratio is only 106:100, which indicates a greater male susceptibility to perinatal complications such as anoxia [Stevenson,

1966; Stevenson and Bobrow, 1967]. Throughout life males remain more vulnerable to a variety of disorders, e.g., cerebral palsy, viral infections, ulcers, coronary thrombosis and some forms of mental illness [Taylor and Ounsted, 1972; Garai, 1970]. In fact the male's longevity is so curtailed that by the 6th and 7th decades of life the sex ratio is reversed in favour of the females. The sex-linked recessive disorders like haemophilia and colour-blindness predominantly affect the males; the recessive genes being carried on the X chromosome, males manifest the disorder even in the heterozygotic condition, whereas females are protected, other than in the homozygous condition, by the normal allele on the other X chromosome. The adage of the male being the stronger sex requires a very literal interpretation indeed.

At birth, males are heavier and longer than females [Ounsted, 1972]. From infancy on boys have a consistently higher basal metabolism and greater vital capacity, develop proportionately larger hearts and lungs, and have a higher concentration of haemoglobin, notably after puberty [Hutt, 1972]. Moreover, the male hormone facilitates protein synthesis whereas the female hormones have no such direct action. All these features characterise the male for a more active and strenuous life.

In sharp contrast to his physical advantages, however, is the male's developmental retardation: growth velocity lags nearly 2 years behind the female's [Tanner, 1970], bone ossification is completed much later [see Hutt, 1972b] and puberty is attained about 2½ years after the girl [Nicholson and Hanley, 1953]. The onset of walking and talking, as well as aspects of dentition occur earlier in girls than in boys. In terms of maturity the newborn girl is equivalent to a 4- to 6-week-old boy [Garai and Scheinfeld, 1968].

Behaviour Differences in Infancy

MOTOR ACTIVITY AND
SENSORY CAPACITIES

In general, male newborn infants exhibit more spontaneous motor activity and this consists predominantly of gross movements, whereas the activity of the female infants consists typically of finer movements, largely of the facial area, e.g., mouthing, smiling or sucking [Korner, 1969]. Female neonates have lower tactual and pain thresholds [Lipsitt and Levy, 1959] and this sex difference very probably obtains throughout the lifespan since Galton observed it in adults and specifically commented upon it as early as 1894. Female infants also react more irritably to tactual stimulation [Bell and Costello, 1964].

There is now substantial evidence that the visual acuity of males is superior to that of females, at least from adolescence on [Burg and Hulbert, 1961], whereas females have better auditory discrimination and localisation [Corso, 1959; Schaie et al., 1964]. The results obtained by Lewis suggest that such sensory proficiency and preferences may be evident even in early infancy: he found that male infants showed greater interest in visual patterns generally, while female infants attended more to auditory sequences [Kagan and Lewis, 1965]; of visual patterns female infants found *facial* configurations most interesting and at 3, 6 and 9 months of age they were able to differentiate between such patterns more effectively than the males [Lewis, 1969].

On the basis of results obtained from 3-month-old infants, Moss and Robson [1970] concluded that, whereas social experience and learning appeared to have a strong influence upon the visual behaviour of females, that of the males was more a function of endogenous attributes like state. These several results illustrate not merely the sex-dependent sensory capacities but also the differences in those influences to which they are amenable. Such differences, however, are not peculiar to the human species—very similar behaviour is shown by monkeys [Mitchell and Brandt, 1970].

The early dependence on particular sensory modalities has the consequence that auditory and visual stimuli have different reinforcing properties, depending on the sex of the subject. For instance, Watson [1969] found that visual fixation on a target could be operantly conditioned in 14-week-old infants, the effective reinforcers being visual for males and auditory for females. Moreover, the boys failed to learn under conditions of auditory reinforcement. This reliance of males and females on visual and auditory channels, respectively, is observable throughout childhood and adolescence [Stevenson et al., 1963] and persists in adulthood [Miller, 1963; Pishkin and Shurley, 1965].

MOTHER-INFANT INTERACTION

The earliest social behaviour displayed by the human infant is in the context of the mother-infant interaction. Many studies reporting differences in the way mothers handle their male and female infants, or for that matter, any sex differences in human behaviour, tend to account for such differences in terms of the mothers' expectations of a son or a daughter, of her greater affinity for the same-sex infant, or else in terms of the reinforcement of sex-appropriate behaviours. A study by Moss [1967] is notable, therefore, for the demonstration that considerable differences in the behaviour of male and female infants exist at the age of 3 weeks. The differential reactions of the mother are very probably contingent upon these behaviours and not contrariwise, as commonly supposed. Two of Moss' findings seem particularly significant, especially since they were also apparent at the age of 3 months: mothers stimulated their infant sons more, and imitated the vocalisations of their daughters more. The first of these raises the interesting possibility that we may have here the human analogue of the 'early-handled' animals described by Levine [1960], Denenberg [1964] and others. If such findings are replicated, we may seriously have to inquire whether the early experience of male infants in any way contributes to their subsequent lower emotionality [Gray, 1971a; Gray and Buffery, 1971; Buffery and Gray, 1972]. Secondly, the fact that mothers imitated, and thereby very probably reinforced, their daughters' vocalisations is surprising, since the actual amounts of vocalisation by boys and by girls were almost identical. Since a similar finding was also reported by Goldberg and Lewis [1969], it immediately raises the question as to what parameters of infants' vocal behaviour the mothers were responding. May this fact also explain, in part, the earlier acquisition of speech in girls?

Goldberg and Lewis [1969] were able to demonstrate striking sex differences in infants of 13 months, both in their behaviour towards their mothers as well as in the character of their play. Girls were more reluctant than boys to leave their mothers, tended to stay near them when playing and sought physical reassurance more frequently.

FEAR

Analysing data from the Berkeley Growth Study, Bronson [1969] found sex-differences in the onset of the fear-of-stranger reaction: fear at 10–15 months was positively correlated with fear and shyness at a later age in *boys* but not in girls. This was chiefly due to a sub-group of boys who showed a precocious onset of fear (4–6 months) and remained so throughout childhood. Thus, an early onset of fear-of-novelty in male infants was predictive of fearfulness during the entire pre-school period.

Behavioural Differences in Childhood

SOCIAL INTERACTIONS

In an investigation of the types of activity boys and girls generally engaged in [Brindley et al., 1972], it was found that girls engaged in social interactions much more frequently than boys— a dramatic illustration of the early differentiation of masculine and feminine interests, boys being interested in objects or 'things' and girls in people [Little, 1968]. Honzik [1951] and Hattwick [1937] observed very similar differences in older children, as did Farrell [1957].

More specifically, *aggression* is an aspect of social behaviour that has interested many students of child behaviour and a number of studies have shown boys to be more aggressive than girls [Green, 1933; Dawe, 1934; Jersild and Markey, 1935; Hattwick, 1937; Walters et al., 1957; Jegard and Walters, 1960; Bandura et al., 1963; Digman, 1963; Pederson and Bell, 1970]. Many of these results, however, were interpreted in terms of sex-role expectations and conventions, with no reference made to the fact that the males of most mammalian species are more aggressive than the females, nor was surprise expressed at the apparent universality of male aggression—despite differences in culture-patterns, conventions and social norms. In our own study of nursery school children [Brindley *et al.,* 1972], we found that two thirds of all aggressive acts were initiated by boys. Moreover, not only did boys *display* more aggression, but they also *elicited* aggression. Many of such disputes arose over the possession of toys, equipment or territory. Girls, whose aggression generally found verbal expression, were equally aggressive to other girls, boys, teachers or objects. Boys retaliated more and hence prolonged such encounters whereas the girls usually submitted or else employed more devious strategies to secure their objectives [McCandless *et al.,* 1961]. These sex-dependent features of aggression are observable in older children as well as in adults. In experiments which allowed subjects to mete out punishment to a mock opponent, adults males gave bigger shocks when they thought their opponent was a male than when they thought it was a female [Buss, 1963; Taylor and Epstein, 1967]. In a similar experiment 10- and 11-year-olds, using noise as punishment, behaved exactly as the adults had done [Shortell and Biller, 1970].

Male monkeys engage in threat displays while the females show fear grimaces, and in a male monkey group the dominance hierarchy is established by the aggressive behaviour and threat displays of the ascendant male while in female groups the hierarchy is established and maintained by the submissive behaviours of the nondominant females [Angermeier *et al.,* 1968]. Thus, when the human results are considered in the general context of primate social behaviour, any purely cultural or environmental sex-role theory of sexual differentiation becomes difficult to countenance. Elsewhere [Hutt, 1972a, b] I have also presented the experimental evidence for regarding aggressive behaviour as primarily a function of the early sexual differentiation of the brain, and secondarily as an effect of circulating hormone levels.

Another aspect of early social behaviour that we studied was cooperative or mutual behaviour [Brindley *et al.,* 1972], where children joined each other, either spontaneously or at the request of one of them, to engage in some mutual activity. Girls initiated such acts much more than boys, and directed their attention in this respect predominantly towards *younger* children (chiefly girls), thus manifesting their proclivities for fulfilling a nurturant and protective role [Mischel, 1970]. This is evident in many ways: readiness to help younger ones carry things, to button pinafores or tie aprons, and to comfort a hurt or distressed child. The boys appear to show a remarkable indifference to a peer's discomfort or distress. McGrew [1972] has also described the characteristic tendency of the girls to shepherd and care for a new entrant to the nursery group, whereas boys manifest their customary indifference to such a newcomer. The boys in our study tended to direct their cooperative acts primarily towards other *older* boys, usually attempting to join a game or excursion already in progress. Similar sex-typical behaviours have been described in many infra-human primate groups too [DeVore and Jay, 1963; Harlow, 1962; Goodall, 1968].

In general, there is a marked tendency in humans—children and adults alike [Hutt, 1972; Tiger, 1969]—to interact with others of their own sex. The men's club, the officers' mess, the women's institute, all clearly have their ontogenetic origins in the kindergartens and their phylogenetic origins in diverse primate groups.

EXPLORATION AND PLAY

In the study of 13-month-old infants by Goldberg and Lewis [1969], boys were active, frequently banged toys, and showed an interest in manipulating the fixtures; girls were more sedentary, interested in combining toys and showed a preference for the toys with faces. Results essentially similar were obtained in our study of nursery school children in Reading [Brindley *et al.,* 1972]: girls chiefly engaged in sedentary activities like crayonning, cutting-out or plasticene work; boys were much more active—running, jumping and showing a marked preference for push/pull toys. Many of these sex-dependent differences were also observed by Clark *et al.* [1969] in Cambridge nursery schools.

In studies of the exploratory behaviour of

nearly 200 nursery school children, a striking finding that emerged was that boys and girls, after investigating a new toy, went on to use it in very different ways [Hutt, 1970a, b]. Boys more frequently engaged in inventive or creative play with this toy, whereas more girls than boys failed to explore at all. Objections regarding the neutrality of the toy were shown to be invalid on several grounds [Hutt, 1970b, 1972]. To a certain extent these differences are comprehensible in the context of early sexual differentiation in psychological and cognitive faculties. Girls, being advanced developmentally in many respects, at the age of 3 and 4 years are becoming increasingly proficient in verbal and social skills while boys are still actively manipulating and exploring their environment. Nevertheless, there was one other question that concerned us: were we witnessing in this situation some characteristic expression of the originality of the future creative artist or scientist? A follow-up study of these children with tests of creativity was thus indicated. Prior to this study, however, a pilot investigation was carried out, with a view to seeing how children of 7–9 years of age in British primary schools performed on such tests.

CREATIVITY AND DIVERGENT THINKING

On creativity tests like those described by Wallach and Kogan [1965], two measures can be derived: (1) the *total* number of responses given to any item, i.e., fluency; and (2) the number of *unique* responses offered for any item, i.e. originality. On testing 60 boys and 60 girls between the ages of 7 and 10 years, girls were found to score unequivocally higher than boys on the fluency measure [Bhavnani and Hutt, 1972; Hutt, 1972a]. When, however, the unique responses alone were considered there were no differences between the sexes. This was surprising in view of the fact that the number of unique responses is dependent to some extent on the total number of responses, since the former tend to be given when the more conventional responses have been exhausted [Wallach and Kogan, 1965]. Wallach and Kogan themselves make no mention of sex differences despite the fact that they obtained a significant difference in favour of the boys on one of the uniqueness measures. Hudson

[1968], on the other hand, found that sixth form boys (16 years) were more fluent than girls, but he omits any mention of the result on the originality measure. Thus, the evidence for sex-typical performances on both the fluency and originality measures is equivocal. But certainly no study has demonstrated greater originality or uniqueness in the responses of girls.

This conclusion, moreover, is concordant with other evidence, both empirical and circumstantial, which shows adult males to be considerably more divergent and creative than females. Shouksmith [1970] for instance, carried out an extensive factorial study of intelligence, reasoning, problem solving and creativity, and on the basis of his results concluded that:

'. . . males and females do not think alike. Factorially the female group is more complex than the male . . . For females a much greater range of behaviour patterns appear to be mutually exclusive categories . . . for example, we see that "creative associating" is opposed to "deductive reasoning" in women, whereas it is not so clearly opposed in men . . . true creativity depends on an ability to switch from one to the other of these as and when necessary. On this argument, one would expect to find fewer women among the ranks of truly inventive geniuses or scientific discoverers.' (pp. 188, 189.)

Again, Maccoby [1966] reported a study of Radcliffe College academics who, though of equal professional status with their male colleagues, were nevertheless considerably less productive. More circumstantially, Hudson [1966] noted that the proportion of men to women in the Royal Society (Britain's select and august scientific body) was 40 to 1. Klein [1966] found that in the physical and applied sciences the male: female ratio was considerably in excess of 50 to 1. In the aesthetic fields too, despite several decades of relative feminine liberation, it is a lamentable fact that women have not figured more prominently among the creative artists. The domestic bondage of women cannot eternally be proffered as an excuse—after all, even in less auspicious times women contributed to the literary fields.

INTELLECTUAL FUNCTIONS

The performance of the 8- and 9-year-olds on the tests of creativity also indicated that, despite their greater verbal fluency, girls were not necessarily more original than boys. Other studies suggest that verbal fluency is an aspect of language function that is dissociated from other more conceptual aspects like reasoning and comprehension. Garai and Scheinfeld [1968] for instance, provocatively concluded that though girls may acquire language earlier than boys—chiefly due to their maturational advancement—and are superior in terms of verbal fluency as well as in reading, writing and spelling, they are certainly inferior in matters of verbal comprehension, verbal reasoning, and even vocabulary. In general agreement with this conclusion, the relevant evidence was documented in an earlier review [Hutt, 1972a]. Thus, although girls are indubitably superior in the *executive* aspects of language, they seem to be less adequate in manipulating and relating verbal concepts. Very striking evidence for such a conclusion is readily obtained from the norms for verbal reasoning, spelling, and sentence length, on the differential aptitude test [Bennet *et al.*, 1959] given in Table I.

Although the position is rather more ambiguous with respect to intellectual capacities, once again the available evidence suggests that males achieve a higher verbal IQ on the WAIS and WISC than females, whereas females obtain a higher performance IQ than males. Tyler's [1965] summary statement is even more affirmative:

'Most of the available evidence seems to indicate . . . that it is in the verbal *fluency* (what Thurstone has called W) rather than in the grasp of verbal meanings (V) that females are superior . . . Comparisons of various groups of males and females on various tests, however, has also made it fairly clear that girls and women do *not* have larger vocabularies than boys and men do.' (p. 244.)

Results very similar to those noted above were also observed in younger children [Heilman, 1933; Hobson, 1947]. Even Wechsler [1941] who originally maintained that there were no sex differences, having discarded those items which differentiated between the sexes, eventually [Wechsler, 1958] conceded that:

'Our findings do confirm what poets and novelists have often asserted, and the average layman long believed, that men not only behave but *think* differently from women.'

The similarity of Shouksmith's [1970] conclusion, almost 13 years later and based on very different performances, to Wechsler's is indeed striking.

DETERMINANTS OF IQ

On the basis of data obtained from 26 boys and 27 girls in the Berkeley Growth Study, Bayley and Schaefer [1964] concluded that, whereas the intellectual capacities of boys were susceptible to environmental influences, those of girls were more genetically determined. This conclusion was based on the finding that the IQ of girls showed a higher correlation with those of their parents than boys with their parents, as well as a correlation between early maternal behaviour and child's IQ for boys but not for girls. Bayley [1966] subsequently reported other studies which had also

Table I. Norms for 3 sub-tests of the differential aptitude test for boys and girls of 2 age-groups

Age	Sex	Verbal reasoning	Language usage I, spelling	Language usage II, sentences
13	Boys	15.8	25.9	20.2
	Girls	14.6	37.9	28.6
17	Boys	29.3	59.1	40.9
	Girls	25.2	72.1	45.8

demonstrated higher parent-daughter than parent-son correlations in intellectual capacities. Maccoby [1966] regarded the Bayley and Schaefer [1964] conclusion circumspectly in the absence of other supportive evidence. From a follow-up study of 231 boys and 254 girls born in Hawaii, Werner [1969] concluded that her data did not support the Bayley-Schaefer hypothesis, but indicated a sex difference in rate of maturation in favour of the girls as well as 'a greater responsiveness of the girls to achievement demands and educational stimulation in the home in middle childhood'.

It seems to me, however, that the emphases of both Bayley and Schaefer [1964] and Werner [1969] are misplaced for the following reasons. First, the earlier maturation of the girls would determine that a polygenic ability as IQ will be fully manifested earlier in girls than in boys, thereby yielding a higher daughter-parent correlation at any age prior to adolescence. Secondly, much evidence indicates that girls lateralise many cerebral functions earlier and more effectively than males [Taylor, 1969; Buffery, 1971] and hence acquire greater proficiency in them initially. Werner's [1969] data, in fact, corroborates both these points: the discrepancy in parent-child correlations at 20 months and at 10 years was far greater for boys than for girls. Moreover, at 10 years girls showed a significant correlation on all 11 of the parental and environmental variables and boys on 10 of the 11 variables. Thirdly, evidence from longitudinal studies like those of Moore [1967] have demonstrated that in the first 8 years girls are more constrained and more predictable in their intellectual development, which takes place primarily through linguistic channels. Since the principal environmental factor associated with the IQ of the girls in Werner's [1969] study was educational stimulation, a characteristic property of which was 'enlargement of vocabulary', the higher parent-daughter correlation is predictable. The boys in Moore's study, on the other hand, showed an almost haphazard course of development—no earlier score reliably predicted any later one. There was evidence too that non-verbal experiences and skills contributed more to the IQ of boys than to that of girls. In view of all these considerations there seems little need to postulate a different genetic contribution to the IQ of girls and boys, or a differential responsiveness of boys and girls to environmental influences. It is sufficient to state the empirical observations that: (1) the IQ of girls and boys are differently constituted; (2) that the girls' IQ is manifested largely in terms of verbal skills and is, therefore, sensitive to linguistic influences; (3) that since girls mature earlier, the several genes contributing to intelligence are all expressed by an earlier age —this being evident in a more stable IQ—thus yielding a higher parent-daughter correlation during childhood than the comparable parent-son correlation.

There are many other respects in which males and females are characteristically different, but since these have been adequately outlined or discussed elsewhere [Tyler, 1965; Maccoby, 1966; Garai and Scheinfeld, 1968; Hutt, 1972a, b], enumeration of them here seems superfluous.

Concluding Discussion

The foregoing discussion of the process of sexual differentiation and the phenomena of sex differences has been an attempt to reiterate the many biological and psychological differences that characteristically differentiate males and females in our species. These particular properties have clearly been selected in accordance with, on the one hand, certain morphological features, and on the other, with the particular roles human males and females fulfil. That these morphological and functional requirements are not unique to a particular society, nor even to the human species, is evident in the fact that very similar differences are demonstrable in infra-human primate species. This fact alone makes an exclusively environmental theory of sex differences difficult to countenance. Moreover, as Buffery and Gray [1972] point out, such similarities behove us to seek a more appropriately biological explanation for the phenomena. Gray himself has discussed the endocrinological, neural and adaptive bases for sex differences in mammals generally [Gray, 1971a, b; Gray and Buffery, 1971; Buffery and Gray, 1972]. The evidence reviewed by both Gray and myself [Hutt, 1972] shows that not only is behaviour affected by circulating hormones, but that these hormones have an important formative and organisational influence on brain function and structure.

It is a common, but nonetheless fallacious, assumption that the recognition of individual differences, be they sex- or personality-dependent, is to commit oneself to a psychological or behavioural determinism. On the contrary, the recognition of such differences and their possible determinants enables individuals to modify and/or exploit environmental circumstances to profitable advantage.

The conformity and consistency of the female's behaviour in fulfilling a predominantly nurturant role, makes her a stable and reliable support for the dependent infant. Even her distractability [Garai and Scheinfeld, 1968] appears to be adaptive. In her intellectual faculties too the human female seems to have exploited those facets that ensure the optimal execution of her primary role—the maternal role. For more effective communication increasing reliance is placed on linguistic skills, and it is noteworthy that in verbal functions as in non-verbal ones, it is in *execution* that the female excels. The male on the other hand, and necessarily, excels in spatial and numerical abilities, is divergent in thought and action, and is generally superior in *conceptualisation*. The fact that such functional dimorphism exists may be unacceptable to many, but it is a dimorphism that has been uniquely successful.

REFERENCES

ANGERMEIER, W. F.; PHELPS, J. B.; MURRAY, S. and HOWANSTINE, J. Dominance in monkeys: sex differences. Psychon. Sci. *12:* 344 (1968).

BANDURA, A.; ROSS, D. and ROSS, S. A. Transmission of aggression through imitation of aggressive models. J. abnorm. soc. Psychol. *63:* 575–582 (1961).

BAYLEY, N. Developmental problems of the mentally retarded child; in PHILIPS Prevention and treatment of mental retardation (Basic Books, New York 1966).

BAYLEY, N. and SCHAEFER, E. S. Correlations of maternal and child behaviours with the development of mental abilities: data from the Berkeley Growth Study. Monogr. Soc. Res. Child Develop. *29:* 1–80 (1964).

BELL, R. Q. and COSTELLO, N. S. Three tests for sex differences in tactile sensitivity in the newborn. Biol. Neonat. *7:* 335–347 (1964).

BENNETT, G. K.; SEASHORE, H. G. and WESMAN, A. G. Differential aptitude tests. Manual, 3rd ed. (Psychological Corporation, New York 1959).

BHAVNANI, R. and HUTT, C. Divergent thinking in boys and girls. J. child Psychol. Psychiat. (1972, in press).

BONGIOVANNI, A. M. and ROOT, A. W. The adrenogenital syndrome. New Eng. J. Med. *268:* 1283 (1963).

BRINDLEY, C.; CLARKE, P.; HUTT, C.; ROBINSON, I. and WETHLI, E. Sex differences in the activities and social interactions of nursery school children; in MICHAEL and CROOK Comparative ecology and behaviour of primates (Academic Press, London 1972, in press).

BRONSON, G. W. Fear of visual novelty: developmental patterns in males and females. Develop. Psychol. *1:* 33–40 (1969).

BUFFERY, A. W. H. Sex differences in cognitive skills. Paper Ann. Conf. Brit. Psychol. Soc., Exeter; in Symp. on Biological bases of psychological sex differences (1971).

BUFFERY, A. W. H. and GRAY, J. A. Sex differences in the development of perceptual and linguistic skills; in OUNSTED and TAYLOR Gender differences—their ontogeny and significance (Churchill, London 1972).

BURG, A. and HULBERT, S. Dynamic visual acuity as related to age, sex and static acuity. J. appl. Psychol. *45:* 111–116 (1961).

BUSS, A. H. Physical aggression in relation to different frustrations. J. abnorm. soc. Psychol. *67:* 1–7 (1963).

CARLSON, E. R. and CARLSON, R. Male and female subjects in personality research. J. abnorm. soc. Psychol. *61:* 482–483 (1960).

CLARK, A. H.; WYON, S. M. and RICHARDS, M. P. Freeplay in nursery school children. J. child Psychol. Psychiat. *10:* 205–216 (1969).

CORSO, J. F. Age and sex differences in pure-tone thresholds. J. acoust. Soc. Amer. *31:* 489–507 (1959).

DAWE, H. C. An analysis of 200 quarrels of preschool children. Child Develop. *5:* 139–156 (1934).

DENENBERG, V. H. Animal studies on developmental determinants of behavioural adaptability; in HARVEY Experience, structure and adaptability, pp. 123–147 (Springer, New York 1966).

DE VORE, I. and JAY, P. Mother-infant relations in baboons and langurs; in RHEINGOLD Maternal behaviour in mammals (Wiley & Sons, 1963).

DIAMOND, M. A critical evaluation of the ontogeny of human sexual behaviour. Quart. Rev. Biol. *40:* 147–175 (1965).

DIGMAN, J. M. Principal dimensions of child personality as inferred from teachers' judgments. Child Develop. *34:* 43–60 (1963).

FARRELL, M. Sex differences in block play in early childhood education. J. educ. Res. *51:* 279–284 (1957).

FEDERMAN, M. D. Abnormal sexual development (Saunders, Philadelphia 1967).

GALTON, F. The relative sensitivity of men and women at the nape of the neck by Webster's test. Nature, Lond. *50:* 40–42 (1894).

GARAI, J. E. Sex differences in mental health. Genet. Psychol. Monogr. *81:* 123–142 (1970).

GARAI, J. E. and SCHEINFELD, A. Sex differences in mental and behavioural traits. Genet. Psychol. Monogr. *77:* 169–299 (1968).

GLENISTER, T. W. Determination of sex in early human embryos. Nature, Lond. *177:* 1135 (1956).

GOLDBERG, S. and LEWIS, M. Play behaviour in the year-old infant: early sex differences. Child Develop. *40:* 21–31 (1969).

GOODALL, J. L. VAN. The behaviour of free-living chimpanzees in the Gombi Stream Reserve. Anim. Behav. Monogr. *1:* 161–311 (1968).

GORSKI, R. A. and WAGNER, J. W. Gonadal activity and sexual differentiation of the hypothalamus. Endocrinology *76:* 226–239 (1965).

GOY, R. W. Role of androgens in the establishment and regulation of behavioural sex differences in mammals. J. anim. Sci. *25:* suppl., pp. 21–35 (1966).

GOY, R. W. Organising effects of androgen on the behaviour of rhesus monkeys; in MICHAEL Endocrinology and human behaviour (Oxford University Press, London 1968).

GRAY, J. A. Sex differences in emotional behaviour in mammals including man: endocrine bases. Acta psychol., Amst. *35:* 29–46 (1971a).

GRAY, J. A. The psychology of fear and stress (Weidenfeld and Nicolson, London 1971b).

GRAY, J. A. and BUFFERY, A. W. H. Sex differences in emotional and cognitive behaviour in mammals including man: adaptive and neural bases. Acta psychol., Amst. *35:* 89–111 (1971).

GREEN, E. H. Friendships and quarrels among preschool children. Child. Develop. *4:* 236–252 (1933).

HAMBURG, D. A. and LUNDE, D. T. Sex hormones in the development of sex differences in human behaviour; in MACCOBY The development of sex differences (Tavistock, London 1966).

HARLOW, H. F. Development of affection in primates; in BLISS Roots of behaviour (Harper, New York 1962).

HARRIS, G. W. Sex hormones, brain development and brain function. Endocrinology *75:* 627–648 (1964).

HARRIS, G. W. Hormonal differentiation of the developing central nervous system with respect to patterns of endocrine function. Philos. Trans. B *259:* 165–177 (1970).

HATTWICK, L. A. Sex differences in behavior of nursery school children. Child Develop. *8:* 343–355 (1937).

HEILMAN, J. D. Sex differences in intellectual abilities. J. educ. Psychol. *24:* 47–62 (1933).

HOBSON, J. R. Sex differences in primary mental abilities. J. educ. Res. *41:* 126–132 (1947).

HONZIK, M. P. Sex differences in the occurrence of materials in the play constructions of pre-adolescents. Child Develop. *22:* 15–35 (1951).

HUDSON, L. Contrary imaginations (Methuen, London 1966).

HUDSON, L. Frames of mind (Methuen, London 1968).

HUTT, C. Specific and diversive exploration, in REESE and LIPSITT Advances in child development and behaviour, vol. 5 (Academic Press, London 1970a).

HUTT, C. Curiosity in young children. Sci. J. *6:* 68–72 (1970b).

HUTT, C. Neuroendocrinological, behavioural and intellectual aspects of sexual differentiation in human development; in OUNSTED and TAYLOR Gender differences—their ontogeny and significance (Churchill, London 1972a).

HUTT, C. Males and females. Penguin Books (1972b, in press).

JEGARD, S. and WALTERS, R. H. A study of some determinants of aggression in young children. Child Develop. *31:* 739–747 (1960).

JERSILD, A. T. and MARKEY, F. V. Conflicts between preschool children. Child Develop. Monogr. 21 (1935).

KAGAN, J. and LEWIS, M. Studies of attention in the human infant. Behav. Develop. *11:* 95–127 (1965).

KLEIN, V. The demand for professional Woman I power. Brit. J. Sociol. *17:* 183 (1966).

KORNER, A. F. Neonatal startles, smiles, erections, and reflex sucks as related to state, sex and individuality. Child Develop. *40:* 1039–1053 (1969).

LEVINE, S. Stimulation in infancy. Sci. Amer. *202:* 80–86 (1960).

LEVINE, S. Sex differences in the brain. Sci. Amer. *214:* 84–90 (1966).

LEWIS, M. Infants' responses to facial stimuli during the first year of life. Dev. Psychol. *1:* 75–86 (1969).

LIPSITT, L. P. and LEVY, N. Electrotactual threshold in the neonate. Child Develop. *30:* 547–554 (1959).

LITTLE, B. Psychospecialisation: functions of differential interest in persons and things. Bull. Brit. psychol. Soc. *21:* 113A (1968).

MACCOBY, E. E. (ed.). The development of sex differences (Tavistock, London 1966).

MC CANDLESS, B. R.; BILOUS, B. and BENNETT, H. L. Peer popularity and dependence on adults in preschool age socialisation. Child Develop. *32:* 511–518 (1961).

MC GREW, W. C. Aspects of social development in nursery school children with emphasis on introduction to the group; in BLURTON-JONES Ethological studies of child behaviour (Cambridge University Press, London 1972).

MICHAEL, R. P. The endocrinological bases of sex differences. Paper Ann. Conf. Brit. Psychol. Soc., Exeter, in Symp. Biological bases of psychological sex differences (1971).

MILLER, A. Sex differences related to the effect of auditory stimulation on the stability of visually fixed forms. Percept. Mot. Skills *16:* 589–594 (1963).

MISCHEL, W. Sex-typing and socialisation; in MUSSEN Carmichael's manual of child psychology, vol. 2 (Wiley, London 1970).

MITCHELL, G. and BRANDT, E. M. Behavioural differences related to experience of mother and sex of infant in the rhesus monkey. Develop. Psychol. *3:* 149 (1970).

MONEY, J. and EHRHARDT, A. A. Prenatal hormonal exposure: possible effects on behaviour in man; in MICHAEL Endocrinology and human behaviour (Oxford University Press, London 1968).

MOORE, T. Language and intelligence: a longitudinal study of the first 8 years. I. Patterns of development in boys and girls. Human Develop. *10:* 88–106 (1967).

MOSS, H. Sex, age and state as determinants of mother infant interaction. Merrill-Palmer Quart. *13:* 19–36 (1967).

MOSS, H. A. and ROBSON, K. S. The relation between the amount of time infants spend at various states and the development of visual behaviour. Child Develop. *41:* 509–517 (1970).

NICOLSON, A. B. and HANLEY, C. Indices of physiological maturity: derivation and interrelationships. Child Develop. *24:* 3–38 (1953).

OUNSTED, C. and TAYLOR, D. C. The Y chromosome message: a point of view; in OUNSTED and TAYLOR Gender differences—their ontogeny and significance (Churchill, London 1972).

OUNSTED, M. Sex differences in intrauterine growth; in OUNSTED and TAYLOR Gender differences—their ontogeny and significance (Churchill, London 1972).

PEDERSEN, F. A. and BELL, R. Q. Sex differences in preschool children without histories of complications of pregnancy and delinquency. Develop. Psychol. *3:* 10–15 (1970).

PISHKIN, V. and SHURLEY, J. T. Auditory dimensions and irrelevant information in concept identification of males and females. Percept. Mot. Skills *20:* 673–683 (1965).

SCHAIE, K. W.; BALTES, P. and STROTHER, C. R. A study of auditory sensitivity in advanced age. J. Geront. *19:* 453–457 (1964).

SHORTELL, J. R. and BILLER, H. B. Aggression in children as a function of sex of subject and sex of opponent. Develop. Psychol. *3:* 143–144 (1970).

SHOUKSMITH, G. Intelligence, creativity and cognitive style (Batsford, London 1970).

STEVENSON, A. C. Sex chromatin and the sex ratio in man; in MOORE The sex chromatin (Saunders, Philadelphia 1966).

STEVENSON, A. C. and BOBROW, M. Determinants of sex proportions in man, with consideration of the evidence concerning a contribution from x-linked mutations to intrauterine death. J. med. Genet. *4:* 190–221 (1967).

STEVENSON, A. C. and MC CLARIN, R. H. Determination of the sex of human abortions by nuclear sexing the cells of the chorionic. Nature, Lond. *180:* 198 (1957).

STEVENSON, H. W.; KEEN, R. and KNIGHTS, R. W. Parents and strangers as reinforcing agents for children's performance. J. abnorm. Soc. Psychol. *67:* 183–186 (1963).

TANNER, J. M. Physical growth; in MUSSEN Carmichael's manual of child psychology, 3rd ed. (Wiley, New York 1970).

TAYLOR, D. C. Differential rates of cerebral maturation between sexes and between hemispheres. Lancet *iii:* 140–142 (1969).

TAYLOR, D. C. and OUNSTED, C. The nature of gender differences explored through ontogenetic analyses of sex ratios in disease; in OUNSTED and TAYLOR Gender differences—their ontogeny and significance (Churchill, London 1972).

TAYLOR, S. P. and EPSTEIN, S. Aggression as a function of the interaction of the sex of the aggressor and sex of the victim. J. Personality *35:* 474–486 (1967).

TIGER, L. Men in groups (Nelson, London 1969).

TYLER, L. The psychology of human differences, 3rd ed. (Appleton-Century-Crofts, New York 1965).

WALLACH, M. A. and KOGAN, N. Modes of thinking in young children (Holt, Rinehart & Winston, New York 1965).

WALTERS, J.; PEARCE, D. and DAHMS, L. Affectional and aggressive behaviour of preschool children. Child Develop. *28:* 15–26 (1957).

WATSON, T. S. Operant conditioning of visual fixation in infants under visual and auditory reinforcement. Develop. Psychol. *1:* 508–516 (1969).

WECHSLER, D. The measurement of adult intelligence (Williams & Wilkins, Baltimore 1941).

WECHSLER, D. The measurement and appraisal of adult intelligence, 4th ed. (Williams & Wilkins, Baltimore 1958).

WERNER, E. E. Sex differences in correlations between children's IQ and measures of parental ability, and environmental ratings. Develop. Psychol. *1:* 280–285 (1969).

WHALEN, R. E. Differentiation of the neural mechanisms which control gonadotropin secretion and sexual behaviour; in DIAMOND Reproduction and sexual behaviour (Indiana University Press, Bloomington 1968).

WILKINS, L. Adrenal disorders. II. Congenital virilizing adrenal hyperplasia. Arch. Dis. Childh. *37:* 231 (1962).

Patterns of Response to Physical Contact in Early Human Development

H. R. Schaffer   Peggy E. Emerson

Introduction

It has long been assumed that physical contact plays an important part in early human development and that all normal infants actively seek and enjoy this mode of interaction with their social environment. To be rocked, fondled, held, stroked and cuddled is to writers such as Ribble (1944) an essential precondition to psychological growth, and not to achieve close contact with the body of the mother is regarded by them as a form of deprivation with possibly serious consequences. This view has been reinforced by the findings of Harlow and his co-workers (1958, 1959), which have demonstrated the importance of contact comfort in the establishment of the young monkey's social attachments. For human infants experimental proof is, of course, difficult to obtain, and as even systematic field observations are as yet lacking, our conclusions about the role of physical contact in the development of the young child are still largely of a speculative and con-

troversial nature. Rheingold (1961), for instance, has reminded us of the inability of the infant in the early months to cling, and has put forward her belief that visual, not physical, contact is at the basis of human sociability; yet writers such as Casler (1961) continue to maintain that the effects of tactile and kinaesthetic stimulation received through handling are essential to proper developmental progress.

Some material bearing on this problem arose in the course of a longitudinal investigation concerned with the formation of social attachments in infancy (Schaffer, 1963, Schaffer and Emerson, 1964). While carrying out this study it was noted that not all infants eagerly seek physical contact in the way that the literature might lead one to expect—indeed that a considerable proportion of the subjects actively resisted and protested at certain types of such interaction. It had not originally been one of the aims of the project to study contact behavior, but as spontaneous reports from the mothers of the infants repeatedly forced our

H. R. Schaffer and Peggy E. Emerson, "Patterns of Response to Physical Contact in Early Human Development," *Journal of Child Psychology and Psychiatry*, 5, 1964, pp. 1–13. Published by Pergamon Press by permission.

attention in this direction, it was decided that a more systematic analysis of this aspect was called for.

Procedure

The sample from which data concerning reactions to physical contact were obtained comprised 37 infants, mostly from working-class families, living in their own homes and of normal developmental status. Contact with the families was, in the first place, made through a Child Welfare Clinic in the early weeks of the infant's first year. Once the mother's agreement to participate in the project had been obtained, all subsequent interviews took place in the family's home. Interviews were spaced at four-weekly intervals throughout the first twelve months, after which one more interview at eighteen months took place. The main purpose of the interviews was to obtain data regarding the development of social attachments: this material and the relevant methodology will be described in the appropriate section below when the attachment data will be treated as dependent variables.

While casual observations and reports concerning the infants' reactions to various forms of physical contact had been gathered throughout the follow-up period, the data to be presented here are based on the mothers' answers to an interview schedule specifically concerned with this aspect. The schedule was administered at two points: at the end of the infant's first year (in order to obtain information about the whole of the first twelve months) and again at eighteen morths (to cover behavior in the preceding six months). The questions in the schedule dealt with the following aspects:

(a) the infant's behavior in a number of commonly occurring contact situations, such as being cuddled, carried, held on lap, stroked, kissed, fed on knee, and swung or bounced;

(b) the consistency of these reactions with age, person offering the contact, and the infant's internal condition (i.e., the effect of pain, illness, fatigue or fear);

(c) evidence for contact-seeking in relation to inanimate objects or the self;

(d) the mother's behavior in contact situations

and her reactions to any contact avoidance on the infant's part.

Though guided by the schedule, interviews assumed a largely unstructured form, the mothers being encouraged to give as free and full a description of the infant's reactions in the relevant situation as possible. These descriptions were frequently illustrated by spontaneous demonstrations which the mothers enacted with the infant before the interviewer.

The Contact Groups: Descriptive Data

The maternal reports made it evident that considerable and consistent individual differences could be found in response to certain forms of physical contact. This applied in particular to those situations where the contact involved a close and direct form of interaction, being most clearly in evidence in the cuddling situation. Thus a number of mothers found that from an early age their infants unfailingly protested at, resisted and avoided, this form of interaction, whatever the circumstances and whatever the condition of the child. A group of 9 such "Non-Cuddlers" was isolated by using as our criteria of classification (1) the consistency with age throughout the entire period of eighteen months with which the infant responded negatively to cuddling, and (2) the failure to modify this behavior at any time when tired, frightened, ill, or in pain. In the rest of the sample acceptance of cuddling was reported, yet here too some variation occurred. A group of 19 infants were said to accept, enjoy, and (once their motor development enabled them to do so) actively seek physical contact in all forms, under all circumstances, and at all ages. We shall refer henceforth to these infants as the "Cuddlers." The remaining 9 infants may be said to form an intermediate group, in that acceptance of cuddling was reported but with certain reservations, e.g., only when the infant was tired, ill, etc., or only within a limited age range. For the sake of clarity of presentation we shall only be concerned here with the "pure" cases, i.e., the "Cuddlers" and the "Non-Cuddlers," and describe our findings in terms of the contrast between these two groups. Their sex and birth order distribution are given in Table 1.

TABLE 1.   SEX AND BIRTH ORDER DISTRIBUTION AMONG CONTACT GROUPS

| | Sex | | Birth Order | |
	Male	Female	First Born	Others
"Cuddlers"	8	11	7	12
"Non-Cuddlers"	6	3	4	5
$p*$		N.S.		N.S.

*Fisher exact test, two-tailed (Latscha, 1953).

To illustrate the difference between the two groups, the following phrases may be quoted from the reports given by the mothers of the Non-Cuddlers regarding the infant's reaction to cuddling, i.e., that form of physical contact where the baby is picked up, held with both arms in an upright position on the adult's lap, pressed against her shoulder and usually given some skin-to-skin contact such as kissing or cheek stroking.

"Gets restless when cuddled, turns face away and begins to struggle."
"Will not allow it, fights to get away."
"Has never liked this since able to struggle, squirms, and whimpers."
"Gets restless, pushes you away."
"Wriggles and arches back, and only stops when put down again."
"Restless and whiny until allowed back in cot."
"Will kick and thrash with his arms, and if you persist will begin to cry."

These phrases may be contrasted with the following from the mothers of the Cuddlers:

"Cuddles you back."
"Snuggles into you."
"Holds quite still and puts on a soppy face."
"Loves it."
"Laps it up."
"Would let me cuddle him for hours on end."

The two groups are similarly differentiated by their behavior when the mother merely held the infant quietly on her lap, i.e., cradling or supporting him with her arms while having him lie or sit on her knee:

"Not fond of being held, cries until put down."
"Never has liked sitting on knee, it is easier to play with him by sitting beside him on the floor."
"When on your knee will fight to get down again."
"Arches back and slides off."
"Asks to be lifted, yet the moment you hold him on your lap he pushes against you till he is down again."
"Won't sleep in your arms, has to be put down in cot."

Again the Cuddlers provide a striking contrast:

"Will sit on your knee for ages and play."
"Loves being handled, is always asking to be really close to you."
"Has to be nursed in your arms for half an hour before going to bed, else cries."
"Would be up on my lap all day if I let her."
"I have to rock him in my arms every night till he falls asleep."

All Non-Cuddlers were said to have shown their peculiarities from the early weeks—initially through restlessness and subsequently through more purposive struggling. At 9 or 10 m*, when such locomotor skills as crawling and walking first appeared, opening up a much wider environmental range for exploration, resistance to handling became still more pronounced.

At times of distress, while the Cuddlers found relief in close contact, the Non-Cuddlers needed different forms of comfort:

* Editor's note: throughout, m = months.

"You can't calm him by picking him up even when he is teething—wheeling him round in his pram is much more effective."

"Stops crying most quickly if put back on floor and diverted."

"Even when poorly will settle much better in her cot."

"Most easily comforted by walking him round and showing him things."

"Holding her up on her feet is the best way of calming her."

In general, diversion techniques such as walking or carrying the child around, playing with him, or giving him a biscuit or a bottle were found to be the most effective means of dealing with the Non-Cuddlers when ill or in pain. This does not mean that this group of infants showed a lack of orientation towards the mother: she was still regarded as a "haven of safety" and when frightened (as, for instance, by the approach of a stranger) the Non-Cuddlers too sought her proximity. Their means of establishing proximity was, however, different, for instead of the close physical contact which the other infants sought for reassurance, the Non-Cuddlers either made visual contact with the mother by looking away from the frightening object and turning towards her, or established a much less close physical contact such as holding on to the mother's skirt or hiding their face against her knee.

Feeding on the mother's lap did not produce the same clear-cut differentiation. Two of the Non-Cuddlers were said to protest even then, and to accept food only when sitting in a high chair or standing next to the mother's knee. This, however, applied only from the age of 6 or 7 m on, and no cases of propped bottles due to the infant's resistance to handling were reported for the first half-year.

From the above descriptions it can be seen that, while marked differences exist between the Cuddlers and the Non-Cuddlers, the latter do not by any means resist *all* forms of physical contact. Their protests, it appears, are elicited only by those types of interaction which involve a *close* physical contact, as seen at its clearest in the cuddling situation. Skin contact alone, such as occurs when the child is kissed or has his face stroked without being picked up, when he is tickled, or when "skin games" are played with him, failed to differentiate the two groups, for none of the infants was reported as avoiding or protesting at these forms of interaction. Handling also does not appear to be the crucial factor: the Non-Cuddlers not only tolerated but actively enjoyed being swung, bounced, danced around or romped with, in any way which involved contact but not restraint. As soon as restraint was applied, however, i.e., the infant was not merely supported but also had his movements actively restricted, struggling and resistance occurred.

We must conclude, therefore, that it is not contact per se that is avoided by the Non-Cuddlers but only the restriction of movement that is involved in certain of the contact situations. However, because of their resistance in situations in which contact tends to be most commonly offered, the total amount of physical contact obtained by the Non-Cuddlers is likely to be considerably reduced in comparison with the Cuddlers. We will proceed to ask, in the first place, whether this reduction is associated with differences in the manner in which the first social attachments were formed by the two groups and, in the second place, whether any aetiological factors can be isolated to account for the phenomena described.

The Formation of Social Attachments by the Two Contact Groups

The attachment function (defined as the tendency of the young to seek the proximity of certain other members of the species) may be described in terms of three parameters:

(a) age at onset, i.e., the age when the capacity to form attachments to specific individuals is first manifested;

(b) its intensity at any given age point;

(c) its breadth at these various points, i.e., the number of objects towards whom it is directed.

In infancy it may be most suitably assessed by the reaction to the object's withdrawal in any of the separation situations which tend to occur in the everyday life of all infants. The following 7 such situations were examined in this project: left alone in a room; left with other people; put down in cot at night; passed by while in cot or chair; put down after being on adult's knee; left in pram outside house; and left in pram outside shops. From maternal reports the infant's amount of protest in each situation as it occurred in the preceding four-weekly period was ascertained at every interview and rated on a four-point scale: (0) no protest reported; (1) protests occur, but there are qualifications in respect of *both* their intensity and their regularity; (2) protests occur, but there are qualifications in respect of *either* intensity or regularity; (3) protests occur and there are no qualifications as to intensity or regularity. The combined ratings for all 7 situations yielded, for any given age point investigated, a quantitative measure of the intensity of each infant's attachment function. The identity of the individuals towards whom protests were directed was also ascertained for each situation, breadth being defined as the total number of objects reported for any given age point. Age at onset was defined as the point midway between the interview which first yielded information as to the establishment of attachments to specific individuals and the previous interview.

It has been shown (Schaffer and Emerson, 1964) that the majority of infants first provide evidence of a need for the proximity of certain specific individuals (rather than an indiscriminate need for company and attention in general) some-time during the third quarter of the first year. Investigating the influence of contact group on age at onset (see Table 2), the Non-Cuddlers are found to reach this developmental milestone somewhat later than the Cuddlers. Due to the very much greater variance among the Non-Cuddlers, however, the difference fails to reach statistical significance and gives no basis for rejecting the null hypothesis.

As to the intensity with which specific attachments are manifested, comparison may be made at two points, namely for the first year (taking the mean of all intensity scores obtained by each infant up to 12 m) and at 18 m. For the former, the Non-Cuddlers are found to show specific attachments to a significantly less intense degree than the Cuddlers (Table 2). The tie to particular individuals, when first established, is thus weaker in those infants who experienced reduced physical contact with other people. At 18 m, however, although the Non-Cuddlers are still showing less intense specific attachments than either of the other two groups, they appear to have made up a considerable part of the leeway and no longer differ to a significant degree from the Cuddlers in this respect.

For the third parameter of the attachment function investigated here, namely, breadth, no differences were found between the two groups, in that all showed attachments to a similar number of objects both in the first year and at 18 m.

Reduced physical contact is thus associated to only a minor degree with the manner in which

TABLE 2.   AGE AT ONSET AND INTENSITY SCORE OF SPECIFIC ATTACHMENTS RELATED TO CONTACT GROUP

	Age at onset		Intensity scores up to 12 m		Intensity scores at 18 m	
	Mean (Weeks)	Range (Weeks)	Mean	Range	Mean	Range
"Cuddlers"	33·63	22–50	5·19	1·15–9·00	6·68	3·00–15·40
"Non-Cuddlers"	41·77	26–65	2·33	1·33–5·83	4·31	2·30– 9·30
*p**	N.S.		<0·02		N.S.	

*Based on Mann-Whitney U-test. A non-parametic technique was used as, for age at onset, a significantly different variance was found for the two groups and, in the case of the intensity scores, the assumption of equal scale intervals was avoided.

social attachments are established. The association is seen most clearly in the earliest stages of attachment formation to specific individuals, but there is no indication that the Non-Cuddlers are in any way severely or more than temporarily affected.

Aetiological Considerations

In seeking an explanation for the observed differences in reactions to physical contact, two alternative hypotheses may be examined. According to the first, a need for physical contact is potentially present in all infants, but in certain cases environmental conditions (with particular reference to early maternal handling) do not permit the full expression of this need which therefore becomes blocked and frustrated. According to the second hypothesis, congenital rather than environmental forces provide the crucial explanation, there being a factor in the infant's inherent make-up which impels some subjects to seek close physical contact while preventing others from doing so. We shall, as far as the data permit, investigate each of these two hypotheses in turn.

For the most likely environmental force responsible for blocking the contact need we may look to the mother-infant relationship. Observing the sensuous way in which mothers often interact with their infants, one is struck by the fact that it is not only infants but also adults who can have such a need. There are, however, some who prefer not to handle their infant more than is necessary and who will, whenever possible, interact with him through means other than physical contact. On the basis partly of observations of casual interaction sequences between mother and child taking place during interviews, and partly of reports from the mothers as to the method of dealing with the child's demands for attention, each mother was allocated by two judges, who had read through all the relevant material gathered in the course of the project, according to her *preferred* mode of interaction with the infant to one of three categories: personal-handling (interaction takes place mainly through physical contact), personal non-handling (stimulation is provided by the mother mainly through visual and auditory means), and impersonal (toys, food, etc., are used to "divert" the child's demands for attention away from the mother herself). Combining the last two categories as representing Non-Handlers and comparing them with the first category, the Handlers, the distribution for the two contact groups is as given in Table 3. These figures provide no support for the hypothesis that contact type is a direct function of the mother's customary mode of handling: though most of the Non-Cuddlers had mothers who preferred other than physical means of interaction, the prevalence of non-handling mothers amongst the Cuddlers suggests that this variable cannot, in itself, be regarded as the crucial aetiological condition.

Table 3 does, however, raise the interesting problem of non-matching couples. Pursuing this point in interview, it was found that the Cuddlers with non-handling mothers obtained the desired contact comfort either from other members of the family or occasionally from the mother herself, in that the latter found that she just had to give way to the infant's demands from time to time.

TABLE 3.   ASSOCIATION OF MATERNAL HANDLING TYPE WITH CONTACT GROUP

| | Maternal types | |
	Handlers	Non-Handlers
"Cuddlers"	9	10
"Non-Cuddlers"	2	7

$p > 0.10$, Fisher exact test.

Complete rigidity and utter failure to bring about mutual adjustment was therefore not observed in this group. The same applies to the two Non-Cuddlers with handling mothers: although this situation might well be the first step in the development of a pathological relationship, in this sample the mothers were able to adjust to the infant's peculiarities and relate to him by using alternate modes of interaction. The mothers' comments on the child's dislike of cuddling varied: some expressed considerable surprise, while others had encountered it before in other children; some regretted it, others asserted that they did not mind as it was "less bother" for them. None of the mothers regarded it as a form of rejection, as all felt that the child was able to show his affection in other ways. One or two interpreted this phenomenon as showing "independence of mind," "self-will," or an indication that "he is not soft." Their explanations also varied: the mothers with non-cuddling sons mostly believed that this was a characteristic of boys generally, whereas the same explanation with regard to girls was heard from the mother of a non-cuddling daughter. Heredity was also invoked as a cause, mainly on the basis of similar reactions having been observed in other members of the family (one might include here the somewhat wistful comment from one mother: "He is just like his father —not one for a bit of love!").

One of our questions referred to the reactions of older siblings to close physical contact in infancy. Insofar as this involved retrospective data, we were only able to distinguish two categories: those who had accepted and those who had resisted this type of stimulation. As Table 4 shows,

a close similarity in reaction is found between siblings, with none of the older children in the families of Non-Cuddlers being reported as having been Cuddlers.

However, neither these nor any of the other findings quoted above can provide conclusive evidence as to the influence of maternal handling practices. Similarity in reaction of older siblings, for instance, may be as much due to innate factors as to identical modes of child-rearing. The possibility that early learning produced through "contagion" (Escalona's [1953] term for the process whereby maternal feelings are transmitted to the infant through physical interaction) is responsible for the child's resistance to cuddling can only be confirmed or denied by an observational approach applied very much more intensively and earlier than had been the case in this study. The cruder indices which we used to describe early maternal practices failed to differentiate between the contact groups: method of feeding, for instance, was very similar, in that all infants except one Cuddler were bottle- rather than breast-fed after the first month; rigidity of feeding schedule, which might produce associations of tension with handling, also did not differentiate between the groups; and the same applies to the degree of maternal responsiveness to the infant's crying for attention, in that Non-Cuddlers were not left to cry any longer than Cuddlers.

There is, however, another, though more indirect, means of investigating the frustration hypothesis. If some maternal force were indeed blocking the Non-Cuddler's inherent contact need, one might expect to observe some sign of the frustrated need seeking other outlets. There are

TABLE 4.   ASSOCIATION OF SIBLINGS' REACTIONS TO PHYSICAL CONTACT
WITH CONTACT GROUP

| | Siblings' reactions | |
	Accepted	Resisted
"Cuddlers"	14	4
"Non-Cuddlers"	0	5
*p**	0·05	

*Fisher exact test. The figures in this table refer to number of siblings, not to number of subjects.

three main ways in which this could take place, involving respectively people other than the mother, inanimate objects, or the self.

As to the other people, it was reported by all mothers of the Non-Cuddlers that the infant behaved similarly with everybody. While we have no way of confirming the veracity of this statement, casual observations during interviews produced no contradictory evidence. Some of the mothers indeed mentioned their embarrassment when doting relatives and other visitors would attempt to cuddle an otherwise friendly child and be confronted with a violently negative reaction on his part. It may also be recalled in this connection that the two contact groups did not differ with regard to number of attachment objects, suggesting that the Non-Cuddlers did not seek satisfaction from a wide range of other figures in the environment.

Soft toys and other contact-providing objects are another source to which a frustrated child might be expected to turn. The number of infants in each group who, up to the age of 18 m, had at any time in the first 18 m made use of "favorite cuddlies" (most often bits of sheet or blanket which were taken to bed or resorted to at times of pain and illness) is given in Table 5. The trend revealed there goes in the opposite direction to that predicted by the frustration hypothesis.

The same table also gives the incidence in the sample of those autoerotic activities which, according to the mothers, had become established habits at any time during the first 18 m. None of our infants was a confirmed rocker, rubber, or masturbator, and the autoerotic activities refer therefore mainly to oral habits such as thumb-sucking.

Once again the distribution gives no evidence of a frustrated need seeking other outlets—on the contrary, the interesting conclusion is indicated that the more contact a child receives the more is he likely to show other sensual responses too.

We turn now to the second hypothesis concerning aetiology, namely that an infant's reactions to close physical contact is a function of certain inherent characteristics present in the child from the beginning. In attempting to isolate such a characteristic, one may begin with a theme which recurs constantly in the reports of the Non-Cuddlers' behavior, namely the restlessness which these infants generally display over a wide range of situations. The following are some of the descriptions taken from the mothers' reports of the child's behavior on their knees:

"Not content just to sit on your lap, likes to move around."

"Loves being bounced up and down, but otherwise just would not sit still on your knee."

"Enjoys being swung in your arms but not to sit still."

"Will only sit for a couple of seconds on your lap, then struggles to get down."

"Wriggles constantly on knee, likes movement."

"Won't keep still on your knee, walks up you or rocks backwards and forwards."

The Cuddlers, on the other hand, emerge on the whole as far more placid, quiet and content. Activity ratings on a five-point scale, based on

TABLE 5. USE OF "CUDDLY TOYS" AND INCIDENCE OF AUTOEROTIC ACTIVITIES RELATED TO CONTACT GROUP

| | Use of "Cuddly Toys" | | Autoerotic Activities | |
	Reported	Not Reported	Reported	Not Reported
"Cuddlers"	10	9	9	10
"Non-Cuddlers"	1	8	0	9
p*		0·10		0·10

*Fisher exact test.

TABLE 6.   REACTIONS OF CONTACT GROUPS IN TWO RESTRAINT SITUATIONS—DRESSED AND TUCKED INTO BED

| | Dressed | | Tucked into bed | |
	Protest	No Protest	Protest	No Protest
"Cuddlers"	3	16	2	17
"Non-Cuddlers"	6	3	5	4
p*		0·05		0·05

*Fisher exact test.

observations of the infant's behavior during all the interviews held in the course of the study, give quantitative form to this impression. The mean ratings for the Cuddlers and Non-Cuddlers were, respectively, 3.11 and 3.75, indicating a difference only just short of statistical significance ($t = 1.83$, $p < 0.10$).

It is possible, therefore, that the two contact groups may be differentiated on some such basis as the congenital activity types described by Fries (1953). Hyperactive, restless infants would be more likely to resist those forms of physical contact which involve restraint of their movements, and it is this element which, as we have seen, appears to be the crucial one in calling forth their protests in the cuddling situation. We attempted further to pinpoint this difference in reaction to restraint by asking about the infants' behavior in relation to two other situations also involving motor restraint: being dressed and being tucked into bed (see Table 6). In both instances a clear difference is shown between the contact groups when mothers were asked whether or not the child had consistently protested in the relevant situation from the age of at least 6 months on: thus the Non-Cuddlers are far more often reported as showing dislike of being wrapped, changed, or having their clothes put on than the Cuddlers, and the same difference also emerges for behavior in bed in that struggling when tucked into bed, kicking off blankets, and general restlessness when actually asleep were characteristics found to a significantly greater extent amongst the Non-Cuddlers than the Cuddlers. Even the actual amount of sleep differentiates the two groups: when asked to detail the number of hours which the infants spent asleep per 24 hr (the infants being 9-10 m old at the time this information was sought), the

mothers of the Non-Cuddlers reported a mean value of 11.89 hr as compared with the 13.16 hr reported by the mothers of the Cuddlers ($t = 4.12$, $p < 0.001$).

The restlessness of the Non-Cuddlers appears to have one further consequence which is illustrated in Table 7. In their motor development these infants appear to be well ahead of the Cuddlers, reaching such milestones as the ability to sit unsupported, to stand holding on, and to crawl, considerably sooner than the Cuddlers (the failure to obtain a significant difference with regard to the onset of walking may well be due to the fact that in many cases the relevant information was not obtained until the 18 m visit, i.e., 6 m after the last interview compared with the four-weekly intervals between interviews in the first year, and consequently many mothers tended to give the vague answer "at about a year" to our question about onset). The Cattell Infant Scale (Cattell, 1940) was administered to all infants around the age of 6 m and here too a significant difference was obtained between Cuddlers and Non-Cuddlers. As the items composing the test around this age are mainly concerned with motor, particularly manipulative, functioning, further confirmation is given to the association between contact type and early locomotor development. The Non-Cuddlers' restlessness thus appears to provide a drive to motor functioning which results in increased achievement in this sphere when compared with the more placid infants of the Cuddler group.

We may conclude that the Non-Cuddlers' avoidance of close physical contact is concerned with a phenomenon that is not peculiar to the relationship with the mother or indeed to social relationships in general. These children, it appears, were distinguished by a general behavioral characteristic

TABLE 7. AGE AT ONSET OF MOTOR SKILLS AND DEVELOPMENTAL QUOTIENTS IN THE TWO CONTACT GROUPS

	Sitting		Standing		Crawling		Walking		D.Q.	
	Mean (Wks)	S.D. (Wks)	Mean (Wks)	S.D. (Wks)	Mean (Wks)	S.D. (Wks)	Mean (Wks)	S.D. (Wks)	Mean	S.D.
"Cuddlers"	30·11	2·91	37·18	5·01	43·43	5·17	55·08	7·02	110·36	9·76
"Non-Cuddlers"	27·80	1·85	31·33	4·35	36·83	3·89	51·72	4·66	122·50	12·74
t	1·82		2·26		2·12		1·15		2·43	
p	<0·10		<0·05		<0·05		N.S.		<0·05	

affecting a wide range of functions and apparent in non-social as well as social situations. In the absence of any positive evidence that the mothers of the two contact groups could be clearly distinguished according to a criterion aetiologically associated with the infants' reaction to contact, and in view of our failure to find signs of a frustrated need seeking other outlets, we are inclined to regard the congenital explanation as the more likely of the two hypotheses considered. Only further investigation will, however, provide a conclusive answer.

Discussion

For some infants, it appears, contact is not comforting. Certain forms of it may be sought for the sake of obtaining extra stimulation ("rough play," carrying around, etc.), but the closer, more intimate kind of physical contact which is so satisfying to some infants is resisted and actively avoided by others. As a result, the total amount of handling received by the latter will be very much less than that received by more cuddly infants and, furthermore, the nature of their interaction with the mother will tend to assume a less direct form.

Comparison with recent animal studies on the role of contact comfort cannot easily be made. Due to the non-experimental nature of the study, with its lack of direct control over the independent variable, the difference between the groups in terms of the amount of contact received was not as extreme as one would like for a crucial test, for the Non-Cuddlers did not by any means experience a total lack of handling and in the feed-

ing situation, for instance, could not be distinguished at all from the rest of the sample. Moreover, the initiative for the reduction of contact came from the infants themselves, not from an experimenter. It is quite possible that externally imposed deprivation of this type of stimulation could have more serious consequences for some infants than for others, and that the Cuddlers in particular require physical contact for satisfactory developmental progress. Yet, despite these qualifications, it is apparent that, in the case of human infants in general, caution is needed before one can ascribe to contact comfort the overwhelming importance that this variable has been found to assume in certain lower species. Our examination of the development of social attachments bears out this conclusion: reduced physical contact is associated with less intense attachments, but the difference between Cuddlers and Non-Cuddlers appears to be only a temporary one found in the initial stages of attachment formation. The reason, we may assume, lies in the greater flexibility of the human being in comparison with lower animals: prevented from obtaining the usual amount of close physical contact, both mother and child are able to use alternative ways of relating to one another. Rough play, carrying or walking around, and interaction through toys and other material objects were the most frequent examples quoted to us by the mothers of the Non-Cuddlers. Insofar as some of these modes of relating involved interaction through other objects, rather than direct interaction as occurs in cuddling, the initially less intense degree of attachment of the Non-Cuddlers becomes readily understandable. Support is thus given to the notion that what appears to matter in the establishment of primary social bonds is the type of more general mechanism of social arousal advocated by Scott (1962), rather than one particular mode of achieving such arousal. The aim of the attachment function is to obtain the proximity of the object, but such an aim can be attained in many ways, and if one way is blocked (as happens, for instance, in blind babies), other means are still possible. It is thus unlikely that in *all* human infants a great deal of physical contact is a *sine qua non* for early social development.

Aetiologically, we have not been able to produce conclusive evidence for either of the two hypotheses advanced, though, despite our inability to discount totally the effects of certain subtle interaction processes occurring early on between mother and child, a congenital origin appears to us the more likely explanation. Of particular significance here is the suggestion that resistance to close physical contact is not primarily a social phenomenon at all but an expression of a more primitive and more general aspect of the infant's personality, to be observed above all in the level of his activity drive. Schaefer and Bayley (1963) have recently reported evidence pointing to the genetic origin of an individual's activity level and have indicated the need to find out more about its behavioral correlates and consequences. The data presented here suggest that one of these consequences refers to the manner in which the infant's interpersonal behavior is shaped. Thus the avoidance of close physical contact may be interpreted as stemming from a pervasive innate response tendency which will affect the initial development of social behavior and which may, in some cases, even be responsible for imposing a considerable strain on the mother-child relationship. From a clinical point of view, however, it seems unlikely that the non-cuddling pattern is per se a bad sign prognostically. In only those instances where a mother is too rigid to use alternate ways of relating, or where she interprets the infant's behavior as "rejection," may one be confronted with the first step in the development of a pathological relationship.

Summary

In the course of a longitudinal investigation covering the first eighteen months of life, data regarding the infants' reactions to naturally occurring physical contact situations were systematically obtained through maternal reports. On the basis of their behavior two groups of infants were isolated: those who accepted close physical contact under all conditions and those who actively resisted it at all times. Descriptive data, highlighting the behavioral differences between the two groups, are presented, comparisons are made with regard to the manner in which each group forms the first social attachments, and some aetiological considerations to account for the differences between the groups are put forward.

REFERENCES

CASLER, L. (1961). Maternal deprivation. *Monogr. Soc. Res. Child Develpm., 26,* No. 2 (Serial No. 80).

CATTELL, P. (1940). *The measurement of intelligence of infants and young children.* New York: The Psychological Corporation.

ESCALONA, S. (1953). Emotional development in the first year of life. In M. J. E. Senn (Ed.), *Problems of infancy and childhood: transactions of the sixth Josiah Macy Conference.* New York: Macy.

FRIES, M. E., and WOOLF, P. J. (1953). Some hypotheses on the role of the congenital activity type in personality development. *Psychoanal. Stud. Child, 8,* 48–62.

HARLOW, H. F. (1958). The nature of love. *Amer. Psychol., 13,* 673–685.

HARLOW, H. F., and ZIMMERMAN, R. R. (1959). Affectional responses in the infant monkey. *Science, 130,* 421–432.

LATSCHA, R. (1953). Tests of significance in a 2 × 2 contingency table: extension of Finney's table. *Biometrika, 40,* 74–86.

RHEINGOLD, H. L. (1961). The effect of environmental stimulation upon social and exploratory behavior in the human infant. In B. M. Foss (Ed.), *Determinants of Infant Behaviour.* London: Methuen.

RIBBLE, M. A. (1944). Infantile experience in relation to personality development. In J. McV. Hunt (Ed.), *Personality and the behaviour disorders.* New York: Ronald Press.

SCHAEFER, E. S., and BAYLEY, N. (1963). Maternal

behaviour, child behaviour and their intercorrelation from infancy through adolescence. *Monogr. Soc. Res. Child Develpm., 28,* 3 (Serial No. 87).

SCHAFFER, H. R. (1963). Some issues for research in the study of attachment behavior. In B. M. Foss (Ed.), *Determinants of Infant Behaviour: II.* London: Methuen.

SCHAFFER, H. R., and EMERSON, P. E. (1964). The development of social attachments in infancy. *Monogr. Soc. Res. Child Develpm., 29,* 3 (Serial No. 94).

SCOTT, J. P. (1962). Critical periods in behavioural development. *Science, 138,* 949–958.

Self, Other, and Fear:
The Reaction of Infants to People

Michael Lewis   Jeanne Brooks-Gunn

The fears of infants is an important area of inquiry, for it sits squarely on the domains of affect, cognitive and social development.[1] The infant's reactions to other persons may be said to have an affective component: fear of strangers may be an index of attachment. Although attachment usually is defined by a positive approach to the mother, as measured by proximal and distal behaviors (Coates, Anderson & Hartup, 1972; Lewis & Ban, 1971), or by separation from the mother as measured by distress (Ainsworth & Bell, 1970; Goldberg & Lewis, 1969; Schaffer & Emerson, 1964), attachment may also be explored by examining the infant's responses to other persons, either when the mother is or is not present.

Fear of the strange may also be related to cognitive development. Indeed, the theoretical work of Hebb (1946, 1949), as well as of Piaget (1952) and others (Schaffer, 1966), has argued for a relationship between fear and novelty. Moreover, there may be a more indirect relationship, such as increased cognitive capacity leading to greater differentiation, thus producing more strange.

While the strange can include objects and events as well as people, most of the work on fear of the strange has involved people. We will only mention in passing that loud noises, in fact, intensity in general, have the possibility of frightening the infant (see Scarr & Salapatek, 1970). It is not our intention to deal with this dimension of stimulus events. As we have stated before (Lewis, 1971) this stimulus dimension adds little to our understanding of the infant's cognitive development since it acts *upon* the infant, and, as James (1895) has stated, the infant's response is

[1] Paper presented at Eastern Psychological Association meetings, Symposium on *Infants' Fear of the Strange,* Boston, April 1972. This research was supported in part by a Grant from the Spencer Foundation and by the National Institute of Child Health and Human Development, under Research Grant 1 P01 HD01762. Thanks are due to Marcia Weinraub and Gina Rhea who helped to formulate the problem and collect the data.

Michael Lewis and Jeanne Brooks-Gunn, "Self, Other and Fear: The Reaction of Infants to People," Educational Testing Service, May 1972. Paper presented at Eastern Psychological Association symposium on *Infants' Fear of the Strange,* Boston, April 1973.

an immediate passive sensorial response. Rather, we are interested in stimuli that are defined by the interaction of the organism and the stimulus event (novelty and familiarity are examples of such interaction). We shall restrict our discussion further to include only the infant's social world, leaving out the study of nonsocial stimuli.

Fear of strangers or stranger anxiety has been studied, most of the work growing out of the ethological-attachment literature (Ainsworth & Bell, 1970; Schaffer & Emerson, 1964). Fear of strangers usually appears in the second half of the first year and extends, for some, long into the second year. While the ethological-imprinting position would argue for fear of strangers as a way of binding the infant to his caregivers, we recognize, as do Rheingold and Eckerman (1971), that not all infants exhibit fear of strangers. Some infants may show only signs of wariness or differential smiling towards unfamiliar people.

For all the current research on fear in infancy, there has been relatively little effort directed toward the social dimensions which elicit fear. Thus far, age of onset, number of infants exhibiting fear, and specific fears of animate objects have received the most attention. We are interested in the infant's fearful response to people, that is, it is the dimension of humanness that we wish to study. While humans and masks have been studied, only one study, that of Morgan and Ricciuti (1969), touches upon the dimensions that interest us. In this study a male and female stranger were used, and the data reveal that the infants were more frightened of the male. No information about the strangers was given. We do not know the sizes and shapes of each, but yet the data suggest differential fear as a function of the nature of the social event. It is to this point that our study is directed. More concretely, our current study comes from an observation of an 8-month-old female. We observed that an approach by an adult stranger produced extreme fear. The infant screamed, cried, and tried desperately to escape. How different when a stranger 3 or 4 years old approached her: smiling, cooing, and reaching behavior was then exhibited. Why should this be —they were equally strange? Would this hold for children who were generally fearful? What does this mean for the cognitive functioning of the infant, let alone its significance for any theory of attachment? As a first step, this casual observation had to be repeated and extended.

In this study we were interested in the infants' responses to five different social events: a strange adult male and female of the same physical size, a strange female child 4 years of age, the infant's mother, and the infant itself. Twenty-four infants, 7-19 months old, were each placed in a pleasant room which was carpeted and had a few pieces of furniture and pictures on the wall. Only infants who were first-born or who had siblings over 5 years of age were included; 20 were first-born. The infant was seated in an infant tenda facing a door about 15 feet away. The mother sat next to the child. Each of the three strangers, one at a time, would first knock on the door. The mother would say "come in," and each would enter at the far end of the room. The stranger slowly walked toward the infant. Having reached the infant, the stranger would touch the infant's hand. Throughout the episode the stranger smiled but did not vocalize. Movements were deliberately slow to avoid eliciting startle responses. After touching the infant, the stranger slowly turned, walked to the door and left the room. The second and third strangers followed the same procedure. There was approximately a 2-minute wait between visits or until the infant was quiet. After the strangers, the mother went to the door and walked toward the infant in the same manner as the strangers. For the infant-itself condition it was necessary for the infant to see itself. A mirror was used, and to avoid the effect of novelty, the mirror did not approach the infant (mirrors do not walk); rather, the infant approached the mirror. To do this, the mother moved the tenda so that it was directly in front of a mirror placed at the opposite end of the room. She slowly moved the tenda toward the mirror so that the infant was able to see his reflection without observing his mother. When the tenda touched the mirror, the mother moved away. The order was balanced for the three-stranger conditions and between the mother and self conditions.

Three behavioral scales—facial expression, vocalization, and motor activity—were used to rate the infants' reactions to the stranger conditions. The checklist (see Figure 1) is similar to the one developed by Morgan and Ricciuti (1969). The infants' responses were measured at four distances.

Figure 1

SCALES

	Child				Mother			
	Far	Middle	Close	Touch	Far	Middle	Close	Touch
FACIAL								
+2 Smile broad								
+1 Smile slight								
0 Neutral express.								
-1 Slight frown								
-2 Puckering, cry								
MOTOR ACTIVITY								
+2 { Reaches to E / Touches E								
+1 { G.B.M. to E / Looks at E								
0 { Inattention / Explores room / Att. directed away								
-1 { Neg. express. to E / Avoids E glance / Pulls hand away from E								
-2 { Attempts to escape E / Reaches to M								

Distance 1, the farthest distance, was when the stranger entered; distance 2 (middle) was when the social event was in the middle of the room; distance 3 (close) was when the event was 3 feet from the infant; and distance 4 (touch) was when the event touched the infant. Observer reliability was measured by the proportion of agreements for two observers who were hidden behind a one-way mirror. The mean percentage of agreement across both the facial and motor scales was .90.

The vocalization scale proved worthless in that there was almost no vocalizing, crying, or fretting. The data to be presented are those for the facial and motor scales, the results of which were almost identical.

The mean data for the five social events are

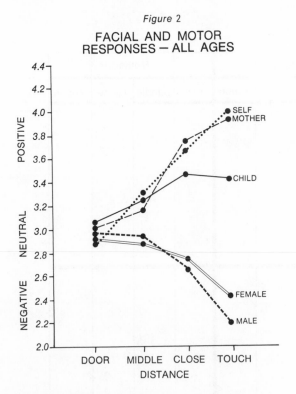

Figure 2

FACIAL AND MOTOR
RESPONSES — ALL AGES

Figure 3

FACIAL RESPONSE
ALL AGES

shown in Figure 2. A score of 3 indicates a neutral response, with 1 being the most negative and 5 being the most positive responses possible. This figure is a combination of the two scales. For the facial expression scale this varied from a broad smile to a puckering crylike expression, while for the motor scale this varied from reaching toward the social event to twisting away from the event and reaching to mother.

The data are rather obvious. Affective social differentiation increases with proximity. Thus, there are no affect differences toward the various social events at the farthest point and affect increases with approach. Social stimuli differ in their effect on the positive and negative affect of the infant. The male and female strangers elicit the most (and only) negative response, while the child stranger elicits a positive response. Moreover, the mother and self elicited the most positive responses. In an analysis of variance with social events and distance as the principal effects, stimulus distance, and stimulus $\times$ distance interaction were highly significant ($F = 11.25$, p <

.001, $F = 16.10$, p < .001, $F = 18.04$, p < .001 respectively).

These findings are consonant with Morgan and Ricciuti's (1969) data and indicate that infants do not exhibit either negative or positive responses until the social event approaches or is in close proximity. This makes good sense since it is a compromise between the need to flee (something strange can hurt) and the need to experience newness in order to alter cognitive structures. The rule might be *stay and attend as long as the event does not get close; if it approaches, withdraw.* Fear and negative affects may be in the service of this escape behavior. Why, though, does the infant not show the positive affect earlier? In order to maintain a parsimonious explanation, we would need to postulate that the intensely positive affects may also interfere with cognitive processes so that they too are only elicited at approach or proximity when social interaction becomes necessary. Of course, a simpler explanation would be related to a time lag notion, wherein the expression of affect, either positive or negative, takes more time. If the social event had waited at the door, would not the same affect have occurred? Morgan and Ricciuti (1969) controlled for this time effect and found it not relevant. On the strength of their results we must reject this hypothesis.

Differentiation of responses to the various social events is also related to age as well as to distance. When the sample is divided by median age, 12 *S*s are between 7 and 11.5 months of age and 12 *S*s are 12-19 months old. We realize that the small sample size and the arbitrary division of the infants into two age groups limits generalization; however, interesting age differences emerge (see Figure 4). While the patterns for the two age levels are similar, older infants exhibit a greater range of responses than do the younger ones. The older infants are more positive to the self, mother, and child, and are more negative toward the female and male strangers. It is only in amount of negative affect that the two ages are significantly different by t-test (p < .05 for male plus female strangers) although there is a trend indicating

that they also exhibit more positive affect (p < .10). It is interesting to note that these age differences are only found when the social event is in close proximity. The greater age and presumably greater cognitive development of the infants more than one year old did not result in prompter affective response. Approach determines the timing, while age affects the intensity of the response.

Age differences in the intensity of fear responses have also been found by others (Morgan & Ricciuti, 1969; Scarr & Salapatek, 1970) and may be influenced by perceptual-cognitive development. However, Scarr and Salapatek (1970) and Schaffer (personal communication) found no relationship either between fear of a female stranger and object permanence (when the age variance was controlled) or between fear of strangers and attention. While these may not be the relevant perceptual cognitive dimensions necessary for eliciting fear, these failures raise the question of what cognitive capacities are relevant to affective responses to social events. While dis-

Figure 4

FACIAL AND MOTOR RESPONSES

UNDER TWELVE MONTHS

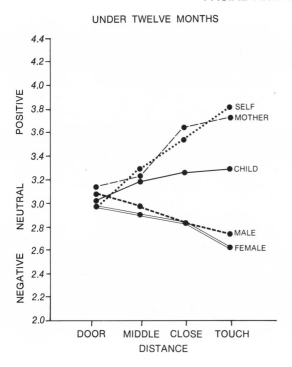

OVER TWELVE MONTHS

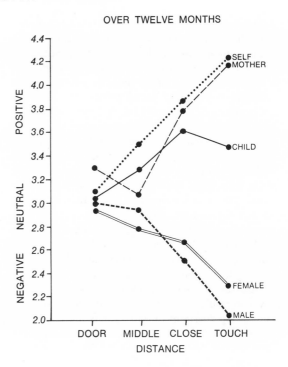

Figure 5

Figure 5

FACIAL RESPONSE

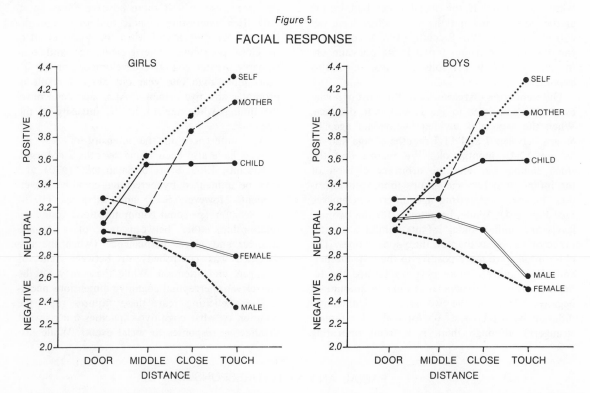

crimination between familiar and strange is essential, this may be so low a level of cognitive skill that all infants are capable of it and it is not really relevant to the study of the affective responses.

The sex of the infant may be related to the affective response to social events. The negative and positive responses of the boy and girl infants are remarkably similar except for their response to the male stranger. While the infants in general are more frightened of the male stranger, this effect is mostly produced by the girls. It is the girls who seem most frightened by the strange male. This is interesting in light of recent findings in our laboratory (Ban & Lewis, 1971). When one-year-old infants were seen in a playroom with both their mothers and fathers, the girl children appeared to be more reluctant to interact with their fathers than the boys—especially in terms of the distal mode of looking! Although these present results are not significant, they raise the interesting questions of why infants are frightened more of a male stranger and why this is more true of females. No explanation based solely on

low levels of paternal interaction as compared to mother's interaction can account for this latter sex difference.

How are we to account for the negative affect directed toward the adult strangers and the positive affect directed toward child stranger and to the mother and self? We would expect fear of the stranger; thus, the negative expression toward the adult strangers comes as no surprise. However, if it is strangeness alone that elicits fear or negative affect, why no fear (in fact, a positive affect) toward the child stranger? This brings into question the whole incongruity hypothesis. Consider the incongruity argument in relation to affect.[2] Briefly, it states that events that are highly incongruent will be those which produce fear, while those that are only partially incongruous will pro-

[2] The effect of incongruity on attentive behavior is still being explored. It is important to note that incongruity may produce little attention not because of any cognitive reason but because it produces fear which might result in withdrawal. Gaze aversion is one type of withdrawal.

duce little fear. For example, the head of a monkey shown to other monkeys produces extreme fear because of its incongruity (Hebb, 1946). If the judgment of congruity is made with the mother as the referent, then the strange female is least incongruent, the strange male more so, and the strange female child most. Thus, the child stranger should produce the most fear. In fact, the child stranger produces no fear but positive affect. Incongruity may not be the sole determinant of fear. On the other hand, the mother may not be the only referent for the infant in his observation of social events. Recall that infants also show positive affect to themselves. We will return to this issue of self shortly.

These data also suggest that we reconsider our formulation about the fear of strangers in infants. It now becomes clear that we cannot state that all strange social events that approach infants will elicit the same degree of negative affect. That is, strangeness *per se* is not a sufficient dimension. The social dimensions or space that elicits fear is multidimensional. Strangeness is necessary, but not sufficient. What are the characteristics of the child stranger that *do not* elicit fearful responses? Two appear most likely; the first is size. Clearly, the child stranger is smaller than the adults; also, the child stranger is closer in size to the infant, especially one sitting in a baby tenda. Ethologically it makes sense to postulate that organisms should be more frightened of strange things that are bigger, than of same size or smaller strange things. Same size or smaller things are less likely or able to hurt. The second dimension is the differential facial configuration between a young child and an adult. Perhaps this is the cue. Observation of the verbal responses of a 12-month-old as she looks through magazines and newspapers containing pictures of adults (these pictures were, of course, mixture) reveals the widely used word "baby" as she points to the figures, suggesting that she was responding to the size of the picture rather than the facial configuration. Whatever the explanation of why the infants were not upset by the child stranger, it is clear that a simple incongruity explanation fails to satisfy the data and that the space of social strangeness is multidimensional, unfamiliar being just one dimension.

The infant's highly positive response to the mother is as we expected; however, the equally positive response to themselves in the mirror is somewhat more interesting. By using the term self we have been making an explicit assumption, one which was quite intentional. There is relatively little information on infants' responses to mirrors, but the anecdotal evidence that does exist all indicates that even at earlier ages there is an intense positive affective response to the mirror. In a recent study of 4-month-olds by Rheingold (1971), further evidence for the positive effect of seeing oneself in the mirror was reported. These infants showed more smiling to a mirror image than to either motion pictures or slides of an infant or to nonsocial stimuli.

Can one talk about the concept of the self at such early ages? Consider two aspects of the self: the first and most common is the categorical self (I am female, or I am intelligent, or I am big or small, or I am capable); the second, and by far the more primitive, is the existential statement "I am." The basic notion of self—probably as differentiated from other (either as object or person, the mother being the most likely other person)—must develop first. There is no reason not to assume that it develops from birth and that even in the early months some notion of self exists. We would argue that this nonevaluative, existential self is developed from the consistency, regularity, and contingency of the infant's action and outcome in the world. Self is differentiated by reafferent (or information) feedback; for example, each time a certain set of muscles operate (eyes close), it becomes black (cannot see). That is, the immediacy, simultaneity, and regularity of action and outcome produces differentiation and self. The action of touching the hot stove and the immediacy of the pain tells me it's my hand that is on the stove. This self is further reinforced if, when I remove my hand, the pain ceases. The infant's world is full of such relationships and they vary from its own action on objects to its relationship with a caregiver. In these social interactions, the highly directed energy of the caregiver (touch, smile, look, etc.) is contingent and specific to infant action (smile, coo, etc.).

The relationship of self to the mirror is, likewise, related. Looking in the mirror is pleasurable because of the consistency, regularity, and contingency of the viewer's action and the viewed outcome. In no other situation is there such consistent action-outcome pairing. In other words, the mirror experience contains those elements that generally make up the fabric of the infant's growing concept of self. It is not possible for us to know if the infant is aware that the image is himself. Awareness is a difficult concept to study in nonverbal organisms, but it is clear that by the time one-word utterances emerge, such as "self" or "mine," the year-old infant has the concept of self. It is reasonable to assume that the concept existed prior to the utterance. In fact, if we consider the research on the development of object permanence (for example, Charlesworth, 1968), we find that, for the most part, object permanence has been established by 8 months of life, in many cases even earlier. If the infant has the cognition available to preserve memory of objects no longer present, how can we deny them the ability to have self-permanence? Indeed, is it reasonable to talk of object-permanence capacity without self-permanence capacity? Given that this first self-other distinction is made very early, the various categorical dimensions of self may also proceed to unfold. The unfolding of the categories, whether sequential, hierarchical, etc., and the dimensions of the various categories are uncertain.

Is our understanding of the phenomenon of fear helped by evoking the concept of self? We would argue, yes. For example, Hebb's (1949, p. 243) study on the fear of monkeys could be explained by this concept. Consider the monkeys were fearful because they saw a monkey without a body and they were aware that they, too, were monkeys. Maybe they too could lose their heads to a mad professor. Would not humans placed in a similar situation show fear for *their* lives or safety?[3] In terms of our data, the notion of self also helps in explaining the data. Perhaps female infants are more frightened than male infants of male adult strangers because, while they are equally strange, the male infant recognizes that the male adult is more like himself. The specific category of self in this case may be gender. The Money, Hampson and Hampson (1957) data on sexual identity sug-

gest that a year-old infant may already possess this category.

That there was a positive response to the child stranger and negative responses to the adult strangers is difficult to explain in any incongruity hypothesis unless we consider that the referent for the social comparison does not always have to be the infant's mother. There could be multiple referents, one of them being the mother, another being the self. Perhaps the positive response to the child stranger is produced because infants find the child like themselves; that is, they use themselves as referent and find the child like them and are therefore not afraid. In this case the categorical dimension of self may have to do with size. I am small vis-à-vis other social events and the child is also small, therefore, like me.[4]

The present data are clear; at least for the social events used, there was significantly different affect elicited as these events approached. The dimensions on which these social events can be ordered are not at all clear. The most likely candidate for the differences between adults and child is size, but since both adults were the same size, the male-female differences cannot be accounted for by this dimension alone. We view this experiment, then, as a beginning in the study of the dimensions and consequences of social events. Clearly more work is necessary.

In this discussion of fear two major theoretical positions have been evoked, and it would help to clarify the discussion by stating them explicitly. These are the ethological and cognitive approaches. The ethological position rests less (if at all) on a cognitive and more on an imprinting, IRM, instinctual approach. The argument for the present data would be as follows: infant imprinted

---

[3] The Gardners report that in their study of sign language in the chimpanzee, the animal exhibits the concept of self. When shown a mirror Washoe responded with the signs "me Washoe." Thus, it is not unreasonable to attribute the concept of self to other primates.

[4] While there is no direct data to support this, there is a strong suggestion to be found in the data. A correlation matrix was obtained by comparing the children's response consistency across the five social events at the touch distance. As was to be expected, infants who were very fearful of the male stranger were also fearful of the female stranger ($r = .71$, $p < .001$); however, there was no significant relationship between the self and mother ($r = .12$). Thus, while the two strangers were treated alike, the self and mother were not. Moreover, as expected, high negative responses to the adult strangers were associated with more positive responses to both mother and the self; however, they were on the average more than twice as highly associated for the self ($r = -.47$, $p < .05$) than for mother ($r = -.22$).

on parents; all others, strange. Strange at a distance→observe, but do not flee. Strange approach→flee. The only caveat would be that strange has to be bigger than the organism. This model requires the use of no or little cognitive process, and following the ethological approach is rather mechanistic in nature.

The cognitive approach, on the other hand, invokes concepts such as incongruity, novelty and familiarity, and schema. These all rest on the interaction between the organism's past and its present experiences. Moreover, the cognitive approach requires the introduction of such processes as object permanence, at least in terms of remembering the mother. This approach stresses that the child's response to strange is a part of the larger emerging cognitive functions. We would extend this position by considering the concept of self and using it as an additional referent in terms of social interactions and cognitions. While the ethological approach has intrinsic appeal—especially since it evokes a biological simplicity—it is difficult for us to consider infants not responding through the use of the elaborate cognitive functions which we know are already available to them.

Before concluding this paper, we should like to return to the most interesting of our findings, that of the infant's response to the child. The positive response of the infants to the child stranger is consistent with other primate evidence, all of which suggests that infant-peer interactions may have a special quality. It is well known that infants often follow and learn faster from an older sibling (peer) than from their parents. In fact, peers may serve quite well as adult substitutes in the early attachment relationships (for example, Chamove, 1966; Freud & Dann, 1951). Infants not only show little or no fear toward peers, but, in fact, can engage in a meaningful attachment behavior. We would suggest that these facts have importance for a general theory of interpersonal relationships.

The following speculations are based on these considerations. Phylogenetically, attachment relationships have changed from infant-peer to infant-adult dyads. Phylogenetically lower organisms' attachment behaviors are between peers of the specie. This is especially true if we consider that at the lower end of the scale most information

the organism needs for survival is prewired into the system. All that is necessary for the developing specie is to practice these skills as they unfold. It would be more logical to practice these skills with someone also somewhat less proficient, for the skills of the adult would be too overwhelming. Moreover, since the adult has little or nothing to teach the infant, there needs to be little attachment to an adult. This would suggest that among birds, for example, the young could be as easily or more easily imprinted on a peer than on an adult member. Whom are the ducklings imprinted on as they swim single file on the pond? The "mother" or the young duckling in front of them? As we proceed along the phylogenetic scale, learning becomes more important for the survival of the organism. As such, peers who are good for practicing present skills are no longer sufficient, and adults who are good in teaching new skills are needed. Thus, attachment on adults rather than peers becomes increasingly important. Single births and long periods of relative helplessness facilitate the infant-adult relationship; however, the data make clear that if infant-peer relationships can be sustained (as, for example, in laboratory colonies) infant-peer relationships satisfy many of the socioemotional requirements (Harlow & Harlow, 1969; Harlow, Harlow & Suomi, 1971). Its effect on learning, however, should be inhibiting.

The implication for caregiving is vast. We might argue that infant-peer relationships are not substitutes for infant-adult, but rather, are more basic, at least older in a phylogenetic sense. Small families isolated from one another may constitute a rather unique and new experience, not only for the caregivers, but for the infants themselves.

We have come a long way from the observations of the terrified 8-month-old. But we have collected information to indicate that infants of this age are not frightened of young children and often seek and are sustained by their company. In some sense they appear to be attached to all peers, familiar and strange. The social commerce with adults, however, is restricted to those that are familiar, and even then they often prefer their peers. Any theory of interpersonal relationships and fear of social events must come to grips with these facts.

REFERENCES

AINSWORTH, M. D. S., & BELL, S. M.   Attachment, exploration, and separation: Illustrated by the behavior of one-year-olds in a strange situation. *Child Development*, 1970, *41*, 49–67.

BAN, P., & LEWIS, M.   Mothers and fathers, girls and boys: Attachment behavior in the one-year-old. Paper presented at Eastern Psychological Association meetings, New York City, April 1971.

CHAMOVE, A. S.   The effects of varying infant peer experience on social behavior in the rhesus monkey. Unpublished M.A. thesis, University of Wisconsin, 1966.

CHARLESWORTH, W. R.   Cognition in infancy: Where do we stand in the mid-sixties? *Merrill-Palmer Quarterly*, 1968, *14*, 25–46.

COATES, B., ANDERSON, E. P., & HARTUP, W. W.   Interrelations in the attachment behavior of human infants. *Developmental Psychology*, 1972, *6*(2), 218–230.

FREUD, A., & DANN, S.   An experiment in group upbringing. In *The psychoanalytic study of the child, Vol. VI.* New York: International University Press, 1951.

GOLDBERG, S., & LEWIS, M.   Play behavior in the year-old infant: Early sex differences. *Child Development*, 1969, *40*, 21–31.

HARLOW, H. F., & HARLOW, M. K.   Effects of various mother-infant relationships on rhesus monkey behaviors. In B. M. Foss (Ed.), *Determinants of infant behavior, Vol. IV.* London: Methuen Press, 1969.

HARLOW, H. F., HARLOW, M. K., & SUOMI, S. J.   From thought to therapy: Lessons from a primate laboratory. *American Scientist*, 1971, *59*, 538–549.

HEBB, D. O.   On the nature of fear. *Psychological Review*, 1946, *53*, 259–276.

HEBB, D. O.   *The organization of behavior.* New York: Wiley, 1949.

JAMES, W.   *The principles of psychology.* New York: Dover Publications, 1950 (1895).

LEWIS, M.   State as an infant-environment interaction: An analysis of mother-infant behavior as a function of sex. Paper presented at the Merrill-Palmer Conference on Research and Teaching of Infant Development, Detroit, February 1971. *Merrill-Palmer Quarterly*, in press.

LEWIS, M., & BAN, P.   Stability of attachment behavior: A transformational analysis. Paper presented at Society for Research in Child Development meetings, Symposium on *Attachment: Studies in Stability and Change*, Minneapolis, April 1971.

MONEY, J., HAMPSON, J. G., & HAMPSON, J. L.   Imprinting and the establishment of gender role. A.M.A., *Archives of Neurology and Psychology*, 1957, *77*, 333–336.

MORGAN, G. A., & RICCIUTI, H. N.   Infants' responses to strangers during the first year. In B. M. Foss (Ed.), *Determinants of infant behavior, Vol. IV.* London: Methuen Press, 1969.

PIAGET, J.   *The origins of intelligence in children.* New York: International University Press, 1952.

RHEINGOLD, H. L.   Some visual determinants of smiling in infants. Unpublished manuscript, University of North Carolina, Chapel Hill, 1971.

RHEINGOLD, H. L., & ECKERMAN, C. O.   Fear of the stranger: A cultural examination. Paper presented at Society for Research in Child Development meetings, Minneapolis, April 1971.

SCARR, S., & SALAPATEK, P.   Patterns of fear development during infancy. *Merrill-Palmer Quarterly*, 1970, *16*, 53–90.

SCHAFFER, H. R.   The onset of fear of strangers and the incongruity hypothesis. *Journal of Child Psychology and Psychiatry*, 1966, *7*, 95–106.

SCHAFFER, H. R., & EMERSON, P. E.   The development of social attachments in infancy. *Monographs of the Society for Research in Child Development*, 1964, *29*(3, Serial No. 94).

Developmental and Motivational Concepts in Piaget's Sensorimotor Theory of Intelligence

Peter H. Wolff, M.D.

In the introduction to his Edinburgh lectures on natural religion, William James (1902) wrote:

Medical materialism seems indeed a good appellation for the too simple-minded system of thought which we are considering. Medical materialism finishes up Saint Paul by calling his vision on the road to Damascus a discharging lesion of the occipital cortex, he being an epileptic. It snuffs out Saint Theresa as an hysteric, Saint Francis of Assisi as an hereditary degenerate. . . . Carlyle's organ-tones of misery it accounts for by a gastro-duodenal catarrh [p. 14]. A more fully developed example of the same kind of reasoning is the fashion, quite common nowadays among certain writers, of criticizing the religious emotions by showing a connection between them and the sexual life.

The First Academic Lecture of the American Academy of Child Psychiatry, delivered on October 13, 1962 at the Edgewater Beach Hotel, Chicago, Ill.

Conversion is a crisis of puberty and adolescence. The macerations of saints, and the devotion of missionaries, are only instances of the parental instinct of self-sacrifice gone astray. For the hysterical nun, starving for natural life, Christ is but an imaginary substitute for a more earthly subject of affection [p. 11f.].

In this manner James prepared his audience for the psychological exploration of religious experience that was to follow in subsequent lectures, by indicating that he would not attempt to reduce complex human experiences to neural excitations or to neurotic instability and other disorders of the mind; in later passages he proposed that such explanations might yield necessary, but could not yield sufficient, explanations of the phenomena in question.

What was fashionable among certain writers in James's time has become an established *Weltanschauung* among some schools of clinical psychiatry, which look to a unitary causal explanation of behavior. Regardless of our particular theoretical persuasion, as clinical psychiatrists many of us are sometimes inclined to view behavior as if it were determined only by motivational causes and completely reducible to genetic sources.

My primary assignment today is an exposition of Piaget's sensorimotor theory of development, but I shall also use the opportunity to focus your attention on his causal conception of behavior, to show how a comprehensive psychological system which does not postulate inherent internal forces or motives accounts for behavior and development in an internally consistent manner. To highlight those features of Piaget's causal conception that distinguish it from our clinical mode of thinking, I have chosen David Rapaport's definition of motivation because it transcends parochial arguments among schools of motivational psychology, and abstracts the formal characteristics that are apposite to all motivation concepts. His definition states: *"motives are appetitive internal forces.* The defining characteristics of the concept of appetitiveness as I am using it here are the following: (a) peremptoriness, (b) cyclic character, (c) selectiveness, and (d) displaceability" (1960, p. 187). Within the context of Piaget's theory I will try to show that under some conditions of internal equilibrium, and with respect to particular kinds of action, Piaget's conception may broaden our general understanding of the causes of behavior and development.

By intention Piaget is a philosopher of science and not a psychologist. His empirical writings culminate in the formulation of a genetic epistemology and a demonstration that the perennial philosophical question, *how man knows the world,* may be fruitfully studied by the empirical methods of developmental psychology.

The fundamental assumptions which Piaget set out to demonstrate are:

1. Intelligence is only one aspect of a general biological adaptation to the environment.

2. Intellectual adaptation is the progressive differentiation and integration of inborn reflex mechanisms under the impact of experience.

3. From the simplest symbolic play to the most complex logical thought, *mental* functions are derived from *motor* actions on concrete objects;

the growth of intelligence may be viewed as the progressive transformation of motor patterns into thought patterns, the latter transcending the concrete circumstances out of which they arise.

4. The defferentiation of reflex structures and of their function gives rise to the mental operations by which man conceives of object, space, time, and causality, and of the logical relationships which constitute the basis of scientific thought.

Piaget sought to answer, for example, how the newborn infant, equipped with stereotyped reflex behaviors, grows into an eighteen-month-old child capable of searching for an object after it has disappeared from vision, of inferring unobserved causes from observed results, of constructing spatial relations in thought, and of arranging sequences of action into means-ends relations. He sought to answer how the eighteen-month-old child, equipped for the first time with representational thought patterns, develops into an adolescent who can formulate abstract problems in the absence of concrete objects, and can solve these by reversible mental functions that approximate the logical operations of algebra.

To outline the model of behavior that is implicit to Piaget's theory, let me first consider the normal newborn infant who is capable of sucking, grasping, auditory and visual pursuit, and other stereotype behavior patterns. The patterns are primed so that they will be activated by nonspecific stimuli in the average expectable environment. After a reflex behavior has been achieved by accidental encounters a sufficient number of times, it is repeated spontaneously, or without additional external stimulation. In the case of reflexes, the act itself serves as a sufficient stimulus to propagate the behavior. In the case of acquired behavior patterns, the infant seeks to renew contact with novelties after he has encountered them; apparently he seeks to repeat newly discovered actions. Action patterns conserved by self-repetition are called *circular reactions;* as each of the reflexes is repeated through circular reaction, behavior corresponding to it is executed with increasing efficiency. Although at birth the child is able to suck at the breast, practice improves his facility and gradually coordinates the ensemble of components making up the sucking act into a stable action adapted to its goal of taking nourishment; but without such practice the component parts present at birth would not be integrated.

At a later stage in development the hand, while moving at random by reflex circular reaction, contacts the mouth and initiates sucking movements. The mouth, already adapted to the breast and to nonnutritive empty sucking, now sucks the hand, and the infant makes repeated efforts to suck his hand. Although the initial efforts are clumsy, the new object (the hand) is not so foreign as to disrupt sucking activity, yet it is sufficiently novel to create a relation of *disadaptation* between the infant's behavior and his environment. After the hand has been brought to the mouth repeatedly by chance, the arm is directed to the mouth, the mouth shapes itself to "receive" the hand before actual contact, and the hand prepares itself to fit the mouth aperture. Gradually a new circular reaction of thumb sucking emerges and persists until the infant sucks his thumb skillfully. After thumb sucking becomes an established form of behavior, the child retains the capacity for empty, nonnutritive sucking and nutritive sucking at the breast. Thus, when two or more behavior patterns coordinate to give rise to a new unit of behavior, the component parts are retained and may still be applied under appropriate circumstances.

From examples like these we can infer the basic model of Piaget's theory of sensorimotor development. The observations show that at least some of neonatal behavior is *organized* as distinct and repeatable action patterns. From this we infer the existence of psychological structures which insure that behavior will be repeated in relatively stable form. The psychological structures existing at birth we call the *reflex schemata*. For each newly acquired motor pattern, such as hand sucking, and for each later thought pattern, we postulate comparable acquired structures or *schemata proper*. In each case the schema is conceptualized as the central guarantee that behavior will be stable and repeatable.

With each repetition behavior changes by an imperceptible increment in the direction of greater adaptation. From this we infer that each activation of a circular reaction alters the behavior to some degree, and that the change is cumulative

rather than abrupt. Since the new motor patterns that emerge with practice are also repeatable in stable form, we deduce that the reflex schema itself undergoes change through experience, and that some actual properties of the encounter must also accrue to the schema to change it in the direction of greater adaptation. The function by which each encounter between infant and environment accrues to the schema is defined as *assimilation*. It represents the incorporation of novel encounters into the assembly of all past experiences of the same kind. The function by which the schema changes as the result of assimilation is defined as *accommodation*. It represents the active reorganization of past experiences of one kind which brings the past into closer correspondence with the assimilated novelty. Development is therefore a constant interplay of assimilatory and accommodative functions. Only when the assimilation of a novelty no longer forces a further modification in behavior will we consider that the behavior is adapted or that a balance between assimilation and accommodation has been struck.

Sensorimotor theory postulates assimilation as the universal function that characterizes all living organisms, the function that selectively incorporates specific material substances into organ systems at the organic level, and at the psychological level incorporates sensorimotor data and ideas into already existing mental structures. Assimilation thus broadens the organism's contact with its environment by differentiating the existing internal structure and producing a more accurate inner representation of the relation between individual and environment. It is the intrinsic developmental factor of Piaget's theory.

Fundamental to the concept of assimilation is the notion that new structures are built *because* the organism actively renews contact with specific stimulus situations and integrates these into the already existing structures, and not because the world of stimuli impinges upon a passive organism. The external stimulus plays a vital role since it determines the direction of adaptation, but assimilation is not identical with the reflex response to stimulation. Only those stimuli are assimilated for which an approximating internal structure already exists, and the organism imposes an order on its surroundings in terms of the structures at its disposal. Nor is accommodation identical with response; rather it refers to the organism's constant restructuring of past experiences in keeping with present circumstances. The schema that is generated by assimilatory activity is therefore in no sense an association chain of discrete sensory stimuli and motor responses.

Sir Frederick Bartlett, among the first to introduce the concept of schema to psychology, defined it as:

> . . . an active organization of past reactions, or of past experiences which must always be supposed to be operating in any well-adapted, organic response. Whenever there is any order or regularity of behaviour, a particular response is possible only because it is related to other similar responses which have been serially organized, yet which operate not simply as individual members coming one after another, but as a unitary mass [Bartlett, 1932, p. 201].

Whatever the schema assimilates is defined as *aliment;* the nature and complexity of aliment that can be assimilated at a given stage is always determined simultaneously by the child's developing structures and by the "action potentialities" of the object encountered—whether the action is concrete behavior or mental activity, whether the object is a concrete thing or an idea.

Aliment does not mean the same as stimulus, which by definition remains identical to itself at successive development levels and is defined independent of the organism, while aliment can only be defined in terms of the relation between organisms and object at a particular stage in development. The newborn infant, for example, assimilates the breast, the bottle, or the finger, as something to suck or to see or to grasp, because he is endowed only with reflex schemata which can encompass such global action properties of objects; and his corresponding accommodation consists simply of sucking or looking or grasping all those objects which suit the action. By three months, when grasping and looking are coordinated, the appropriate object (e.g., the bottle) also offers aliment for looking and grasping, although the stimulus object has not changed from the "objective" point of view. At eight months the child assimilates not only the action properties of

objects but also their spatial and causal characteristics; then his accommodations will include the effort to see what is on the other side of the bottle, and what happens when he drops it. Thus the meaning which the child attributes to objects and to their interrelations constantly changes as he develops, and is determined neither exclusively by the object's stimulus properties nor exclusively by his apperceptions.

So far I have considered only the mechanisms of action but not the causation of behavior in Piaget's sensorimotor theory. We have seen that as long as an action is not adapted to the stimulus object, each repetition slightly alters the behavior pattern; from this we inferred that assimilation and accommodation had not completed their adaptive work. Until the repetition of an act no longer changes behavior, the corresponding schema is said to be in a state of *disequilibrium,* or the action pattern is said to be in a state of *disadaptation.* The theory assumes that disequilibrium (at the level of mental constructs) or disadaptation (at the level of behavioral descriptions) gives rise to a *need to function,* or a need to repeat action to the point of adaptation.

The need to function is the exclusive concept of causation in sensorimotor theory. It refers to all occasions when assimilation of an aliment and accommodation of the schema to it are not in balance. The term does not imply an *a priori* need of the organism to adapt ubiquitously and without specification to any and all objects, as do terms like the instinct for mastery, need achievement, and competence motivation; need to function is a generic term that acquires specific definition only in each particular context of action. For example, when the child who is able to suck at the breast encounters a new object with his mouth which he can suck, the cause of action is the need to suck, but now in the new way already experienced; when two or more action patterns are coordinated into a new circular reaction, the need is created by the fact that the two separate action patterns have intersected while using the same object and it consists, for example, of the "need to see what is grasped and to grasp what is seen." When the child discovers for the first time that a ball will roll down an inclined plane all by itself, he repeats this experiment out of the need to explore the causal properties of objects that he now experiences as being independent of himself. In each case the need arises within a context of action and persists until a full assimilation of the specific datum encountered and a corresponding accommodation are achieved. Since every circular reaction on one object exposes the child to a variety of new circumstances, each of which he can partially assimilate and to which he is not fully adapted, the state of adaptation always remains an ideal goal which gives direction to development, but a goal which is never achieved.

Having now considered Piaget's concept of the causation of behavior, we can contrast it with the concept of motivation as defined by Rapaport.

1. Unlike motives, which are conceptualized as *internal* forces, the need to function is neither generated within the organism nor imposed on the organism as an external force (that is, as a stimulus of academic and Pavlovian learning theory). Both the goal and the aim of action are determined by the context of the encounter, and the cause is located simultaneously in the environment—the novelty, and in the organism—the tendency to assimilate all possible aliment. The child is "caused" to act, or has a need to repeat his contact with specific objects, because he has already acted on them. Encounter with novelty motivates repetition or circular reaction, and it is the *action* which engenders the *need* for further contact rather than the internal *need* which prompts the *action*.

2. Unlike the motivation, need to function is not cyclical; functional need for activity is not terminated by consummatory action. It arises in the course of action and abates after the appropriate modification within the psychic structure has taken place.

3. The need to function is not peremptory. If circular reaction is disrupted before adaptation is completed, the behavior remains in a state of disadaptation until appropriate environmental conditions allow for the necessary practice. Disruption or interference with action, therefore, does not result in increasing internal tension, as is the case with motivational forces.

4. The need to function, unlike motivation, cannot be displaced from one goal to another. Therefore it does not give rise to substitute action on substitute objects when the intended object is not available. Although the child may alternatively

perfect his global sucking schema by acting on his lips, his thumb, or the breast, each object serves as aliment for the stabilization of the global schema of sucking to the extent that the different objects are suckable and for the child identical at this stage of development. Later, distinct objects will generate their own specific action schemata, thereby differentiating the global schema. The concept of object permanence will be assimilated equally from action on disappearing dolls, disappearing faces, or disappearing fingers, since object permanence is a property universal to and therefore abstractable from all of them. But the child will also elaborate differentiated schemata for recovering the doll, the fingers, or the face of another person, since the recovery of these different objects requires distinct means of action.

According to Rapaport's definition (1960), as he has pointed out, Piaget's *need to function* is not a motivation in the true sense, but rather another psychological causation of behavior. I shall now consider the role of this cause in intellectual development in relation to Piaget's observations and experiments.

I have already referred briefly to the data of the first stage. The child simply repeats and strengthens the reflex patterns given at birth. By repetition the reflexes are stabilized. Slight degrees of differentiation in sucking patterns do occur, and as a result the child can for the first time make practical judgments about various related objects in terms of the differentiated actions which he applies to them. During this first stage the need to function is, however, primarily the need to repeat inborn behavior patterns as such. As long as the child does not distinguish between action and object he has no knowledge of objects except while he acts on them, and they exist for him only as something to suck, or something to see, or something to grasp, but not as something to grasp *and* to see at the same time. Since action is hardly differentiated from object, and since action is both the adaptive action and the source for further aliment at the same time, the need to repeat is identical with the act itself.

During the second stage reflex patterns are coordinated into new actions or *primary circular reactions*. Until now the hand has moved independent of visual control; grasping movements developed in a sequence which was similar to that of sucking, while the eyes practiced visual pursuit and began to accommodate to near and far objects. While the hand is repeatedly brought to the mouth, it will sooner or later pass before the eyes, and then it becomes an object for the eyes to follow as well as for the mouth to suck. As the chance encounters between sucking, visual and grasping activities are coordinated, the hand begins to linger in the visual field before going to the mouth, while the eyes adapt themselves by keeping the hand in the visual range in order to observe the different movements of the fingers. Eventually a new behavior pattern emerges in which everything that the child grasps is brought to the eyes, and everything he sees evokes an effort to grasp. This intersection of two behavior patterns creates a new need and an anticipation of looking whenever the hand grasps something, and of directed grasping whenever the eyes see something. The child becomes aware that the object is something distinct from action in progress when he learns to anticipate those other actions which experience and coordination have linked to the action in progress. Thereafter, when he sucks on something, the object exists for him not only by virtue of its "suckability" but also by its visual and graspable properties, although he "knows" of the latter two properties only by an anticipation or a readiness for appropriate sequences of action to follow. In subsequent stages as he acquires more diverse ways of acting on objects, and as these actions are linked into complex anticipation patterns, he will eventually regard the object as something that is entirely independent of action and therefore external to him.

Between the fifth and eighth months (the third stage of sensorimotor development), the child directs his action to the novelties as if they were somewhat separate from although still dependent on his action and as yet he does not adapt his action to the spatial, objective, and causal properties of the events. While kicking for the sake of repetition, for example, the child happens to kick a toy suspended from his crib. He stops kicking, looks at the toy as long as it moves, and when it stops he kicks again while looking intently at the toy. His attitude of expectancy clearly suggests that he anticipates seeing the toy move again after he kicks. He appears to act in order to repeat events which are independent of his action, and for this end uses *procedures* or motor anticipation patterns. However, as *procedures to make interesting spectacles last* are stabilized, the child generalizes them indiscriminately to all other novelties he perceives, and thereby betrays the extent to which for him object permanence still depends on action. He kicks his feet to make a noise recur, or to repeat the movement of a distant window curtain that is causally unrelated to his action, and expects that it will recur. Such observations show that procedures, although they have become ready-made action pattern or a "practical concept" which can be generalized to various circumstances, still have a "magical" quality, and that the child still considers his action to be sufficient cause for all external events, or that the object is still at the disposal of his action ("magical" conception of causality).

During the eighth through the twelfth month, the child actually accommodates his action pattern to real circumstances. He abandons "magical omnipotence" (that is the subordination of all causes to his action) for the intention to achieve actual results by intelligent action. For example, when he wants to reach a doll but the path to it is blocked by a pillow, he discovers in the course of his groping that he can displace the obstacle and reach the doll by striking at the pillow. Unlike in previous stages, he is no longer distracted by the spectacle of displacing the pillow, nor does he rely on magical procedures which will not yield the desired result in "reality." He uses the removal of the pillow as a mediation between his wish and his final goal. In time, means such as displacing one object to obtain another can be linked to various goal actions in sequences appropriate to the causal-temporal-spatial context of the total situation. Then the motor anticipation pattern of striking becomes a stable tool of behavior independent of the specific context in which it was learned and capable of unlimited adaptive generalization as a *mobile schema*.

When the child executes one movement as the intermediary to achieving a goal by a distinctly different movement, we infer that during the delay the child remains aware of both the goal and the goal-directed action, even though he is not acting directly on the goal; and that he must literally "keep the goal in mind" while engaged in detour behavior. Piaget considers such awareness of the goal independent of action as the hallmark of all intelligent action, and calls it *intentional* or *purposive* behavior. As the schemata themselves have differentiated during the first four stages of sensorimotor development, so the simple need to repeat inborn reflex patterns has evolved into a complex, psychological causation that is identical with purpose.

As in earlier stages, the source of a complex cause such as intention resides simultaneously in the novel situation and in the child's tendency to assimilate. But now as the child is able to assimilate the goal, the obstacle, and the relation between them at the same time, his functional need encompasses the goal object as well as its spatial-causal context.

Throughout the first four stages the need to function has been directed by the past, and it resulted simply in the repetition of action discovered by chance. Even during the fourth stage, although the situation was novel, the child used only familiar behavior patterns in new sequences. During the fifth stage when the child encounters a novelty, he acts as if his purpose, instead of repeating what he has already seen, were to explore possible variations which he has not yet perceived. For example, when he pushes with his finger on the matchbox and discovers that it tilts, he systematically pushes the box from various angles at various points, and causes it to tilt in different ways, each novelty leading him to discover a new way of pushing. He may not know what the result will be, but in some primitive sense he must be aware that there are unrealized possibilities of tilting the matchbox, otherwise he would be engaged in repetitive movements or random behavior.

What *causes* the child to invent new variations by trial and error rather than repeating old ones? The need to repeat can no longer provide a sufficient explanation since the child actively creates novelties. Nor can concepts like the instinct for mastery, need achievement, or competence motivation do more than describe the behavior in general terms, since they tell us nothing about the direction which a particular action will take once a novelty is encountered, and therefore nothing about the purpose which directs this action. Piaget argues that the child now explores what the object can do by itself precisely because he has acquired a partial concept of object permanence which is independent of his action; because he has acquired a partial concept of physical causality which is independent of his participation; and because he has acquired a concept of physical space in which he can anticipate the placement of objects independent of his action. The child assimilates the novelty to a whole array of internalized action patterns (mobile schemata) and subordinates these in means-end relationship to the discovery that a matchbox can be tilted by pushing. Each latent action pattern subordinated to the controlling schema of tilting the box then suggests to the child a new way of tilting. Because ready-made anticipation patterns through generalization were freed from their initial context of origin, they are applied freely in entirely new circumstances, but are now applied so as to fit into the spatial-causal context of the present and therefore no longer as magical procedures. The functional need is still generated by the encounter with novelty, but the greater differentiation between self and outside allows the child to explore the properties of objects rather than repeating actions on them.

During the sixth stage the child invents new procedures and discovers new combinations in almost the same way as in the fifth stage, although inventions now take place in thought and by spontaneous rearrangment, rather than by concrete action and by trial and error. Slowly, during the preceding five stages, motor actions have become internalized as thought patterns; at the second stage actions became motor anticipation patterns, at the third stage novel spectacles activated ready-made anticipation patterns or procedures; and during the fourth stage these internalized anticipation patterns became the tools for means-end behavior. During the fifth stage the internal anticipation patterns were sufficiently liberated from their context of origin to engender a systematic creation of novelties.

The complementary roles of assimilation and accommodation remain the same, although in the sixth stage the intermediate steps between the initial desire and the final goal are no longer directly observable. For example, when the child loses sight of a ball as it rolls under a couch, he walks around the couch to retrieve the ball on the other side rather than crawling under it. From such directed behavior we infer that the child invents a new spatial displacement which he relates to the ball's projected displacement so as to bring himself and the ball to the same end point, in thought prior to action. From this it follows that the child is able to represent the ball to himself although he no longer sees it; and that he has acquired the concept of object permanence. It follows that he can represent to himself a space in which various objects, including himself, can be displaced in relation to each other, and that he has acquired a mental representation of space. Finally, it follows that he attributes independent motion to the ball, and that he has differentiated psychological from physical causality.

The end of sensorimotor intelligence marks only the first step in the total sequence of intellectual growth. What was achieved within a context of immediate action on concrete objects must now be repeated at the level of mental representations. When the child acquires language, and as linguistic symbols replace motor anticipation patterns, he must distinguish all over again between himself—in this case his mental representations or *signifiers*—and the things and relations that are represented—or the *significations*. The differentiation between symbolic signifier and signification, and the socialization of differentiated signifiers into a system of communicable signs, are the work of intellectual growth still before the child. At the level of mental representations we can again measure the progress of intelligence in terms of the differentiation between assimilation and accommodation. Now, however, this process is reflected in thought rather than in concrete action. Although we still infer the work of intelligence from its end product in adaptive action, action is no longer the direct expression of intelligence, but simply the observable index of representational thought; in subsequent stages motor action will further be replaced by verbal behavior as the index of intelligent adaptations.

1. To the extent that the two functions are undifferentiated and accommodation has primacy over assimilation, the child responds to novelty without integrating his action fully into the totality of past experiences. He acts in the present without relating his action to his (inner) past, and as a result imitates the models in his environment without comprehending their veridical implications. Like intelligence in general, imitation has its roots in sensorimotor behavior of the first two years. At one year, for example, the child watches his father open and close a matchbox. Then he opens and closes his fist while keeping his eyes on the box; he makes a sound which resembles the scratching of the matchbox, and at the same time opens and closes his mouth. The strange matchbox has created in the child a functional need to encompass in some way what he saw but did not yet understand. In contrast to intellectual adaptation proper, the child does not assimilate the spatial properties of the object to his thought schemata of space and causality, in order to understand them, but imitates the model as he has perceived it. His primary aim appears to be to reconstitute the novelty to himself, to conserve it without seeking to comprehend it. At this stage imitation is still motor action related to objects in his presence, and there is nothing in his behavior to suggest that he has an internal image of the model. One year later, after the symbol has been fully divested of its action context, the child imitates the action of a servant he has observed scrubbing the floor several days before, or he pretends to sew with a thread and needle as he observed his mother do on a previous day. Such *deferred* imitations imply that the child has at his disposal an image of the model to project it as an independent representation which has an inner and therefore an external constancy; and that he can reproduce it at will when the model itself is no longer present. It is imitation rather than intelligent adaptation in so far as the child does not understand the significance of the model he imitates.

2. To the extent that the two functions remain undifferentiated and assimilation has primacy over accommodation, the child incorporates novelties into his private world without modifying that inner world in correspondence to the real properties of the novelty. Thus, the present acquires meaning for him only as he relates it to his inner past; he relates the outside world to himself but does not relate himself to the outside. Thereby

he engages in *play*. Like imitation, play has its roots in early sensorimotor behavior, and becomes symbolic after thought schemata replace motor anticipations. At fourteen months the child engages in practical make-believe games that utilize the sensorimotor actions at his disposal. He pretends to drink or eat although there is nothing in his hands. The nature of his play suggests the child's dawning awareness of "pretending" and suggests the concomitant first realization of the difference between the object as idea and the object as thing. He uses pebbles at one time as if they were candy, at another time as if they were building blocks. He disregards the physical properties of objects to make them fit into his play of the moment, and does not change the action to adapt it to the real properties of the thing with which he is playing. By four years the child makes up stories by organizing fragments of conversations he has heard on previous days into coherent accounts. Although the story may have no basis in reality and is constructed to fit the child's need of the moment, it employs freely interchangeable linguistic symbols. Such use of symbols is "ludic" or playful rather than intelligent adaptation in so far as the child manipulates ideas in disregard of the veridical world that he is capable of perceiving. Only after the child can clearly differentiate between the idea as subjective reality and the thing or phenomenon as objective reality, will intellectual thought become capable of the unlimited combinations and generalizations that characterize abstract logic. In all its developmental manifestations, play therefore serves a crucial function in intellectual growth because it allows for new combinations and inventions that are not bound by the concrete realities of the present.

3. To the extent that assimilation and accommodation are differentiated and integrated, the child assimilates novelties to his representational schemata, and at the same time alters these to make them correspond with the veridical world and its social conventions. Not only does he assimilate the present to symbolic representations of his experiences (as in play), but now he accommodates his inner world to coordinate it with the realistic aspects he has perceived. Thus, at

two and a half, the child adapts his reasoning process to observed events. When he calls his father who does not answer, he concludes that his father did not hear. When he sees his father preparing hot water he infers that the father is going to shave. By four years, adaptive intelligence allows him to classify objects into categories, although such categorizations still often lead to incorrect solutions. When he acquires a concept of classes, he identifies an animal as a horse because it has a mane, on the proposition that all four-legged animals with manes are horses; but because he cannot differentiate logically between horses and mules, he is confused by the fact that mules also have manes. Later as he acquires the mental operations of class inclusion and class multiplication, his class concepts acquire an objective permanence. Then he can decide that the universal class of four-legged animals with manes includes both horses and mules, each constituting a subclass with special attributes (by class multiplication) and both subordinated under the universal class (by class inclusion).

Imitation, symbolic play, and cognitive representation are only three aspects of a general process of intellectual adaptation. Since imitation always combines assimilatory with accommodative functions and can never be pure accommodation, it always increases the child's understanding of real circumstances, although the focus of action is on the reproduction of models rather than on the assimilation of their meanings. Since symbolic play always combines accommodative with assimilatory functions and can never be pure assimilation, it always increases the child's understanding of the real world by altering his mental representation of it, although the focus of action and thought is to subordinate new experiences to already acquired private meanings.

At every new phase in development, the causation of intellectual function remains the same as during the sensorimotor stage. The need to function arises when the child encounters a novelty which he is able to integrate in part but to which his actions or thoughts are not fully adapted. Whether the result is imitation, symbolic play, or cognitive representation, the child is caused to assimilate and to accommodate all novelties he encounters, and the cause resides simultaneously in his fundamental tendency to assimilate, and in the world of objects to which his intellectual structures are partially adapted.

I have devoted so much time to discussing a limited segment of Piaget's general theory of intelligence to show how it accounts for the causation of behavior without invoking the concept of motivation. As a ubiquitous explanation of all behavior, *functional need* is surely as insufficient as other unitary concepts of causation, whether these invoke a classical stimulus-response sequence or one of various motivational forces. From clinical experience we have learned that a concept like the need to function cannot account for all observable behavior, and that motivational factors which antedate experience (that is, causal forces which do not arise in the course of action) are significant and powerful determinants of behavior and organizers of experience. Clinical experience also suggests that without dynamic and economic considerations we cannot adequately account for the peremptory quality of some behavior and for the phenomena subsumed under concepts like directed attention and altered levels of consciousness, for which Piaget's theory provides only *ad hoc* explanations. Clinical data suggest that contrary to Piaget's assertion, affects *are* structure-building forces which give rise to semipermanent emotional predispositions (e.g., moods, character traits, etc.), and that when so structured, affects may also serve as defenses to ward off other affective experiences. The clinical investigations of individual life histories have shown that specific variations of early social experience individualize the person's social, intellectual, and affective adaptive pattern and style. The need to function as the exclusive concept of causation cannot easily account for the fact of individual differences. Finally, clinical experience teaches us that the need to function and the intellectual structures that such a causation generates are always indissociably linked to motivational factors, to defensive organizations, and to the derivative discharge modes arising from defense formations; and that adaptive mechanisms are always only *relatively* but never *absolutely* autonomous from motivation and conflict. The indissociability of affective and

cognitive-perceptual development is a truism postulated both by comprehensive motivational theories of development and by Piaget, although neither theory has studied this interaction systematically. For developmental psychology, the significant question regarding the relative autonomy of structures is not so much whether affects speed up or slow down the *rate* of cognitive development, as it is whether affective forces (and more generally motivational forces) *change* the sequence of developmental steps, *modify* the nature and content of cognitive structures elaborated in the course of adaptation, and thereby *alter* the direction of the need to function.

Piaget did not intend to study the relation between affective and intellectual development. It might be argued that a study of cognitive development which does not pay systematic attention to emotional influence cannot yield valid results. Such an extreme view does not seem justified in view of the complexity of developmental phenomena. It would be equally just or unjust to assert that a study of emotional development, which does not at the same time systematically study cognitive mechanisms, will not yield valid results. To arrive at first approximations of personality development, it is apparently necessary to make an arbitrary division of its affective-motivational and cognitive-perceptual aspects, and then to integrate the partial results. The task remains for us to study *how* motivated behavior, which has been the primary concern of clinical psychiatry, and nonmotivated behavior, which has been the primary concern of some cognitive theories, exercise their mutual influence. Far from achieving such an integration, I have only tried to show how Piaget's data suggest that at least under conditions of relative internal equilibrium, and at least with respect to certain sequences of total development, the psychological causation of behavior resides in the encounter between the individual and the real circumstances on which he acts.

In conclusion, I would like to remind you of Freud's admonition to his circle of students, which states in seven simple words the point for which I took an hour—namely, that sometimes a cigar is also a cigar.

REFERENCES

BARTLETT, F. C. (1932). *Remembering.* Cambridge: Cambridge University Press, 1961.

JAMES, W. (1902). *The Varieties of Religious Experience.* New York: Modern Library.

PIAGET, J. (1936). *The Origins of Intelligence in the Child.* New York: International Universities Press, 1952.

————— (1937). *The Construction of Reality in the Child.* New York: Basic Books, 1954.

————— (1945). *Play, Dreams and Imitation.* New York: Norton, 1951.

RAPAPORT, D. (1960). On the psychoanalytic theory of motivation. In: *Nebraska Symposium on Motivation.* Lincoln, Nebraska: University of Nebraska Press.

Part 3

*Family Influences on
Personality Development*

Current research on the family is moving in a number of new directions. Whereas earlier interest was primarily focused on the ways in which mothers affect their children, today's work is much broader in scope. It takes in a concern for the father and his role, a concern for the ways in which siblings in the family affect one another and the family as a whole, and a concern, too, for the ways in which children affect their parents. The family now is seen as a complex cluster of such influences, and current research is attempting to understand these more sophisticated mutual interactions.

In the articles in this section, Ainsworth and Bell trace the patterns of influences on both the mother and child in the feeding situation, and Sutton-Smith and Rosenberg examine the changing effects of siblings on each other and the family, as the children pass through different developmental stages. Rothbart and Maccoby consider the differences in the ways in which parents react toward boys and girls, and the effects of these differential parent behaviors on sex-typing. Harlow, who has become famous for his work with infant monkeys and the effects of maternal and social deprivation, explores, with Suomi, the possibilities for rehabilitating monkeys damaged by a lack of mothering or family contact, and thereby casts light on conditions of child-rearing as well.

Some Contemporary Patterns
of Mother-Infant Interaction
in the Feeding Situation

Mary D. Salter Ainsworth   Silvia M. Bell

Reviews of research into the effects of methods of infant care (e.g., Orlansky, 1949; Caldwell, 1964) present no clear evidence that the way an infant is fed—whether by breast or bottle, on schedule or demand, with early or late weaning— significantly affects his development.[1] As Caldwell points out, reseach methodology in most of these studies was inadequate to handle the complexity of the variables and the interactions between them. Among the obvious shortcomings were: use of second-hand and often retrospective reports of feeding variables; crude classifications which masked what might have been significant variations in practices; and isolation of a specific practice from its context—its context of maternal attitudes and style, of other infant-care practices, and

of mother-infant interaction to which the infant himself makes a significant contribution.

Most of the studies examined in these reviews were concerned with long-term effects of early feeding practices rather than with the infant's responses to them at the time. Exclusive interest in long-term effects was due undoubtedly to the psychoanalytic hypothesis (Freud, 1905; Abraham, 1921) that fixation, attributable to early frustration or overgratification of instinctual drives, resulted in the formation of character traits which resisted modification through later experiences.

Within the past decade or two research into the effects of early experience upon later personality development has shifted from preoccupation with the fixation hypothesis and towards an examination of mother-infant interaction. Impetus for this shift has come from several sources—from new developments in the study in animal behavior, from Piagetian cognitive theory (by extrapolation), from developments within psychoanalytic theory itself, and also as a consequence of studies

[1] An earlier version of this paper was presented at the biennial meeting of the Society for Research in Child Development in New York, March 29, 1967. The extended project which yielded the data for this study has been supported by Grant 62-244 of the Foundations' Fund for Research in Psychiatry, and by U.S.P.H.S. Grant 1 R01 HD 01712.

Mary D. Salter Ainsworth and Silvia M. Bell, "Some Contemporary Patterns of Mother-Infant Interaction in the Feeding Situation," in A. M. Ambrose, *Stimulation in Early Infancy*, London Academic Press, 1969. Reprinted by permission of the Developmental Sciences Trust, Bedford College.

of the responses of infants and young children to mother-child separation and deprivation of maternal care. The implication is still that there is continuity of development from infancy to later years and that patterns of reaction established in infancy may profoundly influence later development; but there has been a subtle shift from an hypothesis that an inalterable personality structure is fashioned through experience in the earliest years to an hypothesis that neonatal neurophysiological and behavioral structures are transformed through the infant's earliest transactions with his environment and so bias his perceptions and action patterns that subsequent situations are responded to, at least initially, in the light of the earlier experience. Although these inner structures are assumed to be more or less modifiable through experience, experience itself is held to be influenced by inner structure. It cannot therefore be assumed either that early structuring is the sole or major determiner of later outcomes or that its influence is so attenuated through later transformations as to be negligible.

This shift of emphasis has made it seem worthwhile to examine infant behavior carefully and in rich detail, in the belief that the starting point influences what comes afterwards and that the significant endeavor is to understand how it is that different patterns of experience set up different patterns of perceiving and behaving— rather than to prove that early experiences have long-term effects massive enough to resist blurring by the multifarious experiences of intervening years.

This present report deals with mother-infant interaction in the first three months of life, and focuses especially on interaction pertaining to feeding. This focus does not imply an hypothesis that the hunger drive or oral gratification is prepotent in structuring the basis for interpersonal interaction. It reflects the fact that during the earliest weeks the largest proportion of interaction between an infant and his mother has reference to feeding. Moreover, as Brody (1956) suggests, ". . . most things that a mother does with her infant, however unrelated in style they may be to each other, are related to her style of feeding behavior with him."

In examining mother-infant interaction in the feeding situation we were guided specifically by several considerations stemming from earlier research. Levy's (1959) study of mother-neonate interaction strongly suggested that the baby's arousal level at the time he was brought to his mother for feeding determined not only his feeding activity, but also his mother's response to him, and hence their interaction. Sander (1962) specified that the first issue to be resolved in the course of development of mother-infant interaction is the regulation of the baby's rhythms—an issue which is normally resolved by the end of the first three months of life. His (1966) study of infant rhythms further suggested the hypothesis that the points at which feeding interventions occur in the baby's rhythmic cycle of activity-quiescence might do much to regularize or to disorganize the rhythms themselves. Ainsworth's study of the development of the attachment of Ganda infants to their mothers (1963, 1964, 1967) suggested that differences between infants fed on thoroughgoing demand in contrast to those fed otherwise might be attributable in part to the different degrees of initiative permitted to them in feeding. Later work with American infants (Ainsworth and Wittig, in press) led to the hypothesis that the degree of the mother's sensitivity and responsiveness to the baby's signals, both in feeding and more pervasively, was potent in influencing the course of development of his attachment to her.

General Procedures

The larger project which yields the findings reported here is a short-term longitudinal study of the development of infant-mother interaction during the first year of life, with particular focus on the development of infant-mother attachment. The sample to date consists of 26 babies of white, middle-class, Baltimore families—the participating families having been reached through pediatricians in private practice. These babies have been observed in their own homes in the course of repeated visits, and their mothers have been interviewed about their infant-care practices. The first fifteen in the sample were visited for four hours every three weeks, beginning at three weeks of age. The remaining eleven were visited at weekly intervals for the first month, then at six weeks, and every three weeks thereafter, with the first four visits being of about two hours duration. Four of the babies were breast fed at least three months, the rest bottle fed. Two of the mothers had part-time work during part of the early period; the rest were full-time mothers.

The raw data consist of narrative reports of observations and interview findings obtained in each visit.[2] These narrative reports are being subjected to analysis by a variety of procedures, including codings, ratings, and classifications. It is the classification of patterns of interaction in feeding that concerns us here—a classification which deals with the first three months only.

Classification of Patterns of Mother-Infant Interaction in Feeding

As may be seen in Table 1, the classification was based on a cluster analysis of a multiplicity of features of the feeding interaction. These may be reduced to four chief aspects:

1. *The timing of feedings.* When did the mother feed her baby, how often, and at what intervals? Did she time the feeding in response to the baby's signals? After how much delay? Was the period of delay filled with interventions intended to "stave the baby off" and, if so, what kind of interventions? If there was a schedule, was it "rigid or flexible." Would the mother wake the baby to feed him? Would she advance the feeding if the baby were obviously hungry, and, if so, how much?

2. *Determination of the amount of food ingested and the end of the feeding.* Was the baby allowed to determine the amount of food he ingested, and to terminate his own feedings? Or did his mother try to determine both—by coaxing or by forcing? Or was she impatient, discontinuing feeding at the first sign of dawdling? Finally, did she overfeed or underfeed the baby, and if so, with what intent?

[2] Grateful acknowledgment is made to Barbara A. Wittig, George D. Allyn, and Robert S. Marvin II, who conducted the visits and prepared the narrative reports for 21 of the 26 infants.

3. *Mother's handling of the baby's preference in kind of food.* When solids were introduced, how tactfully did the mother present them? How did she handle rejections of new or disliked foods?

4. *Pacing of the rate of the baby's intake.* To what extent did the mother allow the baby to proceed at his own rate? Did she permit him to slow down or drowse during sucking? Did the milk come too fast for him to swallow it easily? To what extent was spoonfeeding geared to his pace, and to what extent was he allowed to be an active participant in feeding?

Nine patterns of mother-infant interaction pertinent to feeding were identified. Four patterns are designated as feeding on demand, four as feeding according to schedule, and one as arbitrary. But the patterns are ordered below and in the tables in accordance with an intuitive judgment of the extent to which the baby was permitted to determine the timing of the feedings, the amount he ingested, the order in which solids were given, and the pacing of his rate of intake. Needless to say, this order is considered a first rough approximation. In the patterns at the top of the list the baby was an active partner; in those toward the end of the list the mother was more and more the dominant one in their transactions.

I. DEMAND: THOROUGHGOING AND CONSISTENT

There was only one pair in this sample characterized by thoroughgoing and consistent demand feeding—a pair with breast feeding. This mother consistently fed her little girl when her signals suggested that she wished the breast—and sometimes this was merely for comfort. No consideration was given to the lapse of time since the last feeding. Perhaps because breast fed, the baby did not get too much. She was allowed to drowse at the breast and then to resume sucking. By six weeks of age she could release the nipple voluntarily and find it again, and she was very active in her participation in feeding. Her mother was vague in her recall of timing, but, by the end of the first quarter, her impression was that the baby usually signalled for the breast about every four hours.

TABLE 1. PATTERNS OF MOTHER-BABY INTERACTION IN THE FEEDING SITUATION

Case No.	Sex	Birth Order	Type of Feeding	Timing of Feedings	Determination of Amount of Food and End of Feeding	M's Handling of B's Preferences in Kind of Food	Pacing of Baby's Intake	Problems Related to Feeding
I. DEMAND: THOROUGHGOING AND CONSISTENT								
#1	F	2	Breast Cereal (5 wks)	Feeds on slight signals and for comfort; never wakes to feed	Terminated by B	B disliked solids; M tactful, did not press	B paces self; can pause and drowse; initiative discouraged	Some colic to 9 weeks
II. SCHEDULE: FLEXIBLE								
#8	M	3	Bottle Cereal (6 wks)	Staves off tactfully; will advance feeding. Sometimes wakes, not at night; installment feedings	M gently persists in coaxing B. Very prolonged feedings	No information	Many pauses while B drowses	None
#10	M	4	Bottle Cereal (2 wks)	Staves off tactfully; will advance feeding. Often wakes, not at night	M coaxes little; stops on B's cues	Bottle first; new solids introduced tactfully: flexible interspersion of bottle and solids	B can loaf, drowse M feeds solids so B has initiative	None
#19	M	1	Breast Cereal (?8 wks)	Staves off tactfully; will advance feeding or give "snacks," yet presses schedule	M coaxes little; feeding seems to end naturally	Breast (or relief bottle first; solids no problem	B can loaf, drowse M feeds solids very skillfully	Colic for first week or so
#21	F	2	Bottle Cereal (5 wks)	Rigid schedule till 7 wks; then flexible. Occasionally wakes to feed; not at night	Amount small and controlled till 7 weeks; M avoids overfeeding	Solids introduced very gradually and in small quantities "to learn the taste"	B very eager; protests interruptions to 7 weeks. Frequent long burping necessary	Neonatal pyloric spasm; much improved by 7 wks; overcome later

II. SCHEDULE: FLEXIBLE (continued)

Case No.	Sex	Birth Order	Type of Feeding	Timing of Feedings	Determination of Amount of Food and End of Feeding	M's Handling of B's Preferences in Kind of Food	Pacing of Baby's Intake	Problems Related to Feeding
#22	M	8	Bottle Cereal (3 wks)	Staves off briefly. Sometimes will advance; sometimes wakes; installment feedings	M coaxes slightly; stops on B's cues	Bottle first; new solids introduced tactfully; flexible interspersion of bottle and solids	B can loaf, drowse. B paces self. B has initiative in taking solids	Slightly overweight
#23	M	1	Bottle Cereal (7 wks)	Staves off briefly. Often wakes to feed. Demands feeding at night	M stops on B's cues	Bottle first; new solids interspersed tactfully; disliked food not given	M very delicate in pacing feeding to B's cues	None

III. DEMAND: OVERFEEDING TO GRATIFY THE BABY

Case No.	Sex	Birth Order	Type of Feeding	Timing of Feedings	Determination of Amount of Food and End of Feeding	M's Handling of B's Preferences in Kind of Food	Pacing of Baby's Intake	Problems Related to Feeding
#6	M	3	Bottle Cereal (2 wks)	Demand; little delay. Never wakes to feed; installment feedings	M coaxes and feeds soon again; overfeeding to gratify B	Solids fed first; B likes them	B feeds very fast and M complies	Colic to 6 wks; spitting up; oversleeping; overweight; irregularity
#14	F	3	Bottle Cereal (6 wks)	Demand; short delay. Never wakes to feed; installment feedings	M coaxes and feeds soon again; overfeeding to gratify B	M switches to bottle if B fusses with solids	Delicate pacing to B's slight signals; B wants solids very fast; M complies	Spitting up; gastric distress; oversleeping; overweight; irregularity

IV. SCHEDULE: OVERFEEDING TO GRATIFY THE BABY

Case No.	Sex	Birth Order	Type of Feeding	Timing of Feedings	Determination of Amount of Food and End of Feeding	M's Handling of B's Preferences in Kind of Food	Pacing of Baby's Intake	Problems Related to Feeding
#2	M	2	Bottle Cereal (4 wks)	Usually wakes to feed; some installment feedings; 3 meals by 9 wks	B falls asleep; M coaxes; very long feedings; overfeeding to gratify B	Solids first; some struggle with disliked foods; sometimes B takes too fast and chokes	B can loaf, drowse. B protests all interruptions. Pacing of solid foods fairly good	Spitting up Oversleeping Overweight

TABLE 1 (continued)

Case No.	Sex	Birth Order	Type of Feeding	Timing of Feedings	Determination of Amount of Food and End of Feeding	M's Handling of B's Preferences in Kind of Food	Pacing of Baby's Intake	Problems Related to Feeding
IV. SCHEDULE: OVERFEEDING TO GRATIFY THE BABY (continued)								
#25	M	4	Bottle Cereal (4 wks)	Usually wakes to feed; 3 meals by 4 wks	B falls asleep; M coaxes long; long feedings; overfeeding to gratify B	Bottle first, then solids, then bottle again	B can loaf, drowse. B very hungry and wants solids very fast	Spitting up; over-sleeping; overweight
V. SCHEDULE: TOO MUCH STAVING OFF								
#3	M	2	Bottle Cereal (4 wks)	Prolonged staving off; many inter-ventions. M denies B's hunger. Occa-sionally B falls asleep; wakes to feed	M coaxes bottle, forces solids	Bottle first; intersperses it with force feeding solids; much struggle	Good pacing of bottle feeding; bad pacing solids. B protests all interruptions.	Unhappy feedings; spitting up; M finds schedule inconvenient
#7	M	3	Breast Cereal (6 wks)	Prolonged staving off; many inter-ventions. M shifts schedule about; M resents B's demands	M impatient; ter-minates breast feeding too soon. Brief feedings	Breast first. B takes solids well	B can't loaf; M interrupts for so-cial interaction; B protests all in-terruptions	Unhappy feedings; spitting up; M finds schedule inconvenient
#24	M	2	Bottle Cereal (1 wk)	Fairly prolonged staving off; occa-sionally B falls asleep; wakes to feed	M coaxes bottle, oral stimula-tion; sometimes forces solids	Disliked food fed first and persistently; restrains B who struggles	Milk comes too fast; B protests burping; M coaxes when B loafs	Unhappy feedings
VI. PSEUDO-DEMAND: MOTHER IMPATIENT								
#9	F	5	Bottle Cereal (6 wks)	B must cry to be fed and must cry to be fed enough; install-ment feedings	M impatient; dis-continues feed-ing; then feeds again. Brief feedings. Under-feeding	Solids inter-spersed with bottle, but not tactfully	Pacing very bad; B can't loaf; nipple too fast; B chokes. Interruptions	Much spit-ting up; unhappy feedings; underfed

VI. PSEUDO-DEMAND: MOTHER IMPATIENT (continued)

Case No.	Sex	Birth Order	Type of Feeding	Timing of Feedings	Determination of Amount of Food and End of Feeding	M's Handling of B's Preferences in Kind of Food	Pacing of Baby's Intake	Problems Related to Feeding
#11	F	2	Bottle Cereal (8 wks)	B fed briefly when B fusses; fed off and on in installments; prolonged delays and B falls asleep and must be wakened	M distracted; forgets feeding till B fusses again. Brief feedings. Underfed	B sometimes rejects solids; struggles, gags, and is too upset to take bottle	Pacing very bad; nipple too fast; B chokes; interruptions	Spitting up; unhappy feedings; underfed
#15	M	1	Breast Relief bottle Cereal (6 wks)	B must cry to be fed; sometimes prolonged delay; installment feedings	M discontinues too soon; B cries again and is fed again	B is eager for food; order does not matter	M won't tolerate pauses but often interrupts herself. Relief bottle too fast; B chokes	Spitting up; unhappy feedings
#16	F	3	Bottle Cereal (8 wks)	Usually long crying before feeding; M sometimes wakes B. Some installment feedings	M impatient; discontinues too soon. Brief feedings. Underfeeding	Solids first; B can't get them fast enough	Pacing bad; interruptions; nipple too fast; burpings too long; M won't tolerate pause	Thumb-sucking; spitting up; underweight; gastric distress

VII. PSEUDO-DEMAND: OVERFEEDING TO MAKE BABY SLEEP LONG

Case No.	Sex	Birth Order	Type of Feeding	Timing of Feedings	Determination of Amount of Food and End of Feeding	M's Handling of B's Preferences in Kind of Food	Pacing of Baby's Intake	Problems Related to Feeding
#13	F	4	Bottle Cereal (2 wks)	M feeds after B wakes; delay usual, sometimes long. Never wakes to feed	M coaxes bottle, forces solids. Very long feedings. Overfeeding to make B sleep long	Solids first. B struggles and chokes; M force feeds	M paces bottle feeding well. Forces solids. B not allowed to be active	Oversleeping; irregularity; unhappy feedings
#17	F	2	Bottle Cereal (2 wks)	M feeds "on demand" but interprets all fussing as hunger. Some staving off with pacifier	M coaxes bottle, forces solids. Long feedings. Overfeeding to make B sleep long plus phenobarb	Solids first. B struggles; M force feeds and intersperses bottle in forcing way	M stimulates to speed sucking; forces solids; B not allowed to be active	Overweight; spitting up; gastric distress; unhappy feedings

TABLE 1 (continued)

Case No.	Sex	Birth Order	Type of Feeding	Timing of Feedings	Determination of Amount of Food and End of Feeding	M's Handling of B's Preferences in Kind of Food	Pacing of Baby's Intake	Problems Related to Feeding
VIII. SCHEDULE: RIGID, BY THE CLOCK								
#26	M	1	Bottle Solids (27 wks)	Wakes to feed or staves off; 3 meals by 10 weeks	At first M impatient; discontinues too soon; later much coaxing	Bottle first; solids disliked and discontinued; later B liked them	Pacing smooth at first; M later impatient with pauses	Thumb-sucking
IX. ARBITRARY FEEDING								
#4	F	2	Bottle Cereal (6 wks)	Prolonged delays; sometimes very prolonged; M doesn't perceive B's hunger; M detached; teases with pacifier; 3 meals by 9 weeks	M sometimes coaxes to noxious point; sometimes M tries to discontinue too soon and B struggles for more	Solids first; B struggles, cries, chokes, spits up; M forces	Pacing very arbitrary; M forces solids, forces pace of bottle feeding; M teases by withholding bottle	Gastric distress; much spitting up; feeding is a battle
#5	M	4	Bottle Cereal (3 wks)	Very prolonged delays, B must cry frantically; M denies B's crying; M distracted, fragmented; arbitrary, irregular feeding	M reports little coaxing or forcing. At 18 wks both coaxing and forcing were observed	M reports B screams with solids; feeding not observed till 18 weeks; solids forced	At 18 weeks milk came too fast; solids forced	Gastric distresses; feeding at 18 weeks unhappy
#12	F	2	Bottle Cereal (9 wks)	Very prolonged delays; M doesn't perceive B's hunger; M fragmented; arbitrary, erratic feedings, sometimes in installments	B can consume but little; falls asleep. M coaxes to noxious point	Bottle first; coaxes solids, intersperses bottle tactlessly	Pacing fair with bottle feeding; poor with solids	Gastric distress; very underfed; very underweight

IX. ARBITRARY FEEDING (continued)

Case No.	Sex	Birth Order	Type of Feeding	Timing of Feedings	Determination of Amount of Food and End of Feeding	M's Handling of B's Preferences in Kind of Food	Pacing of Baby's Intake	Problems Related to Feeding
#18	M	1	Bottle Cereal (6 wks)	Sometimes long delays; sometimes wakes to feed; M denies B's hunger; installment feedings; erratic schedule; arbitrary 3 meals by 9 weeks plus juice	M keeps B awake by noxious stimulation; forcing	Solids first, with forced feeding and forcing kind of interspersing with bottle	Pacing extremely bad; M forces pace of bottle feeding as well as solids	Feeding is a battle; spitting up
#20	M	1	Bottle Cereal (8 wks)	Sometimes delays; sometimes wakes to feed; M feeds at her time; plays music to drown out B's crying; M teases hungry B with fingers in mouth	B terminates own feeding; M tried to wake by noxious stimulation, but B wouldn't wake	Disliked foods first; B gags; Intersperses bottle and solids	B saves milk in cheeks; M forces to swallow; B protests burpings; M teases during feeding; M does not force but B gags, cries, swallows; M can't give liked solids fast enough	Gastric distress; spitting up; unhappy feedings

II. SCHEDULE: FLEXIBLE

Six babies were fed according to a schedule flexibly regulated by mothers highly sensitive to their signals. All of these mothers intended from the beginning to establish a schedule, but there were gentle nudgings toward regularity rather than rigid control. The least flexible of the group were mothers #19 and #21. While giving prime emphasis to gratifying the baby, mother #19 was striving for spacing that would suit her working hours later, and mother #21 had been cautioned not to feed her baby oftener than every three hours because of a congenital gastric disorder.

These mothers sometimes woke their babies to feed them, and sometimes tried to stave them off. The staving-off activities were in themselves intended to give the baby pleasure and often were sociable in nature. If the baby could not be beguiled into happy activity, then he would be fed without further delay. Yet none of these mothers hesitated to let their babies fuss a little. They believed it good for the baby to wait long enough to be genuinely hungry so that he would enjoy his food. But none ever wittingly let tension mount until the baby was frantic.

The most conspicuous feature of the feeding interaction of these mother-infant pairs was the pacing of the feeding, especially the feeding of the solid food. These mothers had skillful techniques of spoonfeeding which presented the food so that the baby could take it easily and yet needed to show some initiative in sucking or gumming it from the spoon. All of them built up the feeding interaction into a smooth and harmonious process—and an occasion for reciprocal exchanges of smiling and vocalization.

Finally, it should be noted that three of the six mothers used some version of installment feeding—in which an unfinished bottle or juice would be given if the baby seemed to want something between scheduled feedings. Without a statement of the mother's intent it would have been difficult to distinguish between flexible schedule feeding and demand feeding.

III. DEMAND: OVERFEEDING TO
GRATIFY THE BABY

There were two feeding patterns, labelled "demand feeding" by the mothers, in which the babies were conspicuously overfed—pattern VII and this one. In pattern III the babies were overfed in an attempt to gratify them; in pattern VII the mothers had the explicit intent to stuff the baby so full that he would sleep a long time and demand little attention. The distinction in intent seems important.

The two mothers of pattern III wanted their babies to be happy, but tended to treat too broad a spectrum of cues as signals of hunger. Each held her baby for a long time after he seemed finished feeding, herself enjoying the contact, and occasionally she coaxed him to take more. If he did not, she played with him, and then came back to the feeding later—a kind of installment feeding. If he did not finish his bottle even then, but later began to move his mouth or to fuss, his mother reheated his bottle and offered it again. When the baby was finally satiated completely, after having taken a very large amount of food over an extended period, he slept for an excessively long time. Both mothers worried about these long sleeps, but neither ever woke the baby in an attempt to get his rhythms more regular. When the baby finally awoke after a marathon sleep he was ravenous, demanding, and protested any delay in feeding. These babies fed fast at first—and probably they fed too fast as well as ingesting too much, for both had considerable gastric discomfort and spitting up.

IV. SCHEDULE: OVERFEEDING
TO GRATIFY THE BABY

The two babies of pattern IV both seemed constitutionally to have a high threshold for arousal. Throughout most of the first three months they slept virtually all the time that they were not being fed. Their spontaneous awakenings were so erratic and after such long intervals that their mothers abandoned demand feeding, and awoke them according to a schedule—but the schedule was a widely spaced one, for both were down to three meals a day in short order. Once awake, both babies were eager for food and fed fast. After solids had been begun the mothers complied with fast spoon feeding. But during bottle feeding both babies tended to fall asleep before they had finished the bottle. The mother let the baby drowse for a while, but then repeatedly coaxed him to take more, interpreting any mouth movement as a sign of hunger. Consequently, the babies were overfed, although both mother and baby seemed to enjoy the prolonged contact. It seems likely that the overfeeding interacted with the constitutional disposition to make for oversleeping.

V. SCHEDULE: TOO MUCH
STAVING OFF

The three mothers who showed this pattern of interaction would have been delighted to get their babies down to three meals a day—and indeed strove constantly to do so—but their babies did not oblige them by oversleeping. On the contrary, these were alert babies who slept little and seemed hungry and fussy much of the time. These mothers all declared their intention to feed on demand—meaning they would not wake the baby to feed him, which seemed to be the chief criterion of demand feeding for the mothers in this sample. But they referred frequently enough to their hopes that the baby would get onto a schedule that it is no real distortion to class this pattern as schedule feeding. They maintained the fiction of demand feeding by mechanisms of denial. They refused to recognize hunger signals when they occurred. Their "staving off" activities often began within two hours of the previous feeding and lasted sometimes as long as three more hours; meanwhile the baby fussed intermittently. The mother—saying, "I can't imagine what he wants" —tried a series of interventions—pacifier, change of position, toys, nap, bath, and sometimes social interaction—but ended by feeling frustrated and irritable when the baby refused to cooperate in a sustained way. These were mothers who later proved themselves capable of delight in reciprocal exchanges of vocalization and smiling—and they would have been pleased to make feeding a happy time. But, probably because the babies were too hungry and upset when they were finally fed, feedings were tense and unhappy.

VI. PSEUDO-DEMAND: MOTHER
IMPATIENT

The mothers in the four pairs who showed this pattern used feeding practices which had some of the characteristics of demand feeding, but these departed enough from a sensitive responsiveness to the baby's signals that the pattern has been labelled "pseudo-demand"—as was pattern VII also.

The babies were fed when they were hungry and cried, after more or less delay—but the feedings were disorganized and inconsistent because of the mother's failure to satisfy the baby. None of the four women could tolerate pauses, and all discontinued the feeding far too soon. In truth, none of the four was patient enough in any transactions with the baby to get sustained chains of interaction. The baby behaved as though the feeding situation was an occasion for social interaction—for the looking, smiling and vocalizing for which the mother otherwise had too little time. When the baby smiled and paused in feeding, his mother concluded that he was finished. The baby, having been put down half fed, soon fussed again, and if he was insistent enough, his mother would feed him in a second or even third installment. Perhaps as an unconscious reflection of the mother's desire to have the feeding over quickly, all these babies had bottles with nipple holes so large that the milk came too fast. Unless the baby swallowed very quickly he would choke, cough or gag—and this, in itself, made for a pause, and an excuse for the mother to discontinue. Spitting up was a great problem with all four babies, and three were underfed enough to cause the pediatrician concern.

VII. PSEUDO-DEMAND: OVERFEEDING
TO MAKE BABY SLEEP LONG

Two mothers, who also claimed to feed according to demand, deliberately stuffed their babies so full that they would sleep a long time and demand little attention. The feedings were very long. In one, for example, the baby, aged three weeks, was induced to ingest seven ounces of formula over a period of two hours. Both babies were given cereal almost from the beginning, but neither accepted it well. They spat it out, struggled, and tried to avert their heads, but both mothers were determined to get the food in and they did. Needless to say, the feedings were tense and anxious. Neither baby was well regulated in rhythms by the end of the first three months, and neither was permitted to be an active participant in feeding.

VIII. SCHEDULE: RIGID, BY THE CLOCK

Only one mother in this sample fed strictly by the clock. She adhered to a progressively more stringent and more widely spaced schedule of feedings, until by the time the baby was ten weeks old he was on three meals a day. He adapted himself reasonably well to this regime during his first three months. On the face of it, it seemed a fairly harmonious partnership. But this pattern is placed low on the list because this mother was almost completely impervious to the baby's signals, and her care was taken almost entirely at her timing rather than at his.

IX. ARBITRARY FEEDING

Finally, there were five cases in which feeding was arbitrary either in the time of feedings or in the pacing of intake or both. In each case, the pattern of feeding stemmed directly from the mother's disturbed personality. The mother in pair #4 had a postpartum reaction; she was detached and very insensitive to the baby's signals —although she improved suddenly when the baby was about twelve weeks old. Mothers #5 and #12 were both very anxious and fragmented. They put their babies away for long periods and either "tuned out" the crying or failed to perceive it as a signal of hunger. Mother #18 was anxious, and the only way she could stem her anxiety was to control everything and everybody in a compulsive and sometimes sadistic way. She could not bear the way her baby defied her by refusing to sleep, wake, feed, and smile in accordance with her will. The timing of feedings was erratic, but the most conspicuous feature was the forced nature of the feeding—both of milk and of solids—which had to be witnessed to be believed. Mother #20 was less obviously disturbed, and less arbitrary in her feeding practices than the others. She treated her baby as a plaything—sometimes charming, but sometimes tiresome and to be put away and ignored. Her transactions with him were always at her own whim, and consequently, in her own way, she was as arbitrary as the other more disturbed mothers.

Correlates of the Feeding Patterns

Three sets of correlates of the feeding patterns will be considered here. These have been selected as the only ones which our current stage of data analysis made available, and certainly not as the only ones which might be correlated with early patterns of interaction in feeding. The first two of these are contemporaneous, referring to the first three months of life: (a) the baby's amount and pattern of crying, and (b) the mother's attitudes and infant-care practices. The third correlate, (c), is the baby's behavior in a strange situation experimentally introduced at the end of the first year.

CRYING IN THE FIRST THREE MONTHS

Each episode of crying which occurred during visits in the first three months was coded.[3] This coding was done entirely independently of the other analyses, although it was, of course, based on the same narrative reports. The quantification of the coded crying includes two types of measures: the number of episodes of crying, and the duration of each episode of crying. Precise timing of the duration of a cry was only rarely reported by the visitor, so these measures have had to be rough estimates made by the coder. Consequently, the absolute figures must be taken as very approximate, although the relative figures are of interest. Corrections were made to adjust for the difference between the two subsamples in the schedule of visits, and for the differences between cases in the amount of time that the baby was actually under observation.[4] Some of the measures

[3] Grateful acknowledgment is made to the following for their painstaking efforts in the task of coding: Robert S. Marvin II, John Conklin, Ross Conner, Terence Leveck, and Herbert Markley.

[4] Since eleven of the babies had been visited four times during the first month and the other fifteen but once, the various crying measures for these eleven were adjusted so that crying during the first month (which may well have exceeded later crying in frequency) was given equal weight to crying in the subsequent three visits—as it was for the other fifteen. Each measure then was divided by actual observation time in minutes, and multiplied by 60, and thus expressed in episodes per hour of observation, or duration in minutes for each hour of observation.

dealt with crying specifically related to feeding: some of them dealt with crying which took place at any time during the visit. The three measures of crying related to feeding were: (a) the mean frequency of crying episodes per hour in the period "before feeding"—a period which was deemed to have begun 180 minutes after the previous feeding and having ended when the next feeding began; (b) the mean duration of "prolonged" crying in the period before feeding, in minutes per hour—"prolonged cry" being defined as anything not specified in the narrative report as a brief cry, and in general as a cry lasting twenty seconds or more; (c) the mean frequency per feeding of crying episodes during feeding. The three measures concerned with overall crying were: (d) the mean frequency of crying episodes per hour; (e) the mean frequency of brief crying episodes per hour —a brief cry being defined as one characterized as "brief" or any short burst lasting no more than nineteen seconds; and (f) the mean duration in minutes per hour of "prolonged" crying. (The total number of episodes, (d), includes a few episodes of intermittent crying that could not be classified as either "brief" or "prolonged"; none of these occurred "before feeding," or "during feeding.") These various scores are shown for each of the babies in Table 2, and for each is also given in parentheses the quintile rank of that score.

This table shows that the first two patterns of feeding interaction are the two associated with the least crying. The babies in these two groups— consistent demand feeding and flexible schedule feeding—are conspicuous for having little crying during feeding, and this seems related to the sensitive pacing and the prompt response to signals which characterized their mother's feeding practices. They also tend to have a relatively short duration of crying before feeding, except for #19 whose mother was "pushing a schedule." They had a relatively short duration of crying overall, although some of them had frequent episodes of brief crying. These findings reflect the fact that their mothers intervened promptly and appropriately enough that cries tended to be of short duration, and also suggest that these babies were learning to use brief cries as modes of communication rather than merely as modes of expression of state.

Feeding pattern IX—arbitrary feeding—is especially associated with long duration of prolonged crying before feeding, despite the fact that these babies do not tend consistently to have a high frequency of separate episodes of crying before feeding. This reflects the fact that the mothers of these babies tended to be very slow in responding to hunger cues. They were also slow to respond to crying generally; the overall cries tend to become very prolonged, especially in cases #5, #12, and #20.

The babies in pattern V—in which there was a long period of staving off the feeding with many ineffective interventions—tended to have relatively frequent episodes of crying, especially brief episodes, although they did not have cries of long duration until the period before feeding. These babies also tended to have relatively high frequency of crying during feeding—presumably because they were too hungry and upset when they were finally fed.

Feeding pattern VI, in which the mothers were impatient and discontinued feeding too soon, is characterized by a relatively high frequency of crying during feeding—and this reflects the fact that the feedings tended to come in several installments, the next installment being given in response to the baby's cry.

It is not possible to discuss further details here, but attention is drawn to the last column in Table 2 which lists the mean time per hour spent in prolonged crying. It is evident that the first four feeding patterns, in which the mothers were relatively sensitive and responsive to the babies' signals and communications, are associated with relatively little crying, while the other five feeding patterns in which the mothers were relatively insensitive, inappropriate, or unresponsive, are associated with a relatively large amount of crying.

MATERNAL-CARE VARIABLES: FIRST THREE MONTHS

Twenty-one nine-point rating scales were devised to assess a number of different aspects of maternal care during the first three months of life. Each mother was rated by two or more judges,[5] and the scores given in Table 3 are the

[5] We thank George D. Allyn and Robert S. Marvin II for their ratings and for their participation in the construction of the rating scales, and also Barbara A. Wittig, whose preliminary work was helpful in the construction of the present scales.

TABLE 2. FREQUENCY AND DURATION OF CRYING EPISODES

Feeding Pattern	Case No.	Crying Related to Feeding			Crying Overall		
		Mean frequency of crying episodes per hour before feeding	Mean duration of "prolonged" crying before feeding (min./hr.)	Mean frequency of crying episodes during feeding per feeding	Mean frequency of crying episodes per hour	Mean frequency of brief crying episodes per hour	Mean duration of "prolonged" crying (min./hr.)
I	#1	0.7 (1)*	0.2 (1)	1.0 (2)	2.2 (1)	1.4 (1)	1.8 (1)
II	#8	1.6 (4)	0.5 (2)	0 (1)	2.8 (2)	2.1 (2)	3.1 (2)
	#10	1.1 (3)	0 (1)	0.5 (1)	3.2 (2)	2.5 (3)	1.4 (1)
	#19	1.3 (4)	2.7 (3)	0.7 (2)	3.2 (2)	2.4 (3)	3.3 (2)
	#21	1.6 (4)	0.4 (1)	0.3 (1)	5.4 (5)	4.9 (5)	0.9 (1)
	#22	0.3 (1)	0.2 (1)	1.2 (2)	4.3 (4)	3.6 (4)	3.7 (3)
	#23	0.5 (1)	0.2 (1)	0 (1)	3.6 (3)	2.6 (4)	0.7 (1)
III	#6	0.9 (2)	1.5 (3)	2.0 (4)	3.6 (3)	1.7 (2)	3.2 (2)
	#14	1.2 (3)	2.8 (4)	1.3 (2)	2.8 (2)	1.6 (1)	3.5 (3)
IV	#2	0.4 (1)	0.4 (1)	0.5 (1)	2.2 (1)	1.6 (1)	2.0 (1)
	#25	1.1 (3)	1.1 (2)	1.5 (3)	2.5 (1)	1.6 (1)	3.0 (2)
V	#3	1.3 (4)	3.0 (4)	2.5 (5)	5.1 (5)	3.8 (5)	4.4 (4)
	#7	2.9 (5)	3.4 (4)	2.3 (5)	5.1 (5)	3.7 (4)	5.6 (4)
	#24	1.6 (4)	2.0 (3)	1.8 (3)	5.6 (5)	4.6 (5)	3.0 (2)
VI	#9	0.3 (1)	2.1 (3)	2.0 (4)	3.6 (3)	2.2 (3)	6.6 (4)
	#11	0.9 (2)	0.7 (2)	2.3 (5)	3.7 (4)	2.7 (4)	4.4 (4)
	#15	1.0 (3)	0.9 (3)	3.3 (5)	3.6 (3)	1.8 (2)	6.2 (4)
	#16	3.4 (5)	3.4 (5)	1.4 (3)	7.9 (5)	6.4 (5)	4.3 (3)
VII	#13	0.5 (1)	1.0 (2)	1.5 (3)	2.8 (2)	1.7 (2)	4.2 (3)
	#17	0.8 (2)	1.8 (3)	1.6 (3)	2.3 (1)	1.3 (1)	7.6 (5)
VIII	#26	2.6 (5)	3.0 (4)	0.3 (1)	2.3 (1)	1.4 (1)	5.5 (4)
IX	#4	1.1 (3)	8.9 (5)	2.0 (4)	3.2 (2)	2.4 (3)	8.2 (5)
	#5	0.9 (2)	16.7 (5)	**	3.9 (4)	2.1 (2)	20.6 (5)
	#12	1.7 (5)	14.7 (5)	2.5 (5)	4.7 (4)	2.5 (3)	15.4 (5)
	#18	1.1 (3)	4.6 (5)	2.1 (4)	3.4 (3)	2.7 (4)	4.0 (3)
	#20	3.0 (5)	4.1 (5)	3.6 (5)	9.6 (5)	6.7 (5)	11.5 (5)

* The figures in parentheses refer to quintile ranks.

** This baby was visited only three times in the first three months. Once he was fed by the observer, but twice he was not fed. "Before feeding" time was sampled, but no observations were made of feeding by M.

final ratings agreed on by the judges in conference. Six [6] of the scales have been selected to

[6] The ratings of four variables of feeding practices will not be reported here, since the scales were revised as a consequence of the analysis of feeding interaction reported here, and the cases re-rated. The six scales selected for this report deal with variables not specifically related to feeding, and were devised before the analysis of feeding interaction; ratings on these were entirely independent of that analysis.

illustrate the relationship between the ratings of the mothers and the kinds of interaction these mothers established with their infants in the feeding situation. These six scales deal with the following variables:

1. *Mother's perception of the baby.* The low end of the scale reflects perceptions that are distorted by projection, denial, or other defensive

TABLE 3.   RATINGS OF SELECTED MATERNAL-CARE VARIABLES AND CLASSIFICATIONS OF STRANGE-SITUATION BEHAVIOR

Feeding Pattern	Case No.	M's Perception of B	M's Delight in B	M's Acceptance of B	Appropriateness of M's Interaction with B	Amount of Physical Contact	Effectiveness of M's Response to B's Cry	Classification of B's Behavior in Strange Situation
I	#1	8.0	6.5	9.0	6.5	7.5	8.0	B_1
II	#8	7.0	7.3	8.5	7.5	8.0	6.5	B_2
	#10	9.0	9.0	9.0	9.0	7.8	7.5	B_1
	#19	7.5	9.0	8.0	7.0	7.0	6.0	B_2
	#21	9.0	7.0	8.0	8.0	6.5	7.0	B_2
	#22	9.0	7.0	8.0	6.5	5.0	7.5	B_2
	#23	7.0	5.5	6.0	7.0	6.5	6.5	A_3
III	#6	7.0	6.0	7.5	7.0	7.0	6.0	B_1
	#14	7.0	6.5	7.0	7.0	7.0	6.0	A_3
IV	#2	6.5	7.0	7.0	7.0	5.0	5.5	B_2
	#25	7.0	8.5	8.0	6.0	7.0	7.5	B_1
V	#3	3.0	3.5	3.5	3.5	3.0	3.5	B (unclass.)
	#7	6.5	6.5	5.5	6.0	6.5	3.5	A_2
	#24	4.0	3.0	4.0	3.5	4.5	3.5	A_1
VI	#9	2.5	3.0	3.0	3.5	3.0	4.0	A_2
	#11	2.0	4.0	5.3	3.5	5.0	5.0	C_1
	#15	4.0	4.0	4.5	3.0	4.0	3.5	...
	#16	3.5	3.0	3.0	3.5	2.5	2.0	A_1
VII	#13	4.5	1.0	4.0	3.0	3.5	3.5	C_1
	#17	4.0	2.0	3.0	4.0	4.5	6.0	A_2
VIII	#26	2.5	1.0	3.0	1.5	2.0	2.0	A_1
IX	#4	3.5	4.0	3.5	4.0	4.0	3.0	A_1
	#5	2.0	2.5	3.0	3.5	3.5	2.0	C_2
	#12	1.0	1.5	2.5	1.0	1.0	1.0	C_2
	#18	1.0	1.0	1.0	1.0	1.0	1.0	A_1
	#20	2.5	2.0	1.5	3.0	3.0	1.5	A_1

operations of the mother. The high end of the scale reflects perceptions that are realistic and accurate, because the mother is capable of seeing things from the baby's point of view.[7]

2. *Mother's delight in the baby.* Delight here is defined as situation-specific or behavior-specific, experienced and expressed in response to the baby himself—and to be distinguished from the pleasure of pride.

3. *Mother's acceptance of the baby.* This scale deals chiefly with the mother's degree of acceptance or rejection of the baby in terms of the extent to which he is felt to interfere with her own autonomy.

4. *Appropriateness of mother's interaction with the baby.* This scale refers to social advances and interaction, and appropriateness is deemed a matter of the mother's timing of her interventions to the baby's state and current activity, the matching of stimulation to the baby's capabilities, and knowing when to desist from stimulation. Both

[7] Jan Smedslund suggested the happy phrase "seeing things from the baby's point of view," as the antithesis of "egocentric" perception, in a Piagetian sense.

overstimulation and understimulation are considered inappropriate.

5. *Amount of physical contact* between mother and baby, especially that which occurs outside the context of routine care.

6. *Effectiveness of mother's response to baby's crying.* This scale deals with three chief facets of maternal behavior—heeding the baby's cry, interpreting the cause of the crying correctly, and responding appropriately.

The reliability of these scales seems to fall within acceptable limits.[8]

The ratings of each of the mothers on each of the six scales are shown in Table 3. Inspection shows that the highest ratings are associated with feeding patterns I, II, III, and IV—the thorough-going demand, flexible schedule, and overfeeding-to-gratify patterns. These were all patterns in which sensitivity to the baby's signals and a desire to gratify him were prominent. These mothers tend to be able to see things from the baby's point of view, to take delight in his behavior, and to accept him with little regret over the temporary surrender of autonomy. They tend to respond promptly and appropriately to the baby's crying, thus terminating the cry. They are sensitive to the baby's state and wishes in their social interaction—as well as in their feeding interaction. They tend to give their babies a relatively large amount of physical contact even outside of routine care.

The lower ratings are associated with the other feeding patterns, with patterns VIII and IX having the lowest ratings. The mothers of these last two patterns tend to be distorted in their perceptions of the baby, to take little or no delight in his behavior, and to resent overtly or covertly the infringement on their autonomy provided by his demands. They are unresponsive to the baby's crying, or inappropriate in their response to it. They are similarly inappropriate in their social interactions with him, and tend to grossly understimulate, or to tease or torment, or to be inappropriate in their timing. Finally, they tend to give

the baby little physical contact save in routine care.

BEHAVIOR IN THE STRANGE SITUATION: AT TWELVE MONTHS

At the end of the first year all but one of these 26 babies were introduced to a standardized strange situation, which has been described in detail elsewhere (Ainsworth and Wittig, in press). In brief, we were interested in: (a) exploratory behavior in the strange situation and whether the child could use his mother as a secure base from which to explore it; (b) the responses of the child to two brief separations from his mother, during the first of which he was left with a stranger, and during the second of which he was left alone; (c) his responses to his mother when reunited with her after separation. (We were also interested in the child's responses to the stranger per se, although this is not especially relevant here.)

As reported elsewhere (Ainsworth and Wittig), the first fourteen infants were classified into three groups on the basis of differential responses to the strange situation, and particularly to separation from and reunion with the mother. With the addition of the new subsample of eleven, it was possible to subdivide the three groups, making seven subgroups in all, and leaving one baby unclassified into the subgroups.[9]

Let us briefly summarize the characteristics of the various groups and subgroups.

Group A babies either did not cry at all when separated from their mothers, or else they cried relatively little. *Group A_1* showed minimal or no distress when separated; when the mother returned the babies in this subgroup did not cling to her; if picked up, they showed neither resistance nor protest to being put down again. *Group A_2* babies showed some slight distress when separated from their mothers and some interest in contact with them on reunion, but substantially less than Group B and with more signs of ambivalence. *Group A_3* babies did not cry when separated from their mothers, but in other episodes they showed an active interest in establishing and sustaining con-

---

[8] As an illustration of the reliability of rating—the following are product-moment correlation coefficients of the six scales, based on the twelve cases which the authors both judged: .93, .97, .94, .89, .89, and .86.

[9] This baby, who was ill, resembled Group B, and was classified there, but he did not fit clearly into either of subgroups B_1 or B_2.

tact with their mothers quite comparable to that shown by the babies of Group B.

Group B babies cried when separated from their mothers, but showed no other substantial evidence of behavior disturbance. Babies in this group also characteristically clung to the mother when reunited with her, and resisted any attempt she made to put him down or to release him. *Group B_1* babies cried during the second separation, but little or not at all during the first; *Group B_2* babies were clearly distressed in both. (The unclassified baby was distressed in both separation situations, but was also fussy and inactive throughout other episodes.)

Group C babies resemble Group B_2 babies in being distressed throughout both separation episodes, but in addition they showed passive-aggressive behavior disturbances to a much greater extent than the babies of the other groups. *Group C_1* babies displayed marked aggression (or anger), especially in the separation episodes, but in other episodes as well. They were also relatively passive —especially in their manifestations of attachment to the mother upon reunion. *Group C_2* babies showed unusual passivity in the strange situation, with striking fragments of aggressive behavior now and then.

Table 3 shows that all of the babies classified in the first four feeding patterns fall into one of three groups—Groups B_1, B_2, or A_3—in regard to their behavior in the strange situation at the end of the first year. Babies whose mothers were especially sensitive and responsive to them in the early feeding situation—and indeed generally— manifested attachment to their mothers (without conspicuous behavioral disturbance) either through distress upon separation, or contact-seeking, or both. Babies classified in the other five feeding patterns fall into one of four groups (leaving the unclassified B-group baby out of consideration): A_1, A_2, C_1, and C_2. Babies whose mothers were relatively insensitive and unresponsive to them in the early feeding situation, tend, at the end of the first year, either to show little or no distress upon separation and little or no clinging and contact-seeking after reunion, or to show behavior disturbances in addition to those contingent upon separation-distress. It is especially interesting to note that the two babies of Group C_2, whose passivity was marked at twelve months,

had been fed arbitrarily, cried much, and had mothers with consistently low maternal-care ratings.

Discussion

The cause-effect relations implicit in these findings are by no means clear-cut or unidirectional. This is a study with a multiplicity of variables. Even assuming that we were successful in our effort to be objective in all our ratings and classifications and to keep our judgments of each variable independent of our judgments of the others, there is nevertheless much confounding among the variables. The twenty-one rating scales yield positively correlated measures of the mothers' attitudes and infant-care practices, and some of the correlations are high. The classification of interaction in the feeding situation emphasizes sensitivity of the mother to the baby's rhythms, signals, pacing and preferences as a pervasive theme, but this same sensitivity is reflected in a number of the rating scales, even those having no explicit relationship to feeding. In general, one could say that those mothers who could see things from the baby's point of view tended to adopt infant-care practices which led to harmonious interaction not only in feeding but generally. One could say further that babies whose behavior, social and otherwise, had consistently gratifying or interesting feedback tended to cry less, to learn modes of communication other than hard expressive crying, and to gain more frustration tolerance and more regular and predictable rhythms than babies whose behavior made little or no difference in determining what happened to them.

On the other hand, it is reasonable to believe that it is easier for a mother to interact harmoniously with a baby who is relatively easy to understand and to predict, and who responds with pleasure and interest rather than with frustration and distress. Some of the babies in our sample may have been more difficult from the beginning than others—for example, baby #12 with whom there was perinatal pathology. Certainly, in the case of feeding pattern IV, there were two babies whose high threshold for arousal seemed to interact with overfeeding to produce long periods of sleeping and little fussiness. The mothers of feeding pattern VII, who tried to accomplish the same end by deliberate overfeeding, had much less success, perhaps in part because their babies were different constitutionally, but probably also because the feeding interaction was controlled by the mothers rather than being geared to the babies' signals. Whatever role may be played by the baby's constitutional characteristics in establishing the initial pattern of mother-infant interaction, it seems quite clear that the mother's contribution to the interaction and the baby's contribution are caught up in an interacting spiral, and it is because of these spiral effects—some vicious and some "virtuous"—that the variables are so confounded that it is not possible to distinguish independent from dependent variables.

Let us now turn to a brief discussion of the specifics of feeding practices. The findings here presented suggest that the central issue in the controversy between demand and scheduled feeding is of some significance, and that it is a question of the programming of the whole sequence of interventions in reasonable synchrony with the baby's rhythms, signals, and behaviors. There is no easy rubric for a pediatrician to use when instructing mothers about feeding practices, nor for an interviewer to use to elicit accurate information about method of feeding. There is clear support for the conclusion of previous investigators (e.g., Heinstein, 1963) that the mother's attitude is important—but the present findings suggest that it not only modulates the effect of her practice, but plays a crucial role both in her initial choice of practice and in shaping the specifics of the practice itself.

Feeding practices which have as objectives, explicitly or implicitly, both the gratification of the baby and the regulation of his rhythms seem to succeed in their aims—whether these practices are labelled "demand" or "schedule." They also succeed in a third aim, which seems important, and that is to allow the baby to be an active participant in feeding rather than merely a passive recipient. Active participation in determining timing and pacing of feeding seems very likely to facilitate the establishment of smooth and mutually gratifying mother-infant interaction. Initiative in determining the amount to be ingested and the termination of feeding seems crucial in facilitating the early regulation of rhythms. Furthermore, from

what can be extrapolated from animal research into the mechanisms regulating feeding behavior (e.g., Stellar, 1966), it seems important to allow an infant to pace himself in regard to rate of feeding; it is likely that interference with his own pace tends to disrupt the feedback mechanisms which regulate normal feeding behavior. Finally, this leads us to an hypothesis which has been discussed more fully elsewhere (Ainsworth, 1967, especially pp. 445–449). Through the feedback a baby obtains to his various signals, actions and communications, he may build up confidence in his ability to influence what happened to him, or, in White's (1963) terms, feelings of efficacy would lead to a sense of competence. Although for most of these babies the feeding situation has become a relatively unimportant occasion for mother-infant interaction by the end of the first year, the baby's experience in influencing his mother's behavior through his own actions—an experience which begins in the earliest weeks of life—seems likely to influence the nature of his attachment to her.

This brings us to the impressive relationship in these findings between mother-infant interaction in the first three months and infants' behavior at the end of the first year. This does not necessarily imply that early feeding experience has a direct effect on later attachment behavior. First, it seems entirely likely that the kinds of mother-infant interaction characteristic of the early feeding situation would persist for a longer or shorter time beyond the first three months of life—which was a termination point set arbitrarily by us—and continue to exert an influence. Secondly, it seems very unlikely that nothing else of consequence could happen in the last nine months of the first year to influence the one-year-old's attachment to his mother. Indeed, to demonstrate this kind of relationship between antecedent and consequent does not, of course, prove a cause-effect relationship at all. The important step of tracing through the developmental processes linking antecedent and consequent has yet to be undertaken. In this context, the lack of obvious phenotypical resemblance between antecedent behavior and consequent behavior need not be dismaying. On the contrary, epigenetic considerations lead us to expect that behavior in one phase of development may depend upon the completion of the developmental "task" of an earlier phase without any apparent continuity in the behaviors themselves.

Nevertheless, it is submitted that the findings here presented suggest that early experience can have a significant effect on later development. It is also submitted that early experience effects its influence through setting up patterns of percep-

tion, expectation, and action which interact with further environmental influences, and which, in the absence of gross changes in either the nature of the environment or the structure of the organish, can make for underlying continuities in developmental processes across wide segments of the developmental years.

REFERENCES

ABRAHAM, K.   Contributions to the theory of the anal character (1921). *Selected papers,* 370–392. London: Hogarth Press, 1949.

AINSWORTH, MARY D.   Development of infant-mother interaction among the Ganda. In: B. M. Foss (ed.) *Determinants of infant behaviour II.* London: Methuen, 1963.

AINSWORTH, MARY D.   Patterns of attachment behavior shown by the infant in interaction with his mother. *Merrill-Palmer Quarterly,* 1964, *10,* 51–58.

AINSWORTH, MARY D. SALTER.   *Infancy in Uganda: infant care and the growth of love.* Baltimore: Johns Hopkins University Press, 1967.

AINSWORTH, MARY D. SALTER and WITTIG, BARBARA A.   Attachment and exploratory behavior of one-year-olds in a strange situation. In: B. M. Foss (ed.) *Determinants of infant behaviour IV.* (In press.)

BRODY, SYLVIA.   *Patterns of mothering.* New York: International Universities Press, 1956.

CALDWELL, BETTYE M.   The effects of infant care. In: M. L. Hoffman and L. W. Hoffman (eds.) *Review of child development research, Vol. 1.* pp. 9–88. New York: Russell Sage Foundation, 1964.

FREUD, S.   Three essays on the theory of sexuality (1905). *The standard edition* of the complete psychological works of Sigmund Freud, Vol. 7, pp. 125–245. London: Hogarth Press, 1953.

HEINSTEIN, M. I.   Behavioral correlates of breast-bottle regimes under varying parent-infant relationships. *Monogr. Soc. Res. Child Developm.,* 1963, *28,* No. 4.

LEVY, D. M.   *The demonstration clinic.* Springfield, Ill.: Charles C Thomas, 1959.

ORLANSKY, H.   Infant care and personality. *Psychol. Bull.,* 1949, *46,* 1–48.

SANDER, L. W.   Issues in early mother-child interaction. *J. Amer. Acad. Child Psychiat.,* 1962, *1,* 141–166.

SANDER, L. W. and JULIA, H. L.   Continuous interactional monitoring in the neonate. *Psychosomat. Med.,* 1966, *28,* 822–835.

STELLER, E.   Hunger in man: comparative and physiological studies. *Amer. Psychologist,* 1967, *22,* 105–117.

WHITE, R. W.   *Ego and reality in psychoanalytic theory.* New York: International Universities Press, 1963.

The Sibling

Brian Sutton-Smith   B. G. Rosenberg

Affiliation and Conformity

The studies of affiliation, as well as the current resurgence of ordinal position studies as a viable activity for psychologists, are directly attributable to *The Psychology of Affiliation,* by Stanley Schachter (1959). In this work Schachter pursued some aspects of social comparison theory, a theory which suggested that one basis for people's gregariousness was a need for self-evaluation (Festinger, 1954; Latane, 1966). Schachter's procedure was to induce varying degrees of anxiety about impending experimental events in a group of subjects. He wanted to know whether in these circumstances the subjects would prefer to be with others or to be by themselves while waiting apprehensively for the experiments to begin. Because the subsequent results seem to have a great deal to do with the particular nature of this situation, it is well to recapitulate his fear-inducing instructions at this point; although on the surface, they read like a parody from *Mad* magazine.

In the high anxiety condition, the subjects, all college girls, strangers to one another, entered the room to find facing them a gentleman of serious mien, horn-rimmed glasses, dressed in a white laboratory coat, stethoscope dribbling out of his pocket, behind him an array of formidable electrical junk. After a few preliminaries, the experimenter began: "Allow me to introduce myself, I am Dr. Zilstein of the Medical School's Department of Neurology and Psychiatry. I have asked you all to come today in order to serve as subjects in an experiment concerned with the effects of electrical shock. . . . What we will ask each of you to do is very simple. We would like to give each of you a series of electric shocks. Now, I feel I must be completely honest with you and tell you exactly what you are in for. These shocks will hurt; they will be painful. As you can guess, if, in research of this sort, we're to learn anything at all that will help humanity, it is necessary that our shocks be intense. . . . Again, I do want to be honest with you and tell you that these shocks will be quite painful but, of course, will do no permanent damage [Schachter, 1959, p. 13].

The degrees of anxiety felt by the subjects in these circumstances were assessed on a 1–5 point self-rating scale (from "I dislike the idea of being shocked very much" to "I enjoy the idea very much"). Subjects then indicated whether they wanted to spend the time waiting for the experiment to begin, by themselves, with others, or whether they didn't care. Schachter's findings, which are of importance for the study of ordinal position, were that under conditions of high fear (there was also a low-inducing fear condition in which the experiments were not represented as being harmful), firstborn females showed a stronger desire to wait with others than did later-born females. Asked about a series of ascending electric shocks, only children and firstborn females were less willing to continue than were later born. When highly anxious firstborn and highly anxious later born were compared, the firstborn still showed the greater desire to be with others. There was the suggestion that while only children and firstborn were similar in their desire to affiliate, only children were, in general, less anxious than firstborn. The size of the subject's family made no difference, though the anxiety-affiliation relationship decreased in strength for each subsequent ordinal position. Subsequently, the subjects were told of the subterfuge in this experiment, given an account of the reasons for it, and, of course, no one actually received any electric shock.

"Speculating" on the origins of these differences, Schachter opined that in early childhood firstborn had perhaps been taught to associate the reduction of pain with the presence of others. The inexperienced mother rushing to the baby's side at every whimper, ready to interpret every burp as a death rattle, quickly conditioned the youngster to expect social solace in the presence of pain or fear. As the youngsters grew older and increased the magnitude of their own instrumental responses, they in turn sought out other persons when in states of pain or fear.

By contrast the later born, relatively neglected by the now much busier and wiser mother (who could tell a burp from a death rattle), learned

that in states of pain or anxiety, tension reduction would have to come about mainly as a result of their own efforts. Although Schachter (1959) was most tentative about this developmental speculation—". . . if this sort of proposition amounts to anything [and] we do not seriously wish to defend these particular arguments" (p. 43)—it has become the vaguely held functional assumption in most subsequent work. Schachter continues: "Without examining further the merits of these arguments, this general line of thought does lead to the expectation that under anxiety provoking conditions first born and only children will manifest stronger affiliative needs than later born" (p. 43).

Intrigued by these relationships, Schachter re-examined various other sets of data in the literature and came up with some surprising findings. In a survey of chronic male alcoholics, it was found that they were more likely to be later born. Again, examining data on psychotherapy, it was found that firstborn were more inclined to go into psychotherapy and less inclined to drop out of it (Wolkon, 1968). They were also perhaps more inclined to suicide (Lester, 1966). Finally, in data on effective fighter pilots, it was found that the aces—that is, those with the more awards for destroying enemy planes—were more likely to be later born. Helmreich (1968) has subsequently found that later born also make better aquanauts and Nisbett (1968) that they participate more in dangerous sports. Linking these phenomena to the earlier results on affiliation, Schachter (1959) suggested that firstborn were more likely to seek the help of others when in states of anxiety (thus, resorting to psychotherapy), and the later born were more likely to handle their anxieties in isolation either effectively (as fighter pilots) or ineffectively (as alcoholics).

Developmental Transformations of Dependency and Achievement

There are not actually any developmental studies of affiliation, conformity, and achievement. What we have are a few scattered studies on parallel topics at different chronological age levels, and from these we must draw inferences with respect to Schachter's thesis. Still, it makes more sense to draw inferences about childhood primarily from studies made on children, and secondarily from studies made on adults.

The most relevant study to deal with infant behavior was one carried out by Cushna (1966) at a pediatric clinic in Iowa. His subjects were middle-class children from 16 to 19 months of age. They were observed immediately after an immunization shot in the clinic and observed also in their own homes. The investigators were interested in the children's reaction to the shot, and in their reaction to the mother's going out of the room in the home setting. They observed whether the child cried, whether he sought out his mother when she left the room, and so on. The results were fairly clear: at home the firstborn were more upset by the mother's leaving them, and in the clinic setting the firstborn boys were more upset than the firstborn girls. In both clinic and home settings the children were asked to carry out a variety of verbal and motor tasks, such as throwing a ball, climbing on a chair, responding to a request to jump, and so forth. The mothers were asked to assess the child's performance level on a variety of items drawn from the Vineland test of social maturity. In both cases the mothers' expectations of firstborn far exceeded their expectations for later born. The overassessment was most pronounced with firstborn boys. The mothers' expectations for independence training, for example, for firstborn were two standard deviations above the mean for that age group! And in fact, the firstborn did better at the motor performances than did the later born. In addition the mothers were more active in prompting and helping the firstborn, though in different ways for the two sexes. They were more supportive, strategic, alluring, and more cautious in directing their boys, but (particularly in the home) they were more demanding, exacting, and intrusive in telling their firstborn girls how a solution is reached, a finding similar to that of Rothbart (1967) with 5-year-olds. . . . In another study of infants, Gewirtz and Gewirtz (1965) found that mothers interacted *twice* as much with only children as with the youngest.

Bayley's results with intelligence tests are of a consistent character (1965), as are the recent results of Solomons and Solomons (1964) with motor performances. As long as it is remembered that we are actually talking about tests of motor and sensory performance and that these have not been shown to have a strong predictive relationship to intelligence as it is measured later, then Bayley's results can be treated like those of Cushna, as indices of the way the babies are responding to additional social stimulation at that age level. Bayley's report on 1,409 infants ranging in age from 1 to 15 months showed small but consistent findings in favor of the firstborn in 11 out of the 15 months. They were significantly higher on her "mental" scale in 4 of the 15 months and on the "motor" scale in 5 of the 15 months. The later born were not significantly higher in any of the months.

Bayley (1965) says: "If we assume that there are differences, they could be accounted for if we postulate a greater amount of parent-child interaction with first borns, thus stimulating them to more rapid development" (pp. 391–392). But she goes on to say: "There is, however, no indication of any cumulative effect of such stimulations; the differences between first born and later born for both ages are small, and they tend to be pretty well distributed over the entire age range" (p. 392). Thus it appears that the initial stimulation affects the infant scores but has no subsequent affect on intelligence test scores.

In these initial results, then, we do find, as Schachter suggested, the mothers more concerned with firstborn's performances, but also we find the firstborn performing at higher levels and being made more anxious by separation from the mother. One gets the impression that while the mother's concern for the firstborn might lead the firstborn to refer back to the mother more often, what they get from her is further expectation of higher level performance. If anxieties are assuaged by this mother attention, it appears likely to be only one part of the relationship. Again, one is impressed not so much by the mother's anxious inexperience as by the adultlike demands she is making on her firstborn as compared with her later born. The higher level of expectation by the mothers of the boys' achievement and perhaps of good behavior from girls is worth restating. It could be that the mother's expectations of both are consistent with sex role expectations because the girls are simply more malleable, and the boys more resistant to their expectations (Moss, 1967).

The girls can be ordered about, but the boys must be lured. A psychoanalytic formulation would, of course, explain the same phenomena in terms of the mothers' rivalries and loves.

In addition to Cushna (1966) and Gewirtz and Gewirtz (1965), the only other observational study of what parents actually do (there are a number on what they say they do) with infants was carried out by Lasko (1954) in Ohio. The mothers were observed in their homes and rated on their different treatment of their firstborn and second born. There were 46 pairs of siblings who were the firstborn and second born in their families, and who were observed in a longitudinal study at repeated intervals. This meant that the mother's treatment of the siblings could be compared at the same chronological age for each sibling. Comparisons were made between the ages of one and nine years. There is a striking confirmation of Cushna's observations insofar as the firstborn are the subject of much greater verbal and intellectual acceleration attempts in the observations made during the first two years. The parents prompt more and satisfy their curiosity more. After the age of two, this is no longer the case. Lasko (1954) says: "By the age of three or four, however, the home no longer revolves around him and starting from a much more favored position in the beginning, he is less warmly treated than is his younger sibling at a similar age" (p. 115). In these and subsequent years, furthermore, the firstborn continues to receive more attempts at acceleration and more "disciplinary friction" from the mother. The age correlation data most strongly suggest that the major change for firstborn over the years is the very substantial decrease in the available interaction with their mothers. Understandably enough, the mothers have less time for them. Non-firstborn received more consistent treatment throughout, and Lasko also concludes that as mothers deal with later children—second, third, and so on—they are somewhat warmer and more protective toward them, but also more arbitrary and strict.

There are a number of points here for further discussion. First, Lasko did not find mothers more anxious with their firstborn than with their second born. But like Cushna, she did find them more demanding. Rather than thinking of the parents as always running to the child because of their own inexperience (each burp a death rattle), it might be a simpler thesis to interpret the adults as treating the infants as much like adults as they are able. The parents of firstborn have been used to dealing with other adults; they have seldom had experience with infants. If they simply generalize these customary responses, then they will expect a very high level of performance from their infants and then believe they perceive more problems in their behavior (Shrader & Leventhal, 1968). They may not expect so much from their later born, partly because they have less time, but partly also because by the time the second born arrives, the parents have been educated by their firstborn and have scaled down their expectations. A good illustration of the way in which parents can be educated by their infants, although in a reverse direction, is provided by Harlow's experiments with those monkey mothers who had not themselves benefited from real monkey mothering. They were instead reared on a bottle mechanically manipulated in a wire cage. These monkey mothers with this nonprimate rearing experience so ignored their own firstborn that several of the infants were mutilated and some killed. But the monkey infants were so persistent in seeking feeding opportunities that their mothers forcibly learned a great deal about mothering by association with them. The mothers were, in consequence, much more effective mothers with their own later-born infants. In this example the newborn monkeys had educated their mothers in an upward direction. It is not hard to believe that firstborn humans educate their parents in a downward direction, forcing them to revise unrealistic expectations derived from associating too long with mature people. Of course, it can also follow that the mother's high level of demand makes the firstborn more anxious about pleasing her (even if she herself is not more anxious with the firstborn than with later born). Some have argued, for example, that the firstborn may be much conflicted by the reduction of attention after the first two years (Sears, Maccoby, & Levin, 1957).

Another point to note is that although Lasko and Cushna demonstrate particular additional attention to firstborn in early years, Lasko also demonstrates the continuance of a special type of interaction with firstborn in subsequent years. Unfortunately, her parent-child rating scales are not designed to be sensitive to the later childhood years, but the existence of more "disciplinary" friction between parents and firstborn suggests higher expectations are still being held out for them.

There are a number of reports by parents of the way in which they say they differentially treated their children by ordinal position, but we wish to give these studies a secondary status. It might seem unfair to treat mothers as more subjective observers of themselves and their own children than are such investigators as Cushna and Lasko, but there are, unfortunately, good reasons for putting the mothers on trial and demanding that they first prove their case. Longitudinal studies of mothers' reports of their children's behavior seem to indicate that they are not a particularly reliable source of evidence (Radke-Yarrow, 1963), at least as time goes by, for they appear to distort their earlier accounts in terms of their current attitudes. Still, it has to be admitted that in the current evidences, mothers' reports seem to be consistent with the data already given above. Thus, most investigators have found that the mothers report that they expected more of their firstborn. Gewirtz (1948) found them more concerned with their firstborn. Sears, Maccoby, and Levin (1957), in their very comprehensive interview study with 379 mothers from the New England area, however, reported that the mothers said they were more indulgent of later children only in large-size families, but not in two-child families, a discrepancy which is unresolved at this point, and perhaps has something to do with the higher levels of achievement aspiration in small-size families than in large ones (Rosen, 1961).

This section on parent-infant relations may be summarized by saying that apparently both parents and firstborn are more concerned with each other than are parents and non-firstborn. By concern, we must at this point mean higher expectations by the parents (Lasko, 1954; Cushna, 1966; Stout, 1960; Gewirtz, 1948); higher performances by the children (Cushna, 1966); more anxiety about being separated from the parents by the children (Cushna, 1966); and more sensitivity to pain by the boys (Cushna, 1966). Later we shall cite findings of Rothbart (1967) and of Hilton (1967) that parents also interfere more and are more inconsistent with firstborn. But in addition, we call attention to the suggestions of a continuing "special" relationship between parents and firstborn denoted by greater "disciplinary friction" (Lasko, 1954), "more chores" and "more conscience" (Sears, Maccoby, & Levin, 1957).

When we move beyond infancy, with some exceptions (Hilton, 1967; Rothbart, 1967) there tend not to be studies of what parents do to the children (as this varies with ordinal position). Instead, there are studies of what children of different ordinal positions are like. If one adopts an infant-deterministic thesis—that is, that what parents do to infants molds their personality permanently—then of course the parents' role has already been explained, the child's radarscope has been set, and the parents' subsequent relationship to the child is, therefore, more or less irrelevant. But there are a few studies which suggest that parental influences continue to count, and these are taken up in turn.

But first we shall deal with the other objective studies of children's characteristics as they vary by ordinal position. In 1948 Gewirtz reported an observational study of preschool children at the Iowa Child Welfare Research Station. His hypothesis accords nicely with the observations of Cushna (1966) and Lasko (1954), whose studies nevertheless succeed his in time. The hypothesis was that as parents have more time for only children and early born than they have for later born, they will more often reduce their tensions and thus will become more reinforcing to them. This is not dissimilar from—though broader than—Schachter's (1959) notion that firstborn would find parents (and subsequently others) reinforcing because the parents consistently reduced their infant pain-derived tensions. Both Gewirtz and Schachter see the firstborn reaching out first for the parents and later for others because this reaching out has been rewarded by the parents. Lasko's and Cushna's studies, however, show us mainly the parents' coaxing and urging on the firstborn, which is a form of tension-enhancement, not reduction. Whether such increase of the child's level of aspiration is also accompanied by a decrease of his physical and other tensions through comforting actions, we do not actually know, though comforting actions might well be expected to accompany any such attempts to push the child ahead rapidly if they were to be successful.

In any case, on the basis of his thesis, Gewirtz (1948) predicted that only and firstborn would reach out toward others and that they would have a high succorant need, more often than later born, because this had become one of their most effective instrumental behaviors. From this point of view, such succorant behavior need not be connected with anxiety, as Schachter had postulated.

Gewirtz (1948) made observations on 45 children of ages 4 and 5 years at a nursery school. Over a period of three months, each child was observed some 16 times for 15 minutes each time. Gewirtz classified the observed behaviors into three groups. Positive attention-getting, which was taken to be a direct expression of succorance or help-seeking, was expected to be manifested mostly by firstborns and only children. Seeking reassurance and bodily contact with others was taken to be an indirect expression of succorance and expected to be manifested by later born who had not received so much reinforcement for their direct approaches to the parents. Finally, negative attention-getting was conceptualized as conflict expression of the need for succorance. Here, it was conjectured, the child's need for succorance, being strong but mainly rejected, led the child into a reverse and hostile expression, getting attention from others by rejecting them in turn.

The three categories of succorance were, indeed, found to be statistically independent of each other. The results were that, as predicted, only children showed succorant behavior more often than children with siblings. Firstborn with siblings, however, expressed their need more often by staying near to others and by seeking reassurance. They were also the least aggressive of all the groups. When we recall Lasko's observation that such firstborn received a sudden decrease in attention with the advent of the next siblings, these Gewirtz results appear to show that the firstborn are now (4–5 years) in a rather precarious position: most concerned with adult reassurance, but not willing to express antagonism in any way. The middle born siblings, when compared with the others, showed more negative attention-getting behavior, suggesting that they had had the least attention of all, and were being driven into rather hostile modes to get some minimal attention from adults. The youngest were more like the only children.

Gewirtz' study is particularly important because it introduces differences between the various ordinal positions, and is not just a dichotomous approach as is true of most birth-order studies. Again, it begins to highlight the particular incongruities in the development of the firstborn. The firstborn in Cushna's study (1966), mentioned above, were at that time mainly only children, although most of the mothers said they intended to have more children, and probabilistically most surely did, which means that firstborn, like only children, began by having higher expectations; but then, unlike only children, suffered a shift in parental rewards and were apparently moved themselves in the direction of more precarious expressions of succorance, that is, seeking reassurance but not expressing hostility. The middle born who had never been seduced into believing in parents as rewarding figures (we speculate), but like all infants and preschoolers needed things only adults could give, perhaps struck back less covertly by being a nuisance.

In any case, at this point we develop the propositions that only children (and younger born) will tend to show an uncontaminated expectation of help from others; they will, therefore, use affiliation as an instrumental behavior. But firstborn, having suffered a mild defeat for the same expectations, will seek more reassurance and comfort, so that they come to use affiliation as a consummatory behavior or end state (in itself). And again middle born will show an aggressiveness toward getting attention, rejecting affiliation as a means behavior.

Work similar to that of Gewirtz is reported by Haeberle (1958) and was carried out in 1958 with mildly disturbed New York City children three to six years in age in a therapeutic nursery school. Children were rated by observers for their dependency behavior (touching, attention-seeking, recognition-seeking). The mean scores for boys and girls follow consistently down the ordinal positions in the same way as Gewirtz' scores for succorance. Thus:

	Boys	
0	1B	LB
24.68	19.24	16.16

	Girls	
0	1B	LB
23.48	21.29	20.31

That girls had higher scores in general probably follows from the fact that mothers find that paying attention to girls leads to greater changes in their behavior, which in turn tends to keep the mothers paying more attention to girls than they do to boys. For example, when the baby cries and the mother consoles it, if it is a girl, it is more likely to stop crying; if it is a boy, it is more likely to keep right on crying. Infant girls are more rewarding to their mothers than infant boys (Moss, 1967). On the other hand, if we follow this same line of reasoning, what then is so rewarding about only boys? Why are they so dependent and succorant? Are we to believe that mothers of only boys are particularly persistent in rewarding them, despite their masculine recalcitrance? Later evidence which suggests that the only boy has marked identification with his mother makes this a worthwhile conjecture.

More recently Hilton (1967) has found that in an experimental situation where only children, firstborn, and later-born 4-year-olds worked on puzzles, the mothers of the only children and firstborn were significantly more interfering, extreme, and inconsistent in their behavior than were the mothers of the later born. This is consistent with Rothbart's very similar observational study (1967) with 5-year-olds in which the mothers put more direct pressure for achievement on their firstborn, were more intrusive into the activity of the firstborn (who were trying to solve puzzles), and yet were more likely to help the firstborn. In Hilton's study the mothers of the early born more often signaled to their children to begin work on the puzzles; the mothers of the later born were more likely to wait for the child to start by himself; again, the mothers of the early-born children continued to give more task-oriented suggestions, but they also made more overt demonstrations of love, especially if the child was doing well; if he was not doing well, they markedly decreased both their love and their verbal support. While various interpretations are possible, Hilton (1967) suggests:

When the parent is inconsistent there is no stable guideline for internalizing the correct course of action. The child cannot predict outcomes on the basis of past performance, and must continue to ask for evaluation because the same behavior will elicit a varying response. The effect of excessive interference is to create standards that the child must fulfill. He does not set his own goals but rather achieves the ones set for him [p. 288].

Hilton goes on to say: "Interference and inconsistency both undermine the child's opportunities to develop reference points for internal evaluation" (1967, p. 288), which is to imply that these children are continually in the position of the subjects in Schachter's (1959) social comparison experiments, that is, reaching out for reassurance and information from others. Her type of argument makes social comparison theory once again particularly appropriate to firstborn. Unfortunately, there is no indication as to why the mothers should be so inconsistent. Perhaps their early high expectations followed by their forced reduction in attention, their use of the older sibling as a surrogate, as well as that sibling's continuing dependency—all combine to establish this vacillating pattern in the mothers. In a subsequent study (1968), Hilton has shown that parental interference does not work effectively unless the child is already dependent. A dependent child is comfortable with an interfering adult and works effectively as a result! But an independent child is only disoriented by this interference. Such a view leaves room for Schachter's more primary notion that the dependency is, in the first place, established by the additional attention and expectation (and presumably reinforcement) focused by mothers upon firstborn children.

The studies on early childhood therefore are loosely consistent with Schachter's developmental thesis. The parents may not relate to their firstborn in quite the way he suggested, but it does seem apparent that they do have a special type of relationship with them. To this point, therefore, there is fairly good evidence for believing that the consensus in the adult experimental results and the consensus in these studies of young children are connected. In the adult studies, the firstborn rely upon others and achieve more than the non-firstborn; and in these infant studies the firstborn also reach out for others and in most studies achieve more than do the non-firstborn. Inconsistencies over time (Lasko, 1954) and in immediate treatment (Rothbart, 1967; Hilton, 1967) may increase the importance of achievement as an instrumental behavior, and affiliation as a consummatory behavior for firstborn children.

CHILDHOOD

Even if a special parent relationship is postulated for parents and firstborn in preschool years, such a relationship may not continue subsequently. The evidence suggests, however, that it does. From this it can be argued that if ordinal position differences do persist in affiliation and achievement, this may well be a continuance of the early determinations dealt with above. First, we shall present some of the rather tenuous evidence of continuing special treatment and, second, further evidences of ordinal position differences in affiliation and achievement throughout childhood.

There are a number of studies all of which add up to the view that, in general, the firstborn continue throughout childhood to be the subject of special expectations on the part of the parents and to have a special relationship with them. Thus Stout (1960), using the Berkeley Guidance data (chiefly ratings based on interviews with parents), found that each parent was more directive of firstborn than later born. Parents tended to act jointly toward the firstborn but differentially toward the later born. Koch (1956a) found that firstborn at the age of 6 years spoke more clearly and articulated more adequately than second born, a difference that she put down to their more consistent modeling after and interaction with adults rather than siblings. She also found firstborn more concerned about parental alignments, relations, and favoritism. Bossard's transcripts of family table talk (1945) demonstrated that younger children "tend to be ignored . . . the family seems to adjust its age level to the older children, and to ignore the younger ones, especially if the age differential is not large. Questions on word meanings raised by the younger children are given less consideration, even in our most intelligent families" (p. 230). McArthur (1956) quoted a series of studies involving interviews, anecdotal observations, and content analyses of interviews, all of which also added up to a continuing "special" relationship of firstborn and parents. He began by citing the anecdotal and unpublished observations of Lantis concerning 134 children of Harvard students upon whom she collected life history data. Lantis summarized her impressions as follows: "The eldest child is adult-oriented. He is more likely to be serious, sensitive (that is, his feelings are hurt easily and he doesn't need much punishment), conscientious, 'good,' fond of books or fond of doing things with adults. . . . The second child is not so anxious to get adult approval; in this sense he is tougher" (McArthur, 1956, p. 48). In a subsequent study reported in the same paper (McArthur, 1956) in which the parents of these children checked the elements of these descriptions which were most characteristic of each birth order, a significant number concurred in attributing the characteristics in much the same way as Lantis had done. Later, in a still further interview with the parents of these parents (grandparents of the original subjects) which was also scored for the same descriptive items, first children were described by both generations as serious and adult-oriented and second children were described by both as nonstudious, cheerful, placid, and easygoing. The trait "shy" was characteristic of firstborn and "friendly" of second born. A majority of McArthur's parents reported being more relaxed in their handling of the later born, but there were no significant associations between specific child training procedures and birth order differences. He suggested that despite important historical changes in child training over recent years, "the resulting personalities in each generation seem to have been the same, the first child was adult-centered, the second child was peer-oriented" (1955, p. 52).

To test whether firstborn children of grade school age did in fact perceive themselves as interacting to a greater extent with parent figures, Houston used the Bene-Anthony Family Relations Test (Sutton-Smith, Rosenberg, & Houston, 1968). Subjects were 40 New Zealand boys of ages 5 through 11 years of differing sibling positions but matched for age, intelligence, and socioeconomic status. All were members of two-child families (M1M, M1F, MF2 or MM2). An adapted version of the test (1957) consisting of 40 items—ten of positive outgoing feelings from the child to his family; ten negative outgoing; ten positive incoming; ten negative incoming—was used (see Table 1). Each item was printed on a card, read to the child, and given to him. First, however,

TABLE 1. Items in Adaptation of the Family Relations Test

Positive Outgoing Feelings:

1. This person is always very nice.
2. This person is nice to play with.
3. This person is kind hearted.
4. This person is jolly.
5. This person often helps the others.
6. This person is lots of fun.
7. This person deserves a present.
8. I love this person very much.
9. I would like to keep this person always near me.
10. I would like to sit on this person's knee.

Positive Incoming Feelings:

11. This person likes to play with me.
12. This person is very kind to me.
13. This person makes me feel very happy.
14. This person likes to help me.
15. This person thinks I am a nice boy.
16. This person smiles at me.
17. This person often wants to be with me.
18. This person always listens to what I say.
19. This person likes me very much.
20. This person likes to give me things.

Negative Outgoing Feelings:

21. This person spoils other people's fun.
22. This person is bad tempered.
23. This person is not very patient.
24. This person is sometimes too fussy.
25. This person sometimes makes me feel very angry.
26. This person sometimes grumbles too much.
27. Sometimes I don't like this person.
28. Sometimes I hate this person.
29. Sometimes I would like to spank/smack/hit this person.
30. This person is a nuisance.

Negative Incoming Feelings:

31. This person hits me.
32. This person teases me.
33. This person scolds me (tells me off).
34. This person won't play with me when I feel like it.
35. This person won't help me when I am in trouble.
36. This person is too busy to have time for me.
37. This person is always complaining about me.
38. This person makes me feel sad.
39. This person gets cross with me.
40. This person makes me feel foolish.

SOURCE: B. Sutton-Smith, B. G. Rosenberg, & S. Houston, *Sibling Perception of Parental Models.* Paper presented at Eastern Psychological Association, Washington, D.C., April 20, 1968.

from an array of 20 line-drawn figures (four men, four women, five boys, five girls, a toddler, and a baby) the child selected figures representing his family. An extra box, Mr. Nobody, was added by the investigator. The items read to the child in random order were mailed by him in the mailbox behind each of the family figures he had chosen.

The results indicated, as predicted, that the firstborn boys placed more messages in the parent boxes than did the second-born boys. Specifically the firstborn recorded more positive intake from the father ($p > .05$), and more negative intake from the mother ($p < .05$). The second born for their part showed more interactions with their older siblings than vice versa. They received a more negative intake ($p < .01$), and gave more negative responses ($p < .01$) to the siblings. For both sibling orders where there was the greatest interaction, therefore, there was also the greatest conflict. This study, like a number of others, again points to the involvement of the parents and the firstborn.

Let us turn to our second question: Does the differential parental treatment lead to continuing differences in affiliation and achievement? The answers available indicate that indeed ordinal position differences continue. But they seem to imply also that the relationships between these variables may change. We shall begin the discussion with an experiment by Gilmore and Zigler (1964), the complexities of which serve to heighten the contradictions that occur if one stays with the view that the dependency responses of infancy will simply persist in a similar form throughout development. In a study with five- to eight-year-olds, Gilmore and Zigler (1964) proposed that as firstborn "have been continually satiated on social reinforcers early in their lives, they will be less effortful in a situation where they can take these for granted and more effortful in a situation where they cannot" (p. 193). From the studies of Gewirtz (1948) and Haeberle (1958), above, this is a proposition which we might expect to be more true of only children, firstborn, and non-firstborn, in that order. Unfortunately, Gilmore and Zigler tested it with only 20 firstborn and late-born boys and girls. More important, where Gewirtz argued that the preexistence of an abundance of social reinforcement would lead to more succorance be-

havior in the firstborn three- and four-year-olds, Gilmore and Zigler were saying that the same condition would lead to less effortful behavior in the five- to eight-year-old firstborn.

Gilmore and Zigler used the "marble hole game," which is nomenclatural doublethink for a monotonous and repetitive procedure, in which the subject sorted 300 marbles of two different colors into two different holes in a boxtop for as long a period of time as he wished to continue. The experimenter said: "Now in this game you can put as many marbles in the hole as you want to. You tell me when you want to stop." Under one condition of playing the game, half the firstborn and later born were given no encouragement while they proceeded. In the other condition they were encouraged: "You really know how to play this game." "Fine." "Good." The results were that the firstborn played for a longer period of time when they received no encouragement than when they were encouraged. Later born played longer when they were given encouragement than when they were not given any. The nonencouragement condition stimulated the later born to greater effort. Gilmore and Zigler concluded that "firstborns evidenced less need for social reinforcement than did later borns when such reinforcers were readily available" (1964, p. 199). Later born who accelerated their performances when the reinforcers were available were said to have done so because they were relatively deprived in earlier years.

These results should perhaps be taken seriously because there is partially corroborative data in Koch's complex study of the 8 two-child family positions at age six. She had teachers rate her subjects on various traits including their relationships to the teachers (1955b). One of her traits, "response to sympathy and approval from adults," may be equated with the encouragement condition in the Gilmore and Zigler study. If we follow Gilmore and Zigler's line of reasoning, then under normal conditions the second born would show more of such a response, being hungrier for any available reinforcements than were the firstborn. The rank order of the levels of response for the various two-child ordinal positions at the different age spacings are indicated in Table 2, an adaptation from a table by Koch (1955b, p. 20).

It will be noticed in this table that only under

TABLE 2. Average Ratings on Response to Approval

Ordinal Categories	Age Differences between Siblings		
	7–24 months	25–48 months	49–72 months
MM2	5	3	2
FM2	8	4	8
MF2	3	1	7
FF2	1	2	3
M1M	4	8	5
M1F	6	6	4
F1M	2	7	1
F1F	7	5	6

SOURCE: Adapted from Koch, H. L. Some personality correlates of sex, sibling position, and sex of sibling among five and six year old children, *Genetic Psychological Monographs*, 1955b, **52**, 3–50.

the intermediate age spacing does the expected difference between firstborn and second born hold up. In that spacing, second born are always more responsive after receiving the rewards of sympathy and approval from adults. This is an important substantiation of the expectation that second borns will be more susceptible to immediate rewards because this two- to four-year-age gap is the one in which a definite contrast will occur between the mother's handling of the two children. This contrast between the siblings is muted in both the nearer and further spacings. It is noticeable that the effect seems to work most consistently across the various age spacings when the second born is one of the same sex as the firstborn (FF2 and MM2). Here, sex of sibling is not a complicating variable as it seems to be in the other second-born cases. The virtue of these supplementary findings from Koch is that although they can give only partial support, or partial refutation (whichever way you choose to look at it) to the Gilmore and Zigler material presented earlier, they do introduce examples of the type of sibling position complexities with which research in this area must actually deal. Still having conceded that Gilmore and Zigler have some partial corroboration in Koch, how then are their findings to be reconciled with those of Gewirtz and Haeberle? Are the differences due to the different age levels? Do younger firstborn children, because of their immaturity, express their need for reinforcement more directly? Or is the nursery school, with the inevitable competitiveness for the teacher's approval and help we especially associate with four- and five-

year-olds, really more like the nonreward condition in Gilmore and Zigler's experiment? If both situations are indeed comparably frustrating, then we might say that at both age levels the firstborn make a greater effort—the younger in Gewirtz and Haeberle by reaching out for succorance, and the older in Gilmore and Zigler by working longer when not rewarded. It might make sense to equate both the nursery school and the marble game in the nonencouraging condition because they are both slightly frustrating situations, and make sense also to see direct appeal (four- to five-year-olds) and appeal through effort (five- to eight-year-olds) as differential age responses to a similar stimulus complex.

Whatever the case, with the adolescent studies it is possible to argue that the relationship between these variables has taken yet a further shift. In the Becker, Lerner, and Carroll experiment (1966) . . . it was shown that the firstborn boys conformed more in an Asch perceptual judgment situation, agreeing that the size of the line was the same as had been stated by the accomplices. In one of the conditions in the 1966 experiment, however, there was no resulting difference between the ordinal positions in yielding to accomplices. Subjects were told: "I'll give you a chance to win some money here. You will get a bonus of $.05 for each accurate answer you give" (p. 321). The experimenters had already established that this was regarded as a not very significant amount of money by these boys. Second-born responses here were like their responses in the earlier control conditions. They did not take much notice of the accomplices. But now the firstborn also ignored the accomplices. Why? Did the desire for $.05 make them rely on themselves more? Did the money now make their own achievement more salient for them than the opinion of the accomplices? Unfortunately, Becker, Lerner, and Carroll also shifted their instructions slightly. They now stated the task not as a perceptual judgment of matching lines, but as a matter of accuracy of judgment. It is possible that this shift in instruction shifted the meaning of the experiment to a concern with a psychological function (judgment rather than perception), about which the first might feel more personally involved. There is some evidence that firstborn are less competent at perceptual judgments (Koch, 1954; Steward, 1967).

In two other experimental conditions, the firstborn showed less conforming behavior than the later born: first, when the reward offered was 25 cents, and second, when the judgments had to be made after the cards were taken away and the subjects had to rely on their own memory in the face of the incorrect statements of the accomplices.

Partial resolution of some of these differences has been provided in a recent study by Rhine (1968). He hypothesized that in low achievement conditions the firstborn would be more conforming (after Schachter, 1959), but in high achievement conditions where they could profit by independence of judgment they would be nonconforming (Sampson & Hancock, 1967). In an experimental situation where the subject had to judge the number of clicks in a series that he had heard after hearing the judgments of others, the firstborn followed the others when they were not rewarded for accuracy, but stayed with their own judgment when they were. That is, under nonachievement conditions they were conforming, but under achievement conditions they were nonconforming.

While there are too many differences among these various studies to be certain that the varying results are not produced by varying instructions, the psychological functions involved, or the social roles of accomplices and experimenters (Carrigan & Julian, 1966; Helmreich & Collins, 1967; Erlich, 1958), there does seem to be some merit in the view that with increasing age, the relationships of affiliation and achievement shift. Perhaps affiliation or dependency has a primary role with young children, so that achievement is a means to that end; whereas, with the passage of time, achievement becomes a more important motive in its own right. It stands to reason that when one's own career is paramount (as in adolescence) rather than one's relationship to parents, the need for achievement would take on a more autonomous role in human behavior. At the same time the particular success of the firstborn and only born in becoming eminent might well imply that they may ultimately use their affiliative skills in service of their achievement. Possibly the relationship between the two variables is reversed during development, so that dependency as a form of "servility" in childhood gives way to dependency as a form of "sensitivity" in adulthood (Alexander, 1967).

Parents' Differential Reactions
to Sons and Daughters

Mary K. Rothbart

Eleanor E. Maccoby

The existence of sex differences in psychological functioning has been repeatedly documented in psychological literature. Often the differences have been unexpected and have taken complex forms (Oetzel, 1966). Any theory of sex typing that attempts to understand the sources of these differences must consider the possible effects of differential parent pressures occurring as a function of the sex of the child. Few studies have as yet explored the nature of differential parent behaviors toward boys and girls, and any complete study of this kind would have to consider sex of parents as another important source of variation. The present study therefore attempts to examine

The authors would like to express their gratitude to Clarene Dong, Carol Spielman, and Paul Wick, who assisted in the development and administration of the initial pilot study, and to Aimée Leifer, who worked on all phases of the final study. This research was financed in part by Public Health Service Predoctoral Fellowship No. 5 F1 MH–20, 971–02, National Institute of Mental Health.

parent behavior toward a child as a function of (*a*) sex of the parent, and (*b*) sex of the child.

Previous studies of mother-father differences in treatment of boys and girls have been of two major types. The first involves children's perceptions of their parents' behavior; the second involves parents' perceptions of their own behavior and attitudes toward their children. Numerous studies of children's perceptions of their parents have been carried out, and the literature is summarized and briefly criticized by Droppleman and Schaeffer (1963). Considering only studies with preadolescent children, a common finding has been that both boys and girls "prefer" the mother to the father and find her friendlier and easier to get along with (Hawkes, Burchinal, & Gardner, 1957; Kagan, 1956; Simpson, 1935).

Cross-sex findings suggesting an interaction between sex of parent and sex of child have also been reported. When Simpson (1935) questioned children ranging in ages from 5 to 9, the boys said

Mary K. Rothbart and Eleanor E. Maccoby, "Parents' Differential Reactions to Sons and Daughters," *Journal of Personality and Social Psychology, 4,* 1966, pp. 237–243. Copyright © 1966 by the American Psychological Association, and reproduced by permission.

they were punished (spanked) more by their fathers than their mothers. Girls said mothers spanked them more, but the inference from their projective responses was that the father punished more. Kagan and Lemkin (1960) interviewed children ages 3–8 and found few sex differences in reports of parent practices. Both boys and girls reported that the opposite-sex parent "kissed the most." Girls saw the father as more punitive and affectionate than the mother, while boys saw him only as more punitive. Kagan (1956) interviewed first-, second-, and third-grade children on four issues: Who (the mother or the father) would be on the child's side in an argument; who punishes; who is the boss of the house; who is more feared. With children of all ages combined, there was little cross-sex difference in response. When the younger and older children were treated separately, the older children showed a consistent tendency to see the same-sex parent as less benevolent and more frustrating.

In studies involving parents rather than children, Aberle and Naegele (1952) and Tasch (1952) used only fathers as subjects. Fathers reported different expectations for sons and daughters and said that they participated in different activities with their sons than with their daughters. Sears, Maccoby, and Levin (1957) used only mothers as subjects, interviewing at length mothers of nursery school children. Mothers reported that they permit more aggressiveness from boys when it is directed toward parents and children outside the family, no difference in permissiveness of aggression against siblings. No differences in severity of punishment for aggression nor in permissiveness for dependency were found. Mothers reported they did most of the disciplining of both sexes, but that the father took a larger role in disciplining his son when both parents were at home. In a study with both parents, Goodenough (1957) found that mothers were less concerned about their child's appropriate sex typing than were fathers. Fathers also reported they were actively involved in implementing sex typing of their children, while mothers reported they did not consciously attempt to influence sex typing.

Emmerich (1962) gave questionnaires for assessing nurturance and restrictiveness to parents of children ages 6–10, defining nurturance as reward for positive behavior and dependency, and restrictiveness as punishment for negative behavior. The two scales were combined as a measure of power. Mothers were found to be more nurturant and less restrictive toward children of both sexes. A marked trend was also found for fathers to exert more power toward their sons than their daughters, and a similar but less powerful trend for mothers to exert more power toward their daughters than toward their sons. Emmerich's data are suggestive of differences between mothers and fathers in their treatment of boys and girls, but only on a very general dimension. The questions asked of parents were also quite amorphous, for example, rating the extent to which he compliments his daughter "when she does what she knows she should do," or gives her "something at the time she wants it."

The present experiment is an attempt to study parents' reactions to specific child behaviors, including some regarded as sex typed, for example, dependency and aggression.

We are also interested in a test of a hypothesis proposed by social learning theorists to account for sex differences in behavior. Mischel (in press) suggests:

> The greater incidence of dependent behaviors for girls than boys, and the reverse situation with respect to physically aggressive behavior, seems directly explicable in social learning terms. Dependent behaviors are less rewarded for males, physically aggressive behaviors are less rewarded for females in our culture, and, consequently there are mean differences between the sexes in the frequency of such behaviors after the first few years of life.

Assuming that the family constitutes the major "culture" to which the preschool child is exposed, we might predict from this learning-theory interpretation that both parents would consistently reinforce dependency more strongly in girls and aggression more strongly in boys. The present study is designed to test this prediction.

Parents were put in a hypothetical situation with a child and were asked to record their immediate reactions to what the child said and did. To avoid the additional variables that would compound an adult's reaction to an actual boy or girl, the recorded voice of a single child constituted the stimulus material. The voices of a number of 4-year-olds were recorded, and one was chosen which judges could not readily identify as to sex. Some of the parents were informed that it was a boy's voice, some that it was a girl's voice, and differences in their responses were examined. A questionnaire was also used to measure the extent to which a parent differentiates between the sexes by either (*a*) feeling boys and girls are different on selected characteristics, or (*b*) feeling boys and girls *should* differ on these characteristics. It was hypothesized that parents showing high differentiation between boys and girls would show greater differences in reaction to the boy's voice compared with the girl's voice than would parents who differentiated little between the sexes.

Method

This study was preceded by an initial individual testing of 58 mothers. A small pilot group of both mothers and fathers was then tested in a group-administered procedure, and the coding categories and questionnaire were revised. The final testing involved both fathers and mothers in a group administration.

SELECTION OF THE STIMULUS VOICE

The child speaker was chosen by recording nine nursery school children reciting a prepared script. Six adult judges rated the sex of each child after hearing the tape recordings. The voice selected (that of a boy) was judged to be a boy by half the judges and a girl by the other half. In the actual study, none of the parent subjects questioned the sex attributed to the voice they heard.

The statements comprising the script were adaptations of actual statements of 3- and 4-year-old children recorded in the same locality approximately a year before the final study. An attempt was made to make the script as realistic as possible, and a number of mothers in the individually administered pretest remarked that the recorded child sounded very much like their own nursery school child.

SUBJECTS

Subjects were 98 mothers and 32 fathers of children enrolled in a parent-education nursery school. These parents came from a range of socio-economic status levels, with a concentration of upper-middle-class families.

Of these parents, 60 mothers and 21 fathers were told that the voice was a girl's, 38 mothers and 11 fathers that it was a boy's. The reason for a larger number of parents hearing the girl's than the boy's voice was that only the number of parents expected to attend had been matched according to sex and age of the nursery school child and assigned to the two groups. More parents attended than had been anticipated, and the extra parents all heard the girl's voice.

The group hearing the boy's voice and the group hearing the girl's voice proved to be matched according to sex of nursery school age child, but it was later found that the two groups were not well matched with respect to whether the parent had children of only one or of both sexes. Our sample was divided according to this variable, and no differences in a direction that would influence our results were found.

PRESENTATION OF THE STIMULUS VOICE

Parents were tested in four separate groups (fathers-girl's voice, fathers-boy's voice, mothers-girl's voice, mothers-boy's voice), with female experimenters. Each experimenter introduced the parents to the situation represented by the tape-recorded voice. The subject was asked to imagine that he (or she) was at home reading, with his 4-year-old boy, Johnny (or girl, Susan), playing with a puzzle in an adjacent room. With the child is the 1-year-old baby. Subjects were asked to give their immediate reactions to the 4-year-old's statements by writing down what they would say or do in response to each statement. The child's statements were as follows. (Due to some lack of clarity in the tape, each statement of the child was repeated by the experimenter to assure that it was understood by all subjects.)

1. Daddy (or Mommy), come look at my puzzle.
2. Daddy, help me.
3. Does this piece go here?
4. Baby, you can't play with me. You're too little.
5. Tell him he can't play with my puzzle—it's mine!
6. Leave my puzzle alone or I'll hit you in the head!
7. I don't like this game—I'm gonna break it!
8. I don't like this game. It's a stupid game. You're stupid, Daddy.
9. Ow! Baby stepped on my hand!
10. Daddy—it hurts.
11. Daddy, get me another puzzle.
12. It's not raining now—I'm going across the street and play.

After each statement, the experimenter stopped the tape while subjects recorded their reactions.

Parents' responses were coded for each item, and items were grouped according to 7 different scales: Help Seeking (Items 1, 2, 3, 11), Comfort Seeking (9, 10), Dependency (Help and Comfort Seeking scales combined), Aggression (6a, 7a, 8a), Allowing Child to Stop Game (7, 8), Siding with Child versus Baby (4, 5, 6), and Autonomy (12). Scores on all scales ranged generally from permissiveness for the child (low score) to nonpermissiveness for the child's actions (high score). For example, in response to the child's statement 9 ("Ow! Baby stepped on my hand!"), a rating of high comfort was given to the response, "Here, Mommy will kiss it," while a rating of low comfort was given to the response, "Keep your hand away from the baby's foot." In response to Statement 5 ("Tell him he can't play with my puzzle—it's mine!"), a parent who said,

"That's right. Let's find the baby something else," was rated as siding with the child. A response of "Johnny, let your brother help you" was rated as siding with the baby. All protocols were coded by one rater, and 25 were coded independently by a second rater. Reliabilities ranged from .83 to 1.00, with a mean scale correlation of .90.

QUESTIONNAIRE

The parent questionnaire, administered immediately after the tape-recorded script, measured two aspects of parents' attitudes about sex differences. Part 1 asked parents' opinions about differences they felt actually existed between boys and girls. The items included were taken from statements given by mothers to open-ended interview questions about sex differences from the files of the Sears et al. (1957) study. The format for the questionnaire was adapted from Sherriffs and Jarrett (1953). A sample from the 40-item list is as follows:

More likely to be obedient are: $\overline{G}$ $\overline{B}$ $\overline{X}$.

Here, G represents girls, B boys, and X no sex differences. The measure of sex-role differentiation for this part of the scale was the total number of X responses, with a large number of X responses indicating low sex-role differentiation.

Part 2 of the questionnaire measured what differences parents felt *should* exist between boys and girls. Boys and girls were rated separately on how important it was to the parent that his child be described by each characteristic. A sample item is:

Very important *not* to	Fairly important *not* to	Unimportant to	Fairly important to	Very important to

be obedient.

As a measure of sex-role differentiation for Part 2 of the questionnaire, absolute differences between ratings of an item's importance for girls and importance for boys were summed. The higher this difference (D) score, the higher the sex-role differentiation that was indicated.

Results

PARENTS' RESPONSE TO THE CHILD'S VOICE

When the direction of differences for all scales are considered, a general trend emerges. Mothers tend to be more permissive for the boy's voice and fathers more permissive for the girl's voice (see Table 1). While only one main effect was significant (Scale 7—fathers allowed more autonomy than mothers, $p < .05$), interactions were significant for Scale 2 (Comfort Seeking, $p. < .05$), Scale 3 (Dependency, $.05 < p < .10$), Scale 5 (Allowing Child to Stop Game, $.05 < p < .10$), and Scale 6 (Siding with Child Versus Baby, $p < .01$) as shown in Table 2. On all of these scales, the interaction was in the direction of mothers showing more permissiveness and positive attention to their sons than to their daughters, fathers showing more permissiveness and positive attention to their daughters than to their sons.

Our failure to find a significant interaction for the Aggression scale was somewhat surprising, since in the initial pilot study we had found a strong tendency for mothers to allow more aggression from their sons than from their daughters. In the pilot study, our measure of aggression had been composed chiefly of aggression directed against the parent. For this reason, item 8a (Aggression Toward Parent) was examined separately from the rest of the Aggression scale. Item 8a showed a significant interaction ($p < .05$), with fathers allowing more aggression from their daughters than from their sons and mothers allowing more aggression from their sons than from their daughters.

QUESTIONNAIRE

Parents' X scores on the questionnaire (extent to which parent felt differences *do* exist between boys and girls) were correlated with parents' D scores (extent to which parent felt differences *should* exist between boys and girls). The correla-

TABLE 1

MOTHERS' AND FATHERS' REACTIONS TO BOY'S VERSUS GIRL'S VOICE

Voice	Help Seeking (High score-refuses help)		Comfort Seeking (High score-refuses)		Dependency (High score-refuses)		Aggression (High score-does not permit)	
	Mothers	Fathers	Mothers	Fathers	Mothers	Fathers	Mothers	Fathers
Boy's								
M	8.71	8.45	4.24	5.82	12.95	14.18	4.95	5.64
SD	1.71	1.51	1.73	2.18	2.32	2.92	1.29	2.16
N	38	11	38	11	38	11	37	11
Girl's								
M	9.15	8.39	5.02	4.84	14.17	13.12	4.91	4.86
SD	1.93	1.61	1.86	1.56	3.05	2.55	1.32	1.62
N	59	18	59	19	59	17	56	21
	Allowing Child to Stop Game (High score-does not)		Siding With Child versus Baby (High score-sides with baby)		Autonomy (High score-does not permit)		Aggression toward Parent (High score-does not permit)	
Boy's								
M	3.62	4.18	6.13	7.64	1.97	2.27	1.59	2.27
SD	1.09	1.17	1.43	1.43	.64	.64	1.76	1.01
N	37	11	37	11	37	11	38	11
Girl's								
M	4.00	3.62	6.76	6.20	2.10	2.40	1.75	1.67
SD	1.09	1.16	1.47	1.61	.47	.60	1.16	1.11
N	57	21	59	19	60	20	60	21

Note.—Mean scores.

TABLE 2

SUMMARY OF ANALYSES OF VARIANCE INTERACTION
TESTS BETWEEN SEX OF PARENT
AND SEX OF CHILD'S VOICE

Variable	Interaction (MS)ᵃ	Error (MS)	F
Help Seeking	1.81	3.24	.56
Comfort Seeking	16.29	3.28	4.97**
Dependency	27.06	7.67	3.53*
Aggression	3.13	2.11	1.48
Allowing Child to Stop Game	5.54	1.31	3.70*
Siding with Child versus Baby	24.94	2.16	11.55***
Autonomy	.04	.32	.12
Aggression toward Parent	4.02	1.02	3.94**

* $p < .10$, $df = 1/121$, $1/122$.
** $p < .05$, $df = 1/123$, $1/125$.
*** $p < .01$, $df = 1/123$.

tion between X and D scores for mothers was
—.53; the correlation for fathers was —.40.
Since a high D score and a low X score both
represent high sex-role differentiation, these findings indicate a positive correlation between the
two measures.

There were no significant differences between
mothers' and fathers' sex-role differentiation scores,
but parents who had heard the girl's voice tended
to have higher sex-role differentiation scores than
parents who had heard the boy's voice. This trend
appeared in mothers' X and D scores and in
fathers' D scores, but was significant only for
mothers' D scores ($p < .05$). This finding is difficult to explain, and it suggests that questionnaire scores may be influenced by situational variables.

Finally, parents with high sex-role differentiation scores were separated from parents with low
sex-role differentiation scores. Both X and D
scores for mothers and fathers were standardized,
and divided approximately at the median for the
high- and low-differentiation groups. Since not
all parents received the questionnaire, Ns for the
fathers' group were quite small. Parents' responses
to the child's voice were then compared, with the
expectation that high-differentiation parents would
show larger differences between their treatment of
boys and girls than would low-differentiation parents. It was also expected that these differences
would be in the direction of promoting sex-typed
behavior. The first part of this prediction received

some support in this study; the second part did
not. When scores for all scales were standardized
and summed for each subject, giving a general
permissiveness score toward the child, high-differentiation parents tended to show greater permissiveness to the opposite-sex child (see Table
3). High sex-role differentiation parents showed
larger differences between treatment of boys and
girls than did low-differentiation parents for
fathers separated on the basis of D scores ($p
< .02$) and for mothers separated on the basis
of X scores ($p < .05$). The differences were in
the same direction but not significant for mothers
separated according to D scores and fathers separated according to X scores.

In testing the hypothesis that differences would
run in a sex-stereotyped direction, parents' responses on the Dependency and Aggression scales
were more closely examined. On the basis of all
parents' responses to the D questionnaire, it was
expected that high-differentiation parents would
act to promote dependency in girls and assertive-
ness in boys. When these scales are examined,

TABLE 3

MEAN STANDARD SCORES REPRESENTING DEGREE
OF OVERALL PERMISSIVENESS FOR HIGH-
AND LOW-DIFFERENTIATION PARENTS

Voice	Mothers		Fathers	
	High diff.	Low diff.	High diff.	Low diff.
	Groups assigned according to D scores			
Boy's				
M	48.74	47.72	56.75	50.92
SD	4.90	2.15	2.40	4.74
N	15	12	5	6
Girl's				
M	53.05	49.23	47.63	50.48
SD	5.45	4.09	4.49	4.57
N	10	11	8	9
	Groups assigned according to X scores			
Boy's				
M	48.62	48.52	55.15	53.05
SD	4.53	3.95	2.78	4.67
N	14	15	7	4
Girl's				
M	53.26	47.60	49.93	49.90
SD	4.81	5.12	3.85	4.52
N	11	9	9	10

Note.—High scores = nonpermissiveness.

however, the differences seem rather to be for high-differentiation parents to show greater relative permissiveness to the opposite-sex child than low-differentiation parents. These differences were significant only in Scales 1 and 3 for mothers separated according to D scores (high-differentiation mothers more permissive of dependency in boys, $p < .05$ for both scales), and Scale 3 for fathers separated according to X scores (high-differentiation fathers more permissive of dependency in girls, $p < .05$). The direction of these results suggests that high-differentiation parents do not necessarily promote sex-role stereotypes; they rather show an intensification of the kinds of differences found for parents as a whole. When the scores of all high-differentiation parents (regardless of which voice they heard) were compared with those of low-differentiation parents, there was an additional tendency for low-differentiation parents to show more general permissiveness than high-differentiation parents, but in no case was this difference significant.

Discussion

Although previous studies have found clear differences between the behavior of mothers and fathers independent of the sex of the child, the present study found only one difference (permissiveness for autonomy) to be independent of the child's sex. A source of this discrepancy may be that earlier studies relied on verbal reports of children and parents; these reports might be expected to be influenced by the cultural stereotypes of the mother and the father. The present study differed from the earlier ones in that a measure more closely approaching the behavior of a parent in an actual situation was used. Also, the fact that the fathers in this study were attending a meeting concerning their children indicates an involvement with the child that may not be found in the father population as a whole.

Another interesting discrepancy exists between some of the current findings and the predictions expected on the basis of common-sense notions of sex typing. For example, the mothers in this study were more likely to allow aggression toward themselves from their boys, as expected in sex-role stereotypes, but they were also more ac-

ceptant of comfort seeking in their sons than in their daughters, an entirely unexpected finding. Fathers, on the other hand, were more acceptant of their daughters' comfort seeking, but also allowed more aggression to be directed toward themselves from their daughters than from their sons. In short, the sex of parent seems to be a better predictor of his differential response to boys and girls than does a sex-role stereotype.

This finding presents some difficulties for the social learning theory interpretation of sex differences outlined at the beginning of this paper (Mischel, in press). Rather than consistent reinforcement of sex-typed behavior by both parents, inconsistency between parents seems to be the rule, and while a parent may treat his child in a manner consistent with the cultural stereotype in one area of behavior, in another he may not.

It is, of course, possible that the only reinforcement counter to the cultural stereotype comes from the child's parents, and that reinforcement from other sources serves to counteract inconsistent parental pressures. It is also possible that parents shift their reinforcing behaviors as their children become older. These possibilities might apply to sex differences in dependency, which seem to emerge late enough to be affected by influences outside the home or later shifts in parental behavior. However, sex differences in aggression have been observed early, while the family is still the primary influence, and our findings fail to support the interpretation that differential reinforcement from both parents is of a kind to promote these differences at this early age level. Perhaps there is a biological component in these sex differences which is of importance either in its own right or in interaction with socialization practices.

There are several possible sources of the cross-sex interaction. In instances of permissiveness for the child's dependent behavior, the parent may be simply responding to the young child as a member of the opposite sex, reacting more favorably to the actions of the child who most resembles his marital partner. Or, reflecting the other side of the Oedipal coin, the parent may react less favorably to the same-sex child because of feelings of rivalry with this child. Another hypothesis, this one concerned with parents' differential responses to negative behavior in the child, suggests that parents may tend to punish the expression of impulses that they do not allow in themselves. As a child, the parent has been punished for certain actions and thoughts, and he may react negatively when he sees expression of these actions and thoughts in his child. When the child is of the same sex as himself, the parent may be more strongly reminded of the situation in which he had been punished, and more negative feelings are evoked. The parent is therefore more likely to punish the same-sex child for negative actions than the opposite-sex child.

This list of possibilities suggests that family interaction springs from multiple motivations, and that any tendency parents may have to reinforce culturally stereotypic behavior in their children may be outweighed by other determinants of their behavior. Parent behavior, then, may not always be consistent with preparing children for the social roles they will fill. Indeed, the child may acquire some aspects of his appropriate role behavior in spite of, rather than because of, what at least one of his parents does as a reinforcing agent.

Although the questionnaire results are by no means conclusive, they suggest a pattern of differences for high-differentiation parents that is simply a stronger statement of the general findings of the study. Perhaps parents with high-differentiation scores are more aware of the differences that distinguish their sons and daughters, but tend to react in a sex-specific way to these sex differences rather than actively promoting sex-typed behavior in their children.

Parents taking the questionnaire for the most part had fairly low sex-role differentiation scores. If this study were replicated with a lower-class sample of parents, we would expect a wider range of sex-role differentiation scores and even stronger interaction effects than were found in this study.

REFERENCES

ABERLE, D. F., & NAEGELE, K. D. Middle class fathers' occupational role and attitudes toward children. *American Journal of Orthopsychiatry*, 1952, *22*, 366–378.

DROPPLEMAN, L. F., & SCHAEFFER, E. S. Boys' and girls' reports of maternal and paternal behavior. *Journal of Abnormal and Social Psychology*, 1963, *67*, 648–654.

EMMERICH, W. Variations in the parent role as a function of the parent's sex and the child's sex and age. *Merrill-Palmer Quarterly*, 1962, *8*, 3–11.

GOODENOUGH, E. W. Interest in persons as an aspect of sex differences in the early years. *Genetic Psychology Monographs*, 1957, *55*, 287–323.

HAWKES, G. R., BURCHINAL, L. G., & GARDNER, B. Pre-adolescents' views of some of their relations with their parents. *Child Development*, 1957, *28*, 393–399.

KAGAN, J. The child's perception of the parent. *Journal of Abnormal and Social Psychology*, 1956, *53*, 257–258.

KAGAN, J., & LEMKIN, I. The child's differential perception of parental attributes. *Journal of Abnormal and Social Psychology*, 1960, *61*, 440–447.

MISCHEL, W. A social learning view of sex differences in behavior. In E. E. Maccoby (Ed.), *The development of sex differences*. Stanford: Stanford University Press, 1966.

OETZEL, R. M. Selected bibliography on sex differences. In E. E. Maccoby (Ed.), *The development of sex differences*. Stanford: Stanford University Press, 1966.

SEARS, R. R., MACCOBY, E. E., & LEVIN, H. *Patterns of child rearing*. Evanston, Ill.: Row, Peterson, 1957.

SHERRIFFS, A. C., & JARRETT, R. F. Sex differences in attitudes about sex differences. *Journal of Psychology*, 1953, *35*, 161–168.

SIMPSON, M. Parent preferences of young children. *Teachers College of Columbia University Contributions to Education*, 1935, No. 652.

TASCH, R. G. The role of the father in the family. *Journal of Experimental Education*, 1952, *20*, 319–361.

Social Rehabilitation
of Isolate-Reared Monkeys

Stephen J. Suomi   Harry F. Harlow

The devastating effect of total social isolation upon monkey behavior is an exceptionally well-documented finding in primate behavioral research. Although 3 months of total social isolation from birth has yielded only transient and reversible behavioral effects (Boelkins, 1963; Griffin & Harlow, 1966), isolation for the first 6 months of life or more has consistently resulted in profound and permanent psychopathology (Harlow, Dodsworth, & Harlow, 1965; Harlow

This research was supported by United States Public Health Service Grants MH–11894 and RR–00167 from the National Institutes of Health to the University of Wisconsin Primate Laboratory and Regional Primate Research Center, respectively. The authors express their appreciation to S. David Kimball and Hal Treharne who collected most of the data, to Carole Mohr who helped to summarize the data, and to Helen Lauersdorf who supervised the final preparation of the manuscript. Reprint requests should be sent to Stephen J. Suomi, University of Wisconsin Primate Laboratory, 22 North Charter Street, Madison, Wisconsin 53706.

& Harlow, 1962; Harlow, Harlow, Dodsworth, & Arling, 1966; Mason, 1963; Rowland, 1964; Sackett, 1968a; Senko, 1966). Upon emergence from total social isolation, monkeys fail to exhibit age-appropriate social and exploratory behavior. Instead, their behavioral repertoire is dominated by self-directed activities, including self-clasping, self-mouthing, huddling, and stereotypic rocking. Such abnormalities persist as the subjects mature. Appropriate sexual responses are virtually absent among adult isolate-reared monkeys, and those females artificially inseminated typically display inadequate maternal behavior toward their initial offspring. Aggressive behavior of isolate-reared monkeys is commonly self directed or, when it occurs in social situations, inappropriately directed.

In contrast, isolation rearing apparently has little effect upon monkey learning capability. Although isolates are slower to adapt to most learning test situations (Harlow, Schiltz, & Harlow, 1969) and to extinguish certain nonreinforced behaviors previously operantly conditioned (Gluck, 1970), these deficits may be attributed to performance rather than intellectual variables. Once properly adapted to a Wisconsin General Test Apparatus, isolate-reared subjects solve complex learning problems as readily as do feral-born monkeys (Singh, 1969).

Two theoretical explanations for the socially destructive effects of isolation for monkeys have dominated the literature, although neither has had its origin in primate research. The "critical period" approach (Scott, 1962), initially an embryological concept and more recently applied by ethologists to avian attachment behavior (e.g., Lorenz, 1965), postulates that subjects progress through critical periods of social development. According to a strict interpretation of the theory, a subject denied appropriate social stimulation during a critical period will be rendered incapable of subsequent normal social development. A second theoretical position, stemming from research using canine subjects (Fuller & Clark, 1966), maintains that the bizarre behavior patterns exhibited by monkeys removed from isolation is the result of "emergence trauma," that is, a shock precipitated by an abrupt shift from an unstimulating environment to one of relatively high complexity.

In view of the apparent discrepancy between intellectual and social effects of isolation rearing and of the alternative theoretical explanation posited, numerous attempts to rehabilitate isolate-reared monkeys have been initiated. Virtually all of these efforts have been summarily unsuccessful, a result consistent with critical period theory. For example, researches designed to shape appropriate social behavior in isolate-reared monkeys via aversive conditioning procedures produced only limited behavioral changes which failed to generalize beyond the experimental situation (Sackett, 1968b). Efforts to alleviate postulated emergence trauma via gradual introduction to environments of increasing complexity did not achieve significant rehabilitation of isolate social behaviors (Clark, 1968; Pratt, 1969). Repeated exposure to socially competent age-mates also had little apparent therapeutic success (Harlow, Dodsworth, & Harlow, 1965). In fact, such exposure may have actually exaggerated isolate disturbance behavior. By 6 months of age, well-socialized monkeys have developed complex patterns of social interaction, including vigorous play and socially directed aggression. They will typically attack any stranger monkey introduced to their social group, and only if the stranger reciprocates the attack will it be "accepted" and mutual play follow. The monkey that does not fight back continues to be the victim of aggression. In retrospect, it is not surprising that isolate-reared subjects were consistently attacked when exposed to well-socialized peers, nor is it surprising that these isolates failed to exhibit significant social recovery.

However, there exist data suggesting that isolate-reared subjects may be responsive to certain social agents and that exposure to such agents may have positive therapeutic value. Isolate-reared mothers who eventually submitted to their infants' efforts to maintain ventral contact usually exhibited adequate maternal behavior toward subsequent offspring (Harlow & Harlow, 1968). Also, monkeys exposed to heated surrogates upon emergence from isolation showed significant decreases in disturbance behavior after contacting the surrogates.[1] In neither case was social rehabilitation complete. The isolate mothers continued to exhibit incompetent sexual behavior, and the isolates exposed to surrogates failed to develop a sophisticated social repertoire.

It seems obvious that any experimental effort designed to rehabilitate isolates via social exposure requires effective social agents or "therapists." What types of monkeys could be appropriate therapists? In view of the above data, one might select animals who would predictably initiate social contact with an isolate without displaying social aggression, and who themselves would exhibit simple social responses which gradually would become more sophisticated. Such requirements are fulfilled by socially experienced monkeys only 3 or 4 months old, for at this age clinging responses still form an integral part of their social repertoire, play is in the primary stage of development, and aggressive behavior has not yet matured. In accord with these fundamental social considerations, the following rehabilitation study was initiated.

[1] H. F. Harlow and S. J. Suomi, manuscript in preparation.

Method

SUBJECTS

Isolates. Isolate subjects were four male rhesus monkeys (*Macaca mulatta*) born within a 2-week period. They were separated from their mothers at birth and maintained in the laboratory nursery (see Blomquist & Harlow, 1961) until their mean age was 10 days, when they were placed in individual isolation chambers (see Rowland, 1964) which effectively denied them physical and visual access to all social agents. The isolate subjects remained in the chambers until their mean age was 6 months.

Therapists. Therapist subjects were four female rhesus monkeys, also born within a 2-week period, but 3 months subsequent to the isolates. They were separated from their mothers at birth and maintained in the laboratory nursery for the first 30 days. They were then placed in individual quadrants of a quad cage, described by Suomi and Harlow (1969), and each monkey was provided with a heated simplified surrogate (see Harlow & Suomi, 1970). In addition, the therapists were permitted 2 hours of mutual social interaction 5 days per week. During three sessions per week they interacted as pairs within the quad cage; during the remaining two 2-hour sessions per week they interacted as a group of four in a social playroom, described by Rosenblum (1961).

PROCEDURE

Postisolation base-line period. When the mean ages of the isolates and therapists were 6 and 3 months, respectively, the isolates were removed from their chambers. All subjects were then placed in individual quadrants of two quad cages, with two isolates and two therapists in each cage. The therapists retained their surrogates and continued to receive 2 hours of social interaction 5 days per week as described above, while the isolates were not permitted to interact socially with other monkeys or with surrogates. The postisolation base-line period lasted 2 weeks.

Postisolation therapy period. Immediately after the base-line period, the following therapy proce-

dure was initiated: (*a*) In therapy weeks 1–4, each isolate was allowed to interact with the therapist monkey adjacent to its quadrant for 2 hours per day, 3 days per week. (*b*) In therapy weeks 5–6, pair interaction (one isolate-one therapist) continued as described in *a*. In addition, the isolates were placed in the playroom with the therapists 1 hour per day, 2 days per week, in groups of four (two isolates, two therapists). (*c*) In therapy weeks 7–11, pair interaction (one isolate-one therapist) was reduced to two 2-hour sessions per week. The playroom sessions were expanded to three 1-hour sessions per week. (*d*) In therapy weeks 12–26, pair interaction was discontinued and replaced by two 2-hour sessions per week during which time all four members of each quad cage (two isolates, two therapists) were permitted free interaction within the quad cage. Playroom interaction continued as in *c*.

To summarize, following removal from isolation, the isolates were housed individually for a period of 2 weeks in order to assess postisolation behavioral levels. Twenty-six weeks of therapy followed. The first 4 weeks of therapy consisted of isolate-therapist interaction within the quad cage. Beginning at the fifth week, the isolates were also permitted social interaction with therapist and with each other in the playroom.

DATA COLLECTION

Beginning at 30 days of age, every subject was observed for two 5-minute periods, 5 days per week. Subject behaviors falling into each of 14 categories were measured for presence or absence during each of the twenty 15-second intervals which comprised the 5-minute session. The following behavioral categories were employed: self-groom (discrete, self-directed picking and/or spreading of the fur), self-mouth (oral contact, exclusive of biting, with any part of own body), self-bite (specific, vigorous, self-directed biting), self-clasp (clasping of any part of own body with hand[s] and/or foot [feet]), huddle (self-enclosed, fetallike position, incorporating any or all patterns of self-clasp, self-embrace, or lowered head), rock (repetitive, nonlocomotive forward and backward movement), spasm (single or repetitive convulsive jerk involving a major part of the body), stereotypy (identical body movements maintained in a rhythmic and repetitive fashion for at least three cycles), locomotion (ambulation of one or more full steps), environmental exploration (tactual and/or oral manipulation by subject or inanimate objects), vocalization (any sound emitted by subject), ventral cling (contact of own ventral body surface with another subject and/or surrogate), social contact (tactual and/or oral contact with another subject and/or surrogate, exclusive of ventral cling or play), and play (any socially directed play activity, including rough and tumble, approach-withdraw, and noncontact play). For each observation session, data consisted of 14 modified frequency scores, one for every behavioral category, each representing the total number of 15-second intervals during which behavior encompassed by the category was observed.

The observations were made between 9:00 A.M. and 5:00 P.M. by one of four testers, each of whom had been trained to a rigorous laboratory reliability criterion prior to the beginning of the experiment. Each subject's two daily observations were distributed as follows:

For isolate subjects (*a*) at 1–6 months there were two observations of each subject in the isolation chamber; (*b*) at 6–6½ months (postisolation base line) there were two observations of the subject in the individual quadrant of the quad cage; (*c*) at 6½–12½ months (therapy period) there was one observation of each subject in the individual quadrant of the quad cage and one observation of each subject in the social situation (either the quad cage or playroom) to which it had been assigned that day.

For therapist subjects at 1–9½ months there was one observation of each subject in the individual quadrant of the quad cage, the other of the subject in the social situation (either the quad cage or playroom) to which it had been assigned that day.

DATA ANALYSIS

Inspection of the data indicated that behaviors encompassed by four categories—self-groom, self-bite, spasm, and vocalization—were infrequently exhibited by any subjects, and therefore these categories were not analyzed statistically. Subject scores of the remaining 10 categories—self-

mouth, self-clasp, huddle, rock, stereotype, locomotion, environmental exploration, and the social categories of ventral cling, social contact, and play—were analyzed in three stages.

First, behaviors of all subjects were traced from the end of the first to the sixth month of life in order to assess isolation effects during the period of confinement. For each of the above seven nonsocial categories, individual subject scores were summed over three 7-week periods, representing behaviors observed from 30 to 80 days, from 80 to 130 days, and from 130 to 180 days of age. Category means for each subject were calculated for each time period, representing the average number of 15-second intervals per observation session during the time block that behaviors encompassed by the category were observed. For each category the above means were subjected to a two-way repeated-measures analysis of variance, with group (isolate versus therapist) as the independent variable and time block as the repeated measure. The means were then compared by use of Duncan's new multiple-range test (Duncan, 1955), employing the Time Block × Subjects Within Groups mean square from the analysis of variance as the test denominator variance term. For the sake of parsimony, only the results of the Duncan tests are presented in this article.[2]

Second, behavioral levels exhibited by the isolate subjects during the 2-week postisolation base line were directly compared to those observed during the final 50 days of isolation in order to determine possible "emergence trauma" effects. Two-tailed *t* tests were employed, one for each of the above nonsocial categories, to test for differences between category means calculated for the two time periods.

Finally, behavioral changes transpiring during the therapy period were examined. Home-cage behaviors of each isolate and control subject were summed for every category over each of the three 60-day projects which comprised the therapy period. Category means were calculated for each subject as above, and the means were subjected to two-way repeated-measures analyses of variance, with group as the independent variable and time block as the repeated measure, then compared by use of Duncan tests. Behaviors recorded during

[2] The analysis of variance summary tables may be obtained from the authors upon request.

the quad cage interaction periods and during the playroom interaction sessions were separately analyzed in a similar fashion. Again, only the results of the Duncan tests are presented, although the complete analyses may be obtained from the authors upon request.

Results

Three unequivocal findings emerged from the data analysis. First, isolate subjects developed significant behavioral abnormalities during the period of social isolation. Second, the isolate subjects exhibited virtually no trace of "emergence trauma" upon removel from isolation. Third and most important, the isolates showed significant recovery, in terms of both nonsocial and social behaviors, in all testing situations during the course of the therapy period.

ISOLATION PERIOD BEHAVIORS

As shown by Table 1, which presents the group means obtained from isolation period observations and the results of the Duncan tests, during the first 2 months of life isolate and therapist monkeys failed to differ significantly on any measure except locomotion, with the isolates locomoting less than the controls ($p < .05$). During the third and fourth months, the only significant group difference was in self-mouthing, with the therapists exhibiting higher levels ($p < .05$). However, during the final 2 months of the isolation period marked behavioral differences between isolates and therapists became evident. The isolates exhibited significantly higher levels of self-clasping ($p < .01$), rocking ($p < .05$), and stereotypy ($p < .01$) than the therapists, changes which reflected increases over previous levels by the isolates rather than decreases by the therapists. These behaviors have consistently been found in the past to differentiate isolate-reared monkeys from more adequately socialized controls. During this time period the isolates also exhibited lower levels of exploration than the therapists ($p < .05$). Thus, although the analysis disclosed few differences between isolate and therapist levels of behavior early in life, by 6 months of age the isolates were clearly exhibiting

TABLE 1

DUNCAN TEST ANALYSIS FOR ISOLATION PERIOD

Category	I	T
Self-mouth		
Period 1	9.5	7.7
Period 2	7.4	10.7
Period 3	10.2	9.0
Self-clasp		
Period 1	.8	.1
Period 2	3.1	.5
Period 3	5.8	.7
Huddle		
Period 1	1.1	.6
Period 2	4.2	.7
Period 3	4.9	1.9
Rock		
Period 1	.1	.6
Period 2	.3	.6
Period 3	2.2	.4
Stereotypy		
Period 1	.2	.1
Period 2	1.2	.1
Period 3	2.6	.0
Locomotion		
Period 1	10.2	13.3
Period 2	11.4	13.4
Period 3	11.4	13.3
Environmental exploration		
Period 1	7.4	8.9
Period 2	8.6	10.9
Period 3	8.1	11.5

Note.—I = isolate subjects, T = therapist subjects; Period 1 = 30–80 days, Period 2 = 81–130 days, Period 3 = 131–180 days of age. Significant differences: Self-mouth—T − 2 > T − 1, I − 2, $p < .05$. Self-clasp—I − 3 > I − 1, T − 1, T − 2, T − 3, $p < .01$; I − 3 > I − 2, $p < .05$. Huddle—I − 3 > I − 1, $p < .05$. Rock—I − 3 > I − 1, I − 2, T − 1, T − 2, T − 3, $p < .05$. Stereotypy—I − 3 > I − 1, T − 1, T − 2, T − 3, $p < .01$; I − 3 > I − 2, $p < .05$; I − 2 > T − 3, $p < .05$. Locomotion—I − 1 < T − 1, T − 2, T − 3, $p < .05$. Environmental exploration—T − 3 > T − 1, I − 1, I − 2, I − 3, $p < .05$; T − 2 > I − 1, $p < .05$.

gross behavioral abnormalities in comparison with their therapist controls.

POSTISOLATION BASE-LINE BEHAVIORS

Comparison of the isolates' postisolation behavioral levels with their counterparts during the immediately preceding isolation period gave little indication of significant change following removal from isolation. No significant differences for any category were disclosed by the *t* tests.

Thus, the data failed to substantiate the occurrence of measurable emergence trauma among the isolate subjects in this experiment. Rather, the isolates' abnormal behaviors, having developed during the period of isolation, remained at existing levels when the monkeys were removed from isolation.

THERAPY PERIOD BEHAVIORS

The data from all three testing situations offered convincing evidence that significant gains were achieved by the isolate subjects during the therapy period. When first removed from their isolation chambers they exhibited high levels of disturbance behaviors and low levels of social behaviors, typical for monkeys socially isolated for the first 6 months of life. By the end of the therapy period, however, their behavioral levels were virtually indistinguishable from those of the socially competent therapist monkeys.

Behavior during quad cage therapy. That the isolates exhibited significant recovery in the quad cage interaction situation during the therapy period was evident from the results of the appropriate Duncan tests, listed in Table 2. During the first 60 days of the therapy period, isolate subjects exhibited significantly higher levels of self-mouthing ($p < .05$), self-clasping ($p < .01$), huddling ($p < .05$), and rocking ($p < .05$) behaviors and lower levels of locomotion ($p < .05$), clinging ($p < .05$), social contact ($p < .01$), and play ($p < .05$) than the therapist monkeys. These differences disappeared as the therapy period progressed, largely resulting from changes in isolate rather than therapist levels of behavior. From the sixty-first to the one hundred and twentieth day of therapy the two groups of monkeys differed significantly only with respect to locomotion, with the isolates exhibiting lower levels ($p < .05$). During the final 60 days of the therapy period there were no significant group differences on any of the category measures in the quad cage interaction situation.

Behavior during playroom therapy. As in the quad cage interaction sessions, the isolate subjects exhibited significant behavioral recovery during the playroom therapy sessions. Initially in the playroom they showed significantly higher levels of self-mouth, self-clasp, huddle, and rock and significantly lower levels of locomotion, exploration, clinging, social contact, and play than the therapist monkeys (all $ps < .01$). During the fifty-first to the one hundredth day of the therapy period detectable group differences vanished except for the categories of self-clasp, for which the isolates showed higher levels than the therapists ($p < .01$) and locomotion, clinging, and play, for which the therapists exhibited higher levels ($p < .05$, $p < .05$, and $p < .01$, respectively). During the final 50 days of playroom therapy the only category to yield significant group differences was self-clasp, with isolates showing higher levels ($p < .05$). These findings are summarized in Table 2, which indicates that the convergence of isolate-therapist behavioral levels over time resulted primarily from changes in isolate rather than therapist levels. Thus, although 9 behavior categories differentiated isolates from therapists during the first days of playroom therapy, the groups were behaviorally equivalent by the end of the therapy period save for the isolates' elevated levels of self-clasping, and for this behavior the isolates showed a significant decline during the therapy period (0−50 days of therapy > 51−100 days of therapy > 101−150 days of therapy, $ps < .01$).

Behavior in home quadrants. Except for the specific interaction sessions, all subjects were individually housed in quadrants of the quad cages during the 6 months of the therapy period. Analysis of home quadrant behavioral levels during this period indicated that the isolates' recovery in the presence of the therapist monkeys generalized to home-cage behaviors in the absence of physical contact with the therapists. The analysis is summarized in Table 2.

During the first 60 days of the therapy period isolates displayed significantly higher levels of self-mouth ($p < .05$), self-clasp ($p < .01$), huddle ($p < .01$), rock ($p < .01$), and stereotypy ($p < .01$) and significantly lower levels of locomotion ($p < .05$) and exploration ($p < .01$) than the therapist monkeys. During the middle 60 days of the therapy period, group differences were evident only for the behaviors of self-mouth ($p < .05$) and self-clasp ($p < .01$), with isolates exhibiting higher levels of both behaviors.

TABLE 2

DUNCAN TEST ANALYSES FOR QUAD CAGE THERAPY, PLAYROOM THERAPY, AND HOME QUADRANT BEHAVIORS

Category	Quad cage therapy[a]		Playroom therapy[b]		Home quadrant behavior[c]	
	I	T	I	T	I	T
Self-mouth						
Period 1	7.8	6.1	5.9	2.6	12.2	10.3
Period 2	3.6	4.0	2.7	2.0	11.6	9.3
Period 3	3.1	4.0	2.2	1.3	9.7	8.8
Self-clasp						
Period 1	7.3	.2	15.9	.4	6.1	.7
Period 2	3.3	1.7	6.6	1.3	4.4	1.1
Period 3	2.6	.8	3.6	.4	3.3	2.3
Huddle						
Period 1	4.4	.1	4.7	.0	5.2	.3
Period 2	2.0	.0	2.1	.0	2.6	1.1
Period 3	.1	.0	.5	.0	.8	.9
Rock						
Period 1	2.7	.8	5.6	.2	2.7	.6
Period 2	.7	.3	2.7	.2	.8	.3
Period 3	.4	.2	1.2	.0	.3	.4
Stereotypy						
Period 1	.1	.0	.4	.0	1.8	.0
Period 2	.6	.0	.0	.0	.5	.0
Period 3	.4	.4	.0	.0	.2	.1
Locomotion						
Period 1	13.2	16.1	9.4	19.0	10.3	12.8
Period 2	15.4	19.2	15.1	18.9	12.6	13.0
Period 3	17.6	18.3	17.3	18.4	13.6	14.2
Environmental exploration						
Period 1	11.0	12.0	6.7	10.5	7.8	10.8
Period 2	9.7	9.1	9.2	11.3	9.8	10.3
Period 3	10.3	9.7	10.3	12.0	10.3	9.9
Ventral cling						
Period 1	.3	1.0	.3	2.0		
Period 2	.1	.6	.0	.8	—	—
Period 3	.0	.3	.0	.3		
Social contact						
Period 1	4.7	7.5	1.2	4.5		
Period 2	4.9	5.9	2.5	4.1	—	—
Period 3	6.0	5.4	2.8	2.8		
Play						
Period 1	3.6	6.6	1.1	3.6		
Period 2	6.1	7.0	3.9	5.3	—	—
Period 3	6.8	7.2	2.0	2.8		

[a] Period 1 = 1–60 days, Period 2 = 61–120 days, Period 3 = 121–180 days of therapy. Significant differences: Self-mouth—I − 1 > I − 2, I − 3, T − 2, T − 3, $p < .01$; I − 1 > T − 1, $p < .05$; T − 1 > I − 2, I − 3, T − 2, T − 3, $p < .05$. Self-clasp—I − 1 > I − 2, I − 3, T − 1, T − 2, T − 3, $p < .01$; I − 2 > T − 1, $p < .05$. Huddle—I − 1 > I − 3, T − 1, T − 2, T − 3, $p < .05$. Rock—I − 1 > I − 2, I − 3, T − 1, T − 2, T − 3, $p < .05$. Stereotypy—no significant differences. Locomotion—I − 1 < I − 3, T − 2, T − 3, $p < .01$; I − 1 < T − 1, $p < .05$; I − 2 < T − 2, T − 3, $p < .05$; T − 1 < T − 2, $p < .05$. Environmental exploration—no significant differences. Ventral cling—T − 1 > I − 1, I − 2, I − 3, $p < .05$. Social contact—I − 1 < T − 1, $p < .01$; I − 2 < T − 1, $p < .01$; T − 3 < T − 1, $p < .05$. Play—I − 1 < I − 2, I − 3, T − 1, T − 2, T − 3, $p < .01$.

[b] Period 1 = 1–50 days, Period 2 = 51–100 days, Period 3 = 101–150 days of therapy. Significant differences: Self-mouth—I − 1 > I − 2, I − 3, T − 1, T − 2, T − 3, $p < .05$. Self-clasp—I − 1 > I − 2, I − 3, T − 1, T − 2, T − 3, $p < .01$; I − 2 > T − 1, T − 2, T − 3, $p < .01$; I − 2 > I − 3, $p < .05$; I − 3 > T − 1, T − 3, $p < .05$. Huddle—I − 1 > I − 3, T − 1, T − 2, T − 3, $p < .01$; I − 1 > I − 2, $p < .05$. Stereotypy—no significant differences. Locomotion—I − 1 < I − 2, I − 3, T − 1, T − 2, T − 3, $p < .01$; I − 2 < T − 1, T − 2, $p < .05$. Environmental exploration—I − 1 < I − 3, T − 1, T − 2, T − 3, $p < .01$; I − 1 < I − 2, $p < .05$; T − 2 < T − 3, $p < .05$. Ventral cling—T − 1 > I − 1, I − 2, I − 3, $p < .01$; T − 2, T − 3, $p < .05$; I − 1 < I − 3, T − 2, T − 3, $p < .05$. Social contact—T − 1 > I − 1, $p < .01$; T − 1 > T − 3, I − 2, T − 3, $p < .05$; I − 1 < I − 3, T − 2, T − 3, $p < .05$. Play—I − 1 < I − 2, T − 1, T − 2, $p < .01$; I − 1 < T − 3, $p < .05$; T − 2 > T − 1, T − 3, I − 1, I − 2, $p < .05$.

[c] Period 1 = 1–60 days, Period 2 = 61–120 days, Period 3 = 121–180 days of therapy. Significant differences: Self-mouth—I − 1 > I − 3, T − 1, T − 2, T − 3, $p < .05$; I − 2 > I − 3, T − 2, T − 3, $p < .05$. Self-clasp—I − 1 > I − 2, I − 3, T − 1, T − 2, T − 3, $p < .01$; I − 2 > I − 3, T − 2, T − 3, $p < .01$; I − 3 > T − 1, T − 3, $p < .01$; T − 2 > T − 1, $p < .05$. Huddle—I − 1 > I − 3, T − 1, T − 2, T − 3, $p < .01$; I − 1 > I − 2, $p < .05$. Rock—I − 1 > I − 2, I − 3, T − 1, T − 2, T − 3, $p < .01$. Stereotypy—I − 1 > I − 2, I − 3, T − 1, T − 2, T − 3, $p < .01$. Locomotion—I − 1 < T − 3, $p < .01$; I − 1 < I − 3, T − 1, T − 2, $p < .05$. Environmental exploration—I − 1 < I − 2, I − 3, T − 1, T − 2, T − 3, $p < .01$.

During the final 60 days of the therapy period, no significant group differences for any category were disclosed by the analysis.

Discussion

The primary finding of this experiment was that monkeys reared in total social isolation for the first 6 months of life exhibited significant recovery of virtually all behavioral deficits across all testing situations after appropriate therapeutic treatment. Reversal of the isolation syndrome to an equivalent degree over such a range of situations had not been previously achieved or approached via any experimental procedures.

Some previous rehabilitative attempts used social agents but failed to reverse the isolation syndrome. We feel that the crucial factor for successful rehabilitation in the present study was intrinsic to the nature of the social agents employed. As well as the fact that they were members of the same species as the isolates, these agents were chosen specifically in terms of behaviors they could be predicted to exhibit consistently and spontaneously at appropriate stages of the therapy program. Behavioral predictions were based upon years of research examining the normal social development of the rhesus monkey.

A sequential, subjective account of the actual rehabilitative process early in the therapy period illustrates the appropriateness of the therapist choice. The isolate subjects did not exhibit spontaneous recovery during initial exposures to the younger, socially normal monkeys, a fact that is not surprising since no isolate monkey had shown spontaneous recovery in previous experimental situations. Rather, the therapist monkeys actively initiated the first social interactions, and only then did the isolates gradually exhibit improvement. Specifically, the therapist monkeys' initial responses to the isolates were to approach and cling, while the isolates were typically immobile and withdrawn. Only after clinging had been initiated did the isolates reciprocate, and only when the therapists had directed play responses toward the isolates did isolate play behavior emerge. Once these interaction patterns were established, the isolates themselves initiated play bouts with progressively increasing frequency.

Although the process of rehabilitation was essentially continuous, it is possible to delineate two stages of isolate recovery. The first stage involved breaking down previously established patterns of abnormal, self-directed behaviors such as self-huddling and stereotypic rocking. This was achieved primarily through the clinging efforts of the therapist monkeys. An isolate receiving intimate social contact cannot effectively continue to rock and self-huddle. The breaking down of entrenched self-directed activity permitted the isolate subjects to engage in alternative behaviors, which took the form of elementary social contact, exploration, and locomotion.

The second stage involved developing the simple behaviors described above into a more complex, socially appropriate behavioral repertoire. Again, the therapists apparently provided the crucial stimulation as they themselves developed a complex social repertoire in the course of normal maturation. With respect to these behavior patterns, isolate recovery was substantial.

Previous rehabilitative attempts which initially exposed isolate subjects to complex social stimulation failed to break down self-directed activity exhibited by the isolates, and recovery did not follow. Also, exposure to a surrogate was demonstrated to reduce isolate disturbance behavior, but because a surrogate cannot provide complex social stimulation those isolate subjects never developed complex social behaviors in the presence of a surrogate. In contrast, the present study provided the isolate subjects with a set of social stimuli designed to reduce self-directed activity, followed by a set of stimuli gradually increasing in social sophistication. In this case, the same group of therapist monkeys provided both types of stimulation and provided them in the appropriate temporal sequence during the course of their own normal social maturation.

These results suggest that a reexamination of traditional theoretical interpretations of isolation-rearing effects is required. The data from the present study are inconsistent with a strict interpretation of the critical period position, which implies that once a so-called critical period has transpired without social stimulation, normal social behaviors can never develop. The present results yield empirical testimony that relatively normal social development can occur following

6 months of total social isolation from birth provided that the isolates are exposed to appropriately selected social stimulation. One can conclude that either the first 6 months of life do not constitute a critical period for socialization of the rhesus monkey or that strict critical periods do not exist for this species. We prefer the latter interpretation. While it is obvious from numerous researches that the first 6 months of life are indeed critical for socialization under usual circumstances, a more apt terminology for this chronological span might be "sensitive period" or "sensitive phase" (Hinde, 1966).

Also, the postisolation base-line data do not specifically support an emergence trauma interpretation of isolation-rearing effects. Rather, the monkeys socially isolated in this study had developed obvious behavioral anomalies prior to emergence, but the data analysis disclosed no significant increments in these abnormalities following emergence. We do not claim that emergence from isolation has no behavioral consequences. The actual analysis compared preemergence behavioral levels with those encompassing a 2-week period following removal from isolation and may well have masked actual effects exhibited during the initial postisolation hours. However, acknowledgement of behavioral changes resulting from shifts in the environment is a far cry from attribution of persisting behavioral deficiencies to the process of environmental change.

It is appropriate at this point to express a certain degree of caution regarding the findings of this study, particularly in light of the absence of a group of control isolate-reared monkeys not exposed to therapists, although, in a sense, a decade of isolation research using monkeys provides an impressive body of control data. The above procedures resulted in a reversal of the isolation syndrome during the course of the experiment. However, since the isolate subjects have not yet reached physical maturity, assessment of their adult social capability is not possible at the present time. Further, the exact procedure described above may not be appropriate for monkeys subjected to longer periods of social isolation, nor will the procedure necessarily be effective if not instituted soon after the period of isolation.

Nevertheless, the fact that the isolates in this study did show marked social gains suggests that the *potential* for adequate social development is not necessarily destroyed by the isolation experience. Rather, the actual relationship between isolation rearing and social behavior may, in fact, be similar to the relationship between isolation rearing and learning capability. Previous researches have demonstrated the while isolation produces performance deficits in learning situations, intellectual capability remains relatively intact in monkey subjects. Apparently, adequate adaptation is required for adequate performance. With respect to social behavior, it may well be that previous studies have reported performance deficits only, that social capability remains viable despite the isolation experience, and that the requirement for rehabilitation is merely appropriate social stimulation. If this finding generalizes not only to other forms of early experience but also to other species, then the implications of the present experimentation for reversal of psychopathological behavior attributed to inadequate early experience become enormous.

REFERENCES

BLOMQUIST, A. J., & HARLOW, H. F.   The infant rhesus monkey program at the University of Wisconsin Primate Laboratory. *Proceedings of the Animal Care Panel*, 1961, 11, 57–64.

BOELKINS, R. C.   The development of social behavior in the infant rhesus monkey following a period of social isolation. Unpublished master's thesis, University of Wisconsin, 1963.

CLARK, D. L.   Immediate and delayed effects of early, intermediate, and late social isolation in the rhesus monkey. Unpublished doctoral dissertation, University of Wisconsin, 1968.

DUNCAN, D. B.   Multiple range and multiple *F* tests. *Biometrics*, 1955, 11, 1–42.

FULLER, J. L., & CLARKE, L. D.   Genetic and treatment factors modifying the postisolation syndrome in dogs. *Journal of Comparative and Physiological Psychology*, 1966, 61, 251–257.

GLUCK, J. P.   Successive acquisitions and extinctions of bar pressing: The effects of differential rearing in rhesus monkeys. Unpublished master's thesis, University of Wisconsin, 1970.

GRIFFIN, G. A., & HARLOW, H. F.   Effects of three months of total social deprivation on social adjustment and learning in the rhesus monkey. *Child Development,* 1966, **37,** 533–547.

HARLOW, H. F., DODSWORTH, R. O., & HARLOW, M. K. Total social isolation in monkeys. *Proceedings of the National Academy of Sciences,* 1965, **54,** 90–96.

HARLOW, H. F., & HARLOW, M. K.   The effect of rearing conditions on behavior. *Bulletin of the Menninger Clinic,* 1962, **26,** 213–224.

HARLOW, H. F., & HARLOW, M. K.   Effects of various mother-infant relationships on rhesus monkey behaviors. In B. M. Foss (Ed.), *Determinants of infant behavior.* Vol. 4. London: Methuen, 1968.

HARLOW, H. F., HARLOW, M. K., DODSWORTH, R. O., & ARLING, G. L.   Maternal behavior of rhesus monkeys deprived of mothering and peer associations in infancy. *Proceedings of the American Philosophical Society,* 1966, **110,** 58–66.

HARLOW, H. F., SCHILTZ, K. A., & HARLOW, M. K.   Effects of social isolation on the learning performance of rhesus monkeys. In C. R. Carpenter (Ed.), *Proceedings of the Second International Congress of Primatology.* Vol. 1. New York: Karger, 1969.

HARLOW, H. F., & SUOMI, S. J.   The nature of love—simplified. *American Psychologist,* 1970, **25,** 161–168.

HINDE, R. A.   *Animal behavior.* New York: McGraw-Hill, 1966.

LORENZ, K.   *Evolution and Modification of behavior.* Chicago: University of Chicago Press, 1965.

MASON, W. A.   Social development of rhesus monkeys with restricted social experience. *Perceptual and Motor Skills,* 1963, **16,** 263–270.

PRATT, C. L.   The developmental consequences of variations in early social stimulation. Unpublished doctoral dissertation, University of Wisconsin, 1969.

ROSENBLUM, L. A.   The development of social behavior in the rhesus monkey. Unpublished doctoral dissertation, University of Wisconsin, 1961.

ROWLAND, G. L.   The effects of total isolation upon learning and social behavior of rhesus monkeys. Unpublished doctoral dissertation, University of Wisconsin, 1964.

SACKETT, G. P.   Abnormal behavior in laboratory reared rhesus monkeys. In M. W. Fox (Ed.), *Abnormal behavior in animals.* Philadelphia: Saunders, 1968. (a)

SACKETT, G. P.   The persistence of abnormal behavior in monkeys following isolation rearing. In R. Porter (Ed.), *The role of learning in psychotherapy.* London: Churchill, 1968. (b)

SCOTT, J. P.   Critical periods in behavioral development. *Science,* 1962, **138,** 949–958.

SENKO, M. G.   The effects of early, intermediate, and late experiences upon adult macaque sexual behavior. Unpublished master's thesis, University of Wisconsin, 1966.

SINGH, S. D.   Urban monkeys. *Scientific American,* 1969, **221,** 108–115.

SUOMI, S. J., & HARLOW, H. F.   Apparatus conceptualization for psychopathological research in monkeys. *Behavioral Research Methods and Instrumentation,* 1969, **1,** 247–250.

Part 4

Language Development

The two most innovative changes in developmental research over the past decades have been concerned with language development in early childhood and cognitive development in general. The first area of research has been influenced mainly by Chomsky, and the second by Piaget.

The three papers in this section trace, in effect, several steps in the revolution currently underway in the linguistics field. The first step clarifies the position that speech, as it is spoken by the child, cannot be accounted for solely by the theory that the child learns language through the process of being rewarded by his parents for appropriate imitations of their speech. Lenneberg's case study gives us some of the information that was relevant to this critique.

The paper by Brown and Bellugi indicates some of the earliest efforts made to provide a grammar for the way in which young children actually speak. Unfortunately, as Lois Bloom points out in her paper, this grammar does not fit the phenomena as well as it might. Merely treating the language alone is not sufficient; one must understand the cognitive and perceptual levels of the child's development as well in order to understand how he uses his language.

Understanding Language Without Ability to Speak: A Case Report

Eric H. Lenneberg

Infants' random babbling is generally considered to play a major—by some, an essential—role in the acquisition and development of language. In fact, many psychologists believe that the main reason for the failure of mammals other than man to learn to speak or even to bring their vocalizations under new and varied stimulus control is due to their scanty random vocalizations. Recently it was discovered that dolphins make a great variety of vocal tract produced noises and, to be sure, the hope was soon expressed that these animals may with proper training learn to converse with their trainers in English. Incidentally, this hope was shared by Dr. Doolittle, Hugh Lofting's charming literary creation.

Our understanding of human behavior is often greatly enlightened by careful investigations of clinical aberrations and in many instances disease or congenital abnormalities provide conditions that may replace the crucial experiments on children that our superego forbids us to plan and perform. No psychological theory on verbal behavior can be successful unless it takes into consideration and accounts for the pathological variations that may be observed clinically. In the present paper I will present the case of a child who is typical of a large group of children with deficits in their motor execution of language skills but who can learn to understand language even in the total absence of articulation. This and similar clinical material forces us to review our theoretical formulations concerning the role of babbling and echoic responses in the acquisition of language and to review once more the relationship between understanding and speaking a language.

Case Report

This is an 8-year-old boy who has a congenital disability for the acquisition of motor speech skills

This paper was written while the author was a National Institute of Mental Health Career Investigator (Grant M–2921).

Eric H. Lenneberg, "Understanding Language without Ability to Speak: A Case Report," *Journal of Abnormal and Social Psychology, 65,* 1962, pp. 419–425. Copyright © 1962 by the American Psychological Association, and reproduced by permission.

(anarthria) which, however, has not impaired his ability to learn to understand language.

MEDICAL HISTORY

The mother, at the time of subject's birth, was a para I, gravida II white housewife who had enjoyed good health. Throughout her second pregnancy she suffered from a mild chronic bronchitis but gestation was otherwise unremarkable. The baby was born 2 weeks prematurely by dates. Delivery was spontaneous, preceded by 6 hours of labor though the birth was precipitous. No other complications were recorded. The birth weight was 4 pounds 10 ounces. Good respiration was established within half a minute at which time the baby cried vigorously. He had good color and was at no time cyanotic or jaundiced. The following abnormalities were noted at birth: he had bilateral club feet (talipes equino varus on left and metatarsus varus on right) and a fine white line in a sagittal direction on the upper lip. Otherwise the physical examination was reported to be within normal limits. The mother was told that the placenta had been too small to nourish the fetus adequately but no pathological report is available. The baby was placed in an incubator for 2 weeks and remained in the newborn nursery at the hospital for 2 months. He sat at 9 months and walked only at 2 years of age, earlier development having been handicapped by casts and corrective shoes. He has never been heard to use any words. He has had the usual complement of inoculations and there have been no severe diseases. At age 2 he fell on his head and required two stitches; the incident had no sequelae. The first pediatric examination recorded in the hospital chart (age 2 years) revealed anomalies of the eyes in addition to the anomalies of feet and lip. There was a right ptosis and a convergent strabismus.

FAMILY HISTORY

The family history is noncontributory. The subject is the second of three children: both siblings are intelligent and well. The mother is now divorced and lives with the subject's grandmother. A home visit revealed a warm and socially adequate climate.

PHYSICAL AND LABORATORY EXAMINATIONS

When first seen by the author the child had been brought to a neurological service with a chief complaint of failure to develop speech. He was then 3 years and 9 months, of markedly small stature but with a head circumference normal for his chronological age (49.6 centimeters). Anomalies of the eyes had been corrected surgically. He had single palmar creases in both hands but no other mongoloid stigmata. The only other abnormal finding on examination was an enlarged heart; no murmurs were heard. His oral cavity was of normal configuration and he had no difficulties in chewing, swallowing, sucking, blowing, or licking. Laryngoscopy was negative. On radiological evidence his bone age was 2:8 according to Todd's standards. A skull series was normal. All laboratory tests were negative, and there were no signs of hypothyroidism or inborn errors of metabolism. An electroencephalogram was read as nondiagnostic though it was noted that activity in the right temporal area was less rhythmic than in the left.

PSYCHOLOGICAL TESTS

Tests were performed at 4, 5, and 8 years. Merrill-Palmer, WISC, Bender Visual Motor Gestalt, and Leiter International Performance tests were used, the examinations being administered by three different psychologists and at two different clinics. The subject always related easily to the examiner and gave no signs of emotional disturbance or psychiatric disease. IQs were consistently in the 72–83 range but might have been consistently biased by the subject's inability to express himself verbally. He always gives an alert impression, reacts quickly to verbal instructions, and has always shown an adequate concentration span with little signs of distractibility or hyperactivity. At his most recent test no evidence of "organic" deficits was obtained although some "immaturity in his drawings" was noted. He is slightly retarded in his mental development but the deficit is definitely in the educable range and cannot explain his inability to speak.

VOICE AND SPEECH

The child's crying and laughter have always sounded normal. He is also able to make other noises, for instance short cough-like grunts accompanying his pantomimed communications. While playing alone he will readily make noises that sound somewhat like Swiss yodeling (though he has never had any experience with these sounds!) and which do not resemble any kind of vocalization heard among normal American children. (Samples of these sounds are reproduced in a documentary film.) When the author first saw him he appeared to have some difficulty in bringing his voicing mechanism under voluntary control. For instance, he was unable to make the pointer of the VU meter in an Ampex tape recorder jump by emitting grunts into a microphone even though he was fully aware of the logical connection between sound and deflection of the pointer and was fascinated by it. He would hold on to the microphone and move his head and lips toward it as if to prompt himself for the action; after a few futile attempts and with signs of rising frustration he would in desperation end up gesturing to the examiner's mouth inviting him to make the needle jump, or else simply resort to clapping his hands and accomplish his end this way. In recent years he seems to have learned to control his vocal apparatus to a greater extent. He has had speech training for a considerable length of time and can now repeat a few words after the speech therapist or his mother but the words are still barely intelligible and are never produced without the support from the speech correctionist or the mother (samples are reproduced in the film).

Some of the spontaneous sounds emitted by the patient at 4 years were analyzed spectrographically.[1] The spectrograms are grossly abnormal for a child of this age and resemble those of a neonate in a number of respects, such as the unsteadiness in the formant pattern, the intermittent bursts of nonharmonic overtones, and the almost random change in resonance distribution over the spectrum (Lenneberg, 1961). The spectrograms may be interpreted either as grossly immature or as evidence of a fixed central nervous system abnormality implicating the basic mechanisms for speech synergism.

From the patient's first visit to the clinic it has been obvious that he had a normal and adequate understanding of spoken language. He has been seen more than 20 times since then and the finding of full comprehension has been confirmed by neurologists, psychologists, speech therapists, medical residents, and other hospital personnel. A number of tape recordings have been made of interviews including a visit to the patient's home. Most of the examinations were done without the presence of his mother. At one time a short series of instructions were tape recorded and transmitted to the patient through earphones. He followed the instructions without being able to see the examiner.

DEMONSTRATION FILM

At age 8 years his capacity to comprehend was fully documented in a 16-millimeter sound film which is publicly available.[2] The film was not rehearsed and the examiner had been known to the patient by sight only. The demonstration includes the following items: ability to chew, swallow, and suck; sounds emitted while playing at age 4; tape recordings of mother's "conversation" with subject, recorded during a home visit; following commands and answering questions by nodding; a short story is told followed by questions on it which are couched in complex grammatical constructions such as the passive voice.

INTERPRETATION

It is tempting to explain the patient's responses to verbal instructions by extralinguistic means. Perhaps he is merely responding to visual cues given by the examiner and has, in fact, not

[1] A 5-page table giving a transcript of commands, questions, and statements with classification of subject's response and a figure showing frequency cycles per second have been deposited with the American Documentation Institute. Order Document No. 7317 from ADI Auxiliary Publications Project, Photoduplication Service, Library of Congress; Washington, D. C. 20540, remitting in advance $2.50 for microfilm or $6.25 for photocopies. Make checks payable to: Chief, Photoduplication Service, Library of Congress.

[2] *The Acquisition of Language in a Speechless Child,* 16-millimeter sound film. Running time 18 minutes, distributed by Psychological Cinema Register, Pennsylvania State University.

learned to understand English! Could children with his type of abnormality develop perceptual skills such as were observed in von Osten's famous horse, der kluge Hans, who supposedly could stamp his hoof in response to questions posed to him in German, but who, upon close examination by the psychologist Pfungst, had merely learned to observe the questioner, picking up minute motor cues related to posture and respiratory patterns which signaled to him whether to stop or to continue to stamp his hoof? There is direct evidence against this hypothesis. The child described can react to tape recorded instructions in the absence of any observer. Further, his responses do not merely consist of nodding but also of doing things which could under no circumstance be conveyed by inadvertent motor cues. In the film which documents the case, it is clear that the child frequently follows commands without looking at the examiner. Out of the 45 responses only 3 times was there vacillation between correct and incorrect answers and the last answer in each case is correct. On the other hand, there was no hesitation in the 3 instances when incorrect answers were given. There is no reason to assume that this child has superhuman ability to respond to visual cues instead of assuming that he has learned what every other child of his age has learned, namely, to understand English. Table 1 summarizes the child's performance. It is the result of a panel of three judges who scrutinized the film, viewing each command and its execution individually and with as many repetitions as was necessary in order to determine by unanimous agreement whether there was any likelihood of extralinguistic cuing.

Finally, we must consider the possibility that this patient had no understanding of syntactic connections but merely responded to key words in the commands and questions. This possibility is extremely unlikely in the face of his understanding of such sentences as "Take the block and put it on the bottle." "Is it time to eat breakfast now?" "Was the black cat fed by the nice lady?"

DIAGNOSIS

The hospital's clinical diagnosis is multiple congenital anomalies, which, however, is a wastebasket classification and of no heuristic value. Certainly it does not explain the absence of motor speech. The two most common causes for this deficit, peripheral deafness and severe emotional disturbance, may be readily ruled out on clinical evidence. Nor may we assume that the patient's mental retardation is a sufficient cause since the degree of deficiency revealed in his psychological tests is not ordinarily accompanied by any marked speech deficit. Patients with an IQ as low as 25 to 35 have a wide repertoire of sounds and frequently use a vocabulary of 50 or more words. Some authorities would clasify this patient as having congenital or developmental motor aphasia. I am not in favor of such a classification on terminological grounds. Aphasia has come to designate loss of speech in persons who had been fluent before the onset of disease or trauma. The condition occurs in children (Guttmann, 1942) as well as in adults and presents a symptomatology that is distinct from any developmental condition. However, the most important reason for rejecting the term aphasia for cases such as described here is that aphasia has tradi-

TABLE 1

NUMBER OF SUBJECT'S CORRECT, INDECISIVE, AND INCORRECT RESPONSES

Type of response required	Classification of subject's response						
	Correct		Indecisive		Incorrect		
	No cue possible	Cue possible or certain	No cue possible	Cue possible or certain	No cue possible	Cue possible or certain	Total
Action	19	5	0	0	2	2	28
Yes-No nodding	2	11	0	3	0	1	17
Total	21	16	0	3	2	3	45

tionally been applied to cortical and subcortical lesions. The present case, on the other hand, gives every indication of an abnormality on a lower level, probably mesencephalic, because of the association with the ocular abnormalities and the discoordination as seen in the spectrograms. The term congenital anarthria better characterizes the condition. Psychological tests make cortical or subcortical damage also unlikely and his excellent understanding of language supports this view.

Discussion

FAILURE TO LEARN TO UNDERSTAND DESPITE BABBLING AND IMITATIVE FACILITY

The case reported makes it clear that hearing oneself babble is not a necessary factor in the acquisition of understanding; apparently, hearing oneself babble is also not a sufficient factor. In a language acquisition study on home-raised mongoloid children (research in progress) I have gathered empirical evidence that these children are excellent imitators who babble abundantly and freely. In all cases they have a speaking command of at least single word utterances; yet their understanding of complex commands and questions (such as used in the demonstration film) is frequently defective (usually if their IQ is about 50 or below). Here the vocal play is present and motivation is provided through interaction with parents, but it does not enable these children to overcome their inborn cerebral deficit.

RELATIONSHIP BETWEEN SPEAKING AND UNDERSTANDING

We must now pose the problem: if the secondary reinforcement provided by hearing oneself babble is neither necessary nor sufficient for an acquisition of understanding of language, could learning to speak be an entirely independent task, justifying a theory that applies to it alone, but not to the learning of understanding? We will see that the answer to this question is a qualified *no*.

The case presented here—by no means unique

—is particularly dramatic because of the vast discrepancy between understanding and speaking; a similar phenomenon in more attenuated form is extremely common. Understanding normally precedes speaking by several weeks or even months. The discrepancy is regularly increased in literally all types of developmental speech disorders and is best illustrated in a condition known in the profession as Delayed Speech. Pertinent are also those children who have structural deformities in the oral cavity or pharynx and who produce unintelligible speech for years—sometimes throughout life—without the slightest impairment of understanding. Congenitally deaf children also learn to comprehend language in the absence of vocal skills. Understanding in all of these circumstances is definitely prior to and in that sense independent from speaking.

However, there is no clear evidence that speaking is ever present in the absence of understanding. Speaking is to be understood here as the production of utterances that are bona fide examples of a natural language (such as English) with presumptive evidence of autonomous composition of grammatically acceptable sentences. An empirical test of speaking without understanding might be as follows: a child acquires nothing but words that have no meaning to him (by blind imitation) and learns the formal principles governing the generation of sentences. He will now utter sentences out of context and irrelevant to situations by established common sense standards; he would also have to be demonstrably incapable ever to respond appropriately to commands formulated in natural language. My assertion is that such a condition has never been described as a congenital, developmental problem (Mark, 1962). (Adventitious conditions such as sensory aphasia in the adult are problems in *partial loss,* not *partial acquisition* of language and are therefore not relevant to this discussion. Nor could case reports of psychotic children be adduced reliably because even if their utterances are primarily echolalic, there are usually indications that the child does understand, at least at times, what is said to him. In fact, this is usually the basis of the therapy given them.) It is thus likely that the vocal production of language is dependent upon the understanding of language but not vice versa. Though there is no conclusive proof of this hypothesis, there are theoretical considerations that make this likely. In order to make this latter point clear, a few general remarks on the nature of grammar are indispensable. My discussion will lean heavily on Chomsky's (1957) and Chomsky and Miller's (1962) work.

Wherever the word *imitation* is used in connection with language learning it is assumed that subjects learn more than passive mirroring of sentences heard. The novel creation of sentences is a universally accepted fact. At first it was thought that this phenomenon could be accounted for by postulating that grammar simply reflected transitional probabilities between words. In this model the learning of grammar was thought to be like the learning of probabilities. Such learning has been demonstrated to occur for a great many mammals. If this model were acceptable, a child's exposure to certain contingencies should enable him to learn grammar in the absence of "understanding" the relationship between words. Chomsky has offered formal proof against left-to-right probabilistic models, and has shown how a different model can overcome some of the basic difficulties encountered by Markovian grammars. We shall not concern ourselves here with the mathematical detail but shall merely demonstrate by a few examples (most of them suggested by Chomsky) that grammar simply cannot be explained in terms of learned sequential contingencies, and that therefore the understanding and producing of sentences cannot be equated with probability learning.

Consider the following two strings of words, (*a*) colorless green ideas sleep furiously, (*b*) furiously sleep ideas green colorless. In terms of transitional probabilities they are indistinguishable. Both sentences can only occur in a zero order of approximation to English. However, we can discriminate between them from the point of view of grammaticality. Sentence *a* strikes us as a possible sentence, whereas *b* does not. The difference between *a* and *b* could not possibly be due to association by contiguity for obvious reasons. (Miller, Galanter, & Pribram, 1960). Nor is the sequence of form class markers *-less*, *-s*, *-ly* the hallmark of grammaticalness as shown by the sentence, (*c*) friendly young dogs seem harmless, which is grammatical though it reverses the order of the markers.

In order to account for the difference in our perception of *a* and *b* we might try to see whether sequential contingencies do exist, but instead of on the level of words, on the level of parts of speech (actually proposed by Jenkins & Palermo, 1961). If this were so the essence of the transitional probability model would be saved and the principal underlying the formation of sentences would still be simple enough to allow of the possibility of speaking without understanding. Unfortunately this model is no more successful in accounting for "sentencehood" than any other Markovian device. If we compare the strings, (*d*) occasionally call warfare useless, (*e*) useless warfare call occasionally, we find that now *d* is perceived as more grammatical than *e* though the order of parts of speech in *d* is that of *b* above which we rejected as less grammatical. This example shows that the traditional categorization in terms of parts of speech is certainly not successful in reinstating a Markovian model.[3]

Mowrer (1960) has proposed that simple contiguity of words is sufficient explanation for the complex meaning that is conveyed by a sentence. Osgood (1957) on the other hand believes that grammatical order can be set aside by motivational factors and that with an increase of motivation word order would correlate with order of importance of words. Doubt is cast on both views, however, by comparison of sentences such as, (*f*) the fox chases the dog, (*g*) the dog chases the fox, which clearly make either position untenable. A child whose task it is to learn to produce sentences such as *f* and *g* in the appropriate physical environment must necessarily learn some principal of concatenation which goes *beyond* recognition of contiguity. It would be tempting to maintain that the principle to be learned is something like "First noun phrase is the actor or subject in a sentence." Yet, the patterning involved must be more complex and in a sense more abstract still, for even a preschool child would understand the sentence, (*h*) the fox is chased by the dog, as belonging to *g* and not to

---

[3] Nor is there any hope that eventually more efficient categories might be discovered since Chomsky's (1957) criticism is leveled against all finite state sentence generating devices. Compare his argument concerning mirror-image languages, and Miller's (1960) argument.

f. To explain this phenomenon we would now have to postulate that in addition to the principle above, the child would also have to learn that the presence of the morphemes *is, -ed, by* signals a reversal of the original principle. But sentence (*i*) the fox is interested by virtue of his nature in chasing the dog, eliminates this possibility because this sentence is understood as similar in meaning to *f* instead of *g* despite the presence of morphemes *is, -ed, by* occurring in essentially the same sequential order as in *h*. In other words, if we must learn to compose sentences that conform to English grammar, we can only learn to apply the structural principles of sentence formation by first learning to understand and to group sentences in accordance with similarity or differences in meaning. It is not possible to explain the grammatical phenomena demonstrated in the test sentences above by assuming that the entire sentence is in one way or another associated with the complex natural situation to which it refers. Sentences without any referential meaning such as, (*j*) A v's C, (*k*) C v's A, (*l*) C is v'ed by A, (*m*) A is v'ed by C, can easily be grouped in terms of similarity and dissimilarity of meaning. Therefore, the word *meaning* in this context refers to grammatical understanding and not to an association between a symbol and a physical stimulus.

Obviously, we do not yet have a satisfactory model that might explain how grammar is learned. All we can say is that a child learns to produce novel sentences after hearing a number of utterances which were produced by formal laws of generation in addition to a number of other determining factors: he must be able to abstract the formal laws through observation (or be equipped to accept sentences as an input and recognize invariant patterns of complex relationship) before he can apply them to the production of new sentences. It is particularly important to realize that what the child learns during acquisition of grammar is the peculiar formal relationship that obtains between a number of different grammatical patterns, i.e., the relationship between active-passive, declarative-interrogative-negative, and many other similar relationships called *rules of transformation* (Chomsky, 1957; Harris, 1957). It is this latter ability—and only this—that enables any speaker of English to group the sentences *f* through *i* according to similarity in meaning. The psychological process involved here is more similar to the operations by which we know that:

and

$$w \left(\sqrt{w} \times \sqrt{w} \right)$$

$$\frac{w^6}{w^4}$$

can both be represented by w^2 than to an operation by which we know that the symbol S_4 is next in line to be generated after a train of symbols S_1, S_2, S_3, has been produced. This point is illustrated by Chomsky's examples of structural ambiguity. There are rules of transformations which convert sentences of the form (*n*) one visits relatives, (*o*) relatives are visiting, into a phrase, (*p*) visiting relatives. Because of the two different transformational origins this phrase is ambiguous and, when used in a sentence, may render that entire sentence ambiguous: (*q*) visiting relatives can be a nuisance.

The conclusion of this discussion is that *knowing a language* may be, and ordinarily is, manifested by two distinct behavioral manifestations: understanding and speaking. Upon careful analysis, however, both of these manifestations depend upon the application and use of a single set of grammatical rules; in the case of understanding, the rules are applied to the analysis, i.e., processing and organizing of input data; in the case of speaking, the same rules are applied to the organization of output data or responses. In the process of language learning, the acquisition of grammatical rules must occur first in connection with analysing incoming sentences; then with producing outgoing sentences. The most important point here is, however, that *knowing* a natural language is dependent upon the *acquisition of a single set of organizing principles* and that this set of principles is merely reflected in understanding and speaking but is not identical with these skills.

Summary

A case was presented, typical of a larger category of patients, where an organic defect prevented the acquisition of the motor skill necessary for *speaking a language,* but evidence was presented for the acquisition of grammatical skills as required for a complete *understanding of language*. Theories on the acquisition of speech and language must account for both motor and grammatical skills. Present theories assert that babbling, hearing oneself vocalize, and imitation are the cornerstones of speech development. These phenomena primarily relate to the development of the motor skills involved which, however, never develop in isolation, i.e., without simultaneous acquisition of grammatical skills. The case presented together with the language deficit in certain Mongoloids clearly shows that babbling, hearing oneself talk, and imitation are neither sufficient nor necessary factors in the acquisition of grammar and since the motor skills alone are never shaped into "speaking without grammar," i.e., parroting without understanding, it is concluded that the present theories are inadequate.

REFERENCES

CHOMSKY, N. *Syntactic structures.* Hague: Mouton, 1957.

CHOMSKY, N., & MILLER, G. A. Introduction to the formal analysis of natural languages. In D. Luce, E. Galanter, & R. Bush (Eds.), *Mathematical psychology.* 1962.

GUTTMANN, E. Aphasia in children. *Brain,* 1942, **65**, 205–219.

HARRIS, Z. S. Co-occurrence and transformation in linguistic structure. *Language,* 1957, 33, 283–340.

JENKINS, J. J., & PALERMO, D. S. Mediation processes and the acquisition of linguistic structure. Paper read at SSRC conference in Cambridge, Massachusetts, October 1961.

LENNEBERG, E. H. Speech as a motor skill with special reference to nonaphasic disorders. Paper read at SSRC conference in Cambridge, Massachusetts, October 1961.

MARK, H. J. Elementary thinking and the classification of behavior. *Science,* 1962, **135**, 75–87.

MILLER, G. A. Plans for speaking. In G. A. Miller, E. Galanter, & K. H. Pribram (Eds.), *Plans and the structure of behavior.* New York: Holt, 1960. Pp. 139–158.

MILLER, G. A., GALANTER, E., & PRIBRAM, K. H. *Plans and the structure of behavior.* New York: Holt, 1960.

MOWRER, O. H. *Learning theory and the symbolic processes.* New York: Wiley, 1960.

OSGOOD, C. E. Motivational dynamics of language behavior. In M. R. Jones (Ed.), *Nebraska symposium on motivation: 1957.* Lincoln: Univer. Nebraska Press, 1957. Pp. 348–424.

Three Processes in the Child's Acquisition of Syntax

Roger Brown   Ursula Bellugi

Some time in the second six months of life most children say a first intelligible word. A few months later most children are saying many words and some children go about the house all day long naming things (*table, doggie, ball*, etc.) and actions (*play, see, drop*, etc.) and an occasional quality (*blue, broke, bad*, etc.). At about eighteen months children are likely to begin constructing two-word utterances; such a one, for instance, as *Push car*.

A construction such as *Push car* is not just two single-word utterances spoken in a certain order. As single-word utterances (they are sometimes called holophrases) both *push* and *car* would have primary stresses and terminal intonation contours. When they are two words programmed as a single utterance the primary stress would fall on *car* and so would the highest level of pitch. *Push* would be subordinated to *car* by a lesser stress and a lower pitch; the unity of the whole would ap-

pear in the absence of a terminal contour between words and the presence of such a contour at the end of the full sequence.

By the age of thirty-six months some children are so advanced in the construction process as to produce all of the major varieties of English simple sentences up to a length of ten or eleven words. For several years we have been studying the development of English syntax, of the sentence-constructing process, in children between eighteen and thirty-six months of age. Most recently we have made a longitudinal study of a boy and girl whom we shall call Adam and Eve. We began work with Adam and Eve in October of 1962 when Adam was twenty-seven months old and Eve eighteen months old. The two children were selected from some thirty whom we considered. They were selected primarily because their speech was exceptionally intelligible and because they talked a lot. We wanted to make it as easy as possible to transcribe accurately large quantities of child speech. Adam and Eve are the children of highly-educated parents, the fathers were gradu-

This investigation was supported in whole by Public Health Service Research Grant MH7088 from the National Institute of Mental Health.

ate students at Harvard and the mothers are both college graduates. Both Adam and Eve were single children when we began the study. These facts must be remembered in generalizing the outcomes of the research.

While Adam is nine months older than Eve, his speech was only a little more advanced in October of 1962. The best single index of the level of speech development is the average length of utterance and in October, 1962, Adam's average was 1.84 morphemes and Eve's was 1.40 morphemes. The two children stayed fairly close together in the year that followed; in the records for the thirty-eighth week Adam's average was 3.55 and Eve's, 3.27. The processes we shall describe appeared in both children.

Every second week we visited each child for at least two hours and made a tape recording of everything said by the child as well as of everything said to the child. The mother was always present and most of the speech to the child is hers. Both mother and child became very accustomed to our presence and learned to continue their usual routine with us as the observers.

One of us always made a written transcription, on the scene, of the speech of mother and child with notes about important actions and objects of attention. From this transcription and the tape a final transcription was made and these transcriptions constitute the primary data of the study. For many purposes we require a "distributional analysis" of the speech of the child. To this end the child's utterances in a given transcription were cross classified and relisted under such headings as: "*A* + noun"; "Noun + verb"; "Verbs in the past"; "Utterances containing the pronoun *it*," etc. The categorized utterances expose the syntactic regularities of the child's speech.

Each week we met as a research seminar, with students of the psychology of language,[1] to discuss the state of the construction process in one of the two children as of that date. In these discussions small experiments were often suggested, experiments that had to be done within a few days if they were to be informative. At one time, for instance, we were uncertain whether Adam understood the semantic difference between putting a noun in subject position and putting it in object position. Consequently one of us paid an extra visit to Adam equipped with some toys. "Adam," we said, "show us the duck pushing the boat." And, when he had done so: "Now show us the boat pushing the duck."

Another week we noticed that Adam would sometimes pluralize nouns when they should have been pluralized and sometimes would not. We wondered if he could make grammatical judgments about the plural, if he could distinguish a correct form from an incorrect form. "Adam," we asked, "which is right, 'two shoes' or 'two shoe'?" His answer on that occasion, produced with explosive enthusiasm, was "Pop goes the weasel!" The two-year-old child does not make a perfectly docile experimental subject.

The dialogue between mother and child does not read like a transcribed dialogue between two adults. Table 1 offers a sample section from an early transcribed record. It has some interesting properties. The conversation is, in the first place, very much in the here and now. From the child there is no speech of the sort that Bloomfield called "displaced," speech about other times and other places. Adam's utterances in the early months were largely a coding of contemporaneous events and impulses. The mother's speech differs from the speech that adults use to one another in many ways. Her sentences are short and simple; for the most part they are the kinds of sentences that Adam will produce a year later.

Perhaps because they are short, the sentences of the mother are perfectly grammatical. The sentences adults use to one another, perhaps because they are longer and more complex, are very often not grammatical, not well formed. Here for instance is a rather representative example produced at a conference of psychologists and linguists: "As far as I know, no one yet has done the in a way obvious now and interesting problem of doing a in a sense a structural frequency study of the alternative syntactical in a given language, say, like English, the alternative possible structures, and how what their hierarchical probability of occurrence structure is."[2] It seems unlikely that

[1] We are grateful for intellectual stimulation and lighthearted companionship to Dr. Jean Berko Gleason, Mr. Samuel Anderson, Mr. Colin Fraser, Dr. David McNeill, and Dr. Daniel Slobin.

[2] H. Maclay and C. E. Osgood, "Hesitation phenomena in spontaneous English speech," *Word,* XV (1959), 19–44.

TABLE 1

A Section from Adam's First Record

Adam	Mother
See truck, Mommy.	
See truck.	
	Did you see the truck?
No I see truck.	
	No, you didn't see it?
	There goes one.
There go one.	
	Yes, there goes one.
See a truck.	
See truck, Mommy.	
See truck.	
Truck.	
Put truck, Mommy.	
	Put the truck where?
Put truck window.	
	I think that one's too large to go in the window.

a child could learn the patterns of English syntax from such speech. His introduction to English ordinarily comes in the form of a simplified, repetitive, and idealized dialect. It may be that such an introduction is necessary for the acquisition of syntax to be possible but we do not know that.

In the course of the brief interchange of Table 1 Adam imitates his mother in saying: "There go one" immediately after she says "There goes one." The imitation is not perfect; Adam omits the inflection on the verb. His imitation is a reduction in that it omits something from the original. This kind of imitation with reduction is extremely common in the records of Adam and Eve and it is the first process we shall discuss.

Imitation and Reduction

Table 2 presents some model sentences spoken by the mothers and the imitations produced by Adam and Eve. These were selected from hundreds in the records in order to illustrate some general propositions. The first thing to notice is that the imitations preserve the word order of the model sentences. To be sure, words in the model are often missing from the imitation but the words preserved are in the order of the original. This is a fact that is so familiar and somehow reasonable that we did not at once recognize it as an empirical outcome rather than as a natural necessity. But of course it is not a necessity, the outcome could have been otherwise. For example, words could have been said back in the reverse of their original order, the most recent first. The preservation of order suggests that the model sentence is processed by the child as a total construction rather than as a list of words.

In English the order of words in a sentence is an important grammatical signal. Order is used to distinguish among subject, direct object, and indirect object and it is one of the marks of imperative and interrogative constructions. The fact that the child's first sentences preserve the word order of their models partially accounts for the ability of an adult to "understand" these sentences and so to feel that he is in communication with the child. It is conceivable that the child "intends" the meanings coded by his word orders and that, when he preserves the order of an adult sentence, he does so because he wants to say what the order says. It is also possible that he preserves word order just because his brain works

TABLE 2

Some Imitations Produced by Adam and Eve

Model Utterance	Child's Imitation
Tank car	*Tank car*
Wait a minute	*Wait a minute*
Daddy's brief case	*Daddy brief case*
Fraser will be unhappy	*Fraser unhappy*
He's going out	*He go out*
That's an old time train	*Old time train*
It's not the same dog as Pepper	*Dog Pepper*
No, you can't write on Mr.	*Write Cromer shoe*
Cromer's shoe	

that way and that he has no comprehension of the semantic contrasts involved. In some languages word order is not an important grammatical signal. In Latin, for instance, "Agricola amat puellam" has the same meaning as "Puellam amat agricola" and subject-object relations are signalled by case endings. We would be interested to know whether children who are exposed to languages that do not utilize word order as a major syntactic signal, preserve order as reliably as do children exposed to English.

The second thing to notice in Table 2 is the fact that when the models increase in length there is not a corresponding increase in the imitation. The imitations stay in the range of two to four morphemes which was the range characteristic of the children at this time. The children were operating under some constraint of length or span. This is not a limitation of vocabulary; the children knew hundreds of words. Neither is it a constraint of immediate memory. We infer this from the fact that the average length of utterances produced spontaneously, where immediate memory is not involved, is about the same as the average length of utterances produced as immediate imitations. The constraint is a limitation on the length of utterance the children are able to program or plan.[3] This kind of narrow span limitation in children is characteristic of most or all of their intellectual operations. The limitation grows less

restrictive with age as a consequence, probably, of both neurological growth and of practice, but of course it is never lifted altogether.

A constraint on length compels the imitating child to omit some words or morphemes from the mother's longer sentences. Which forms are retained and which omitted? The selection is not random but highly systematic. Forms retained in the examples of Table 2 include: *Daddy, Fraser, Pepper,* and *Cromer; tank car, minute, briefcase, train, dog,* and *shoe; wait, go,* and *write; unhappy* and *old time.* For the most part they are nouns, verbs, and adjectives, though there are exceptions, as witness the initial pronoun *He* and the preposition *out* and the indefinite article *a.* Forms omitted in the samples of Table 2 include: the possessive inflection *–s,* the modal auxiliary *will,* the contraction of the auxiliary verb *is,* the progressive inflection *–ing,* the preposition *on,* the articles *the* and *an,* and the modal auxiliary *can.* It is possible to make a general characterization of the forms likely to be retained that distinguishes them as a total class from the forms likely to be omitted.

Forms likely to be retained are nouns and verbs and, less often, adjectives, and these are the three large and "open" parts-of-speech in English. The number of forms in any one of these parts-of-speech is extremely large and always growing. Words belonging to these classes are sometimes called "contentives" because they have semantic content. Forms likely to be omitted are inflections, auxiliary verbs, articles, prepositions, and conjunctions. These forms belong to syntactic

[3] Additional evidence of the constraint on sentence length may be found in R. Brown and C. Fraser. "The acquisition of syntax," C. N. Cofer and Barbara Musgrave, eds., *Verbal Behavior and Learning* (New York: McGraw-Hill, 1963).

classes that are small and closed. Any one class has few members and new members are not readily added. The omitted forms are the ones that linguists sometimes call "functors," their grammatical *functions* being more obvious than their semantic content.

Why should young children omit functors and retain contentives? There is more than one plausible answer. Nouns, verbs, and adjectives are words that make reference. One can conceive of teaching the meanings of these words by speaking them, one at a time, and pointing at things or actions or qualities. And of course parents do exactly that. These are the kinds of words that children have been encouraged to practice speaking one at a time. The child arrives at the age of sentence construction with a stock of well-practiced nouns, verbs, and adjectives. Is it not likely then that this prior practice causes him to retain the contentives from model sentences too long to be reproduced in full, that the child imitates those forms in the speech he hears which are already well developed in him as individual habits? There is probably some truth in this explanation but it is not the only determinant since children will often select for retention contentives that are relatively unfamiliar to them.

We adults sometimes operate under a constraint on length and the curious fact is that the English we produce in these circumstances bears a formal resemblance to the English produced by two-year-old children. When words cost money there is a premium on brevity or to put it otherwise, a constraint on length. The result is "telegraphic" English and telegraphic English is an English of nouns, verbs, and adjectives. One does not send a cable reading: "My car has broken down and I have lost my wallet; send money to me at the American Express in Paris" but rather "Car broken down; wallet lost; send money American Express Paris." The telegram omits: *my, has, and, I, have, my, to, me, at, the, in.* All of these are functors. We make the same kind of telegraphic reduction when time or fatigue constrain us to be brief, as witness any set of notes taken at a fast-moving lecture.

A telegraphic transformation of English generally communicates very well. It does so because it retains the high-information words and drops the low-information words. We are here using "in-formation" in the sense of the mathematical theory of communication. The information carried by a word is inversely related to the chances of guessing it from context. From a given string of content words, missing functors can often be guessed but the message "my has and I have my to me at the in" will not serve to get money to Paris. Perhaps children are able to make a communication analysis of adult speech and so adapt in an optimal way to their limitation of span. There is, however, another way in which the adaptive outcome might be achieved.

If you say aloud the model sentences of Table 2 you will find that you place the heavier stresses, the primary and secondary stresses in the sentences, on contentives rather than on functors. In fact the heavier stresses fall, for the most part, on the words the child retains. We first realized that this was the case when we found that in transcribing tapes, the words of the mother that we could hear most clearly were usually the words that the child reproduced. We had trouble hearing the weakly stressed functors and, of course, the child usually failed to reproduce them. Differential stress may then be the cause of the child's differential retention. The outcome is a maximally informative reduction but the cause of this outcome need not be the making of an information analysis. The outcome may be an incidental consequence of the fact that English is a well-designed language that places its heavier stresses where they are needed, on contentives that cannot easily be guessed from context.

We are fairly sure that differential stress is one of the determinants of the child's telegraphic productions. For one thing, stress will also account for the way in which children reproduce polysyllabic words when the total is too much for them. Adam, for instance, gave us *'pression* for *expression* and Eve gave us *'raff* for *giraffe;* the more heavily-stressed syllables were the ones retained. In addition we have tried the effect of placing heavy stresses on functors which do not ordinarily receive such stresses. To Adam we said: "You say what I say" and then, speaking in a normal way at first: "The doggie will bite." Adam gave back: "Doggie bite." Then we stressed the auxiliary: "The doggie *will* bite" and, after a few trials, Adam made attempts at reproducing that auxiliary. A science fiction experiment comes to mind. If these were parents who stressed functors rather than contentives would they have children whose speech was a kind of "reciprocal telegraphic" made up of articles, prepositions, conjunctions, auxiliaries, and the like? Such children would be out of touch with the community as real children are not.

It may be that all the factors we have mentioned play some part in determining the child's selective imitations; the reference-making function of contentives, the fact that they are practiced as single words, the fact that they cannot be guessed from context, and the heavy stresses they receive. There are also other possible factors: for example, the left-to-right, earlier-to-later position of words in a sentence, but these make too long a story to tell here.[4] Whatever the causes, the first utterances produced as imitations of adult sentences are highly systematic reductions of their models. Furthermore, the telegraphic properties of these imitations appear also in the child's spontaneously produced utterances. When his speech is not modeled on an immediately prior adult sentence, it observes the same limitation on length and the same predilection for contentives as when it is modeled on an immediately prior sentence.

Imitation with Expansion

In the course of the brief conversation set down in Table 1, Adam's mother at one point imitates Adam. The boy says: "There go one" and mother responds: "Yes, there goes one." She does not exactly reproduce the model sentence of the child but instead adds something to it or expands it. What she adds is a functor, the inflection for third-person on the verb, the very form that Adam had omitted when he imitated his mother.

One of the first things we noticed when we began to study child speech several years ago was the frequency with which adults imitated children. Indeed they seemed to imitate more often than did the children themselves. We later came to realize that adult imitations are seldom exact reproductions; they are usually expansions. The mothers of Adam and Eve responded to the speech of their children with expansion about thirty per cent of the time. We did it ourselves

when we talked with the children. Indeed we found it very difficult to withhold expansions. A reduced or incomplete English sentence seems to constrain the English-speaking adult to expand it into the nearest properly formed complete sentence. Table 3 lists a few sample expansions from the hundreds in the records.

The first thing worthy of attention in the expansions of Table 3 is the fact that the words spoken by the mother preserve the order of the words in the child's sentences. To be sure, words and inflections are added but they are fitted in—before, and after and between the words the child used; they are not generally permitted to disturb the order of the child's words. It is as if these latter were taken as constants by the mother, constants to which some sentence had to be fitted. She acts as if she were assuming that the child means everything he says, all the words and also their order, but as if he might also mean more than he says. From the mother's point of view an expansion is a kind of communication check; it says in effect: "Is this what you mean?"

The second thing to notice about Table 3 is the character of the forms added to the child's utterances. They include the auxiliaries *is* and *will;* the prepositions *in, on, to,* and *up;* the verb forms *is, have, had,* and *having;* the articles *a* and *the;* the pronouns *her, he,* and *it.* For the most part, the words added are functors and functors are of course the words that the child omits in his reductions.

The interaction between mother and child is, much of the time, a cycle of reductions and expansions. There are two transformations involved. The reduction transformation has an almost completely specifiable and so mechanical character. One could program a machine to do it with the following instructions: "Retain contentives (or stressed forms) in the order given up to some limit of length." The expansion accomplished by Adam's mother when she added the third-person inflection to the verb and said "There goes one" is also a completely specifiable transformation. The instructions would read: "Retain the forms given in the order given and supply obligatory grammatical forms." To be sure this mother-machine would have to be supplied with the obligatory rules of English grammar but that could be done. However, the sentence "There

4 Brown and Fraser, *ibid.*

TABLE 3

Expansions of Child Speech Produced by Mothers

Child	Mother
Baby highchair	*Baby is in the highchair*
Mommy eggnog	*Mommy had her eggnog*
Eve lunch	*Eve is having lunch*
Mommy sandwich	*Mommy'll have a sandwich*
Sat wall	*He sat on the wall*
Throw Daddy	*Throw it to Daddy*
Pick glove	*Pick the glove up*

goes one" is atypical in that it only adds a compulsory and redundant inflection. The expansions of Table 3 all add forms that are not grammatically compulsory or redundant and these expansions cannot be mechanically generated by grammatical rules alone.

In Table 3 the topmost four utterances produced by the child are all of the same grammatical type; all four consist of a proper noun followed by a common noun. However, the four are expanded in quite different ways. In particular the form of the verb changes: it is in the first case in the simple present tense; in the second case the simple past; in the third case the present progressive; in the last case the simple future. All of these are perfectly grammatical but they are different. The second set of child utterances is formally uniform in that each one consists of a verb followed by a noun. The expansions are again all grammatical but quite unlike, especially with regard to the preposition supplied. In general, then, there are radical changes in the mother's expansions when there are no changes in the formal character of the utterances expanded. It follows that the expansions cannot be produced simply by making grammatically compulsory additions to the child's utterances.

How does a mother decide on the correct expansion of one of her child's utterances? Consider the utterance "Eve lunch." So far as grammar is concerned this utterance could be appropriately expanded in any of a number of ways: "Eve is having lunch"; "Eve had lunch"; "Eve will have lunch"; "Eve's lunch," etc. On the occasion when Eve produced the utterance, however, one expan-

sion seemed more appropriate than any other. It was then the noon hour, Eve was sitting at the table with a plate of food before her, and her spoon and fingers were busy. In these circumstances "Eve lunch" had to mean "Eve is having lunch." A little later when the plate had been stacked in the sink and Eve was getting down from her chair the utterance "Eve lunch" would have suggested the expansion "Eve has had her lunch." Most expansions are not only responsive to the child's words but also to the circumstances attending their utterance.

What kind of instructions will generate the mother's expansions? The following are approximately correct: "Retain the words given in the order given and add those functors that will result in a well-formed simple sentence that is appropriate to the circumstances." These are not instructions that any machine could follow. A machine could act on the instructions only if it were provided with detailed specifications for judging appropriateness and no such specifications can, at present, be written. They exist, however, in implicit form in the brains of mothers and in the brains of all English-speaking adults and so judgments of appropriateness can be made by such adults.

The expansion encodes aspects of reality that are not coded by the child's telegraphic utterance. Functors have meaning but it is meaning that accrues to them in context rather than in isolation. The meanings that are added by functors seem to be nothing less than the basic terms in which we construe reality: the time of an action, whether it is ongoing or completed, whether it is presently relevant or not; the concept of possession and such relational concepts as are coded by *in, on, up, down,* and the like; the difference between a particular instance of a class ("Has anybody seen *the* paper?") and any instance of a class ("Has anybody seen *a* paper?"); the difference between extended substances given shape and size by an "accidental" container (*sand, water, syrup,* etc.) and countable "things" having a characteristic fixed shape and size (*a cup, a man, a tree,* etc.). It seems to us that a mother in expanding speech may be teaching more than grammar; she may be teaching something like a world-view.

As yet it has not been demonstrated that expansions are *necessary* for learning either grammar or a construction of reality. It has not even been demonstrated that expansions contribute to such learning. All we know is that some parents do expand and their children do learn. It is perfectly possible, however, that children can and do learn simply from hearing their parents or others make well-formed sentences in connection with various nonverbal circumstances. It may not be necessary or even helpful for these sentences to be expansions of utterances of the child. Only experiments contrasting expansion training with simple exposure to English will settle the matter. We hope to do such experiments.

There are, of course, reasons for expecting the expansion transformation to be an effective tutorial technique. By adding something to the words the child has just produced one confirms his response insofar as it is appropriate. In addition one takes him somewhat beyond that response but not greatly beyond it. One encodes additional meanings at a moment when he is most likely to be attending to the cues that can teach that meaning.

Induction of the Latent Structure

Adam, in the course of the conversation with his mother set down in Table 1, produced one utterance for which no adult is likely ever to have provided an exact model: "No I see truck." His mother elects to expand it as "No, you didn't see it" and this expansion suggests that the child might have created the utterance by reducing an adult model containing the form *didn't.* However, the mother's expansion in this case does some

violence to Adam's original version. He did not say *no* as his mother said it, with primary stress and final contour; Adam's *no* had secondary stress and no final contour. It is not easy to imagine an adult model for this utterance. It seems more likely that the utterance was created by Adam as part of a continuing effort to discover the general rules for constructing English negatives.

In Table 4 we have listed some utterances produced by Adam or Eve for which it is difficult to imagine any adult model. It is unlikely that any adult said any of these to Adam or Eve since they are very simple utterances and yet definitely ungrammatical. In addition it is difficult, by adding functors alone, to build any of them up to simple grammatical sentences. Consequently it does not seem likely that these utterances are reductions of adult originals. It is more likely that they are mistakes which externalize the child's search for the regularities of English syntax.

We have long realized that the occurrence of certain kinds of errors on the level of morphology (or word construction) reveals the child's effort to induce regularities from speech. So long as a child speaks correctly, or at any rate so long as he speaks as correctly as the adults he hears, there is no way to tell whether he is simply repeating what he has heard or whether he is actually constructing. However, when he says something like "I digged a hole" we can often be sure that he is constructing. We can be sure because it is unlikely that he would have heard *digged* from anyone and because we can see how, in processing words he has heard, he might have come by *digged.* It looks like an overgeneralization of the regular past inflection. The inductive operations of the child's mind are externalized in such a creation. Overgeneralizations on the level of syntax (or sentence construction) are more difficult to identify because there are so many ways of adding functors so as to build up conceivable models. But this is difficult to do for the examples of Table 4 and for several hundred other utterances in our records.

The processes of imitation and expansion are not sufficient to account for the degree of linguistic competence that children regularly acquire. These processes alone cannot teach more than the sum total of sentences that speakers of English have either modeled for a child to imitate or built

TABLE 4

Utterances Not Likely to be Imitations

My Cromer suitcase	*You naughty are*
Two foot	*Why it can't turn off?*
A bags	*Put on it*
A scissor	*Cowboy did fighting me*
A this truck	*Put a gas in*

up from a child's reductions. However, a child's linguistic competence extends far beyond this sum total of sentences. All children are able to understand and construct sentences they have never heard but which are nevertheless well-formed, well-formed in terms of general rules that are implicit in the sentences the child has heard. Somehow, then, every child processes the speech to which he is exposed so as to induce from it a latent structure. This latent rule structure is so general that a child can spin out its implications all his life long. It is both semantic and syntactic. The discovery of latent structure is the greatest of the processes involved in language acquisition and the most difficult to understand. We will provide an example of how the analysis can proceed by discussing the evolution in child speech of noun phrases.

A noun phrase in adult English includes a noun but also more than a noun. One variety consists of a noun with assorted modifiers: *The girl; The pretty girl; That pretty girl; My girl*, etc. All of these are constructions which have the same syntactic privileges as do nouns alone. One can use a noun phrase in isolation to name or request something; one can use it in sentences, in subject position or in object position or in predicate nominative position. All of these are slots that nouns alone can also fill. A larger construction having the same syntactic privileges as its "head" word is called in linguistics an "endocentric" construction and noun phrases are endocentric constructions.

For both Adam and Eve, in the early records, noun phrases usually occur as total independent utterances rather than as components of sentences. Table 5 presents an assortment of such utterances at Time 1. They consist in each case of some sort of modifier, just one, preceding a noun. The modifiers, or as they are sometimes called the

"pivot" words, are a much smaller class than the noun class. Three students of child speech have independently discovered that this kind of contruction is extremely common when children first begin to combine words.[5, 6, 7]

It is possible to generalize the cases of Table 5 into a simple implicit rule. The rule symbolized in Table 5 reads: "In order to form a noun phrase of this type, select first one word from the small class of modifiers and select, second, one word from the large class of nouns." This is a "generative" rule by which we mean it is a program that would actually serve to build constructions of the type in question. It is offered as a model of the mental mechanism by which Adam and Eve generated such utterances. Furthermore, judging from our work with other children and from the reports of Braine and of Miller and Ervin, the model describes a mechanism present in many children when their average utterance is approximately two morphemes long.

We have found that even in our earliest records the M + N construction is sometimes used as a component of larger constructions. For instance, Eve said: "Fix a Lassie" and "Turn the page" and "A horsie stuck" and Adam even said: "Adam wear a shirt." There are, at first, only a handful of these larger constructions but there are very many constructions in which single nouns occur in subject or in object position.

Let us look again at the utterances of Table 5 and the rule generalizing them. The class M does

5 M. D. S. Braine, "The ontogeny of English phrase structure: the first phrase," *Language*, XXXIX (1963), 1–13.

6 W. Miller and Susan Ervin, "The development of grammar in child language," Ursula Bellugi and R. Brown, eds., *The Acquisition of Language, Child Developm. Monogr.* (1964).

7 Brown and Fraser, *op. cit.*

TABLE 5

Noun Phrases in Isolation
and Rule for Generating Noun Phrases at Time 1

A coat	*More coffee*
A celery*	*More nut**
A Becky*	*Two sock**
A hands*	*Two shoes*
The top	*two tinker-toy**
My Mommy	*Big boot*
That Adam	*Poor man*
My stool	*Little top*
That knee	*Dirty knee*

$$N P \rightarrow M + N$$

M $\rightarrow$ a, big, dirty, little, more, my, poor, that, the, two.
N $\rightarrow$ Adam, Becky, boot, coat, coffee, knee, man, Mommy, nut, sock,
stool, tinker-toy, top, and very many others.

* **Ungrammatical for an adult.**

not correspond with any syntactic class of adult English. In the class M are articles, a possessive pronoun, a cardinal number, a demonstrative adjective or pronoun, a quantifier, and some descriptive adjectives—a mixed bag indeed. For adult English these words cannot belong to the same syntactic class because they have very different privileges of occurrence in sentences. For the children the words do seem to function as one class having the common privilege of occurrence before nouns.

If the initial words of the utterances in Table 5 are treated as one class M then many utterances are generated which an adult speaker would judge to be ungrammatical. Consider the indefinite article *a*. Adults use it only to modify common count nouns in the singular such as *coat, dog, cup,* etc. We would not say *a celery,* or *a cereal,* or *a dirt; celery, cereal,* and *dirt* are mass nouns. We would not say *a Becky* or *a Jimmy; Becky* and *Jimmy* are proper nouns. We would not say *a hands* or *a shoes; hands* and *shoes* are plural nouns. Adam and Eve, at first, did form ungrammatical combinations such as these.

The numeral *two* we use only with count nouns in the plural. We would not say *two sock* since *sock* is singular, nor *two water* since *water* is a mass noun. The word *more* we use before count nouns in the plural (*more nuts*) or mass nouns

in the singular (*more coffee*). Adam and Eve made a number of combinations involving *two* or *more* that we would not make.

Given the initial very undiscriminating use of words in the class M it follows that one dimension of development must be a progressive differentiation of privileges, which means the division of M into smaller classes. There must also be subdivision of the noun class (N) for the reason that the privileges of occurrence of various kinds of modifiers must be described in terms of such subvarieties of N as the common noun and proper noun, the count noun and mass noun. There must eventually emerge a distinction between nouns singular and nouns plural since this distinction figures in the privileges of occurrence of the several sorts of modifiers.

Sixteen weeks after our first records from Adam and Eve (Time 2), the differentiation process had begun. By this time there were distributional reasons for separating out articles (*a, the*) from demonstrative pronouns (*this, that*) and both of these from the residual class of modifiers. Some of the evidence for this conclusion appears in Table 6. In general one syntactic class is distinguished from another when the members of one class have combinational privileges not enjoyed by the members of the other. Consider, for example, the reasons for distinguishing articles (Art)

TABLE 6

Subdivision of the Modifier Class

A) PRIVILEGES PECULIAR TO ARTICLES

Obtained	Not Obtained
A blue flower	*Blue a flower*
A nice nap	*Nice a nap*
A your car	*Your a car*
A my pencil	*My a pencil*

B) PRIVILEGES PECULIAR TO DEMONSTRATIVE PRONOUNS

Obtained	Not Obtained
That my cup	*My that cup*
That a horse	*A that horse*
That a blue flower	*A that blue flower*
	Blue a that flower

---

from modifiers in general (M). Both articles and modifiers appeared in front of nouns in two-word utterances. However, in three-word utterances that were made up from the total pool of words and that had a noun in final position, the privileges of *a* and *the* were different from the privileges of all other modifiers. The articles occurred in initial position followed by a member of class M other than an article. No other modifier occurred in this first position; notice the "Not obtained" examples of Table 6A. If the children had produced utterances like those (for example, *blue a flower, your a car*) there would have been no difference in the privileges of occurrence of articles and modifiers and therefore no reason to separate out articles.

The record of Adam is especially instructive. He created such notably ungrammatical combinations as "a your car" and "a my pencil." It is very unlikely that adults provided models for these. They argue strongly that Adam regarded all the words in the residual M class as syntactic equivalents and so generated these very odd utterances in which possessive pronouns appear where descriptive adjectives would be more acceptable.

Table 6 also presents some of the evidence for distinguishing demonstrative pronouns (Dem) from articles and modifiers. (Table 6B). The pronouns occurred first and ahead of articles in three-and-four-word utterances—a position that

neither articles nor modifiers ever filled. The sentences with demonstrative pronouns are recognizable as reductions which omit the copular verb *is*. Such sentences are not noun phrases in adult English and ultimately they will not function as noun phrases in the speech of the children, but for the present they are not distinguishable distributionally from noun phrases.

Recall now the generative formula of Table 5 which constructs noun phrases by simply placing a modifier (M) before a noun (N). The differentiation of privileges illustrated in Table 6, and the syntactic classes this evidence motivates us to create, complicate the formula for generating noun phrases. In Table 7 we have written a single general formula for producing all noun phrases at Time 2 [NP → (Dem) + (Art) + (M) + N] and also the numerous more specific rules which are summarized by the general formula.

By the time of the thirteenth transcription, twenty-six weeks after we began our study, privileges of occurrence were much more finely differentiated and syntactic classes were consequently more numerous. From the distributional evidence we judged that Adam had made five classes of his original class M: articles, descriptive adjectives, possessive pronouns, demonstrative pronouns, and a residual class of modifiers. The generative rules of Table 7 had become inadequate; there were no longer, for instance, any combinations like

TABLE 7

Rules for Generating Noun Phrases at Time 2

$NP_1 \rightarrow Dem + Art + M + N$
$NP_2 \rightarrow Art + M + N$
$NP_3 \rightarrow Dem + M + N$
$NP_4 \rightarrow Art + N$
$NP_5 \rightarrow M + N$
$NP_6 \rightarrow Dem + N$
$NP_7 \rightarrow Dem + Art + N$

$NP \rightarrow (Dem) + (Art) + (M) + N$

( ) means class within
parentheses is optional

"A your car." Eve had the same set except that she used two residual classes of modifiers. In addition nouns had begun to subdivide for both children. The usage of proper nouns had become clearly distinct from the usage of count nouns. For Eve the evidence justified separating count nouns from mass nouns, but for Adam it still did not. Both children by this time were frequently pluralizing nouns but as yet their syntactic control of the singular-plural distinction was imperfect.

In summary, one major aspect of the development of general structure in child speech is a progressive differentiation in the usage of words and therefore a progressive differentiation of syntactic classes. At the same time, however, there is an integrative process at work. From the first, an occasional noun phrase occurred as a component of some larger construction. At first these noun phrases were just two words long and the range of positions in which they could occur was small. With time the noun phrases grew longer, were more frequently used, and were used in a greater range of positions. The noun phrase structure as a whole, in all the permissible combinations of modifiers and nouns, was assuming the combinational privileges enjoyed by nouns in isolation.

In Table 8 we have set down some of the sentence positions in which both nouns and noun phrases occurred in the speech of Adam and Eve. It is the close match between the positions of nouns alone and of nouns with modifiers in the speech of Adam and Eve that justifies us in calling the longer constructions noun phrases. These longer constructions are, as they should be, endocentric; the head word alone has the same syntactic privileges as the head word with its modifiers. The continuing failure to find in noun phrase positions whole constructions of the type "That a blue flower" signals the fact that these constructions are telegraphic versions of predicate nominative sentences omitting the very form *is*. Examples of the kind of construction not obtained are: "That (that a blue flower)"; "Where (that a blue flower)?"

For adults the noun phrase is a subwhole of the sentence, what linguists call an "immediate constituent." The noun phrase has a kind of psy-

TABLE 8

Some Privileges of the Noun Phrase

Noun Positions	Noun Phrase Positions
That (flower)	*That (a blue flower)*
Where (ball) go?	*Where (the puzzle) go?*
Adam write (penguin)	*Doggie eat (the breakfast)*
(Horsie) stop	*(A horsie) crying*
Put (hat) on	*Put (the red hat) on*

TABLE 9

Pronouns Replacing Nouns or Noun Phrases and Pronouns Produced Together with Nouns or Noun Phrases

Noun Phrases Replaced by Pronouns	Pronouns and Noun Phrases in Same Utterances
Hit ball	*Mommy get it ladder*
Get it	*Mommy get it my ladder*
Ball go?	*Saw it ball*
Go get it	*Miss it garage*
Maae it	*I miss it cowboy boot*
Made a ship	*I Adam drive that*
	I Adam drive
Fix a tricycle	*I Adam don't*
Fix it	

chological unity. There are signs that the noun phrase was also an immediate constituent for Adam and Eve. Consider the sentence using the separable verb *put on*. The noun phrase in "Put the red hat on" is, as a whole, fitted in between the verb and the particle even as is the noun alone in "Put hat on." What is more, however, the location of pauses in the longer sentence, on several occasions, suggested the psychological organization: "Put . . . the red hat . . . on" rather than "Put the red . . . hat on" or "Put the . . . red hat on." In addition to this evidence the use of pronouns suggests that the noun phrase is a psychological unit.

The unity of noun phrases in adult English is evidenced, in the first place, by the syntactic equivalence between such phrases and nouns alone. It is evidenced, in the second place, by the fact that pronouns are able to substitute for total noun phrases. In our immediately preceding sentence the pronoun "It" stands for the rather involved construction from the first sentence of this paragraph: "The unity of noun phrases in adult English." The words called "pronouns" in English would more aptly be called "pro-noun-phrases" since it is the phrase rather than the noun which they usually replace. One does not replace "unity" with "it" and say "The *it* of noun phrases in adult English." In the speech of Adam and Eve, too, the pronoun came to function as a replacement

for the noun phrase. Some of the clearer cases appear in Table 9.

Adam characteristically externalizes more of his learning than does Eve and his record is especially instructive in connection with the learning of pronouns. In his first eight records, the first sixteen weeks of the study, Adam quite often produced sentences containing both the pronoun and the noun or noun phrase that the pronoun should have replaced. One can here see the equivalence in the process of establishment. First the substitute is produced and then, as if in explication, the form or forms that will eventually be replaced by the substitute. Adam spoke out his pronoun antecedents as chronological consequents. This is additional evidence of the unity of the noun phrase since the noun phrases *my ladder* and *cowboy boot* are linked with *it* in Adam's speech in just the same way as the nouns *ladder* and *ball*.

We have described three processes involved in the child's acquisition of syntax. It is clear that the last of these, the induction of latent structure, is by far the most complex. It looks as if this last process will put a serious strain on any learning theory thus far conceived by psychology. The very intricate simultaneous differentiation and integration that constitutes the evolution of the noun phrase is more reminiscent of the biological development of an embryo than it is of the acquisition of a conditional reflex.

Why Not Pivot Grammar?

Lois Bloom

Recent studies of language development have focused attention on the early stages of emerging syntax—the use of two-word and three-word sentences sometime during the second half of the second year of life. A number of investigators have reported similar distributional phenomena in samples of early child speech. When children begin to use two words in juxtaposition there are often a small number of words that occur frequently, in relatively fixed position, in combination with a large number of other words, each of which occurs less frequently. Braine (1963) named this first group of words "pivots"; children's speech has since been described in the literature as "pivotal," and an account of the systematic productivity of early utterances is often referred to in terms of "pivot grammar." The apparent convergence on this point in the literature (in particular, Bellugi and Brown, 1964; McNeill, 1966a) has led to its application to programs for language disorders (see, for example, McNeill, 1966b). However, more recent research (Bloom, 1970) and a careful examination of earlier studies, such as the

classic diary study of Leopold (1949), indicate that the time is at hand for a reevaluation of the phenomenon. How real is pivot grammar?

This paper will begin with a review of the original evidence. Subsequently, several important questions will be raised concerning the adequacy of the notion of pivot grammar as an account of what children know about grammar as they begin to use syntax in their speech. Recent evidence of the underlying conceptual relations in children's early speech will be reported, and, finally, this information will be discussed as it relates to possible approaches to language disorders in children.

The Original Evidence

The studies of Braine (1963), Miller and Ervin (1964), and Brown and Fraser (1963) were essentially distributional studies. They viewed children's speech as evidence, potentially, of a distinctive language, and for this reason they were admirably motivated to avoid the classes and

Lois Bloom, "Why Not Pivot Grammar?" *Journal of Speech and Hearing Disorders, 36,* 1971, pp. 40–50.

categories of adult speech in their accounts. As a linguist would approach an exotic language in order to describe its grammar, these investigators looked at large numbers of children's utterances, and described what they saw in terms of classes of words based on their privileges of occurrence. What they found was essentially an orderly arrangement of at least two, possibly three, classes of words. Certain words, such as "no," "no more," "all gone," "more," "this," "that," "here," "there," "off," "on," occurred frequently, in fixed position as either the first or second constituent in a two-word utterance, and shared contexts with a larger number of words that occurred relatively less frequently. Braine (1963) referred to the classes as "pivots" and "x-words," Brown and Fraser (1963) referred to "functors" and "contentives," and Miller and Ervin (1964) referred to "operators" and "non-operators."

Only Braine (1963) was discussing a relatively complete corpus. His data consisted of (1) the records kept by the mothers of two boys of all of their first two-word utterances over a period of several months, and (2) tape recorded samples of a third boy's speech during play sessions. Brown and Bellugi (1964) described only the constituents of noun phrases and the developmental differentiation of the initial position modifier class. Brown and Fraser (1963) and Miller and Ervin (1964) presented for discussion lists of two-word and three-word utterances that demonstrated the distributional phenomenon—for example, utterances with "this" and "that" or "Mum" and "Dad."

McNeill (1966a), using some of Brown's data, presented an extended account of the "pivotal" nature of children's speech. He viewed the original classes of pivots and x-words, or, as he named them, "open" words (because of the apparent tendency of the class to admit new members freely), as the original generic classes from which all the category classes of the adult model ultimately develop, through some sort of differentiation. McNeill (1970) has since refined his distinction between pivot forms and other forms further, in terms of their syntactic features with respect to occurrence with noun forms. Essentially, his account specifies all noun forms as an unmarked class in the child's lexicon—the class of "open" words. All other words are marked forms—marked, in the sense that they are identi-

fied as occurring only with nouns—the verbs, modifiers, and determiners which constitute the originally undifferentiated "pivot" class.

At least two critical questions can be raised about the adequacy of the pivot grammar notion as an account of children's early speech. First, how does pivot grammar relate to the grammar of the adult, model language? Large enough samples of adult speech would undoubtedly reveal similar kinds of distributional evidence based on relative frequency of occurrence (see Zipf, 1965). Certain words such as determiners, pronouns, and other function words or syntactic markers occur more frequently and in more varied linguistic environments in adult speech than do verbs, adjectives, and nouns. However, such rules of grammar as "pivot + open," "open + pivot," or "open + open" have no real analog among the syntactic structures of the adult model. How does the child progress from using pivotal utterances to using utterances that reflect the complex interrelation of rules that is the essence of adult phrase structure? McNeill, in both of the foregoing accounts, attempted to deal with this question. However, his conclusions are based upon certain assumptions—for example, that pivot forms do not occur in isolation, and that two nouns cannot occur together—that simply are not supported in the data.

The second question concerns the adequacy of the pivot grammar account for describing and explaining children's early speech. What does the notion of pivot grammar tell us about what children know about grammar when they begin to use syntax in their speech?

The Adequacy of a Pivot Grammar Account

The studies just discussed focused attention on the formal syntax of children's speech—on the arrangements of words in utterances. However, such descriptions of the form of speech provide minimal information about the child's intuitive knowledge of a linguisitc code. Linguistic expression is intimately connected with cognitive-perceptual development and the child's interaction in a world of objects, events, and relations. The goal of the research discussed here (and reported at length in Bloom, 1970) was to investigate the development of linguistic behavior in relation to aspects of experience related to the speech children use.

The subjects of the study—Kathryn, Eric, and Gia—were the first-born children of white, college-educated, American English-speaking parents. They were each visited in their homes for approximately eight hours over a period of several days. Each sample of spoken language (at six-week intervals) was obtained during the child's (1) play with a selected group of toys, (2) eating, dressing, and toileting, and (3) play with a peer. The syntactic components of generative grammars were proposed for the earliest texts with mean length of utterance less than 1.5 morphemes. The syntactic and semantic development of negation was described until mean length of utterance was approximately 3.0 morphemes (in Bloom, 1970). Kathryn was 21 months old when the study began; Eric and Gia were each 19 months, one week old.

Judgments were made of the semantic intent of utterances, based upon clues from the context and behavior in the speech events in which utterances occurred. Using this kind of information, an attempt was made to propose rules of grammar to account for the inherent semantic relations that underlie the juxtaposition of words in early sentences. The notion of sentence structure implies a pattern of organization—an arrangement of otherwise independent parts that is based on the relationship of the parts to each other—which is something more than simply a sequence of words. The semantic relations that were coded in the children's speech were essentially of two kinds: functional relations with invariable grammatical meaning, and grammatical relations with variable grammatical meaning between constituents in subject-predicate relationship.

FUNCTIONAL RELATIONS: SEMANTICS OF CERTAIN PIVOT FORMS

To begin with, the data from Kathryn, Eric, and Gia contained utterances that were similar to those reported in the earlier studies and described as pivotal: Kathryn's utterances with "no," "this," "that," "more," and "hi"; Gia's utterances with "more" and "hi"; and Eric's utterances with "no," "another," "there," and "it." The children's use of these forms, in terms of semantic intention, could be described with some confidence. "No" most often signaled the non-existence of the referent named by the second constituent (as in "no pocket"), where there was some expectation of its existence in the context of the speech event. "More" or "another" was used to comment on or to request the recurrence or another instance of an object or event (as in "more raisin" and "more read"). "This" and "that," and "there" were not contrastive in proximal-distal reference, and were used to point out an object or event in the environment (as in "this book," or "this cleaning"). "Hi," which occurred less frequently, was used in a nonsalutatory way as the child took notice of an object, person, or picture (as in "Hi shadow," "Hi spoon," "Hi Jocelyn"). The forms occurred frequently, in fixed syntactic position, with a number of different words, and they shared contexts. All occurred as single-word utterances as well. However, they occurred with specific semantic intent, either in relation to the words with which they were juxtaposed or with inherent relation to something not specified, in the case of single-word utterances. Their use was motivated by their semantic function; they occurred in speech events that shared features of context and behavior. This last point is of considerable importance; certain words occur often in children's speech apparently because of the nature of their referential function. Description of such utterances as pivotal is only a superficial description of relative frequency of occurrence and syntactic position.

Moreover, it turned out that the utterances described as pivotal, in the limited sense just indicated, proved to be a small percentage of the total number of utterances that were obtained from Gia and Kathryn. Only Eric's speech—during the period of time under discussion, when mean length of utterance was less than 1.5 morphemes—contained a preponderance of utterances such as have been so far described. The majority of the utterances of Kathryn and Gia presented certain critical problems for a pivot grammar account.

There were certain words in the children's speech that met all the distributional criteria for specification as pivots. The most frequent of these was either "Mommy" or reference to self—either by first name or, in Kathryn's case, "Baby" as well. However, not only did syntactic utterances with "Mommy" occur frequently, but it was also the case that "Mommy" occurred in relatively fixed position. For example, in 32 sentences with "Mommy" in the first speech sample from Kathryn (when mean length of utterance was 1.32), "Mommy" occurred in sentence-initial position 29 times. Moreover, "Mommy" also shared contexts with other forms, for example, "Mommy sock" and "no sock," "Mommy haircurl" and "more haircurl."

One immediate objection to "Mommy" as pivot is that "Mommy" is a form having lexical status as a substantive or content word rather than a function word or syntactic marker. There is something intuitively wrong about classing "Mommy" as a function word, and, indeed, there has been a general inclination to avoid such characterization in the literature (see, for example, the discussion in Smith and Miller, 1966).

However, more important reasons for arguing against the distributional evidence that would class "Mommy" as a pivot or function form had to do with the fact that different utterances with "Mommy" meant different things. For example, in the first sample from Kathryn, the utterance "Mommy sock" occurred twice in two separate contexts:

(1) Kathryn picking up her mother's sock
(2) Mommy putting Kathryn's sock on Kathryn

It appeared that the difference in semantic interpretation between the two utterances (1 and 2) corresponded to a structural difference in grammatical relationship between the constituents "Mommy" and "sock." In one instance the structure was a genitive relation and in the other the relation between subject and object.

GRAMMATICAL RELATIONS

Constructions with two substantive forms (the 32 utterances with "Mommy" and 24 utterances with "Baby" or "Kathryn," for example) were described by Braine (1963) and McNeill (1966a) as the juxtaposition of two x-words or open class words, respectively. But whether such utterances

are classed together as "pivot + open" or "open + open," the two instances of "Mommy sock" would have the same structural description in either case, because the surface form of each is the same. Rules that account for utterances in terms of the juxtaposition of pivots and open words cannot account for differences in semantic interpretation. And yet there was strong evidence in the data for ascribing different structural descriptions to utterances with similar surface form but different underlying relationship between constituents. The full argument regarding the correct structural representation of such utterances has already been presented (Bloom, 1970). For the purpose of this paper, it will be pointed out that interpretation of the semantic intent of utterances with two substantive forms provided evidence that the children knew more about grammar at this early stage than merely rules for permitted juxtaposition of two different kinds of words.

There were a number of potential interpretations of the utterances that occurred with "Mommy" in constructions with nouns. The first possibility was that the child had simply named two aspects of a referent, or two referents, within the bounds of a single utterance—a conjunction (for example, "Mommy" and "sock"). If one interpreted children's use of single-word utterances (before and during the emergence of syntax) as labeling or naming behavior, then this would be an intuitively appealing interpretation of the juxtaposition of two noun forms within an utterance. If such were the case, and the two noun forms were simply conjoined without connection or with any possible connection between them, one could reasonably expect the constituents to be named in variable order. If the child had simply named two referents, or two aspects of a referent, there would be no motivation for naming them in a particular order. But the occurrence of "Mommy" in sentence-initial position 29 times in the 32 utterances that included "Mommy" was impressive evidence that the motivation for the order of the constituents was strong.

In addition to the utterances with "Mommy," there were 37 other noun + noun constructions in the first sample of Kathryn's speech and 66 utterances that juxtaposed two nouns in the second sample of Gia's speech (when mean length of utterance was less than 1.5 for each). Clearly, this utterance type was one of the most productive constructions in the speech of both children. Of the total of 135 noun + noun utterances, there were only seven that occurred with no other interpretable relationship between the forms than simple conjunction, for example, "umbrella boot" from Kathryn as her mother walked into the room carrying her umbrella and boots, and "Mommy Gia" from Gia as she looked at a photograph of Mommy and Gia. All of the remaining utterances appeared to present constituents with an inherent relationship between them, although in some instances the relationship was equivocal.

The utterances with two noun forms specified the following grammatical relations (given here in order of frequency): subject-object ("Mommy pigtail"), the genitive relation ("Kathryn sock"), the attributive relation ("bread book"), subject-locative ("sweater chair"), and, marginally, conjunction ("umbrella boot"). However, it was not the case that any two words could occur with any possible relation between them. There were no instances of such other possible relations that could hold between two noun forms as identity ("Mommy lady"), disjunction (either-or relation), or direct-indirect object. If it could be assumed that the unobtained relations existed in the child's experience, for example, giving something to someone (direct-indirect object), then the children's utterances were not merely reflections of nonlinguistic states of affairs. Such selectivity in expression and the impressive consistency of word order provided evidence for assuming that the children's utterances were motivated by an underlying cognitive-linguistic rule system.

The most frequently expressed relationship between two nouns was subject-object. All three children produced verb forms in predicate relation to noun forms in subject-verb and verb-object strings in the early two-word utterances, when subject-verb-object strings occurred only rarely. Utterances that have been described in the literature as simply the occurrence of two substantive words (x-word + x-word by Braine [1963], or two open-class words by McNeill, [1966a]) could thus be explained in terms of the inherent semantic relationship between the constituents. It was apparent that the children in the study were talking about the relations between actors or agents, actions, or states, and objects or goals, and that the order of constituents reflected the underlying order of basic sentence relations with remarkable consistency—subjects and verbs preceded objects or goals.

The possible grammatical relations were not equally represented in the data. Not only were certain relations more productive than others—that is, they occurred more often in different situations with different words—but the children differed in their use of each. For example, Eric used the verb-object relation first, and utterances expressing this relation were dominant in his speech before he began to use subject nouns in relation to verb forms. The most productive early relationship for Gia and Kathryn was subject-object; Eric never produced such utterances. I. M. Schlesinger (in press) reported the productivity of this structural relationship between two nouns in the early speech of two Hebrew-speaking Israeli children, and Leopold (1949) described its frequent occurrence in the speech of his daughter Hildegard. In the speech of Kathryn, Eric, and Gia, verb-object strings appeared earlier and were more productive than subject-verb strings.

Summary

The children's earliest sentences could thus be seen as expressing two kinds of conceptual relations. In grammatical relations, substantive words such as "Mommy" and "sock" enter into variable grammatical relationship with other words in sentences. Such words are not in themselves relational terms in the sense that they have independent lexical meaning. The children's earliest sentences also expressed functional relations, where inherently relational words such as "more" and "no" operate in linear structure with other (substantive) words to specify a particular relational aspect of such words (or their referents). Spoken alone as single-word utterances, such words manifestly imply such a semantic relationship to some unspecified aspect of experience.

It is not the case that the words the children used—for example, "no" and "more"—have only one meaning. All of the children used "no" subsequently to signal rejection, as in "no dirty soap" (I don't want to use the dirty soap) and, still later, denial, as in "no truck" (that's not a truck, it's a car). In the adult model, "more" is used to express the partitive notion (here is sand—and here is an addition to the quantity of sand, or "more sand"), and the comparative notion as well. The partitive may be a derivative of recurrence, but it is clear that the notion of comparative "more" is a relatively late development. Similarly, substantive forms with essentially constant semantic meaning vary in grammatical meaning in relation to other words in sentences, for example, *"Mommy* push," "push *Mommy,"* "*Mommy's* shoe," and "my *Mommy."* The function or use of certain forms is not implicit for the child in the word itself.

Given that children comment on the notions of existence, nonexistence, and recurrence of objects and events, one might well wonder why they should talk about anything else—in the light of what we know to be the achievements of sensory-motor intelligence. Piaget (1960) has described a major achievement in the child's development of thought with the realization of the endurance of objects when removed in space and time. The child learns that objects and events exist, cease to exist, and recur, and so he talks about it. The important conclusion about the development of grammar appears to be that children do not simply use a relatively uncomplex syntactic frame (such as pivot + open); they talk about something, and syntax is learned by the child in his efforts to code certain conceptual relations.

There is a necessary distinction between a speaker-hearer's knowledge of grammar and the notion of grammar as a linguistic account of that knowledge. The nature of the underlying rules that the child uses to speak and understand utterances cannot be described directly. A generative grammar represents a formal linguistic account of how such rules specify the inherent relations in sentences. Such an account specifies the syntax of utterances (the arrangements of forms) that accounts for the semantic relations among the forms, and in this sense there is a crucial relationship between linguistic structure and underlying cognitive function. Indeed, it is difficult to distinguish between cognitive and linguistic categories when accounting for the expressed relations between actors or agents, actions or states, and objects or goals.

It appears that the notion of pivot grammar

describes children's early speech in only the most superficial way. Although the notion of pivot speech describes certain distributional phenomena in early utterances, it is clear that children know more about grammar, that is, more about the inherent relationships between words in syntactic structure, than could possibly be accounted for in terms of pivot and open class analysis. If treatment for language disorders in children is ultimately to be derived from a model of normal language development, there is evidence to indicate that a pivot grammar is not the model of child speech to use.

Treatment of Language Disorders

Several conclusions from this discussion may be applicable to planning treatment of language disorders in children. There are necessary limitations in the extent to which the conclusions of this study pertain to all children learning language, and it would follow that similar limitations apply as well to using these results in evaluating and treating language pathology. Whether or not, and how, the normative data on language development in the literature can or should be directly applied to treating children with delayed language development are important questions (see Bloom, 1967). However, certain observations can be made at this time that should provide hypotheses for research directed toward evaluating procedures for treating language disorders.

First, the results of this study confirmed a conclusion that has been reached in every study of language development of children in the earliest stages of acquiring grammar. Children learn the syntax of language—the arrangements of words in sentences—before they learn influences of noun, verb, and adjective forms. Although there may be alternation of certain forms from the beginning —"block," "blocks," and "sit," "sits"—the different forms of a word do not occur in contrast. For example, in the early samples, "-s" did not signal a meaningful difference, such as marking reference to more than one block as opposed to reference to only one block without expression of "-s." Thus, children learn word sequences (for example, "throw block") before morphological contrasts (as between "block," singular, and "blocks," plural).

Second, Kathryn, Eric, and Gia did not produce constructions that were potentially analyzable as noun phrases as their first (or most productive) syntactic structures. Rather, the most productive structures they produced (after utterances with initial /ə/) were those which, in the adult model, express the basic grammatical relations: subject-object, subject-verb, and verb-object strings. Although the grammars of Kathryn and Gia specified a noun phrase constituent (with attributive adjectives in Kathryn's lexicon only), this structure was far less productive than others which occurred, and Eric did not produce noun phrases at all. Based on these two observations, children appear to learn the expressions "throw block" or "Baby (subject) block (object)" before the expressions "big block," "red block," or "blocks."

Finally, the results of this study indicated that (1) the status of the referent in the context in which an utterance occurs, and (2) the child's relation to the referent in terms of behavior are critically important as influences on language performance. There were four contextual variables which characterized the occurrence of early syntactic utterances: (1) existence of the referent within the context, (2) recurrence of the referent or addition to the referent after its previous existence, (3) action upon the referent, and (4) nonexistence of the referent in the context where its existence was somehow expected.

The manifestation of the referent in the contexts of speech events was most significant. Utterances most often referred to objects or events which the child was able to see, and functioned as comments or directions, where the referent was manifest or imminent in the context of the speech event, as opposed to reports of distant past or future events. All of the children used a relational term, "more" or "another," to signal another instance of the referent or recurrence of the referent after previous occurrence. The productivity of verb-object and subject-object strings reflected the tendency for the children to talk about objects being acted upon. And, finally, as might be expected given the foregoing observations, their first negative sentences signaled the nonexistence of the referent. On the simplest level, children appear to learn to perceive and to discriminate (and, ultimately, to communicate) (1) such aspects of a referent as its existence, recurrence, or nonexistence, and (2) such relational aspects of events as between agent, action, and object before, among other things, such features of objects as relative size, color, or other identifying attributes.

It might be said that children learn to identify particular syntactic structures with the behavior and context with which they are perceived and then progress to reproducing structures in similar, recurring contexts. To use a structure in a new situation, the child needs to be able to perceive critical aspects of the context of the situation. Thus, the sequence in which the child learns syntactic structures may be influenced as much by his ability to differentiate aspects of situational context and to recognize recurrent contexts as by such factors as frequency of exposure to structures or their relative complexity.

Programs for language therapy that present children with linguistic structure (for example, pivot grammar) without attention to content ignore the very nature of language. It appears that learning a linguistic code depends upon the child's learning to distinguish, understand, and express certain conceptual relations. It would follow that children with language disorders need to learn more than simply the permitted cooccurrence of different words in their efforts at the analysis and use of language.

Acknowledgment

The research described in this paper was supported by PHS grant 5-F1-MH-30,001,03 from the National Institute of Mental Health.

REFERENCES

BELLUGI, U., and BROWN, R. (Eds.) *The Acquisition of Language.* Monograph No. 29, Chicago, Ill.: Society for Research in Child Development (1964).

BLOOM, L. A comment on Lee's developmental sentence types: A method for comparing normal and deviant syntactic development. *J. Speech Hearing Dis.*, 32, 294–296 (1967).

BLOOM, L. *Language Development: Form and Func-*

tion in Emerging Grammars. Cambridge, Mass.: MIT Press (1970).

BRAINE, M. D. S. The ontogeny of English phrase structure: The first phase. *Language, 39,* 1–13 (1963).

BROWN, R., and BELLUGI, U. Three processes in the child's acquisition of syntax. *Harv. Educ. Rev., 34,* 133–151 (1964).

BROWN, R., and FRASER, C. The acquisition of syntax. In Charles N. Cofer and Barbara S. Musgrave (Eds.), *Verbal Behavior and Learning.* New York: McGraw-Hill (1963).

LEOPOLD, W. F. *Speech Development of a Bilingual Child.* (Vol. III.) Evanston, Ill.: Northwestern Univ. (1949).

MC NEILL, D. Developmental psycholinguistics. In Frank Smith and George A. Miller (Eds.), *The Genesis of Language.* Cambridge, Mass.: MIT Press, 15–84 (1966a).

MC NEILL, D. The capacity for language acquisition. *Volta Rev.,* reprint no. 852, 5–21 (1966b).

MC NEILL, D. *The Acquisition of Language: The Study of Developmental Psycholinguistics.* New York: Harper (1970).

MILLER, W., and ERVIN, S. The development of grammar in child language. In Ursula Bellugi and Roger Brown (Eds.), *The Acquisition of Language.* Monograph No. 29, Chicago, Ill.: Society for Research in Child Development (1964).

PIAGET, J. *The Psychology of Intelligence.* Paterson, N. J.: Atherton (1960).

SCHLESINGER, I. M. Learning grammar: From pivot to realization rule. In Dan I. Slobin (Ed.), *The Ontogenesis of Grammar: Some Facts and Several Theories.* New York: Academic.

SMITH, F., and MILLER, G. A. (Eds.). *The Genesis of Language.* Cambridge, Mass.: MIT Press (1966).

ZIPF, G. K. *The Psychobiology of Language; An Introduction to Dynamic Philology.* Cambridge, Mass.: MIT Press (1965).

Part 5

Cognition

Although Piaget's name has become almost synonymous with cognitive theory, this field is much broader than simply the area of Piaget's research, extensive though it is. There is no doubt, however, that Piaget has been the major modern influence in developmental psychology. In the first article in this section, Whiteman attempts to trace that influence to the area of defense mechanisms, often considered a classic reserve of psychoanalytic theory.

Probably Piaget's greatest impact, however, in a practical sense, has resulted from his description of how children gain their understanding of number, mass, weight, and length. Many researchers have attempted to teach children these concepts, but it has not been an easy task. Piaget has always indicated that we might well find the roots of such learning in the arguments that children have with each other. Proceeding on this basis, Murray has been successful in inducing these concepts in children, a finding that holds important implications for the use of peers in education. (In Section VII, School and Intelligence, an article by Gagné outlines another approach to the acquisition of these concepts, from a learning theory perspective.) Rubenstein looks to properties in the inanimate environment and considers their effects on cognitive development. Piaget's article recapitulates his views and indicates the direction of some of his current work.

Children's Conceptions of Psychological Causality

Martin Whiteman

Piaget's pioneering explorations have brought forth a number of investigations of the child's conception of physical causality. However, there has been relatively little investigation of the child's conceptions of psychological causality. It would

This research was supported by a grant from the National Institute of Mental Health (No. MH-10578-01). Grateful acknowledgment is made to Anita G. Bardin, Judith F. Levine, Sherrie F. Miller, and Judith L. Ryan for their contribution to the interviewing and to the coding of the data gathered in phase 2. Dr. Lassar K. Gotkin of the Institute for Developmental Studies, Department of Psychiatry, New York Medical College, was most helpful in securing the cooperation of the teachers and of the administration of the public schools in which the work was done. Miss Jean Lloyd and Mrs. Goldie Haile, kindergarten teachers, are thanked for their cooperation in expediting the interviewing of the children.

The scoring criteria, the interview guide, item analyses, and reliability data have been deposited with the American Documentation Institute. Order Document No. 9148, remitting $1.75 for 35-mm microfilm or $2.50 for 6 × 8-inch photocopies.

Author's address: Columbia University School of Social Work, 2 East 91st Street, New York, New York 10028.

seem as appropriate to ask a child, "What makes people angry?" as it is to ask him, "What makes clouds move?" Yet, systematic explorations of the child's developing awareness of the causes of another person's behavior are lacking. This lack is particularly poignant since, as adults, we are continually making inferences about the causes of other people's behavior. An important problem, then, is how and when such causal inferences are learned.

A major set of concepts used by people in explaining behavior comprises the so-called mechanisms of adjustment. People, in their everyday behavior, do seem to use as explanatory devices those behaviors that psychologists have conceptualized as rationalizations or displacements or projections, for example, rationalization ("He's using that as an excuse"), displacement ("He's just taking out all his troubles on me"), projection ("Well, that's the way he is himself and he thinks everybody is that way"). From a theoretical point of view, it is important to understand how and

Martin Whiteman, "Children's Conceptions of Psychological Causality." Paper presented at the 1965 meeting of the Eastern Psychological Association, Atlantic City, New Jersey.

when such explanatory ideas become part of the conceptual repertoire of the child. Psychologists of such widely differing theoretical persuasion as Anna Freud (1946) and Hilgard (1949) have pointed to the importance of such mechanisms for maintenance of self-esteem. However, there has been no attempt to study directly the cognitive development of such notions, which are as important in their own right as the development by the child of conceptions of space, time, and physical causality.

Piaget has drawn a basic distinction between the preoperational intuitive stage (around 4–7 years) and the concrete operational stage (around 7–11 years). According to Piaget (1950) and Flavell (1963), there is a major revision in the child's thought at around 7 years, enabling him to conceptualize certain types of relations and classes. A major achievement of the operational child is his ability to decenter from a focus on the perceptually dominant to an emphasis on the more invariant but less salient properties of stimulus displays, as illustrated by the operational child's ability to conserve conceptually an object's substance or length despite changes in the object's appearance or location. Similarly, one would expect that the operational as compared to the younger preoperational child should have greater ease in decentering from the more obvious overt behaviors to the less obvious underlying motivations as described by the adjustment mechanisms. Furthermore, Laurendeau and Pinard (1962), replicating early Piaget investigations (1929; 1930), have shown striking differences between these two age levels in their ability to apprehend physical causality. It becomes pertinent, therefore, to explore the differences between such contrasting age groups in their explanations of psychological causality as well as to relate such differences to conceptions of physical causality.

The general aim of this study is to explore the feasibility of using interviews with children at two age levels, the 5–6-year range and the 8–9-year-old span, in order to study developing conceptions of psychological causality.

The study comprised two separate phases. The specific aims of phase 1 were to (a) devise usable categorizations and scoring systems for the assessment of psychological causality, (b) study the homogeneity among items in order to determine whether reliable and meaningful indexes might be formed, and (c) study developmental and intellectual differences with respect to such indexes of psychological causality. The second phase had as its purposes: (a) the objectification and standardization of the interviewing procedure devised in phase 1, (b) the replication of phase 1 with comparable but somewhat larger samples to assess the reliability of phase 1 findings with respect to developmental and intellectual differences in the understanding of psychological causality, and (c) the extension of phase 1 results through the study of the relation between grasp of psychological causality and understanding of physical causality.

Phase 1

METHOD

Subjects. The subjects comprised 42 children. The 21 younger children comprised an experimental kindergarten class in Harlem, New York City. Stanford-Binet IQ's were available for these children. For each kindergarten child, a separate roster of third-grade children from the same school was prepared. The third graders on each roster had been matched with the kindergarten child with respect to sex and IQ as assessed by group test. For each kindergarten child, a third grader was then selected from the appropriate roster by random sampling. For each grade, the average IQ was 101 with a standard deviation of 10. All children were Negro or Puerto Rican. The kindergarten children were in the 5–6-year range, while the third graders fell in the 8–9-year span.

The interview. The interviews were conducted by the writer and dealt with the child's tape-recorded responses to questions about each of seven stories. Each story read to the child exemplified in rudimentary form a different mechanism of adjustment, that is, displacement, wishful dreaming, projection, regression, repression, rationalization, and denial. The instructions to the child and the stories themselves were as follows:

"I'm going to tell you some stories about a little girl called Jane. In each of these stories

Jane does something different from what she usually does. I want you to tell me why she did it. Here's the first story." (For boys, "Johnnie" was substituted for "Jane" in the stories, and "toy soldiers" for "dolls" in the first story.)

1. Displacement: "There was once a little girl named Jane. One day her mother promised that Jane's favorite dessert, ice cream, would be served at supper. But Jane's mother forgot to buy the ice cream, and so there wasn't any ice cream for dessert. Jane didn't say anything to her mother about the ice cream. After supper Jane went to play with her dolls and did something she never did before. She spanked her dolls. Why did she spank her dolls?"

2. Wishful dreaming: "One day Jane looked at T.V. and saw a girl who had a wonderful bicycle. Jane herself didn't have a bicycle and couldn't even ride one. That night Jane dreamed that her father bought her a bicycle and that she was riding all over the block on it. How come she had such a dream?"

3. Projection: "Jane was a good girl, but there was one thing she never liked to do. She didn't like to share her toys with the other kids. She always wanted to keep her toys to herself and not let the other kids use them. One day Jane's mother told her that they were going to visit another family where there was another little girl who was Jane's age. Jane and this other little girl could play together. But Jane looked unhappy and said, 'I bet she won't want to share any of her games and toys.' Why did Jane say this when she didn't even know the other little girl?"

4. Regression: "One day Jane didn't feel well. She had a headache and didn't want to eat. She began to act just like her baby brother. She talked baby talk; she wanted to suck her baby brother's milk bottle; and she even wanted to be held in her mother's arms just like a baby. Why did she act this way?"

5. Repression: "One day Jane's mother bought her a new pair of gloves. She warned Jane not to lose the gloves, because Jane had lost the last pair. One afternoon Jane lost her gloves coming back from school. She knew she had to tell her mother. But when she got home, she forgot to tell her. When Jane went out to play

in the afternoon, she told her friends about the lost gloves. But that night she forgot to tell her mother. The next morning at breakfast Jane again forgot to tell her mother. Why did she keep forgetting to tell her mother about the lost gloves?"

6. Rationalization: "One day Jane's mother gave her a big bowl of spinach. Jane said, 'I'm not going to eat the spinach because it makes you very fat!' Why did Jane say that about the spinach when she liked to eat fattening things like ice cream and candy?"

7. Denial: "Jane wanted very much to go to her friend's birthday party. On the day of the party she fell sick and couldn't go. But Jane said, 'I didn't want to go to that party anyway!' Why did Jane say that?"

There was an attempt in each story to focus questions or probes on certain key elements, for example, whether the child grasped the role of the ice cream disappointment in arousing anger in the displacement story, or whether the child saw Jane as really wanting to go to the party in the denial story.

In order to gain some control on memory and language differences, an attempt was made to pose alternatives, to recapitulate part of the stories in the questions, and in some cases to suggest causal possibilities as a kind of testing-of-the-limits procedure.

Each story was coded according to the degree in which the motivation of the child in the story situation was grasped. Thus, in the displacement story, the highest score was given to the children who attributed the spanking of the doll to the ice cream deprivation, who spontaneously or in response to probes cited an appropriate emotional reaction to the ice cream deprivation, that is, being mad or sad, and had some psychological explanation for spanking the doll rather than the mother. A lower score was assigned to sequences which related the ice cream deprivation to the spanking, but offered no psychological reason for spanking the doll rather than the mother. At a lower level, the spanking was conceived as the doll's fault, with no apprehension of the possible causal role of the ice cream incident. Thus, the doll was conceived as bad or dirty or ugly or jumping too much.

Statistical treatment. The feasibility of combining the responses to the various stories into an index was explored. A Motivation Index was constructed by cumulating weights for each of the seven stories. For the entire group, this total index score was then correlated with each of the subscores derived from particular stories. Each of the groups of seven subscores was dichotomized at the median and correlated with the highest and lowest trichotomies of the index. A χ^2 analysis based on correlated proportions was used to evaluate the significance of the differences between age groups for each of the stories. In addition, a three-way analysis of variance was performed on the Motivation Index using the method of unweighted means for unequal cell frequencies as described by Winer (1962).

RESULTS

The individual stories. Table 1 indicates that the stories proved difficult even for the older children. The percentage of older children showing the highest level of understanding (level 4 in Table 1) ranges from 5 per cent for the rationalization story to 38 per cent for the displacement

TABLE 1. DISTRIBUTION OF 21 YOUNGER CHILDREN (AGES 5 AND 6) AND MATCHED OLDER CHILDREN (AGES 8 AND 9) IN RESPONSE CATEGORIES OF PHASE 1 STORIES

Story and Age Group	Level of Understanding					χ^{2a}
	0	1	2	3	4	
Displacement:						
Younger	...	3	15	3	0	
Older	...	0	5	8	8	11.08***
Wishful dreaming:						
Younger	3	10	3	5	0	
Older	0	4	5	8	4	2.77
Projection:						
Younger	4	4	12	1	0	
Older	0	0	9	9	3	9.09**
Regression:						
Younger	6	6	4	5	0	
Older	0	5	12	2	2	4.08*
Repression:						
Younger	...	...	10	10	1	
Older	...	...	6	8	7	.75
Rationalization:						
Younger	2	18	1	0	0	
Older	0	11	8	1	1	4.90*
Denial:						
Younger	...	14	3	4	0	
Older	...	8	3	6	4	2.08

[a]Corrected for discontinuity. Adjacent scoring categories for each story combined to form median dichotomies for the χ^2 analysis.
   * Significant at .05 level.
  ** Significant at .01 level.
 *** Significant at .001 level.

story, with a median of 19 per cent. The repression and displacement stories proved the easiest for the older children, while the rationalization and regression stories proved the most difficult. For the younger children, the highest level could be reached only in the case of the repression story, and this with only one child. With more lenient criteria (success at levels 3 or 4), the percentage of success for the younger children ranged from 48 per cent in the case of the repression story to 0 per cent for the rationalization story, with a median of 10 per cent. Rationalization and projection were the most difficult stories for the younger children while repression, regression, and wishful dreaming proved relatively easier. Most of the older children (71 per cent as compared to 10 per cent of the younger children) were able to show comprehension of Jane's underlying motivation in at least three stories (using the more lenient level 3 or 4 criterion). The application of more rigorous criteria for comprehension, with greater concentration on the spontaneous answers of the child (level 4), disclosed that 76 per cent of the older children were able to reach the highest level on at least one story as compared to 5 per cent of the younger group.

Table 1 also indicates that, when the scores for each story were dichotomized at the median, significant age differences appeared in the case of the displacement, projection, regression, and rationalization stories.

With respect to the displacement story, the older children tended to attribute the spanking to the ice cream deprivation. The younger children tended to attribute the spanking to the intrinsic naughtiness of the doll. In the projection story, some of the older children tended to attribute Jane's statement about the other girl's not sharing to Jane's own behavior. Thus, Jane's remark is seen as a projection of her own disinclination to share. As one child put it: "Just because she don't share her things, she might believe that girl would be as evil as she." More usually, however, Jane's remark was seen as occasioned by the other girl's reaction to Jane's own habit of not sharing. The younger children had difficulty seeing Jane's own nonsharing as the direct or indirect cause of her thinking the other child would not share. The younger children tended to refer more to the other

girl as directly causing Jane's remark, for example: "Jane says the other girl won't share because the girl was strange." In the regression story, the older children more readily perceived the advantages of acting like a baby. The younger children may have mentioned the illness as cause, but had difficulty in seeing the child wanting to be treated as a baby when ill. Finally, in the rationalization story, the younger child was more prone to believe that Jane said she would not eat the spinach because it makes you very fat because Jane actually thought that the spinach made you very fat, that she did not just say it but really believed it. The older child tended to attribute Jane's saying that spinach makes you very fat because she didn't want to eat it.

Item homogeneity. For each of the individual stories, the weighted responses were significantly associated with the cumulative index derived from all the stories. The ϕ coefficients ranged from .41 (for the repression story) to .66 (for the projection story), with a median ϕ of .57.

The Motivation Index. The analysis of variance of the Motivation Index revealed the expected and highly significant age differences. Ninety per cent of the younger children scored below the median score of the older children. The more intelligent children tended to score significantly higher when the dichotomies of those above 100 IQ and those at 100 or below were used. Rhos of .40 and .15 between IQ and Motivation Index were found for the older and younger children, respectively. Neither of these coefficients is significant. However, the analysis of variance revealed a significant interaction between grade and IQ. Thus, IQ differences on the Motivation Index were stronger among the older children than among the younger children. Sex differences on the Motivation Index were not significant, but there was a significant interaction between sex and intelligence. Differences between intelligence levels were more clearly related to the Motivation Index in the case of the boys, with the less intelligent boys scoring lower. However, among the girls, the difference between intelligence levels on the Motivation Index was minimal and in a reversed direction, with the less intelligent girls scoring slightly but not significantly higher.

TABLE 2.   ANALYSIS OF VARIANCE OF MOTIVATION INDEX 1

	SS	df	MS	F	P
Between-subject pairs:					
IQ	60.9892	1	60.99	17.48	<.01
Sex	1.8992	1	1.90	1.90	
IQ and sex	21.6072	1	21.61	6.19	<.05
Subject pairs within groups	59.5400	17	3.49	...	...
Within-subject pairs:					
Age	368.9690	1	368.97	25.62	<.001
Age and IQ	66.1540	1	66.15	4.59	<.05
Age and sex	1.0723	1	1.07	<1	...
Age and IQ and sex	.5247	1	.52	<1	...
Age and subject pair within groups	244.8375	17	14.40	...	...

Phase 2

METHOD

Subjects. The phase 2 subjects comprised seventy children—36 kindergarten children and 34 third graders. As in phase 1, the younger children were in the 5–6-year range, the older in the 8–9-year span, and all children were Negro or Puerto Rican. Two kindergarten classes were used, both taught by the same teacher. Of the 47 kindergarten children interviewed, the records of 11 children were not used either because of difficulty in comprehending their answers or, more frequently, because they simply replied "don't know" to most of the questions on the psychological causality interview. The 34 third-grade children were randomly selected from the entire third-grade roster of this particular school. The IQ data based on group tests were available for 27 of the 34 third graders. The mean IQ was 97, with a range from 75 to 133. For the kindergarten group, Stanford-Binet IQ data were available, but only for 24 out of the 36 children. However, these IQ's were based on a random sample of children from the two kindergarten classes. For the kindergarten group, the mean IQ was 94, with a range from 71 to 116. Forty-two per cent and 53 per cent of the kindergarten and third graders, respectively, were male. In order to replicate an analysis performed on 21 matched pairs in phase 1 (see Table 2), twenty pairs of kindergarten and third-grade children matched in IQ were selected. The mean IQ of the twenty phase 2 kindergarten and twenty matched third graders was 93.

Procedure. Six of the seven stories used in phase 1 were administered to the two groups. The repression story was omitted in order to shorten the administration time. In addition, the projection story was revised so as to impress upon the respondent that Jane did not know the other child. However, the paramount change in phase 2 was the use of a standardized interview with standardized probes and a standard sequence of probes. The standardized probes were explicit wordings of questions to be asked the child. The sequence of such probes was also specified for the interviewers. Directions were given to the interviewers about when to probe for a new element of the concept in question and when to stay with the same point, altering the question in order to see whether the child could succeed with more information. The stories were administered in a randomized order.

In contrast to phase 1, the interviews were not conducted by the writer but by four graduate students of the Columbia University School of Social Work. A number of sessions were devoted to a discussion of the specific rationales of the study, of underlying theoretical issues, and of methodological problems in interviewing young children. Pilot interviewing was conducted by three of the students at a neighboring day-care center, after which further discussion was held regarding ambiguities or difficulties arising in the interviewing situation.

Scoring categories were devised, both for the initial responses to the story and the responses to questions by the interviewer. As in phase 1, there was an attempt to arrange the categories in each story hierarchically, with the higher-numbered categories including more of the elements of the concept studied. The scoring system involved categorizing the children for each story at three levels. Level 3 was assigned to children whose responses at any point in the interview included all of the elements of the concept for any particular story, whether or not the grasp of the concept was maintained or lost following further questioning. Level 2 included children whose responses at any point showed comprehension of some but not all elements of the concept, while level 1 was assigned to children whose responses at no point showed an understanding of any of the key elements of the explanatory concept.

In addition to the questionnaire on psychological causality, a series of questions dealing with physical causality was also posed. These questions dealt with the attribution of life to various objects and were designed to reveal animistic tendencies in the child. The questionnaire was originally constructed by Laurendeau and Pinard (1962) in their replication of Piaget's work on physical causality. The child was asked whether each of 21 objects was alive. In the present study, the score of this Animism Scale was the number of correct responses given by child. The reliability of this measure for the combined group was .84, as assessed by the Kuder-Richardson Formula 20 (Gulliksen, 1950, pp. 220–227).

RESULTS AND DISCUSSION

The individual stories. The stories were scored independently by two sets of raters. For the coding of the elements of each story based on the initial response of 36 children, the percentage of agreement was 96 per cent. The percentage of agreement ranged from 89 per cent for the denial story to 100 per cent for the dream wishing story. For the coding of the elements of each story based on both initial and probed-for responses of 28 chil-

dren, the overall percentage of agreement was 85 per cent, with a range from 75 per cent for rationalization to 93 per cent for the wishful dreaming story. Table 3 reveals that the older children consistently scored higher than the younger group, with five of the six items significant at least on the .01 level. The failure of the rationalization story to yield significant differences between the two graders may be due to the relatively low interrater reliability of coding for this item. From the point of view of age differentiation, the new interview procedure seems at least as effective as the one reported on in phase 1. However, the increment in significant age differentiation on the part of the stories may be at least partly due to the increased sample size in phase 2. The displacement, projection, and regression stories which were significant differentiators between age levels in phase 1 also show significant differentiation in phase 2. Additionally, the denial and wishful dreaming stories which did not yield significant differences in phase 1 do so in phase 2.

Item homogeneity. The ϕ coefficients, representing the associations between particular item scores and the composite score derived from all six items, were all significant and ranged from a high of .89 in the case of the projection story to .35 for rationalization. The median ϕ was .45 as contrasted with a median ϕ of .57 derived from the item analysis of stories in phase 1. The writer has been unable to find a test of significance of difference between ϕ coefficients. However, it is doubtful whether the difference between the two ϕ cofficients is significant with these sample sizes.

The reliability of Motivation Index 2, as assessed by the Kuder-Richardson Formula 20, was .68 as compared with the comparable coefficient of .76 derived from the phase 1 sample. Again, it is quite likely that this discrepancy is attributable to sampling error rather than to real differences between the two indexes. The reliability of the Motivation Indexes was attenuated when computed within grade because of restriction in range. Although there is a drop in the reliability within age groups as compared to the total group, the error of measurement which is relatively independent of heterogeneity of talent remains at a moderately consistent level as we move from total group to younger and to older age groups for each of the

TABLE 3. PERCENTAGES OF 36 YOUNGER CHILDREN (AGES 5 AND 6) AND 34 OLDER CHILDREN (AGES 8 AND 9) IN RESPONSE CATEGORIES OF PHASE 2 STORIES

Story and Age Group	Level of Understanding[a]			χ^2
	1	2	3	
Displacement:				
Younger	31	69	0	7.52*
Older	3	79	18	df = 1
Wishful dreaming:				
Younger	30	61	9	17.83**
Older	3	50	47	df = 2
Projection:				
Younger	78	8	14	25.41**
Older	15	15	70	df = 1
Regression:				
Younger	25	67	8	10.59*
Older	12	47	41	df = 2
Rationalization:				
Younger	36	64	0	.75
Older	26	65	9	df = 1
Denial:				
Younger	50	42	8	13.70**
Older	24	29	47	df = 2

[a]For displacement, projection, and rationalization, scoring categories 2 and 3 were combined in the χ^2 analysis, with correction for discontinuity.
   * Significant at the .01 level.
  ** Significant at the .001 level.

Motivation Indexes. This indicates a fairly consistent pattern of measurement reliability for the Motivation Indexes as groups of children within the 5–8-year-old range are being compared. It also suggests, however, that increased reliability may be required for differentiation among individuals within age-grades as compared to the differentiation of individuals between age-grades.

Focusing on the most significant results in both phases, we find that the items most sharply differentiating between the two ages (significant at the .001 level) are displacement (from phase 1), and wishful dreaming, projection, and denial (from phase 2). The projection story is the only one which is significant, at least at the .01 level, in both phases and at the same time shows the highest correlation with the Motivation Index in each sample.

The special difficulty of the projection story for the younger children may be traceable to the confluence of two factors. First, the story involves the difficult perception of incongruence between overt behavior and inner intent; Jane says that Mary will not share where her intent is really the reverse—she does not want to share with Mary. Second, the projection story also demands a difficult shift from a given locus of effect (Mary's not sharing) to a new causal locus (Jane's own nonsharing). A similar factor appears in the displacement story where the younger child finds it more difficult to assume a cause (the mother and her behavior) which is distal to behavior located elsewhere (child spanking doll).

Motivation Index 2: Table 4 reveals that the age differences on Motivation Index 2 were highly significant. As anticipated, the older children scored considerably higher than the younger. Ninety-four per cent of the kindergarten group fell below the median score of the third graders, which parallels the comparable figure of 90 per cent found with Motivation Index 1. However, this and a separate analysis of variance (not shown) failed to reveal significant IQ differences, nor IQ interactions with age and sex—contrary to the results of phase 1. The younger children were significantly more animistic than the older ones. Twice as many kindergarten children as third graders fell into a high animism group ($P < .01$). The above analyses suggest that conceptions of psychological causality (as assessed by Motivation Index 2) and of physical causality (as assessed by the Animism Scale) both develop with age. However, the limited relation between the two measures points to independence in the rate and timing of their respective development within the individual child.

The relation between age and conceptions of psychological causality appears stronger than the relation between age and conceptions of physical causality (see Table 5). Thus when one selects children who are relatively homogeneous with respect to the Motivation Index, the relation between age and the Animism Scale is not statistically significant. However, when the selection is of children who are relatively homogeneous on animism score, the relation between age and Motivation Index is still highly significant. Simi-larly, a comparison of the five kindergarten children and eight third graders with comparable MA's (about 7 years) revealed that the younger children averaged about four points *below* the older on the Motivation Index but about four points *above* the older on the Animism Scale. This suggests the importance of chronological rather than mental age in the development of conceptions of psychological causality.

SOME CONCLUDING POINTS

The relative difficulty of the younger child in (*a*) differentiating between observed locus of effect and inferred locus of cause and (*b*) de-centering from a focus on overt behavior to a more covert intent would not be inconsistent with Piaget's distinction between the "intuitive" child (ages 4–7) and the "concrete operational" child (ages 7–11). It would, therefore, be worthwhile to explore the Motivation Index scores of children who have and have not attained conservation of substance, for example, since the latter is a criterion for the concrete operation stage. However, the operation of more specific experiential factors is suggested by the differential ease of the items within age groups, the lack of strong or consistent correlations of the Motivation Indexes with IQ, the importance of chronological age over and above mental age differences, the relative independence of the Motivation Indexes from the Animism Scale, and the sex differences on Motivation Index 1. It is also possible that age differences in psychological causality may take a different form within groups of higher socio-economic standing where the child's linguistic

TABLE 4.   ANALYSIS OF VARIANCE OF MOTIVATION INDEX 2 AS RELATED TO IQ AND AGE

	SS	df	MS	F	P
IQ	10.00	1	10.00	2.86	...
Error	63.00	18	3.50	...	...
Age	129.60	1	129.60	26.56	<.001
Age X IQ	3.60	1	3.60	<1	...
Error	87.80	18	4.89	...	...

TABLE 5.   RELATIONS BETWEEN AGE AND (a) ANIMISM SCALE, WITH
MOTIVATION INDEX 2 CONTROLLED; (b) MOTIVATION
INDEX 2, WITH ANIMISM SCALE CONTROLLED

| | AGE GROUP | | | | | |
| | 5 and 6 years | | 8 and 9 years | | | |
	N	%	N	%	χ^2	P
Animism Scale[a]:						
Higher	9	64	8	35		
					1.98	>.05
Lower	5	36	15	65		
Motivation Index 2[b]:						
Higher	0	0	14	82		
					14.97	<.001
Lower	11	100	3	18		

[a]Higher and lower levels, defined by score ranges on the Animism
Scale of 5-12 and 13-21, respectively. The 37 subjects are all
within the 11-14 range on the Motivation Index 2.

[b]Higher and lower levels defined by score ranges on the Motivation
Index of 13-16 and 7-12, respectively. The 28 subjects are all
within the 16-19 range on the Animism Scale.

experiences and explanatory encounters with
adults are differently patterned.

Behavioral correlates need exploration. Certain
patternings of responses to the stories may be related to particular behavioral patterns. Thus,
ease in grasping projection stories, where blame
is externalized, may be related to acting-out behavior. The Motivation Index might be correlated
with measures of ability to shift role, to understand the other's viewpoint, and with avoidance
of what Piaget (1932) has conceptualized as objective morality. One would expect the growth
of understanding of psychological causality to
parallel the growth of moral judgments based on
the other's underlying intentions, rather than on
his overt behaviors.

REFERENCES

FLAVELL, J. The developmental psychology of Jean
Piaget. Princeton, N.J.: Van Nostrand, 1963.

FREUD, ANNA. The ego and the mechanisms of de-
fence. New York: International Universities Press,
1946.

GULLIKSEN, H. Theory of mental tests. New York:
Wiley, 1950.

HILGARD, E. Human motives and the concept of the
self, American Psychologist, 1949, 4, 374–382.

LAURENDEAU, MONIQUE, & PINARD, A. Causal thinking
in the child. New York: International Universities
Press, 1962.

PIAGET, J. The child's conception of the world. New
York: Harcourt, Brace, 1929.

PIAGET, J. The child's conception of physical causality. London: Kegan Paul, 1930.

PIAGET, J. The moral judgment of the child. London: Kegan Paul, 1932.

PIAGET, J. The psychology of intelligence. New
York: Harcourt, Brace, 1950.

WINER, B. J. Statistical principles in experimental
design. New York: McGraw-Hill, 1962.

Acquisition of Conservation through Social Interaction

Frank B. Murray

That so many reasonable attempts to train nonconservers in conservation have been surprising failures raises the question of how children normally acquire conserved concepts. In the *Language and Thought of the Child*, Piaget suggested originally that a necessary condition for the movement from the stage of preoperational or egocentric thought to more mature stages of thought was the occurrence of repeated communication conflicts between children. These conflicts would require the young child to attend to another child's point of view and perspective, and the ability to maintain a perspective of another or to take another's role appears to be related to operational modes of thought (Flavell, 1967) and

The assistance of Anne Matthews at the University of Minnesota and Virginia Flynn at the University of Delaware and the cooperation of the children and staff at the Bloomington Elementary School and the St. Mary Magdalan Elementary School is greatly appreciated.

Requests for reprints should be sent to the author, College of Education, Willard Hall Education Building, University of Delaware, Newark, Delaware 19711.

to the opportunities for social interaction (Neale, 1966). Since nonconservation is the salient mode of preoperational thought, one would expect that an effective conservation training procedure would be one in which the child was confronted with opposing points of view. This expectation was investigated in an experiment and a replication experiment in which the child's point of view was brought into conflict with other children's points of view. Specifically it was expected that the young child's ability to give conservation judgments, and to support those judgments with adequate reasons, would improve after he had been subjected to the contrary arguments and viewpoints of other children.

Method

SUBJECTS

In Experiment I, there were 57 white children, 28 boys and 29 girls, whose mean age was 6.70

years ($SD = .72$ years) from kindergarten and first grades of a suburban Minneapolis elementary school. In Experiment II, there were 51 white children, 28 boys and 23 girls, with a mean age of 6.74 ($SD = .31$ years) from the first grade of a suburban parochial elementary school in Wilmington, Delaware. The data were collected by female experimenters in a vacant classroom in the child's school during the months of November and December.

PROCEDURE

In the first of three sessions of both experiments, all subjects were given Form A of the Concept Assessment Kit (Goldschmid & Bentler, 1968), which provided a standardized and individual testing procedure for six conservation problems (two-dimensional space, number, substance, continuous quantity, weight, and discontinuous quantity). Two points were given for each correct problem, one point for a correct judgment and one point for an explanation that noted reversibility, compensation, or invariant quantity. In Experiments I and II, one nonconserver (subjects with scores from 0–4 on Form A) was grouped with two conservers (subjects with scores from 10–12 on Form A).

In a second session of both experiments, each group of three subjects was given the same problems from Form A of the Concept Assessment Kit. In each group, subjects were told that they could not receive a score until all of them agreed on the answer to each problem. Subjects were given 5 minutes to solve each problem. The experimenter started with the lowest scorers on Form A, and asked each child in a group to answer a problem, and when there was disagreement between children, they were directed to discuss the problem, and explain to each other why they had said what they had. Subjects were allowed to manipulate the conservation stimuli, but the experimenter gave no information or reinforcement for correct or incorrect answers.

One week later in the critical third session each subject was tested alone, as in the first session. Conservation problems from Form B, Form C, and lastly Form A of the Concept Assessment Kit were presented. Form B consisted of parallel problems on the same six concepts as Form A, but

different conservation stimuli or different conservation transformations were used. Form C tested the conservation of two new concepts, length and area, with three area and three length conservation problems. As on Form A, each problem on Forms B and C, was scored one point for the correct judgment and a second point for the appropriate explanation of that judgment. Thus the maximum score on any form was 12.

Results

Scores between 0 and 6 were taken to indicate nonconservation on that form, and scores between 7 and 12 were taken to indicate conservation. This somewhat arbitrary division preserved all the data and required that all children labeled as conservers give at least one acceptable reason for their conservation judgments. Since less than 9% of the children earned scores of 5, 6, 7, or 8 on any form, the dichotomy and labeling of the subjects was not inappropriate. The effect of the conflict situation on the nonconservers was evident in both experiments from the significant numbers of nonconservers on Pretest Form A who conserved on Posttest Form A, Posttest Form B, and Posttest Form C. In both experiments, the shifts from nonconservation to conservation were all significant at the .001 level by the McNemar test between Pretest Form A and Posttest Form A, between Pretest Form A and Posttest Form B and between Pretest Form A and Posttest Form C (Table 1).

The effects of the conflict situation upon the nonconservers was also evident in both experiments in the comparison of their mean scores on the pretest with those on the posttests, which are presented in Table 2. The difference between the mean score of these subjects on Pretest Form A and the mean scores of subjects on Posttests Forms A, B, and C were all significant at the .001 level by the t test (Experiment I, $t = 14.79$, $t = 11.57$, and $t = 7.99$, respectively; Experiment II, $t = 6.74$, $t = 7.32$, and $t = 7.51$, respectively).

Of special interest are 11 firm nonconservers in Experiment II who had scores of zero on Pretest Form A. Their mean scores on Posttests Form A, Form B, and Form C are presented in Table 2, and by the t test these differences be-

TABLE 1

Numbers of Conservers (Cs) and Nonconservers (NCs) Who Shifted or Were Consistent in Experiments I and II between Pretest Form A and Posttests Forms A, B, and C, and the Chi-Square for Each Comparison

Pretest	Posttest					
	Form A		Form B		Form C	
Form A	Cs	NCs	Cs	NCs	Cs	NCs
Exp. I ($N = 57$)						
Cs	40	0	40	0	38	2
NCs	16	1	15	2	14	3
x^2	14.06**		13.06**		7.56*	
Exp. II ($N = 51$)						
Cs	25	0	25	0	24	1
Ns	18	8	19	7	21	5
x^2	16.06**		17.05**		16.40**	

* $p < .01$.
** $p < .001$.

tween the pretest mean and posttest means were significant at the .01 level. The remaining 15 nonconservers in Experiment II (scores between 1 and 6) had a mean score of 2.80 on Pretest Form A. The mean scores of these subjects on Posttest Forms A, B, and C are also presented in Table 2, and the differences between the pretest mean and posttest means were all significant at the .001 level by the t test ($t = 7.11$, $t = 6.98$, and $t = 11.09$, respectively). Gains in conservation from pretest to posttest were compared for those subjects ($N = 11$) who had exhibited no conservation on the pretest and those ($N = 15$) who had exhibited some conservation on it. None of the contrasts was significant (Form A, $t = .54$, $p > .05$; Form B, $t = .24$, $p > .05$; Form C, $t = .89$, $p > .05$).

Another indicator of the effect of the conflict situation upon children's ability to conserve was found in the comparison of their performance on the pretest and posttests with the performance of an appropriate control group on Forms A, B, and C. Since the norms for the standardized sample are separated by sex for the Concept Assessment Kit, the appropriate boy and girl mean scores from the norms are presented in Table 3 for Forms A, B, and C along with the boy and

TABLE 2

Mean Scores and Standard Deviations for Pretest A and Posttests A, B, and C for Conservers (Cs) and Nonconservers (NCs) on Pretest A in Experiments I and II, and for Nonconservers Who Scored Zero or More Than Zero on Pretest A in Experiment II

Experiment	Test							
	Pretest A		Posttest A		Posttest B		Posttest C	
	M	SD	M	SD	M	SD	M	SD
Exp. I								
Cs	10.77	1.3	11.90*	.4	11.55*	.8	11.40	1.9
NCs	2.35	1.9	11.41*	1.4	10.18*	1.9	8.82*	2.6
Exp. II								
Cs	10.37	1.8	11.91*	.4	11.87*	.4	11.08	1.9
NCs	1.61	1.8	8.08*	4.4	8.38*	4.2	8.19*	3.9
NCs who scored 0	.00	.0	6.00*	4.9	7.09*	5.1	5.73*	4.7
NCs who did not score 0	2.80	1.6	9.60*	3.2	9.33*	3.1	10.00*	1.8

* Compared to Pretest A, $p < .01$.

TABLE 3

COMPARISON OF MEAN SCORES OF EXPERIMENTAL SUBJECTS ON PRETEST A AND POSTTESTS A, B, AND C WITH
MEAN SCORES OF STANDARDIZED SAMPLE ON FORMS A, B, AND C

Group	Test							
	Pretest Form A		Posttest Form A		Posttest Form B		Posttest Form C	
	Girls	Boys	Girls	Boys	Girls	Boys	Girls	Boys
Standarized	7.15*	5.15*	7.15**	5.15**	7.37**	7.64**	6.82**	5.03**
Experimental	7.72*	6.77*	10.52**	11.25**	10.48**	10.66**	10.38**	10.03**

* $p > .05$.
** $p < .01$.

girl mean scores from the experimental subjects for Pretest Form A and Posttests Forms A, B, and C. As they should be, the differences between the norm mean scores on Form A and experimental mean scores on Pretest Form A were insignificant by the t test (girls, $t = .48$, $p > .05$; boys, $t = .97$, $p > .05$). However, all other differences between the norm mean scores on Forms A, B, and C and experimental mean scores on Posttests Form A, B, and C were significant at the .01 level (Form A: girls, $t = 3.06$, $p < .01$; boys, $t = 5.00$, $p < .01$; Form B: girls, $t = 2.66$, $p < .01$; boys, $t = 2.29$, $p < .01$; Form C: girls, $t = 4.24$, $p < .001$; boys, $t = 6.02$, $p < .001$).

Not only did the social conflict situation influence the nonconservers' performance on the posttests, it influenced as well the performance of the conservers. The mean scores of the conservers in both experiments on Pretest Form A and Posttests Forms A, Form B, and Form C are presented in Table 2. The differences between these mean scores were significant between Pretest Form A and Posttest Form A, between Pretest Form A and Posttest Form B, but not between Pretest Form A and Posttest Form C (Experiment I: $t = 5.17$, $p < .001$; $t = 3.15$, $p < .01$; $t = 1.70$, $p > .05$, respectively; Experiment II: $t = 3.99$, $p < .001$; $t = 3.88$, $p < .001$; $t = 1.29$ $p > .05$, respectively).

In Experiment II, some of the first graders had attended kindergarten where it might be expected that the opportunities for social interaction and conflict would be greater than it would be for those children who had not attended kindergarten. This expectation was not supported by any significant difference in mean performance on Pretest Form A between those who had (6.06) and those who had not (5.81) attended kindergarten ($t = .18$, $p > .05$).

In both experiments there were no significant differences in the proportions of conservers and nonconservers on Pretest Form A between boys and girls (Experiment I, $\chi^2 = .53$, $p > .25$; Experiment II, $\chi^2 = .49$, $p > .25$). However there were the usual differences in these proportions between older and younger children in Experiment I, but not in Experiment II. In Experiment I, there were significantly fewer conservers and more nonconservers in the group below 6.66 years (median age) than in the group above it ($\chi^2 = 6.06$, $p < .02$); in Experiment II, there were insignificant differences in these proportions between the group above and below the sample's median age of 6.50 years ($\chi^2 = .94$, $p > .25$).

Although the principal findings of Experiment I were replicated in Experiment II, there were significant differences in the proportions of conservers and nonconservers in Experiment I and conservers and nonconservers in Experiment II on Pretest A ($\chi^2 = 4.18$, $p < .05$). The mean score for subjects in Experiment I was 8.16 and the mean score for subjects in Experiment II was 5.85 on Pretest Form A, and the difference in these means was significant ($t = 2.67$, $p < .02$).

Discussion

The issue of whether or not conservation development can be accelerated is complicated in the research literature by theoretical doubts of its possibility, conflicting empirical results, and ambiguity in the criterion of conservation. Theoretically, conservation is taken to be one of many symptoms of concrete operational thought, and in a sense the manipulation of responses which indicate conservation is as trivial as any exercise that manipulates the symptom and not the disease. Although the acceleration of conservation responses without an attending presence of other aspects of operational thought may be an empty accomplishment in developmental theory, it is not one in education. The conservation response, regardless of its theoretical status, is an important behavior in itself for educational psychology. Procedures, like the present social conflict procedure, that induce or facilitate conservation behavior, and also have classroom applications constitute an important part of the psychology of curriculum and instruction.

The data indicate that social conflict or interaction is an important mediator of cognitive growth. Virtually all the children made significant gains in conservation performance after the social conflict situation. Since there were no significant differences in conservation performance between the children in the standardized sample and the children in both experiments on Pretest A, the standardized sample can serve as a control group. Performance on Posttests A, B, C was significantly higher than that of the standardized children on these tests, and indicates that the training effect cannot be attributed to retesting or maturation effects, although the effect may have been due to modeling and not the communication interaction (Waghorn & Sullivan, 1970), or to the efficacy of Lancastrian or peer instruction (Rothenberg & Orost, 1969). In general, conservation training studies have been most successful with nonconservers who were close to the threshold of conservation. However, there were no significant differences in the gains in conservation between those nonconservers who exhibited no conservation on the pretest and those who exhibited some conservation on the pretest. In fact, of 15 children from Experiments I and II who scored 0 on the pretest, 8 had scores of 11 or 12 on the posttests. It should be noted that these gains include the more demanding conservation criterion of an appropriate explanation for the conservation judgment. It should also be noted that there was considerable transfer to different forms of the same concepts and to different concepts.

Brison (1966) was able to induce some form of conservation in one-half of a group of nonconservers with a combination social training procedure and conflict-reversibility instruction. Since there was no deliberate instruction in the present experiments, the data emphasize the effectiveness of social interaction even in the absence of any systematic instructional effort. It was the case that the children often resorted to reversibility explanations to persuade their lagging colleagues, and that in the social situations nonconservers acquiesced and generally gave conservation responses after the third problem ($M = 2.76$) on Form A and generally (80%) did not give a nonconserving response after they had once given a conserving one.

It is not clear what the nonconservers learned in the social situation that sustained them in the individual situation. It probably was not a set to say, "the same," since all forms contained items in which the stimuli were unequal before the conservation transformation. The reversibility explanation for the conservation judgment, although strictly speaking incorrect (Murray & Johnson, 1969), and the invariant quantity explanation ("You did not add or subtract anything"; "they were the same before, and you didn't change the weight, etc.") could be used as rules that would lead to the correct response on all forms if the child had grasped the initial relationship (equal or unequal) between the stimuli before they were transformed. If these rules or algorithms were acquired, and the children's reasons indicate that in some sense they were, they would account for the very high level of performance on the transfer tasks, Forms B and C.

Smedslund (1966) in a review of the research on the many conditions that have been found to be inconsistently related to the acquisition of operational thought concluded that "the occurrence of communication conflicts is a necessary condition for intellectual decentration" and recommended that the key interaction needed for the growth of intelligence was not so much between the individual and the physical environment as it was between the individual and those about him. The present data support his hypothesis and emphasize, as Piaget has (Sigel, 1969), the educational role of social interaction in the transition from egocentrism to operational thought.

REFERENCES

BRISON, D. W.   Acceleration of conservation of substance. *Journal of Genetic Psychology,* 1966, **109**, 311–322.

FLAVELL, J.   Role-taking and communication skills in children. In W. Hartup & N. Smothergill (Eds.), *The young child.* Washington, D. C.: National Association for the Education of Young Children, 1967.

GOLDSCHMID, M., & BENTLER, P.   *Concept assessment kit-conservation manual.* San Diego: Educational and Industrial Testing Service, 1968.

MURRAY, F. B., & JOHNSON, P. E.   Reversibility in the nonconservation of weight. *Psychonomic Science,* 1969, **16**, 285–287.

NEALE, J. M.   Egocentrism in institutionalized and non-institutionalized children. *Child Development,* 1966, **37**, 91–101.

ROTHENBERG, B.B., & OROST, J. H.   The training of conservation of number in young children. *Child Development,* 1969, **40**, 707–726.

SIGEL, I. E.   The Piagetian system and the world of education. In D. Elkind & J. H. Flavell (Eds.), *Studies in cognitive development. Essays in honor of Jean Piaget.* New York: Oxford University Press, 1969.

SMEDSLUND, J.   Les origines sociales de la centration. In F. Bresson & M. de Montmalin (Eds.), *Psychologie et épistémologie génétiques.* Paris: Dunod, 1966.

WAGHORN, L., & SULLIVAN, E.   The exploration of transition rules in conservation of quantity (substance) using film mediated modeling. *Acta Psychologica,* 1970, **32**, 65–80.

Dimensions of Early Stimulation and Their Differential Effects on Infant Development

Judith L. Rubenstein   Leon J. Yarrow

Frank A. Pedersen   Joseph J. Jankowski

To some extent experimental studies have confirmed the general premise that marked trauma and extreme deprivation can have significant effects. The impact of less extreme variations in experiences, experiences within the "normal" range, is much less clear. This is due in part to a lack of differentiation of environments, and to our difficulties in describing and measuring with any degree of precision the dimensions of natural environments. In this study we have looked at a range of variation in experiences of five- to six-month-old infants on a concrete behavioral level, and have conceptualized these discrete behaviors.

Our major objectives in this study were (a) to differentiate the natural environment in conceptually meaningful terms through detailed analysis of caretaker's behavior and properties of the proximal inanimate stimuli in the infant's environment; (b) to determine whether inanimate stimulation on the one hand, and social stimulation on the other, are related to different facets of the infant's development; and (3) to determine the extent to which separate dimensions or components of these variables (e.g., variety, complexity, and responsiveness of inanimate stimuli; level and variety of social stimulation; and the expression of positive affect) have different orders of relationships to the development of early infant functions.

This study represents a convergence of applied and theoretical interests. We were especially interested in assessing the impact on development of so-called "disadvantaged" environments in early infancy. Limited observational data are available on mother-infant interaction in disadvantaged groups. Moreover, we thought environmental effects might be highlighted in these settings. Our

This paper is a condensation of four papers presented at a symposium at the biennial meeting of the Society for Research in Child Development, April 4, 1971, Minneapolis, Minnesota.

We are indebted to Mrs. Myrna Fivel and Miss Joan Durfee for their assistance in the development of the observation scale and their dedicated work in the collection of data; and to Mr. Richard Cain for his arduous labor on the data analyses.

Judith Rubenstein, Leon Yarrow, Frank Pedersen and Joseph Jankowski, "Dimensions of Early Stimulation and Their Differential Effects on Infant Development," *Merrill Palmer Quarterly of Behavior and Development,* *18,* 1972, pp. 205–218. Reprinted by permission of the Merrill Palmer Institute.

sample, however, represents a wide continuum on environmental variables. Therefore, the implications of this research go beyond disadvantaged or depriving environments; the findings have relevance for understanding a broad range of environmental influences on development.

Method

The sample consisted of 41 black infants, 21 boys and 20 girls, who had been cared for by a stable "primary caretaker." The mother was the primary caretaker in 30 cases, a relative (usually the maternal grandmother) in 6 cases, and an unrelated babysitter in 5 cases. Of this group, 34 were recruited through two public well-baby clinics. Their fathers had completed from 6 to 12 years of school, with a mean of 10.9 years. They were engaged in primarily semi-skilled and unskilled occupations. To extend the range on the environmental variables, 7 black infants were obtained through a private group medical program. These families were all intact, and the fathers' education ranged from one year of college through graduate school; the mean educational level was 14.6 years. All infants were of normal birth weight, were free from gross complications in pregnancy or delivery, and were screened by a pediatrician to eliminate cases in which there were any indications of neurological damage.

The basic data were obtained through time-sampling observations in the home when the infants were five months of age.[1] The mother or baby's caretaker was encouraged to go about her usual activities. Two home observations about a week apart were conducted; each involved three hours of time-sampling while the baby was awake. The time-sampling cycle consisted of a 30 second observation period and a 60 second recording period repeated through 120 cycles each day. There are a total of 240 time-sample units, or six hours, for each child and caretaker.

Approximately 60 categories of events were monitored in each interval. Selected infant behaviors observed included positive vocalizations, fussing or irritable vocalizations, and whether the infant was engaging in focused manipulation of

play objects or directing his visual attention to the mother. Approximately 45 categories of caretaker behavior were recorded describing aspects of social stimulation. There were in addition several time-sample measures of the proximal inanimate environment. The categories of social stimulation can be classified in the following areas: (a) *Sensory modality* of social stimulation (e.g., visual, auditory, tactile, and kinesthetic stimulation, as exemplified by looking at, talking to, and holding the baby); (b) The *intensity* or rate of stimulus change (for example, passive holding is distinguished from active touching or moving the baby); (c) Whether stimulation is *contingent* on certain infant behaviors (for example, social soothing in response to distress states, contingent vocal response to the infant's positive vocalizations); and (d) The *type* or class of behavior the caretaker is attempting to evoke (for example, the attainment of motor skills such as postural control or locomotion, or fostering interest in play materials by highlighting the properties of toys or positioning them for the baby). In addition, ratings were made of the caretaker's expression of positive affect toward the infant, and contingency of response to distress.

To measure perceptual-sensory stimulation from the proximal inanimate environment, the observers recorded all play materials and household objects within reach of the infant during each time-sampling interval. At a later time similar objects were obtained and rated in terms of their complexity and responsiveness.

Three young women served as observers; one with a doctorate in developmental psychology; one with an M.A. degree; and one with a B.A. degree. Observer reliability was established on 20 cases before data collection was initiated. The correlations ranged from .96 to .99 on the time-sampling variables, and from .72 to .91 on the ratings.

ENVIRONMENTAL VARIABLES

Our basic strategy in choosing variables for differentiated analysis of the natural environment was to order the infant's experiences in terms of a conceptual framework. The selection of the parameters of the environment was guided by concepts from several theoretical orientations, such as, information theory, adaptation level

---

[1] The manual describing the observation categories is available from the authors.

theory, operant learning theory, and Piagetian developmental theory.

The inanimate environment was analyzed in terms of three major dimensions: variety, responsiveness, and complexity. Although the deprivation literature has particularly emphasized quantity of sensory or social stimulation, theoretical thinking and some experimental studies in recent years have pointed to the crudeness of sheer amount of stimulation. Several theoretical positions, especially information theory, have emphasized the importance of variety. Variety in this study was measured in terms of the number of different objects within reach of the infant during the six hours of observation. The interobserver reliability was .99.

Our second dimension, responsiveness, an index of the feedback potential inherent in objects, derives from several theoretical sources. In a loose sense it is related to the contingency concept in operant learning theory; it is also related to Hunt's (1965) thinking about intrinsic motivation. The basic hypothesis is that an object that changes in response to some action on the part of the infant may affect the infant's rudimentary sense of mastery, the conviction that he can have an effective impact on the environment. This variable was measured in terms of the extent to which objects change in visual, auditory, and tactile properties as a result of the infant's behavior. There are four subscales: moving parts, change in shape and contour, reflected image, and noise production. The subscale scores for each toy were added; a subject's score was the average for all his toys. Interrater reliability on this measure was .90.

The third dimension of the inanimate environment, complexity, derives its meaning from information theory, particularly Berlyne's (1960) theoretical formulations. Theories regarding complexity emphasize a golden mean, that is, an optimal degree of complexity based on the organism's capacity to assimilate the information provided. Complexity represents the extent to which objects provide information through various modalities. Criteria of complexity include number of colors, number of different shapes and variation in contour, the amount of visual and tactile pattern, and the degree of responsiveness of the object. A subject's score is the average for his toys (interrater reliability .83).

Theories regarding the influence of social stimulation are more diverse, more wide-ranging, and less explicit than theories about the inanimate environment. In this study, the social environment was observed at the level of discrete behaviors of the mother, for example, talking to the infant, smiling, touching him, moving him, etc. These behaviors formed the basis for higher order categories similar to some of the dimensions of the inanimate environment, such as level of social stimulation and variety of social stimulation. Other dimensions like contingency of maternal response and expression of positive affect were more distinctive to the human environment.

Level of social stimulation was a composite of the amount and intensity of stimulation by the caretaker. We obtained through time-sampling the frequency with which the mother was within view or within reach of the infant; and the frequency with which she talked to the infant, touched or held him, or engaged him in vigorous play. These discrete behaviors were weighted on a five-point scale so that vigorous play involving intense stimulation and several modalities received a higher score than stimulation of low intensity in one modality, such as touching the baby (composite reliability.99).

Variety of social stimulation is an unweighted sum of different types of social stimulation. Examples of these are play, encouraging motor responses, presentation of play objects, the range of affect which the caretaker exhibited, and the number of different physical settings in which stimulation occurred (composite reliability .95).

Two indices of contingency were used: (a) frequency of contingent responses to positive vocalizations by the infant obtained through time-sampling (interobserver reliability .96); and (b) contingency of response to distress, a five-point rating scale based on latency of response to the infant's distress signals (interrater reliability .91). These variables are derived from operant learning theory (Gewirtz, 1969), and other formulations (Ainsworth, 1967; Lewis & Goldberg, 1968) emphasizing the importance of early intervention in distress states.

The variable, expression of positive affect, was based on ratings by the observers following the time-sampling observations. It is a measure of the characteristic level of demonstrativeness of the mother or caretaker (interrater reliability .72).

THE INFANT VARIABLES

The dependent variables were derived from two procedures, a research from the Bayley Scales of Infant Development (administered in the fifth month) and a structured situational test measuring exploratory behavior and preference for novel stimuli (administered in the sixth month). In addition to the Mental Developmental Index and Psychomotor Developmental Index which the Bayley yields, eight more differentiated clusters were developed. Items were grouped on the basis of their apparent conceptual coherence. Split-half and part-whole analyses provided a statistical basis for further refinement. The final split-half reliabilities ranged from .74 to .92. The clusters include: *Social Responsiveness, Language, Fine Motor, Gross Motor*, and four measures that we considered indices of cognitive-motivational functions—*Goal Orientation, Reaching and Grasping, Secondary Circular Reaction*, and *Object Permanence*. Another cluster, *Problem Solving*—a measure of rudimentary means-ends relationships—was developed from four supplementary items administered after the Bayley Test.

The procedure to measure exploratory behavior and preference for novel stimuli, functions that we also labelled cognitive-motivational, has been described in detail by Rubenstein (1967). Essentially it involves presenting the baby with an attractive, novel toy—a bell—for ten minutes. The amount of exploratory interest shown by looking and manipulating was recorded; then a series of ten new toys was presented one at a time for one minute intervals paired with the bell, which had become more familiar. Preference for novel stimuli was expressed by measures of differential looking or manipulation, that is, the difference between time directed to the novel toy vs. the more familiar bell.

Results

DIFFERENTIATION OF THE ENVIRONMENT

Table 1 indicates the interrelationships among the social and inanimate variables. Among the social variables, level, variety, and positive affect

TABLE 1

Interrelationships Among the Social and Inanimate Variables

	Social				Inanimate		
	Variety	Positive Affect	Cont. R. to Pos. Voc.	Cont. R. to Distress	Responsiveness	Complexity	Variety
Social							
Level	.76	.62	.64	.53	—	—	—
Variety		.64	.45	.48	.33	—	.29
Positive Affect			.51	.23	.23	—	.20
Contingent Response to Positive Vocalization				.31	—	—	—
Contingent Response to Distress					—	—	.31
Inanimate							
Responsiveness						.70	—
Complexity							--
Variety							

For *p* = .05, one-tailed test, *r* = .26.
— indicates *r* less than .20

are all rather strongly interrelated. In fact, level has considerable generality with all other social stimulation variables. In regard to the two contingency measures, there is a relatively low relationship between the frequency measure, contingent response to positive vocalization and the latency measure, contingent response to distress ($r = .31$). This suggests that maternal responsiveness is itself not a highly general trait.

Within the dimensions of inanimate stimulation, variety of play objects is independent of responsiveness and complexity. On the other hand, the correlation between responsiveness and complexity is .70, in part because responsiveness is one of the components of the complexity scale.

Perhaps the most important generalization to be made from Table 1 is that the dimensions of the social environment are largely independent of dimensions of the inanimate environment. This differentiation suggests that global characterizations of environments as "depriving" or "stimulating" are oversimplified.

RELATIONS BETWEEN THE SOCIAL ENVIRONMENT AND INFANT FUNCTIONING

Both Level and Variety of social stimulation are thought of as having an arousal function, serving to activate the infant and increase his responsiveness to the environment. The general pattern of relationships seen in Table 2 is quite similar for these two variables, although a greater number of significant correlations are found with variety.

The variables were defined quite differently. Level is defined in terms of characteristics of the stimuli themselves, amount weighted by different degrees of intensity. Variety was defined in terms of the types of behavior elicited by the caretaker and the different physical settings where interaction occurred. It is the frequency of interactive play, motor training, presentation and highlighting of play objects, and the number of changes in the location of interaction with the baby, such as an infant seat, the caretaker's lap, or the floor. The essence of variety is the encouragement of more differentiated responses on the part of the

infant, whereas level is defined in terms of the stimulus characteristics.

As with level and variety, contingent response to distress is also significantly related to the Mental Development Index and to the measures of goal-directed behavior. These results seem to support the Ainsworth (1967) or the Lewis and Goldberg (1968) interpretation of what happens when one responds to the infant's cry; relatively early intervention in distress states may have a general facilitating effect, either by freeing the infant to respond to external stimuli or by making him aware of a contingent relationship with the caretaker.

There are two language measures. Vocalize to Bell is a measure of *amount* of vocalization obtained during the test of exploratory behavior, the ten minute period when the infant had the interesting toy. Its significant relationship with the mother's contingent response to infant vocalization has special conceptual interest. This relationship found in the natural environment adds to the generalizability to life settings of the operant laboratory studies of the social reinforcement of vocalization rates (Rheingold, Gewirtz, & Ross, 1959; Weisberg, 1963; Todd & Palmer, 1968). Another measure, the mother's spontaneous vocalizations (that is, total vocalization minus contingent vocalization), was not related to the infant's vocal output. This finding, as well as the lack of relationship to the other measure of contingency, underscores the specificity of this effect and buttresses the operant learning interpretation.

The second language measure is a cluster of eight Bayley items dealing with the qualitative aspects of language. The measure was not related to any environmental variables. Although language quality at five to six months may be more important conceptually than amount of vocalization, it is probably too unstable developmentally or too complex to measure adequately with a few test items.

More evidence of differential effects is seen in relation to social responsiveness. This cluster of eight Bayley items includes vocalizing to a social stimulus, anticipatory adjustment to lifting, enjoying frolic play, and approaching and smiling to a mirror image. Instigating stimuli, that is, level, variety, and expression of positive affect, are all significantly correlated with social respon-

TABLE 2

Correlations Between Social Stimulation Variables and Infant Functioning

Infant Functioning	Social Stimulation Variables				
	Level	Variety	Positive Affect	Cont. R. Pos. Voc.	Cont. R. Distress
General Status					
Mental Dev. Index	.32*	.34*	.23	—	.32*
Psychomotor Dev. Index	—	.23	—	—	.37*
Social Responsiveness	.35*	.34*	.26*	.22	—
Language					
Vocal. to Bell	—	.31*	.24	.30*	—
Language Quality	—	—	—	—	—
Motor Development					
Gross	—	—	—	—	.28*
Fine	—	.26*	—	—	.33*
Goal-Directed Behaviors					
Goal Orientation	.45**	.48**	.30*	—	.38**
Reaching & Grasping	.25	.28	—	—	.29*
Secondary Circular					
Reaction	.32*	.35*	.30*	—	.30*
Cognitive Functions					
Problem Solving	.21	.20	—	—	—
Object Permanence	.31*	.47**	—	—	—
Exploratory Behavior					
Looking at Bell	—	—	—	−.37	—
Manipulating Bell	—	.32*	—	—	.21
Looking at Novel	—	—	—	—	—
Manipulating Novel	—	—	.28*	.31*	.24

* $p < .05$; one-tailed test.
** $p < .01$; one-tailed test.
— indicates *r* less than .20.

siveness; whereas the soothing stimuli, contingent response to distress, are unrelated to social responsiveness.

The strongest grouping of significant relationships is in the cognitive-motivational set called goal-directed behaviors. *Goal orientation* is a cluster of six Bayley items, primarily motivational in nature, including such behaviors as persistent and purposeful attempts to secure objects just out of reach. This measure has very high generality with many other dependent variables; it correlates .86 with the total Bayley Mental Developmental Index, higher than any other cluster. The results suggest that motivational differences in infants are particularly sensitive to the social environment.

The cluster *Reaching and Grasping* consists of nine Bayley items and emphasizes especially visual-motor coordination and fine motor skills in transactions with play objects. It probably has more of a skill emphasis than other variables in this group, and that may account for the weaker relationships.

Secondary Circular Reaction, as defined by Piaget, is the repetition of behavior which produces interesting results. It reflects an intentionality to maintain interesting activities, and it is thought of as a precursor of instrumental behavior requiring an appreciation of means-ends relationships. The cluster consisted of only two items, banging in play and enjoying sound production. Despite the sharp restriction in range of the dependent variable, there are four correlations significant at the .05 level. A supplementary test item with high face validity was also devised for measuring secondary circular reactions; the results were essentially the same as for the Bayley cluster.

RELATIONS BETWEEN THE INANIMATE ENVIRONMENT AND INFANT FUNCTIONING

Table 3 presents the results. A striking specificity of effect is seen for properties of the inanimate environment. Variety, responsiveness, and complexity show no significant relationships with language or social responsiveness. In contrast, there are many significant relationships with the cognitive-motivational and fine motor variables, all measures which involve responses to inanimate objects.

Responsiveness, which is defined in terms of the feedback potential of objects, is most highly related to the variable that specifically tests the infant's repeated efforts to evoke feedback from objects, namely secondary circular reactions. Responsiveness is also related to goal orientation and reaching and grasping; to fine motor development; and to a measure of exploratory behavior, preference for looking at novel stimuli. Our findings suggest that the responsiveness of objects in the infant's natural environment may facilitate both motivational and skill components of development.

Consistent with expectations, complexity is related to infant measures that reflect receptivity to stimulation: preference for novel stimuli; reaching and grasping objects; and repeating actions which produce changes in stimulation, that is, secondary circular reactions. Contrary to expectation, complexity is not significantly related to the Bayley Mental Developmental Index, goal orientation, or problem solving ability.

Of the three dimensions of the inanimate enviroment, variety of inanimate objects is the strongest antecedent, in terms of both the number of significant relationships with developmental outcomes and the magnitude of these correlations. Variety is related to nearly all the infant measures dealing with inanimate objects, and it correlates more highly than does complexity or responsiveness with most of them.

Variety is the one parameter of inanimate objects that is significantly related to object permanence and problem solving. Both these measures involve the infant's reaction to inanimate objects that are not immediately available or easily accessible. At this developmental level object permanence measures primarily the baby's tendency to look for an object that is out of reach and going out of view; problem solving measures his efforts and ability to use one object as a means to another that is in view but out of reach. The results suggest that it is the variety of objects with which the baby comes in contact, rather than complexity or feedback potential, that relates to the ability to secure and follow visually objects not immediately accessible.

Variety of inanimate objects also shows strong relationships with exploratory behavior. The high relationship between variety and manipulating novel objects ($r = .48$) is consistent with several theoretical views. Piaget emphasizes that assimilating and accommodating to varying properties of objects is instrumental in differentiating basic schemata. Variety may also affect the arousal level of the infant keeping him alert and ready to "tune in" to the environment (Schaffer & Emerson, 1968); and it may lead to an adaptation level (Helson, 1964) for more novel input, strengthening the infant's motivation to maintain high degrees of variation in stimulation.

SEX DIFFERENCES

Although results have been reported for the group as a whole, the data have also been analyzed separately for males and females. Generally, the direction of the relationships tends to be similar for boys and girls. However, the mag-

TABLE 3

Relations Between Dimensions of Inanimate Stimulation and Infant Functioning

Infant Functioning	Inanimate Stimulation		
	Responsiveness	Complexity	Variety
General Status			
Mental Developmental Index	.27*	—	.36*
Psychomotor Developmental Index	.28*	—	.51**
Social Responsiveness	.21	—	—
Language			
Voc. to Bell	—	—	—
Language Quality	—	—	—
Motor Development			
Gross	.27*	.22	.42**
Fine	.33*	—	.37*
Goal-Directed Behaviors			
Goal Orientation	.30*	—	.41**
Reaching and Grasping	.46**	.32*	.38*
Secondary Circular Reaction	.51**	.46**	.33*
Cognitive Functions			
Problem Solving	—	—	.50**
Object Permanence	—	—	.30*
Exploratory Behavior			
Looking at Bell	—	—	—
Manipulating Bell	.21	—	.40**
Looking at Novel	.28*	.30*	.35*
Manipulating Novel	—	.35*	.48**

* $p < .05$.
** $p < .01$.
— indicates r less than .20.

nitude of relationships between environmental and infant variables is higher for females. Among the girls there are 23 correlations that are .50 or higher. In contrast, no correlation as high as .50 is found for the boys.

Discussion

Several issues important for development theory and research are highlighted by these findings. We have shown that the natural environment of the young infant can be differentiated into many discrete behaviors of the caretaker, and the properties of objects available to the infant can be subjected to very detailed analyses.

We have shown that events in the natural environment can be coordinated with theoretical concepts. We have isolated specific variables in the natural environment and we have explored their relationships to specific aspects of infant development, for example, the relationship between responsiveness of objects in the home and the emergence of secondary circular reactions; the relationship between the mother's contingent responsiveness to the infant's vocalizations and rate of vocalization in the exploratory behavior situation. These findings suggest that some relationships found in the laboratory can be generalized to life settings.

Another issue highlighted by the findings of this study concerns the level at which one characterizes environments. The findings underscore the inadequacy of global characterizations of environments, and emphasize the value of differentiating the dimensions and characteristics of stimulation. The relatively low relationships between variables of the inanimate environment and variables of the social environment suggest that, for this particular sample at least, it may not be very meaningful to label environments grossly as depriving.

A third issue, a very complex and controversial one, concerns the relative importance of human and inanimate stimulation. There has been a tendency in recent years in theory and in experimental research to focus on cognitive stimulation variables, and to deemphasize the affective components of the mother-infant relationship. Our findings of a relative independence of the inanimate and the social environments, in conjunction with the specific relationships between social stimulation and social responsiveness and language, on the one hand, and between properties of inanimate stimulation and exploratory behavior, on the other hand, emphasize the importance of both the human and the inanimate environment.

A fourth issue has to do with the simple correlational model we have used. We recognize that looking at relationships between single variables is a very simple model that ignores the realities of environment-child interaction. Although there are many significant correlations between environmental variables and infant characteristics, the magnitude of many of the correlations is not very high. These associations exceed chance expectations and, in general, are consistent with theoretical assumptions, but they do not permit predictions with any high degree of accuracy. It is likely that these environmental variables interact in many complex ways. We cannot conclude that any single variable alone is decisive for any particular infant function. It is meaningful, however, to ask to what extent a given environmental variable makes a special contribution to some aspect of infant functioning.

We also need to ask more complex questions,

such as, whether certain environmental variables may be interchangeable; whether certain combinations of variables are additive in their effects; and to what extent certain variables interact to strengthen or diminish each other's impact. We must also recognize that the relationship between environmental variables and infant behavior is not a simple unidirectional one. There is a reciprocal interaction between infant characteristics and environmental events. It is likely that an active and responsive infant elicits more social response from others as well as greater inanimate stimulation than a lethargic withdrawn infant.

We have been particularly interested in the group of infant behaviors that we have called cognitive-motivational functions. One striking finding of this study is the extent to which these functions seem to be amenable to environmental influences in early infancy. These results support Provence and Lipton's (1961) impressions that motivational functions may be more vulnerable to depriving institutional environments than are specific emerging skills.

Motivation, as we have used it, is not an abstract intervening variable. It refers to clearly specified behaviors, such as reaching persistently for objects, attempting to have an effect on and elicit responses from objects, showing preferential attention to and manipulation of novel objects. These behaviors might be considered expressions of the infant's motivation to assimilate, to learn about, and to master the environment. They may be viewed as an early expression of a competence or an effectance motive (White, 1959). The importance of these relationships lies in their convergence with a number of theoretical formulations based primarily on laboratory studies. Lewis and Goldberg (1969) have formulated a "generalized expectancy model," emphasizing the role of contingent mother-infant interaction in the development of the child's belief that he can affect his environment, that he can bring about reinforcement by his actions. Watson (1966) speaks of "contingency awareness" as a precondition for later learning. The common thread in these formulations is the active, information processing organism, initiating transactions with the environment and in turn being influenced by these transactions.

One last point in regard to the significance of motivational functions. It is likely that the infant's orientation to objects and to people very early becomes part of a feedback system with the environment. His smiling, vocalizing, and reaching out to people; his visually attending to and manipulating objects tend to be self-reinforcing and thus, to some extent, self-perpetuating. These behaviors become part of a system of reciprocal interactions which may characterize a given infant's transactions with the environment over a long period of time. This orientation to the world may be a more consistent and more significant characteristic of the young infant than any specific cognitive ability. We might speculate that the infant's orientation to his environment adds to the continuity of his experiences. If this is so, then the fact that these aspects of functioning seem to be related to identifiable aspects of the environment during the first six months may have great significance not only for developmental theory, but for intervention programs as well.

REFERENCES

AINSWORTH, M. *Infancy in Uganda: Infant care and the growth of love.* Baltimore: Johns Hopkins, 1967.

BERLYNE, D. *Conflict, arousal and curiosity.* New York: McGraw-Hill, 1960.

GEWIRTZ, J. Mechanisms of social learning: Some roles of stimulation and behavior in early human development. In D. Goslin (Ed.), *Handbook of socialization theory and research.* Chicago: Rand McNally, 1969.

HELSON, H. *Adaptation level theory.* New York: Harper & Row, 1964.

HUNT, J. MC V. Intrinsic motivation and its role in psychological development. In D. Levine (Ed.), *Nebraska symposium on motivation.* Lincoln: University of Nebraska Press, 1965. Pp. 189–282.

LEWIS, M. & GOLDBERG, S. Perceptual-cognitive development in infancy: A generalized expectancy model as a function of the mother-infant relationship. *Merrill-Palmer Quarterly,* 1969, Vol. 15, 81–100.

PROVENCE, S. & LIPTON, R. *Infants in institutions.* New York: International Universities Press, 1961.

RHEINGOLD, H., GEWIRTZ, J., & ROSS, H. Social conditioning of vocalizations in the infant. *Journal of Comparative and Physiological Psychology,* 1959, Vol. 52, 68–73.

RUBENSTEIN, J. Maternal attentiveness and subsequent exploratory behavior. *Child Development,* 1967, Vol. 38, 1089–1100.

SCHAFFER, H. & EMERSON, P. The effects of experimentally administered stimulation on developmental quotients of infants. *British Journal of Social and Clinical Psychology,* 1968, Vol. 7, 61–67.

TODD, G. & PALMER, B. Social reinforcement of infant babbling. *Child Development,* 1968, Vol. 39, 591–596.

WATSON, J. The development and generalization of contingency awareness in early infancy: Some hypotheses. *Merrill-Palmer Quarterly,* 1966, Vol. 12, 123–135.

WEISBERG, P. Social and nonsocial conditioning of infant vocalizations. *Child Development,* 1963, Vol. 34, 377–388.

WHITE, R. Motivation reconsidered: The concept of competence. *Psychological Review,* 1959, Vol. 66, 297–323.

Intellectual Evolution
from Adolescence to Adulthood

J. Piaget

We are relatively well informed about the important changes that take place in cognitive function and structure at adolescence. Such changes show how much this essential phase in ontogenic development concerns all aspects of mental and psychophysiological evolution and not only the more 'instinctive', emotional or social aspects to which one often limits one's consideration. In contrast, however, we know as yet very little about the period which separates adolescence from adulthood and we feel that the decision of the Institution FONEME to draw the attention of various research workers to this essential problem is extremely well founded.

A French version of the article was presented at *FONEME*, 3rd International Convention, Milan 1970, and published in the proceedings (FONEME, Institution for Studies and Research in Human Formation, 20135, Via Bergamo 21, Milan, Italy). The English translation was prepared by JOAN BLISS and HANS FURTH, to whom special thanks are due. The editors of Human Development gratefully acknowledge permission by the author and FONEME to publish the English version.

In this paper we would first like to recall the principal characteristics of the intellectual changes that occur during the period from 12–15 years of age. These characteristics are too frequently forgotten as one tends to reduce the psychology of adolescence to the psychology of puberty. We shall then refer to the chief problems that arise in connection with the next period (15–20 years); firstly, the diversification of aptitudes, and secondly, the degree of generality of cognitive structures acquired between 12 and 15 years and their further development.

The Structures of Formal Thought

Intellectual structures between birth and the period of 12–15 years grow slowly, but according to stages in development. The order of succession of these stages has been shown to be extremely regular and comparable to the stages of an embryogenesis. The speed of development, however, can vary from one individual to another and also

Jean Piaget: Intellectual Evolution from Adolescence to Adulthood. *Human Development, 15:* 1–12 (1972).

from one social environment to another; consequently, we may find some children who advance quickly or others who are backward, but this does not change the order of succession of the stages through which they pass. Thus, long before the appearance of language, all normal children pass through a number of stages in the formation of sensorimotor intelligence which can be characterized by certain 'instrumental' behavior patterns; such patterns bear witness to the existence of a logic which is inherent to the coordination of the actions themselves.

With the acquisition of language and the formation of symbolic play, mental imagery, etc., that is, the formation of the symbolic function (or, in a general sense, the semiotic function), actions are interiorized and become representations; this supposes a reconstruction and a reorganization on the new plane of representative thought. However, the logic of this period remains incomplete until the child is 7 or 8 years old. The internal actions are still 'preoperatory' if we take 'operations' to mean actions that are entirely reversible (as adding and subtracting, or judging that the distance between A and B is the same as the distance between B and A, etc.). Due to the lack of reversibility, the child lacks comprehension of the idea of transitivity ($A \leqq C$, if $A \leqq B$ and $B \leqq C$) and of conservation (for a preoperatory child, if the shape of an object changes, the quantity of matter and the weight of the object change also).

Between 7–8 and 11–12 years a logic of reversible actions is constituted, characterized by the formation of a certain number of stable and coherent structures, such as a classification system, an ordering system, the construction of natural numbers, the concept of measurement of lines and surfaces, projective relations (perspectives), certain general types of causality (transmission of movement through intermediaries), etc.

Several very general characteristics distinguish this logic from the one that will be constituted during the pre-adolescent period (between 12 and 15 years). Firstly, these operations are 'concrete', that is to say, in using them the child still reasons in terms of objects (classes, relations, numbers, etc.) and not in terms of hypotheses that can be thought out before knowing whether they are true or false. Secondly, these operations, which involve sorting and establishing relations between or enumerating objects, always proceed by relating an element to its neighboring element— they cannot yet link any term whatsoever to any other term, as would be the case in a combinatorial system: thus, when carrying out a classification, a child capable of concrete reasoning associates one term with the term it most resembles and there is no 'natural' class that relates two very different objects. Thirdly, these operations have two types of reversibility that are not yet linked together (in the sense that one can be joined with the other); the first type of reversibility is by inversion or negation, the result of this operation is an annulment, for example, $+A -A = 0$ or $+ n - n = 0$; the second type of reversibility is by reciprocity and this characterizes operations of relations, for example, if $A = B$, then $B = A$, or if A is to the left of B, then B is to the right of A, etc.

On the contrary, from 11–12 years to 14–15 years a whole series of novelties highlights the arrival of a more complete logic that will attain a state of equilibrium once the child reaches adolescence at about 14–15 years. We must, therefore, analyze this new logic in order to understand what might happen between adolescence and full adulthood.

The principle novelty of this period is the capacity to reason in terms of verbally stated hypotheses and no longer merely in terms of concrete objects and their manipulation. This is a decisive turning point, because to reason hypothetically and to deduce the consequences that the hypotheses necessarily imply (independent of the intrinsic truth or falseness of the premises) is a formal reasoning process. Consequently the child can attribute a decisive value to the logical form of the deductions that was not the case in the previous stages. From 7–8 years, the child is capable of certain logical reasoning processes but only to the extent of applying particular operations to concrete objects or events in the immediate present: in other words, the operatory form of the reasoning process, at this level, is still subordinated to the concrete content that makes up the real world. In contrast, hypothetical reasoning implies the subordination of the real to the realm of the possible, and consequently the linking of all possibilities to one another by necessary implications that encompass the real, but at the same time go beyond it.

From the social point of view, there is also an important conquest. Firstly, hypothetical reasoning changes the nature of discussions: a fruitful and constructive discussion means that by using hypotheses we can adopt the point of view of the adversary (although not necessarily believing it) and draw the logical consequences it implies. In this way, we can judge its value after having verified the consequences. Secondly, the individual who becomes capable of hypothetical reasoning, by this very fact will interest himself in problems that go beyond his immediate field of experience. Hence, the adolescent's capacity to understand and even construct theories and to participate in society and the ideologies of adults; this is often, of course, accompanied by a desire to change society and even, if necessary, destroy it (in his imagination) in order to elaborate a better one.

In the field of physics and particularly in the induction of certain elementary laws (many experiments have been carried out under the direction of B. Inhelder on this particular topic), the difference in attitude between children of 12–15 years, already capable of formal reasoning, and children of 7–10 years, still at the concrete level, is very noticeable. The 7- to 10-year-old children when placed in an experimental situation (such as what laws concern the swing of a pendulum, factors involved in the flexibility of certain materials, problems of increasing acceleration on an inclined plane) act directly upon the material placed in front of them by trial and error, without dissociating the factors involved. They simply try to classify or order what happened by looking at the results of the co-variations. The formal level children, after a few similar trials stop experimenting with the material and begin to list all the possible hypotheses. It is only after having done this that they start to test them, trying progressively to dissociate the factors involved and study the effects of each one in turn—'all other factors remaining constant'.

This type of experimental behavior, directed by hypotheses which are based on more or less refined causal models, implies the elaboration of two new structures that we find constantly in formal reasoning.

The first of these structures is a combinatorial system, an example of which is clearly seen in 'the set of all subsets', ($2n^2$ or the simplex structure). We have, in fact, previously mentioned that the reasoning process of the child at the concrete level (7–10 years old) progresses by linking an element with a neighboring one, and cannot relate any element whatsoever to any other. On the contrary, this generalized combinatorial ability (1 to 1, 2 to 2, 3 to 3, etc.) becomes effective when the subject can reason in a hypothetical manner. In fact, psychological research shows that between 12 and 15 years the pre-adolescent and adolescent start to carry out operations involving combinatorial analysis, permutation systems, etc. (independent of all school training). They cannot, of course, figure out mathematical formulas, but they can discover experimentally exhaustive methods that work for them. When a child is placed in an experimental situation where it is necessary to use combinatorial methods (for example, given 5 bottles of colorless, odorless liquid, 3 of which combine to make a colored liquid, the fourth is a reducing agent and the fifth is water), the child easily discovers the law after having worked out all the possible ways of combining the liquids in this particular case.

This combinatorial system constitutes an essential structure from the logical point of view. The elementary systems of classification and order observed between 7 and 10 years, do not yet constitute a combinatorial system. Propositional logic, however, for two propositions 'p' and 'q' and their negation, implies that we not only consider the 4-base associations (p and q, p and not q, not p and q, not p and not q) but also the 16 combinations that can be obtained by linking these base associations 1 to 1, 2 to 2, 3 to 3 (with the addition of all 4-base associations and the empty set). In this way it can be seen that implication, inclusive disjunction and incompatibility are fundamental propositional operations that result from the combination of 3 of these base associations.

At the level of formal operations it is extremely interesting to see that this combinatorial system of thinking is not only available and effective in all experimental fields, but that the subject also becomes capable of combining propositions: therefore, propositional logic appears to be one of the essential conquests of formal thought. When, in fact, the reasoning processes of children between 11–12 and 14–15 years are analyzed in detail it is easy to find the 16 operations or binary functions of a bivalent logic of propositions.

However, there is still more to formal thought: when we examine the way in which subjects use these 16 operations we can recognize numerous cases of the 4-group which are isomorphic to the Klein group and which reveal themselves in the following manner. Let us take, for example, the implication $p > q$, if this stays unchanged we can say it characterized the identity transformation I. If this proposition is changed into its negation N (reversibility by negation or inversion) we obtain $N = p$ and not q. The subject can change this same proposition into its reciprocal (reversibility by reciprocity) that is $R = q > p$; and it is also possible to change the statement into its correlative (or dual), namely $C = $ not p and q. Thus, we obtain a commutative 4-group such that $CR = N$, $CN = R$, $RN = C$ and $CRN = I$. This group allows the subject to combine in one operation the negation and the reciprocal which was not possible at the level of concrete operations. An example of these transformations that occurs frequently is the comprehension of the relationship between action (I and N) and reaction (R and C) in physics experiments; or again, the understanding of the relationship between two reference systems, for example: a moving object can go forwards or backwards (I and N) on a board which itself can go forwards or backwards (R and C) in relation to an exterior reference system. Generally speaking the group structure intervenes when the subject understands the difference between the cancelling or undoing of an effect (N in relation to I) and the compensation of this effect by another variable (R and its negation C) which does not eliminate but neutralizes the effect.

In concluding this first part we can see that the adolescent's logic is a complex but coherent system that is relatively different from the logic of the child, and constitutes the essence of the logic of cultured adults and even provides the basis for elementary forms of scientific thought.

The Problems of the Passage from Adolescent to Adult Thought

The experiments on which the above-mentioned results are based were carried out with secondary school children, 11–15 years, taken from the better schools in Geneva. However, recent research has shown that subjects from other types of schools or different social environments sometimes give results differing more or less from the norms indicated; for the same experiments it is as though these subjects had stayed at the concrete operatory level of thinking.

Other information gathered about adults in Nancy, France, and adolescents of different levels in New York has also shown that we cannot generalize in all subjects the conclusion of our research which was, perhaps, based on a somewhat privileged population. This does not mean that our observations have not been confirmed in many cases: they seem to be true for certain populations, but the main problem is to understand why there are exceptions and also whether these are real or apparent.

A first problem is the speed of development, that is to say, the differences that can be observed in the rapidity of the temporal succession of the stages. We have distinguished 4 periods in the development of cognitive functions (see beginning of part 1): the sensorimotor period before the appearance of language; the preoperatory period which, in Geneva, seems on the average to extend from about 1½–2 to 6–7 years; the period of concrete operations from 7–8 to 11–12 years (according to research with children in Geneva and Paris) and the formal operations period from 11–12 to 14–15 years as observed in the schools studied in Geneva. However, if the order of succession has shown itself to be constant—each stage is necessary to the construction of the following one—the average age at which children go through each stage can vary considerably from one social environment to another, or from one country or even region within a country to another. In this way Canadian psychologists in Martinique have observed a systematic slowness in development; in Iran notable differences were found between children of the city of Teheran and young illiterate children of the villages. In Italy, N. Peluffo has shown that there is a significant gap between children from regions of southern Italy and those from the north; he has carried out some particularly interesting studies indicating how, in children from southern families migrating north, these differences progressively disappear. Similar comparative research is at present taking place in Indian reservations in North America, etc.

In general, a first possibility is to envisage a difference in speed of development without any modification of the order of succession of the stages. These different speeds would be due to the quality and frequency of intellectual stimulation received from adults or obtained from the possibilities available to children for spontaneous activity in their environment. In the case of poor stimulation and activity, it goes wthout saying that the development of the first 3 of the 4 periods mentioned above will be slowed down. When it comes to formal thought, we could propose that there will be an even greater retardation in its formation (for example, between 15 and 20 years and not 11 and 15 years); or that perhaps in extremely disadvantageous conditions, such a type of thought will never really take shape or will only develop in those individuals who change their environment while development is still possible.

This does not mean that formal structures are exclusively the result of a process of social transmission. We still have to consider the spontaneous and endogenous factors of construction proper to each normal subject. However, the formation and completion of cognitive structures imply a whole series of exchanges and a stimulating environment; the formation of operations always requires a favorable environment for 'co-operation', that is to say, operations carried out in common (e.g., the role of discussion, mutual criticism or support, problems raised as the result of exchanges of information, heightened curiosity due to the cultural influence of a social group, etc.). Briefly, our first interpretation would mean that in principle all normal individuals are capable of reaching the level of formal structures on the condition that the social environment and acquired experience provide the subject with the cognitive nourishment and intellectual stimulation necessary for such a construction.

However, a second interpretation is possible which would take into account the diversification of aptitudes with age, but this would mean excluding certain categories of normal individuals, even in favorable environments, from the possibility of attaining a formal level of thinking. It is a well-known fact that the aptitudes of individuals differentiate progressively with age. Such a model of intellectual growth would be comparable to a fully expanded hand fan, the concentric layers of which would represent the successive stages in development whereas the sectors, opening wider towards the periphery, correspond to the growing differences in aptitude.

We would go so far as to say that certain behavior patterns characteristically form stages with very general properties: this occurs until a certain level in development is reached; from this point onwards, however, individual aptitudes become more important than these general characteristics and create greater and greater differences between subjects. A good example of this type of development is the evolution of drawing. Until the stage at which the child can represent perspectives graphically, we observe a very general progress to the extent that the 'draw a man' test, to cite a particular case as an example, can be used as a general test of mental development. However, surprisingly large individual differences are observed in the drawings of 13- to 14-year-old children, and even greater differences with 19–20 year olds (e.g., army recruits): the quality of the drawing no longer has anything to do with the level of intelligence. In this instance we have a good example of a behaviour pattern which is, at first, subordinate to a general evolution in stages [cf. those described by LUQUET and other authors for children from 2–3 until about 8–9 years] and which, afterwards, gradually becomes diversified according to criteria of individual aptitudes rather than the general development common to all individuals.

This same type of pattern occurs in several fields including those which appear to be more cognitive in nature. One example is provided by the representation of space which first depends on operatory factors with the usual 4 intellectual stages—sensorimotor (cf. the practical group of displacements), preoperatory, concrete operations (measure, perspectives, etc.) and formal operations. However, the construction of space also depends on figurative factors (perception and mental imagery) which are partially subordinated to operatory factors and which then become more and more differentiated as symbolical and representative mechanisms. The final result is that for space in general, as for drawing, we can distinguish a primary evolution characterized by the stages in the ordinary sense of the term, and then a growing diversification with age due to gradually differentiating aptitudes with regard to imaged representation and figurative instruments. We know, for example, that there exist big differences between mathematicians in the way in which they define 'geometrical intuition': Poincaré distinguishes two types of mathematicians: the 'geometricans', who think more concretely and the 'algebrists', or 'analysts', who think more abstractly.

There are many other fields in which we could also think along similar lines. It becomes possible at a certain moment, for example, to distinguish between adolescents who, on the one hand, are more talented for physics or problems dealing with causality than for logic or mathematics and those who, on the other hand, show the opposite aptitude. We can see the same tendencies in questions concerning linguistics, literature, etc.

We could, therefore, formulate the following hypothesis: if the formal structures described in part 1 do not appear in all children of 14–15 years and demonstrate a less general distribution than the concrete structures of children from 7–10 years old, this could be due to the diversification of aptitudes with age. According to this interpretation, however, we would have to admit that only individuals talented from the point of view of logic, mathematics and physics would manage to construct such formal structures whereas literary, artistic and practical individuals would be incapable of doing so. In this case it would not be a problem of under-development compared to normal development but more simply a growing diversification in individuals, the span of aptitudes being greater at the level of 12–15 years, and above all between 15 and 20 years, than at 7–10 years. In other words, our fourth

period can no longer be characterized as a proper stage, but would already seem to be a structural advancement in the direction of specialization.

But there is the possibility of a third hypothesis and, in the present state of knowledge, this last interpretation seems the most probable. It allows us to reconcile the concept of stages with the idea of progressively differentiating aptitudes. In brief, our third hypothesis would state that all normal subjects attain the stage of formal operations or structuring if not between 11–12 to 14–15 years, in any case between 15 and 20 years. However, they reach this stage in different areas according to their aptitudes and their professional specializations (advanced studies or different types of apprenticeship for the various trades): the way in which these formal structures are used, however, is not necessarily the same in all cases.

In our investigation of formal structures we used rather specific types of experimental situations which were of a physical and logical-mathematical nature because these seemed to be understood by the school children we sampled. However, it is possible to question whether these situations are, fundamentally, very general and therefore applicable to any school or professional environment. Let us consider the example of apprentices to carpenters, locksmiths, or mechanics who have shown sufficient aptitudes for successful training in the trades they have chosen but whose general education is limited. It is highly likely that they will know how to reason in a hypothetical manner in their speciality, that is to say, dissociating the variables involved, relating terms in a combinatorial manner and reasoning with propositions involving negations and reciprocities. They would, therefore, be capable of thinking formally in their particular field, whereas faced with our experimental situations, their lack of knowledge or the fact they have forgotten certain ideas that are particularly familiar to children still in school or college, would hinder them from reasoning in a formal way, and they would give the appearance of being at the concrete level. Let us also consider the example of young people studying law—in the field of juridical concepts and verbal discourse their logic would be far superior to any form of logic they might use when faced with certain problems in the field of physics that involve notions they certainly once knew but have long since forgotten.

It is quite true that one of the essential characteristics of formal thought appears to us to be the independence of its form from its reality content. At the concrete operatory level a structure cannot be generalized to different heterogenous contents but remains attached to a system of objects or to the properties of these objects (thus the concept of weight only becomes logically structured after the development of the concept of matter, and the concept of physical volume after weight): a formal structure seems, in contrast, generalizable as it deals with hypotheses. However, it is one thing to dissociate the form from the content in a field which is of interest to the subject and within which he can apply his curiosity and initiative, and it is another to be able to generalize this same spontaneity of research and comprehension to a field foreign to the subject's career and interests. To ask a future lawyer to reason on the theory of relativity or to ask a student in physics to reason on the code of civil rights is quite different from asking a child to generalize what he has discovered in the conservation of matter to a problem on the conservation of weight. In the latter instance it is the passage from one content to a different but comparable content, whereas in the former it is to go out of the subject's field of vital activities and enter a totally new field, completely foreign to his interests and projects. Briefly, we can retain the idea that formal operations are free from their concrete content, but we must add that this is true only on the condition that for the subjects the situations involve equal aptitudes or comparable vital interests.

Conclusion

If we wish to draw a general conclusion from these reflections we must first say that, from a cognitive point of view, the passage from adolescence to adulthood raises a number of unresolved questions that need to be studied in greater detail.

The period from 15 to 20 years marks the beginning of professional specialization and consequently also the construction of a life program corresponding to the aptitudes of the individual. We now ask the following critical question: Can one demonstrate, at this level of development as at previous levels, cognitive structures common to all individuals which will, however, be applied or used differently by each person according to his particular activities?

The reply will probably be positive but this must be established by the experimental methods used in psychology and sociology. Beyond that, the next essential step is to analyze the probable processes of differentiation: that is to say, whether the same structures are sufficient for the organization of many varying fields of activity but with differences in the way they are applied, or whether there will appear new and special structures that still remain to be discovered and studied.

It is to the credit of the FONEME Institution to have realized the existence of these problems and to have understood their importance and complexity, particularly as, generally speaking, developmental psychology believed that its work was completed with the study of adolescence. Fortunately, today, certain research workers are conscious of these facts and we can hope to know more about this subject in the near future.

Unfortunately the study of young adults is much more difficult than the study of the young child as they are less creative, and already part of an organized society that not only limits them and slows them down but sometimes even rouses them to revolt. We know, however, that the study of the child and the adolescent can help us understand the further development of the individual as an adult and that, in turn, the new research on young adults will retroactively throw light on what we already think we know about earlier stages.

Part 6

Imaginative Processes

Fantasy, play, and forms of aesthetic expression are becoming increasingly recognized as important components of the child's development. While this is not a well-studied field in developmental psychology, these readings are offered because of the author's belief in the value of exploring the child's imagination and art. The child's fantasy development—his daydreams, make-believe play, and night dreams —is explored in the first article by Singer.

The next three papers explore the child's development in the arts—his dramatic improvisations, paintings, and drawings. The arts are, in effect, mediated structures of the imagination. Without this kind of knowledge about how human beings grow, the knowledge that we do have—in terms of intellectual, social, and physical competence—is one-sided. Because human beings live primarily within their imaginative experience of the world around them, we need to know more about that world.

Toward a Theory of Daydreaming: Childhood Origins

Jerome L. Singer

Some Experimental Studies with Children

Before moving to a more speculative integration of the experimental data and clinical evidence concerning fantasy development, it may be appropriate to describe some findings from our own investigations with children. The major emphasis in these studies was toward an initial approach to the function of daydreaming in children and toward a study of the relations of fantasy play to background factors in the child's experience. In one study of this group, for example, Lesser (1962) found that children who are characterized as imaginative by Rorschach and Thematic Apperception Test criteria played most vigorously and aggressively in a free play situation before and after experimental frustration. They "bopped" Bobo and shot off the "burp gun" more often than less imaginative children. In the same study, given a choice of expensive toys as a reward for a task, the more imaginative children chose toys requiring minimal motor activity and greater fantasy interpolation (for example, a fort with soldiers or a science kit), while the less imaginative group more often chose toys that involved physical activity for its own sake (for example, a baseball bat or basketball). In effect, then, the data suggest that vigorous motor play is not a suitable basis for distinguishing between children of differing degrees of imagination but that the more imaginative have the greater option or inclination to introduce "make-believe" elements into their activities.

Another study sought to obtain additional evidence of the correlates in children of a consistent disposition to include fantasy elements in their play. In this investigation (Singer, 1961), children ages six through nine were questioned in a structured interview about their play patterns, imaginary companions, and "pictures in their heads," and then were classified into high- and low-fantasy play groups.

All the children also underwent a series of other procedures. They were questioned in some detail about parental interaction and family background factors, were asked to do some doodling after being given a choice of one crayon to use (red, yellow, green, or blue) and to make up original stories which were subsequently rated for creativity, achievement, and other motivational themes. Of particular interest was the rocket ship game. Informed that experimenters were looking for spacemen of the future, the children were asked to sit quietly in chairs for as long as they possibly could. It should be noted that care was taken not to mislead the children into believing this was an actual selection procedure; they were merely given a notion of what kinds of conditions were necessary for space flight. They were told that sitting quietly simulated the relative isolation and cramped space conditions prevailing in space capsules. The children were permitted under the first delay condition to indicate when they could no longer sit in place. In the second condition they were asked to stay in place for their estimate of fifteen minutes. Data on both measures indicated a moderately high individual consistency in waiting ability.

The results were fairly clear-cut. High-fantasy children were able to sit longer in place than the children who showed little indication of daydreams or make-believe elements in their play. The high-fantasy group proved likely to turn the delay into a quasi-fantasy situation and through some slight motor activity or mouth noises made it clear that they were pretending an actual flight.

The two groups differed on other variables as well. High-fantasy children were rated as higher in creativity for their stories by independent judges who had no knowledge of experimental objectives. Similarly, in making crayon choices they showed a significant preference for blue and green, the so-called "cool" colors, whereas the low-fantasy children often chose red or yellow, the "warm" colors. Some literature has supported the notion that the "cool" end of the spectrum is more often associated with measures of control, intellectuality, and achievement-motivation (Colvin, 1953; Atkinson, 1958). When interview and test protocols were rated by a clinician unfamiliar with the objectives of the study, children

in the low-fantasy group were significantly far more often classified as hysterical personalities, high-fantasy children as obsessional personalities.

Some interesting results emerged as well from questions about background factors. The high-fantasy group reported considerably more interaction along fantasy lines (storytelling, fantasy games) with parents and indicated particular preference for or more extended association with one parent. The low-fantasy group more often indicated a nondiscriminating attitude towards their parents and considerably less personal interaction. Children in the high-fantasy group also proved to be more often either the oldest or only child or to have fewer older siblings than the low-fantasy children.

In effect, then, the results of this investigation led to at least the tentative conclusion that greater parental contact, less involvement with siblings, and greater storytelling creativity characterize children who report that they engage in more fantasy play. The ability to engage in fantasy play served to enable these children to sustain themselves more effectively when circumstances called for a long period of delay or waiting. A much earlier study (Riess, 1957) had also found that children with more imagination (Rorschach M responses) showed greater motor restraint during a waiting period.

An attempt to determine whether training children to play fantasy games might enhance their delaying ability foundered because of the technical difficulties of developing suitable controls (Singer and Chipman, 1961). Some results may be cited, however, since an effort was made to inquire more directly about daydreaming through a verbally administered form of the daydream questionnaire used with adults. A test and retest carried out several weeks apart with a sample of twenty-three children of ages seven through nine yielded a correlation of .83, suggesting a satisfactorily high degree of consistency in response to this instrument. The daydream score for this sample correlated significantly with the two measures of delay in the rocket ship test. In a subsequent study with a larger group, it was found that children who indicated a greater degree of daydreaming also provided more internal "entertainment" or stimulation for themselves during the waiting period, while children who showed less disposition to daydream were also the ones who made more direct perceptual responses and seemed to depend more heavily on what Piaget has called the "stimulus nutriment" of the environment.

An outgrowth of these studies was an investigation by Singer and Streiner (1965) of the imaginative behavior of congenitally blind children. In view of the strong visual component in most reports of daydreaming and imagination, it appears that blind children may be doubly handicapped. Not only are they shut off from direct visual perceptual contact with the world but a whole realm of visual imagery is not available to them. Lacking such environmental stimulus nutriment they may be less likely to practice a variety of make-believe situations. One might surmise that young children born blind would show less make-believe play than an otherwise comparable sighted group. Formal studies suggest that when blindness occurs before age six, visual imagery is unlikely to persist into later life. The dreams of the blind, although utilizing auditory and kinesthetic imagery, tend to be somewhat reality oriented, traceable to specific day-residues or material recently read, and generally involve less variety in main character or type of conflict (McCartney, 1913; Kimmins, 1923; Blank, 1958). While some clinical observers have attributed greater fantasy disposition to the blind (Rowley, 1922; Cutsforth, 1933; Deutsch, 1928), none of their studies included comparison with comparable sighted subjects; lacking such comparisons these investigators may have overevaluated data that the blind do indeed engage in fantasy behavior.

In the Singer and Streiner (1965) study, a structured interview was carried out with each child pertaining to the structure and the content of the child's play habits, daydreams, and night dreams. Degree and nature of parental contact were examined, as were favorite games, any imaginary playmates, thoughts before going to sleep, and interior monologues. An actual recurrent fantasy, a new story, and an actual recalled dream were elicited from each child. The rocket-ship-waiting situation was also employed. The interview content was transcribed from tape recordings and rated by judges who were unfamiliar with the sighted status of the subjects or with the separate sections of the protocol.

The results made clear that blind children do engage in daydreams, make-believe play, and night dreams. Yet quite significant differences were obtained for each of the variables—namely, imaginative play, storytelling creativity, and creativity of dream content. In effect, in all cases the content of the material presented by the sighted children was rated as more make-believe, imaginative, or creative. Sighted children were also able to give significantly more specific examples of fantasies and had considerably more recall of dreams. In one respect only did the blind children show a greater fantasy disposition. This was in their more frequent reliance upon an *imaginary companion*, almost invariably a sighted person more capable than the blind child. In the waiting situation the long-standing habituation of the blind to remaining passive or controlling their motility counteracted the results found in the earlier studies with sighted children.

An examination of the content of the daydream and night-dream material corroborated the general rating idea. The blind children's daydream and night-dream content was more concrete, more closely related to immediate personal experiences, and somewhat more dependent in orientation. The sighted children brought in many more fantastic or impossible elements and their stories were freer of reference to family or to daily routine activities.

An example of the contrast emerges in the stories told by two children of quite comparable age and background. Both involved a trip to the airport. The blind child's story focused on the little boy's reaction to the plane, his having a nice trip, and enjoying going places with his mother. The sighted child, however, described an adventure in which the pilot was knocked unconscious when the plane hit an airpocket so that the parents had to fly the plane back to the airport. The parents taught the children to fly and the children became famous pilots in the war and shot down many planes. They were rewarded by receiving as gifts from the Air Force two personal jet planes. The blind child's fantasy thus appears to be a more direct reflection of recent experiences, while the daydream and dream content of the sighted child represents a more complex pattern of interwoven associations leading to a product that is more original or abstract.

While it is obvious that blind children, through

reading Braille and listening to talking story-books, radio, and TV, can make up some of the imaginative decrement resulting from lack of visual imagery, nevertheless the overall gap remains large. "Blindisms" (repetitive rocking or eye-rubbing motions) and immersion in other concrete kinesthetic or auditory experiences may somewhat replace the visual and provide a degree of stimulus nutriment, but it is unlikely that such stimuli are as conducive to evoking fantasy patterns as visual stimuli are.

In general, the series of studies and observations as part of our general research program on daydreaming raise the question of the importance of varied environmental stimulation in forming the basis for fantasy development. The impression gained seems contrary to the classical psychoanalytic formulations which stress imagination as arising from instinctual sources that have been blocked from expression. It seems more likely that the child who engages in fantasy play is not necessarily withdrawing from "real" life or responding defensively to inner instinctual promptings. It may be more likely that he is actively exploring his environment visually and then continuing this exploration in play. Curiosity, pleasure in development of imaginative skill, and some defensiveness may all combine to foster fantasy play as a strong disposition in a given child.

Daydreaming as a Cognitive Skill

Let us now consider some of the significant implications of the body of research we have summarized so far in this volume. The position to be presented here represents both the fruits of personal investigation and thought and the opportunity to examine other positions which will be cited here.

The position to which I refer represents a somewhat groping effort to move beyond behaviorist reductionism which focuses too much on overt response and the psychoanalytic reductionism which (even with the development of ego psychology) overemphasizes drives and neglects the subtle interplay of external stimulation with ongoing inner states. Hebb's (1949, 1959) influential theoretical and experimental work must be acknowledged as one force that has opened the way

for a deeper look both at the ongoing reverberatory activity of brain process and at the motivating properties of the environment in its complexity and unfamiliarity. White (1959, 1964) and Schachtel (1959), working somewhat more closely to psychoanalytic theory and clinical observation, have pointed out a position which stresses the importance of organismic development *for its own sake,* so to speak, rather than in the service of specific erotic or aggressive drives. In this respect their work also reflects some of the influence of the thought of Lois and Gardner Murphy, Piaget, and Werner. Quite recently Tomkins (1962, 1963) has also presented a point of view which emphasizes the great significance of affects or emotions as motivating properties of behavior and attempts to show the relation of affect to both the complex regulatory and feedback processes within the organism and to the density of neural stimulation provided by the complexity or novelty of environmental stimuli.

Within the framework of this "third force" in psychology—this cognitively oriented approach with its avoidance of drive-reduction theory—the phenomenon of daydreaming can be viewed as a more general capacity of the organism—a potential skill in Bartlett's (1958) sense—available for development in particular directions and under specific enhancing circumstances. The daydream is one manifestation of an ability to attend to internally produced stimuli or to use those stimuli to construct a new stimulus source less monotonous or less threatening than some external stimulus patterns.

If we assume that the brain is indeed continuously active, then the organism is constantly confronted with a competing source of stimulation from within. The feedback from the ongoing activity of the body itself must also be considered. At any given moment, just in sitting and other postures, there is stimulation of kinesthetic and tactual modalities. Smells and sounds from one's own body (for example, the gurglings of one's stomach) are all fed into central organizing areas of the brain and, in effect, compete with the reverberatory associational stream. The latter consists of recently perceived stimuli as well as associations from long-term storage which emerge either by linkage with recent stimulation or, very likely, almost randomly by the very nature of the activity of the brain. As Tomkins has put it: ". . . The central assembly is at best an untidy aggregate. It has none of the orderliness of our present-day [computer] programs. It is perpetually vulnerable to interference, drift, disassembly . . . it is more like an information stew than it is like a program. . . . As nature is said to abhor a vacuum, so psychologists have been loathe to look entropy full in the face" (Tomkins, 1963, p. 41).

The important work of Witkin and his associates (1962) suggests that long-standing differences in perceptual orientation may develop which represent important stylistic differences in perceptual and motor priorities. Similar important stylistic differences in attention to internal or external stimulus channels may develop which have unique value to a given individual or turn out to be adaptive to very special environments. Barron (1955), for example, found that Rorschach M-perceivers were consistently rated as different personality types from persons who saw few Rorschach M, but that these differences were not manifested in test performances and certain skills as much as in the impression the M-perceivers made on others. Similarly, one of the implications of the Singer and Antrobus (1963) factor analysis of daydream scales is that persons may differ strikingly in their style of response to inner experience without necessarily manifesting greater neurotic tendencies in one or the other pattern.

In essence, then, it is argued that the relative reliance on priority assigned to various channels of stimulus information, grossly termed inner and outer, is an individually developed skill pattern which may or may not have long-run adaptive import. The person disposed to creating pleasurable stimulation by attention to his own thoughts may well withdraw some attention from the external environment but he may have also learned to make certain modifications in his behavior to manage this. The daydreamer may "see" less when he drives but he may have learned to drive more slowly in general than the person whose pleasure comes from his active involvement in the speed or physical experience of wind on the face, the flashing by of scenery, or his catching up to and passing another car.

As with any skill, the response to inner stimulation may be put to a variety of uses or serve purposes which are not always desirable. Daydreaming might well serve a defensive function, as originally noted by Freud, so that an individual could avoid awareness of sexual fears or doubts through fantasied prowess in semi-disguised form. As such a defensive reliance on fantasy persisted, the skill might be overvalued. Its once defensive utility no longer advantageous, daydreaming might persist as a withdrawal state or obsessional substitutive symptom. A patient in psychoanalysis impressed by a newly discovered ability to track down a sudden fear or affective response through examination of an associative chain may turn into a bore at parties or may use the technique to avoid confronting a more serious personality problem. Whatever the uses to which daydreaming may be put, however, it seems best regarded as a capacity available to most persons for assigning priorities to particular sets of spontaneous internally produced cognitive stimuli.

Tomkins (1962, 1963) has offered some cogent arguments for assigning to the less specific affect system a more important role in motivation than to the specific drives. He has also suggested that there are certain innate activities of the positive (surprise, interest, joy) and negative (rage, fear, distress) affects. Briefly, he has argued that negative affects are aroused by a persisting high level of density of neural firing which can be produced either by an unpleasant or unfamiliar external situation—or, I might add, by a series of internal associations or memories, for example, the details of the death of a loved one. A reduced density of neural firing produces laughter, smiling, and the experience of joy. Here the conception verges close on Freud's concept of drive reduction, but it is extended by Tomkin's emphasis on surprise and interest as positive affects activated by a gradual rise in stimulation. Thus the individual, in striving to maximize pleasurable affect, may seek and welcome new stimulation. To the extent that new stimulation can be produced by attention to inner ongoing reverberatory activity or by construction of new internal environments through organized daydreaming, the individual has available an additional dimension for achievement of positive affect.

Once a long-standing disposition has been developed for assigning a high priority to internal channels, however, there may not be any turning back. The internally sensitive person may have to confront not only pleasant, but unpleasant memories, not only familiar or welcome associations, but also awareness of doubts, fears, and hatreds. This may account for the generally significant correlations obtained between daydream frequency measures and various anxiety scales. The penalty of self-awareness and introspection is the direct confrontation of anxiety. The extrovert or represser may well experience the same degree of anxiety symptomatically or in the form of insomnia and somatic ailments. For many persons who have developed priority for internal channel response and who also have serious personality problems, self-awareness may take the form of repetitive anxious fantasies which maintain the high level of density of stimulation, creating despair and distress. Such negative fantasies may also be used as repetitive obsessional substitutions preventing attention to a more seriously disturbing psychological problem; for example, a persistent hypochondriacal fantasy may prevent awareness of sexual inadequacy or of irresponsibility and failure in a significant social obligation.

The Internalization of Play

THE FUNCTION OF FANTASY

It may be possible to understand the implications of the cognitive-skill approach to daydreaming if we begin by speculating somewhat as to its development in childhood. Piaget (1962), in forty years of careful observation of the development of thought and language in children, has been struck by the interaction of two general processes which he terms *accommodation* and *assimilation*. The child must on the one hand accommodate his perceptual and motor apparatus to the outside world—he must make appropriate differentiations of figures and grounds, of colors, of shapes, and also of the significance or utility of certain perceptual objects or of certain motor responses. This adaptation to the "real" world is, of course, limited by the actual inherent skills and maturation level of the child, and by (a factor rather neglected by Piaget) the particular interaction patterns established by parents. On the other hand, whatever is available from the outside world is

assimilated in the cognitive and affective system which is already functioning for its own sake *within* the child. Thus the information which the outside world makes available to the child becomes a part of the child's own internal sphere and plays perhaps quite a different role there than might be anticipated by the adults. This conception has been elaborated upon by Schachtel (1959), who has noted how material that is obvious to adults, for example, a story like "The Three Bears," takes on for a child quite a different significance in its own right and forms a much different associational pattern in the young child's memory storage system.

When we observe a young child imitating a sound or a gesture and we laugh in a positive way, he strives to repeat this act and to adapt his motor and perceptual apparatus to ours. Yet, when alone, he may repeat the word or gesture and begin to work it into a pattern that bears no discernible relationship to the adjustment he made for the sake of having contact with the adults. The inherent reward qualities attained by increasing emotional experiences of interest and joy lead the child when alone to attempt to use the material he has incorporated through his imitative accommodation to create new sources of change and pleasure. This assimilative process, free of any constraints to reproduce exactly the external world, permits a freer combination of associations and accounts both for the bizarre and the creative quality we discern in children's play. Later the child may take the fruits of what he has practiced for its own sake and bring these back again to some accommodation to the outside world. In this case, as Piaget notes, the combination of creative inner activity with an awareness of the demands of the outer world leads to effective thought or what Piaget calls "operations." But even in later life the continuation of assimilative activity plays an important role in developing creative thought, while accommodation results in careful recall or imitation of what is appropriate in a social circumstance.

The picture I have been striving to present is of an active, curious, almost endlessly inventive child, given, however, material from without, with which he can deal. For the very young infant little enough is needed, and his own body, his own movements, the appearance and disappearance of his own hands—all these can suffice. As he masters these simpler perceptual, motor, or imaginal integrations, he requires more complex material, and this must be provided in part by his parents. The reader familiar with the psychoanalytic model of development of thought presented by Rapaport (1951) . . . will sense that Rapaport's portrayal is of a passive, helpless infant in whom a hunger need arises, a hallucinatory image of the breast occurs, temporarily delaying distress over failure of gratification, gratification is available, and then activity subsides. By contrast, the emphasis here is upon a more actively curious child, who enjoys play for its own sake. As both White (1959) and Schachtel (1959) have pointed out, the child who is under great drive pressure is less likely to explore or play. Instead, observation suggests that the child's more creative learning occurs under states of relative biological satisfaction.

Although the internalization of spontaneous play into symbolism and the daydream is largely completed by early adolescence, it is undoubtedly a very gradual process that probably continues through life. Let us consider some of the conditions particularly conducive for an earlier, more extensive, and more differentiated skill in fantasy or daydreaming. We must begin by accepting the possibility of very real difference in constitutional predispositions in children. Some are more motorically active than others, some apparently more prone to anxiety under pressure of need; for some the build-up of what Tomkins calls density of neural stimulation is too rapid and its reduction too slow to permit easy smiling or joy. When an infant fails to respond with a ready smile, the onlooking parents' disappointment feeds back further distress to the child. This can create a dangerous circle of anxiety which allows only brief periods of reduced stress and emotions of joy or interest. Under such circumstances, spontaneous play or exploration may be much less than in other children and opportunities for fantasy development may be hindered. We may assume that, while man seems by natural selection uniquely capable of complex symbolism and imagery, such capacities are not uniform and internalization of play into imagination and a fluid associative stream may come more easily to some than to others.

The capacities for image formation and symbolization and for adopting an "attitude towards the possible," as Goldstein (1940) has put it, may well be a product of natural selection and are available for man's development. The growing child takes pleasure in his very use of these capacities—as White (1959) has argued in developing his notion of the sense of competence. At earliest stages this pleasure is evident in simple peek-a-boo games, in which the child is delighted by the rise and fall of tension in the "now it's here, now it isn't, now I can bring it back." The sense of efficacy which a child obtains from this capacity to hide or uncover his own hand or a rattle he is holding undoubtedly furthers his inclination to try other types of make-believe play. And, it may be noted, this capacity for control may be one step in the child's learning to differentiate between himself and his environment —"*I* can make my rattle go away and come back!"

The self-actualizing tendencies, the play for its own sake, the sense of efficacy that comes from realizing that one can have an effect upon the environment, undoubtedly develop into the capacities for symbolization, imagery, and as-if behavior. The child still has to learn how to exercise some of his make-believe skills. Here early individual differences may play an important role. I have observed children who show tendencies towards organized play well before the age of two and for whom the disruption of a line-up of toy cars or blocks is quite upsetting. These children play well alone and are no "trouble" to parents until put into social situations such as the playground of an apartment house or nursery school. There, the more kaleidoscopic play patterns of other children who cannot sustain the game or continue the line of toys or blocks lead to great distress for the child who tends towards "organized" play.

THE INTERNALIZATION PROCESS

At first, lacking sufficient perceptual differentiation, the child is content to use sticks for guns and blocks for cars, just as he may continue for some time to be undifferentiated in his verbal patterns. But as perceptual differentiation increases, the child may not be as satisfied with using any stick as a gun and any block as an airplane. His urge to play is great and he will make do, particularly if he has already shown some skill at make-believe. There is no question, however, that beyond the preschool age, the excitement of having more realistic-appearing toys is very great. Whether such realistic toys impede further fantasy development is an intriguing question.

As the child plays during the preschool period he combines considerable overt motor activity, running around, jumping, galloping like a horse, with much verbal expressiveness. Some verbalization involves imitation of sounds, for example, the engine-roar of a plane, or the narrative description of his game in the telegraphic, limited vocabulary of so young a child. One thinks of Piaget's (1932) charming description of the egocentric speech of nursery school children at play, in which two children, side-by-side, verbalize at length about their individual games without, however, really attempting to communicate.

At a later age, verbalization may be more elaborate and motor play more differentiated, reflecting increased sophistication and environmental imitation and differentiation. Erikson (1963) has employed a delightful excerpt from *Tom Sawyer* to exemplify the play of the nine- or ten-year-old. As Tom paints the fence, along comes Ben Rogers munching an apple, hop-skipping and jumping and engaging in a rather elaborate verbal and motor imitation of the steamship the *Big Missouri*, full of sound imitations, "Ting-a-ling," "Chow-ow-ow," and barked orders, "Get out that head-line! Lively now!"

Erikson goes on to say: "My clinical impression of Ben Rogers is a most favorable one and this on all three counts: organism, ego, and society. For he takes care of the body by munching an apple, he simultaneously enjoys imaginary control over a number of highly conflicting items (being a steamboat, and parts thereof, as well as being the captain of said steamboat, and the crew obeying said captain); while he loses not a moment in sizing up social reality when, on navigating a corner, he sees Tom at work. By no means reacting as a steamboat would he knows immediately how to pretend sympathy though he undoubtedly finds his own freedom enhanced by Tom's predicament" (Erikson, 1963, p. 210).

It seems clear that gradually less and less play is verbalized or expressed in gross motor fashion. By the ages of ten to twelve, many boys still seem eager to continue such activity but it now takes a social form with as much equipment— toy guns, packs, helmets—as is feasible. Solitary play of this type is less often verbal, and drawing may be used as a vehicle. As the child continues to play but inhibits overt motor activity, he may gradually, if Werner's theory of sensory-tonic vicariousness is correct, be sensitizing his brain for apparent motion perception—one basis for the stuff of imagery. His drawings or his television-watching provide him with content which he partially enacts and then inhibits motorically. Similarly his verbalizations, which in preschool age were sketchy for lack of content and elaborate during the ages five through nine, as Ben Rogers's were, now again become telegraphic, so that observing the fantasy play of an older child one catches only whispers of sound imitation or conversation. What seems to be happening is that the child, no longer able for various reasons to recreate his game each time through elaborate motor activity and vocalization, is finding a means for storage of the associational content in a form readily available on demand but not requiring public manifestation.

What I am suggesting is that for the younger child who can play publicly there is little need to store content from a previous day. Each fantasy game is *almost* a new one, with the overt motor activity and verbalization presenting through feedback a new environment of interest to the child. Obviously some gradual storage of content does occur, and phrases, sounds, and motor content of the game come more readily to the child with a bit of practice. But before social pressure or ridicule forces inhibition of overt play, any storage of previous play content is evident only in the greater elaborateness of overt fantasy play. As pressure for internalization increases, however, storage becomes more essential. A fairly systematic, if perhaps unwitting, effort is made by the child to transform his motor and verbal reactions into a form available on demand, without the elaborate overt feedback of self-produced kinesthesia, sight, and sound.

Tomkins (1963) has provided the beginnings of a theory of memory which may suggest how fantasy play material can become stored as a series of images or conversations available more or less on demand without overt reconstruction. According to Tomkins's view, which makes use of computer terminology, the technique of storage of specific material involves ". . . a process of informational compression in which the individual produces more and more miniaturized copies of the original information. This he does by using the original to produce a more miniature copy, which in turn is miniaturized in a series which in turn is miniaturized in a series. . . ." (Tomkins, 1963, p. 42).

This transformation of an overtly reproduced response, whether motor or verbal or quasi-perceptual, by miniaturizing for storage seems to some extent what may happen in the internalization of fantasy play. The child slowly and with many repetitions compresses the content of his play and verbal material. His motoric inhibition, following Werner's sensory-tonic theory, may lay a groundwork for a particularly movement-oriented perceptual sensitivity. At the same time he gradually compresses the content of his play, reducing it to miniature both by speeding up content into more and more telegraphic verbalization and more controlled motor patterns (for example, drawing as against overt movement) and by speaking more and more softly. The compression of the fantasy response into a miniature form probably takes years of effort. My experience in observation as yet suggests no clear hierarchy of order for the various modalities, although obviously the greater degree of motor activity is first to be internalized. A child between ten and twelve may show a little overt motor exemplification of fantasy play but one can still see him providing visual stimulation through drawings, and an occasional hushed "Bang-bang" or "5-4-3-2-1-blast off!" may leak out in public. One cannot avoid the thought that such compression not only miniaturizes specific components of fantasy play but also leads to compression of a whole pattern of approach to fantasy material or verbalization, so that there is increased tendency to transform conversation or visual content into comparable internalized form. Undoubtedly there are individual differences of great consequence in the sequence of miniaturization for modalities, in the systematic effort at miniaturization itself,

and in the subsequent continuation of internalized fantasy play as a valued personality dimension. What has been described so far is the more general process which may reflect the way in which at least the minimal degree of internalization occurs for most children.

Let us next consider some of the more specific conditions which may strongly influence great individual differences in the internalization process and in the assignment of priorities to inner or outer channels.

The Role of Parental Interaction in Fantasy Play

RELIEF FROM NEED-PRESSURE

Although Piaget refers to imitation as a manifestation of accommodation and White makes much of effective environmental response and curiosity, neither investigator has commented to any extent on the interpersonal interactions which form a crucial part of the child's environment. The theoretical position of Sullivan (1953b), and what may loosely be called his school of thought, has forced upon psychology a much more careful consideration of the ways in which parental attitudes and patterns of parent-child interaction play a critical role in personality development. In relation specifically to child development and patterns of imitation and identification, the recent experimental work of Bandura and Walters (1963) has also called attention to the extensive influence of the parental model. As one might surmise from the earlier section on experimental work with children, there has as yet been relatively little formal study of parental influences on the development of daydreaming or inner experience. What follows, therefore, represents a speculative construction gleaned from hints in research findings, clinical observation, and the experience of being both a parent and a child.

As White (1959) and Schachtel (1959) have noted, the manifestations of exploratory or creative play are most likely to appear under conditions in which biological drives are reasonably well satisfied and anxiety kept to a minimal level. The early experience with a benign and effective parent who can anticipate the infant's and young child's needs and maintain a reasonably natural and consistent schedule of feeding, sleeping, cleansing, and social stimulation will prevent the excessive persistence of unpleasant affective experience. Under such benign circumstances the child will be freer to begin the exploration of its body, of its motor control, and of the environment that is essential for effective ego development as well as more specifically for the development of make-believe and "as-if" games. It is this active play and interest in seeking stimulation that leads the child to construct new environments or new play situations when the novelty of a given toy has been lost. Once a child has explored a set of blocks as blocks and has determined the properties of the set, such as what stands on what and how high the tower may go, the next step may be to convert the blocks into a city or a schoolhouse or army fort. This crucial next step towards the development of an "as-if" play pattern is most likely to occur when the child has enough *time* to explore thoroughly the more direct perceptual-motor aspects of his contact with blocks. If he is hungry or frightened, the recurrent awareness of the unpleasant affect amplifying the drive signal (as Tomkins puts it) might break up sustained attention to his blocks.

I do not mean to deny that children work out unresolved conflicts through play or to say that their play cannot manifest anxieties or sexual orientations. Erikson (1963) has ably exemplified some of these manifestations through play of the problems of the child's world. What I am suggesting is that such uses of play to deal with fears of loss of love, sibling rivalry, or traumatic experiences can come only after the initial skill of as-if behavior has been developed to a reasonable level. The children who can "work out" or show signs of problems in their play are children who have already sufficiently learned how and had the opportunity to engage in make-believe. And such opportunity can come only if there has been at least some degree of parental attentiveness or consistent satisfaction of basic needs and affectional strivings. The children whose play is generally cited in case reports to exemplify evidence of conflict expression are usually middle-class children whose early basic needs were indeed cared for, even though particular areas of conflict with parents or siblings emerged later. It is quite likely that children whose early experiences involved greater direct frustration of biological need or who lacked a consistent and reasonably benign parental figure have never sufficiently mastered the art of as-if play or, later, the internalization of such play into daydreaming. Such children often are seen clinically as hyperactive, anti-social, impulse-ridden—the "acting-out" child so disruptive to the routine of the residential treatment center.

Although more systematic study is obviously rather urgent, some scanty evidence is available to support this view. Goldfarb's (1949) work with children reared in institutions during their very early years has yielded indications that they are in adolescence hyperactive, incapable of delay, and lacking in ability to rely on inner experiences, as evidenced by poor planning and lack of Rorschach M responses. Unpublished data obtained by Ralph Colvin at the Astor House for Children also have indicated that children institutionalized shortly after birth are more likely by ages nine through twelve to be rated high on impulsiveness and hyperactivity and lack of imagination than are otherwise comparable children who had even a few early years of some experience either with their own family or a foster family. A study by Singer and Sugarman (1955) indicated that schizophrenic patients who show more Rorschach M also present significantly fewer negative accounts of parental figures or indicate greater accessibility of parents in their TAT stories.

THE MOTHER'S ROLE

Thus far I have stressed perhaps the most essential features of parenthood in the early years —the maintenance of a benign atmosphere for early child development. But other important aspects of the parental role must be considered. The mother carries on a subtle affective interaction with the child as well as providing for its basic needs. Sullivan (1953b) has written with great sensitivity about how parental anxiety may be communicated to the child. More recently Tomkins (1962) has dealt in detail with the interplay of the smiling response between mother and child and its importance in establishing a basic communication system. In the pleasurable contacts which come with an interested (and interesting) mother, the child may be more likely to attempt an accommodating imitation of her sounds, her smiles, her movements.

Mowrer (1960) and Lair (1949) have dealt in detail with the role of a benign relationship between mother and child or even master and pet in eliciting imitative responses. Such stimulation is undoubtedly especially important in the learning of language and of culturally appropriate affective behavior. Its role in the development of fantasy play may come in the absence of the parent, when the child in its assimilative phase uses the motor and verbal responses of the parent in its own play by itself. The child's efforts may reflect an attempt not only to reinstate the absent parent (as Freud has implied) but probably to create through its own use of these gestures or sounds the positive affects experienced before with the parent.

The mother's role is not just one of familiarity, although regularity and frequency are of tremendous importance to a child to establish the degree of familiarity which adults attain with each other at a glance (Hebb, 1949; Schachtel, 1959). By saying funny things, by playing peek-a-boo games, by lightly bouncing the baby, the mother creates an *atmosphere* novel yet not startling, hence arousing the positive affect of interest (Tomkins, 1962). She creates an atmosphere of play itself as a means by which the child learns to obtain positive affective experience. For the child past infancy, the mother's play more clearly fosters the "as-if" attitude. Her singing and rudimentary storytelling, the use of games like "Where did the cereal go?" as a technique for getting the child to eat, all establish a stimulus complex which the child will attempt to imitate when the mother is present to elicit her smile (accommodation) and will engage in when alone to amuse itself (assimilation). Needless to say, mothers differ in the flexibility of their own behavior with the child, and the hungry, harried, anxious, or rejecting mother will herself be less capable of the playful exploration and creativity in the nurturing of her child which is one of the greatest arts of femininity.

To some extent Western civilization and most of its subcultural groups have left to the mother the role of fostering language development, storytelling, and inner experiences such as religion. Goethe, for instance, has made poetic reference to his mother's encouragement of making up stories. Folk lore in America also emphasizes the feminine schoolmarm, Abe Lincoln learning his letters from his mother, and the general role of the woman as the culture-bearer to frontier towns, introducing theaters and lectures. Without minimizing the many individual instances, such as the training of geniuses (McCurdy, 1960), where the fathers were important in fostering the imaginative tendencies of children, the statistically greater possibility at least for earlier generations has been that a positive early relationship with the mother is more likely to lead in both men and women to a greater disposition towards fantasy skill. A poignant account of a mother's fostering of such a fantasy development in her child appeared in "Stories," a *New Yorker* short story by Robert Hemenway. Quite recently the poet W. H. Auden has also in a *New Yorker* magazine memoir reported his mother's role in molding his imaginative inclinations. The data of the Singer and Mc-Craven (1961) and Singer and Schonbar (1961) studies seem to support this finding to some extent. Where the mother goes further and establishes some kind of confidante relationship with her children, such internalized activity may be fostered even more. Sharaf (1959) found that male college students who had developed much closer relationships with their mothers were inclined to be higher in intraception, using Murray's term, a tendency towards awareness and analysis of inner experience. Clinically, observation indicates that excessive fostering of such an intimate relationship may lead to Oedipal difficulties and to serious neurotic problems, along with encouraging imaginative development.

GENERAL PARENTAL INFLUENCES

Establishment of a confidante relationship may be only one of many ways in which close parental contact fosters imaginative development. The general atmosphere of the home, the emphasis on reading and literacy, the degree to which the parents are tolerant of children's fantasy games and encourage exploratory play—all of these undoubtedly must play a role in the enhancement of daydreaming as a skill. Parents who talk freely of stories or plays, who occasionally engage in bits of play acting themselves, or who, on occasion, even if briefly, are willing to engage in make-believe games with children, may provide the stimulation and stimulus content for the fantasy play the children will engage in later when alone.

The importance of the stimulus content provided by parents should not be overlooked. Parents whose conversation either with each other in the child's presence or directly with the child is limited only to the most immediately experienced content—"the lateness of supper," "time for bed," "the window shade needs fixing," "keep quiet so we can hear the TV!"—are offering little material which the child can weave into fantasy play later. Parents who read and tell each other or the children about the material read or who discuss significant events not immediately available to the child—international affairs, their business or work situations, or even gossip—are providing a greater variety of material. Even when much of this is not well understood by the children, it can be woven into their solitary play; indeed, the very strangeness of some of the material or the names or events may challenge the child's interest and lead to what looks to adults like a somewhat bizarre or comical fantasy creation.

Enforced precocity may also lead to a greater degree of fantasy activity. Parents who discuss more adult subjects with their children or who bring the children along on trips, to theaters, or social engagements intended for adults, are providing some degree of more complex material which children, in imitation initially, and later during assimilative activity, will include in play. Of course, such enforced precocity may not be an optimally healthy situation for a child psychologically. Parents who enforce early social maturity often do so out of coldness, egocentricity, or impatience with childhood's limitations. At the same time, considerable anecdotal evidence indicates that children subjected to such situations often show greater fantasy development. On the other hand, enforced precocity *without* the opportunity for solitary play and practice of fantasy will not lead to an inner development. Children led into professional careers as actors or entertainers have considerable pressure on them for "grown-up" behavior and contact with adults. In their free time, however, they are likely to be required to engage in pre-established training routines, with only very little opportunity for solitary play and imaginative development.

Daydreaming skill is probably closely associated with exploratory tendencies. Parental attitudes that inhibit such activities are also more likely to limit the use of new-found content for fantasy play or the use of fantasy play itself as a technique for creating new environments. Exploration and as-if play both depend on the individualized activity of the child. If excessive parental anxiety, punitive restriction, or contempt block a child's exploration, whether of his body, his environment, or his assimilative play activity, then there is a greater likelihood that he will avoid or be unable to enjoy or attend to private experiences.

For persons whose exploration has been restricted or who are from early years intimidated about assimilative activity, one might expect less discriminating sensitivity even to sensuous experience, as Schachtel (1959) has suggested. Kaplan and Singer (1963) have carried this conception further and argued that what they term a "self-alienated man" would "de-emphasize . . . autocentric modalities and in doing so reduce subjective experience and awareness of self." They hypothesized that a person who rated high on the Rokeach Dogmatism Scale, indicating that "the individual . . . is closed to or unaware of his feelings, tendencies, impulses, or reactions" (Kaplan and Singer, 1963, p. 487), would also reveal less sensory acuity than a person in a contrasted low-dogmatism group. The investigators' results clearly supported their hypothesis that the less dogmatic at the ideational level were also more discriminating at all sensory levels, but particularly in the senses least capable of objective expression, that is, smell, taste, and touch.

This investigation appears to support the view presented here that development of sensitivity to inner experience may be linked with an early opportunity for free exploration, and play may be linked with the opportunity for the utilization of a variety of sensory modalities. A widespread popular point of view, often cited by clinicians as well, holds that the daydreamer or inner-oriented person is less capable of enjoying sensual or physical experience. This notion may have arisen because such persons, who allot greater priority of responding to internal channels, may not overtly manifest their sensual interests to the same degree as persons minimally concerned with inner experience. That such introversive persons are acutely aware of many kinds of sensual experience seems undeniable, however, and in the realm of the creative the great introspectionists have excelled because they were capable of describing with clarity a great variety of subtle taste, smell, and touch experiences, as well as auditory and visual ones. Recall the imagery of Keats's *Eve of St. Agnes,* Joyce's detailed communication of smell and bodily sensation, and, perhaps most strikingly, that the creator of Hamlet also created Falstaff.

The parent, then, in permitting free play and free exploration, establishes a basic atmosphere in which the child can maximize his affective experiences of interest and joy through a series of detailed discriminations. If such discriminations are also incorporated in fantasy play, they become more and more the stuff of a richly sensitive inner experience. Certain areas of experience may be more or less emphasized, of course, by idiosyncratic factors. For example, parents who prevent sexual exploration may be more tolerant of other types of physical exploration. In many subtle ways the parents do indeed play a role in shaping the degree to which exploratory behavior and as-if play will be combined eventually into the cognitive skills of daydreaming and self-awareness.

Opportunity for Practice and Daydream Development

The development of a skill as subtle as the ability to respond to inner spontaneous cognitive processes without necessarily seriously impairing adaptive environmental awareness undoubtedly takes considerable practice. Because of its nature, such a skill must as a rule be practiced alone. The literature on the imaginative, sensitive child has indeed stressed his loneliness, and Schachtel's (1961) work on affiliation motivation seems to bring out clearly that first-born or only children do indeed show a craving for company in their fantasy and in some of their actions. Yet children will often show signs of a need to withdraw from a group in order to carry on fantasy activity or some form of solitary play or, later on, to read or to engage in a hobby. Our present American society in many ways offers little such opportunity, however; the great emphasis on organized activity —the round of Brownies or Cub Scouts, music lessons, dance lessons, Little League games, father-son dinners—precludes the privacy a child needs for solitary play and fantasy development.

Quite apart from any active part played by parents, other factors may significantly affect the opportunity for practice of fantasy. An only or first-born child may, of course, have the greatest opportunities for solitary play since even doting parents must spend some time on adult preoccupations. But the second-, third-, or fourth-born child (except in cases of a great age gap with other siblings) is in quite a different psychological situation. Other children represent a constant element in his life space, and the likelihood of his being left alone is greatly reduced. The active play of other children has a strong appeal and leads a child to give up solitary play rather readily. The level of imagination in play groups tends as a rule towards that of the least imaginative unless there are older children in leadership or unless the more imaginative children are also particularly forceful personalities. Observing attempts at organizing more elaborate fantasy play games among groups of five- through eleven-year-old children can be painful for adults who see the efforts of the children trying to plan the game interrupted by sudden laughter or irrelevant teasing and chasing. The experience of such group situations has unquestioned value for a child in preparing him for the comparable ebb and flow that occurs in adult conversations and social behavior, but it may be destructive of the development of imaginative skills.

Indeed, such a realization undoubtedly affected the thinking of parents intent on producing genius children, for a number of them insisted on the child's complete separation from peer groups (McCurdy, 1960). John Stuart Mill has written with sadness of the social harm done him by his father's early intellectual program for him, but it is quite clear that the program did have its effect of producing an active intraceptive capacity. Bertrand

Russell has also described a long period of social isolation in childhood when he lived with his grandmother and found most of his stimulation in self-created games and his library (Egner and Dennon, 1962).

The opportunity for privacy thus permits time for practice of self-generated play or later daydreaming skill. Such private activity also must play a great part in leading to a highly differentiated sense of self or of "me-ness." The very act of observing one's own inner processes or of creating play situations in which no others are sharing makes for a more sharp differentiation of the I-thou dimension, and, incidentally, of the dimension of inner experience as a clearly delineated sphere of activity. In moderation such separation of self may be an essential feature of a healthy development of self-awareness and individuality. Of course, it can be carried too far—to the point of a schizoid solipsism. At the other extreme, the child who is never alone may later in life find it difficult to be in situations in which he is socially isolated and may be startled when he is made aware of his ongoing inner spontaneous processes. The finding cited by Mendelson (West, 1962) that hallucinators showed less daydreaming predisposition than did nonhallucinators, suggests that one adaptive advantage of the practice of daydreaming is that it prepares the adult to accept his own inner processes and to differentiate fantasy from reality more precisely.

The accident of birth into the middle of a large family, the fate of growing up in conditions of lower socioeconomic status or severe poverty, where crowded conditions prevail, may impede development of sensitivity to inner experience. The so-called inability to delay gratification, impulsivity, and lack of basic trust manifested by many children from culturally disadvantaged groups may in part reflect the lack of inner continuity and integrated self-differentiation which an opportunity for the development of an inner fantasy life might have been able to provide. Growing up in an atmosphere where parents themselves present models of aggressive, uneducated, impulsive, or distrustful behavior (Mischel, 1965), children may be less likely to internalize long-range goals or fantasy play content. In this connection the influence of television as a stimulant of fantasy may be quite significant, but,

unless the material provided is assimilated when the child is alone, the TV content may ultimately be available only when he directly confronts the set itself.

Cultural Stimulation of Imagination

Reading, radio serials, television, movies, and popular music undoubtedly all play an important role in stimulating fantasy play in young children and daydreaming in later childhood and adolescence. These media undoubtedly encourage the actual engagement in as-if behavior. Thus the very young child, even in watching a TV cowboy movie, may arise and begin to play his own cowboy game with shouts and "giddyaps" and "bang-bangs," soon losing contact with what is actually transpiring on the screen. The popular entertainment media make available scenes of interpersonal behavior, places, and events ordinarily beyond the intellectual grasp of younger children but exciting enough to suggest imitation or assimilative play. For the child from a family which presents a drab or even noxious model, such popular fantasy stimuli present dramatic alternatives. The models presented by television and movie stars or popular singers undoubtedly influence styles of dress, speech patterns, and to some extent, personality characteristics. The exotic or luxurious settings of movies and television and the interesting characters portrayed provide basic content for fantasy activity.

An interesting question is whether reading is more stimulating to the development of imaginative skill and reliance on inner experience than, say, radio, movies, and television, in approximately that order. In general, adolescents who show active and varied fantasy lives tend to be more extensive readers but we cannot be sure whether a causal aspect is involved. One might speculate that a medium such as reading, which permits greater reliance on the various imagery modalities, leads to more development and skill at reliance on inner channels. I believe radio played an immediate role in this regard, since visual imagery had to be developed somewhat to follow the direct auditory stimulation of the story. The tremendous power of the movies and of television in exciting fantasy activity cannot be denied, however. The ready availability of television and movies leads also to the young person's reliance on them *instead* of carrying on individual fantasy activity. In that case, the extensive practice and time required to miniaturize perceptual and motor imagery into forms suitable for extended storage does not take place and the capacity for a self-generated daydream does not develop to the same extent as it does for a reader who takes time to think about the material in a page and run it through a "mental screen."

Popular songs may be mentioned briefly. Much has been written about their content as a reflection of adolescent fantasies and as a stimulant for such fantasies. While my introspections as a music lover make it clear that much daydreaming occurs during music listening, it is also the case that when an extended daydream is touched off a good deal of the music is missed! The popular song to which most adolescents listen word for word with concurrent dancing or foot-tapping or active singing calls forth a direct perceptual-motor reaction. Such direct motor responses do not seem especially conducive to developing inner fantasy skills. The definite psychological values of music lie, I believe, not so much in the encouragement of inner-directed orientation as in the very direct physical, perceptual, aesthetic response.

Although we have little formal evidence, it seems quite likely that subcultural group experience plays a significant role in imaginative development. If the cultural atmosphere reflects hostility towards imaginative play, it may affect the way in which a child sees such activity as ego-syntonic. Studies by Singer and Opler (1956) and Opler and Singer (1956) yielded some indications that anthropological suggestions concerning the support of fantasy in Irish and Italian cultures were upheld in a group of schizophrenics. McArthur's (1955) study of the fantasies of upper-class and middle-class adolescents also revealed differences in value orientation and in relative emphasis on past versus future, but little evidence on the effect of class status on degree of fantasy is available.

A fairly general trend in the American ethos has been a distrust of the fantastic and highly imaginative, perhaps as one aspect of a strong anti-intellectual facet of our society. Such a trend has never been completely dominant, however,

despite viewers-with-alarm in every generation. After all, America has produced such highly imaginative writers as Poe, Hawthorne, Melville, and Faulkner. It remains to be seen whether the great upsurge of respect for the scientist as a man of great inner capacity will affect the anti-imaginative facets of our society. Since the orbiting of Sputnik, the PTA's and school boards and congressmen have become more interested in "creativity," most especially of the type exemplified by the thinking-man, engineer, or scientist daydream pattern described in the Singer and Antrobus (1963) factor analysis.

Since teachers, counselors, fellow-students, and others still reflect the dominant distrust of daydreaming in our society, one might expect the adolescent to be less developed in this skill and to quell any tendency in himself toward fantasy. Complex forces are at work in our society, however, and the great recent interest of the brighter high-school students in the "beat," in existential concepts or "Zen," undoubtedly reflects an effort to assert their right to develop their own imaginations without the contempt from others usually forthcoming to the dreamer. The very fact that in psychology there has been enough recent interest in such inner processes so that experimental papers on dreaming or fantasy processes (outside of strictly clinical concerns) are beginning to appear, undoubtedly reflects some small inward turn of the mores!

Suggestions for Further Research

It should be obvious to a critical reader that what has been asserted in this chapter remains far too general and that much greater precision in theoretical formulation and experimental study is necessary. The use of inner and outer channels . . . meshes with concepts such as Piaget's *assimilation* and *accommodation,* or Schachtel's *autocentric* and *allocentric* perceptual modes. All of these formulations involve dichotomies that may be too gross to describe the cognitive dimension in question. By defining fantasy play carefully, for example, in terms of relative nonperceptual elements, we could observe children under specified conditions of drive or affective arousal and ascertain whether fantasy play does indeed occur most often under minimal biological drive pressure. The degree of fantasy introduced into children's play during a period of hunger (prior to lunch, for example) compared with such elements manifested following a meal, might be observed systematically with suitable controls. Or one might study the manner in which systematically presented novel elements in an otherwise very familiar environment are integrated into fantasy play. A more systematic study of birth position and the degree of as-if elements in play would be most desirable, too.

Female readers may be aware that most examples in this book describe boys' experiences. Girls usually play games such as "house" and "school" that prepare them for normal adult roles, while the boys' games more often involve unreal possibilities. Both types of play call for as-if elements but have different implications for socialization. Adult data suggest no sex differences in frequency or even in content except for the most obvious ones of heroism for males versus fashion interest for females. Much needs to be done in this field with children, however.

A whole area as yet unexplored is that of trying to train children to play fantasy games and observe the degree to which internalization does occur. Ideally it would be desirable to see whether a long-term plan of such training would lead to greater internalization and sensitivity to inner channels in adolescence. One might also set up a graded series of such training for children and early adolescents and observe closely how the different age groups go about learning to fantasize. One might predict greater motor and perceptual behavior in the younger groups and increased evidence of compression and miniaturization in the fantasy-play learning of the adolescents. By careful observation of actual play and then comparison with the children's behavior in suitably modified monitoring or vigilance situations, we might begin to catch hold of the degree to which an ongoing inner stream of imagery is already present well before adolescence. It would also be possible to compare the degree of motor elements in spontaneous play with the degree of imagery manifested under reduced sensory stimulation.

Age Differences in Dramatic Improvisation

Brian Sutton-Smith   Gilbert Lazier

Douglas Zahn

A review of the literature on child drama (Mc-Caslin, 1968; Siks, 1958; Slade, 1968; Ward, 1948) reveals that there is no research on the developmental ordering of improvisational phenomena. Unlike the abundant stage studies of children's spontaneous art (Harris, 1963), there are no parallel treatments of children's dramatic improvisation. Whether this is due to the relative scarcity of dramatic programs for children in schools, the dominance of "cathartic" theories, or the difficulty of obtaining records of this very complex subject-matter is not certain. The existence of video-taping procedures removes the latter handicap. The present study represents a first attempt to collect a sample of improvisations from children of different age levels in order to see if these do in fact exhibit a developmental character.

Method

The Ss were 34 children (22 female, 12 male) ages 7–12 yr. who were voluntary participants in an after-school creative dramatics program. The type of program in which they had participated for 6 mo. prior to this study is described by Siks (1958). It has a heavy emphasis on improvisation. All the prior activity as well as the study in question were carried out in a small (2 × 15 ft.) carpeted and soundproofed room. Two sides of the room were viewable through one-way mirrors. The area was monitored by three ceiling microphones as well as a permanently installed wide-angle ½-in. video camera, and a portable ½-in. camera with zoom lens operated manually from one of the booths.

As all the texts in the field of creative drama agree that a fundamental skill is the ability to react to something imaginary as if it were existent, the children were presented with a series of such tasks involving, for example, reacting to an imaginary object within a larger specified environment, and reacting to object and environment while interacting with another character. The larger study included 10 such activities. The present report deals with only these first three. In each

Brian Sutton-Smith, Gilbert Lazier, and Douglas Zahn, "Age Differences in Dramatic Improvisation," *Proceedings, 79th Annual Convention,* American Psychological Association, 1971.

case the teacher introduced the solitary child to the tasks with instructions such as the following:

> I'd like you to imagine something for me, if you will. Right here where my fingers are touching the floor, I want you to suddenly find a large brown wallet. Now, the wallet has 21 bills in it. I'd like you to do three things with it, first of all find it. Do whatever you think you might do with it if you really found a wallet. Your cue to begin is when I sit down. Do you understand everything?

Scene 2 added to finding the wallet the introduction of a city park, sandbox, and swings. Scene 3 added the further complication of a policeman who entered the scene after the wallet was found and challenged the child's right to its possession.

Many categories were developed for the analysis and quantification of the video records obtained. The present report includes: *duration:* of the child's improvisation following the instructions; *space:* the amount traversed; *stops:* the number of times the child stopped during his enactment; *incidents:* an integral unit in which the motivational pattern remained unchanged; *novel incidents:* an incident for which there was no precedent in the instructions; *acts:* the smallest units of represented behavior. These included details of body and gestural movement where these were intended; *repeats:* the number of times the same acts were repeated; *characters:* the number of imaginary characters created by the child during his improvisation; *resistant acts and verbalizations:* this category was relevant only to the third scene and the appearance of the policeman; *resistance time:* the amount of time spent resisting the policeman.

Each category was scored from the videotapes by two separate teams working independently. Reliabilities varied from 73% for acts to 98% for time (taken by a stopwatch).

Results

The data were subject to analysis of variance for repeated measures to compare two age groups (7–8 yr. vs. 9–12 yr.) and the two sexes. There were no sex differences, no Sex $\times$ Age interactions, but there were the following age differences.

The two age groups did not differ in the amount of time devoted to the scenes, which were approximately 40, 60, and 70 sec. in each successive scene. The younger age group, however, traversed almost twice as much space in every scene ($p < .05$) and made twice as many stops in the first two scenes ($p < .05$; $p < .01$). The last scene, which was controlled to a greater extent by the preset dialogue of the policeman, led to a general attenuation of differences between the two age groups. There were no significant differences between the two groups in the number of incidents. Most children found the wallet in the first scene, played on the swings, played in the sandbox, and found the wallet in the second scene, then repeated these for the third scene until the policeman appeared with his challenge. However, the younger age group did invent almost four times as many novel incidents in the first and second scenes ($p < .01$; $p < .01$). They also created about three times as many imaginary characters in both of those scenes ($p < .01$; $p < .01$). Again, while there were no differences between the number of acts created within each scene, the older age group repeated its acts twice as much in the first two scenes ($p < .01$; $p < .01$). What this means is that the younger group had more incidents and fewer details for each incident. The older group had fewer incidents and more details for each. Given that the younger group also traversed more space, made more stops, and created more novel characters and incidents with this same lack of detail, we might say they displayed about twice as much action and half as much communication as the older group.

When the policeman interfered in the third scene the younger group spent an average of 30 sec. resisting him, as compared with the older group's 12 sec. ($p < .01$). They also made more resistant acts and verbalizations, but not significantly so.

Discussion

The basic finding of this study is that there are clear-cut age differences in improvisation during childhood, at least as measured by the above categories. While this will not appear as a surprise to some, it must be considered in the light of the more prevalent view in the theatre world that acting is a cathartic exercise or a matter of individual talent, not a phenomenon particularly suitable for developmental analysis. Yet if such differences are replicated (and the authors are currently proceeding with such replications) there are very important implications for the teaching of drama to children and for the understanding of why and how they react to the materials presented to them. The discovery of such age differences in children's drawings 50 yr. ago contributed to a revolution in the teaching and appreciation of children's art.

The likelihood that the present differences in improvisation are particular to this population is lessened by the parallel with many other developmental studies. Younger children generally respond with more diffuseness (or more noise) to any given stimulus (Graham, Berman, & Ernhart, 1960). The present instructions triggered off a wider variety of responses in the younger age group; they brought in more people, they moved more, they added more novelty, and, not shown in these results, they insisted on talking about it more afterwards. This is similar to earlier findings on children's responses to thematic apperception tests where this younger age group (7–8 yr.) was found to be more prolific, expressive, and original in fantasy than the older group, which was in turn more concerned with technique, form, and order (Sanford, Adkins, Millier, & Cobb, 1943). There are parallels too with children's art at this younger age which has the same highly schematic quality (Harris, 1963). We have been inclined to term the hectic action of the 7–8-yr.-olds (more novel incidents and more movement) and the lack of communications (fewer repeated acts) the *keystone effect*. One paradox presents itself, however. In a parallel study involving the content analysis of the drawings and stories of these same children, it was found that the older children had both more novel incidents and more details in those art forms. That is, the older children showed increased signs of complexity in both respects, not just in terms of details within the incidents. Our present interpretation of these differences across artistic media is that the drawing and stories with which the children have had consistently more experience over the years are actually at a higher developmental level. There was, in contrast, something quite playlike (and not actorlike) in the way our 7- and 8-yr.-olds interrupted their acting to make comments to the teacher, and in the way they resisted the policeman. It was often more like a game of tag than the representation of a story (Avedon & Sutton-Smith, 1971; Herron & Sutton-Smith, 1971). The older children, on the other hand, treated the task much more clearly as one of portrayal and communication to the teacher. Questions related to these "expressive profiles" across art forms have been dealt with elsewhere (Sutton-Smith, in press).

The categories chosen for this first analysis were drawn from Kenneth Burke's (1952) dramatic pentad (time, space, actors, acts, and agencies). What they do is call attention to structural, or, if you will, the cognitive, aspects of representation. What they do not do is focus in upon the actor's competence in an affective sense. Some of our children who showed quite sketchy representation were nevertheless felt to be highly effective communicators of appropriate feeling. To evaluate this phenomenon we require measures with more empathic focus. We are currently proceeding with studies of this sort.

REFERENCES

AVEDON, E., & SUTTON-SMITH, B. *The study of games.* New York: Wiley, 1971.

BURKE, K. *A rhetoric of motives.* New York: Prentice-Hall, 1952.

GRAHAM, F. K., BERMAN, P., & ERNHART, C. B. Development in preschool children of the ability to copy forms. *Child Development,* 1960, 31, 339–359.

HARRIS, D. B. *Children's drawings and measure of intellectual maturity.* New York: Harcourt, Brace & World, 1963.

HERRON, R. E., & SUTTON-SMITH, B. *Child's play.* New York: Wiley, 1971.

MC CASLIN, N. *Creative dramatics in the classroom.* New York: McKay, 1968.

SANFORD, R. N., ADKINS, M. M., MILLIER, R. B., & COBB, E. A. Physique, personality and scholarship. *Monographs of the Society for Research in Child Development,* 1943, 8, Serial No. 34.

SIKS, G. B. *Creative dramatics: An art for children.* New York: Harper & Row, 1958.

SUTTON-SMITH, B. *The folkgames of children.* Austin: University of Texas Press, in press.

SLADE, P. *An introduction to child drama.* London: University of London Press, 1967.

WARD, W. *Play acting with children.* New York: Appleton-Century-Crofts, 1947.

Developmental Trends in Sensitivity to Painting Style and Subject Matter

Howard Gardner   Judith Gardner

The Problem and Its Background

Which of the diverse aspects of pictorial displays are noticed and which are preferred by children of different ages has long interested psychologists and educators. Reliable information about children's sensitivity to color, form, subject matter, or overall composition is needed if one wishes to understand perceptual development or to use pictorial materials appropriately in the classroom. Several general findings have emerged from earlier research on such perceptual sensitivities. It has been established that from earliest infancy children notice and prefer to attend to edges, contours, and contrasts,[1, 2] but that the capacity to pick out and discriminate various forms from one another increases dramatically throughout childhood.[3] Children can interpret representations in pictures by the age of two [4] even when they have had little or no prior experience with pictorial materials.[5] Sensitivity to specific colors and forms increases in the preschool years,

with older children tending increasingly to sort by form.[6] Interest in the subject matter represented in pictorial displays is strong throughout childhood,[7] with children tending to look for and discern objects in a variety of perceptual forms.[8, 9]

To insure clarity and experimental precision, previous research has employed simple stimuli, frequently prepared by the experimenter himself, and has concentrated upon the stimulus dimensions of color and dominant figure or form. Researchers have employed either geometrical shapes, abstract patterns, or simple line representations of objects. As a consequence, little is known about children's reactions to the more complex pictures produced by artists and about children's capacities to discern and evaluate more subtle features of pictures, such as texture, composition, or style. Though findings based on simplified patterns have been suggestive, it is clearly important for art educators that investigators probe children's reactions to the kinds of pictures ordinarily encountered in schools, museums, or homes and

Howard Gardner and Judith Gardner, "Developmental Trends in Sensitivity to Painting Style and Subject Matter." Reprinted from *Studies in Art Education, 12,* Fall 1970, publication of the National Art Education Association, Washington, D.C., pp. 11–16.

to those aspects of pictures which are valued by artists and connoisseurs.

An area consistent with these specifications and susceptible to analysis is children's sensitivity to painting styles. Though style may be conceptualized in a number of ways,[10, 11] it has proved reasonable and convenient to operationalize style sensitivity as the capacity to recognize that certain works have common properties indicating that they were produced by the same individual. Apart from scattered anecdotal material[4, 12] little is known about children's ability to recognize or to sort paintings by style. Walk and Tighe have investigated ability to form the concept of a painter's style, but their studies have been restricted to individual painters rather than to generalized style sensitivity and have not examined developmental trends.[13, 14] A few reports have noted that children do not spontaneously speak about style until adolescence,[15, 16] and such findings have been interpreted as suggesting that style sensitivity involves the kind of hypothetical thinking unavailable to preadolescents. Yet there is no reason to postulate that the ability to classify by style need be predicated on the ability to speak of style. Accordingly a series of studies has been undertaken in an effort to determine whether style sensitivity as well as sensitivity to other, equally subtle properties of pictorial materials, may exist at an earlier stage of development.

In the initial study, children were exposed to two reproductions of works by artist A and were then asked to select the additional work by A from an array containing single works by A, B, C, and D. Twenty sets employing different painters from diverse schools were employed. *Ss* averaging 6, 8, and 11–12 years of age did not perform significantly different from 14 year-olds on those items where subject matter was either controlled for (portraits) or absent (abstract works). Younger *Ss* did perform significantly poorer than adolescents on those items (heterogeneous) where the strategy of focusing on the subject matter *per se* rather than on the technique by which it was depicted could lead to an incorrect response. Thus, if shown two paintings of horses by Degas and then asked to choose the additional Degas from an array containing a ballerina by Degas and a horse by Dufy, younger *Ss* tended to equate represented subject matter with painting style and

to choose the Dufy. The adolescents were more likely to take into account those aspects of composition, balance, fine detail, and overall expressiveness thought to be central in style detection. The study suggested that, for younger *Ss*, sorting by style was synonymous with sorting by similarity and that subject matter was their principal means of assessing similarity. Adolescents had a more flexible method of judging similarity and so were able to look beyond what was being represented to the manner in which it was represented.

Questions and Hypotheses

The original study suggested a program of research which might illuminate the natural classificatory tendencies and the degree of flexibility available to various populations of different ages.[18, 19] Two questions of particular interest arose: 1) Do children at different ages and developmental stages ordinarily employ the same criteria in making judgments about similarities among paintings? 2) How are the natural sorting tendencies of children of various ages affected by instructions directing them to attend to stylistic features? To resolve these questions, sets of paintings were constructed which would pit subject matter and dominant figure against style as possible modes of classification. In these sets subject matter always coincided with dominant perceptual figure: i.e., not only were the objects represented in the two paintings characterizable by the same label (two trees) but they also had similar contours and perceptual Gestalts (two long narrow isosceles triangular masses with vertices at the top). It was hypothesized that older *Ss* would have a stronger tendency to group paintings spontaneously by style and would show greater sensitivity to instructions in their classifications.

Procedure

SUBJECTS

Forty first graders (average age 6) and forty sixth graders (average age 11) were selected at random from an elementary school in an upper middle class suburban community. Forty college sophomores (average age 19) at Harvard and Radcliffe Colleges volunteered to participate. A slightly larger number of males were included in the study.

MATERIALS

Eight sets of stimuli, each containing four post-card-sized reproductions of paintings, were assembled. Each set consisted of two paintings by one artist and two paintings by a second artist. The two paintings by the first artist always portrayed the same two kinds of subject matter (with the same dominant figures) as did the two paintings by the second artist. For example, set 7 consisted of a still life by Von Gogh, a still life by Matisse, a landscape by Van Gogh and a landscape by Matisse. The artists' names were never visible. A set could be sorted into pairs on the basis of subject matter represented or the style of the artist; an anomalous third grouping which cut across these dimensions was also possible.

STUDY 1

The four reproductions in a set were placed in front of the subject who was asked to make two piles of two paintings each, grouping together the paintings which he found "most similar." If a subject pressed for further instructions, he was told only to "place together those pairs which seem most alike to you." All subjects were asked to paraphrase the instructions and could do so. Twenty subjects at each age level participated in Study 1.

STUDY 2

The same procedure as in Study 1 was followed, except that subjects were told that two of the paintings were done by one artist and the other two by a second artist. Subjects were then asked to sort according to artist, placing together each pair which they thought had been painted by the same artist. Twenty subjects at each age level participated in this study.

Results

Each subject's score was the number of sortings by style on the eight items. A two-way analysis of variance (Age by Instructions) was performed on the scores, with both of the factors and the interaction being significant at the .01 level (cf. Table 1).

Additional analyses indicated that there was no significant difference between the scores of the various age groups when they were instructed simply to group by similarity ($F = 2.88$, $df = 2$, 57, N.S.) but that the performance of the age groups diverged greatly when subjects were instructed to group according to painting style ($F = 87.26$, $df = 2$, 57, p. $< .01$). First graders gave almost the same number of style responses irrespective of instructions ($F = .5$, $df = 1$, 38, N.S.) while sixth graders and college students dramatically increased style response under the second set of instructions (sixth graders: $F = 32.72$, $df = 1$, 38, p. $< .01$; sophomores: $F = 69.14$, $df = 1$, 38, p. $< .01$).

Table 1. Analysis of Variance: Scores in the Two Studies

Source	df	MS	F
Instructions	1	187.50	85.23*
Ages	2	98.24	44.65*
Age x Instruction	2	45.30	20.59*
Error	114	2.20	

*p $<$ .01

In addition to overall performance differences between groups, the sorting tendencies of individual subjects were also examined. Table 2 lists the number of subjects at each age level and condition who sorted five or more of the eight pairs according to style.

Chi-square tests indicated that the number of subjects with a strong tendency toward style sorting did not differ significantly across age groups in the first study ($\chi^2 = 2.70$, $df = 2$, N.S.) but differed markedly in the second study ($\chi^2 = 44.57$, $df = 2$, p. $< .01$). While the sophomores had a somewhat stronger tendency to sort by style under the style instruction than did the sixth graders ($\chi^2 = 3.52$, $df = 1$, p. $< .07$), a far larger gap existed between the first and the sixth graders ($\chi^2 = 25.48$, $df = 1$, p. $< .01$).

At no age level or condition were significant sex differences noted. The third anomalous grouping was rarely favored by any subject.

Discussion

Both of the questions raised above are illuminated by the results. When subject matter and painting style are alternative means of grouping paintings, subjects at different age levels tend to group by the subject matter represented. Only a few idiosyncratic or aesthetically sophisticated subjects appear willing or able to suspend this strong classificatory tendency. When subjects are explicitly instructed to group by style, however, most at or above the sixth grade level are able to take into account aspects other than the subject matter. Only the first graders appear insensitive to the new set of instructions.

Contrary to what was hypothesized, older subjects do not evince a stronger natural tendency to classify by style. These results seem attributable to the pervasive tendency in our culture to group according to membership in a class of objects, which may have its origin in the mother's handling of picture-books and is strongly reinforced in most school systems. Only when a powerful alternative or an explicit set of counter-instructions are offered may this tendency be suspended. A second possibility is that since the terms "similar" or "alike" so frequently pertain to class membership, the instructions in Study 1 created a set to sort by objects. Yet even if subjects were allowed to sort in whatever way they chose, classification by subject matter would probably be the most popular strategy.

The ability of older subjects to counteract this tendency indicates their flexibility, alertness to instructions, and awareness that a person may leave consistent traces throughout his works even though manifest subject matter and figure are radically altered. Apparently the youngest subjects are lacking in one or more of these capacities. The initial study did indicate that when subject matter was not available as a miscue, young subjects responded much like older ones. Thus it is conceivable that younger subjects have the potential to perceive style but that they are impeded by their proclivity toward noting subject matter and deeming it a sufficient (or even a necessary) basis for classification. In addition, instructions referring to works by a painter may well be devoid of meaning for young children; in efforts currently underway to train children to sort by style rather than by dominant figure, verbal instructions have been avoided.

The performance of the sixth graders is among the most suggestive aspects of the study. Their

Table 2. Number of Subjects Giving Five or More Style Responses

Instructions	Grade Level		
	First	Sixth	Sophomore
By Similarity	1	2	4
By Style	0	15	20

scores, closer to college students' than to first graders', are particularly notable since the college population may have been of a somewhat higher intelligence. Other studies have indicated that the sixth graders are on the verge of becoming sensitive to painting style,[17,18] either because they have attained greater familiarity with the arts, are undergoing certain neurological changes associated with puberty, or have become able to perform those logical operations which permit the consideration of hypothetical alternatives.[20] The impressive ability of the sixth graders to sort by style might conceivably be due to their conscious realization that subject matter was being pitted against style, and their resulting decision to disregard subject matter. Yet, the absence of comments by either the sixth graders or sophomores to this effect even in the post session interview makes it unlikely that either group was explicitly aware of the construction of the arrays. More probable, and of greater theoretical interest, is the possibility that inclusion of subject matter as an alternative induced the subjects to confront directly the question of which criteria are relevant to style. Even as the subject matter made it impossible for the youngest subjects to respond to stylistic qualities, it may have encouraged those individuals in the process of learning about style to avoid facile groupings and to direct their focus instead to those attributes more likely to reveal the characteristic features of particular artists. Perhaps, then, the sixth graders epitomized in their performance these trends toward greater flexibility and organization as well as the increased capacity to note relevant aspects of a situation which are thought to characterize the process of development.[21, 22]

Implications

Those concerned with education in the arts may find the present results unsettling yet hopeful.

While individuals intimately involved with art may naturally think of paintings in terms of their aesthetic or stylistic qualities, the study indicates that most individuals consider paintings initially and perhaps primarily in terms of the subject matter represented. Many of the subjects appear to regard paintings simply as objects to be identified and then dispensed with; they seem insufficiently aware that there are other, equally valid, bases on which to view and evaluate pictorial displays. Though these studies suggest that style is not a natural means of grouping, they also indicate that, by the time of adolescence and perhaps earlier, children have the potential to transcend the "identification set" and to take into account more subtle properties of pictorial materials. The practice of contrasting subject matter or dominant figure with style appears to encourage flexibility in classification; at any rate the present sixth grade class showed relatively more style sensitivity than have comparable groups.[17] Direct confrontation of alternative ways of classification and active manipulation of sets of stimuli may encourage the student to look beyond the most ready means of classification and seem to be useful teaching techniques. Teachers might assemble sets of paintings or other kinds of pictorial materials and guide students to consider the various plausible and implausible groupings; employment of different kinds of rules, instructions, or games might also encourage flexibility in a child's responses while deepening his discriminative and evaluative powers. While it seems unlikely that children under sixth grade age will learn to classify by style simply by being so directed, it remains possible that, when confronted over a period of time with such sets of contrasting pairs, children of a younger age may be able to learn to sort by styles. A training study currently underway will hopefully reveal the lower limits of style sensitivity and may also indicate whether the kinds of perceptual proclivities probed here have relevance outside the arts.[23]

REFERENCES

1. FANTZ, R. "The Origin of Form Perception," *Scientific American,* Vol. 204, No. 5, 1961, pp. 66–72.

2. KESSEN, W. "Sucking and Looking: Two Or-

ganized Congenital Patterns of Behavior in the Human Newborn," in H. Stevenson, ed., *Early Behavior.* New York: Wiley, 1967.

3. GIBSON, E., GIBSON, J., PICK, A., and OSSER, H.

"A Developmental Study of the Discrimination of Letterlike Forms, *Journal of Comparative and Physiological Psychology,* Vol. 55, No. 6, 1962, pp. 897–906.

4. BUEHLER, K. *The Mental Development of the Child.* London: Routledge and Kegan Paul, 1949.

5. HOCHBERG, J., and BROOKS, V. "Pictorial Recognition as an Unlearned Ability: A Study of One Child's Performance," *American Journal of Psychology,* Vol. 75, 1962, pp. 624–28.

6. KAGAN, J., and LEMKIN, J. "Form, Color and Size in Children's Conceptual Behavior," *Child Development,* Vol. 32, 1961, pp. 25–28.

7. MARCHAL, G. "Contribution a l'etude du sentiment esthetique," *BINOP,* Vol. 14, 1958, pp. 82–93 (Abstract).

8. LOWENFELD, V. *Creative and Mental Growth,* New York: Macmillan, 1947.

9. LORENZ, K. "The Role of Gestalt Perception in Animal and Human Behavior," in L. L. Whyte, ed., *Aspects of Form,* Bloomington, Ind.: Midland Press, 1966, pp. 157–78.

10. SCHAPIRO, M. "Style," in S. Tax. ed., *Anthropology Today,* Chicago: University of Chicago Press, 1962, pp. 278–303.

11. GARDNER, H. "The Development of Sensitivity to Artistic Styles," *Journal of Aesthetics and Art Criticism,* 1971, in press.

12. SHINN, M. *The Biography of a Baby,* Boston: Houghton Mifflin, 1900.

13. WALK, R. "Concept Formation and Art: Basic Experiment and Controls," *Psychonomic Science,* Vol. 9, 1967, pp. 237–8.

14. TIGHE, T. "Concept Formation and Art: Further Evidence on the Applicability of Walk's Technique," *Psychonomic Science,* Vol. 12, 1968, pp. 363–4.

15. MACHOTKA, P. "Le developpement des criteres esthetiques chez l'enfant," *Enfance,* Vol. 4–5, 1963, pp. 357–379.

16. GARDNER, H., and GARDNER, J. "Children's Literary Skills." Unpublished paper.

17. GARDNER, H. "Children's Sensitivity to Painting Styles," *Child Development,* Vol. 41, 1970, pp. 813–821.

18. GARDNER, H. "Effects of Stimulus Rearrangement on the Development of Sensitivity to Painting Styles." Paper delivered at the American Psychological Association Convention, September, 1970, reprinted in Proceedings, II, pp. 495–496.

19. GARDNER, M. "Art Sensitivity and Discrimination in the Emotionally Disturbed." Unpublished master's essay, University of Pittsburgh, 1969.

20. INHELDER, B., and PIAGET, J. *The Growth of Logical Thinking from Childhood to Adolescence,* New York: Basic Books, 1958.

21. VYGOTSKY, L. *Thought and Language,* Cambridge, Mass.: MIT Press, 1962.

22. WERNER, H. *The Comparative Psychology of Mental Development,* New York: Wiley, 1962.

23. This research was supported by grants from the Department of Social Relations, Harvard University, and the National Science Foundation. Preparation of the manuscript was aided by Project Zero. We want to thank members of the Newton, Massachusetts, school system for their assistance.

Graphic Representations of a Motivated Act: An Ontogenetic Study

George Rand   Seymour Wapner

Our purpose in this study was to elicit information about the nature of the schemata or organizational capacities that are present in children of different ages, for conceiving of events as directed or motivated acts, e.g., "the act of searching."

The pictorial representation of motivated or goal-oriented activities is usually conveyed through a series of pictures (as in a comic-strip or motion picture) where the frames are either ordered or somehow marked in time. To condense these successive views into a single frame, while retaining the manner in which the act unfolds, provides something of a logical paradox. Past, present, and future have to be conveyed as three faces or perspectives of the same occurrence, i.e., they have to be condensed into the same image or presentational view. With multiple frames, it is possible to convey the directional movement of behavior by "mere" juxtaposition of one state with the next, wherein the viewer deduces the nature of the act from the changes that have occurred between frames. Condensation into a single frame forces the person doing the drawing to expose his characteristic conceptual focus, i.e., what is central and what is peripheral in his orientation toward events.

As we will see, the adult represents a general theme through selective depiction of a very specific, momentary state of affairs. The child, on the other hand, manages to include more things and relations in his representation, and yet the product is far more concrete and particularized. To see the general in the specific, as the adult does, is perhaps the highest level of symbolization.

With this introduction we may now turn to the data. We tested 19 boys and 19 girls in each of six age groups from 7 to 16 years. Each subject was asked to draw two pictures—"Themselves, looking for a lost penny in the grass," and a standard of comparison, "Themselves, standing

This investigation was supported, in whole, by a Public Health Service Research Grant, MH 00348, from the National Institute of Mental Health.

George Rand and Seymour Wapner, "Graphic Representations of a Motivated Act: An Ontogenetic Study." Reprinted from *Studies in Art Education, 12,* Fall 1970, publication of the National Art Education Association, Washington, D.C., pp. 25–30.

a. 210105 (Age 7)

b. 210107 (Age 7)

Fig. 1a,b

a. 210106(Age 7)

b. 110114(Age 7)

c. 110123(Age 7)

Fig. 2a,b,c

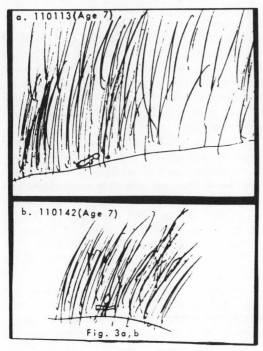

a. 110113(Age 7)

b. 110142(Age 7)

Fig. 3a,b

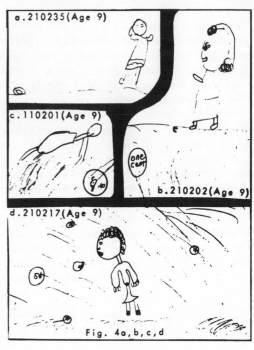

a.210235(Age 9)

c.110201(Age 9)

b.210202(Age 9)

d.210217(Age 9)

Fig. 4a,b,c,d

in the grass." The major focus will be on the "Looking for the lost penny" drawing.

We looked at the drawings through a set of categories that seemed particularly appropriate for analyzing the event-structure conveyed in the representation. These were borrowed from Kenneth Burke's analysis of the dramatic act (cf. *The Grammar of Motives*). These categories include: the *act* (what took place in thought and deed); the *scene* (situation in which act occurred); the *agent* (kind of person performing the act); the *agency* (means or instruments employed); and the *purpose* (goal or objective).

In the drawings we are about to present, the concept of "Searching for the penny" is generally conveyed, though in a number of different ways. Burke's categories will help to distinguish the conceptual orientation that governs these representations.

For example, in Figure 1 a and b, note the drawings of 7-year-old children with the penny embedded deeply in the grass. The conceptual focus here is the lack of psychological contact between "agent" and "object." Incidentally, the agent is almost unchanged from the way it ap-

pears in the "Standing in the grass" picture. You might say that the children hear these instructions as *"Bury or hide the penny,"* rather than "I am searching."

The drawings in Figure 2 a, b and c show a different focus. Object (the penny) and Agent are much more accessible to one another. The conceptual focus is really a change in state of the agent, or a modification of the *agent-object* relationship. It is as if the child hears, "I am missing the penny" vs. "The penny (it) is lost."

The drawings in Figure 3 a and b show an obviously different focus—the agent-object relationship is not a significant feature of the event. "Lostness" diffuses throughout the whole representation, and the concept is carried almost entirely by modification of the scene. It is as if the child hears only *Lost in grass.* Incidentally, that certain children do this may well be based on an emotional characteristic of the child, e.g., anxiety, but the focus on the scenic content is clear.

In the drawings by 9-year-old children in Figure 4 a, b, c and d, the focus is on the *object* at the expense of other aspects of the event. Duplication and enlargement of the penny implies that the

Fig. 5 a, b, c, d

Fig. 6 a, b, c

child is hearing, "A penny shouldn't be lost, it is very, very, valuable." With the onset of symbolization in puberty (see Figure 5) we see heightened concern with the ambiguity of any visual representation. Artificial and conventional graphic mechanisms are introduced to compensate for the limited ability to communicate inner states within the vocabulary of the rendering.

Now let us move on to some more subtle aspects of the representations. These have to do with the *agencies* or *instrumentalities* of search. In the children's drawings in Figure 6 a, b, c, the primary focus is on the *posture* of searching, as if the child hears *"draw someone on the ground."*

In Figure 7 a, b, c, d and e, we notice the beginnings of trying to convey different instrumentalities of search and also how difficult it is to integrate one instrumentality, e.g., palpation, getting on the floor with another, e.g., vision. The universality of this difficulty is depicted in the drawings in Figure 8 a, b, c, d and e, which include children of all ages.

In drawings by 13-year-old children in Figure 9 a, b and c there appears a very interesting transitional stage in which both vision and palpation become specialized or differentiated. Note the

tool-like construction of the hands designed to subserve this "searching" function.

At 14 years of age we see a radical shift in focus which is only to be fully resolved in adult and artistically oriented individuals. It is around 14 years when the conceptual focus becomes integrative. The drawings in Figure 10 a-k show how an action is represented through drawing a particularized activity. The subject is now beginning to integrate all aspects of the event with a focus on what it would look like to be searching for a penny. Of course, the penny is now represented as truly *lost* or not in view as it would be in reality, that is, the object is subordinated to the activity.

Finally the drawings in Figure 11 a-e show how older subjects subordinate the nature of the instrumentality, the scene, and the object, to the motivational state of the agent. Though our "captions" may not match your own, we append them only to indicate that the drawings have a focus on an inner, motivational state of affairs, rather than on a concretely depicted relationship between an agent and an object.

By way of summary we present some generalizations from the quantitative data.

Fig 7a, b, c, d, e

Fig. 8a, b, c, d, e

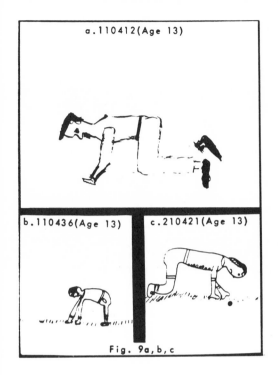

a. 110412 (Age 13)

b. 110436 (Age 13)

c. 210421 (Age 13)

Fig. 9a, b, c

a. 220504 (Age 14)

b. 120516 (Age 14)

c. 220541 (Age 14)

d. 220507 (Age 14)

e. 120530 (Age 14)

f. 120538 (Age 14)

g. 220528 (Age 14)

h. 220520 (Age 14)

i. 220513 (Age 14)

j. 120523 (Age 14)

k. 220505 (Age 14)

Fig. 10a-k

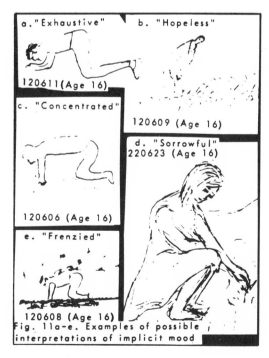

a. "Exhaustive"

120611 (Age 16)

b. "Hopeless"

120609 (Age 16)

c. "Concentrated"

120606 (Age 16)

d. "Sorrowful"
220623 (Age 16)

e. "Frenzied"

120608 (Age 16)

Fig. 11a-e. Examples of possible interpretations of implicit mood

1. There is an increase with age in representation of the theme (searching) through focus on the inner motivational state of the *agent*.

2. In the youngest groups, the "object" of the search is depicted in concrete form (i.e., by including the penny in the drawing). With age, the primary concern shifts to delineation of the activity of the agent (purpose) so that the particular object of search is of subordinate significance and the penny need not be included. In children's drawings the relation of agent and object is represented by juxtaposition of child and penny. In the older group the purpose or intent underlying the act becomes one aspect of the representation of the *agent*.

3. With age there is increasing independence of the scene or context. The young children focus the event more on the "lostness" of the penny and therefore increase the size of the grass or shrubbery. Older *Ss* focus their representation on the "state of deprivation" of the agent so that manipulation of the context does not add to the

poignancy of the image. In a way, the represented act in drawings of older *Ss* has a more universal quality, applying, as it were, to all agents, all times, in all contexts.

4. With age the instrumentality or agency employed in the "search" is increasingly subordinated to visual searching. The postural disposition of the agent becomes increasingly determined by its suitability for a visual act. In the drawings of young children the standing figure is often merely rotated in space so that it faces the ground.

5. There are numerous paradoxical findings. First, some young children do focus on the internal "state of deprivation" of the agent as opposed to the "lostness of the penny." When this is done, however, the mood seems to be represented in concrete form, e.g., by drawing tears or a sad expression. Second, many of the older *Ss* persist in representing the activity of searching by mere juxtaposition of agent and object as if they are really not able to manipulate the posture of the agent adequately.

Part 7

School and Intelligence

The modern era in psychology is remarkable both for the greater understanding that has been gained of the ways in which social background or problems of personal adjustment can jeopardize intellectual and academic performance, and for the growing refinement of knowledge about the components of the learning process itself.

The article by Gagné represents the search for an even more precise understanding of the learning process; Gagné's approach is that of the behaviorist, rather than the cognitive theorist or Piagetian, whose views were outlined in Part Five, Cognition. The Kagan paper discusses some of the conditions that may interfere with intellectual development and performance and also looks at the I.Q. test and some of its shortcomings as a measure of intellectual capacity. A tutorial language program to develop abstract thinking skills in disadvantaged children is discussed by Blank and Solomon.

Contributions of Learning to Human Development

Robert M. Gagné

One of the most prominent characteristics of human behavior is the quality of change. Among those who use the methods of science to account for human behavior are many whose interest centers upon the phenomena of behavioral change, and more specifically, on change in behavior capabilities. Sometimes, changes in behavior capabilities are studied with respect to relatively specific forms of behavior, usually over relatively limited periods of time—hours, days, or weeks. In such instances, the investigator names the processes he studies *learning* and *memory*. Another major class of phenomena of capability change comprises general classes of behavior observed over longer periods of time—months and years. The latter set of events is usually attributed to a process called *development*.

This article is a slightly modified version of the Address of the Vice President, Section I (Psychology), American Association for the Advancement of Science, Annual Meeting of the Association, Washington, D. C., December 1966.

The reality of these two kinds of capability change is obvious in everyday experience, and requires no special experimentation to verify. The capabilities of the young child, for example, change before our eyes every day, as he learns new names for things, new motor skills, new facts. In addition, his more general capabilities develop, over the months, as he becomes able to express his wants by means of word phrases, and later to communicate in terms of entire sentences and even longer sequences of ideas, both in oral and printed form. From these common observations one can distinguish in at least an approximate sense between the specific short-term change called learning, and the more general and long-term change called development.

To distinguish learning and development is surely a practically useful thing, for many purposes. At the same time, the two kinds of processes must be related to each other in some way. The accumulation of new names for things that the child learns is quite evidently related to the capability he develops for formulating longer and more complex sentences. The specific printed letters he learns to discriminate are obviously related to the development of his skill in reading. The question is, how? What is the nature of the relation between the change called learning, on the one hand, and the change called development, on the other?

Over a period of many years, several different answers have been proposed for this question of the relation between learning and development. Investigators in this field have in general been concerned with accumulating evidence which they interpret as being consonant or dissonant with certain theories, or models. Usually the model they have in mind is fairly clear, even though it may not be explicitly represented in their writings.

Models of Human Behavioral Development

It is my purpose here to consider what certain of these models are, and what their implications are for continuing research on human learning and development. Specifically, I am interested in contrasting certain features of models which appear to be of commanding interest in present-day research. I hope by this means to clarify some issues, so that they may, perhaps, be subjected to experimental testing in a manner that will allow us to sharpen and strengthen our inferences about the nature of human behavioral development.

It is inevitable that the theme of genetically determined growth, or maturation, as opposed to influences of the environment, will run through any discussion of the nature of behavioral development. Everyone will agree, surely, that development is the result of an interaction of growth and learning. There are enormous practical consequences associated with this issue—for example, in designing education for the young. If growth is the dominant theme, educational events are designed to wait until the child is ready for learning. In contrast, if learning is a dominant emphasis, the years are to be filled with systematically planned events of learning, and there is virtually no waiting except for the time required to bring about such changes.

It will be clear enough that my own views emphasize the influence of learning, rather than growth, on human behavioral development. But this is not because I deny the importance of growth. Rather it is because I wish to come to grips with the problem of what specific contributions learning can make to development, and by inference, what kinds of learned capabilities enter into the process of development. I want particularly to contrast a model of development which attempts to account specifically for learning effects with certain other models that do not do so. When I describe this model, you will perhaps agree that it can be conveyed briefly by means of the statement: Within limitations imposed by growth, *behavioral development results from the cumulative effects of learning.*

To set the stage for a model of this sort, it seems desirable first to mention two other models that are more or less in current use, and which have been in existence for some time. The first of these may be called the *growth-readiness model,* which has been associated in previous times with such theorists as G. Stanley Hall (1907) and Arnold Gesell (1928), among others. Briefly, it states that certain organized patterns of growth must occur before learning can effectively contribute to development. Major evidence for this theory comes primarily from studies of the development of physical and motor functions in young children. A prototype study in this field (Gesell & Thompson, 1929) involved special training in stair-climbing for one of a pair of identical twins at the age of 46 weeks, no special training for the other twin. At 53 weeks, the untrained twin did not climb as well as the trained twin. But after 2 weeks of training, one-third as much as the total given to the trained twin, she actually surpassed the trained twin in performance. What this and many similar studies are usually interpreted to mean is that training for a motor performance might as well wait, in fact had better wait, until the child is maturationally "ready," before beginning the specific regime of training leading to the desired proficiency. The findings are consistent with this model. Other writers have pointed out that giving the untrained twin no special training doesn't mean that the child is learning nothing during this period. Unfortunately, the study is not therefore a truly critical one for testing predictions from the theory. Actually, it must be said that much other evidence bearing upon this model suffers from this kind of defect.

A second model of considerable importance, particularly because it has attracted much attention, is that of Piaget. Although the interaction of the child with his environment is given a specific role in this theory, it is well to recognize that it is in some fundamental sense a theory which assigns only a contributory importance to the factor of learning (Flavell, 1963, p. 46; Sonstroem, 1966, p. 214). The model may be summarized, briefly and therefore not without some injustice, in the following statements:

1. Intellectual development is a matter of progressive internalization of the forms of logic. The sequence of development manifests itself at first through motor action, later through concrete mediation of ideas, and still later through complete symbolic representation.

2. Progress in development is affected by the interaction of the child with his environment. New experiences are *assimilated* into existing cognitive structures, and newly acquired structures in turn make possible *accommodation* to the demands imposed by the environment. The total process, as Flavell (1963, p. 47) points out, may be considered one of *cognitive adaptation.*

This theory has been accompanied by a great mass of observational evidence, gathered over a period of many years, by Piaget and his colleagues in Geneva. They have observed children's performance of a variety of tasks, including those having to do with number, quantity, time, movement, velocity, spatial and geometrical relations, the operations of chance, and reasoning, among others. Generally speaking, the method has been to present the child with a concrete situation, say, two arrays of beads differing in spatial arrangement, and to ask probing questions in the attempt to determine the nature of the child's understanding of the situation. The behavior of the same child may then be tested again at a later age; or his behavior may be compared with that of older children on the same task.

There have been a number of confirming studies of Piaget's findings carried out by several in-vestigators in various countries of the world (Dodwell, 1961; Elkind, 1961; Lovell, 1961; Peel, 1959). More important for present purposes, however, are the several studies which have attempted to induce particular kinds of intellectual development by means of specific instruction (or learning). Many of these are described by Flavell (1963, p. 370 ff.), and need not be reviewed here. One prototype investigation, by Wohlwill and Lowe (1962), took the following form: Kindergarten children were tested on a task dealing with "conservation of number," requiring them to recognize that the rearrangement of a set of objects in space does not alter their number. Three different groups of the children were given three different varieties of training, each designed to provide them with a mediational way of arriving at conservation of number. A fourth group served as a control, and was given no training. The results were that no effects could be shown of any of the kinds of training. The groups improved their performance somewhat, but the experimental groups gained no more than the control group. Other experiments by Smedslund (1961a, 1961b, 1961c, 1961d, 1961e) lead to much the same conclusion.

Another example is provided by a recent experiment reported by Roeper and Sigel (1966), this time concerned with the tasks of conservation of quantity, using standard situations described by Piaget and Inhelder (1964) for conservation of substance, liquid substance, weight, and volume. In this case the trained groups of 5-year-old children were given fairly extensive general training in classifying, in reversibility, in seriation, three mental operations identified by Piaget as involved in the development of ideas of conservation in children. To summarize individual results very briefly, it was found that some trained children *did* improve on some tasks, but not on all of them. In contrast, the untrained control children showed no improvement. But the effectiveness of training was by no means general—one child might achieve a success in conservation of weight, but not in conservation of volume.

There have been quite a number of experiments using conservation-type tasks, and I have only mentioned here what seem to me a couple of representative examples. Generally speaking, the results seem to be summarizable as follows. Tasks which require young children to respond to situations reflecting conservation of substance, volume, weight, and number do not appear to be readily modifiable by means of instruction and training which is aimed rather directly at overcoming the typical deficiencies exhibited by children. Where such training has been shown to have some effect, it is usually a very specific one, tied closely to the situation presented in training, and not highly generalizable. On the whole, any impartial review of these studies would doubtless be forced to conclude that they do not contradict Piaget's notions of cognitive adaptation, and in fact appear to lend some support to the importance of maturational factors in development.

It is my belief that there is an alternative theory of intellectual development to which many students of child behavior would subscribe. In particular, it is one which would be favored by those whose scientific interest centers upon the process of learning. Naturally enough, it is one which emphasizes learning as a major causal factor in development, rather than as a factor merely involved in adaptation, as is true in Piaget's theory; or rather than a strictly incidental factor, as in the theory of maturational readiness. It is easy enough to identify the philosophical roots of such a theory in American psychology. Perhaps the proponents who most readily come to mind are John B. Watson (1924) and B. F. Skinner (1953), both of whom have given great weight to the importance of environmental forces, of learning, in the determination of development.

But philosophy is not enough. As Kessen (1965, p. 271) points out, for some reason not entirely clear, those theorists who have generally emphasized the influences of environment, as opposed to growth, have also generally espoused a rather radical type of associationism. Thus, they have maintained not only that learning is a primary determinant of intellectual development, but also that what is learned takes the form of simple "connections" or "associations." To account for how a child progresses from a stage in which he fails to equate the volume of a liquid poured from one container into a taller narrower container, to a stage in which he succeeds in judging these volumes equal, seems to me quite impossible to accomplish on the basis of learned "connections." At the least, it must be said that there is no model which really does this. Furthermore, the experi-

ments which have tried to bring about such a change, largely on the basis of "associationistic" kinds of training, have not succeeded in doing so.

In contrast to a weak and virtually empty "associationistic" model, it is not surprising that a theory like Piaget's has considerable appeal to students of development. It tells us that there are complex intellectual operations, which proceed generally from stages of motor interaction through progressive internal representation to symbolic thought. As an alternative, we may choose a theory like Bruner's (1965), which conceives the developmental sequence to be one in which the child represents the world first enactively (through direct motor action), then ikonically (through images), and finally symbolically. These are models with a great deal of substance to them, beside which the bare idea of acquiring "associations" appears highly inadequate to account for the observed complexities of behavior.

The Cumulative Learning Model

The point of view I wish to describe here states that learning contributes to the intellectual development of the human being because it is *cumulative* in its effects. The child progresses from one point to the next in his development, not because he acquires one or a dozen new associations, but because he learns an ordered set of capabilities which build upon each other in progressive fashion through the processes of differentiation, recall, and transfer of learning. Investigators of learning know these three processes well in their simplest and purest forms, and spend much time studying them. But the cumulative effects that result from discrimination, retention, and transfer over a period of time within the nervous system of a given individual, have not been much studied. Accordingly, if there is a theory of *cumulative learning,* it is rudimentary at present.

If one cannot, as I believe, put together a model of cumulative learning whose elements are associations, what will these entities be? What is it that is learned, in such a way that it can function as a building block in cumulative learning? Elsewhere (Gagné, 1965) I have outlined what

I believe to be the answer to this question, by defining a set of learned capabilities which are distinguishable from each other, first, as classes of human performance, and second, by their requirements of different conditions for their acquisition. These are summarized in Figure 1.

The basic notion is that much of what is learned by adults and by children takes the form of complex rules. An example of such a rule is, "Stimulation of a neural fiber changes the electrical potential of the outer surface of the neural membrane relative to its inner surface." I need to emphasize that "rule" refers to what might be called the "meaning" of such a statement, and not to its verbal utterance. These ideas are learned by individuals who have already learned, and can recall, certain simpler rules; in this instance, for example, one of these simpler rules would be a definition of electrical potential. Simple rules, in their turn, are learned when other capabilities, usually called concepts, have been previously learned. Again, in this instance, one can identify the presence of concepts like "stimulation," "fiber," "electric," "surface," and "membrane," among others. In their turn, the learning of concepts depends upon the availability of certain discriminations; for example, the idea of surface has been based in part on prior learning of discriminations of extent, direction, and texture of a variety of actual objects. In the human being, multiple discriminations usually require prior learning of chains, particularly those which include verbal mediators. And finally, these chains are put together from even simpler learned capabilities which have traditionally been called "associations" or "S-R connections."

The identification of what is learned, therefore, results in the notion that all these kinds of capabilities are learned, and that each of them is acquired under somewhat different external conditions. By hypothesis, each of them is also learned under different *internal* conditions, the most important of these being what the individual already has available in his memory. It is clear that associations, although they occupy a very basic position in this scheme, are not learned very frequently by adults, or even by 10-year-olds. Mainly, this is because they have already been learned a long time ago. In contrast, what the 10-year-old learns with great frequency are rules and con-

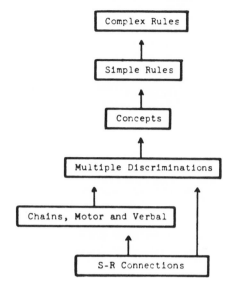

FIG. 1. A general sequence for cumulative learning.

cepts. The crucial theoretical statement is that the learning of such things as rules and concepts depends upon the recallability of previously learned discriminations, chains, and connections.

Examples of Cumulative Learning

Some verification of the idea of cumulative learning has come from studies of mathematics learning, an example of which is Gagné, Mayor, Garstens, and Paradise (1962). Seventh-grade students acquired a progressively more complex set of rules in order to learn the ultimate performances of adding integers, and also of demonstrating in a logical fashion how the addition of integers could be derived from number properties. The results of this study showed that, with few exceptions, learners who were able to learn the capabilities higher in the hierarchy also knew how to do the tasks reflected by the simpler rules lower in the hierarchy. Those who had not learned to accomplish a lower-level task generally could not acquire a higher-level capability to which it was related.

These results illustrate the effects of cumulative learning. They do so, however, in a very restricted manner, since they deal with a development period of only 2 weeks. Another form of restriction arises from the fact that only rules were being learned in this study, rather than all of the varieties of learned capabilities, such as concepts, discriminations, chains, and connections. In another place (Gagné, 1965, p. 181) I have attempted to spell out in an approximate manner a more complete developmental sequence, applicable to a younger age, pertaining to the final task of ordering numbers. In this case it is proposed that rules pertaining to the forming of number sets depend upon concepts such as joining, adding, and separation; that these in turn are dependent upon simpler capabilities like multiple discriminations in distinguishing numerals; while these depend upon such verbal chains as naming numerals and giving their sequence. Following this developmental sequence to even earlier kinds of learning, it is recognized that children learn to draw the numerals themselves, and that at an even earlier stage they learn the simplest kinds of connections such as orally saying the names of numerals and marking with a pencil.

It should be quite clear that this cumulative learning sequence is only a suggested, possible one, and not one which has received verification, as was true of the previous example. I doubt that it is at all complete. It attempts to show that it is possible to conceive that all of the various forms of learned capabilities are involved in a cumulative sense in the first-grade task of ordering numbers—not only the specific rules that are directly connected with the task, but also a particular set of concepts, discriminations, chains, and connections which have been previously learned. Normally, such prior learning has taken place over a period of several years, of course. And this means that it would be quite difficult to establish and verify a cumulative learning sequence of this sort in its totality. If such verification is to be obtained, it must be done portion by portion.

A Cumulative Learning Sequence in Conservation

Can a cumulative learning sequence be described for a task like the conservation of liquid, as studied by Piaget (cf. Piaget & Inhelder, 1964)? Suppose we consider as a task the matching of volumes of liquids in rectangular containers like those shown in Figure 2. When the liquid in A is poured into Container B, many children (at some particular age levels) say that the taller Container B has more liquid. Similarly, in the second line of the figure, children of particular ages have been found to say that the volume in the shallower Container B, exhibiting a larger surface area, is the greater.

What is it these children need to have learned, in order to respond correctly to such situations as these? From the standpoint of the cumulative learning model, they need to have learned a great many things, as illustrated in Figure 3.

First of all, you may want to note that "conservation of liquid" is not a behaviorally defined task; accordingly I have attempted to state one that is, namely, "judging equalities and inequalities of volumes of liquids in rectangular containers." However, such behavior is considered to be rule-based, and could be restated in that form.

"Nonmetric" is also a word requiring comment. What this diagram attempts to describe is a cumulative learning sequence (in other words, a developmental sequence), that obtains approximate volume matchings without the use of numbers, multiplication, or a quantitative rule. I believe such a learning sequence can occur, and perhaps sometimes does occur, in children uninstructed in mathematical concepts of volume. Choosing this particular sequence, then, has the advantage of application to children who are more like those

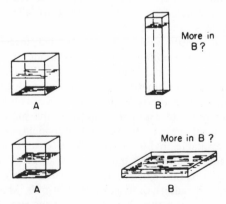

Fig. 2. Two tasks of "conservation of liquid" of the sort used by Piaget and other investigators.

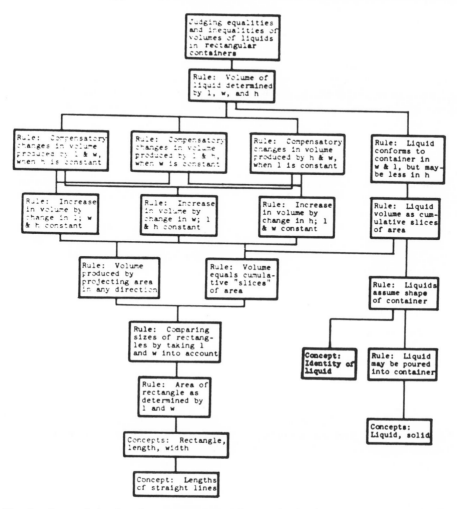

FIG. 3. A cumulative learning sequence pertaining to the development of nonmetric judgments of liquid volume.

on whom Piaget and others have tried the task. But let it be clear that it is by no means the *only* learning route to the performance of this task. There must be at least several such sequences, and obviously, one of them is that which *does* approach the final performance through the multiplication of measured quantities.

The first subordinate learning that the child needs to have learned is the rule that volume of a liquid (in rectanglar containers) is determined by length, width, and height. A change in any of these will change volume. This means that the child knows that any perceived change in any of these dimensions means a different volume. Going

down one step in the learnings required, we find three rules about compensatory changes in two dimensions when another dimension remains constant. That is, if the height of a liquid remains the same in two different containers one can have the same volume if a change in width is compensated by a change in length. Similarly for the other instances of compensatory change.

Now, in order for a child to learn these compensatory rules, the model says, he must have previously learned three other rules, relating to change in only one dimension at a time. For example, if length is increased while width and height remain constant, volume increases. Again, similarly for the other single dimensions. These rules in turn presuppose the learning of still other rules. One is that volume of a container is produced by accumulating "slices" of the same shape and area; and a second is that volume can be projected from area in any direction, particularly, up, to the front or back, and to the right or left. Finally, one can work down to considerably simpler rules, such as those of comparing areas of rectangles by compensatory action of length and width; and the dependence of area upon the dimensions of length and width. If one traces the development sequence still farther, he comes to the even simpler learned entities, concepts, including rectangle, length, width, and an even simpler one, the concept of length of a straight line.

Just to complete the picture, the model includes another branch which has to do with liquids in containers, rather than with the containers themselves, and which deals in simpler levels with rules about liquids and the concept of a liquid itself. This branch is necessary because at the level of more complex rules, the child must distinguish between the volume of the liquid and the volume of the container. Of particular interest also is the concept of liquid identity, the recognition by the child that a given liquid poured into another container is still the same liquid. Such a concept may fairly be called a "logical" one, as Piaget does. Bruner (1966) presents evidence tending to show that identity of this primitive sort occurs very early in the child's development, although its communication through verbal questions and answers may be subject to ambiguities.

Having traced through the "stages" in learning which the model depicts, let me summarize its characteristics as a whole, and some of their implications.

1. First, it should be pointed out that this model, or any other derived in this manner, represents the hypothesis-forming part of a scientific effort, not the verification part. This specific model has not been verified, although it would seem possible to do so. In the process of verification, it is entirely possible that some gaps would be discovered, and this would not be upsetting to the general notion of cumulative learning.

2. According to this way of looking at development, a child has to learn a number of subordinate capabilities before he will be able to learn to judge equalities of volume in rectangular containers. Investigators who have tried to train this final task have often approached the job by teaching one or two, or perhaps a few, of these subordinate capabilities, but not all of them in a sequential manner. Alternatively, they may have given direct practice on the final task. According to the model, the incompleteness of the learning programs employed accounts for the lack of success in having children achieve the final task.

3. In contrast to other developmental models, some of them seemingly based on Piaget's, the cumulative learning model proposes that what is lacking in children who cannot match liquid volumes is not simply logical processes such as "conservation," "reversibility," or "seriation," but concrete knowledge of containers, volumes, areas, lengths, widths, heights, and liquids.

Generalization and Transfer

There is still another important characteristic of a cumulative learning model remaining to be dealt with. This is the fact that any learned capability, at any stage of a learning sequence, may operate to mediate other learning which was not deliberately taught. Generalization or transfer to new tasks, and even to quite unanticipated ones, is an inevitable bonus of learning. Thus the child who has been specifically instructed via the learning sequence shown in the previous figure has actually acquired a much greater learning potential than is represented by the depicted sequence itself.

Suppose, for example, we were to try to get a child who had already learned this sequence to learn another requiring the matching of volumes in cylindrical containers. Could he learn this second task immediately? Probably not, because he hasn't yet learned enough about cylinders, volumes of cylinders, and areas of circles. But if we look for useful knowledge that he *has* acquired, we find such things as the rule about liquids assuming the shapes of their containers, and the one about volumes being generated by cumulative "slices" of areas. The fact that these have been previously learned means that they do not have to be learned all over again with respect to cylinders, but simply recalled. Thus a cumulative learning sequence for volumes of liquids in cylinders could start at a higher "stage" or "level" than did the original learning sequence for rectangular containers. Cumulative learning thus assumes a built-in capacity for transfer. Transfer occurs because of the occurrence of specific identical (or highly similar) elements within developmental sequences. Of course, "elements" here means rules, concepts, or any of the other learned capabilities I have described.

It will be noted that the final tasks of the developmental sequences I have described are very specific. They are performances like "matching volumes in rectangular containers." Does the existence of transfer imply that if enough of these specific tasks are learned, the child will thereby attain a highly general principle which might be called *substance conservation?* The answer to this question is "no." The model implies that an additional hierarchy of higher-order principles would have to be acquired before the individual might be said to have a principle of substance conservation. Transferability among a collection of such specific principles will not, by itself, produce a capability which could be called the principle of substance conservation, or the principle of conservation.

What *is* possible with a collection of specific principles regarding conservation, together with the transfer of learning they imply, is illustrated in Figure 4.

Suppose the learner, making use of transfer of learning where available, has acquired all four of the specific conservation principles shown in the bottom row—dealing with conservation of number, conservation of liquid volumes in both rectangular and cylindrical containers, and conservation of solid volumes. Others could be added, such as conservation of weight, but these will do for present purposes. The property of learning transfer makes possible the ready acquisition of still more complex principles, such as the example given here—judging the volumes of liquids in irregularly shaped containers. It is easy to see that by *combining* the principles applicable to volume of rectangular containers, and others applicable to cylindrical containers, a learner could easily acquire a capability of estimating volumes of irregularly shaped containers. Other kinds of combinations of previously acquired knowledge are surely possible. As I have pointed out, this is the kind of generalizing capability made possible by the existence of learning transfer.

In contrast to this new entity in the develop-

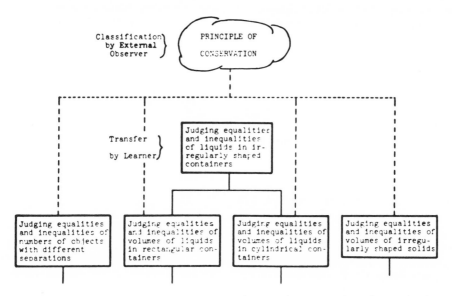

Fig. 4. The contrast between a principle acquired by the learner through transfer from previously learned principles, and a "principle of conservation" used as a classificatory aid by an external observer.

mental sequence, an external observer may, if he wishes, look at the *collection* of what the individual has learned about conservation, and decide he will call this collection the principle of conservation. An external observer is perfectly capable of doing this, and he may have legitimate reasons for doing so. But what he achieves by so doing is still an abstraction which exists in his mind, and not in the mind of the learner. If the external observer assumes that because he can make this classification of such an entity as a principle of conservation, the same entity must therefore exist as a part of the learner's capabilities, he is very likely making a serious mistake. The learner has only the specific principles he has learned, along with their potentialities for transfer.

I believe that many of the principles mentioned by Piaget, including such things as reversibility, seriation, and the groupings of logical operations, are abstractions of this sort. They are useful descriptions of intellectual processes, and they are obviously in Piaget's mind. But they are not in the child's mind.

Another example of how such abstractions may be useful for planning instructional sequences, but not as integral components of intellectual development, may be seen in exercises in science for elementary school children, titled *Science— A Process Approach,* developed by the Commission on Science Education of the American Association for the Advancement of Science (1965). One of the processes these exercises intend that young school children learn is called Observation. But it would be incorrect to think that the designers of this material believe that something like the Principle of Observation is to be directly taught to children as an intellectual entity. Observation in this case is an abstraction, which exists in the minds of the designers, but not in the minds of children. What the children *do* learn is a rather comprehensive collection of specific capabilities, which enable them to identify several fundamental properties of the world of objects—tastes, odors, sounds, the solid-liquid distinction, color, size, shape, texture, as well as changes in these. Each is a fairly specific capability, applying to a class of properties only one step removed in abstraction from the objects themselves. At the same time, transfer of learning makes it possible for the child to build upon these things he has learned, and to learn to identify objects or changes in them in a manner which requires the use of several senses at once.

These instructional materials make it clear that the specific capabilities of observation are considered to have transfer value to other kinds of things which are learned later on—to classifying and measuring and predicting and inferring, as well as to other activities involved in scientific experimentation. Transfer of these specific capabilities takes place in many ways and in many directions. But the processes themselves are not acquired as a part of the child's mental constitution. They are merely external names for a collection of capabilities, as well as for the developmental sequences on which these are built.

Returning to the general theme, it should be clear that the various kinds of capabilities that children learn cumulatively, despite their relative specificity, provide a totality of transferable knowledge that is rich in potentialities for further learning. New combinations are possible at any time between principles acquired, let us say, in a context of containers of water, on the one hand, and in the very different context of exchanges of money, on the other. Furthermore, it is recognized that such generalizations can readily occur when the individual himself initiates the intellectual activity; the new learning does not have to be guided by external instruction. The process of cumulative learning can involve and be contributed to by the operations of inductive and deductive thinking. The cumulative learning model obviously does not provide a theory of thinking; but it suggests the elements with which such a theory might deal.

Summary

What I have attempted to describe is a model of human intellectual development based upon the notion of cumulative learning, which contrasts in a number of respects with developmental theories whose central theme is maturational readiness, as well as with those (of which the best known is Piaget's) of cognitive adaptation. It is a model which proposes that new learning depends primarily upon the combining of previously acquired and recalled learned entities, as well as upon their potentialities for transfer of learning.

As for the entities which are learned, the model assumes that complex principles are formed from combinations of simpler principles, which are formed by combining concepts, which require prior learning of discriminations, and which in turn are acquired on the basis of previously learned chains and connections. The "stage" in which any individual learner finds himself with respect to the learning of any given new capability can be specified by describing (*a*) the relevant capabilities he now has; and (*b*) any of a number of hierarchies of capabilities he must acquire in order to make possible the ultimate combination of subordinate entities which will achieve the to-be-learned task. In an oversimplified way, it may be said that the stage of intellectual development depends upon what the learner knows already and how much he has yet to learn in order to achieve some particular goal. Stages of development are not related to age, except in the sense that learning takes time. They are not related to logical structures, except in the sense that the combining of prior capabilities into new ones carries its own inherent logic.

The entities which are acquired in a cumulative learning sequence are relatively specific. They are specific enough so that one must specify them by naming the class of properties of external objects or events to which they will apply. At the same time, they possess great potential for generalization, through combination with other learned entities by means of a little understood, but nevertheles dependable, mechanism of learning transfer.

This kind of generalization through learning transfer is internal to the learner, and thus constitutes a genuine and measurable aspect of the learner's intellectual capability. Another kind of generalization is not necessarily a part of the learner. This is the classification an external observer may make of a collection of learned capabilities. While the observer naturally has the capability of making such a generalization (and often does so), the learner may not have such a capability. Thus, an external observer may classify a collection of learner capabilities as "the conservation principle," or "the principle of reversibility." Such abstractions have a number of uses in describing intellectual capabilities. Because they are so described, however, does not mean that the learner possesses them, in the same sense that the external observer does.

Intellectual development may be conceived as the building of increasingly complex and interacting structures of learned capabilities. The entities which are learned build upon each other in a cumulative fashion, and transfer of learning occurs among them. The structures of capability so developed can interact with each other in patterns of great complexity, and thus generate an ever-increasing intellectual competence. Each structure may also build upon itself through self-initiated thinking activity. There is no magic key to this structure—it is simply developed piece by piece. The magic is in learning and memory and transfer.

REFERENCES

BRUNER, J. S. The growth of mind. *American Psychologist,* 1965, **20**, 1007–1017.

BRUNER, J. S. On the conservation of liquids. In Bruner, J. S., et al., *Studies in cognitive growth: A collaboration at the Center for Cognitive Studies.* New York: Wiley, 1966.

COMMISSION ON SCIENCE EDUCATION. *Science—A process approach,* 3rd experimental edition, Parts 1–7. Washington: American Association for the Advancement of Science, 1965.

DODWELL, P. C. Children's understanding of number and related concepts. *Canadian Journal of Psychology,* 1961, **15**, 29–36.

ELKIND, D. Children's discovery of the conservation of mass, weight, and volume: Piaget replication study II. *Journal of Genetic Psychology,* 1961, **98**, 219–227.

FLAVELL, J. H. *The developmental psychology of Jean Piaget.* Princeton: Van Nostrand, 1963.

GAGNÉ, R. M. *The conditions of learning.* New York: Holt, Rinehart & Winston, 1965.

GAGNÉ, R. M., MAYOR, J. R., GARSTENS, H. L., & PARA-

DISE, N. E. Factors in acquiring knowledge of a mathematical task. *Psychological Monographs,* 1962, 76(7, Whole No. 526).

GESELL, A. *Infancy and human growth.* New York: Macmillan, 1928.

GESELL, A., & THOMPSON, H. Learning and growth in identical twin infants. *Genetic Psychology Monographs,* 1929, 6, 1–124.

HALL, G. S. *Aspects of child life and education.* New York: Appleton, 1921.

KESSEN, W. *The child.* New York: Wiley, 1965.

LOVELL, K. *The growth of basic mathematical and scientific concepts in children.* New York: Philosophical Library, 1961.

PEEL, E. A. Experimental examination of some of Piaget's schemata concerning children's perception and thinking, and a discussion of their educational significance. *British Journal of Educational Psychology,* 1959, 29, 89–103.

PIAGET, J., & INHELDER, B. *The early growth of logic in the child.* New York: Harper & Row, 1964.

ROEPER, A., & SIGEL, I. Finding the clue to children's thought processes. *Young Children,* 1966, 21, 335–349.

SKINNER, B. F. *Science and human behavior.* New York: Macmillan, 1953.

SMEDSLUND, J. The acquisition of conservation of substance and weight in children. I. Introduction. *Scandinavian Journal of Psychology,* 1961, 2, 11–20. (a)

SMEDSLUND, J. The acquisition of conservation of substance and weight in children. II. External reinforcement of conservation of weight and of the operations of addition and subtraction. *Scandinavian Journal of Psychology,* 1961, 2, 71–84. (b)

SMEDSLUND, J. The acquisition of conservation of substance and weight in children. III. Extinction of conservation of weight acquired "normally" and by means of empirical controls on a balance scale. *Scandinavian Journal of Psychology,* 1961, 2, 85–87. (c)

SMEDSLUND, J. The acquisition of conservation of substance and weight in children. IV. An attempt at extinction of the visual components of the weight concept. *Scandinavian Journal of Psychology,* 1961, 2, 153–155. (d)

SMEDSLUND, J. The acquisition of conservation of substance and weight in children. V. Practice in conflict situations without external reinforcement. *Scandinavian Journal of Psychology,* 1961, 2, 156–160. (e)

SONSTROEM, A. M. On the conservation of solids. In J. S. Bruner, et al., *Studies in cognitive growth.* New York: Wiley, 1966.

WATSON, J. B. *Psychology from the standpoint of a behaviorist.* Philadelphia: Lippincott, 1924.

WOHLWILL, J. F. & LOWE, R. C. An experimental analysis of the development of the conservation of number. *Child Development,* 1962, 33, 153–167.

Personality and IQ Change

Jerome Kagan

Charles T. Baker

Lester W. Sontag

Virginia L. Nelson

Research on mental development during the last twenty years has indicated that a child's IQ score does not necessarily remain constant with age (2, 3, 4, 10). Several reports (9, 10, 12) suggest that changes in environmental conditions can depress or raise IQ level and it is sometimes implied that these changes may be explained by recourse to personality variables. The purpose of this paper is to demonstrate that changes in IQ during childhood are correlated with certain personality predispositions as inferred from projective test data. The personality variables under study include (a) need for achievement, (b) competitive strivings, (c) curiosity about nature, and (d) passivity.

Performance on an IQ test is assumed to be a

function of at least two major variables; the variety of skills and abilities the person brings to the test situation and his motivation to perform well on the test (2, 6). Since the IQ scores of some children change markedly during the school years, it seems plausible to assume that those children who show marked increases in IQ have a very strong motivation to acquire or develop the various intellectual skills tapped by an IQ test and to perform well in a testing situation. It is suggested that need for achievement, competitive strivings, and curiosity about nature motivate the acquisition and improvement of cognitive abilities and by so doing facilitate increases in tested IQ.

The social environment often awards praise and recognition for intellectual accomplishment, and school age children with a high need for achievement might seek to gratify this need through intellectual activity. Thus it was predicted that children showing marked increases in IQ would produce more achievement imagery

This investigation was supported in part by a research grant (PHS M 1260) from the National Institute of Mental Health of the National Institutes of Health, United States Public Health Service. The writers wish to thank Dr. Seymour B. Sarason for his critical reading of the manuscript.

259

on the TAT than those with minimal gains in IQ.

Secondly, the school environment emphasizes competitive intellectual activity, and children with strong competitive needs would be highly motivated to acquire the intellectual skills which result in successful competition with one's classmates. Thus it was predicted that children showing IQ gains would show more competitive strivings than children displaying minimal gains in IQ. In choosing an index of competitive strivings, besides the related measure of TAT achievement fantasy, it was decided to use aggressive content on the Rorschach. The bases for this choice rested on the assumptions that (a) incidence of aggressive imagery reflected degree of aggressive motivation and (b) competition was a socially accepted form of aggressive behavior. For in competition, as in aggression, the child desires to defeat another individual and assert his superiority over him. The population of children in this study is predominantly middle class and apt to place strong inhibitions on direct, overt expression of aggression. Therefore, there would be a tendency for the individual with high aggressive motivation to seek socially accepted channels for aggressive expression such as competitive activity with peers. Thus it was predicted that children showing IQ gain would report more Rorschach aggressive content than those with minimal gain because of their greater competitive predisposition.

A third motive that might facilitate a child's acquisition of knowledge and skills in dealing with the environment could be curiosity about nature. Interest in birth, death, sexual anatomy, and other processes of nature is a frequent phenomenon in young children. It is suggested that the more intense this curiosity the greater the motivation to acquire the habits which would gratify this motive. Since reading, questioning, and manipulating the environment are effective behavioral methods of gratifying one's curiosity, it might be expected that the highly curious child would be more likely to develop these skills and therefore apt to gain in IQ score. The TAT measure used to evaluate curiosity was presence of themes of interest in nature and its phenomena. For the Rorschach, it was hypothesized that concern with the body might reflect, in part, heightened interest in natural processes, and it was suggested that anatomy content might be more frequent for children who showed marked IQ gains than for those with minimal increases in IQ. It is recognized that many clinical psychologists regard anatomy content in adults as indicative of psychopathology. This study is concerned with the correlates of IQ gain rather than psychopathology, and it is not implied that children who show increases in IQ are completely free of conflict. Secondly, it was felt that the determinants of anatomy content for children might be different from those which produce this content in adults.

A final prediction dealt with the predisposition to behavioral passivity. The children who show IQ gains have been characterized as having high need achievement, competitive strivings, and curiosity about the environment. This constellation of motives implies that when these children are confronted with a problem, they would have a tendency to attack and attempt to solve the problem rather than withdraw from the situation or seek help. On this basis, it was predicted that children who showed IQ gains would be less likely than those with minimal IQ increases to characterize their TAT heroes as passive in attitude or behavior.

The Fels Research Institute is uniquely equipped to test these ideas about IQ change since it has continuous longitudinal information on the development of a sample of normal children. These data include intelligence and projective tests, observations of the children, and reports on the parent-child interaction. In a recent study, Sontag, Baker, and Nelson (11) related personality information on a sample of children with changes in IQ and found that those children who showed marked increases in IQ were rated as more competitive, more likely to display self-initiated behavior and less passive than those who showed decreases in IQ. The TAT and Rorschach protocols were not utilized in making these personality ratings, and the results from this study served as a major stimulus for the present investigation.

Method

A sample of 140 Fels subjects (Ss), 70 of each sex, were chosen for study because a fairly complete record of test information was available on them. From ages 2½ to 6, the Stanford-Binet intelligence test (1916 or 1937 revision) was administered to most *S*s twice yearly, on their birthdays and six months after their birthdays. From ages 6 to 12, most *S*s received alternately Form L or Form M of the 1937 revision annually on or near each *S*'s birthday. All of the tests were administered by one of the authors (VLN). The mean IQ of the Fels population is near 120, with standard deviation varying from 14 to 20 IQ points.

In order to obtain groups of *S*s who showed the most change in IQ score from ages 6 to 10, a smoothed longitudinal plot of each *S*'s IQ was prepared by averaging the mean of three consecutive test scores around each age. This procedure is explained in detail in other reports (1, 10, 11). This technique tends to eliminate erratic variations in IQ and hopefully furnishes a more valid measure of IQ changes. Then each *S*'s smoothed IQ at age 6 was subtracted from his smoothed IQ at age 10, and this distribution of differences, positive if *S* gained in IQ and negative if *S* lost in IQ, was divided into quartiles. This report deals with the projective test information on those *S*s in the two extreme groups; those who increased and those who decreased the most in IQ score. These will be called Group A, the IQ ascenders, and Group D, the IQ descenders, respectively. There was no significant difference between the mean IQ of the two extreme quartiles at age six, the means being 119 and 116 for Groups A and D respectively. The average amount of increase in IQ for Group A was larger (plus 17 points) than the corresponding decrease for the members of Group D (minus 5 points) and while 46 per cent of Group D lost five or more points, every child in Group A gained 10 or more points during the years 6 through 10. The mean IQ of the entire sample of 140 tends to increase slightly from ages 6 to 10, probably as a result of practice effects with the same test. Since every *S* in Group D showed a decrease in IQ, it might be inferred that the members of Group D did not benefit from practice and familiarity with the test, and it is probably more accurate to view Group D *S*s in this light rather than as *S*s who showed marked decreases in IQ score.

The projective tests used in the analysis were the Rorschach and selected TAT pictures. Two factors governed the choice of the TAT cards which were analyzed. Because the protocols were gathered over a period of years, there was not complete comparability for all *S*s for the number of cards administered. Secondly, the specific hypotheses of the study dictated the cards chosen for analysis and Cards 1, 3 BM, 3 GF, 5, 6 BM, 12 F, 14, and 17 BM were selected for analysis. The age at which the TAT protocols were administered ranged from 8–9 to 14–6 with median at 11–6 and 80 per cent of the protocols obtained between the age of 11 and 12. The age at which the Rorschachs were administered ranged from 6–5 to 13–6 with median at 10–5 and 63 per cent of the sample having had the test between ages 10 and 11. Since the Rorschach and TAT were administered by different examiners there was no comparability with respect to inquiry or probing. Thus, the analysis of both the Rorschach and TAT was restricted to the *S*'s spontaneous verbalization to the stimulus before any questions or inquiry were conducted by the examiner. The protocols were scored for the following fantasy categories.

1. *Need achievement on the TAT.* Achievement imagery on the TAT was scored according to the definition of McClelland et al. (8); and themes involving a reference to competition with a standard of excellence were scored achievement imagery.

2. *Rorschach aggression.* The definition of aggressive content on the Rorschach included (*a*) people, animals, or creatures engaged in physical or verbal aggression, e.g., fighting or quarreling, (*b*) explosive objects or explosions, e.g., volcanoes, bombs exploding, fireworks, and (*c*) objects or animal parts normally regarded as instruments of aggression, e.g., spears, rifles, clubs, guns, knives, horns, and claws.

3. *Intellectual curiosity about nature.* For the TAT, curiosity was defined in terms of themes in which someone is interested in the processes or phenomena of nature. Curiosity on the Rorschach was restricted to anatomy or X-ray responses of internal organs or boney parts, e.g., stomach, backbone, ribs.

4. *Passivity.* Because of the limited amount of thematic material in the spontaneous performance, themes of passivity were limited to stories in which the central figure was described as sleepy, tired, or resting.

The fantasy categories were independently scored by the senior author and an assistant without knowledge of the *S*'s IQ scores.[1] Reliability was very high because of the limited amount of content scored for each response and the objectivity of the definitions. Percentage of agreement for the three TAT categories was 95 per cent and for the two Rorschach categories 99 per cent.

Results

Although there was a total of 70 *S*s in the two extreme quartiles, not all of the *S*s had Rorschach or TAT data for the age range under study. Table 1 shows the distribution of *S*s, by sex and direction of IQ change, for the TAT and Rorschach analyses. Because there are approximately twice as many boys as there are girls in Group A, all comparisons were first made separately by sex and results were only combined if the direction of the result for both boys and girls in the same IQ group was in the predicted direction.

1. *Need achievement.* All achievement themes, save one, occurred to Cards 1 and 17 BM. The typical achievement story to Card 1 concerned a boy who wanted to master the violin and/or become a famous violinist, while the typical achievement theme to 17 BM involved competitive activity with regard to rope climbing. Table 2 shows the percentage of *S*s in each group reporting achievement imagery plots to Cards 1, 17 BM, and to both pictures.

For both Cards 1 and 17 BM, more male and female *S*s in Group A report achievement imagery than the boys or girls of Group D. For Card 1, the difference between Group A and Group D girls is reliable at the .03 level; the difference for boys is in the predicted direction but not significant. For Card 17 BM, the difference between Group A and Group D boys is significant (P = .03) and in the predicted direction for girls. All P values are for one tail and were evaluated

[1] The writers wish to thank Mary Schnurer for her assistance in assessing the reliability of the scoring.

TABLE 1
DISTRIBUTION OF *S*s BY SEX AND DIRECTION OF IQ CHANGE USED IN THE ANALYSIS OF THE TAT AND RORSCHACH

Group	TAT		Rorschach	
	Boys	Girls	Boys	Girls
Group A	22	11	22	10
Group D	10	20	9	18
Both groups	32	31	31	28

using the exact method suggested by Fisher (5). When the sexes were pooled, comparisons between Groups A and D were significant not only for Cards 1 and 17 BM separately but also for the number of *S*s telling achievement imagery to both Cards 1 and 17 BM (P < .10, .03, and .01 respectively). Thus, the *S*s who showed increases in IQ were more prone to structure Cards 1 and 17 BM in terms of achievement oriented behavior than the *S*s in Group D.

2. *Aggressive content on Rorschach.* There was no significant difference between Groups A and D or between boys and girls with respect to the mean number of responses per protocol, and the mean for the entire sample was 27 responses. There was no difference between Group A and Group D girls with respect to percentage of each group reporting one or more aggressive responses per protocol (30.0 per cent for Group A versus 33.0 per cent for Group D). However, the difference between Group A and D boys approached significance with 59.1 per cent of the former and 22.2 per cent of the latter reporting one or more aggressive images (P = .07). Thus, the prediction of a correlation between IQ increase and

TABLE 2
PERCENTAGE OF *S*s REPORTING ACHIEVEMENT IMAGERY TO CARDS 1 AND 17 BM

TAT Card	Group A			Group D		
	Boys	Girls	Boys and Girls	Boys	Girls	Boys and Girls
Card 1	36.4	50.0	40.6	27.3	15.0	19.4
Card 17 BM	36.4	30.0	34.4	0.0	15.0	9.7
Cards 1 and 17 BM	22.7	10.0	18.8	0.0	0.0	0.0

aggressive imagery held only for the boys. Because of the tentativeness of this result and the more speculative nature of the hypothesis relating competitive striving and aggressive content, an attempt was made to validate this finding by analyzing a later Rorschach protocol for the boys in Groups A and D. Not all of the boys had Rorschachs administered to them at a later age, and only 15 Ss in Group A and five in Group D were available for analysis. The median ages at the time of administration were 13–8 and 15–0 for Groups A and D respectively, and there was no significant difference in the lengths of the protocols of the two groups. The results were in the same direction for 86.7 per cent of Group A, and 20.0 per cent of Group D reported one or more aggressive images, and this difference is highly significant ($P = .01$).

3. *Intellectual curiosity.* The only TAT card eliciting curiosity plots was Card 14, and the typical theme described a person gazing at or interested in the stars or the heavens. Table 3 shows the percentage of each group telling such themes to Card 14.

Both the boys and girls in Group A told more themes of interest in the stars or heavens than the males and females in Group D ($P = .14$, $P = .10$, respectively) and combining of the sexes yielded a highly significant difference between Groups A and D ($P < .01$).

4. *Anatomy and X-ray responses on the Rorschach.* There was no difference between Group A and Group D girls reporting one or more anatomy responses (30.0 per cent versus 38.9 per cent for Groups A and D respectively). For the boys, 31.8 per cent of Group A and 0.0 per cent of Group D reported anatomy or X-ray imagery, a difference that approached significance ($P = .06$). This finding was also validated on the same sample of 20 boys that was used to

check the differences in aggressive content. The results were in the same direction with 60.0 per cent of Group A and 20.0 per cent of Group D reporting anatomy content ($P = .15$).

5. *Passivity.* Card 3 BM accounted for most of the passivity themes and the groups were compared with respect to the incidence of stories to Card 3 BM in which the central figure was sleepy, tired, or resting. Table 4 shows the percentage of each group telling such themes. Both the boys and girls in Group D showed more passivity themes than the boys and girls in Group A. Although only the difference for the girls was significant ($P = .06$), when the sexes were pooled the difference was highly reliable ($P < .03$).

Cards 3 GF, 5, 6 BM, and 12 F did not furnish data relevant to the hypotheses under test and these results are not summarized.

Discussion

In the main, the hypotheses about the differences between Groups A and D have been verified. Boy and girl ascenders produced more TAT achievement imagery and curiosity about nature than Group D children and male ascenders displayed more aggressive content on the Rorschach than the boys in Group D. The higher incidence of aggressive imagery for the boys who gained in IQ was interpreted as reflecting stronger competitive motivation. Finally, the Ss in Group D were presumed to have a more passive orientation since they were more likely to perceive the ambiguous figure on Card 3 BM as sleeping or tired. The relation between Rorschach anatomy content and IQ gain was the most tentative finding.

The results are interpreted as indicating that

TABLE 3

PERCENTAGE OF Ss REPORTING THEMES OF CURIOSITY TO CARD 14

Sex	Group A	Group D
Boys	40.9	18.2
Girls	30.0	5.0
Boys and girls	37.5	9.7

TABLE 4

PERCENTAGE OF Ss REPORTING THEMES OF PASSIVITY TO CARD 3 BM

Sex	Group A	Group D
Boys	9.1	27.3
Girls	10.0	45.0
Boys and girls	9.4	38.7

high motivation to achieve, competitive strivings, and curiosity about nature may motivate the acquisition of intellectual skills and knowledge which, in turn, facilitates increases in tested IQ. If one accepts the generally assumed notion that boys are more competitive and achievement oriented than girls, the fact that there were twice as many boys in Group A as there were girls supports the present interpretation. A recent study using the Edwards Personal Preference Schedule found that high school boys obtained higher need achievement scores than high school girls (7).

These results are not interpreted as indicating that strong achievement, competitive, and curiosity motives are the only variables involved in producing gains in IQ. The Ss in this study are all average or above in IQ and there is not adequate sampling of children with lower IQ levels. One would not expect Ss with low IQs or language handicaps to suddenly show an interest in reading despite achievement needs or intellectual curiosity. The child who spends increased time reading because of a heightened interest in natural processes must have already learned the basic reading skills so that this behavior is not a difficult or unlikely choice for him.

Similarly, needs for achievement and successful competition should only motivate attempts at improvement of intellectual abilities in a social milieu where praise, recognition, and superior status are awarded for such accomplishment. That is, achievement-oriented children from homes in which intellectual activity was praised would probably be more likely to master intellectual skills than achievement-oriented children from homes in which such accomplishment was not rewarded. In a cultural environment where athletic ability, fighting prowess, or success with the opposite sex was highly valued, one might expect the child to choose these behavioral channels to gratify his achievement and competitive needs. The parents in the Fels population are predominantly middle class and tend to place importance on intellectual accomplishment. A large majority of the parents have attended college, and since enrollment in the Fels program is voluntary it might be inferred that only parents who valued knowledge and scientific pursuits would be predisposed to become part of the research population. Thus, the children under study

tend to come from homes which value intellectual ability.

Study of the educational attainment of the parents of the Ss in Groups A and D revealed no significant difference between the groups with respect to the percentage of families in which both parents attended college (57.1 per cent for Group A versus 42.9 per cent for Group D; $P > .30$). Although there is a slight difference favoring the educational level of Group A families, the difference was not dramatic. There may be important differences between Groups A and D with respect to the differential encouragement of intellectual achievement, but measurement of these differences would probably require variables more refined than educational level of the parents. However, even though parental emphasis on intellectual activity may increase the child's desire to improve his cognitive skills, the child's predisposition to adopt or rebel against parental values should selectively influence his motivation to strive for intellectual accomplishment. Thus, the type of relation between parent and child may be an important factor in this process.

Finally, there is the possibility that genetic and/or constitutional variables may play a role in facilitating marked IQ changes. There is considerable data indicating that genetic factors influence general IQ level but less evidence relevant to the role of these variables in producing childhood increases in IQ score. For most of the children in our population, IQs tend to level off during the ages 6–10 and most of the marked changes in level occur during the preschool years. However, the exact relationship between genetic variables and IQ change has yet to be determined. The phenomenon of IQ increase during the school years is admittedly complex and it is not implied that the child's motives are the major factor. However, it is suggested that personality needs may influence this process. Perhaps the most accurate generalization is that for middle-class children with average or above IQ levels, strong achievement, competitive, and curiosity needs may facilitate IQ gains by motivating the child to master intellectual skills.

A final implication of these findings is that they add indirect evidence for the usefulness of the Rorschach and TAT as research instruments. Validation of a predicted relationship between TAT achievement imagery and IQ gain increases one's confidence in the hypothesis that TAT plots can serve as an index of achievement-oriented tendencies. The results of the Rorschach analysis suggest that aggressive content may be an index of an individual's aggressive predispositions but not necessarily a measure of his tendency to express direct, physical aggression. Although Sontag, Baker, and Nelson (11), using behavioral observations, rated the boys in Group A as more competitive than those in Group D, were was no difference between these groups with respect to intensity or incidence of direct verbal or physical aggression or destruction of property. We have assumed that competition is a socially approved form of aggressive behavior and the higher incidence of aggressive content for Group A boys was presumed to be a result of their more intense competitive strivings. Some clinicians who use projective tests are too prone to focus on predictive statements about direct, physical aggression when confronted with a protocol containing aggressive content. One is apt to overlook the fact that the individual may have alternative behavioral channels for expression of aggressive motives.

Summary

For a group of 140 boys and girls in the Fels Research population on whom continuous Binet IQ data were available, a distribution of IQ change was obtained by subtracting each *S*'s smoothed IQ at age 6 from his smoothed IQ at age 10. This distribution of differences was divided into quartiles, and the Rorschach and TAT protocols of the upper (maximum increase in IQ) and lower (maximum decrease in IQ) quartiles were analyzed and compared. The results showed that in comparing the *S*s who showed IQ increases with those showing IQ decreases, the former had, on the TAT, significantly more (*a*) achievement imagery on Cards 1 and 17 BM and (*b*) themes of curiosity about nature on Card 14, and significantly fewer themes of passivity on Card 3 BM. For the boys only, more of the *S*s who increased in IQ had anatomy responses and aggressive imagery on the Rorschach. The results were interpreted as indicating that high need achievement, competitive striving, and curiosity about nature are correlated with gains in IQ score because they may facilitate the acquisition of skills that are measured by the intelligence test.

REFERENCES

1. BAKER, C. T., SONTAG, L. W., & NELSON, VIRGINIA L. Specific ability in IQ change. *J. consult. Psychol.,* 1955, **19**, 307–310.

2. BAYLEY, NANCY. Mental growth in young children. *Yearb. Nat. Soc. Stud. Educ.,* 1940, **39**, (II), 11–47.

3. BAYLEY, NANCY. Consistency and variability in the growth in IQ from birth to eighteen years. *J. genet. Psychol.,* 1949, **75**, 165–196.

4. BRADWAY, KATHERINE. IQ constancy on the Revised Stanford-Binet from the preschool to the junior high school level. *J. genet. Psychol.,* 1944, **65**, 197–217.

5. FISHER, R. A. *Statistical methods for research workers.* (5th ed.) Edinburgh: Oliver & Boyd, 1934.

6. HAGGARD, E. A., DAVIS, A., & HAVIGHURST, R. J. Some factors which influence performance of children on intelligence tests. *Amer. Psychol.,* 1948, 3, 265–266.

7. KLETT, C. J. Performance of high school students on the Edwards Personal Preference Schedule. *J. consult. Psychol.,* 1957, **21**, 68–72.

8. MC CLELLAND, D. C., ATKINSON, J. W., CLARK, R. A., & LOWELL, E. L. *The achievement motive.* New York: Appleton-Century-Crofts, 1953.

9. RICHARDS, T. W. Mental test performance as a reflection of the child's current life situation: A methodological study. *Child Develpm.,* 1951, **22**, 221–233.

10. SONTAG, L. W., BAKER, C. T., & NELSON, VIRGINIA L. Personality as a determinant of performance. *Amer. J. Orthopsychiat.,* 1955, **25**, 555–562.

11. SONTAG, L. W., BAKER, C. T., & NELSON, VIRGINIA L. Mental growth and personality development. *Monogr. Soc. Res. Child Develpm.,* in press.

12. WELLMANN, BETH L., & MC CANDLESS, B. R. Factors associated with Binet IQ changes of preschool children. *Psychol. Monogr.,* 1946, **60**, No. 2 (Whole No. 278).

A Tutorial Language Program
to Develop Abstract Thinking in Socially
Disadvantaged Preschool Children

Marion Blank   Frances Solomon

Widespread deficiencies ranging across the cognitive, affective, motivational, and social areas have been found in deprived children. Compensatory programs have therefore aimed at exposing the children to a different and wider range of almost every type of stimulus deemed to be beneficial (e.g., better equipment, parent participation, trips, perceptual training). In essence, this approach assumes that all factors contribute an equal amount to the alleviation of the deficits found in the deprived child.

This paper outlines an approach which offers an alternative to the philosophy of total enrichment. The premise of this approach is that, while total enrichment is not without value, it does not diagnose the key deficits of the deprived child. The usual concept of enrichment is also limited by the idea that exposure to the previously absent stimuli is sufficient for learning.

We feel that exposure to an infinite number of ostensibly enriching stimuli does not necessarily overcome the deficits. Presentation alone does not insure that the child will partake of newly available material. If learning is to occur, the child must involve himself actively with the stimuli so as to comprehend their significance. Active involvement refers, not to motor activity, but rather to the internal mental manipulation of experience. The latter applies to skills involving the ability to organize thoughts, to reflect upon situations, to comprehend the meaning of events, and to structure behavior so as to be able to choose among alternatives.

These skills coincide with many of the characteristics defining the abstract attitude (Goldstein, 1959). Research by the senior author (Blank & Bridger, 1964, 1966, 1967) has led us to postulate that the failure to develop this abstract attitude represents the most glaring deficiency of deprived children. *Their behavior reflects the lack of a symbolic system by which to organize the plentiful stimulation surrounding them.*

Marion Blank and Frances Solomon, "A Tutorial Language Program to Develop Abstract Thinking in Socially Disadvantaged Preschool Children," *Child Development, 39,* 1968, pp. 379–386. Reprinted by permission of the authors and the Society for Research in Child Development, Inc.

The problem then arises of what is the most effective means for developing abstract thinking. We feel that an internal symbolic system can best be achieved through the development of abstract language (Vygotsky, 1962). Certain types of language, such as labeling clear, circumscribed objects (e.g., bottle, table, ball), can be grasped easily through illustration and/or imitation. Therefore, no great effort is required to learn these words. By contrast, words referring to properties which are not immediately evident require much elaboration for understanding. For example, a word such as "top" is much more abstract than a word such as "book." The word "top" can refer to such physically different things as the "top" of one's head, the "top" of one's desk, and the "top" of a building. The word unites these instances only when there is an understanding that "top" refers to the highest point on anything, regardless of how different the "anythings" look. Other examples requiring a similar level of abstraction are time (before, after), direction (underneath, between), and relative judgments (warmer, heavier). It is here that an articulate person, be it mother, teacher, or sibling, is required to offer the necessary corroboration or negation of the child's emerging ideas.

This type of feedback is readily available in the middle-class home, but it is rare in the lower-class home (see Freeberg & Payne, 1967). We therefore propose that this lack of an ongoing, elaborated dialogue is the major experiential deficit of the deprived child (Bernstein, 1960).

Previous attempts to transmit this aspect of learning to disadvantaged children have relied on using the group situation (Bereiter & Englemann, 1966; Deutsch, 1964; Gray & Klaus, 1965). A serious question arises of whether early language skills can be fostered in a group situation or whether we must in some way mirror the middle-class one-to-one situation. For example, if given a direction to "place the red block on top of the blue one," a child in the group setting can wait to see what the other children do and simply *imitate* their action. Of course, the child *might* listen to the language and associate it with the key features of the performance he just imitated. However, this method relies on the hope that the child will avail himself of this opportunity to learn. Nothing inherent in the situation requires

him either to heed or to understand the language in order to fulfil the demands placed upon him.

In the latter example, the child at least had to make a response; in many classroom situations, no overt response is required. It is assumed that, when the teacher instructs, the child makes the appropriate inner response even though he is not required to answer overtly. If the inner response is lacking, he cannot follow the dialogue, and the teaching, no matter how well organized, is lost. By contrast, the one-to-one situation can be easily designed so that the child is required to use his language skills, and then he cannot function on a level lower than the goals set by the teacher. In addition, since goals set in individual instruction are designed for the child's specific capabilities, they are more likely to be appropriate.

Although most educators acknowledge that ideal teaching would be a one-to-one relation, this has been deemed impractical because of the costs involved. The conclusion of excessive costs is based on the implicit assumption that individual teaching would or should occupy most of the teaching day. Little consideration has been given to the possible effectiveness of short periods of daily individual instruction, even though such instruction is widely and effectively used in the initial teaching of language to other language-deficient groups, such as deaf children (Blank, 1965). In addition, the limited attention spans of young children suggest that relatively brief sessions involving frequent reinforcement of new (language) skills would theoretically be the most effective means of teaching.

In summary, our assumptions were:

1. Deprived preschool children do not have a firm language base for thinking. They will develop one only if they are given consistent guidance. This leads to the further assumption that the most effective teaching is based on individual tutoring.

2. Language acquisition, like any new complex skill, may be met with some resistance. To prevent resistance from becoming established, the child should not be permitted to leave a task unfinished. If necessary, the task can be simplified, but the child should still be required to fulfil the demands set by the teacher.

Once these initial difficulties have been conquered, the child is able to experience great pleasure both in using this new tool and in knowing that he has this tool to use.

3. Young children have short attention spans and therefore need relatively brief but frequent reinforcement of new skills (i.e., 5 days a week for 15–20 minutes each day, resulting in a total of about 1½ hours of tutoring per week).

4. The new command of language will allow the child to cope more effectively with an otherwise debilitating environment. Therefore, marked improvements in many aspects of maladaptive behavior should occur.

Based on these considerations, an exploratory program was developed which involved brief daily teaching of language skills for abstract thinking. The central hypothesis was that intervention limited to the development of language for reflection would play such a vital role in cognition that it would facilitate not only language but many other aspects of thinking.

Method

TEACHING TECHNIQUES

Even though we are stressing abstract language, we are not deceived into thinking that the young child is capable of the highest level of concept formation. His concepts must still be bound to direct referents because he needs some tangible evidence of the idea being demonstrated. Nevertheless, the young child can be taught to bring to his level of conceptualization the processes of thinking vital to the development of abstraction.

The first goal of the teaching was to have the child recognize that information relevant to his world was not immediately evident but could be and *had* to be sought from his previous experience. Thus he was taught to question, to probe, to investigate. For example, the teacher put on her coat at the end of a session. The child said, "Why are you going home?" The teacher replied, "How do you know I am going home?" to which the child said, "You're not going home?" This response meant that the child had dropped any attempt at reasoning; he had interpreted the

teacher's query to mean that he must negate his earlier inference. To encourage the child to pursue the matter, the teacher said "I *am* going home, but what makes you think I am going home? When you get ready to go home, what do you do?" The child said, "I get my coat." A discussion then followed to solidify the significance of these observations. Thus Socratic dialogue was employed instead of didactic teaching.

Various teaching methods were devised to achieve these goals. A common denominator of all the methods was that the child was confronted with situations in which the teacher used no gestures; to accomplish the task correctly, the child had to understand and/or use language. Another consistent factor was that the child was led to produce an independent response relevant to a situation created by the teacher and to extend the situation set forth by her. This extension focused on having the child discuss situations which did not exist in front of him at the moment but which were relevant to the present situations (e.g., past, future, alternative courses of action, giving explanations of events). By structuring the teaching time in this way, the teacher made maximum use of every opportunity to aid the child in developing his budding ability to think and to reflect. Some of the major techniques used are described below. As the work progresses, we hope to expand and refine this list. It should be noted that each technique is specifically geared to overcome a particular deficiency. This is in contrast to the concept of an enriched environment where the aim is to give a massive dosage that will somehow hit the individual deficiencies. Specifically, the method attempted to develop the following:

a) Selective attention The young child has few guidelines to assist him in discriminating selectively from the plethora of stimuli which surround him. He tends to be drawn to stimuli which may not be of great cognitive importance but which have potent perceptual qualities (e.g., blast of a horn, a whirling disk). The aim of this technique was to teach the child to recognize essential elements by requiring him to compare objects and make choices among them (e.g., if given a group of different-colored blocks, he was asked to take "two red blocks and one green block"). In this example, the higher-level concept of number helps the child restrain his impulse to respond primitively to the sensory impact of color alone.

b) Categories of exclusion When the adult gives specific instructions (e.g., "get a crayon"), the child does not need to reflect upon the characteristics of a particular category; he merely responds to direct commands. When the adult gives no direction, the child works aimlessly. When the child can work within the confines of exclusion, however, it means that he has understood the teacher's frame of reference and can independently make appropriate responses. To develop this skill, the child may be asked to make decisions within the confines set by the teacher. For example, the child may be asked to draw something, and he may draw a circle. To encourage the development of exclusion, he would then be asked to draw something "other than a circle."

c) Imagery of future events The young child can easily describe existing objects and situations. Difficulty arises when he must perceive the meaning of this information relevant to a particular context (see John, 1963). To increase this capacity, the child was required to think through the results of realistically possible but not present courses of action. The child might be first asked to locate a doll that was on the table. After the child completed this correctly, the doll would remain on the table, and the child might be asked, "Where would the doll be if it fell from the table?"

d) Relevant inner verbalization We have found that many deprived children will use language to direct their problem-solving only when asked to; they will not spontaneously use language when these external requirements are not imposed. Thus it is not a matter of not having the words but rather a matter of not voluntarily using these words without specific demands. This technique attempts to train the children to develop inner verbalization by retaining words as substitutes for objects. In this method, the child must use language silently and then express it upon request. He might be asked to

look at a picture, say the name to himself, and then after the picture has been removed tell the name to the teacher.

e) Separation of the word from its referent Young children tend to respond to language automatically without fully recognizing that the word exists independently of the object or action represented. If this separation is not achieved, the child will not generalize the meaning of words beyond the particular contexts in which he hears them. To encourage the ability to reflect upon meaning, the child might be given a command which he must repeat aloud *before* acting out the command—for example, "Jump up two times," "Walk to the door and open it."

f) Models for cause-and-effect reasonings Our research (Blank & Bridger, 1966, 1967) has indicated that the perceptual powers of deprived children are intact; they need help, however, in organizing their observations so as to comprehend their significance. To achieve this comprehension, the child can be led to observe common but not frequently noted phenomena (e.g., "What is the weather outside today?" "Can we go out and play today?"). He can then be asked to draw upon hs previous experience to determine the reasons underlying these observations (e.g., "Why can't we go out and play?" "Where is the rain coming from?").

g) Ability to categorize The place of categorization in thinking has been well documented, and its importance was recognized in this project. To aid the children in this sphere, elementary categories such as food, clothing, transportation, and job functions were taught. Thus, after feeding a doll an imaginary apple, the child was asked to name some other fruits that the doll might eat. Then, utilizing the process of exclusion (*b* above), the child might be asked to name some foods that were *not* fruits.

h) Awareness of possessing language Frequently young children are only passive recipients of instruction. This deficiency means that they are unaware that they can independently invoke language to help order their world. This weakness can be overcome by techniques such as asking the child to give commands to the teacher. The teacher might say to the child, "What shall I do with these pencils?" "Now *you* ask *me* to draw something," "Now tell me what the doll should do this afternoon."

i) Sustained sequential thinking   Just as musical notes attain their full meaning only when heard within a melody, words attain their full potential only when imbedded in context. This is true even at the elementary level of a simple sentence, and it becomes increasingly important as chains of events extending into time and space must be understood. To be able to see objects, events, and words as located within their appropriate framework, the child has to be taught to maintain concentration and to determine all the possibilities of a course of action. For example, in discussing ways in which material can be altered, the discussion might begin with vegetable dyes (their function, their appearance, etc.). The issue can then be raised as to what can happen to these dyes under various conditions (diluting them with water, leaving them in concentrated form, etc.). In each case, the child is required to apply the necessary change (e.g., add the water) so that he can directly and immediately experience the phenomenon being discussed.

These techniques for achieving higher mental processes are in contrast to the language programs stressing concepts as an end in themselves. In our view, concepts were seen as the necessary preliminary tools for thinking; accordingly, they occupied only a segment of the program. The type of concept taught could not be illustrated by simple direct examples or simple labeling. For example, to call an object a "book" may facilitate communication, but it does not serve to abstract anything more of the object than does a gesture. In addition, the child who can label glibly is often deceptive, since his facile use of words gives the false appearance of understanding. Concepts such as number, speed, direction, temperature, and emotions are suitable for stressing the more abstract functions of language. Techniques for teaching these concepts have been well documented by Bereiter and Englemann (1966).

Common inexpensive objects readily available

in the child's environment were the only ones used in the teaching (e.g., papers, crayons, blocks, toy cars, simple books). The materials were used only as points of departure from which the child could discuss increasingly abstract (nonpresently-existing) situations which were relevant to the materials. The same materials, when used alone by the child without supervision, might prove useless in terms of the aims of the study—namely, the avoidance of aimless, scattered, stimulus-bound activity.

SUBJECTS AND PROCEDURES

The subjects were selected from a nursery school in a socioeconomically deprived area in New York City. All 22 children from the youngest classes were tested on the Stanford-Binet Intelligence Test (S-B Test) and the Leiter Scale. The children ranged in age from 3 years, 3 months to 4 years, 7 months. Based on these test results, the children were divided into four groups, two tutored and two untutored, matched as closely as possible for IQ, age, and sex. Each child in the first tutored group received individual teaching for 15–20 minutes daily, five times per week; each child in the second tutored group received the same training only three times a week. This tutoring involved taking the child for this short period from his classroom to a familiar room in the school. Each child in one untutored group had daily individual sessions with the same teacher, but no attempt was made to tutor the child. During this time, the child was exposed to the identical materials and was permitted to engage in any activity of his choice. While the teacher was warm and responsive to the child's questions and comments, she did not initiate or extend any cognitive interchange. This group was included to control for the possible role of individual attention alone in facilitating intellectual performance. Another untutored group of seven children remained in the regular nursery school program with no additional attention.

All the tutoring was conducted by a professional nursery school teacher who was trained in the techniques outlined above. The experiment took place over a 4-month period, after which the children were retested. Both the pre- and posttesting were conducted by two research assistants who did not know to which of the groups the children had been assigned and who had had no contact with the children other than at the time of testing.

Results

The pre- and posttest results on the S-B Test are shown in Table 1. Mean IQ increases in tutored groups 1 and 2 were 14.5 and 7.0 points, respectively; in untutored groups 1 and 2, the changes were 2.0 and 1.3 points, respectively. A Kruskal-Wallis analysis of variance indicated that the changes in the four groups were significantly different ($p < .05$). A Mann-Whitney Test indicated that the rise in the tutored groups was significantly greater than the rise in the untutored groups ($p < .02$). Although the difference was not significant, the gain by the group tutored five times a week was greater than that of the group tutored three times a week. This suggests that improvements in performance may be directly cor-

TABLE 1
PRE- AND POSTTEST STANFORD-BINET SCORES

SEX	AGE[a]	TOTAL HOURS TUTORED	IQ		
			Pre	Post	Change
Tutored group 1 (5 times/wk.):					
F1	3.8	11	70	98	+28
F2	3.11	11	100	109	+9
F3	3.4	13	104	115	+11
M1	3.3	12	111	127	+16
M2	3.11	14	90	109	+19
M3	3.7	14	111	115	+4
Mean			97.7	112.2	+14.5
Tutored group 2 (3 times/wk.):					
F4	3.9	8	89	105	+16
F5	4.7	6	86	98	+12
F6	4.5	7	103	103	0
F7	3.3	6	79[b]	96	+17
M4	3.11	9	94	93	−1
M5	4.0	5	107	105	−2
Mean			93.0	100.0	+7.0
Untutored group 1 (5 times/wk.):					
F8	4.1	13	107	111	+4
M6	4.4	10	101	99	−2
M7	4.2	11	80	84	+4
Mean			96.0	98.0	+2.0
Untutored group 2 (classroom):					
F9	4.6	...	97	99	+2
F10	3.5	...	105	107	+2
F11	3.11	...	105	103	−2
F12	4.2	...	117	114	−3
M8	4.2	...	115	124	+9
M9	4.2	...	88	88	0
M10	3.5	...	93	94	+1
Mean			102.8	104.1	+1.3

[a] Age at beginning of study.
[b] No basal score was achieved; a basal MA of 2 years was assumed for the calculations, thus overestimating the score.

related to the amount of tutoring per week. The lack of a clear difference in gain between the two untutored groups indicates that the element of individual attention from an adult without specialized tutoring was not sufficient to achieve the rise in IQ scores.

The results on the Leiter Scale, though somewhat less marked, are in accord with those on the S-B Test. Thus, tutored groups 1 and 2 showed mean increases of 4.5 and 9.5, respectively, while untutored groups 1 and 2 showed 5.0 and 1.9, respectively. The lower overall gains on the Leiter Scale may also be a reflection of the fact that this test does not require verbal abilities, while the teaching techniques emphasized verbal development. The Leiter scores, however, showed erratic variations. For example, untutored children who remained in the classroom showed spontaneous losses and gains of up to 20 points. This result leads us to believe that the Leiter performance is not a reliable indicator of functioning at this age range.

These IQ changes must also be evaluated in conjunction with the dramatic behavioral changes that accompanied these rises. For example, three of the children were so excessively withdrawn that they had not uttered any coherent verbalizations during their entire time in school. They also exhibited other severe symptoms, such as drooling, "ramlike" headbutting, and bizarre physical coordination. Within 1 month after the program was started, all three were speaking clearly, coherently, and appropriately, and there was a diminution of all symptomatology. No comparable changes were noted in the two children from the control groups who exhibited similar symptomatology.

Even among the children who were relatively well functioning, striking improvements were found. For example, on the S-B Test the pretest response of one girl in describing a picture was "a lady, a horse"; the posttest response was, "The mother is trying to catch the dog with the clothes, the dog takes the clothes, and the mother was trying to get it." This response illustrates the growth from simple labeling to a coordinated, sequential story construction.

The most striking gains in the program were the apparent joy in learning and the feeling of mastery which the children displayed as the tutoring progressed. The untutored children, even

those who received individual attention, showed none of these attitudes. This result is extremely important in that it strongly suggests that exposure to materials, a school-like situation, and an interested adult is not sufficient for learning. Both mastery and enthusiasm for learning will come only when the child can be shown how to become actively involved in the learning process.

Discussion

The program outlined above is offered as a means of teaching those language skills necessary for developing abstract thinking in disadvantaged preschool children. We feel that most enrichment programs, and indeed most nursery school programs, are remiss in this area. It is generally assumed that abstract thinking will evolve naturally by school age from having an enriched environment available in the early years. This expectation is often met in the case of middle-class children, because the skills not taught by the nursery school are learned in the verbally rich home environment. In the case of the lower-class child, these experiences are not available.

Although the disadvantaged child has not been given the necessary tools for thinking, there are implicit expectations when he enters school that he has a well-formulated abstract attitude. For example, multiple-choice questions are common in reading-readiness tests. Aside from the content, this type of question assumes that the child can evaluate a series sequentially, can refocus attention selectively, and can realize that he must make a definitive choice between alternatives. How is this abstract attitude to emerge? Our research indicates that high-level language skills are central to the development of this kind of thinking. Even at the preschool level, there are tasks for which abstract language is the only means of solution (Blank & Bridger, 1964). Therefore, it is risky to hope that the "fallout" from a perceptually enriched environment will encourage the formation of what is the central core of intelligence.

Even where the language deficits of the deprived preschooler are recognized, they are treated through enlarging the vocabulary, since vocabulary is seen as the basic unit of language. Implicit in this approach is that, as in perceptual training, mere exposure to the basic units will "lubricate" the entire language system. It is our thesis that these children do not simply need more and better words; rather, they need to use the language they already have, as well as any new words they learn, to structure and guide their thinking.

Although this approach benefited the children in this study, its full potential needs further exploration. In addition, it is believed that the program would have to be maintained for a considerable period of time, probably for about 2–3 years, for the gain to be maintained independently thereafter by the child. Reasoning is still difficult for these children, and they need continuing guidance for it to become firmly established. However, considering the amount of time (approximately 60–90 minutes per week per child), the low cost of the materials, and the rapid gains in performance, it seems worthwhile to pursue this program as a technique for facilitating cognitive growth in young children from deprived backgrounds.

REFERENCES

BEREITER, C., & ENGLEMANN, S. *Teaching disadvantaged children in the preschool.* Englewood Cliffs, N.J.: Prentice-Hall, 1966.

BERNSTEIN, B. Language and social class. *British Journal of Sociology,* 1960, *2,* 271–276.

BLANK, M. Use of the deaf in language studies: a reply to Furth. *Psychological Bulletin,* 1965, *63,* 442–444.

BLANK, M., & BRIDGER, W. H. Cross-modal transfer in nursery school children. *Journal of Comparative and Physiological Psychology,* 1964, *58,* 277–282.

———. Deficiencies in verbal labeling in retarded readers. *American Journal of Orthopsychiatry,* 1966, *36,* 840–847.

———. Perceptual abilities and conceptual deficiencies in retarded readers. In J. Zubin (Ed.), *Psychopathology of Mental Development.* New York: Grune & Stratton, 1967, 401–412.

DEUTSCH, M. Facilitating development in the preschool child: social and psychological perspectives. *Merrill-Palmer Quarterly,* 1964, *10,* 249–263.

FREEBURG, N. E., & PAYNE, D. T. Parental influence on cognitive development in early childhood: a review. *Child Development,* 1967, *38,* 65–87.

GOLDSTEIN, K. Functional disturbances in brain damage. In S. Arieti (Ed.), *American Handbook of Psychiatry.* Vol. 1. New York: Basic Books, 1959, 770–794.

GRAY, S. W., & KLAUS, R. A. An experimental preschool program for culturally deprived children. *Child Development,* 1965, *36,* 887–898.

JOHN, V. P. The intellectual development of slum children: some preliminary findings. *American Journal of Orthopsychiatry,* 1963, *33,* 813–822.

VYGOTSKY, L. S. *Thought and language.* New York: Wiley, 1962.

Part 8

Social and Moral Development

Just as there has been a shift away from behavioristic explanations of linguistic and cognitive development, there also has been a shift in the study of moral and ego development, as illustrated by the Kohlberg paper.

The developments in this area, however, are much more open to dispute than they are in the areas of linguistic and cognitive functioning. There can be no doubt that there is a cognitive structure of language and logic. Both language and logic, to a certain extent, exist separately from usage, whereas cognitive structures dictate the speech and thought habits of their users. It is questionable, however, whether moral judgments or ego structures maintain quite the same relative degree of autonomy from surrounding influences as do language and logic. It is useful, therefore, to compare the general position of Kohlberg's article with that of Mischel in Section IX, Personality and Prediction. Nevertheless, one cannot deny the tremendous importance of Kohlberg's approach and the revival it has brought to the whole area of moral development, which for many years has been relatively neglected in psychology.

The paper by Maccoby, Modiano, and Lander illustrates an older and more classic view of moral development as shaped by the group structures in which the child participates. It illustrates just how conservative traditional group structures can be. The Freedman paper examines the development of dominance and power hierarchies in group life—a topic having significant implications for societal and world health.

The Development of
Children's Orientations Toward a Moral Order
I. Sequence in the Development of Moral Thought

Lawrence Kohlberg

Since the concept of a moral attitude forms the basic building block of the social psychological theories of *Freud* (1922), *Durkheim* (1906), *Parsons* (1960) and others, there is reason to agree with *McDougall* (1908) that "the fundamental problem of social psychology is the moralization of the individual by the society."

Following the leads of *Freud* and *Durkheim*, most social scientists have viewed moralization as a process of *internalizing* culturally given external rules through rewards, punishments, or identification. Without questioning the view that the end point of the moralization process is one in which conduct is oriented to internal standards, one may well reject the assumption that such internal standards are formed simply through a process of "stamping in" the external prohibitions of the culture upon the child's mind. From the perspective of a developmental psychology such as that of

Piaget (1932) or *J. M. Baldwin* (1906), internal moral standards are rather the outcome of a set of transformations of primitive attitudes and conceptions. These transformations accompany cognitive growth in the child's perceptions and orderings of a social world with which he is continuously interacting.

Directed by this developmental conception of the moralization process, our research has been oriented to the following tasks:

1. The empirial isolation of sequential stages in the development of moral thought.
2. The study of the relation of the development of moral thought to moral conduct and emotion.
3. The application of a stage analysis of moral judgment to subcultural differences as well as pathological deviance in moral orientations.
4. The isolation of the social forces and experiences required for the sequential development of moral orientations.

Part II: Social Experience, Social Conduct and the Development of Moral Thought will appear in a subsequent issue of *"Vita Humana."*

Lawrence Kohlberg: The Development of Children's Orientations Toward a Moral Order. I. Sequence in the Development of Moral Thought. *Vita Humana, 6:* 11–33 (1963).

In the present paper, we shall summarize our findings as they relate to moralization as an age-developmental process, and we shall compare this characterization with that of *Piaget*.

The Isolation of Six Stages of Development in Moral Thought

Our developmental analysis of moral judgment is based upon data obtained from a core group of 72 boys living in Chicago suburban areas. The boys were of three age groups: 10, 13, 16. Half of each group was upper-middle class; half, lower to lower-middle class. For reasons to be discussed in the sequel to this paper, half of each group consisted of popular boys (according to classroom sociometric tests), while half consisted of socially isolated boys. All the groups were comparable in I.Q.

We have also used our procedures with a group of 24 delinquents aged 16, a group of 24 six-year-olds, and a group of 50 boys and girls aged 13 residing outside of Boston.

The basic data were two-hour tape-recorded interviews focussed upon hypothetical moral dilemmas. Both the content and method of the interviews were inspired by the work of *Piaget* (1932). The ten situations used were ones in which acts of obedience to legal-social rules or to the commands of authority conflicted with the human needs or welfare of other individuals. The child was asked to choose whether one should perform the obedience-serving act or the need-serving act and was then asked a series of questions probing the thinking underlying his choice.

Our analysis of results commenced with a consideration of the action alternatives selected by the children. These analyses turned out to shed little light on moral development. Age trends toward choice in favor of human needs, such as might be expected from *Piaget's* (1932) theory, did not appear. The child's reason for his choice and his way of defining the conflict situations did turn out to be developmentally meaningful, however.

As an example, one choice dilemma was the following:

Joe's father promised he could go to camp if he earned the $50 for it, and then changed his mind and asked Joe to give him the money he had earned. Joe lied and said he had only earned $10 and went to camp using the other $40 he had made. Before he went, he told his younger brother Alex about the money and about lying to their father. Should Alex tell their father?

Danny, a working class 10-year-old of I.Q. 98 replied: "In one way it would be right to tell on his brother or his father might get mad at him and spank him. In another way it would be right to keep quiet or his brother might beat him up."

Obviously whether Danny chooses to fulfill his "obligation" to adult authority or to peer loyalty will depend on which action he perceives as leading to the greater punishment. What interests us most, however, is the fact that Danny does not appear to have a conception of moral obligation. His judgments are predictions; they are not expressions of moral praise, indignation, or obligation. From one to the next of the situations presented him, Danny was not consistently "authoritarian" or "humanistic" in his choices, but he was consistent in choosing in terms of the physical consequences involved.

A careful consideration of individual cases eventually led us to define six developmental types of value-orientation. A Weberian ideal-typological procedure was used to achieve a combination of empirical consistency and logical consistency in defining the types. The six developmental types were grouped into three moral levels and labelled as follows:

LEVEL I. PRE-MORAL LEVEL

Type 1. Punishment and obedience orientation.
Type 2. Naive instrumental hedonism.

LEVEL II. MORALITY OF CONVENTIONAL ROLE-CONFORMITY

Type 3. Good-boy morality of maintaining good relations, approval of others.
Type 4. Authority maintaining morality.

LEVEL III. MORALITY OF SELF-ACCEPTED MORAL PRINCIPLES

Type 5. Morality of contract and of democratically accepted law.

Type 6. Morality of individual principles of conscience.

These types will be described in more detail in subsequent sections of this paper. The typology rests upon 30 different general aspects of morality which the children brought into their thinking. One such aspect was the child's use of the concept of rights, another his orientation toward punitive justice, a third his consideration of intentions as opposed to consequences of action, etc. Each aspect was conceived as a dimension defined by a six-level scale, with each level of the scale corresponding to one of the six types of morality just listed.

A "motivational" aspect of morality was defined by the motive mentioned by the subject in justifying moral action. Six levels of motive were isolated, each congruent with one of the developmental types. They were as follows:

1. Punishment by another.
2. Manipulation of goods, rewards by another.
3. Disapproval by others.
4. Censure by legitimate authorities followed by guilt feelings.
5. Community respect and disrespect.
6. Self-condemnation.

These motives fall into three major levels. The first two represent on the verbal level what *McDougall* (1905) termed "the stage in which the operation of the instinctive impulses is modified by the influence of rewards and punishments." The second two correspond to *McDougall's* second stage "in which conduct is controlled in the main by anticipation of social praise and blame." The fifth, and especially the sixth, correspond to *McDougall's* third and "highest stage in which conduct is regulated by an ideal that enables a man to act in the way that seems to him right regardless of the praise or blame of his immediate social environment."

A more cognitive aspect of morality, conceptions of rights, was defined in terms of the following levels:

1. No real conception of a right. "Having a right" to do something equated with "being right," obeying authority.

2. Rights are factual ownership rights. Everyone has a right to do what they want with themselves and their possessions, even though this conflicts with rights of others.
3. Same as the second level concept but qualified by the belief that one has no right to do evil.
4. Recognition that a right is a claim, a legitimate exception, as to the actions of others. In general, it is an earned claim, e.g., for payment for work.
5. A conception of unearned, universal individual or human rights in addition to rights linked to a role or status.
6. In addition to level 5 conceptions, a notion of respecting the individual life and personality of the other.

Each of the 50 to 150 moral ideas or statements expressed by a child in the course of an interview could be assigned to one of 180 cells (30 dimensions × 6 levels per dimension) in the classification system. This classification yielded scores for each boy on each of the six types of thought based on the percentage of all his statements which were of the given type. Judges were able to assign responses to the moral levels with an adequate degree of agreement, expressed by product moment correlations between judges ranging from .68 to .84.

In spite of the variety of aspects of morality tapped by the 30 dimensions, there appeared to be considerable individual consistency in level of thought. Thus 15 boys in our original group of 72 were classified (in terms of their modal response) as falling in the first of our six types. On the average, 45% of the thinking of these 15 boys could be characterized as Type 1.

The differences between our age groups offer evidence concerning the developmental nature of the typology. The age trends for usage of the six types of thought are presented in Figure 1.

It is evident that our first two types of thought decreased with age, our next two types increase until age 13 and then stabilize, and our last two types increase until age 16. Analyses of variance of the percentage usage of each type of thought by the 10-, 13-, and 16-year-old groups were carried out.* The differences between the three

* The means in Figure 1 for age 7 are based on only 12 boys and a limited number of responses per child, compared to the older group.

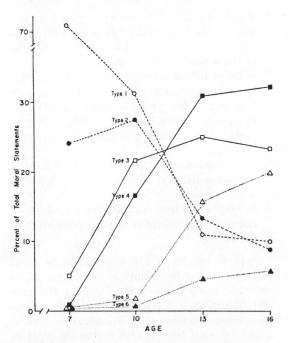

Fig. 1. Use of six types of moral judgments at four ages.

age groups in usage of all types of thought but one (Type 3) were found to be significant beyond the .01 level.

If our stages of moral thinking are to be taken as supporting the developmental view of moralization, evidence not only of age trends, but of sequentiality is required. While the age trends indicate that some modes of thought are generally more difficult or advanced than other modes of thought, they do not demonstrate that attainment of each mode of thought is prerequisite to the attainment of the next higher in a hypothetical sequence.

Because the higher types of moral thought replace, rather than add to, the lower modes of thought, the *Guttman* (1950) scaling technique used by other investigators to establish certain cognitive developmental sequences (*Schuessler and Strauss,* 1950; *Wohlwill,* 1960) is not appropriate for our material. A more appropriate statistical model is derived from *Guttman's* (1954) quasi-simplex correlation matrix. The "simplex" pattern of intercorrelations derives from the expectation that the more two types of thought are separated from one another in a developmental sequence,

the lower should be the correlations between them. This expectation can be compared with the actual intercorrelations obtained among the six types of thought.

Each child had a profile showing the percent of his responses that fell within each of the six types of thought. These profiles permitted us to correlate each of the six types of thought with each of the others across the sample of 72 boys, aged 10 to 16. The resulting product-moment correlation matrix is presented in Table I. Each correlation reflects the extent to which the individuals who use the type of thought identified by the numbers at the left margin of the matrix also use a second type of thought identified by the numbers above the matrix.

The expectation applied to the matrix is that the correlations between two types of thought should decrease as these two types are increasingly separated in the developmental hierarchy. The matrix presented in Table I indicates general agreement with the expectation. The correlations diminish as we move away from the main diagonal entries, whether we go across the columns or down the rows. (The correlations are markedly negative, partially because of the necessity for one percentage score to decrease as another increases.) Furthermore, correlations of types within the three main levels are higher than between levels, supporting our distinction of levels.*

The First Two Stages Compared with Piaget's Stages

Our proposed sequence of stages must have logical as well as empirical support. In characterizing our stages, we shall attempt a logical justification of their location in the hierarchy and at the same time, a comparison of our stages and concepts with *Piaget's* (1932) theory of developmental stages of moral judgment.**

* These cross-sectional findings need to be supplemented by a longitudinal analysis if we are to accept the stages as a genuine developmental sequence. We are presently engaged in a semilongitudinal analysis, in which we have reinterviewed 54 of our original subjects after a three-year interval. The findings will be reported in a subsequent publication.

** There are a number of other recent typologies of moral judgment relevant to our own, briefly discussed elsewhere (*Kohlberg,* 1963).

Table I

Matrix of Intercorrelations between Six Types of Moral Judgment

Type	1	2	3	4	5	6
1	x					
2	55	x				
3	−41	−19	x			
4	−52	−41	18	x		
5	−52	−58	09	00	x	
6	−37	−43	−29	−07	23	x

Piaget (1932) starts from a conception of morality as respect for rules, a respect derived from personal respect for the authorities who promulgate and teach the rules. The young child's respect for authority and rules is originally unilateral and absolutistic, but in the 8- to 12-year-olds, this respect becomes mutual, reciprocal and relativistic. Unilateral respect for adults is said to inspire a *heteronomous* attitude toward adult rules as sacred and unchangeable. This attitude is believed to be supported by two cognitive defects in the young child's thought. One defect, egocentrism, the confusion of one's own perspective with that of others, leads to an inability to see moral value as relative to various persons or ends. The other defect, realism, the confusion of subjective phenomena with objective things, leads to a view of moral rules as fixed, eternal entities rather than as psychosocial expectations. The moral ideology resulting from the interaction of heteronomous respect and cognitive realism is described as "moral realism."

Piaget believes that the development of mutual respect toward other individuals in the 8- to 12-year-olds leads to an "autonomous" regard for the rules as products of group agreement and as instruments of cooperative purposes. "Mutual respect" is believed to be associated with the cognitive capacity to differentiate one's own value perspective from that of others (decline of egocentrism) and both of these trends are believed to arise largely through peer-group interaction.

Several of the thirty dimensions characterizing our six types are based on *Piaget's* conceptions. Our Moral Type 1 shares such characteristics of *Piaget's* heteronomous as concern for consequences rather than intentions, lack of awareness of relativity of value, definition of right as obedience to authority. These and other Type 1 characteristics are illustrated by an excerpt from an interview with Tommy (age 10, working class, I.Q. 128). The excerpt also illustrates how the interview method traces back the child's immediate judgments to the unstated but basic assumptions or "principles" behind them.

This portion of the interview is in response to the third of the 10 moral dilemmas:

In Europe, a woman was near death from a special kind of cancer. There was one drug that the doctors thought might save her. It was a form of radium that a druggist in the same town had recently discovered. The drug was expensive to make, but the druggist was charging ten times what the drug cost him to make. He paid $200 for the radium and charged $2000 for a small dose of the drug. The sick woman's husband, Heinz, went to everyone he knew to borrow the money, but he could only get together about $1000 which is half of what it cost. He told the druggist that his wife was dying and asked him to sell it cheaper or let him pay later. But the druggist said: "No, I discovered the drug and I'm going to make money from it." So Heinz got desperate and broke into the man's store to steal the drug for his wife. Should the husband have done that?

The interview proceeded as follows:

"His wife was sick and if she didn't get the drug quickly, she might die. Maybe his wife is an important person and runs a store and the man buys stuff from her and can't get it any other place. The police would probably blame the owner that he didn't save the wife. That would be like killing with a gun or knife."

(Interviewer: Would it be all right to put the druggist in the electric chair for murder?)

"If she could be cured by the drug and they didn't give it to her, I think so, because she could be an important lady like Betsy Ross, she made the flag. And if it was President Eisenhower, he's important, and they'd probably put the man in the electric chair because that isn't fair."

(Should the punishment be more if she's an important person?)

"If someone important is in a plane and is allergic to heights and the stewardess won't give him medicine because she's only got enough for one and she's got a sick one, a friend, in back, they'd probably put the stewardess in a lady's jail because she didn't help the important one."

(Is it better to save the life of one important person or a lot of unimportant people?)

"All the people that aren't important because one man just has one house, maybe a lot of furniture, but a whole bunch of people have an awful lot of furniture and some of these poor people might have a lot of money and it doesn't look it."

On the one hand we notice Tommy's reasoning ability, his utilitarian calculation of the economics of the greater good. On the other hand we notice that the calculation of value is based on a "primitive" assumption as to the basis of moral values. A prosaic and commendable concern about the wife's life is eventually based on the notion that the value of a life is determined by its "importance" and that such importance is essentially a function of the amount of furniture owned.

Why are we justified in using the term "primitive" in describing the derivation of the value of life from the value of furniture? Awarding moral value to furniture involves a failure to differentiate the self's point of view from that of others, or to differentiate what the community holds as a shared or moral value (the value of life) and what the individual holds as a private value (the desire for furniture). Such a lack of a sense of subjectivity of value is also suggested by Tommy's definition of culpability in terms of consequences rather than intentions (the wickedness of the druggist depends on his causing the loss of an important life).

It seems warranted then to view our Type 1 responses as reflecting cognitively primitive value assumptions.

Type 1 value assumptions, furthermore, are externalized from the motivational point of view, as indicated by definitions of right and wrong in terms of punishment and conformity to power-figures. As an example, Tommy defines the druggist's wrong in terms of a prediction with regard to punishment, and in terms of conformity to the wishes of important persons.

Such an interpretation of Tommy's responses as involving external motives is open to question, however. *Piaget* would see these responses as reflecting the young child's deep respect for authority and rules. *Piaget* sees the young child's morality as externally oriented only in a cognitive sense, not in a motivational sense. According to *Piaget,* the strong emotional respect the young child feels for authority and rules makes him feel unable to judge for himself, and forces him to rely on external adult sanctions and commands to define what is right and wrong. In the *Piaget* view, the child is oriented to punishment only because punishment is a cue to what is disapproved by adults or by the "sacred World-Order."

In contrast to *Piaget's* interpretation, it has seemed to us simpler to start with the assumption that the Type 1 definition of wrong in terms of punishment reflects a realistic-hedonistic desire to avoid punishment, rather than a deep reverence for the adult "World-Order." The children of 10 and older who represent Type 1 morality did not in fact seem to show strong respect for adult authority. A case in point is Danny who, in a situation of conflict between brother and father, defined the right choice in terms of a prediction as to which one would retaliate more heavily. Danny went on to say:

"My brother would say, 'If you tell on me, I'll whip you with my belt real hard.' "

(What would you do then?)

"Well, if I was to tell my Dad if my brother Butchie was still hurting me, my brother Butchie would go find another house to live in."

Danny scores high on various attributes of *Piaget's* "moral realism," but it is hard to see Danny as expressing what *Piaget* terms "the sacredness of rules," "unilateral respect for adults," or a "belief in a World-Order."

We have concluded that it is possible to interpret all our observations with regard to "moral realism" without invoking *Piaget's* notion of the child's sense of the sacredness of authority and rules. This conclusion is consistent with the findings of other studies of *Piaget's* moral judgment dimensions, as is documented elsewhere (*Kohlberg,* 1963).

Regardless of the validity of *Piaget's* interpretation of "moral realism," *Piaget's* assumption that the young child feels a strong idealized moral respect for adult authority requires direct investigation. *Piaget* shares this assumption with psychoanalysts, and some form of the assumption seems critical for widely accepted notions as to the early childhood origins of adult neurotic guilt. In collaboration with *B. Brener,* we attempted a direct study of the validity of the *Piaget* assumption of "heteronomous respect" to explain the moral judgments of children aged four to eight. Earlier work with children of six and seven indicated that these children defined right and wrong mainly by reference to punishment when faced with simplified versions of our moral dilemmas. Did this indicate a basically "hedonistic" view of right or wrong or did it rather reflect a lack of cognitive resources in answering "why" questions in the context of a concern for conformity to sacred authority (*Piaget's* view)?

To investigate this issue, 96 children, aged 4, 5, and 7 were confronted with doll-enactments of stories in which disobedience to a rule (or adult) was followed by reward, and other stories in which obedience to a rule was followed by punishment. One such story was of a boy who was ordered to watch a baby on a couch while his mother left the house. The boy in the story proceeded to run out of the house and play outside. The *S* was asked to complete the story. The *S* was told that the mother returned and gave the disobedient boy some candy. *S* was then asked whether the child-doll had done good or bad, and a series of related questions.

In general, the 4-year-olds defined the story act as good or bad according to the reward or punishment rather than according to the rule or adult command. The older children showed considerable conflict, some of the 7-year-olds defining right and wrong in terms of the rule and showing concern about the "injustice" of punishing good and rewarding evil. These older children, however, still explained the rightness and wrongness of the act in relation to sanctions, but took a long-range or probabilistic view of this relation. Disobedience might have been rewarded in that situation, the children said, but in general it would still lead to punishment.

These results, while not consistent with *Piaget's* assumptions, should not be used to conclude that the moral decisions of 4–5-year-olds are based on crafty hedonism. Only as children reach a level of cognitive development at which the meaning of moral concepts can be differentiated from punishment can they attain either a definite hedonism or a degree of disinterested respect for authority.

The emergence of individualistic hedonism out of such growing cognitive differentiation is suggested by the responses which fall in our Type 2. Just as our first stage of morality coincides descriptively with *Piaget's* "heteronomous stage" but differs from it in interpretation, so our second stage coincides descriptively with *Piaget's* autonomous stage but differs from it in interpretation. Like *Piaget* and others, we found an increase in the use of reciprocity (exchange and retaliation) as a basis for choice and judgment in the years six to ten, though not thereafter. We also found age increases in notions of relativism of value, and in egalitarian denial of the moral superiority of authorities.

These reactions were common enough and well enough associated in our 10-year-olds to help define our Type 2. The tendency to define value relative to private needs is reflected in the response of Jimmy (a 10-year-old working-class boy, I.Q. 105) to our test situation about mercy-killing. The story continues the plight of the wife dying of cancer as follows:

The doctor finally got some of the radium drug for Heinz's wife. But it didn't work, and there was no other treatment known to medicine which could save her. So the doctor knew that she had only about six months to live. She was in terrible pain, but she was so weak that a good dose of a pain-killer like ether or morphine would make her die sooner. She was delirious and almost crazy with pain, and in her calm periods, she would ask the doctor to give her enough ether to kill her. She said she couldn't stand the pain and she was going to die in a few months anyway.

Should the doctor do what she asks and make her die to put her out of her terrible pain?

Jimmy replied, "It's according to how you look at it. From the doctor's point of view, it could be a murder charge. From her point of view, it isn't paying her to live anymore if she's just going to be in pain."

(How about if there were a law against it?)

"It should be up to her; it's her life. It's the person's life, not the law's life."

In this situation Jimmy defines right action instrumentally, as means to individual values; he defines it relativistically, in relation to the conflicting values of various individuals; and he defines it hedonistically, in terms of "paying" in pleasure and pain. The woman has ownership rights over herself, she is her own property. In more mature types of thought rights are defined relative to duties, the law is seen as defending and defining rights, and the law's respect for the woman's rights represents a respect for her personality and life.

Jimmy also relied heavily on reciprocity in defining role relations as indicated by such remarks as the following:

(Why should someone be a good son?)

"Be good to your father and he'll be good to you."

The advance in cognitive differentiation of this type of response over that of Type 1 seems evident. It seems clear that such definition of value in terms of ego-need and reciprocity of needs is in a sense internal; i.e., it is not simply a reflection of direct teaching by others. It reflects rather Type 2's increasing awareness of its own ego-interests and of the exchange of ego-interests underlying much of social organization.

It also seems evident, however, that the Type 2 modes of thought are far from constituting an adequate or mature basis for morality. We find in a number of our older delinquent boys that further intellectual development seems to carry this Type 2 morality to the cynicism which is its logical endpoint. For example, John, a bright 17-year-old working-class delinquent (I.Q. 131), said in response to the story about stealing a drug for one's wife:

"Should the husband steal the drug for his wife? I would eliminate that into whether he wanted to or not. If he wants to marry someone else, someone young and good-looking, he may not want to keep her alive."

John's hedonistic relativism was also associated with a view of rights and law which was the systematic endpoint of Jimmy's views:

(Should the law make a worse punishment for stealing $500 or for cheating that amount by making a personal loan with no intention to repay it?)

"I don't see that they have a right to decide anything? Who are they? They didn't get robbed and they don't do the stealing. It's vanity, they like the feeling of saying what's right. Laws are made by cowards to protect themselves."

Insofar as John was willing to make judgments not based completely on hedonistic relativism, they involved some notion of equality or reciprocity, e.g.:

"If a buddy of mine loans me something I'd do anything for him. If he double-crosses me, I'll do anything against him.*"

From a developmental view, then, the Type 2 morality of need and reciprocity reflects both cognitive advance and a firmer internal basis of judgments than does the Type 1 morality. It does not, however, give rise to any of the characteristics usually attributed to moral judgment, or to a sense of obligation. While possessing the basic attributes stressed by *Piaget* as characterizing the stage of moral autonomy, this type of thought is not based on mutual (or any other type) moral respect (as *Piaget* had hypothesized).

The Intermediate Stages of Moral Development

It is clear that Type 1 and Type 2 children do not express attitudes toward "the good" and "the right" like those we take for granted in adults and which we often regard as moral clichés or stereotypes. These stereotypes first appear in our Type 3 and Type 4 preadolescents, whose verbal judgments and decisions are defined in terms of a concept of a morally good person (the implication of labelling Type 3 as a "good boy" morality).

A fairly typical Type 3 "good boy" response to

---

* Such use of reciprocity by delinquents should not be considered evidence of a genuine morality of peer loyalty or "mutual respect" however. John says elsewhere, "I'm a natural leader. I understand how kids are made and I just pull the right strings and make monkeys out of them."

the story about stealing the drug is the following response by Don (age 13, I.Q. 109, lower-middle class):

"It was really the druggist's fault, he was unfair, trying to overcharge and letting someone die. Heinz loved his wife and wanted to save her. I think anyone would. I don't think they would put him in jail. The judge would look at all sides, and see that the druggist was charging too much."

Don's response defines the issues in terms of attitudes toward the kinds of people involved; "the loving husband," "the unfair druggist," "the understanding judge," "what anyone would do," etc. He assumes that the attitudes he expresses are shared or community attitudes.

Don carries his moral-stereotypical definition of the social world into material not explicitly moral, e.g. into a series of questions we asked concerning the status of various occupational roles. Don tells us:

"President Eisenhower has done a good job and worked so hard he got a heart attack and put himself in the grave, just about, to help the people."

Don sees expected role-performances as expressions of a virtuous self, and bases respect for authority on a belief in the good intentions and wisdom of the authority figure, rather than in his power. It is also clear that his definition of the good and right has moved from a simple classification of outward acts (Type 1) and their need-related consequences (Type 2) to a definition in terms of "intentions," of inner attitudes of liking and "helping other people" (Type 3), or attitudes of "showing your respect for authority" (Type 4). These concerns imply a definition of good and right which involves an active concern for the social goals behind the rules.

In terms of motivation, this second level is one in which conduct is controlled in the main by anticipation of praise and blame. Praise and blame are, of course, effective reinforcers even in the child's earliest years. In these early years, however, disapproval is but one of the many unpleasant external consequences of action that are to be avoided. In contrast, our Type 3 and Type 4 preadolescents attempt to make decisions and define what is good for themselves by *anticipating* possible disapproval in thought and imagination and by holding up approval as a final internal goal. Furthermore, the preadolescent is bothered only by disapproval if the disapproval is expressed by legitimate authorities. This attitude is naively expressed by Andy (age 16, working class, I.Q. 102) in his reply to the second story about telling one's father about one's brother's lie:

"If my father finds out later, he won't trust me. My brother wouldn't either, but I wouldn't have *a conscience* that he (my brother) didn't."

Andy equates his "conscience" with avoidance of disapproval by authorities, but not by peers. The growth of self-guidance in terms of consciously anticipated moral praise or blame seems to be part of a larger process of development expressed in the active use of moral praise and blame toward others expressed at this stage. There is also a close relationship between approval-sensitivity and what is often termed "identification with authority." This is evident with regard to Andy who tells us:

"I try to do things for my parents, they've always done things for you. I try to do everything my mother says, I try to please her. Like she wants me to be a doctor and I want to, too, and she's helping me to get up there."

Unlike the statements of compliance to the wishes of superiors (as in Level I), Andy's statements imply an identification of his own goals wtih his parent's wishes and a desire to anticipate them, somewhat independent of sanctions.

To summarize, we have mentioned the following "cognitive" characteristics of moral definitions at our second level:

a) Moral stereotyping. Definition of the good in terms of kinds of persons and a definition of persons and roles in terms of moral virtues.
b) Intentionalism. Judgments of moral worth based on intentions.
c) Positive, active and empathic moral definition. Duty and moral goodness defined in terms going beyond mere obedience to an actual service to other persons or institutions, or to a concern about the feelings of others.

On the motivational side we have mentioned:

d) Sensitivity to and self-guidance by anticipated approval or disapproval.
e) Identification with authority and its goals.

All of these characteristics imply that moral judgments at this level are based on *role-taking,* on taking the perspective of the other person with legitimate *expectations* in the situation, as these expectations form part of a *moral order.*

For children dominantly Type 3, this order and its associated role-taking is mainly based on "natural" or familistic types of affection and sympathy, as our examples have suggested. For children of Type 4, the moral order is seen as a matter of rules; and role-taking is based on "justice," on regard for the rights and expectations of both rule-enforcers and other rule-obeyers. The distinction between Type 3 and Type 4 styles of role-taking in moral judgment may be illustrated by two explanations as to the wrong of stealing from a store. Carol (13, I.Q. 108, lower-middle class, Type 3) says:

"The person who owns that store would think you didn't come from a good family, people would think you came from a family that didn't care about what you did."

James (13, I.Q. 111, lower-middle class, Type 4) says:

"You'd be mad, too, if you worked for something and someone just came along and stole it."

Both Carol and James define the wrong of stealing by putting themselves in the role of the victim. James, however, expresses the "moral indignation" of the victim, his sense that the rights of a community member have been violated, rather than expressing merely the owner's disapproval of the thief as a bad and unloved person. In both, Type 3 and Type 4, regard for rules is based upon regard for an organized social order. For Type 3, this order is defined primarily by the relations of good or "natural" selves; for Type 4 it is rather defined by rights, assigned duties, and rules.

Moral Orientation at the Third Developmental Level

It is often assumed by psychologists that moral conflicts are conflicts between community standards and egoistic impulses. If this were true, it seems likely that the Type 3 and 4 moral orientations would persist throughout life. The story situations we used, however, placed in conflict two standards or values simultaneously accepted by large portions of the community. Many of the children at stages 3 and 4 went to great lengths to redefine our situations in such a way as to deny the existence of such conflicts between accepted norms, no matter how glaringly this conflict was presented. Both types of children took the role of the authority figure in defining right and wrong, tending to insist that the authority figure would adjust the rule in the interests of the various individuals involved.

In contrast, children of Types 5 and 6 accept the possibility of conflict between norms, and they attempt something like a "rational" decision between conflicting norms. This is most clear in our Type 6 children who attempt to choose in terms of moral principles rather than moral rules. Conventional examples of moral principles are the Golden Rule, the utilitarian principle (the greatest good for the greatest number) and Kant's categorical imperative. A moral principle is an obligatory or ideal rule of choice between legitimate alternatives, rather than a concrete prescription of action (*Dewey and Tufts,* 1936; *Kohlberg,* 1958). Philosophically such principles are designed to abstract the basic element that exists in various concrete rules, and to form an axiomatic basis for justifying or formulating concrete rules.* Moral principles, of course, are not legally or socially prescribed or sanctioned, they are social ideals rather than social realities.

An example of the use of the utilitarian maxim as a moral principle is provided by Tony (age 16, I.Q. 115, upper-middle class). He is replying to a situation involving a choice of leaving or staying at a civilian air-defense post after a heavy bombing raid may have endangered one's family:

"If he leaves, he is putting the safety of the few over the safety of many. I don't think it matters that it's his loved ones, because people in the burning buildings are someone's loved ones too. Even though maybe he'd be miserable the rest of his life, he shouldn't put the few over the many."

Tony says that leaving the post is wrong, not because of the actual consequences, but because

---

* It is historically true that all philosophic formulations of moral principles, such as those just mentioned, are variations of a basic prescription to take the role of all others involved in the moral situations.

he evaluated the situation wrongly, and "put the few over the many." This is not merely a matter of utilitarian economics but of the requirement of justice that all lives be treated as of equal value.

Moral principles are principles of "conscience," and Type 6 children tend to define moral decisions in these terms. When Type 6 children are asked "What is conscience?", they tend to answer that conscience is a choosing and self-judging function, rather than a feeling of guilt or dread.

A more easily attained "rationality" in moral choice than that of Type 6 is embodied in the Type 5 orientation of social contract legalism. Type 5 defines right and wrong in terms of legal or institutional rules which are seen as having a rational basis, rather than as being morally sacred. Laws are seen as maximizing social utility or welfare, or as being necessary for institutional functioning. It is recognized that laws are in a sense arbitrary, that there are many possible laws and that the laws are sometimes unjust. Nevertheless, the law is in general the criterion of right because of the need for agreement.

While Type 5 relies heavily on the law for definitions of right and wrong, it recognizes the possibility of conflict between what is rationally "right" for the individual actor, and what is legally or rationally right for the society. George (16, upper-middle class, I.Q. 118) gives a fairly typical response to the questions as to whether the husband was wrong to steal the drug for his dying wife:

"I don't think so, since it says the druggist had a right to set the price since he discovered it. I can't say he'd actually be right; I suppose anyone would do it for his wife though. He'd prefer to go to jail than have his wife die. In my eyes he'd have just cause to do it, but in the law's eyes he'd be wrong. I can't say more than that as to whether it was right or not."

(Should the judge punish the husband if he stole the drug?)

"It's the judge's duty to the law to send him to jail, no matter what the circumstances. The laws are made by the people and the judge is elected on the basis that he's agreed to carry out the law."

George's belief is that the judge must punish even though the judge may not think the act is wrong. This is quite consistent with his belief

that the act was individually "just," but legally wrong. It reflects a typical distinction made at this level between individual person and social role, a distinction which contrasts with the earlier fusion of person and role into moral stereotypes. The judge's role is seen as a defined position with a set of agreed-upon rules which the role-occupant contractually accepts on entering office. At the level of definition of role-obligation, then, contract replaces earlier notions of helping the role-partner, just as legality replaces respect for social authority in defining more general norms.

All these aspects of a Type 5 orientation seem to be, in part, reactions to a cognitive advance in social concepts to what *Inhelder* and *Piaget* (1958) describe as the level of formal operations. Such a cognitive advance permits a view of normative judgment as deriving from a formal system derived from a set of agreed-upon assumptions. Any given set of norms or roles is then seen as one of many possibilities, so that the major requirement of normative definition becomes that of clarity and consistency.

Implications of the Stages for Conceptions of the Moralization Process

We may now briefly consider some of the implications of our stages for conceptions of the process and direction of moral development. Our age trends indicate that large groups of moral concepts and ways of thought only attain meaning at successively advanced ages and require the extensive background of social experience and cognitive growth represented by the age factor. How is this finding to be interpreted?

From the internalization view of the moralization process, these age changes in modes of moral thought would be interpreted as successive acquisitions or internalizations of cultural moral concepts. Our six types of thought would represent six patterns of verbal morality in the adult culture which are successively absorbed as the child grows more verbally sophisticated.

In contrast, we have advocated the developmental interpretation that these types of thought represent structures emerging from the interaction of the child with his social environment, rather than directly reflecting external structures given by the child's culture. Awareness of the basic prohibitions and commands of the culture, as well as some behavioral "internalization" of them, exists from the first of our stages and does not define their succession. Movement from stage to stage represents rather the way in which these prohibitions, as well as much wider aspects of the social structure, are taken up into the child's organization of a moral order. This order may be based upon power and external compulsion (Type 1), upon a system of exchanges and need satisfactions (Type 2), upon the maintenance of legitimate expectations (Types 3 and 4), or upon the maintenance of legitimate expectations (Type 3 and 4), or upon ideals or general logical principles of social organization (Types 5 and 6). While these successive bases of a moral order do spring from the child's awareness of the external social world, they also represent active processes of organizing or ordering this world.

We have cited two major results from our quantitative analyses which support this developmental interpretation. The first result was the approximation of the matrix of type intercorrelations to a quasi-simplex form. This suggested that individual development through the types of moral thought proceeded stepwise through an invariant sequence. If our moral types form an invariant sequence, acquisition of a higher type is not likely to be a direct learning of content taught by cultural agents, but is rather a restructuring of preceding types of thought. This interpretation is strengthened by the trend toward negative correlations between the higher and lower types of thought. Such negative relations suggest that higher modes of thought replace or inhibit lower modes of thought rather than being added to them. This in turn suggests that higher types of thought are reorganizations of preceding types of thought.

More strongly than the quantitative data, we believe that the qualitative data and interpretations contained in our stage descriptions makes the notion of developmental transformations in moral thought plausible and meaningful. We have described characteristics of the types which suggest that each type is qualitatively different than previous types. Such qualitative differences would not

be expected were development simply a reflection of greater knowledge of, and conformity to, the culture. We have also attempted a logical analysis of the characteristics of the types which allows us to see each type as a conceptual bridge between earlier and later types.

The developmental conception of the moralization process suggested by our analysis of age changes has some definite further implications. Implications as to relations of the development of moral thought to social environmental factors on the one hand, and to the development of moral conduct on the other, will be considered in the sequel to this paper.

Summary

The paper presents an overview of the author's findings with regard to a sequence of moral development. It is based on empirical data obtained mainly from boys aged 10, 13, and 16 in lengthy free interviews around hypothetical moral dilemmas. Ideal-typological procedures led to the construction of six types of moral thought, designed to form a developmental hierarchy. The first two types parallel *Piaget's* heteronomous and autonomous moral stages, but various findings fail to support *Piaget's* view that these stages are derived from heteronomous or mutual respect.

More mature modes of thought (Types 4–6) increased from age 10 through 16, less mature modes (Types 1–2) decreased with age. Data were analyzed with regard to the question of sequence, e.g., to the hypothesis that attainment of each type of thought is the prerequisite to attainment of the next higher type. A quasi-simplex pattern of intercorrelations supported this hypothesis.

Such evidence of developmental sequence in moral attitudes and concepts is believed to be of great importance for conceptions of the process of moralization. It indicates the inadequacy of conceptions of moralization as a process of simple internalization of external cultural rules, through verbal teaching, punishment, or identification. In contrast, the evidence suggests the existence of a series of internally patterned or organized transformations of social concepts and attitudes, transformations which constitute a developmental process.

REFERENCES

BALDWIN, J. M.   Social and ethical interpretations in mental development (Macmillan, New York 1906).

DEWEY, J. and TUFTS, J.   *Ethics* (Holt, New York 1932).

DURKHEIM, E.   Sociology and philosophy (Free Press, Glencoe, Illinois 1953). Originally published 1906.

FREUD, S.   Group psychology and the analysis of the ego (Liveright, New York 1949). Originally published 1922.

GUTTMAN, L.   The basis for scalogram analysis; in Stoufer, S. A. et al., Measurement and prediction; pp. 60–90 (Princeton University Press, Princeton 1950).—In Lazarsfeld, P. (Ed.), Mathematical thinking in the social sciences (Free Press, Glencoe 1954).

INHELDER, B. and PIAGET, J.   The growth of logical thinking (Basic Books, New York 1958).

KOHLBERG, L.   The development of modes of moral thinking and choice in the years 10 to 16; unpublished doctoral dissertation, Chicago (1958).—Moral development and identification; in Stevenson, H. (Ed.), Child psychology, 1963. Yearbook of Nat. Soc. for the Study of Education (University of Chicago Press, Chicago 1963).

MC DOUGALL, W.   An introduction to social psychology (Methuen, London 1905).

PARSONS, T.   The superego and the theory of social systems; in Bell, N. and Vogel, E. (Eds.), A modern introduction to the family (Free Press, Glencoe 1960).

PIAGET, J.   The moral judgment of the child (Free Press, Glencoe 1948). Originally published 1932.

SCHUESSLER, K. and STRAUSS, A. L.   A study of concept learning by scale analysis. Amer. Soc. Rev. *15:* 752–762 (1950).

WOHLWILL, J.   A study of the development of the number concept by scalogram analysis. J. genet. Psychol. *97:* 345–377 (1960).

Games and Social Character in a Mexican Village

Michael Maccoby   Nancy Modiano

Patricia Lander

In studying games and play in a peasant village, we had two general aims. The first was to compare the interpersonal relationships expressed in games, especially those of competition and cooperation, with these relationships as they have been observed by other anthropological and psychological methods. The second was to explore what influence games have on the development of social character in the village and whether the introduction of new games plays a role in social change. The village studied is a mestizo farming community of 850 inhabitants, 65 miles southwest of Mexico City in the state of Morelos.

The meaning and function of games are complicated by the fact that games may both express and form traits of culture. Huizinga has pointed out how play reflects culture and is "culture-creating," the foundation of equity, economy, respect for rules, controlled rivalry, and other civilized and civilizing aspects of society.[1] Caillois has developed this thesis, positing an interdependence of culture and games. He considers games to be a sensitive measure of the social character of a society, serving "to define the society's moral or intellectual character, provide proof of its precise meaning, and contribute to its popular acceptance by accentuating the relevant qualities."[2] For example, Caillois cites golf as a particularly Anglo-Saxon sport in which a player may cheat at will, but does not because the game would then lose all interest for him; "this may be correlated with the attitude of the

This study is part of a larger investigation of the interrelationship of socioeconomic and psychological factors in a Mexican village, directed by Dr. Erich Fromm and supported by a grant from the Foundations Fund for Research in Psychiatry. The senior author's work was supported by a Public Health Service Fellowship (M7888) from the National Institute of Mental Health. An earlier version of this paper was presented at the Congress of Americanists in Mexico City, August, 1962.

[1] Johan Huizinga, *Homo Ludens;* Boston, Beacon Press, 1955.
[2] Roger Caillois, *Man, Play, and Games;* New York, Free Press of Glencoe, 1961; p. 82.

Michael Maccoby, Nancy Modiano, and Patricia Lander, "Games and Social Character in a Mexican Village," *Psychiatry, 27,* 1964, pp. 150–162. Reprinted by special permission of the William Alanson White Psychiatric Foundation, Inc. Copyright © 1964 by the Foundation.

taxpayer to the treasury and the citizen to the state."[3] The analysis might be expanded by tracing the roots of golf in the moral values of nineteenth-century free capitalism. The golfer essentially plays against himself and his own best score; playing against others is a more recent development. The game demands individualism, conscience, and the constant measurement of one's efforts at self-improvement. Even if a player does better than his opponent, his triumph is clouded by an overly high score.

In contrast, one might postulate that American football corresponds to the rise of large organizations, with sharp divisions of labor, regulated by intricate rules. The linemen provide the muscle power for those who carry the ball and who literally must step over the heads of their teammates to score. Those who take fewer knocks receive more glory. Foul play is expected, and penalties are part of the game. Football is brutal, dangerous, surrounded by controversy (for example, over the subsidization of amateur athletes), yet often defended as "character-building." (One might ask, for what?) Baseball more unequivocally expresses the American ideal of cooperation among teammates, each of whom has a turn at bat and the opportunity to score. Unlike the situation in football, scandals in baseball have been rare and their effect on the American public—as in the case of the "Black Sox" scandal—profound. Baseball is the only game exempted by Congress from antitrust legislation. It might be said that while football expresses the reality of the society, baseball expresses its ideal.

On the level of individual psychology, play and games may also serve a dual function, liberating a child from repressed conflicts and helping him to master traumas of helplessness, and also teaching him new attitudes, values, and skills.[4] The

same game which acts as a safety valve or compensation may also be helping to form character. Piaget has suggested a relationship between the games of children and the attitudes of respect for rules, cooperation, and reciprocity, although it is not clear whether games teach or merely reflect this development.[5] George Herbert Mead postulated that games play a role in the growth of the self-concept (the "generalized other"), since in games one must be prepared to exchange roles and attitudes.[6] Games also both reflect and teach attitudes and values considered proper for boys and girls, and it is possible to see the blurring of sex roles in the United States since World War II in the increasing overlap of games preferred by the two sexes.[7]

Of particular interest to us was how character traits of cooperation, individualism, and rational authority develop and whether games might throw light on this question. A problem for the village (and for much of Latin America [8]) is the irrational use of authority and the tendency to produce political systems based on personal relationships of authority rather than on abstract law. The village lacks neither laws nor democratic values. The problem is one of social character.

---

[3] See footnote 2; p. 83.
[4] The analyses of the liberating and mastering functions of play are based, first of all, on Freud's discussion in "Beyond the Pleasure Principle," *Standard Edition of the Complete Psychological Works of Sigmund Freud* 18:7–64; London, Hogarth Press, 1955. It has since been expanded by other psychoanalytic writers, the most original of whom is Erik H. Erikson, who discusses both the liberating aspects of play and its function in helping the child to master not only trauma, but his body and social demands as well (see *Childhood and Society;* New York, Norton, 1950). An analysis of the function of play in cognitive mas-

tery has been made by Jean Piaget in *Play, Dreams and Imitations in Childhood;* New York, Norton, 1951. The first emphasis on play as practice in teaching children skills and behavior needed for maturity is to be found in Karl Groos's work, *The Play of Man;* New York, Appleton, 1919.
[5] See Jean Piaget, *The Moral Judgment of the Child;* Glencoe, Ill., Free Press, 1948.
[6] Mead distinguishes between play that reflects a child's age, tensions, and aspirations and the game which has all these elements but is itself an active socializing experience, molding the child's character. He writes, ". . . the child must be ready to take the attitude of everyone else involved in that game and these definite roles must have a definite relationship to each other." *The Social Psychology of George Herbert Mead,* edited by Anselm Strauss; Chicago, Univ. of Chicago Press, 1956; p. 228.
[7] Brian Sutton-Smith and Benjamin G. Rosenberg, "Sixty Years of Historical Change in the Game Preferences of American Children," *J. Amer. Folklore* (1961) 74:17–46.
[8] See, for example, Richard N. Adams and others, *Social Change in Latin America Today;* New York, Vintage Books, 1960. For a discussion of the more general implications of this problem for peasant societies see George M. Foster, *Traditional Cultures: The Impact of Technological Change;* New York, Harper, 1962.

Social Organization of the Village

As a background to understanding games and the development of social character in the village, it will be useful to have in mind an outline of the socioeconomic structure. As Caillois has written, without such analysis it is impossible to determine which games "are in accordance with, confirm, or reinforce established values, and conversely, which contradict and flout them," [9] as in our contrast between football and baseball in the United States.

For centuries, since a hacienda was constructed in the seventeenth century, sugarcane has been the base of the economic system. Before the Revolution of 1910-20, the villagers lived in peonage, but, as Wolf has written, without even the guarantees of the medieval serf, since the Mexican peon could be whipped, fined, expelled, or executed at will by the *hacendado*.[10] Starting in 1924, the land was partitioned to the peasants under the *ejido* system.[11] Yet the semi-feudal organization was not totally erased by the partition. The *ejiditarios* continue to plant most of their land in cane, under the direction of a large cooperative sugar mill, which for villages in this region has taken over many functions of the old hacienda. It provides social services and loans, and influences the peasant to plant sugar even though profits are low in comparison to what he could

make planting more intensive crops on his small plot, averaging five acres. These garden crops would demand more work and initiative, and involve more risk than does cane. Thus, though he is free and a landowner, the peasant tends to act as a peon in respect to the cooperative, trading independence and the chance of greater profits for security and direction.

Another factor reinforcing the semi-feudal system stems from the fact that while the population has doubled since the original distribution of land to all who wanted it (some families refused land for fear the *hacendados* would return to punish them), the amount of arable land has not. Of 150 heads of families, some 70 are landowners. The others must work as peons at bare subsistence wages, seek employment as migrant laborers in the United States, or leave the village for jobs in the cities. Thus a system instituted to give each peasant an equal stake has led over the years to sharp differences of income. A scale of possessions based on land, capital and consumer goods, and type of house ranges from zero to 343, with 26 percent of the cases at zero and the median at twelve.

Although the village ideology calls for a political system based on equality and democracy without regard to class differences, most often the *ayudante municipal* (mayor) is chosen from the *ejiditarios* (landowners). This is the result not of coercion or institutionalized power, but of lack of energy and interest among those who barely earn enough to live. In addition, as we shall analyze further, the real leaders of the town tend to shun positions of authority, since the villagers distrust and are hostile to all institutionalized authorities. Weak men, whom no one takes seriously, often occupy the most important offices, with the result that little gets accomplished.

The villagers' ideals include democracy and cooperation, in which everyone gives and profits equally. Community decisions are made in town meetings where all adults may vote. Although the sons of the richer villagers are more likely to study beyond primary school than are those of the poor, rich peasants neither live nor dress in a manner much different from the poor. The villagers, with few exceptions, disapprove of a person who tries to be different from the rest, to give himself "class" (*categoría*). Still fresh in the

[9] See footnote 2; p. 66.

[10] See Eric R. Wolf, *Sons of the Shaking Earth;* Chicago, Phoenix Books, 1959; p. 204. Wolf writes, ". . . some writers have called the institution 'feudal,' because it involved the rule of a dominant landowner over his dependent laborers. But it lacked the legal guarantees of security which compensated the feudal serf for his lack of liberty and self-determination." Wolf also describes (p. 209) how the hacienda system produced peons who were submissive to authority and alienated from each other, seeing their fellow workers as rivals for the favor of authority.

[11] For a description of the *ejido* system and its effects on villages such as the one referred to here, see Nathan Whetten's *Rural Mexico;* Chicago, Univ. of Chicago Press, 1948. Foster also describes the social structure of Mexican peasant villages (see footnote 8). See also Michael Maccoby, "Love and Authority, A Study of Mexican Villagers," *The Atlantic,* March, 1964, pp. 121-126. Oscar Lewis in *Life in a Mexican Village* (Urbana, Univ. of Ill. Press, 1951) describes the social structure of Tepoztlán, a village in the same area of Mexico. Although there are many factors in common, Tepoztlán is essentially an Indian village, without the hacienda tradition. However, the attitudes of the Tepoztlán villagers to authority appear to be similar to those described here (see p. 292).

mind of the villagers are the ideals of the Revolution, particularly those of Emiliano Zapata, who lived and fought in this region.

It is not merely differences in wealth that keep the villagers from realizing these ideals. The centuries of the hacienda, of exploitation, of violence, and of scarcity have conspired to cause a mistrust of self and others, a tendency to seek security in submission, a fatalism often leading to alcoholism and apathy.[12]

Method of Study

Three methods were used to investigate games. During two years of work in the village, two of the investigators were participant observers in children's play and in the games of older villagers. A playroom was established where younger children, aged approximately 4 to 10, would come to play, seemingly undisturbed by the investigator taking notes. We also made a point of asking some of the children to describe the games they played and which ones they preferred. Often we would ask children about the rules and variations of games they were playing spontaneously.

The second method employed was a formal questionnaire, administered individually to 76 children. Fifty, 25 boys and 25 girls between the ages of 6 and 12, were chosen randomly from the census lists. The remaining 26, 13 boys and 13 girls aged 13 to 16, were chosen from a larger random sample and interviewed catch-as-catch-can and therefore are representative of the more talkative and less timid teen-agers. The questionnaire asked the child to indicate which games were for boys, which were for girls, and which were played by both sexes. The child was also asked which game he liked best and why.

The third method of study was experimental, the introduction of new games.

In the following sections, the results will be analyzed in terms of age, sex, and cultural differences in games played, and, finally, the effects of introducing new games into the village.

[12] Foster notes that fatalism is common to peasant societies. The peasant is governed and exploited by the city; he cannot control the forces that determine his life, including politicians, disease, or vagaries of the weather that affect his crop. He is fatalistic because that is the way things are. See footnote 8; p. 47.

Age Differences in Play

On the basis of the questionnaire and observation, four age periods characterized by different forms of play were distinguished. The first includes ages 4 through 7; the second, ages 8 through 11; the third, ages 12 through 15; and the fourth describes the play of adults.

Dramatic play or mimicry most characterizes the play of the children under 8. Dolls are rare, but if there are kittens in the household, the children dress them in scraps of cloth and rock them like babies. Little girls seldom lack opportunities to rock real baby siblings. Children of both sexes play a simple version of house, making tortillas from mud, sweeping, and so on, with little spirit of fantasy. Indeed, if one playfully asks a little girl if her mud pies are tortillas, she will in all probability answer, without irony, "No, they're mud."

Children were not observed playing doctor or nurse, even though a doctor and a nurse often visit the village, and they were also not observed playing policeman or fireman, roles which were less familiar to them. Boys play at pistols. (Many of the grown men regularly carry them.) Sometimes a girl will pretend to be a teacher, usually playing at being a disciplinarian quieting an unruly class. One of the few roles often imitated is that of a drunk; for example, once a child fell down and said, "I fell, I'm drunk from two beers." The enjoyment of mimicry does not end with childhood. Adults often mimic others as a form of ridicule, especially against those who aspire to *categoría*.

A form of play common both to the younger (4–7) and older (8–12) children is games of skill, which become more competitive with age. Boys climb trees and aim slingshots. They also play *balero,* the game of cup and stick—a rusty tin can frequently serving as the cup—which may be played either alone or in competition. Boys of this age play marbles with considerable expertise, always following the same pattern of play, the game essentially consisting of knocking the opponent's marble out of a circle drawn in the dirt. When questioned, they express no resistance to changing the rules and playing in new ways. But neither are they actively interested in rules; they are much more concerned with perfecting shots. Only rarely do villagers of any age argue about rules.

Children of ten and older who manage to scrape up a few centavos play a penny-pitching game which combines skill and competition with a new element, chance. The game is called *ante-ojos,* or eyeglasses, which are drawn with a stick in the dirt. Even if one child seems to win by pitching closest to the center of the eyeglasses, the other may still avoid losing by flipping his penny and calling it correctly. It seems as though the moral of the game is that skill is not enough to gain a living in this society; one must have luck also.

By the age of 8, except for games played within the schoolyard (generally tag or volley-ball), girls and boys neither play together nor play the same games. Games of competitive skill played exclusively by girls include jump rope, in which they see who can jump the most times without missing, hopscotch, and bounceball. Neither jump rope nor bounceball is accompanied by chants. When girls play ball, often there is a leader who decides who will be next to catch. Sometimes the ones who miss are eliminated.

The type of game which most characterizes the ages of 9 to 12 is the central-person game, the preferred game of two-thirds of the girls and thirty percent of the boys. We shall discuss more fully how the contents of the village central-person games differ from such games as they are played in the industrialized world. It is sufficient to say here that there are three types of central-person games. One, played mostly by boys, involves phys-ical activity. *La rabia* (tag) is an example (in much of Mexico the game is called *la roña*). The game is often disorganized; sometimes there may be an *it,* but frequently everyone runs around, chasing and being chased according to his whim. A form of hide-and-seek (*escondidas*) is played in which the central person is the one to hide while the others try to find him. The game is also played in its more widespread form in which the *it* searches for the others, but there is no "home-free-all." In *cuero quemado* (burnt leather), a belt is hidden, and the one who finds it chases after the others, who flee to the base line. The one with the belt may whip all those who have not yet reached safety.

Team sports are most popular during the ages 12 to 16. Seventy percent of the boys preferred soccer, which had been taught to them only three years before by a volunteer from the American Friends Service Committee who worked with us. Those girls of this age who have not given up playing games as undignified play either volleyball or central-person games.

The young men over 16 fall into two groups. One group plays basketball, introduced into the village twenty years ago. Most afternoons at about 6 P.M., after work, one can find 15 to 20 young men practicing. A villager feels honored to be chosen for the first team, which plays on Sundays either at home, on the concrete court of the plaza built about 1950, or in a neighboring village. In all, some 30 young men belong to the *Club Deportiva* (Sports Club), which centers about basket-ball but also sponsors dances in order to raise money for basketball equipment. The team boasts of having won the state trophy, which is on display in the municipal building. The other group is made up of young men who, if they play games at all, play cards or billiards.

A form of play that cuts across all types and is enjoyed even by married women is the pure game of chance. Those who can afford it play the national lottery. Others wager smaller sums in fairs that periodically pass through the district. During Easter week the village is host to itinerant proprietors of games of chance.

In summary, the average village child, as he grows up, proceeds from dramatic play to central-person games to team sports. While this develop-ment appears similar to that of industrial societies, a closer analysis will show that the central-person games differ significantly in content, and that team sports are innovations played only by particular villagers.

Sex Differences in Games

The analysis of sex differences, particularly in central-person games, first alerted us to more wide-spread differences in the social character of men and women. The central-person games of boys, such as *cuero quemado,* tag, and *escondidas,* are of two symbolic types. Either the central person has no authority and is chased by the group, or he has full permission to punish the others, who must try to escape. As contrasted with the central-person games of girls, they lack structure, they are more violent, and they conceive of authority only as an irrational punishing force. (When the *it* is chased, he represents the deviant rather than an authority, since he lacks any power.)

Central-person games of girls offer more variety, including those combining competition and chants such as *María Blanca* and *La Monjita* (The Little Nun), pure roundelays such as *Naranja Dulce* (Sweet Orange), and competitive verbal contests, of which *Matarili* is the prime example. What do these games reveal about girls as contrasted to boys?

First of all, the girls' games, which usually demand a circle, are more structured and orderly than those played by boys. The girls take turns being leader, and the others neither rebel nor flee from the authority; they accept it. Second, the content of most games refers to danger from the male world, and especially from the sexually predatory male who threatens to capture and destroy the pure maiden. In *Naranja Dulce* the song tells us that because a girl has asked for an embrace and has lain down, death will carry her away.

Naranja Dulce

Sweet orange, parted lemon,
Give me the embrace I beg.
If my judgment were in vain
Quickly would I forget.
Play the march, my breast cries out,
Goodbye my lady, now I am going.

Sweet orange, celestial lemon,
Tell María not to lie down.
But María has already lain down.
Death came and took her away.

In *María Blanca, El Lobo* (The Wolf), and *La Monjita,* the drama is more explicit. If the girl leaves the protecting circle of women, she is likely to be destroyed by the male.[13] In these games of prepubescent girls, the war between the sexes, often a cold war, has already begun.

In central-person games of this type the wolf who eats a girl "whole" and the devil who wants the pure little nun both appear within the same formal structure and seem interchangeable, suggesting that the threat is more than a simple sexual assault. The unconscious fear seems to be that the male will try sadistically to incorporate the young girl, to use her sexually when he wishes, and, when he is hungry, to eat her. The danger lies not in sex, per se, although the threat may take a sexual disguise, but in the loss of personal integrity, the fear of being used, the extreme of which in a society of material scarcity becomes terror of being incorporated cannibalistically. Once the man has satisfied his impulse, he goes away, as in *Naranja Dulce,* leaving the girl unprotected, to die. *Naranja Dulce* is a verbal warning not to trust romantic love. In *La Monjita* and *María Blanca* the circle tries to protect the girl.

In this society, in which the male often does exploit the woman, treating her alternately as a sexual object and a mother figure who must feed and baby him, the symbolism of girls' games approximates truth. But there is another dimension to the symbolism of wolf and man. The woman not only fears the predatory male; she ambivalently wishes to identify with his strength, to be swallowed whole. In *El Lobo,* the children form a ring with the wolf outside. They walk around singing,

> We'll play in the forest while the wolf's not here,
> For if the wolf appears, he'll eat us whole.

They ask the wolf what he is doing. "Bathing," he answers. They repeat the question. "Putting on my shirt," is the next answer. After each verse he is more fully dressed;[14] and finally he closes the door of his house and says, "Ahí voy" (Here I come). The children flee, and the first one he catches is the new wolf.

Thus the girl who is caught by the wolf (or

---

[13] As a point of interest, Caillois notes that the roundelays of Europe, which are probably the originals of those in the village, sometimes referred to "marriage by capture" (see footnote 2; p. 61).

[14] Speculating on the symbolic meaning of the wolf's dressing, we have thought that it might be a reversal of the latent meaning—that the wolf is actually undressing, preparing for a sexual attack; but it is also possible that the wolf, having satisfied himself sexually, is now hungry.

by the devil in *La Monjita*) in turn *becomes* the aggressor when the game begins anew. The threat to personal integrity stems as much from the desire to identify with the aggressor and trade weakness for strength as it does from the real threat of male exploitation.

In the purely verbal central-person game of *Matarili* (which means nothing, but is like saying, "To kill-ili-ili"), a characteristic weapon of the village women is sharpened through play. One player stands alone and must by her wits force the others, one by one, to her side. She does this by shaming the other girls, by finding such cutting phrases to describe them that they would rather join her than wait for even more devastating descriptions which would expose them to still more ridicule and mirth from the others. *Matarili* is really killing with words. As each new victim joins the leader, she helps in thinking up new verbal attacks on the ones who remain, until all have joined the leader or, again, identified with the aggressor.

While the games of boys arouse open violence, the games of girls are sharpening the subtler weapon that destroys with words. Although *Matarili* is played with a happy and carefree air, as girls grow older the battle of words deepens in intensity. Mature women sometimes openly attack each other in the style of *Matarili* but far more ferociously, until one of them is so shamed that she retreats speechless. In like manner, the woman's weapons against the greater physical strength of her husband are words that undermine his manliness.

Why do words carry so much power to destroy? Two reasons come to mind. The first is the fear of ostracism, of being alone without the ties that keep one alive. Words that ridicule suggest that the victim is less than human, immoral, too ugly to be suffered, beneath contempt, fit only to be cast away by society. Second, the intelligence of the villagers is concrete rather than abstract.[15] Theirs is an astuteness that perceives the person beneath his façade of dignity, manliness, or de-

corum. Their insults fly directly at the victim's most vulnerable targets, his fears, his "secret name," and they are cleverly exaggerated and metaphorically designed to widen the wound. For when such intelligence is combined with malevolence, suggesting to villagers the woman with a penetrating "evil eye," it may seem as though the aggressor respects no limits in her destructiveness, that her words literally can kill.

In older indigenous societies, women often gained respect and mastery through learning the words of songs and rituals. Even in this mestizo village, where Indian rituals, if they were ever known, are long forgotten, some of the women most skilled at insulting also lead the villagers in the Christmas Posadas and church prayers. But there are no women curers in the village; nor are there those traditional dances and liturgical dialogues which might serve as models for different types of central-person games. These games now express and reinforce the female distrust of men and teach the type of force she needs to protect herself from male violence.

What is the true social situation of women? Little girls are expected to obey their parents without question. Little boys are also, but in addition more work and responsibility is demanded of the girls at an earlier age than the boys. It often happened that a mother would allow a boy of 8 or 9 to take books from the small library we founded, but his sister of 10 would state regretfully that her mother insisted that she clean the house or care for the baby and not waste her time reading.

The grown-up woman, according to prevailing ideology, should adopt a submissive role. She has fewer rights than her husband, and, as some villagers put it, should obey him as a new father. Yet the woman is less dominated and stronger than she may seem. Her three ways of responding to the male attack are illustrated in the games. First is solidarity with other girls and isolation from men. When this is undercut by her sexual, romantic, or power-seeking impulses, she may identify with her husband as a second line of defense and obey him, as long as he remains strong. The urge to merge with a stronger power seems the most important factor in dissolving female solidarity, for in the end women distrust each other as rivals. A study by Lola M. Schwartz,

---

[15] This has been shown in tests of cognitive style and intelligence, comparing the village children to both Mexico City and U.S. children. See, for example, Michael Maccoby, Nancy Modiano, and Isidro Galván, "Culture and Abstraction," *VII Congreso Interamericano de Psicologia*, Mexico D.F., Sociedad Interamericana de Psicologia, 1963.

one of our co-workers, of adultery cases brought to the local courts showed that the injured woman invariably blamed her rival and not her husband, whom she did not expect to resist a seductive woman.

The woman's identification with her husband lasts only as long as he demonstrates superior force. Sometimes authority is thrust upon her by his desertion. More often, she takes over when he falters, because of age or alcoholism, sometimes leaving him if he is irresponsible and does not support her. As an authority her hand is more firm than his, since men remain more conflicted over taking command.[16] The village female, even as a child, seeks and enjoys authority much more than the male does. (Some girls said they preferred central-person games because they could be chief, a response never given by a boy.) The female does not hesitate when she sees the opportunity to take charge. One investigator associated with the study, Marta Salinas, related that in one family which she knew well the husband dominated as a tyrant until he reached the age of sexual impotence, when his wife turned on him suddenly, ridiculed him as less than a man, and grabbed the reins of household command.

Cultural Differences in Games

No adequate descriptive and analytic study has been made of the games played at various stages of character development in Western societies. Yet by drawing from various studies one may construct a development from an egocentric attitude, which Piaget has related to the child's obedience

and unquestioning acceptance of adult authority, to a social character which is at once more just (reciprocal) and more independent (autonomous).[17] Piaget has demonstrated, in his study of Swiss children, that changing concepts of rules reflect this process. While the findings of a number of other studies have not lent support to all of Piaget's conclusions, Kohlberg in reviewing the literature on moral development writes, "The age trends for several of the Piaget dimensions are consistent enough to warrant the conclusion that they are genuine developmental dimensions in both American and French-speaking cultures." [18] Among these dimensions, he includes changes in concepts of rules. The data are less clear on the consistency of development to the reciprocal-autonomous "stage," but in all the Western societies studied a high percentage of children do express this attitude, and as Kohlberg found, "A morality of reciprocity and equality was found . . . to be associated with lack of respect for adult authority. . . ." [19]

Piaget does not make clear to what extent games are responsible for this development, but he does report that a greater sense of reciprocity in play *precedes* independence in moral judgment.[20] While it is more demonstrable that games

---

[16] Support for this conclusion has been found by Isidro Galván in the comparison of the Rorschachs of men and women in the village. The women show more control and extensor Ms, while the men combine softer images (such as flowers and butterflies) with explosive outbursts ("Investigación Psico-social sobre el Machismo en Tres Culturas Mexicanas," unpublished master's thesis, National University of Mexico). This analysis is also consistent with the interpretation of Rorschachs in Tepoztlán, reported by Lewis. "As she grows older (over 40) the strict discipline, which has been impressed on the female from childhood in Tepoztlán becomes her strength; it appears that she realizes she can control and manipulate the world around her. She is undisturbed by daydreams, sexual urges and emotional needs. The older woman has somehow discovered that she can now run the show, and does so." See Lewis, in footnote 11; p. 313.

[17] See footnote 5; pp. 190–191. Piaget also writes, "There is, in our opinion, the same relation between mutual respect and autonomy as between unilateral respect and egocentrism, provided the essential qualification be added, that mutual respect far more than unilateral respect, joins forces with the rationality already incipient in the motor stage, and therefore extends beyond the phase that is marked by the intervention of constraint and egocentrism" (p. 89).

[18] Lawrence Kohlberg, "Moral Development and Identification," in *Sixty-second Yearbook of the National Society for the Study of Education, Part I;* Chicago, Univ. of Chicago Press, 1963; p. 317.

[19] See footnote 18; p. 320. Kohlberg questions Piaget's theory that autonomy and group participation are related, pointing to his finding that peer-group relations are not related to a reciprocal orientation. However, Piaget makes it clear that the development of reciprocity and autonomy depends on relations that are free of all constraint (see footnote 5; p. 190), and it must be asked whether the peer-group in the United States today does not at times impose an even greater constraint and demand for conformity than do parents and teachers, who seem to be becoming progressively more permissive. In the village, submission to authority sometimes seems to be directly transferred to become submission to the group, without any development of autonomy or reciprocity.

[20] See footnote 5; pp. 78–79.

reflect social character development, it remains hypothetical how much games influence this development, as compared to the influence of family, the school, folklore, and so on.

From the observations of Piaget, Erikson, and Sutton-Smith, and from our own experiences, we would characterize the path of social character development in terms of games played in industrial societies as follows.

For the egocentric child of 5 or younger, other children can only help or hinder *his* game, which both imitates adults and compensates for his feelings of helplessness. He must be the master and the winner; what other children do matters little. But the games of children aged 6 to 9 reflect a more cooperative spirit. Sutton-Smith has written, "The analysis of all the games played by children in the first three school grades shows that approximately three-quarters of these games are Central Person games. These are games in which one central person plays in opposition to the rest of the group." [21] As they are played in Western Europe, the United States, and Australia and New Zealand, these games share a central person who orders the others or tries to capture them (Giant Steps, Hide-and-Seek, or Red Rover Come Over) while the group has powers to fight back, sometimes banding together, sometimes freeing companions who have been caught.

From ages 9 through 12 this independent-fraternal attitude jells, as children play games with more complicated rules requiring what Piaget calls "reciprocity," which includes a rational respect for rules allotting equal justice to all of the players. During this period, the ethic of fairness is stressed both in games and in daily life. The games or sports that follow generally assume the characteristic of reciprocity, although the emphasis shifts, as we have noted, to winning, or beating the system.[22]

Viewing in this way the games of Western industrialized societies, it is possible to trace through games the development of social and psychological attitudes which underlie democratic, capitalistic social systems, based on a combination of voluntary cooperation, regulated competition, contracts, rational authority, and respect for laws which protect the rights of the weak and powerful alike. Although the system does not always live up to this ideal, it could not function unless these attitudes were formed in its members.

In the village, games and social character are different. A boy does not learn to disengage himself from authority and egocentrism by cooperating with his peers. He does not internalize reciprocal rights and learn the meaning of rational authority. Authority remains dangerous and impulsive, a force he must escape or imitate. The central person is either chased or chases brutally. The group is a mass whose tyranny precludes cooperation to achieve autonomy, regulated competition, or the practice of rational authority. One joins the group to chase an enemy but runs alone without recourse against the tyrant. In both games and village life, the tendency is for atomism rather than cooperation, and the formation of a mass rather than individualism and respect for differences.

Like their elders, the most capable boys shun leadership. Two real leaders refused the presidency of the agricultural club, one admitting privately that he did not want to push others around and be disliked. He did not believe that he or anyone else could act differently. In a more extreme protest, one of the town elders on being elected to office complained of incapacitating weariness and backache, which did not disappear until the village had chosen a substitute.

It is our hypothesis that cultural differences in both games and attitudes toward authority are rooted in socioeconomic differences which determine beliefs about what is necessary for progress and prosperity. In the village both games and social character reflect conservatism, authority relations branded by the feudal past and semi-feudal present, and the distrust of all individualism as a threat to the status quo. There is only so much land, all of it in use. An ingenious new idea or a competitive spirit can only mean one person's gain at the expense of the others. The wish for political authority equals the impulse to exploit.

---

[21] Brian Sutton-Smith, "A Formal Analysis of Game Meaning," *Western Folklore* (1958) 18:13–24; p. 15.

[22] John M. Roberts, Malcolm J. Arth, and Robert R. Bush have demonstrated a relationship between the complexity of a social system and the presence of games of strategy. Such games, they feel, are expressive models of mastering the social system. "Games in Culture," *American Anthropologist* (1959) 61: 597–605.

The boy who plays games does not need to analyze his social system. He experiences adult authority by decree and threat of beatings. His successes are never rewarded, and his failures (to obey) are always punished. He may avoid opposing authority because his fear is too strong and because he lacks both allies and institutions to support his forbidden impulses. An experience which is too frightening or arouses too much hostility is not a subject for play, which demands distance and security. Only when authority is limited and children's rights are respected does it seem likely that the child can become independent without risking total rebellion and can learn how to be a rational authority.[23]

It is true that adolescents play cooperative team sports which are relatively new, despite their older roots in pre-Columbian cultures. Basketball and soccer are imports from the city, and both games are played by the villagers in less structured form than their counterparts in the United States. There is less division of labor, and even in basketball there are no pivot men, playmakers, or organized patterns of play. Whereas American games are based on reciprocity, interest in rules, and individualism, the village team sports are the outgrowth of a more simple group cohesion and cooperation without leaders, individual stars, or complex rules. Village sports also illustrate a more general finding—that villagers cooperate most when they can find an enemy or opponent.

The Effects of New Games

In an effort to study how much games influence culture change, we have tried to analyze the effects of new games introduced into the village, both by local innovators and by ourselves.

Basketball, which was introduced in 1938 by a school director, early became the focal point for a group of young men who believed in "progress" and who opposed older local customs they considered wasteful. As one of the town elders who was among the first basketball players related, the young men used to have only three interests— *jaripeos* (local bullfights), *naipes* (cards), and drinking.[24] The basketball players led the opposition to *jaripeos* and were also responsible for cutting down on costly religious festivals.

Many young men still embrace the cult of *machismo* (maleness), get drunk often, and show off their manliness with pistols or machetes, but for others basketball has become a substitute, a nondestructive way of displaying skill and endurance to the crowds who watch the games. The basketball players are the most productive young men, the best farmers, and the first volunteers to work on community projects. When we helped establish a library, the committee selected by the village for its direction was composed of three basketball players. The first group of players helped to found a community store, which failed later because of opposition from the town's other dominant group, centered around a powerful leader and his more *macho* followers.

Lola Schwartz attempted to form a club of young women, centered around a volleyball team. For a while the club flourished after an auspicious inauguration complete with new uniforms and flower-bearing *madrinas* (godmothers) for each player. But the team dissolved in dissension. Three factors were responsible. First of all, the question of leadership—which has never bothered the basketball players, whose captain only reluctantly accepts the post—was important to the girls. They argued about who would be captain, who would decide on the color of the uniforms, and who would carry the volleyball. Second, the mothers of the girls were from the start suspicious of the club, some feeling that it diverted their daughters from work, others that it was an excuse for the girls to display themselves in front of the young men. Finally, when the leader of the club got married and shortly thereafter became pregnant, the group disintegrated.

[23] The contrast between rational and irrational authority is explained by Erich Fromm in *Escape From Freedom;* New York, Farrar and Rinehart, 1941. Fromm shows how rebellion, of the type characteristic of the village, is an aspect of the authoritarian character and does not represent true independence.

[24] Caillois points out that games of chance reflect passivity and fatalism and are particularly popular in Central America. Games of competition, on the other hand, express the idea that skill and work lead to success. "However, pure games of chance do not develop any physical or mental attitude in the player, since he remains essentially passive. Their moral consequences are also quite formidable, because they detract from work and effort in creating hope for sudden and considerable wealth." See footnote 2; p. 167.

What can be concluded from the experiences with basketball and volleyball? Basketball did not create the desire for cooperation and progress, but it institutionalized and reinforced these impulses. In the case of the girls' team, competition over the role of authority and the disapproval of the mothers destroyed the team before it could work any change on the girls' attitudes.

The fact that volleyball was introduced by an American anthropologist and not by a Mexican may also have contributed to its failure. It is true that soccer, which was enthusiastically accepted by boys of 12 to 16, was taught them by a Friends Service Committee volunteer who stayed in the village only two months and was in no way a charismatic leader. However, the fact that the game was played in nearby villages made the boys eager to form a team, and they may also have accepted the game more readily because they had already joined in a boys' agricultural club. The result of the new game was increased interest in agricultural work, in part to make more money to pay for equipment and for transportation to play teams of other villages. Soccer did not solve the problems of the boys' avoiding responsibility and roles of authority,[25] but it did increase the club's cohesion.

The popularity of a sport reflects in part the range of alternatives open to a society. The village is culturally barren, and the most intelligent and alert people are the first to take advantage of any new stimulus that breaks the monotony of peasant life. But as the battle against the *jaripeo* proved, attitudes toward sports may also reflect a deeper characterological structure or aspiration.

A brief experiment of introducing a new central-person game was aimed at seeing whether a more independent-fraternal attitude could be reinforced through symbolic play. In other words, we wondered whether the children, by banding together against authority in play, might begin to assert themselves more in real life. No such changes were forthcoming, for the experiment turned out far different from our expectations.

The experimenter had lived in the village two months, getting to know the children through her work in starting the library, before she asked the school director's permission to teach a game to children of the third and fourth grades, who share a classroom. The game was a variation of Red Rover Come Over, which Sutton-Smith points out is played with variations in all Anglo-Saxon countries.[26] It is typical of central-person games which demand cooperation against *it*, the authority. Here it was called *Jefe* or Chief of Police, with a chief and thieves. The instructions were given as follows:

Good morning. As some of you know, I'm here to learn your language and help with the library. I also want to see how you play, and I've already seen some of your games.

Today I want to show you a game from my country that perhaps some of you are going to enjoy. It's a game which the children play in the United States during recess or in the afternoons after school. Boys and girls can play together or apart.

In this game there is a person in the center of the field whom we may call the "chief," or "the chief of police," because all the others are "thieves."

There are two bases at the sides of the field and a position in the middle, like this [drawing on the blackboard]:

```
_____Second base
_____Chief of Police
_____First base
```

Everyone begins at first base, standing on this line. The chief in the center calls someone. He says, for example, "Mario, Mario, come here." Then Mario, or whoever the chief calls, has to try to run across the field to second base. The chief of police tries to catch him. If the chief catches the thief, he has to remain in the center with the chief and help him catch the others. But if the thief can run to second base without being caught, then he can say to the other thieves, "Thieves, all of you, come on over here." Then the players, all of them, run to the other side, and the chief and his assistants try to catch all they can. Remember that only when one of the thieves has gotten to the other side can he give permission to run. The rest of the

---

[25] See Maccoby, in footnote 11, for a discussion of the vicissitudes of the boys' club and the results of efforts to stimulate a greater sense of responsibility.

[26] See footnote 21.

time the chief in the center is the one who may say who may run across.

Then the chief calls another name, and another thief tries to run to the other side. The game continues until all the thieves are caught except one. This last one, who doesn't get caught, becomes the new chief for the new game.

As the children played the game, it became expressive of their attitudes toward authority. The first day an attempt was made to combine boys and girls, but the girls left when the male *jefe* called none of their names. At this stage, the game was being played according to the rules. But the boys began to modify the game as they played on. At first they showed their anger against the authority figure. The field notes relate,

I had marked the boundaries with several stones and pieces of wood, which I soon regretted. The boys picked them up as weapons and as each boy was called, several people would run out of the line. Instead of just tagging, boys jumped on each other, and a general hassle arose.

The authority figure punished severely anyone he caught, and the others fought back.

But in the next stage of play, the "thieves" submitted. Instead of trying to escape, they waited patiently to be caught. Perhaps this was a reaction to the experimenter's attempt to calm them after the first game ended in violence. Those few who did get across safely never called to the others to come over. In the final stage of play, the game took on the aspect of a typical village central-person game. The field notes continue,

Those who ran across safely the first time, instead of waiting to be called again, joined the *jefe* and his *ayudantes*. The game soon became an example of the group (*jefe* and *ayudantes*) persecuting the individual (the person named to run across), rather than one of the group against the *jefe*.

In successive stages, the boys demonstrated their reaction to irrational authority—first, they showed anger and violent rebellion; second, they reacted with patient submission; and third, the concept of the leader was lost as the group solidified to persecute the outsider.

Later, when the game was played with girls alone, there was a somewhat different reaction. The girls learned the rules and were much calmer than the boys, but they decided that the object of the game was to be chosen as *ayudante* by the chief. When called, they stepped forth proudly to be caught and to stand with the chief. No matter how many times the game was re-explained, it always became a game of the chief and her helpers, and the girl who was left considered herself an outcast rather than the winner.

It would appear that both boys and girls distorted the game to conform to their attitudes toward authority and to the formal structure of the central-person games they normally play. But before drawing conclusions as to the strength of this assimilating tendency, it is important to be clear to what extent the children understood and were trying to comply with the instructions. The first day, the boys were curious about the new game and seemed bent neither on pleasing nor opposing the experimenter. The second day, several boys who had played the first day declined, but those who did play appeared to do so of their own choosing. Each time they played, the game was explained, and they at first played according to the rules; but each time they soon distorted the game, seemingly not out of spite, but during the heat of action.

Some of the girls appeared eager to win the experimenter's favor, clustering around her and begging to be taught the new game, and during play, they seemed to enjoy the game, expressing their enthusiasm by shouting and jumping. Although the experimenter only played the game with the girls on two mornings, and left the village shortly afterward, she was told on a return visit that the girls had played it on their own a number of times, but it is quite possible this was said with a mind to pleasing her. There is no evidence that the boys ever played it on their own.

Although the instructions were repeated several times and the game was played correctly at first, it is possible that some of the children never understood the instructions. Village children would hesitate to ask for clarification, preferring not to expose themselves to possible ridicule. However, even though it is necessary to exercise caution in drawing conclusions, the forms of distortion that did occur lent support to the analysis of the unconscious attitudes toward authority, and differences between the sexes, a conclusion we did not set out to prove with the experimental game. On the contrary, our purpose was to teach a new game which might stimulate cooperation and in-

dependence—an experiment that would have required continued attempts to teach the game.

To conclude, the analysis of games has enriched the understanding of how social character is formed in the village, of beliefs and attitudes expressed and reinforced through play. New games will not reform character and society, but they appear to support the process of culture change.

The Development of Social Hierarchies

D. G. Freedman

"Power is what makes the world go around." That's probably been said ever since men first reflected on politics. A sampling of language groups indicates a major proportion of vocabulary is generally devoted to power related terms (Osgood, 1963), and the striving for political power is a factor in all lives, whether among the Dani of New Guinea or the Hyde Parkers of Chicago. In other words, it characterizes the hominid species. To give examples, it will doubtless characterize the grouping of invitees in Stockholm, even as it does academic departments and large businesses.

That is, all groups in which persons work together end up in some form of a dominance hierarchy; certain individuals are eventually looked to as the leadership, or, in the words of Chance (1969), the attention structure of a group is directed upwards. While Chance meant this to describe monkeys, there is little doubt that it as well describes human working groups (cf. Freedman, 1967).

Ontogenetically and phylogenetically, how did this come about? Neither question will be fully answered but I will say something about both.

Phylogeny: Dominance-Submission Hierarchies Among Sub-human Primates

To deal briefly with a complex subject, the terrestrial macaques and baboons are the most widely distributed primate groups (Africa, Asia, Japan). They share with man a basically non-arboreal way of life which in turn makes predation a constant problem for them. As a result this terrestrial modality seems to have required high titres of aggression and fully mobile, organized bands (Washburn & DeVore, 1968). For example, tree living langurs in Ceylon are less aggressive and exhibit a looser social hierarchy than do their ground living cousin species. For that matter chimps in the forest are less hier-

Daniel G. Freedman, "The Development of Social Hierarchies." Paper prepared for World Health Organization meetings on *Society, Stress and Disease: Childhood and Adolescence,* Stockholm, June 27–July 3, 1971.

archical and form less physically compact groups than are the *same animals* when in open bush country. As Washburn and DeVore (1968) have pointed out, man as a terrestrial primate may be more like baboons and macaques in his social organization than like the genetically closer arboreal anthropoids because of the selection pressure of a similar ecology.

What about the ontogeny of the dominance hierarchy among the most widely spread terrestrial genus, the macaques? We know more about Macaca fuscata (Japanese monkeys) than any other terrestrial macaque, for they have been closely observed by scientists over the past 20 years. First of all, size of bands. Troops tend to be under 160, and when numbers go far beyond this figure a split in two may be expected. However, under some ecological conditions troops may be as large as 600 individuals, or as small as 20.

Less variable is the course of development of male-female differences in behavior. Even as infants, macaque mother-male pairs interact differently from mother-female pairs (Jensen, 1966). More aggression and independence from one another is seen in mother-male infant pairs. By the first year male infants who wander farther from the mother than females have sought each other out and begin to play. Soon, this rough and tumble play occupies the young males much of the day, and, perhaps because the adult males find this annoying, the young males take their play to the periphery of the troop. The female young do not take to rough and tumble play, and remain close to their mothers as they mature, engaging in mutual grooming and assuming some responsibility for the new infants.

By two and three years of age the peripheral young males are well on the way to establishing a hierarchy of strength and/or courage, and by four, the more brave among them may make forays into the troop's central hierarchy. Depending upon a number of factors, including the hierarchical position of his mother, a young male experiences success or failure in entering the central hierarchy. There one usually finds well established mature males at the top, and often a coalition of two or three appear to lead the troop. The hierarchy, as determined by such measures as who gives way to whom, is rather linear, with females occupying the lower half.

The problem of inter-group contacts is most interesting and important. To summarize it briefly, groups of Japanese macaques who are ecologically forced into frequent contact, as on the island of Koshima (or similarly in rhesus on Cayo Santiago, P.R.), develop a dominance order, usually based on size of troop. Fights, in fact, are rare and the deferent group makes sure to keep out of the way. Even troops which have just formed from a split show the same pattern. As we have seen, sustained aggression is rare at either the intra-troop or inter-troop levels; somehow each animal, each troop, assesses its chances and comes to decision *before* a fight. At least this is true in the majority of encounters, although a number of observations have been made of rare but vicious fights between an established male and a challenger; no one, however, has yet reported analogous sustained combat between monkey troops. In fact, the central males usually do not participate in inter-group threats since the peripheral males, because of their position, take the lead in such contacts.

There are many more facts of interest that might be added, but this will suffice as a model for the dominance-submission hierarchy usually seen in terrestrial sub-human primates, including the lowland baboons.[1]

We may now ask, if these are not comparable patterns in man?

---

[1] In addition to these data on primates, there has been a good deal of speculation on the aggressive nature of our more immediate evolutionary forebears. The first identified linear relative was Australopithecus africanus. These early savannah-living hominines, who according to current estimates were present as recognizable species for about ¾ of a million years beginning 2¼ million years ago, were erect and bipedal, averaged about 4 feet in height, were predacious and wielded bone weapons, and apparently murdered their own kind upon occasion (cf. Dart, 1955). On this last point, their upper Pleistocene successors, Homo erectus, were fairly certainly cannibalistic. This can be judged from the widely dispersed skull remains whose base (around the foramen magnum) had been broken open as if to better extract the meat inside (cf. von Koenigswald, 1962). It is startling, in fact, to note the common agreement on these deductions among our top paleontologists. While this doesn't assure correctness, we may note that some present day New Guinea tribes, who until recently practiced cannibalism, broke open the enemy skulls in the same way, and that weaponry, hunting and predation certainly characterizes the recent hominid adaptation.

Ontogeny: The Development of Dominance Hierarchies in Man

I turn to data based on our work with children between 3 and 9 years of age. The data is as yet unpublished and represents two dissertations (Donald Omark and Murray Edelman), a master's paper (Susan Beekman), and a number of course papers.

Our work began with the common observation that man, like the macaques, frequently engages in intra-group dominance displays, except that among men we call it by the species-specific term of "one-upmanship." Again, it would appear to occupy the male of the species considerably more than the females, and there is no point in cataloging here examples from everyday life, for by now much has been written on the subject (cf. Freedman, 1967). It is similarly evident that man tends to identify with a primary group (family, city, nation, race, religion), and when inter-group competition arises, as over land, resources, markets, etc., groups act in concert vis-à-vis one another in what we can call a modified macaque pattern (adversely modified, we might say), with the weaker group usually giving way to the stronger. Of course there are enormous differences between monkeys and men, but the basic pattern is undeniably similar and seems to be cross-culturally universal.

Given this background, we wondered about the ontogeny of such competitive behavior with individuals, and embarked upon a series of studies of youngsters between 3 and 9 years of age. We started by noting, at a local Montessori school, that when 3- and 4-year-olds went from room to room (they were allowed this freedom), they went alone, or at most by 2's or 3's. By 5 and 6 years, however, boys invariably moved about in groups of 3 and above. While girls continued as before in small groups or couples. On the playground, too, we found that after 5 years, boys formed into swarms and tended to use the entire grounds as their play-area, often keeping in touch as a group through loud shouts and visual signals. The girls, by contrast, occupied smaller and less expansive groups. Their games, for example jump rope, tended to be confined to a small area and tended to involve repetitive activity. Boys games, for example tag, involved unpredictable patterns of movement.

We then began questioning the children about possible competitive feelings, and we found that by 4 years boys were definitely aroused by the question, "which of you is toughest?" A typical 4 year old's response, no matter who the opposition, was "Me!" Girls, on the other hand, were rarely provoked by this question.

By 6 years, something new had been added. When asked the same question, boys now tended to agree with one another on who, in fact, *was* tougher. A hierarchy had been formed! Girls, again, were for the most part less interested in placing themselves in such a hierarchy, although their perception of "toughness" in boys was as accurate as judgments among the boys themselves. Teachers, on the other hand, were generally very poor in making similar judgments.

Following these observations we began to gather more systematic data; we developed a test called, naturally enough, the Hierarchy Test, and administered it to pairs of children in 32 classes at the University of Chicago Laboratory school, ranging from nursery school through grade 3. At the same time, we observed these classes on the playground during recess periods, using a technique borrowed from Hans Kummer (1968) and used with baboons, the "nearest neighbor method." Numbers and ages are listed in Table 1.

TABLE 1.   ALL CHILDREN FROM UNIVERSITY OF CHICAGO LABORATORY SCHOOLS

Classes	Nurs.	Kind.	1	2	3
Playground Observations	2	4	4	4	
Hierarchy Test	2	4	4	4	3
No. of Children	41	116	104	100	74

The Hierarchy Test consisted of two versions, the first for nursery school and kindergarten, and the second for grades one to three. In the first, each child is individually taken out of his class into the hall, and shown photographs of his classmates, placed horizontally on a bench. The photographs were arranged alphabetically by the first name.

The instructions were: "I'm going to ask you some questions about your classmates. The first question is about toughness. Now what is another word for tough?" (If the child had trouble answering, he was told to "do something tough.") "Now let us look at the first child in the row. If the child is tougher than you, turn his picture over." The experimenter made sure the child understood the question, and then said, "Now continue on down the row, turning over the picture of each child that is tougher than you."

By second grade, children could easily read names, so that a paper and pencil version of this test was administered to the entire class. The children's first names were randomly grouped into clusters of approximately six on a sheet of paper, with "ME" placed in a different position in each cluster. The integers from 1 to 6 were printed a few inches from the cluster of names. The administrator read the names of all the children in the cluster and said, "Use your pencil and connect the toughest kid with number one, the next

toughest with number two, and keep on until all numbers and names are connected." Before starting the test, the administrator worked an example on the blackboard. He took care to make sure that all children understood that "ME" refers to the child who was filling out the test.

The nearest neighbor technique consists of a series of 10 second assessments, during recess, of: 1) the first, second and third neighbor of the child being watched, 2) the relative distance between the child and each of his neighbors, 3) the type of interaction, if any, occurring between the child and his neighbors (a first neighbor is defined as the child spatially closest, etc.), and 4) the size and sex composition of the children's groups. All data was collected during free play activities on the playground.

Perception Among Peers of a Hierarchy of Toughness

As can be seen in Table 2, boys were consistently in the top two quintiles (1 quintile = 20%) of a classroom hierarchy of toughness, while the girls were in the bottom two quintiles, with considerable agreement in ranking among children in a class, and we see that by and large children tended to agree on the order. The major source of disagreement, naturally enough, was

TABLE 2. HIERARCHICAL DISTRIBUTION OF CHILDREN BY QUINTILE RANK AT EACH GRADE LEVEL (PERCENT OF EACH SEX)

Grade (age)	Sex	N	Quintile Rank				
			1	2	3	4	5
N (4)	B	22	27	23	23	23	5
	G	19	5	5	26	26	37
K (5)	B	69	29	35	25	10	1
	G	47	-	2	13	34	40
1 (6)	B	54	31	35	22	7	4
	G	50	4	6	12	36	42
2 (7)	B	55	25	38	25	5	5
	G	45	4	-	13	22	49
3 (8)	B	38	32	42	16	8	3
	G	36	-	-	25	33	42

TABLE 3.   PERCENTAGE OF AGREEMENT BETWEEN EACH CHILD AND EVERY OTHER CHILD ON THEIR RELATIVE DOMINANCE

Grade	Class	Pairs of Children			
		Boy-Boy (%)	Girl-Girl (%)	Boy-Girl (%)	Total (%)
1st	A	70.5	60.0	75.3	71.1
	B	60.6	55.5	66.6	62.7
	C	61.8	53.3	67.2	62.8
2nd	A	55.1	67.2	75.5	68.1
	B	75.7	62.2	80.0	75.3
	C,	62.5	42.8	85.9	71.3
3rd	A	74.2	60.0	64.1	66.2
	B	67.0	62.2	91.4	78.6
4th	A	72.7	64.2	74.8	73.0

one's own rank in that children tended to see it higher than general agreement would have it. (It is indeed amusing to watch a pair of 6- or 7-year-old boys ranking their class, for while there was rather easy agreement on the rank of those not present, the placing of one's own name was frequently challenged by the partner as being too high, which in turn led to a good deal of uninhibited banter. Thus, something of the 4-year-old's push towards alpha-ness seems to remain at 6 and 7—and most probably—forever after.)

Besides toughness, children were also asked to rank nicest, and smartest, but neither approached "toughness" in terms of the enthusiasm elicited or in the extent of mutual agreement. We suspect, of course, that in later grades the ranking of "smartest" would become more involving, at least in middle class schools.

Sex-difference on the Playground

After nursery school, the size of boys' groups are larger than are girls' groups (Table 5). This is both in terms of the maximum and average size of the groups (p < .05). The important point about the nursery school figures is that nursery schoolers do not form mutually cooperating groups, but are nevertheless usually playing near someone else. Groups in nursery school, then, are usually noninteracting and rarely goal oriented.

The very large boys' groups usually contained a few girls, and in those classes where the children were well known to the observer, these girls tended to be near the top of the girls' hierarchy.

Tables 6 and 7 demonstrate results of the nearest neighbor method. In Table 6 we see that boys tend to be near boys, while girls tend to be near girls, and in Table 7, we see that boys are more often in groups of boys than are girls in groups of girls. At all ages the girls were also found to be near adults (generally female teachers) more frequently than were the boys (p < .05). Of great interest is the fact that Kummer, in using the same method with baboons, found the same patterns among juveniles; males were near males, females near females as well as adults.

Physical interaction, such as playful wrestling, holding hands, or throwing a ball to one another increased with age for both sexes. Not surprisingly, males showed more aggression and physical interaction of all kinds with their nearest neighbor at all ages, whereas girls were more frequently talking to their nearest neighbor. Furthermore, boys demonstrated this greater physical interaction with the 1st, 2nd and 3rd nearest neighbors, while

TABLE 4. THE PERCENT OF ESTABLISHED DOMINANCE PAIRS WHICH WERE
VIEWED ACCURATELY BY BOYS AND BY GIRLS

| | | Boy-Boy Pairs | |
| | | Accuracy of Boys (%) | Accuracy of Girls (%) |
Grade	Class		
1st	A	87.1	89.4
	B	74.2	71.5
	C	68.3	60.2
2nd	A	56.2	58.7
	B	88.8	86.0
	C	73.3	73.8
3rd	A	79.7	76.3
	B	81.4	81.1
4th	A	77.8	72.7

| | | Girl-Girl Pairs | |
| | | Accuracy of Boys (%) | Accuracy of Girls (%) |
Grade	Class		
1st	A	69.8	79.1
	B	72.3	77.5
	C	69.6	72.9
2nd	A	66.5	68.7
	B	69.0	69.1
	C	61.9	56.9
3rd	A	85.4	77.3
	B	71.1	79.4
4th	A	72.8	64.2

girls demonstrated greater verbal behavior with only the very closest neighbor (Table 7).

Differences in Facial Expression Between Those High and Low in the Toughness Hierarchy

In monkey troops it is commonly observed that individuals of lower status demonstrate a "fear-grin" when passing near a dominant; similarly they spend more time watching the dominant animal than he does watching them—a sort of disdain on the dominant's part and its complement, fearful watchfulness, on the submissive's part. A straight-on stare, in fact, is invariably interpreted as a threat.

Again, there are many observations in print about human groups which read very similarly. Scheinfeld (1970), for example, has observed the

TABLE 5.   MAXIMUM AND AVERAGE NUMBER OF CHILDREN IN GROUPS OF
PREDOMINANTLY ONE SEX (<60%)

Predominant sex of the groups	Grade			
	Nurs.	Kind.	1	2
Boys: Max.	6	10	11	16
Avg.	3.36	2.28	3.46	4.55
No. of Groups	40	200	75	18
Girls: Max.	5	6	5	6
Avg.	3.86	1.92	2.16	3.60
No. of Groups	29	163	118	20

same behavior in street gangs on Chicago's West Side. According to Scheinfeld, alpha males never "bother" to look at low status males—it is up to the latter to make themselves a "name," to gain sufficient value in the eyes of leadership to be worth watching. Further, submissives or strangers never dare stare into the eyes of the higher males.

With these ideas in mind, we videotaped, for later analysis, pairs of children who were asked to draw a picture together. The videotaping also included an interview situation after the drawing was completed. There were 32 children in all, taken from 2 classes of 1st graders and 2 classes of 3rd graders (8 from each class). Only children who were perceived by most of their classmates as being near the top or near the bottom of the toughness hierarchy (for their sex) were used,

and all combinations were paired off (see Fig. 1).

In Table 8 we see that lower status boys and girls did indeed spend more time watching their higher status partner ($p < .044$), and that girls spent more time gazing at boys than vice versa ($p < .05$). Also, as predicted, lower status girls smiled considerably more than higher status boys or girls, but lower status boys did not react this way with higher status boys (Table 9); however, when low status boys were paired with high status girls there was a decided tendency for the boy to do more smiling.

The issue of smiling behavior as a mechanism for facilitating social interaction has been dealt with elsewhere (Freedman, 1964, 1968), so it will suffice here to point out that females, at birth, already exhibit more eyes-closed "reflexive" smil-

TABLE 6.   PERCENT OF CHILDREN OF EACH SEX WHO ARE NEAREST NEIGHBORS
OF BOYS, GIRLS, AND ADULTS

Child being observed	Grade			
	Nurs.	Kind.	1	2
Boys: Boys	48.5	65.2	74.0	66.3
Girls	30.4	28.3	21.9	28.5
Adults	20.1	6.5	4.1	5.2
n	105	211	181	84
Girls: Boys	29.1	40.2	19.6	39.0
Girls	48.8	48.5	69.9	52.4
Adults	22.1	11.3	10.5	8.6
n	95	195	217	86

TABLE 7.   NEAREST NEIGHBOR TEST--SEX DIFFERENCES ACROSS ALL
AGES (4-8 YRS.)

Aggression	Imitation	Physical Interaction (not agg.)	Verbal Behavior
p=.009 hi	N.S.	.005 hi	.0048 hi

	Neighbor		
	1	2	3
Physical interaction	p=.003 ♂	.005 ♂	.0001 ♂
Verbal behavior	p=.04 ♀	N.S.	N.S.
Percent of time with neighbor of same sex	p=.01 ♂	.003 ♂	.01 ♂

ing, and that a series of studies show them to have lower thresholds for social smiling through adulthood (Freedman, 1971). However, as we see here, when a female is dominant over a male there can be a reversal in the relative frequency of smiling: When the boys were subdominant in a cross-sex pair, it was they who smiled more.

Discussion

Thus we have seen evidence for a primate pattern in human affairs: The development of dominance-submission hierarchies based on perceived superiority in a trait that is mutually agreed upon as important, and the related higher frequency of deference behaviors of lower status individuals. I consider these facts as well established and believe this pattern to be universal.

Now all the data presented were concerned with *intra*-group hierarchization whereas in our macaque model we did mention that inter-group

hierarchies work in an analogous way. Unfortunately we have no human data on the ontogeny of inter-group hierarchization, but I should nevertheless like to take this opportunity to speculate about this process in man.[2]

I think the evidence is very strong that people, like macaques, engage in inter-group hierarchization, and that this is one of the greatest sources of stress on people today. A rather obvious hypothesis follows from this assertion: There is least stress within dominant groups and greatest stress within dominated groups.

By stress, I have two levels in mind: (1) Stress at the level of physical well-being, including the

[2] I have discussed elsewhere (Freedman, 1967) some problems arising out of intra-group social hierarchization: For example, the problem of the nonparticipant (often a lone male), problems of psychological "castration" in young males, and problems of women competing with men. These are issues dealt with most extensively heretofore by psychoanalysis, but I believe our zoologically based framework will, in the long run, prove more viable.

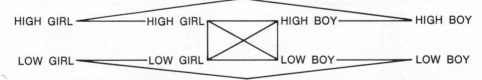

Figure 1
Pairings of high and low status children in assessments of who gazes at whom and who smiles at whom.

TABLE 8

		same-sex, unequal-status pairs mean % gazing at peer	
		high-status child	low-status child
first grade	boys	7.22	19.52
	girls	11.90	16.80
third grade	boys	3.65	8.50
	girls	13.19	27.06
		cross-sex pairs mean % gazing at peer	
		boys	girls
first grade		8.82	17.35
third grade		12.27	18.31

persistent possibility of slaughter, unchecked disease, and/or starvation. (2) Stress at the cultural-psychological level. By this I specifically mean formerly culturally intact peoples in the process of breaking-up (institutions and gene pool) under pressures from the dominant group.

The former inhabitants of what is now called Tasmania are, of course, examples of a people who were slaughtered by Europeans beyond the possibility of rebuilding genetically or culturally. That was also true of some American Indian tribes. There is probably no sound reason to believe that slaughter, starvation and epidemic are part of man's history and not his future, but we can hope and work to that end, for the enemy is most often visible.

On the other hand, genetic and institutional elimination is more subtle, and it takes its major toll on the psyche of physically intact men. (By genetic elimination, I mean simply excessive outbreeding.) Again, under pressure of the European, practically all American Indian tribes, the Polynesian peoples and the Australian Aborigines are on the way out as intact breeding populations or culturally definable groups. How does a young person who belongs to these groups define himself today? That has to be a source of tremendous stress.

But the question of self-definition, one may respond, is a world-wide problem among youth, including European youth. Which are the intact, dominant groups you are speaking of? I have no good answer to that, but I do know, from close at hand experience, that it is less stressful to be a European-American and to identify as best as one can with that amorphous but powerful group, than to be an Afro-American. To illustrate, many Afro-American youth experienced joy and well being for the first time in their lives when, less than a decade ago, the Black Power movement was launched and a new commodity, pride, became available out of that group experience.

It is significant that Stokely Carmichael, the young man who at 25 years of age gave life to the phrase "Black Power," now sees the future of Afro-Americans as tied with the future of Africa. Psychological intactness, he feels, can only be achieved if black men become consciously identified with their source. I find I can only agree. Israel has played just such a role for millions of Jews, and her importance can only be understood as the fulfillment of a deep need all men share, to be proudly part of an intact group which is at the same time part of themselves. Young people who haven't the opportunity for this experience cannot be happy.

TABLE 9

same-sex, unequal-status pairs mean % smiling		
	high-status child	low-status child
first grade boys	51.25	42.54
first grade girls	21.78	47.60
third grade boys	20.50	25.83
third grade girls	34.69	70.34
cross-sex pairs mean % smiling		
	pairs with high-status girls	pairs with low-status girls
first grade boys	21.21	28.11
first grade girls	13.88	39.41
third grade boys	27.91	26.95
third grade girls	25.93	51.55

REFERENCES

CHANCE, M. R. A. (1967). Attention structure as the basis of primate rank orders. *Man,* 2, 503–518.

DART, R. (1955). The cultural status of the South African man-apes. *Smithsonian Report,* pp. 317–338, Washington, D. C.

DEVORE, I. and WASHBURN, S. (1963). Baboon ecology and human evolution, in *African Ecology and Human Evolution,* eds. Howell, F. C. and Bourliere, F., pp. 335–367, Chicago: Aldine Press.

FREEDMAN, D. G. (1964). Smiling in blind infants and the issue of innate vs. acquired. *J. Child. Psychol. Psychiat.* Vol. 5, 171–189.

FREEDMAN, D. G. (1967). A biological view of man's social behavior, in *Social Behavior from Fish to Man,* ed. Etkin, W., pp. 152–188, Chicago: University of Chicago Press.

FREEDMAN, D. G. (1968). Personality development in infancy: a biological view. Reprinted in *Perspectives on Human Evolution,* eds. Washburn,

S. L. and Jay, P., Vol. 1, New York: Holt, Rinehart and Winston.

FREEDMAN, D. G. (1971). An evolutionary approach to research on the life cycle. *Human Development,* (in press).

JENSEN, G. (1966). Sex differences in developmental trends of mother-infant monkey behavior (M. Nemestrina). *Primates,* Vol. 7, No. 3, p. 403.

VON KOENIGSWALD, G. H. R. (1962). *The evolution of man.* Ann Arbor: University of Michigan Press.

KUMMER, H. (1968). Social organization of Hamadryas baboons. University of Chicago Press.

OSGOOD, C. E., MIRON, M. S., and ARCHER, W. K. (1963). The cross cultural generality of affective meaning systems: Progress Report. Center for Comparative Psycholinguistics, University of Illinois.

SCHEINFELD, D. (1970). Report on work in progress, University of Chicago, Department of Anthropology.

Part 9

*Personality and
Prediction*

The question of continuity and change, of stability and instability in individual behavior and personality, is considered in the papers by Mischel, Neugarten, and Emmerich. The prediction of behavior over long periods of time has not been too successful in psychological research. So far, it has not been clear whether this lack of success is due to inadequate measurements or to changeability of human beings.

Increasingly, however, we were learning to see long-term changes as more subtle processes than we once thought them to be. We now understand that underlying continuity in personality may remain even though surface behavior may change. Furthermore, it now seems probable that the more an individual's behavior supports a consistent personality trait, the less apt it is to change; yet personality traits, by and large, are more changeable than intellectual habits. At each age level, also, there appear to be distinctive ways of transforming the expression of personal qualities, as the article by Neugarten shows quite clearly.

Continuity and Change in Personality

Walter Mischel

The question of continuity and change in personality has enduring importance, and the position that one takes on this topic profoundly influences one's approach to most other issues in personality psychology. Almost no psychologist, myself included, would argue with the basic and widely shared assumption that continuity does exist in personality development (e.g., Kagan, 1969). Indeed, few other phenomena seem to be so intuitively self-evident. The experience of subjective continuity in ourselves—of basic oneness and durability in the self—is perhaps the most compelling and fundamental feature of personality. This experience of continuity seems to be an intrinsic feature of the mind, and the loss of a sense of felt consistency may be a chief characteristic of personality disorganization.

Clinically, it seems remarkable how each of us generally manages to reconcile his seemingly diverse behaviors into one self-consistent whole. A man may steal on one occasion, lie on another, donate generously to charity on a third, cheat on a fourth, and still construe himself readily as "basically honest and moral." Just like the personality theorist who studies them, our subjects also are skilled at transforming their seemingly discrepant behavior into a constructed continuity, making unified wholes out of almost anything.

It might be interesting to fantasize a situation in which the personality theorist and his subjects sat down together to examine each subject's data on behavioral consistency cross-situationally or over time. Actually it might not even be a bad idea for psychologists to enact such a fantasy. In inspecting these data the theorist would look for genotypic unities that he is sure must be there;

This article is based on a paper presented at the symposium "Behavioral Continuity and Change with Development," held at the meeting of the Society for Research in Child Development, Santa Monica, California, March 27, 1969. Preparation of this paper was facilitated by Grant M-6830, from the National Institutes of Health, United States Public Health Service. Requests for reprints should be sent to Walter Mischel, Department of Psychology, Stanford University, Stanford, California 94305.

his subject would look for genotypic unities and be even more convinced that they exist and would proceed to find his own, often emerging with unities unknown to the theorist. But the consistency data on the IBM sheets, even if they reached statistical significance, probably would account for only a trivial portion of the variance, as Hunt (1965) has pointed out. A correlation of .30 leaves us understanding less than 10% of the relevant variance. And even correlations of that magnitude are not very common and have come to be considered good in research on the consistency of any noncognitive dimension of personality.

How does one reconcile our shared perception of continuity with the equally impressive evidence that on virtually all of our dispositional measures of personality substantial changes occur in the characteristics of the individual longitudinally over time and, even more dramatically, across seemingly similar settings cross-sectionally. I had the occasion to broadly review the voluminous evidence available on this topic of consistency and specificity (Mischel, 1968). In my appraisal, the overall evidence from many sources (clinical, experimental, developmental, correlational) shows the human mind to function like an extraordinarily effective reducing valve that creates and maintains the perception of continuity even in the face of perpetual observed changes in actual behavior. Often this cognitive construction of continuity, while not arbitrary, is only very tenuously related to the phenomena that are construed.

To understand continuity properly it is necessary to be more specific and to talk about types of variations and the conditions that regulate them. In this regard it may be useful to distinguish between consistency in various types of human activity.

There is a great deal of evidence that our cognitive constructions about ourselves and the world —our personal theories about ourselves and those around us (both in our roles as persons and as psychologists)—often are extremely stable and highly resistant to change. Data from many sources converge to document this point. Studies of the self-concept, of impression formation in person perception and in clinical judgment, of cognitive sets guiding selective attention—all these phenomena and many more document the consistency and tenacious continuity of many human construction systems (Mischel, 1968). Often these construction systems are built quickly and on the basis of little information (e.g., Bruner, Olver, & Greenfield, 1966). But, once established, these theories, whether generated by our subjects or ourselves, become exceedingly difficult to disconfirm.

An impressive degree of continuity also has been shown for another aspect of cognition: These are the features of problem solving called cognitive styles. Significant continuity often has been demonstrated on many cognitive style dimensions (e.g., Kagan, 1969; Witkin, Goodenough, & Karp, 1967). The current prolific cognitive style explorations on this topic provide excellent evidence of developmental continuity. In this case the research also reveals a welcome continuity in our professional developmental history. Research into consistent individual differences in cognition has had deep roots and a long and distinguished history in experimental psychology. Simple cognitive measures like reaction time and response speed and duration have intrigued psychologists since the earliest laboratory work on mental measurement began more than 70 years ago. Individual differences on specific measures of problem solving, such as speed of reaction time and weight judgments, began to be explored in 1890 by James McKeen Cattell and others. Their studies of responses on specific cognitive and ability measures in the early laboratories were neglected when the development of practical intelligence testing started in this century. At that time, Binet and Henri shifted attention to the measurement of generalized intelligence by studying individual differences in more complex global tasks. Now it is refreshing to witness the reawakened interest in such enduringly important topics as reaction time and "conceptual tempo" and it is good to see sophisticated consistency evidence for it (Kagan, 1969). The generality and stability of behaviors assessed by these cognitive measures often have been found to be among the best available in personality research.

Some puzzling problems may arise, however, from the correlations found between some of the most promising new cognitive style measures and the traditional measures of generalized intelligence such as the performance IQ on the WISC. That is, correlations between measures of generalized intelligence and cognitive style such as Witkin's field dependence raise the question of the degree to which the consistency of cognitive styles may be due to their associations with intellectual abilities. The obtained generality and stability, as well as the external personality correlates, of at least some cognitive style measures thus may rest in part on their sizable correlations with indexes of more generalized intelligence and achievement behavior, as has been found in other studies (e.g., Crandall & Sinkeldam, 1964; Elliott, 1961). To illustrate, the Witkin measures of cognitive style are strongly related to performance IQ ability indexes. Indeed the relationship between the Witkin Embedded Figures Test and the Wechsler Intelligence Block Design subtest is so strong that Witkin (1965) has indicated he is willing to use Block Design scores when available as a substitute for other field-dependence measures. When such cognitive styles as field independence and such coping patterns as "intellectualization" are substantially correlated with IQ then the stability reported for them and their correlates (e.g., by Schimek, 1968) may partly reflect the stability of the IQ.

This issue might also constitute a problem in interpreting such cognitive styles as Kagan's conceptual tempo. To the extent that conceptual tempo involves reaction time, and fast reaction time is a determinant of generalized performance IQ, one would have to be alert to their interrelations, as has been pointed out by Campbell and Fiske (1959). It will be interesting to continue to explore exactly how conceptual tempo and other cognitive styles based on performance indexes such as response speed and accuracy take us beyond generalized ability measurement and into the domain of personality traits. Ultimately research on cognitive styles surely will provide a clearer analysis of intellective behavior. The implications of cognitive styles for the concept of general intelligence (as well as the reverse relation) should then become more explicit than they are now. In the course of these explorations the meaning of intercorrelations among diverse cognitive style measures—such as conceptual tempo, field dependence-independence, leveling-sharpen-

ing, and so on—will become clearer. At the same time our understanding of the interactions among cognitive and noncognitive personality dimensions hopefully will improve

When we turn away from cognitive and intellective dimensions to the domain of personality and interpersonal behavior, consistency evidence is generally much harder to establish, at least whenever we use conventional tactics and the correlation coefficient (e.g., Maccoby, 1969). On the basis of past literature on this topic, one should no longer be surprised when consistency correlations for social behavior patterns turn out to be quite low. Theoretically, in my view, one should not expect social behavior to be consistent unless the relevant social learning and cognitive conditions are arranged to maintain the behavior cross-situationally. On theoretical as well as on empirical grounds, much of the time there is no reason to expect great consistency in the social behaviors comprising most of our personality dimensions.

It is not possible to even begin to cite here the extensive evidence that I believe supports this point, namely, that noncognitive global personality dispositions are much less global than traditional psychodynamic and trait positions have assumed them to be (Mischel, 1968). A great deal of behavioral specificity has been found regularly on character traits such as rigidity, social conformity, aggression, on attitudes to authority, and on virtually any other nonintellective personality dimension (Mischel, 1968; Peterson, 1968; Vernon, 1964). Some of the data on delay of gratification with young children, emerging from our current studies at Stanford, are illustrative. In an ongoing longitudinal study on this problem we have obtained evidence that delay of gratification has some developmental consistency and increases with age, up to a point.[1] Much more impressive in my view, however, is our finding that within any child there exists tremendous variability on this dimension. Now we are studying how long preschool children will actually sit still alone in

---

[1] W. Mischel, E. B. Ebbesen, & A. Raskoff. In progress research report, Stanford University, entitled "Determinants of Delay of Gratification and Waiting Behavior in Preschool Children."

a chair waiting for a preferred but delayed out-come before they signal to terminate the waiting period and settle for a less preferred but im-mediately available gratification. We are finding that the same 3½-year-old child who on one occasion may terminate his waiting in less than half a minute may be capable of waiting by himself up to an hour on another occasion a few weeks earlier or later, *if* cognitive and attentional conditions are appropriately arranged. Our con-clusion is that some significant predictions of length of voluntary delay of gratification cer-tainly can be made from individual differences data; but the most powerful predictions by far come from knowledge of the cognitive and in-centive conditions that prevail in the particular situation of interest.

These results are not at all atypical. A tribute to the interaction of person and environment is usually offered at the front of every elementary textbook in the form of Kurt Lewin's famous equation: Behavior is a function of person and environment. In spite of such lip service to the stimulus, most of our personality theories and methods still take no serious account of condi-tions in the regulation of behavior. Literally thousands of tests exist to measure dispositions, and virtually none is available to measure the psychological environment in which development and change occurs.

Evidence on observed instability and incon-sistency in behavior often has been interpreted to reflect the imperfections of our tests and tools and the resulting unreliability and errors of our mea-surements, as due to the fallibility of the human clinical judge and his ratings, and as due to many other methodological problems. Undoubtedly all these sources contribute real problems. Some of these have been excellently conceptualized by Emmerich (1969). His emphasis on the need for considering rate and mean changes over age if one is to achieve a proper understanding of continuity, growth, and psychological differentia-tion is especially important. Likewise, his call for longitudinal, multimeasure, and multivariate stud-ies needs to be heeded most seriously.

I am more and more convinced, however, hope-fully by data as well as on theoretical grounds, that the observed inconsistency so regularly found in studies of noncognitive personality dimensions often reflects the state of nature and not merely the noise of measurement. Of course, that does not imply a capriciously haphazard world—only one in which personality consistencies seem greater than they are and in which behavioral complexities seem simpler than they are. This would, if true, be extremely functional. After all, if people tried to be radical behaviorists and to describe each other in operational terms they would soon run out of breath and expire. It is essential for the mind to be a reducing valve—if it were not it might literally blow itself!

Perhaps the most widely accepted argument for consistency in the face of seeming diversity is the one mentioned so often, the distinction be-tween the phenotypic and the genotypic. Thus most theorizing on continuity seems to have been guided by a model that assumes a set of genotypic personality dispositions that endure, although their overt response forms may change. This model, of course, is the one shared by traditional trait and dynamic dispositional theories of personality. The model was well summarized in the example of how a child at age 12 may substitute excessive obedience to a parent for his earlier phobic re-action as a way of reducing anxiety over parental rejection (Kagan, 1969). At the level of physical analogy Kagan spoke of how the litre of water in the closed system is converted to steam and recondensed to liquid.

This type of hydraulic Freudian-derived per-sonality model, while widely shared by personality theorists, is of course not the only one available and not the only one necessary to deal with phenomena of continuity and change. Indeed, in the opinion of many clinical psychologists the hydraulic phenotypic-genotypic model applied to personality dynamics, psychotherapy, and symp-tom substitution has turned out to be a con-ceptual trap leading to some tragic pragmatic mistakes in clinical treatment and diagnosis for the last 50 years (e.g., Mischel, 1968; Peterson, 1968). I am referring, of course, to the unjustified belief that seemingly diverse personality problems must constitute symptoms of an underlying gen-eralized core disorder rather than being relatively discrete problems often under the control of rela-tively independent causes and maintaining con-ditions.

The analysis of diverse behaviors as if they

were symptomatic surface manifestations of more unitary underlying dispositional forces also is prevalent in our theories of personality development (e.g., Kagan, 1969; Maddi, 1968). But while diverse behaviors often may be in the service of the same motive or disposition, often they are not. In accord with the genotype-phenotype distinction, if a child shows attachment and dependency in some contexts but not in others one would begin a search to separate phenotypes from genotypes. But it is also possible that seeming inconsistencies, rather than serving one underlying motive, actually may be under the control of relatively separate causal variables. The two behavior patterns may not reflect a phenotype in the service of a genotype but rather may reflect discrimination learning in the service of the total organism. Likewise, while a child's fears sometimes may be in the service of an underlying motive, most research on the topic would lead me to predict it is more likely that the fear would involve an organized response system with its own behavioral life, being evoked and maintained by its own set of regulating conditions (e.g., Bandura, 1969; Paul, 1967).

When we observe a woman who seems hostile and fiercely independent some of the time but passive, dependent, and feminine on other occasions, our reducing valve usually makes us choose between the two syndromes. We decide that one pattern is in the service of the other, or that both are in the service of a third motive. She must be a really castrating lady with a facade of passivity —or perhaps she is a warm, passive-dependent woman with a surface defense of aggressiveness. But perhaps nature is bigger than our concepts and it is possible for the lady to be a hostile, fiercely independent, passive, dependent, feminine, aggressive, warm, castrating person all-in-one. Of course which of these she is at any particular moment would not be random and capricious— it would depend on who she is with, when, how, and much, much more. But each of these aspects of her self may be a quite genuine and real aspect of her total being. (Perhaps we need more adjectives and hyphens in our personality descriptions. That is what is meant, I think, by "moderator variables.")

I am skeptical about the utility of the genotype-phenotype distinction at the present level of be-havioral analysis in personality psychology because I fear it grossly oversimplifies the complexity of organized behavior and its often nonlinear causes. The genotype-phenotype oversimplification may mask the complex relations between the behavior and the organism that generates it, the other behaviors available to the organism, the history of the behavior, and the current evoking and maintaining conditions that regulate its occurrence and its generalization.

The question of the nature of the similarity or dissimilarity among the diverse responses emitted by a person is one of the thorniest in psychology. Even when one response pattern is not in the service of another the two of course may still interact. No matter how seemingly separated the various branches of behavior may be, one can always construe some common origins for them and some current interactions. At the very least, all behavior from an organism, no matter how diverse, still has unity because it is all generated from the same source—from the same one person. At the other extreme, incidentally, few response patterns are ever phenotypically or physically identical: Their similarity always has to be grouped on some higher-order dimension of meaning. To make sense of bits of raw behavior one always has to group them into larger common categories. The interesting theoretical issue is just what the bases of these groupings should be. Dispositional theories try to categorize behaviors in terms of the hypothesized historical psychic forces that diverse behaviors supposedly serve; but it is also possible to categorize the behaviors in terms of the unifying evoking and maintaining conditions that they jointly share.

Moreover, few potent response patterns can occur without exerting radical consequences for the other alternatives available to the person. Thus an extremely "fast-tempo" child may be so active that, in addition to fatiguing his parents, he may as Kagan (1969) found, smile less. Perhaps that happens because he is too busy to smile. My comment about how fast-tempo children may be too busy to smile is not really facetious. One of the intriguing features of any strong response syndrome is that it soon prevents all kinds of other intrinsically incompatible behaviors. If a child darts about a lot and is fast there are all sorts of other things he automatically cannot do. His speed in living, his pace, not only automatically influences his other possible behavior, it also soon starts to shape his environment. I now expect my fast-tempo children to be fast tempo, and currently it takes almost no cues from them to convince me I am right about them.

It would have been relatively simple to assess and predict personality if it had turned out to consist mainly of stable, highly generalized response patterns that occur regularly in relation to many diverse stimulus constellations. The degree and subtlety of discrimination shown in human behavior, however, is at least as impressive as is the variety and extensiveness of stimulus generalization. What people do in any situation may be altered radically even by seemingly minor variations in prior experiences or slight modifications in stimulus attributes or in the specific characteristics of the evoking situation. From my theoretical perspective this state of affairs—namely, the enormously subtle discriminations that people continuously make, and consequently the flexibility of behavior—is not a cause of gloom. Instead, the relative specificity of behavior, and its dependence on environmental supports, is the expected result of complex discrimination learning and subtle cognitive differentiation. When the eliciting and evoking conditions that maintain behavior change—as they generally do across settings—then behavior surely will change also. While the continuous interplay of person and condition may have been a surprise for faculty and trait psychology it should come as no upset for us now. If one pays more than verbal tribute to the dependency of behavior on conditions, and to the modification of behavior when situations change, then the so-called negative results of dispositional research on behavioral continuity appear attributable largely to the limitations of the assumptions that have guided the research. From the viewpoint of social behavior theory the findings of behavioral specificity, rather than primarily reflecting measurement errors, are actually congruent with results from experimental research on the determinants and modification of social behavior (Mischel, 1968). When response consequences and valences change so do actions; but when maintaining conditions remain stable so does behavior.

The last decade has seen an exciting growth of research on cognitive styles and many researchers have begun to study the person as an information-processing and problem-solving organism. Generally, however, these processes have been viewed in dimensional and dispositional terms and quickly translated back to fit the consistency assumptions of traditional global trait and psychodynamic theory. Individual differences on dimensions such as conceptual tempo, field dependence, leveling-sharpening, and so on, have been isolated with some promising results. Less progress has been made in applying the concepts and language of information processing and cognitive styles to forming a better theoretical conception of personality structure itself. It has become fashionable to speak of the organism as creating plans, generating rules, and, depending on his needs and situations, devising strategies. These tactics yield payoffs and consequences, and in light of these the person modifies his plans accordingly. But when contingencies change stably, what happens? For example, what happens when the mother-dependent child finds that his preschool peers now consistently have little patience for his whining, attention-getting bids, and instead respect independence and self-confidence? Generally the child's behavior changes in accord with the new contingencies, and if the contingencies shift so does the behavior—if the contingencies remain stable so does the new syndrome that the child now displays. Then what has happened to the child's dependency trait?

One might argue that the basic genotype remained but its manifestation phenotypically has altered. But is this just a "symptom" change leaving unaffected the psyche that generated it and the life space in which it unfolds? A vigorous "No!" to this question comes from much research on behavior change in the last few years (e.g., Bijou, 1965; Fairweather, 1967; Mischel, 1966; Patterson, Ray, & Shaw, 1969).

What would happen conceptually if we treated the organism as truly active and dynamic rather than as the carrier of a stable dispositional reservoir of motives and traits? Might one then more easily think of changes in the developing organism not as phenotypic overlays that mask genotypic unities but as genuinely new strategies in which many of the person's old plans are discarded and replaced by more appropriate ones in the course of development? (Perhaps Gordon

Allport's idea of functional autonomy needs to be rethought.) Can the person even become involved in plans to change what he *is* as well as what he *does*? George Kelly and the existentialists in their search for human nature noted that existence precedes essence. According to that position, to find out what I *am* I need to know what I *do*. And if my actions change do they leave me (the "real me") behind? Or perhaps they just leave some of my discarded psychological genotypes behind?

A search for a personality psychology that has conceptual room for major variability and changes within the individual's dispositions can easily be misinterpreted as undermining the concept of personality itself. That would be an unfortunate misconstruction. Instead, we do need to recognize

that discontinuities—real ones and not merely superficial or trivial veneer changes—are part of the genuine phenomena of personality. If one accepts that proposition, an adequate conceptualization of personality will have to go beyond the conventional definition of stable and broad enduring individual differences in behavioral dispositions. We may have to tolerate more dissonance than we like in our personality theory. To be more than nominally dynamic our personality theories will have to have as much room for human discrimination as for generalization, as much place for personality change as for stability, and as much concern for man's self-regulation as for his victimization by either enduring intrapsychic forces or by momentary environmental constraints.

REFERENCES

BANDURA, A. *Principles of behavior modification.* New York: Holt, Rinehart & Winston, 1969.

BIJOU, S. W. Experimental studies of child behavior, normal and deviant. In L. Krasner & L. P. Ullmann (Eds.), *Research in behavior modification.* New York: Holt, Rinehart & Winston, 1965.

BRUNER, J. S., OLVER, R. R., & GREENFIELD, P. M. *Studies in cognitive growth.* New York: Wiley, 1966.

CAMPBELL, D., & FISKE, D. Convergent and discriminant validation by the multitrait-multimethod matrix. *Psychological Bulletin,* 1959, **56,** 81–105.

CRANDALL, V. J., & SINKELDAM, C. Children's dependent and achievement behaviors in social situations and their perceptual field dependence. *Journal of Personality,* 1963, **32,** 1–22.

ELLIOTT, R. Interrelationships among measures of field dependence, ability, and personality traits. *Journal of Abnormal and Social Psychology,* 1961, **63,** 27–36.

EMMERICH, W. Models of continuity and change. Paper presented at the meeting of the Society for Research in Child Development, March 27, 1969, Santa Monica, California.

FAIRWEATHER, G. W. *Methods in experimental social innovation.* New York: Wiley, 1967.

HUNT, J. MC V. Traditional personality theory in the light of recent evidence. *American Scientist,* 1965, **53,** 80–96.

KAGAN, J. Continuity in development. Paper presented at the meeting of the Society for Research in Child Development, March 27, 1969, Santa Monica, California.

MACCOBY, E. E. Tracing individuality within age-related change. Paper presented at the meeting of the Society for Research in Child Development, March 27, 1969, Santa Monica, California.

MADDI, S. R. *Personality theories: A comparative analysis.* Homewood, Ill.: Dorsey Press, 1968.

MISCHEL, W. A social learning view of sex differences in behavior. In E. E. Maccoby (Ed.), *The development of sex differences.* Stanford: Stanford University Press, 1966.

MISCHEL, W. *Personality and assessment.* New York: Wiley, 1968.

PATTERSON, G. R., RAY, R. S., & SHAW, D. A. Direct intervention in families of deviant children. *Oregon Research Institute Bulletin,* 1969, **8**(9), 1–62.

PAUL, G. L. Insight versus desensitization in psychotherapy two years after termination. *Journal of Consulting Psychology,* 1967, **31,** 333–348.

PETERSON, D. *The clinical study of social behavior.* New York: Appleton-Century-Crofts, 1968.

SCHIMEK, J. G. Cognitive style and defenses: A longitudinal study of intellectualization and field independence. *Journal of Abnormal Psychology,* 1968, **73,** 575–580.

VERNON, P. S. *Personality assessment: A critical survey.* New York: Wiley, 1964.

WITKIN, H. Psychological differentiation and forms of pathology. *Journal of Abnormal Psychology,* 1965, **70,** 317–336.

WITKIN, H. A., GOODENOUGH, D. R., & KARP, S. A. Stability of cognitive style from childhood to young adulthood. *Journal of Personality and Social Psychology,* 1967, **7,** 291–300.

Continuities and Discontinuities of Psychological Issues Into Adult Life

B. L. Neugarten

I have chosen to play the devil's advocate today, for despite the title of the paper assigned to me, I am impressed more by the discontinuities than the continuities in the psychological issues that have thus far been preoccupying developmental psychologists who are concerned with the life span.

We shall not understand the psychological realities of adulthood by projecting forward the issues that are salient in childhood—neither those issues that concern children themselves, nor those that concern child psychologists as they study cognitive development and language development and the resolution of the Oedipal.

Many of those investigators who have been focussing upon infancy and childhood are dealing with issues that are not the salient issues to adults. To illustrate very briefly, and not to dwell upon the obvious:

In the adolescent we are accustomed to thinking that the major psychological task is the formation of identity. For the period that immediately follows, KENNETH KENISTON has re-cently suggested the title 'youth,' distinguishing it from young adulthood, as the time when the major task for the ego is the confrontation of the society, the sorting out of values, and making a 'fit' between the self and society.

In young adulthood, the issues are related to intimacy, to parenthood, and to meeting the expectations of the world of work, with the attendant demands for restructing of roles, values, and sense of self—in particular, the investment of self into the lives of a few significant others to whom one will be bound for years to come.

In middle age, some of the issues are related to new family roles—the responsibilities of being the child of aging parents, and the reversal of authority which occurs as the child becomes the decision-maker for the parent . . . the awareness of the self as the bridge between the generations . . . the confrontation of a son-in-law or daughter-in-law with the need to establish an intimate relation with a stranger under very short notice . . . the role of grandparenthood.

Some of the issues are related to the increased

B. L. Neugarten: Continuities and Discontinuities of Psychological Issues into Adult Life. *Human Development, 12:* 121–130 (1969).

stock-taking, the heightened introspection and reflection that become characteristic of the mental life . . . the changing time-perspective, as time is restructured in terms of time-left-to-live rather than time-since birth . . . the personalization of death, bringing with it, for women, the rehearsal for widowhood, and for men, the rehearsal of illness; and for both, the new attention to body-monitoring.

Some of the issues relate to the creation of social heirs (in contrast to biological heirs) . . . the concomitant attention to relations with the young—the need to nurture, the care not to overstep the delicate boundaries of authority relationships, the complicated issues over the use of one's power—in short, the awareness of being the social*izer* rather than the social*ized*.

And in old age, the issues are different again. Some are issues that relate to renunciation—adaptation to losses of work, friends, spouse, the yielding up of a sense of competency and authority . . . reconciliation with members of one's family, one's achievements, and one's failures . . . the resolution of grief over the death of others, but also over the approaching death of self . . . the need to maintain a sense of integrity in terms of what one has been, rather than what one is . . . the concern with 'legacy' . . . how to leave traces of oneself . . . the psychology of survivorship. . . .

All these are psychological issues which are 'new' at successive stages in the life cycle; and as developmental psychologists we come to their investigation ill-equipped, no matter how sophisticated our approaches to child development.

The issues of life, and the content and preoccupation of the mental life, are different for adults than for children. Furthermore, as psychologists, we deal in a sense with different organisms. Let me illustrate again, only briefly, that which we all know:

As the result of accumulative adaptations to both biological and social events, there is a continuously changing basis within the individual for perceiving and responding to new events in the outer world. People change, whether for good or for bad, as the result of the accumulation of experience. As events are registered in the organism, individuals inevitably abstract from the traces of those experiences and they create more

encompassing as well as more refined categories for the interpretation of new events. The mental filing system not only grows larger, but it is reorganized over time, with infinitely more cross-references. This is merely one way of saying that not only do the middle-aged differ from the young because they were subject to different formative experiences, but because of the unavoidable effects of having lived longer and of having therefore a greater apperceptive mass or store of past experience.

Because of longer life-histories, with their complicated patterns of personal and social commitments, adults are not only much more complex than children, but they are more different one from another, and increasingly different as they move from youth to extreme old age.

More important, the adult is a self-propelling individual who manipulates the environment to attain his goals. He creates his environment, more or less (and varying in degree, of course, by the color of his skin and the size of his own or his father's bank account). He *invents* his future self, just as he recreates or *reinvents* his past self. We cannot go far in understanding adult psychology, then, without giving a central position to purposive behavior, to what CHARLOTTE BUHLER calls intentionality, or to what BREWSTER SMITH has called self-required values, or to what MARJORIE LOWENTHAL refers to as the reassessment of goals as itself the measure of adaptation.

These are not new ideas, but because they are such striking features of the adult as compared to the child, they create special problems for the student of the life cycle when he turns to problems of prediction, for we do not yet know how to capture the phenomena of decision-making.

Another factor is the adult's sense of time and timing. The adult, surely by middle age, with his highly refined powers of introspection and reflection, is continually busying himself in making a coherent story out of his life history. He reinterprets the past, selects and shapes his memories, and reassesses the significance of past events in his search for coherence. An event which, at the time of its occurrence, was 'unexpected' or arbitrary or traumatic becomes rationalized and interwoven into a context of explanation in its retelling 20 years later.

The remembrance of things past is continually

colored by the encounter with the present, of course; just as the present is interpreted in terms of the past. To deal with both the past and the present simultaneously is a unique characteristic of human personality. It is a set of mental processes which vary according to the sensitivity of the individual, probably with his educational level and his ability to verbalize, but a set of mental processes which probably also follow a distinguishable course with increasing age. In a study presently under way in Chicago, for instance, the data seem to show that middle-aged people utilize their memories in a somewhat different fashion than do old people. The middle-aged draw consciously upon past experience in the solution of present problems; the old seem to be busy putting their store of memories in order, as it were, dramatizing some, striving for consistency in others, perhaps as a way of preparing an ending for that life-story.

There is another way in which issues of time and timing are of central importance in the psychology of adulthood: namely, the ways in which the individual evaluates himself in relation to socially-defined time. Every society is age-graded, and every society has a system of social expectations regarding age-appropriate behavior. The individual passes through a socially-regulated cycle from birth to death as inexorably as he passes through the biological cycle; and there exists a socially-prescribed timetable for the ordering of major life events: a time when he is expected to marry, a time to raise children, a time to retire. Although the norms vary somewhat from one socioeconomic, ethnic, or religious group to another, for any social group it can easily be demonstrated that norms and actual occurrences are closely related.

Age norms and age expectations operate as a system of social controls, as prods and brakes upon behavior, in some instances hastening an event, in others, delaying it. Men and women are aware not only of the social clocks that operate in various areas of their lives; but they are aware also of being 'early,' 'late,' or 'on time' with regard to major life events.

Being on time or off time is not only a compelling basis for self-assessment with regard to family events, but also with regard to occupational careers, with both men and women comparing themselves with their friends or classmates or siblings in deciding whether or not they have made good.

Persons can describe ways in which being on-time or off-time has other psychological and social accompaniments. Thus, in a study of Army officers (the Army is a clearly age-graded occupation, where expectations with regard to age and grade are formally set forth in the official Handbook) the men who recognized themselves as being too long in grade—or late in career achievement—were also distinguishable on an array of social and psychological attitudes toward work, family, community participation, and personal adjustment.

When factors such as these are added to the inexorable biological changes, the individual develops a concept of the 'normal, expectable life-cycle'—a phrase which I have borrowed from Dr. ROBERT BUTLER and which owes much, of course, to HARTMANN's 'normal, expectable environment.' Adults carry around in their heads, whether or not they can easily verbalize it, a set of anticipations of the normal, expectable life-cycle. They internalize expectations of the consensually-validated sequences of major life events —not only what those events should be, but when they should occur. They make plans and set goals along a time-line shaped by these expectations.

The individual is said to create a sense of self very early in life. FREUD, for example, in describing the development of the ego; and GEORGE MEAD, in describing the differentiation between the 'I' and the 'me,' placed the development of self very early in childhood. But it is perhaps not until adulthood that the individual creates a sense of the life-cycle; that is, an anticipation and acceptance of the inevitable sequence of events that will occur as men grow up, grow old and die—in adulthood, that he understands that the course of his own life will be similar to the lives of others, and that the turning points are inescapable. This ability to interpret the past and foresee the future, and to create for oneself a sense of the predictable life-cycle differentiates the healthy adult personality from the unhealthy, and it underlies the adult's self-assessment.

The self-concept of the adult has the elements of the past contained within it. The adult thinks of himself in the present in terms of where he has come from; what he has become; how content he is at 50 compared to the time when he was 40.

All this differentiates the adult as subject from the psychologist as observer. The adult has a built-in dimension of thought that is the present-relative-to-the-past—but the psychologist has not yet created dimensions of this type in capturing the psychological realities of the life-cycle and in studying antecedent-consequent relations. In fact, it is the specific aim of most investigators to keep separate Time 1 from Time 2 observations and evaluations, on the premise that to do otherwise is to contaminate the data.

To put this differently, to the subject, the blending of past and present is psychological reality. To the investigator, validity (and therefore, reality) lies in keeping time segments independent of each other.

Thus, to repeat, some of the problems that face us in attempting to build a psychology of the life-cycle stem from the facts that the salient issues of the mental life are different for adults than for children; the underlying relations of the individual to his social environment are different; the relations of the investigator to his subject are different; and the salient dimensions psychologists use to describe and measure mental and emotional life *should* be different.

I am suggesting, then, that our foremost problem in studying the life span is to create a frame of reference and sets of dimensions that are appropriate to the subject-matter, and that are valid in the sense that they are fitting ways of capturing reality. To do this, it might be added, we need first a great wealth of descriptive studies, based on various methods that stem from naturalistic observational approaches.

Let me turn now more specifically to the studies which are emerging in which the attempt is made to relate findings on childhood and adulthood in the lives of the same individual—in short, to longitudinal studies which form the foundation of a psychology of the life cycle.

The longitudinal studies may be seen, in overly simplified and overly dichotomized terms, as being of two major types: first are those I shall refer to as 'trait' or 'dimension' oriented, studies addressed to questions of stability and change along given dimensions of ability and personality; second are those I shall call 'life-outcomes' oriented, those which pose such questions as these: What kind of child becomes the achieving adult? The middle-aged failure? The successful ager? The psychiatric casualty? What constellation of events are predictive of outcomes?

In the first type of research, the investigators have been preoccupied with such problems as whether or not the individual who is aggressive at age 3 is aggressive at age 30, or whether the high IQ child turns out to be the high IQ adult. There are also studies in which the ipsative approach is taken, and in which the stability of personality types is the question being pursued —the difference being, that is, that attention is focussed upon the patterns of traits rather than individual traits, and the degree to which these patterns show stability or change.

In such studies, the investigator is plagued with questions of validity of his measures over time— is the concept of aggression or intelligence the same concept for 3- and 30-year-olds? Are we measuring the same phenomenon? These studies have proceeded without regard to the events of the life-cycle, and the passage of calendar time is itself taken to be the sufficient variable. As in KAGAN and MOSS' studies from birth to maturity or NANCY BAYLEY's studies of cognitive development, or ODEN's latest follow-up of the TERMAN gifted group, the presumption seems to be that the same changes can be expected between age 3 and 30 whether or not marriage has intervened, or parenthood, or job failure or widowhood. 'Time' is treated as independent from the biological and social events that give substance to 'time,' and independent from the events that might be regarded as the probable psychological markers of time.

In studies of life-outcomes, we need, of course, studies of traits and dimensions; but we are in particular need of studies aimed at determining which life events produce change and which do not—which ones leave measurable traces in the personality structure, and which ones call forth new patterns of adaptation.

Let me illustrate: parenthood might be presumed to be an event that has a transforming effect upon the personality, whether one reasons from psychoanalytic theory, or role theory, or learning theory; and whether one conceptualizes the event in terms of elaboration and differentiation of the ego, or in terms of adjustment to a major new set of social roles, or in terms of the development of new sets of responses to the demands of a new significant other. Yet we have no systematic studies of the effects of parenthood upon personality development; and no good evidence that parenthood is more significant, say, than college attendance or marriage or widowhood.

To take another example: some of my own work on middle-aged women has led me to conclude that the menopause is not the transforming event in personality development that puberty is; nor is the departure of children from the home of the same importance as parenthood.

We need to establish which life events are the important ones, but we need to study also when the event occurs, in terms of its social 'appropriateness.' (To marry at age 30 is a different psychological event than to marry at age 16; and to be widowed at age 40 may be more significant than to be widowed at age 65, for in either case, the event comes off-time and does not fit the anticipations of the normal, expectable life-cycle.)

Among the longitudinal and long term follow-up studies presently available, investigators have taken both prospective and retrospective approaches. They begin with a group of infants or young children and follow them forward in time; or they begin with a group of adults and look backward in their life-histories to identify the predictors or antecedents of present adult status. In both instances, what is most striking is the relative lack of predictability from childhood to adulthood with regard to life-outcomes. To mention only a few very recent studies: HOYT's review of the literature indicates that we cannot predict from school success to vocational success . . . ROBINS' study of deviant children grown up shows that while anti-social behavior in childhood is predictive of sociopathic behavior in adults, the withdrawn personality characteristics of childhood are not associated with later adult pathology of any kind . . . ROGLER and HOLLINGSHEAD's study in Puerto Rico indicates that experiences in childhood and adolescence of schizophrenic adults do not differ noticeably from those of persons who are not afflicted with the illness . . . BALLER's follow-up of mid-life attainment of the mentally retarded shows low predictability from childhood, with persons of below-70 IQ faring vastly better than anyone anticipated.

I recognize that, in some ultimate sense, we may never be able to make satisfactory predictions regarding life-outcomes, no matter how well we choose our variables or how well we manage to identify the important and unimportant life events, for we shall probably never be able to predict the changes that will occur in an individual's social environment, nor the particular contingencies and accidents that will arise in an individual life, nor—equally important—the ways his life cycle is affected by those of the significant others with whom his life is intertwined. Furthermore, the psychologist, no matter how sophisticated his methods, will need the sociologist, the anthropologist, and the historian, to say nothing of the developmental biologist, to help him. Thus the study of lives will flourish only to the extent that a truly interdisciplinary behavioral science is created. Perhaps we shall have to leave the field to the creative writer, the philosopher, or the archivist for a long-time still to come, and decide that the life-cycle as a unit of study in the behavioral sciences is one with which we are not yet prepared to deal.

Yet we developmental psychologists are not likely to abandon the subject matter that intrigues us; and in the immediate future, as we work in our own areas, we can probably gain enormously in our ability to predict outcomes if we focus more of our attention upon the things that are of concern to the individuals we are studying—what the subject selects as important in his past and in his present; what he plans to do with his life; what he predicts will happen; and what strategies he elects—in short, if we make greater use of the subject himself as the reporting and predicting agent.

I am reminded in this connection that JEAN MCFARLANE recently told me that after her intensive and intimate study of her subjects over a 30-year period, she was continuously surprised to see how her people turned out. In going back over the data that she and MARJORIE HONZIK had painstakingly amassed, she found that much of what her subjects told her had been important to them when they were children or adolescents was not even to be found in her records—in other words, that which the investigators had regarded as important and had bothered to record was not the same as that which the subjects themselves had regarded as important at the time.

I suggest therefore that in future studies we pay more attention to gathering systematic and repeated self-reports and self-evaluations, and in doing so, to utilize what I shall call the 'clinical' as well as the 'observer's' approach. In the one case, the clinical psychologist tries to put himself into the frame of reference of his patient or client and to see the world through that person's eyes. In the other case, the 'observer' psychologist brings his own frame of reference to the data and interprets according to his own theories.

We need to gather longitudinal data of both types (as by collecting autobiographies from our subjects at repeated intervals, and by creating a set of dimensions and measures that are appropriate to that data). We need, in other words, to use a double perspective: that of the observer and that of the person whose life it is.

In conclusion, I have been drawing attention to the discontinuities between a psychology of childhood and a psychology of adulthood, between the perspectives of the investigator and that of the subject himself, between the stances of the clinician and the psychometrician. If, as our chairmen had in mind in naming this symposium, we have presently available only a few elements of a life-span developmental psychology, I am suggesting a few of the elements that are conspicuously missing.

Continuity and Stability
in Early Social Development:
Teacher Ratings

Walter Emmerich

An earlier study integrated the concepts of behavioral continuity-discontinuity and individual stability-instability into a fourfold scheme for developmental analysis (Emmerich, 1964). This framework was applied to a short-term longitudinal study of early social development, based upon systematic observations of the social behavior of children in the nursery-school setting. The present study extends this approach to a different source of data on the same subjects, that of teacher ratings. First, the dimensionality and continuity of social behavior are examined by means of independent factor analyses of teacher ratings of the same children in each of four semesters of nursery school. The extent of

Presented in part at the biennial meeting of the Society for Research in Child Development, Minneapolis, Minnesota, March 27, 1965. The author wishes to express his appreciation to the research and nursery school staffs of the Purdue Longitudinal Study for collecting and making available the data of this report and to Aaron G. Auerbach for his assistance with the analyses.

trait stability is then determined by looking at the correlations among factors having similar structure in all four semesters. Finally, attention is given to changes over time in factor structure and to an accompanying transformation in the behavior of some children.

Method

SUBJECTS

The subjects were 53 middle-class children who attended four consecutive semesters of nursery school and participated in the Purdue Longitudinal Study (Emmerich, 1964; Martin, 1964). Since subjects were from four groups entering nursery school in successive years, partial control was achieved over factors associated with calendar year of entry. Because of the small sample sizes, separate factor analyses of the 24 girls and 29 boys were not attempted. The

Walter Emmerich, "Continuity and Stability in Early Social Development: Teacher Ratings," *Child Development, 37,* 1966, pp. 17–27. Reprinted by permission of the authors and the Society for Research in Child Development, Inc.

average age was 3.1 years at the beginning of the first semester.

TEACHER RATINGS

At the end of each semester, the head and assistant teachers independently rated the children on 34 social-behavior scales taken from Beller (1948) with only minor modifications. Ratings were made at any point between 1 (low) and 7 (high) on the scales, but final scores were based upon subsequent groupings of these responses to form 7-point scales. The sequence of presentation of scales was varied among raters and subjects. Interjudge reliabilities were estimated from correlations between the head- and assistant-teachers' ratings. Since the four groups did not necessarily have the same teachers in a particular semester, this procedure led to entry in the same column of ratings by different teachers. The resulting coefficients were therefore conservative estimates of reliability, uncorrected for possible systematic judge differences in scale utilization. Final scores were based upon the sums of the ratings by the two teachers, except for a few instances when only one teacher rated a child in a particular semester, in which case the ratings of the single judge were doubled. In order that the summed ratings contribute reliable individual-difference variance to each factor analysis, a scale was included in the study only if interjudge agreement was significant at the 5 per cent level in *all four* semesters. Twenty-four of the scales met this criterion and are given in Table 1, together with their median and highest reliability coefficients for the four semesters.

FACTOR ANALYSES [1]

Scores on the 24 sufficiently reliable scales were intercorrelated (Pearson r) within semesters and subjected to independent factor analyses using the principal factor method with com-

[1] The rating scales, unrotated factor loadings, and rotated factor-score intercorrelations have been deposited with the American Documentation Institute. Order Document number 8609 from ADI Auxiliary Publication Project, Photoduplication Service, Library of Congress, Washington, D.C. 20541, remitting in advance $1.75 for microfilm, or $2.50 for photocopies. Make checks or money orders payable to: Chief, Photoduplication Service, Library of Congress.

munalities estimated by the squared multiple-correlation procedure (Harman, 1960). Factors were obliquely rotated by means of Carroll's biquartimin computer program. Initially, six factors were extracted and rotated in each semester, but this procedure resulted in several highly correlated factors within semesters. In order to clarify the developmental analyses of factor continuity and stability, it was first essential to isolate relatively *independent* sources of variance *within* time periods. Therefore, the strategy was adopted of reducing the number of factors to be rotated until the criterion of factor independence within semesters was achieved. This criterion was met by rotation of the first three factors in each semester, accounting for an average among semesters of 82 per cent of the estimated total common variance. Factor scores were derived by selecting the scales having the five highest loadings on a factor, dividing these loadings by their respective standard deviations, and summing the products of these weights by the subject's scores on the five scales.

Results and Discussion

CONTINUITY AND STABILITY

The same basic factor structures emerged in all four time periods (see Table 1). The first factor, called Aggression-Dominance, accounted for the greatest amount of variance in each semester. The other factors were identified as Dependency and Autonomy. For each factor, six stability coefficients make up the complete longitudinal network (Emmerich, 1964) of relations among the four semesters. All of these stability coefficients were significant (see Table 2). Thus, these three factors exhibited considerable individual stability as well as behavioral continuity throughout this period.

The structural findings replicate in remarkable detail Beller and Turner's (1964) four independent factor analyses of teacher ratings of clinical and non-clinical nursery-school girls and boys, using 14 of the present scales. The great similarity of factor structures in the two studies argues for the generalized salience and unidimensionality of these personality characteristics, at least during

TABLE 1

Rater Reliabilities and Oblique Factor Loadings by Semester[a]

Rating Scales	Semester Reliabilities		Aggression-Dominance Semester				Dependency Semester				Autonomy Semester			
	Median	Highest	1	2	3	4	1	2	3	4	1	2	3	4
Threatens children	.55	.70	.88	.89	.90	.93	−.10	−.01	−.04	−.02	−.16	−.13	−.16	−.22
Bosses children	.63	.68	.86	.89	.90	.79	.06	.00	.06	.03	.07	.09	.17	.27
Derogates children	.53	.70	.86	.84	.86	.88	.10	.10	.03	.05	−.10	−.09	−.13	−.05
Directs children	.51	.66	.84	.86	.72	.74	.02	−.13	.12	.04	.13	.25	.47	.46
Dominates children	.51	.55	.80	.68	.69	.60	.04	−.23	.15	.13	.17	.08	.27	.47
Attacks children physically	.62	.85	.68	.83	.84	.83	−.13	−.10	−.08	−.07	−.44	−.31	−.19	−.21
Threatens teacher	.55	.66	.72	.78	.81	.84	.00	.27	.03	.03	−.02	−.01	−.21	−.25
Insists on own ideas	.45	.58	.77	.69	.79	.80	.17	.22	.03	.19	−.08	.02	.02	.05
Destroys property of other children	.57	.76	.59	.72	.79	.79	−.10	−.05	−.01	−.22	−.55	−.33	−.27	−.28
Derogates teacher	.44	.58	.76	.75	.73	.70	−.02	−.15	.03	.03	.06	−.10	−.15	−.15
Seeks recognition from children	.29	.45	.53	.71	.58	.33	.41	.10	.27	.51	.06	.16	.35	.28
Submits to children when challenged	.30	.68	−.73	−.83	−.64	−.56	.12	.17	.20	.02	.01	−.09	−.30	−.24
Avoids rough activities	.56	.77	−.57	−.73	−.83	−.67	.20	.35	.24	.22	.18	.14	−.12	−.20
Follows teacher's directions without resistance	.55	.61	−.54	−.65	−.71	−.65	.11	−.07	.11	.12	.38	.52	.38	.45
Seeks to be near teacher	.67	.82	−.23	−.34	−.18	−.39	.90	.83	.85	.75	.03	.09	−.14	−.12
Seeks physical contact with teacher	.62	.75	−.13	−.34	−.20	−.27	.88	.77	.81	.77	.03	−.08	−.02	−.09
Seeks recognition from teacher	.37	.42	.07	.22	.14	.12	.87	.74	.83	.84	.18	.32	−.05	−.02
Seeks attention from teacher	.53	.71	.19	.18	.08	−.01	.77	.89	.85	.81	.00	.12	−.11	−.05
Asks teacher for special privileges	.40	.55	.43	.36	.53	.49	.64	.83	.58	.59	−.21	−.14	−.16	−.08
Asks teacher to do what teacher asks child to do	.29	.59	−.06	.08	.14	.19	.84	.82	.33	.46	−.14	−.09	−.69	−.75
Seeks help from teacher	.43	.53	−.08	−.25	.02	−.12	.66	.68	.56	.47	−.35	−.41	−.47	−.67
Completes activities	.47	.69	−.09	−.21	−.16	−.23	−.06	.13	−.23	.07	.88	.84	.77	.74
Gets intrinsic satisfaction from his work	.46	.55	−.07	−.10	−.13	−.01	.01	.05	−.11	.06	.87	.90	.78	.79
Overcomes obstacles by himself	.44	.66	.02	.11	.11	.03	−.21	−.16	−.05	−.08	.76	.80	.73	.81

a Italicized loadings were those used in the computation of factor scores.

TABLE 2
FACTOR-STABILITY COEFFICIENTS*

| | AGGRESSION-DOMINANCE | | | | DEPENDENCY | | | | AUTONOMY | | | |
| | Semester | | | | Semester | | | | Semester | | | |
SEMESTER	1	2	3	4	1	2	3	4	1	2	3	4
1......	...	...	...	...	...	...	...	...	...	...	...	...
2......	.84	...	...	...	.83	...	...	...	.78	...	...	...
3......	.47	.64	...	...	.61	.56	...	...	.44	.63	...	...
4......	.47	.66	.81	...	.48	.45	.69	...	.54	.67	.80	...

* *p* < .001 for all correlations.

this period. Furthermore, the marked individual stability of these dimensions adds to the accumulating evidence for the view that certain attributes of personality become established early in life and tend to be sustained in their original forms (e.g., Emmerich, 1964; Kagan & Moss, 1962; Martin, 1964; Schaefer & Bayley, 1963).

However, several aspects of the present study limit the scope of these conclusions. Factor structures vary according to the range of variables included in them, and alternative factoring procedures could have resulted in different structures.[2] It is also likely that greater discontinuity and instability would occur over longer time spans. And although teachers made their ratings independently, discussions among teachers in carrying out their school responsibilities probably had the effect of increasing consensus with respect to both dimensionality and ratings of individuals. Furthermore, ratings were made in the nursery-school setting only and therefore cannot reveal broad situational variations in trait structure or individual trait scores. Finally, alternative methods of data collection could lead to quite different conclusions. In the case of dependency, for example, there is considerable evidence that systematic observations of child dependency by trained observers do not form a unidimensional trait (Emmerich, 1964; Hartup, 1963; Heathers, 1955b; Sears, 1963). Why ratings should be less complex than observations remains an intriguing problem for investigation. A number of variables would seem to be relevant, including the spatio-temporal scope (molarity) of the unit of observation, the nature of the affective and role

relationships between the observer and the observed, and extent of control over halo effects (Hartup, 1963).

DISCONTINUITY AND STABILITY

The above findings do not support a view of marked discontinuity in social behavior during the nursery-school period, at least as reflected by the procedures of this study. However, the detection of less obvious discontinuities requires a closer examination of variations among semesters in the amount of individual-difference variance contributed by each of the three dimensions. Figure 1 portrays the variance contributed by the factors in each semester, based upon the average of the squared loadings on those scales for which the squared loading on the factor in question was .100 or greater in at least one semester. Not surprisingly, Dependency's importance diminished during this period, whereas Autonomy's increased somewhat, although none of the temporal shifts were statistically significant. Inspection of the loadings did reveal interesting qualitative changes, however (see Table 3). The two scales reflecting *instrumental dependency* (Heathers, 1955a) loaded more heavily on Dependency than on Autonomy during the first year, whereas the converse was more frequent during the second year. This structural change bears on the question of the relations among instrumental dependency, emotional dependency, and independence (Beller, 1955; Hartup, 1963; Heathers, 1955a, b). It indicates that instrumental dependency was initially associated with emotional dependency but then increasingly came to signify an *alternative* to autonomy. For several reasons, it is unlikely that

[2] However, oblique and orthogonal (Varimax) rotations of the first six factors resulted in very similar structures in each semester.

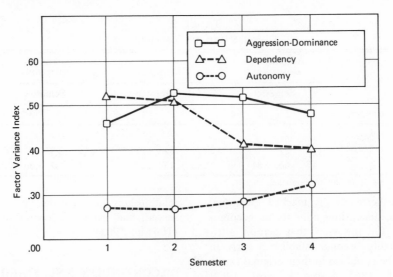

Fig. 1. Factor-variance index by semester.

this age change was confounded with individual differences among teachers in trait structuring: the four groups did not necessarily have the same teachers within the same semester; the over-all clarity and simplicity of the factor structures indicated that rater similarities greatly outweighed any possible differences; and the structural changes themselves were not of the sporadic sort expected if teacher differences had been marked.

The bipolarity of autonomy and instrumental dependency was not anticipated, but Crandall and Sinkeldam (1964) report a pattern of intercorrelations among ratings of emotional dependency, instrumental dependency, and achievement in middle-class children ages 6 to 10 that is similar to the structures found in the second year of the present study. Perhaps, then, self-reliance and help-seeking are early formed stable alternative habits or "strategies" used by the child in his goal-directed and problem-solving efforts.

What might be the origins of this bipolarity between autonomy and instrumental dependency? There is evidence that it could arise from differential maternal-reinforcement histories. Crandall, Preston, and Rabson (1960) intercorrelated ratings of child help-seeking, achievement efforts, and maternal reinforcements of these behaviors in a middle-class nursery-school group. The relevant findings were that help-seeking and achievement efforts were negatively correlated, as were

the maternal rewards for these behaviors, and that the child's achievement efforts were positively correlated with maternal rewards for achievement but negatively (non-significantly) correlated with maternal rewards for help-seeking. On the other hand, a reverse (or mutual) causality explanation is also plausible. Differential maternal reinforcement of autonomy and instrumental dependency could arise from a tendency for mothers to implement the maternal role by supporting whichever of these behaviors happens to be dominant in the child's early repertoire. However, both of these explanations raise the question of why this bipolarity was not present in the first semester, a problem considered later in the discussion.

Another change on the Autonomy factor was a decrease after the first semester in negative loadings on two aggression scales (see Table 3). Taken in conjunction with the above shift of instrumental dependency, this change is evidence for discontinuity in the meaning of autonomy, or more accurately, its bipolar counterpart. The question arises whether this structural shift was accompanied by change in the behavior of the children. In order to evaluate this question, separate scores were computed for both poles of the Autonomy factor in the first and fourth semesters. If the autonomous child remained autonomous while the non-autonomous child's aggression became transformed into instrumental dependency, then the autonomy pole of semester 1 should correlate positively with autonomy and negatively with instrumental dependency in semester 4; while the aggression pole of semester 1 should correlate negatively with autonomy, and positively with instrumental dependency in semester 4. The results for the combined sexes partially supported these expectations (see Table 4). However, it was noted that the autonomy and aggression poles of semester 1 were clearly bipolar in boys ($r = -.77$, $p < .001$) but not in girls ($r = -.17$, not significant), suggesting that the question could be evaluated most meaningfully in boys. As seen in Table 4, this was the case. All the expected correlations were significant in boys, while only the stability coefficient for the autonomy pole was significant in girls.

What brings about this developmental transformation in non-autonomous boys? Since autonomy is positively valued by teachers, the non-autonomous boy's intial failure to meet the teachers' expectations in this respect could result in aggressive attention-seeking outbursts which only gradually become transformed into more acceptable instrumental dependency. This view is supported by the "acting-out" quality of the particular aggression scales that were bipolar to autonomy in the first semester (see Table 3), as contrasted with the more socialized forms of aggression which loaded heavily on the Aggression-Dominance factor (see Table 1). If this transformation includes both a subsiding of frustration-induced hostility and the disinhibition of instrumental dependency, then it could explain why instrumental dependency was subsumed by Dependency rather than being bipolar to Autonomy during the first semester. Also,

such a process suggests that the "sleeper effect" (Kagan & Moss, 1962) may involve not only the temporary inhibition of an earlier- and later-appearing response but also the emergence of an alternative response during the interim.

Perhaps the non-autonomous girl is less likely to go through this process because teachers tolerate more instrumental as well as other forms of dependency in girls (Kagan & Moss, 1962) and/or because girls are generally perceived as more autonomous to begin with. There was empirical support for both these possibilities: girls were higher than boys on the Dependency factor in each semester (all p's $< .01$) and were also more autonomous, but significantly so only in the first semester ($p < .05$).

The present interpretation assumes that socializing agents attempt to bring about greater autonomy in children of this age, especially in those who lack it. But the continued bipolarity of Autonomy throughout the four semesters indicates that such attempts were not very successful. It is of interest that the autonomous child's persistence was also found by Hofstaetter (1954) to be an especially important component of intelligence between 20 and 40 months. There is also evidence that intelligence is a correlate of autonomous-achievement behavior during the elementary-school years (Crandall & Sinkeldam, 1964). Thus, perhaps the less intellectually advanced children were less able to adapt to the autonomy demands made by the teachers. Since all subjects were administered the Stanford-Binet (1937 revision) during the first year of nursery school, it was possible to determine whether the autonomy poles were positively related to IQ and, furthermore, whether the bipolar counterparts of

TABLE 3

Prominent Shifts of Factor Loadings Over Time

	Dependency Factor				Autonomy Factor			
	Semester				Semester			
Scale	1	2	3	4	1	2	3	4
Seeks help from teacher....	.66	.68	.56	.47	−.35	−.41	−.47	−.67
Asks teacher to do what teacher asks child to do..	.84	.82	.33	.46	−.14	−.09	−.69	−.75
Destroys property of other children...............	...	...	...	...	−.55	−.33	−.27	−.28
Attacks children physically.	...	...	...	...	−.44	−.31	−.19	−.21

TABLE 4

INTERCORRELATIONS AMONG AUTONOMY FACTOR POLES IN SEMESTERS 1 AND 4

SEMESTER	FACTOR	SEMESTER 1		SEMESTER 4	
		Autonomy	Aggression	Autonomy	Instrumental Dependency
		Girls			
1	Autonomy.....	....			
	Aggression.....	−.17			
4	Autonomy.....	+.49**	+.21		
	Instrumental Dependency..	−.28	−.29	−.68**	
		Boys			
1	Autonomy.....	....			
	Aggression.....	−.77**			
4	Autonomy.....	+.67**	−.59**		
	Instrumental Dependency..	−.56**	+.40*	−.65**	
		Sexes Combined			
1	Autonomy.....	....			
	Aggression.....	−.58**			
4	Autonomy.....	+.61**	−.30*		
	Instrumental Dependency..	−.43**	+.12	−.65**	

* $p < .05$.
** $p < .01$.

autonomy—aggression in semester 1 and instrumental dependency in semester 4—were *negatively* correlated with IQ. The results generally supported this reasoning, although the relationships were not strong (see Table 5). And, of course, this analysis cannot reveal whether reinforcements of autonomy by parents stimulated intelligence (Crandall, 1963), and/or whether such reinforcements were part of a parental-response pattern elicited by rapid intellectual development in the child.

Conclusions

It can be concluded that Aggression-Dominance, Dependency, and Autonomy are salient personality dimensions having high stability from ages 3 to 5, supporting the view that personality differences arise early in life and are maintained in essentially their original form. However, because of certain methodological limitations, these generalizations should be accepted with caution.

Several factors probably converged in this study

TABLE 5

CORRELATIONS BETWEEN IQ AND THE AUTONOMY FACTOR
POLES OF SEMESTERS 1 AND 4

GROUP	SEMESTER 1		SEMESTER 4	
	Autonomy	Aggression	Autonomy	Instrumental Dependency
Girls...........	.27	−.28	.43*	−.40*
Boys...........	.32*	−.33*	.34*	−.18
Sexes combined...	.32**	−.33**	.39**	−.27*

* $p < .05$.
** $p < .01$.

to exaggerate the picture of behavioral continuity and individual stability. But despite these masking influences, there was also evidence for structural change over time and for an accompanying behavioral change in non-autonomous boys. Therefore, the results also support the view that development involves significant personality change in certain classes of persons during particular time periods.

Instrumental dependency became increasingly bipolar to autonomy throughout this period. This unexpected finding received post hoc conceptual and empirical support, illustrating how the present methodology can lead to plausible hypotheses about structure and discontinuity in development.

Finally, when the present results for rating are compared with those based upon alternative methods of assessment, it becomes apparent that structural equivalence as well as predictability between data sources cannot be taken for granted. Systematic knowledge is needed on how the "perspective" tied to a particular assessment procedure influences substantive conclusions about personality structure and development.

REFERENCES

BELLER, E. K. Dependency and independence in young children. Unpublished doctoral dissertation, State University of Iowa. 1948.

BELLER, E. K. Dependency and independence in young children. *J. genet. Psychol.*, 1955, *87*, 23–25.

BELLER, E. K., & TURNER, J. L. Sex differences: the factorial structure of personality variables in normal and emotionally disturbed preschool children. Paper read at Eastern Psychol. Association, Philadelphia, April, 1964.

CRANDALL, V. J. Achievement. In H. W. Stevenson (Ed.), *Child psychology: the sixty-second yearbook of the national society for the study of education.* Part I. Chicago: Univer. of Chicago Press, 1963. Pp. 416–459.

CRANDALL, V. J., PRESTON, A., & RABSON, A. Maternal reactions and the development of independence and achievement behavior in young children. *Child Develpm.*, 1960, *31*, 243–251.

CRANDALL, V. J., & SINKELDAM, C. Children's dependent and achievement behaviors in social situations and the perceptual field dependence. *J. Pers.*, 1964, *32*, 1–22.

EMMERICH, W. Continuity and stability in early social development. *Child Develpm.*, 1964, *35*, 311–332.

HARMAN, H. H. *Modern factor analysis.* Chicago: Univer. of Chicago Press, 1960.

HARTUP, W. W. Dependence and independence. In H. W. Stevenson (Ed.), *Child psychology: the sixty-second yearbook of the national society for the study of education.* Part I. Chicago: Univer. of Chicago Press, 1963. Pp. 333–363.

HEATHERS, G. Acquiring dependence and independence: a theoretical orientation. *J. genet. Psychol.*, 1955, *87*, 277–291. (a)

HEATHERS, G. Emotional dependence and independence in nursery-school play. *J. genet. Psychol.*, 1955, *87*, 37–58. (b)

HOFSTAETTER, P. R. The changing composition of "intelligence": a study in *t*-technique. *J. genet. Psychol.*, 1954, *85*, 159–164.

KAGAN, J., & MOSS, H. A. *Birth to maturity.* New York: Wiley, 1962.

MARTIN, W. E. Singularity and stability of profiles of social behavior. In C. B. Stendler (Ed.), *Readings in child behavior and development.* New York: Harcourt, Brace & World, 1964. Pp. 448–466.

SCHAEFER, E. S., and BAYLEY, N. Maternal behavior, child behavior, and their intercorrelations from infancy through adolescence. *Monogr. Soc. Res. Child Develpm.*, 1963, *28*, No. 87.

SEARS, R. R. Dependency motivation. In M. R. Jones (Ed.), *Current theory and research in motivation.* Lincoln: Univer. of Nebraska Press, 1963. Pp. 25–64.

Part 10

Cultural Influences

We live in an age that has begun to recognize the extent to which a person's behavior and beliefs are related to his personal background and circumstances. The articles in this section explore the relative effects of cultural influences on the individual. Cole and Bruner examine the effects of ethnic and social-class differences on learning and performance; Coleman considers the phenomenon of adolescent culture and its relationship to the adult society; and Whiting, Kluckhohn and Anthony discuss the function of male initiation rites.

It is interesting to remember, however, that other writers, such as Kohlberg, recently have been attempting to discover universal structures in human development and the human condition, which are independent of cultural influences. In a sense, the universality-relativity argument parallels the differences between the structuralist and behaviorist views. The structuralist seeks the universal sequences in growth and development, whereas the behaviorist looks for particular conditioning influences.

Cultural Differences and Inferences
About Psychological Processes

Michael Cole   Jerome S. Bruner

Deficit Interpretation

Perhaps the most prevalent view of the source of ethnic and social class differences in intellectual performance is what might be summed up under the label "the deficit hypothesis." It can be stated briefly, without risk of gross exaggeration. It rests on the assumption that a community under conditions of poverty (for it is the poor who are the focus of attention, and a disproportionate number of the poor are members of minority ethnic groups) is a disorganized community, and this disorganization expresses itself in various forms of deficit. One widely agreed-upon source of deficit is mothering; the child of poverty is assumed to lack adequate parental attention. Given the illegitimacy rate in the urban ghetto, the most conspicuous "deficit" is a missing father and, consequently, a missing father model. The mother is away at work or, in any case, less involved with raising her children than she should be by white middle-class standards. There is said to be less regularity, less mutuality in interaction with her. There are said to be specialized deficits in interaction as well—less guidance in goal seeking from the parents (Schoggen, 1969), less emphasis upon means and ends in maternal instruction (Hess & Shipman, 1965), or less positive and more negative reinforcement (Bee, Van Egeren, Streissguth, Nyman, & Leckie, 1969; Smilansky, 1968).

More particularly, the deficit hypothesis has been applied to the symbolic and linguistic environment of the growing child. His linguistic community as portrayed in the early work of Basil Bernstein (1961), for example, is characterized by a restricted code, dealing more in the stereotype of interaction than in language that explains and elaborates upon social and material

A version of this article will appear in the 1972 *National Society for the Study of Education Yearbook on Early Childhood Education*. Requests for reprints should be sent to Michael Cole, The Rockefeller University, New York, New York 10021.

events. The games that are played by poor children and to which they are exposed are less strategy bound than those of more advantaged children (Eifermann, 1968); their homes are said to have a more confused noise background, permitting less opportunity for figure-ground formation (Klaus & Gray, 1968); and the certainty of the environment is sufficiently reduced so that children have difficulty in delaying reinforcement (Mischel, 1966) or in accepting verbal reinforcement instead of the real article (Zigler & Butterfield, 1968).

The theory of intervention that grew from this view was the idea of "early stimulation," modeled on a conception of supplying nutriment for those with a protein deficiency or avitaminosis. The nature of the needed early stimulation was never explained systematically, save in rare cases (Smilansky, 1968), but it variously took the form of practice in using abstractions (Blank & Solomon, 1969), in having dialogue where the referent objects were not present, as through the use of telephones (Deutsch, 1967; John & Goldstein, 1964), or in providing secure mothering by substitution (Caldwell et al., 1970; Klaus & Gray, 1968).

A primary result of these various deficits was believed to express itself in the lowered test scores and academic performance among children from poverty backgrounds. The issue was most often left moot as to whether or not this lowered test performance was easily reversible, but the standard reference was to a monograph by Bloom (1964) indicating that cognitive performance on a battery of tests, given to poor and middle-class children, yielded the result that nearly 80% of the variance in intellectual performance was accounted for by age 3.

Difference Interpretation

Such data seem to compel the conclusion that as a consequence of various factors arising from minority group status (factors affecting motivation, linguistic ability, goal orientation, hereditary proclivities to learn in certain ways—the particular mix of factors depends on the writer), minority group children suffer intellectual deficits

when compared with their "more advantaged" peers.

In this section, we review a body of data and theory that controverts this contention, casts doubt on the conclusion that a deficit exists in minority group children, and even raises doubts as to whether any nonsuperficial *differences* exist among different cultural groups.

There are two long-standing precedents for the view that different groups (defined in terms of cultural, linguistic, and ethnic criteria) do not differ intellectually from each other in any important way.[1] First, there is the anthropological "doctrine of psychic unity" (Kroeber, 1948) which, on the basis of the "run of total experience," is said to warrant the assumption of intellectual equality as a sufficient approximation to the truth. This view is compatible with current linguistic anthropological theorizing, which concentrates on describing the way in which different cultural/linguistic groups categorize familiar areas of experience (Tyler, 1970). By this view, different conclusions about the world are the result of arbitrary and different, but equally logical, ways of cutting up the world of experience. From this perspective, descriptions of the "disorganization" of minorities would be highly suspect, this suspicion arising in connection with questions like, Disorganized from whose point of view?

Anthropological critiques of psychological experimentation have never carried much weight with psychologists, nor have anthropologists been very impressed with conclusions from psychological tests. We have hypothesized elsewhere (Cole, Gay, Glick, & Sharp, 1971) that their mutual indifference stems in part from a difference in opinion about the inferences that are warranted from testing and experimentation, and in part because the anthropologist relies mainly on data that the psychologist completely fails to consider: the mundane social life of the people

---

[1] It is assumed here that it is permissible to speak of minority group or poverty group "culture" using as our criterion Lévi-Strauss' (1963) definition: "What is called 'culture' is a fragment of humanity which, from the point of view of the research at hand . . . presents significant discontinuities in relation to the rest of humanity [p. 295]." We do not intend to enter into arguments over the existence or nature of a "culture of poverty," although such an idea seems implicit in the view of most deficit theorists.

he studies. As we shall see, these issues carry over into our criticism of the "deficit" theory of cultural deprivation.

A second tradition that calls into question culturally determined group difference in intelligence is the linguist's assertion that languages do not differ in their degree of development (Greenberg, 1963), buttressed by the transformationalist's caution that one cannot attribute to people a cognitive capacity that is less than is required to produce the complex rule-governed activity called language (Chomsky, 1966).

Although Chomskian linguistics has had a profound effect on psychological theories of language and cognitive development in recent years, psychological views of language still are considered hopelessly inadequate by working linguists. This criticism applies not only to psycholinguistic theory but to the actual description of linguistic performance on which theory is based. Needless to say, the accusation of misunderstanding at the descriptive level leads to accusations of absurdity at the theoretical level.

A third tradition that leads to rejection of the deficit theory has many sources in recent social sciences. This view holds that even when attempts have been made to provide reasonable anthropological and linguistic foundations, the conclusions about cognitive capacity from psychological experiments are unfounded because the performance produced represents a complex interaction of the formal characteristics of the experiment and the social/environmental context that determines the subject's interpretation of the situation in which it occurs. The need for "situation-bound" interpretations of experiments is emphasized in such diverse sources as sociology (Goffman, 1964), psychology (Brunswik, 1958), and psycholinguistics (Cazden, 1970). This is an important issue, which we will return to once illustrations of the "antideficit" view have been explored.

Perhaps the most coherent denial of the deficit position, coupled with compelling illustrations of the resourcefulness of the supposedly deprived and incompetent person, is contained in Labov's attack on the concept of "linguistic deprivation" and its accompanying assumption of cognitive incapacity (Labov, 1970).

It is not possible here to review all of Labov's evidence. Rather, we have abstracted what we take to be the major points in his attack.

1. *An assertion of the functional equality of all languages.* This assertion is applied specifically to his analysis of nonstandard Negro English, which has been the object of his study for several years. Labov provided a series of examples where young blacks who would be assessed as linguistically retarded and academically hopeless by standard test procedures enter conversations in a way that leaves little doubt that they can speak perfectly adequately and produce very clever arguments in the process.

2. *An assertion of the psychologist's ignorance of language in general and nonstandard dialects in particular.* Labov's particular target is Carl Bereiter (Bereiter & Englemann, 1966) whose remedial teaching technique is partly rationalized in terms of the *inability* of young black children to use language either as an effective tool of communication or thinking. Part of Labov's attack is aimed at misinterpretations of such phrases as *"They mine,"* which Labov analyzed in terms of rules of contraction, but which Bereiter made the mistake of referring to as a "series of badly connected words [Labov, 1970, p. 171]." This "psychologist's deficit" has a clear remedy. It is roughly equivalent to the anthropological caveat that the psychologist has to know more about the people he studies.

3. *The inadequacy of present experimentation.* More serious criticism of the psychologist's interpretation of "language deprivation" and, by extension, his whole concept of "cultural deprivation" is contained in the following, rather extensive quote:

> this and the preceding section are designed to convince the reader that the controlled experiments that have been offered in evidence [of Negro lack of competence] are misleading. The only thing that is controlled is the superficial form of the stimulus. All children are asked, "What do you think of capital punishment?" or "Tell me everything you can about this." But the speaker's interpretation of these requests, and the action he believes is appropriate in response is completely uncontrolled. One can view these test stimuli as requests for in-

formation, commands for action, or meaningless sequences of words. . . . With human subjects it is absurd to believe that identical stimuli are obtained by asking everyone the same question. Since the crucial intervening variables of interpretation and motivation are uncontrolled, most of the literature on verbal deprivation tells us nothing of the capacities of children [Labov, 1970, p. 171].

Here Labov is attacking the experimental method as usually applied to the problem of subcultural differences in cognitive capacity. We can abstract several assertions from this key passage: (*a*) Formal experimental equivalence of operations does not insure de facto equivalence of experimental treatments; (*b*) different subcultural groups are predisposed to interpret the experimental stimuli (situations) differently; (*c*) different subcultural groups are motivated by different concerns relevant to the experimental task; (*d*) in view of the inadequacies of experimentation, inferences about lack of competence among black children are unwarranted.

These criticisms, when combined with linguistic misinterpretation, constitute Labov's attack on the deficit theory of cultural deprivation and represent the rationale underlying his demonstrations of competence where its lack had previously been inferred.

One example of Labov's approach is to conduct a rather standard interview of the type often used for assessment of language competence. The situation is designed to be minimally threatening; the interviewer is a neighborhood figure, and black. Yet, the black 8-year-old interviewee's behavior is monosyllabic. He is a candidate for the diagnosis of linguistically and culturally deprived.

But this diagnosis is very much situation dependent. For at a later time, this same interviewer goes to the boy's apartment, brings one of the boy's friends with him, lies down on the floor, and produces some potato chips. He then begins talking about clearly taboo subjects in dialect. Under these circumstances, the mute interviewee becomes an excited participant in the general conversation.

In similar examples, Labov demonstrated powerful reasoning and debating skills in a school dropout and nonlogical verbosity in an acceptable,

"normal" black who has mastered the forms of standard English. Labov's conclusion is that the usual assessment situations, including IQ and reading tests, elicit deliberate, defensive behavior on the part of the child who has realistic expectations that to talk openly is to expose oneself to insult and harm. As a consequence, such situations *cannot* measure the child's competence. Labov went even further to assert that far from being verbally deprived, the typical ghetto child is

bathed in verbal stimulation from morning to night. We see many speech events which depend upon the competitive exhibition of verbal skills —sounding, singing, toasts, rifting, louding— a whole range of activities in which the individual gains status through the use of language. . . . We see no connection between the verbal skill in the speech events characteristic of the street culture and success in the school room [Labov, 1970, p. 163].

Labov is not the only linguist to offer such a critique of current theories of cultural deprivation (see, e.g., Stewart, 1970). However, Labov's criticism raises larger issues concerning the logic of comparative research designs of which the work in cultural/linguistic deprivation is only a part. It is to this general question that we now turn.

Competence and Performance in Psychological Research

The major thrusts of Labov's argument, that situational factors are important components of psychological experiments and that it is difficult if not impossible to infer competence directly from performance, are not new ideas to psychologists. Indeed, a concern with the relation between *psychological processes* on the one hand and *situational factors* on the other has long been a kind of shadow issue in psychology, surfacing most often in the context of comparative research.

It is this question that underlies the oft-berated question, What do IQ tests measure? and has been prominent in attacks on Jensen's (1969) argument that group differences in IQ test performance are reflective of innate differences in capacity.

Kagan (1969), for example, pointed to the work of Palmer, who regularly delays testing until the child is relaxed and has established rapport with the tester. Jensen (1969, p. 100) himself reported that significant differences in test performance can be caused by differential adaptation to the test situation.

Hertzig, Birch, Thomas, and Mendez (1968) made a direct study of social class/ethnic differences in response to the test situation and demonstrated stable differences in situational responses that were correlated with test performance and were present even when measured IQ was equivalent for subgroups chosen from the major comparison groups.

Concern with the particular *content* of tests and experiments as they relate to inferences about cognitive capacity occurs within the same context. The search for a "culture-free" IQ test has emphasized the use of universally familiar material, and various investigators have found that significant differences in performance can be related to the content of the experimental materials. Price-Williams (1961), for example, demonstrated earlier acquisition of conservation concepts in Nigerian children using traditional instead of imported stimulus materials, and Gay and Cole (1967) made a similar point with respect to Liberian classification behavior and learning.

Contemporary psychology's awareness of the task and situation-specific determinants of performance is reflected in a recent article by Kagan and Kogan (1970). In a section of their paper titled "The Significance of Public Performance," they are concerned with the fact that "differences in quality of style of public performance, although striking, may be misleading indices of competence [p. 1322]."

Although such misgivings abound, they have not yet crystallized into a coherent program of research and theory nor have the implications of accepting the need to incorporate an analysis of situations in addition to traditional experimental manipulations been fully appreciated.

Extended Idea of Competence

Labov and others have argued forcefully that we cannot distinguish on the basis of traditional experimental approaches between the underlying competence of those who have had a poor opportunity to participate in a particular culture and those who have had a good opportunity, between those who have not had their share of wealth and respect and those who have. The crux of the argument, when applied to the problem of "cultural deprivation," is that those groups ordinarily diagnosed as culturally deprived have the same underlying competence as those in the mainstream of the dominant culture, *the differences in performance being accounted for by the situations and contexts in which the competence is expressed.* To put the matter most rigorously, one can find a corresponding situation in which the member of the "out culture," the victim of poverty, can perform on the basis of a given competence in a fashion equal to or superior to the standard achieved by a member of the dominant culture.

A prosaic example taken from the work of Gay and Cole (1967) concerns the ability to make estimates of volume. The case in question is to estimate the number of cups of rice in each of several bowls. Comparisons of "rice-estimation accuracy" were made among several groups of subjects, including nonliterate Kpelle rice farmers from North Central Liberia and Yale sophomores. The rice farmers manifested significantly greater accuracy than the Yale students, the difference increasing with the amount of rice presented for estimation. In many other situations, measurement skills are found to be superior among educated subjects in the Gay and Cole study. Just as Kpelle superiority at making rice estimates is clearly not a universal manifestation of their superior underlying competence, the superiority of Yale students in, for example, distance judgments is no basis for inferring that their competence is superior.

We think the existence of demonstrations such as those presented by Labov has been salutary in forcing closer examination of testing situations used for comparing the children of poverty with their more advantaged peers. And, as the illustration from Gay and Cole suggests, the argument may have quite general implications. Obviously, it is not sufficient to use a simple equivalence-of-test procedure to make inferences about the competence of the two groups being compared. In fact, a "two-groups" design is almost useless for making any important inferences in cross-cultural research, as Campbell (1961) has suggested. From a logical view, however, the conclusion of equal cognitive competence in those who are not members of the prestige culture and those who are its beneficiaries is often equally unwarranted. While it is very proper to criticize the logic of assuming that poor performance implies lack of competence, the contention that poor performance is of *no* relevance to a theory of cognitive development and to a theory of cultural differences in cognitive development also seems an oversimplification.

Assuming that we can find test situations in which comparably good performance can be elicited from the groups being contrasted, there is plainly an issue having to do with the range and nature of the situations in which performance for any two groups can be found to be equal.

We have noted Labov's conclusion that the usual assessment of linguistic competence in the child elicits deliberate defensive behavior and that he can respond effectively in familiar nonthreatening surroundings. It may be, however (this possibility is discussed in Bruner, 1970), that he is unable to utilize language of a decentered type, taken out of the context of social interaction, used in an abstract way to deal with hypothetical possibilities and to spell out hypothetical plans (see also Gladwin, 1970). If such were the case, we could not dismiss the question of different kinds of language usage by saying simply that decontextualized talk is not part of the natural milieu of the black child in the urban ghetto. If it should turn out to be the case that mastery of the culture depends on one's capacity to perform well on the basis of competence one has stored up, and to perform well in particular settings and in particular ways, then plainly the question of differences in the way language enters the problem-solving process cannot be dismissed. It has been argued, for example, by Bernstein (1970) that it is in the nature of the very social life of the urban ghetto that there develops a kind of particularism in which communication usually takes place only along concrete personal lines. The ghetto child, who by training is likely to use an idiosyncratic mode of communication, may become locked into the life of his own cultural group, and his migration into other groups consequently becomes the more difficult. Bernstein

made clear in his most recent work that this is not a question of capacity but, rather, a matter of what he calls "orientation." Nevertheless, it may very well be that a ghetto dweller's language training unfits him for taking jobs in the power- and prestige-endowing pursuits of middle-class culture. If such is the case, then the issue of representativeness of the situations to which he can apply his competence becomes something more than a matter of test procedure.

A major difficulty with this line of speculation is that at present we have almost no knowledge of the day-to-day representativeness of different situations and the behaviors that are seen as appropriate to them by different cultural groups. For example, the idea that language use must be considered outside of social interactions in order to qualify as abstract, as involving "cognition," is almost certainly a psychologist's fiction. The work of contemporary sociologists and ethnolinguists (Garfinkle, 1967; Hymes, 1966; Schegloff, 1968) seems conclusively to demonstrate the presence of complex contingent thinking in situations that are all too often characterized by psychologists as consisting of syncretic, affective interactions. Until we have better knowledge of the cognitive components that are part of social interactions (the same applies to many spheres of activity), speculations about the role of language in cognition will have to remain speculations.

In fact, it is extraordinarily difficult to know, save in a most superficial way, on the basis of our present knowledge of society, what is the nature of situations that permit control and utilization of the resources of a culture by one of its members and what the cognitive skills are that are demanded of one who would use these resources. It may very well be that the very definition of a subculture could be put into the spirit of Lévi-Strauss' (1963) definition of a culture:

> What is called a subculture is a fragment of a culture which from the point of view of the research at hand presents significant discontinuities in relation to the rest of that culture with respect to access to its major amplifying tools.

By an amplifying tool is meant a technological feature, be it soft or hard, that permits control by the individual of resources, prestige, and deference within the culture. An example of a middle-class cultural amplifier that operates to increase the thought processes of those who employ it is the discipline loosely referred to as "mathematics." To employ mathematical techniques requires the cultivation of certain skills of reasoning, even certain styles of deploying one's thought processes. If one were able to cultivate the strategies and styles relevant to the employment of mathematics, then that range of technology is open to one's use. If one does not cultivate mathematical skills, the result is "functional incompetence," and inability to use this kind of technology. Whether or not compensatory techniques can then correct "functional incompetence" is an important, but unexplored, question.

Any particular aspect of the technology requires certain skills for its successful use. These skills, as we have already noted, must also be deployable in the range of situations where they are useful. Even if a child could carry out the planning necessary for the most technically demanding kind of activity, he must not do so if he has been trained with the expectancy that the exercise of such a skill will be punished or will, in any event, lead to some unforeseen difficulty. Consequently, the chances that the individual will work up his capacities for performance in the given domain are diminished. As a result, although the individual can be shown to have competence in some sphere involving the utilization of the skill, he will not be able to express that competence in the relevant kind of context. In an absolute sense, he is any man's equal, but in everyday encounters, he is not up to the task.

The principle cuts both ways with respect to cultural differences. Verbal skills are important cultural "amplifiers" among Labov's subjects; as many middle-class school administrators have discovered, the ghetto resident skilled in verbal exchanges is a more than formidable opponent in the battle for control of school curriculum and resources. In like manner, the Harlem youth on the street who cannot cope with the verbal battles described by Labov is failing to express competence in a context relevant to the ghetto.

These considerations impress us with the need to clarify our notion of what the competencies are that underlie effective performance. There has been an implicit, but very general, tendency in

psychology to speak as if the organism is an information-processing machine with a fixed set of routines. The number and organization of these routines might differ as a function of age, genetic makeup, or environmental factors, but for any given machine, the input to the machine is processed uniformly by the routines (structures, skills) of the organism.

Quite recently, psychologists have started to face up to the difficulties of assuming "all things are equal" for different groups of people (concern has focused on difference in age, but the same logic applies to any group comparisons). The study of situational effects on performance has forced a reevaluation of traditional theoretical inferences about competence. This new concern with the interpretation of psychological experiments is quite apparent in recent attempts to cope with data inconsistent with Piaget's theory of cognitive development. For example, Flavell and Wohlwill (1969) sought to distinguish between two kinds of competence: First, there are "the rules, structures, or 'mental operations' embodied in the task and . . . [second, there are] the actual mechanisms required for processing the input and output [p. 98]." The second factor is assumed to be task specific and is the presumed explanation for such facts as the "horizontal decalages" in which the same principle appears for different materials at different ages. The *performance* progression through various stages is presumably a reflection of increases in both kinds of competence, since both are assumed to increase with age.

The same general concern is voiced by Mehler and Bever (1968). They ask,

> How can we decide if a developmental change or behavioral difference among adults is really due to a difference in a structural rule, to a difference in the form of the expressive processes or a difference in their quantitative capacity [p. 278]?

Their own work traces the expression of particular rules in behavior and the way the effect of knowing a rule ("having a competence") interacts with dependence on different aspects of the input to produce "nonlinear trends" in the development of conservation-like performance.

Broadening psychological theory to include

rules for applying cognitive skills, as well as statements about the skills themselves, seems absolutely necessary.

However, the extension contemplated may well not be sufficient to meet all of Labov's objections to inferences about "linguistic deprivation." In both the position expressed by Flavell and Wohlwill and by Mehler and Bever, "competence" is seen as dependent on situational factors and seems to be a slowly changing process that might well be governed by the same factors that lead to increases in the power of the structural rules or competence, in the older sense of the word. Yet in Labov's example, the problem is considerably more ephemeral; Labov gives the impression that the subjects were engaged in rational problem solving and that they had complete control over their behavior. He is claiming, in effect, that they are successfully coping with *their* problem; it simply is not the problem the experimenter had in mind, so the experimenter claims lack of competence as a result of his own ignorance.

Acceptance of Labov's criticisms, and we think they should be accepted, requires not only a broadening of our idea of competence, but a vast enrichment of our approach to experimentation.

Necessity of a Comparative Psychology of Cognition

If we accept the idea that situational factors are often important determinants of psychological performance, and if we also accept the idea that different cultural groups are likely to respond differently to any given situation, there seems to be no reasonable alternative to psychological experimentation that bases its inferences on data from comparisons of both experimental and situational variations.

In short, we are contending that Brunswik's (1958) call for "representative design" and an analysis of the "ecological significance" of stimulation is a prerequisite to research on ethnic and social class differences in particular, and to any research where the groups to be compared are thought to differ with respect to the process under investigation prior to application of the experimental treatments.

Exhortations to the effect that college sophomores with nonsense syllables and white rats in boxes are not sufficient objects for the development of a general psychological theory have produced, thus far, only minor changes in the behavior of psychologists. The present situations seem to *require* a change.

An illustration from some recent cross-cultural research serves as an illustration of one approach that goes beyond the usual two-group design to explore the situational nature of psychological performance.

Cole et al. (1971, p. 4) used the free-recall technique to study cultural differences in memory. The initial studies presented subjects with a list of 20 words divided into four familiar, easily distinguishable categories. Subjects were read the list of words and asked to recall them. The procedure was repeated five times for each subject. A wide variety of subject populations was studied in this way; Liberian rice farmers and school children were the focus of concern, but comparison with groups in the United States was also made.

Three factors of the Kpelle rice farmers' performance were remarkable in these first studies: (a) The number recalled was relatively small (9–11 items per list); (b) there was no evidence of semantic or other organization of the material; (c) there was little or no increase in the number recalled with successive trials.

Better recall, great improvement with trials, and significant organization are all characteristic of performance of the American groups above the fifth grade.

A series of standard experimental manipulations (offering incentives, using lists based on functional rather than semantic classes, showing the objects to be remembered, extending the number of trials) all failed to make much difference in Kpelle performance.

However, when these same to-be-recalled items were incorporated into folk stories, when explicit grouping procedures were introduced, or when seemingly bizarre cuing procedures were used, Kpelle performance manifested organization, showed vast improvements in terms of amount recalled, and gave a very different picture of underlying capacity. Cole et al. (1971) concluded that a set of rather specific skills associated with remembering disconnected material out of context underlies the differences observed in the standard versions of the free-recall experiment with which they began. Moreover, they were able to begin the job of pinpointing these skills, their relevance to traditional activities, and the teaching techniques that could be expected to bring existing memory skills to bear in the "alien" tasks of the school.

Conclusion

The arguments set forth in this study can now be brought together and generalized in terms of their bearing on psychological research that is "comparative" in nature—comparing ages, cultures, subcultures, species, or even groups receiving different experimental treatments.

The central thesis derives from a reexamination of the distinction between competence and performance. As a rule, one looks for performance at its best and infers the degree of underlying competence from the observed performance. With respect to linguistic competence, for example, a single given instance of a particular grammatical form could suffice for inferring that the speaker had the competence to generate such instances as needed. By the use of such a methodology, Labov demonstrated that culturally deprived black children, *tested appropriately* for optimum performance, have the same grammatical competence as middle-class whites, though it may be expressed in different settings. Note that negative evidence is mute with respect to the status of underlying capacity—it may require a different situation for its manifestation.

The psychological status of the concept of competence (or capacity) is brought deeply into question when one examines conclusions based on standard experiments. Competence so defined is both situation blind and culture blind. If performance is treated (as it often is by linguists) only as a shallow expression of deeper competence, then one inevitably loses sight of the ecological problem of performance. For one of the most important things about any "underlying competence" is the nature of the situations in which it expresses itself. Herein lies the crux of the problem. One must inquire, first, whether a competence is expressed in a particular situation and, second, what the significance of that situation is

for the person's ability to cope with life in his own milieu. As we have had occasion to comment elsewhere, when we systematically study the situational determinants of performance, we are led to conclude that cultural differences reside more in differences in the situations to which different cultural groups apply their skills than to differences in the skills possessed by the groups in question (Cole et al., 1971, Ch. 7).

The problem is to identify the range of capacities readily manifested in different groups and then to inquire whether the range is adequate to the individual's needs in various cultural settings. From this point of view, cultural *deprivation* represents a special case of cultural *difference* that arises when an individual is faced with demands to perform in a manner inconsistent with his past (cultural) experience. In the present social context of the United States, the great power of the middle class has rendered differences into deficits because middle-class behavior is the yardstick of success.

Our analysis holds at least two clear implications of relevance to the classroom teacher charged with the task of educating children from "disadvantaged" subcultural groups.

First, recognition of the educational difficulties in terms of a *difference* rather than a special kind of intellectual disease should change the students' status in the eyes of the teacher. If Pygmalion really can work in the classroom (Rosenthal & Jacobson, 1968), the effect of this change in attitude may of itself produce changes in performance. Such difference in teacher attitude seems to be one prime candidate for an explanation of the fine performance obtained by Kohl (1967) and others with usually recalcitrant students.

Second, the teacher should stop laboring under the impression that he must create new intellectual structures and start concentrating on how to get the child to *transfer* skills he already possesses to the task at hand. It is in this context that "relevant" study materials become important, although "relevant" should mean something more than a way to motivate students. Rather, relevant materials are those to which the child already applies skills the teacher seeks to have applied to his own content. It requires more than a casual acquaintance with one's students to know what those materials are.

The Soviet psychologist, Lev Vygotskii (1962), took as the motto of his well-known monograph on language and thought an epigraph from Francis Bacon: Neither hand nor mind alone, left to themselves, amounts to much; instruments and aids are the means to perfection.[2] Psychologists concerned with comparative research, and comparisons of social and ethnic group differences in particular, must take seriously the study of the

[2] *Nec manus nisi intellectus sibi permissus multam valent; instrumentibus et auxilibus res perficitur.*

way different groups organize the relation between their hands and minds; without assuming the superiority of one system over another, they must take seriously the dictum that man is a cultural animal. When cultures are in competition for resources, as they are today, the psychologist's task is to analyze the source of cultural difference so that those of the minority, the less powerful group, may quickly acquire the intellectual instruments necessary for success of the dominant culture, should they so choose.

REFERENCES

BEE, H. L., VAN EGEREN, L. F., STREISSGUTH, A. P., NYMAN, B. A., & LECKIE, M. S. Social class differences in maternal teaching strategies and speech patterns. *Developmental Psychology,* 1969, **1,** 726–734.

BEREITER, C., & ENGLEMANN, S. *Teaching disadvantaged children in the preschool.* Englewood Cliffs, N. J.: Prentice-Hall, 1966.

BERNSTEIN, B. Social class and linguistic development: A theory of social learning. In A. H. Halsey, J. Floyd, & C. A. Anderson (Eds.), *Education, economy and society.* Glencoe, Ill.: Free Press, 1961.

BERNSTEIN, B. A sociolinguistic approach to socialization: With some references to educability. In F. Williams (Ed.), *Language and poverty.* Chicago: Markham, 1970.

BLANK, M., & SOLOMON, F. A tutorial language program to develop abstract thinking in socially disadvantaged preschool children. *Child Development,* 1969, **40,** 47–61.

BLOOM, B. S. *Stability and change in human characteristics.* New York: Wiley, 1964.

BRUNER, J. S. *Poverty and childhood.* Merrill-Palmer Institute Monographs, 1970.

BRUNSWIK, E. *Representative design in the planning of psychological research.* Berkeley: University of California Press, 1958.

CALDWELL, B. M., et al. Infant day care and attachment. *American Journal of Orthopsychiatry,* 1970, **40,** 397–412.

CAMPBELL, D. The mutual methodological relevance of anthropology and psychology. In F. L. K. Hsu (Ed.), *Psychological anthropology.* Homewood, Ill.: Dorsey Press, 1961.

CAZDEN, C. The neglected situation. In F. Williams (Ed.), *Language and poverty.* Chicago: Markham Press, 1970.

CHOMSKY, N. *Cartesian linguistics.* New York: Harper & Row, 1966.

COLE, M., GAY, J., GLICK, J., & SHARP, D. W. *The cultural context of learning and thinking.* New York: Basic Books, 1971.

DEUTSCH, M. *The disadvantaged child.* New York: Basic Books, 1967.

EIFERMANN, R. *School children's games.* Washington, D. C.: Department of Health, Education, and Welfare, 1968.

FLAVELL, J. H., & WOHLWILL, J. F. Formal and functional aspects of cognitive development. In D. Elkind & J. H. Flavell (Eds.), *Studies in cognitive development.* New York: Oxford University Press, 1969.

GARFINKLE, H. *Studies in ethnomethodology.* Englewood Cliffs, N. J.: Prentice-Hall, 1967.

GAY, J., & COLE, M. *The new mathematics and an old culture.* New York: Holt, Rinehart & Winston, 1967.

GLADWIN, T. *East is a big bird.* Cambridge: Belnap Press, 1970.

GOFFMAN, E. The neglected situation. In J. Gumperz & D. Hymes (Eds.), The ethnology of communication. *American Anthropologist,* 1964, **66**(6, Pt. 2), 133.

GREENBERG, J. *Universals of language.* Cambridge: M.I.T. Press, 1963.

HERTZIG, M. E., BIRCH, H. G., THOMAS, A., & MENDEZ, O. A. Class and ethnic differences in the responsiveness of preschool children to cognitive demands. *Monographs of the Society for Research in Child Development,* 1968, **33**(1, Serial No. 117).

HESS, R. D., & SHIPMAN, V. Early experience and socialization of cognitive modes in children. *Child Development,* 1965, **36,** 869–886.

HYMES, D. *On communicative competence.* (Report of a Conference on Research Planning on Language

Development among Disadvantaged Children) New York: Yeshiva University Press, 1966.

JENSEN, A.   How much can we boost IQ and scholastic achievement? *Harvard Educational Review,* 1969, 39, 1–123.

JOHN, V. P., & GOLDSTEIN, L. S.   The social context of language acquisition. *Merrill-Palmer Quarterly,* 1964, 10, 265–275.

KAGAN, J.   Inadequate evidence and illogical conclusions. *Harvard Educational Review,* 1969, 39, 274–277.

KAGAN, J., & KOGAN, N.   Individuality and cognitive performance. In P. Mussen (Ed.), *Manual of child psychology.* New York: Wiley, 1970.

KLAUS, R., & GRAY, S.   The early training project for disadvantaged children: A report after five years. *Monographs of the Society for Research in Child Development,* 1968, 33(4).

KOHL, H.   *36 children.* New York: New American Library, 1967.

KROEBER, A. L.   *Anthropology.* New York: Harcourt, Brace, 1948.

LABOV, W.   The logical non-standard English. In F. Williams (Ed.), *Language and poverty.* Chicago: Markham Press, 1970.

LÉVI-STRAUSS, C.   *Structural anthropology.* New York: Basic Books, 1963.

MEHLER, J., & BEVER, T.   The study of competence in cognitive psychology. *International Journal of Psychology,* 1968, 3, 273–280.

MISCHEL, W.   Theory and research on the antecedents of self-imposed delay of reward. In *Progress in experimental personality research.* Vol. 3. New York: Academic Press, 1966.

PRICE-WILLIAMS, D. R. A.   A study concerning concepts of conservation of quantities among primitive children. *Acta Psychologia,* 1961, 18, 297–305.

ROSENTHAL, R., & JACOBSON, L.   *Pygmalion in the classroom.* New York: Holt, Rinehart & Winston, 1968.

SCHEGLOFF, E. A.   Sequencing in conversational openings. *American Anthropologist,* 1968, 70, 1075–1095.

SCHOGGEN, M.   An ecological study of three-year-olds at home. Nashville, Tenn.: George Peabody College for Teachers, November 7, 1969.

SMILANSKY, S.   The effect of certain learning conditions on the progress of disadvantaged children of kindergarten age. *Journal of School Psychology,* 1968, 4(3), 68–81.

STEWART, W. A.   Toward a history of American Negro dialect. In F. Williams (Ed.), *Language and poverty.* Chicago: Markham Press, 1970.

TYLER, S.   *Cognitive anthropology.* New York: Holt, Rinehart & Winston, 1970.

VYGOTSKII, L. S.   *Thought and speech.* Cambridge: M.I.T. Press, 1962.

ZIGLER, E., & BUTTERFIELD, E.   Motivational aspects of changes in IQ test performance of culturally deprived nursery school children. *Child Development,* 1968, 39, 1–14.

Interpretations of Adolescent Culture

James S. Coleman, Ph.D.

A number of years ago, sociologists began writing about "the adolescent subculture." And as soon as they did so, other sociologists began to question whether there is an adolescent subculture. The debate has continued since that time. I regard the debate as unimportant except insofar as its two sides focus attention on two important facts about adolescents and youth. First, that they are coming to be increasingly distinct from other age groups in a variety of ways—in their clothing fashions, linguistic habits, political beliefs, social values, and association patterns. Second, that their tastes, values, beliefs, habits, are nevertheless formed by the adult society and in some way derivative from it. It is these two facts that must form the starting point of any analysis of the role of adolescents in modern society. More particularly, it is the second of the two—the fact that adolescent culture derives from the adult society—that is the necessary starting point for explaining the first. And there are three ways of doing this.

Rational Response, Cultural Derivation, or Structural Consequence

These are three very different models of explanation that have been proposed to account for those activities described as adolescent culture. The first, a "rational-response" explanation, is perhaps least comprehensive in its aim. It attempts to explain only the social and political alienation of some youth and the sociopolitical movements such as the New Left. Its exponents include Edgar Friedenberg and Paul Goodman, and its general explanatory schema goes something like this: The society is sick, with men occupied in meaningless work directed toward the meaningless goal of accumulation of wealth. In addition, schools are authoritarian and ritualistic institutions, imposing conformity for its own sake upon the young.

Confronted with these harmful institutions, and

James S. Coleman, "Interpretations of Adolescent Culture," in *The Psychopathology of Adolescence*, Grune & Stratton, 1970. Reprinted by permission of Grune & Stratton, Inc. and the author.

seeing before them the meaningless goal of much adult activity, the best youth recognize the authoritarianism and the sham and the triviality and become alienated from it. Some rebel, producing the politics of the New Left. Some withdraw and create a hippie culture, antithetical in every way to the false adult culture they see around them. Still others, the most disenchanted of all, escape into a world of drugs.

This mode of explanation in large part accepts the rhetoric of the youth themselves who make these various responses. In effect, it aligns itself with the alienated youth, sometimes as a spokesman for them, and joins in the indictment of society by these youth. It disregards the large majority of nonalienated youth who are assumed to be unliberated or duped and misled by the corrupt institutions of the sick society.

The distinguishing characteristic of this mode of explanation of youth culture is the nature of the causal connection it sees between the larger society and the youth culture. The connection is an intellectual one: individual youths intellectually comprehend the futility of adult activity and rationally decide not to go along with it. The image of youth is that of a disembodied observer of society, analyzing the society and imposing upon it a judgment intellectually arrived at, but affected by the society in no other way. The organizational and collective aspects of youth culture are largely missing in this explanation, since the response of youth to the society is an individually intellectual one. The collectivities and organizations are the simple outcome of the aggregation of young people who have made the same judgment upon society.

The second model of explanation of adolescent culture I shall term "cultural derivation." In this explanation, the content of adolescent culture is seen as merely a mirror to the adult society. The fascination of youth with automobiles is seen as derivative of the fascination of the adult society with automobiles. The importance of sports to youth is seen as derivative from the importance of sports in adult society. The strength of popular culture, of clothing fashions, and the lack of interest in serious intellectual pursuits are seen as directly derivative from similar characteristics of adult society. In this explanation, there is no real difference between adolescent culture and adult

culture. The only difference is between what adults *say* they want adolescents to be like and what adolescents (and adults) themselves do. The adolescents pay attention not to what the adults say, but to what they do. Thus, in this explanation, all that is necessary to describe the adolescent culture is to describe the adult culture. The fact that adolescents carry out their cultural activities together rather than admixed with adults is not regarded as important or problematic in this explanation. Nor does this explanation attempt to account for very special and distinct phenomena such as the New Left politics or the hippies, for which no specific counterparts in adult society can be found. This explanation attempts to account for the broad, major aspects of adolescent culture and not for these special manifestations.

The image of the adolescent in this explanation is that of a passive adopter of social norms or patterns of activity from adult society. The causal connection is one of direct imitation—the young seen as imitators of the adult world.

The third model of explanation sees adolescent culture as a consequence of the structure of modern society in a somewhat less direct and straightforward way than either of the first two. It first specifies that the very phenomenon of adolescence and youth as a socially distinctive age period is a consequence of changes in the social structure, including: the enforced delay of productive work, the reduced importance of the extended family as a unit of social cohesion and social activity, the separation of adolescents and youth into mass institutions such as high school and college, and the withdrawal of any social function beyond the individualistic goal of "self-improvement" for those in this age group. It further explains the growth and strength of the adolescent culture as depending on the extent of these changes in society. Thus, it would look for an "adolescent culture" to develop among teen agers in a society as the employment rate of teen agers declined, and for a postadolescent youth culture to develop as the employment rate of youth in their twenties declined in that society.

The content of the adolescent culture is explained in this structural approach by certain other structural phenomena. It accounts for the importance of team sports in schools that ostensibly have academic goals by the fact that the academic goals in a school are wholly individualistic and generate no social resonance, whereas athletic achievements are achievements of the school as a unit, and thus do generate a social resonance from all who are identified with the school. It accounts for the importance of clothes and fashion by the structural fact that in a massive matching process where many potential mates are in contact but don't know one another (in contrast to the fixed acquaintanceships in a stable local neighborhood), it is important to attract visual attention. It accounts for the importance of automobiles in the privacy, the autonomy, and the power this allows people at a time of life when they have been largely deprived of privacy, autonomy, and power because of their status as children.

The image of the adolescent provided by this social structural explanation is the image of an individual who forms his social ties and carries out activities through a kind of situational logic, which depends on the situation in which society has cast him, and constitutes a rational response to that immediate situation. It thus may see the "reasons" for his actions not in the reasons he gives but in the structure of the situation that has led him to develop such reasons. In this way, it emphasizes indirect or unintended consequences, with the possibility that certain types of youth culture may derive from structural changes that have no connection at all to the content of that culture.

This explanatory model, which sees adolescent culture as a structural consequence of society, is, I believe, the most satisfactory of the three approaches in accounting for the social phenomena of adolescence. To defend this belief fully, it would be necessary to carry out extensive and rigorous tests of predictions of these three models (for example, predictions about which adolescents would exhibit particular aspects of the culture and which societies would exhibit particular forms of adolescent culture), and I will not pursue that here. Rather, I will explore a further implication of this last model that I regard as most accurate, an implication concerning the phenomenon of the hippies. I regard the hippie movement as a particularly important one because I believe it aids in the diagnosis of certain trends in modern so-

ciety. The hippie movement is, I believe, a response to those trends, in which young people use the movement to satisfy psychological needs that were until recently met in other ways.

The principal element in the hippie ideology is communal love—that is, love that is pervasive and undifferentiated, enveloping all within it. Its antithesis is individualism and isolation, what Emile Durkheim called "egoisme." Durkheim meant by *egoisme* a characteristic of the social structure rather than a personality tendency. He meant the condition in which different individuals' goals are unconnected to one another, so that no collective endeavors, no shared goals, exist.

I want to suggest that on three counts *egoisme* is particularly high among adolescents in American society. The first is a general increase in individualism throughout all parts of society, due partly to affluence, which always allows people to depend less on others, and partly to the increased geographic mobility that characterizes man in modern society. The second is the particularly inividualistic goals imposed on adolescents by the institutions in which they find themselves. These institutions are principally schools, and schools are very peculiar social institutions where neither the nature of the work nor the goals transcend the individual. In schools, students are explicitly entreated to work by and for themselves alone. In a job, by contrast, there is a common product. The joint or interdependent efforts lead to this common product; and although the ultimate goal of each is his own paycheck, the work itself does produce a common product through collective efforts. One's efforts in school are carried out alone, and his achievements are individualistic.

The third structurally isolating element for youth is the absence of a spouse with whom to have shared activities, goals and problems. There are few such areas of shared activities, goals, and problems with his parental family, for he is psychologically further removed from that family than ever before, and until he is married there is nothing to replace it.

Thus, the individual is in a very isolating role as an adolescent. If one were to design a social institution ideally to counter this psychological isolation or *egoisme* in the absence of any common task or goal, it would have qualities of the following sort: barriers between individuals would be lowered as far as possible; individuals would share with others all aspects of their existence, through 24 hours of the day, rather than 8; the guiding ethic of the institution would be love, with each member able to hold the expectation of a diffuse love from any other; and each could expect that the other would share his goods without question. These collectivities or communities would be relatively small, so that, although one had a few others to whom he could feel very close, the processes of differentiation that arise in larger organizations would be absent.

All this is not to say that such an institution as described above is viable over any period of time or has beneficial consequences for its members. It is rather to say that it represents the antithesis of the principal characteristics of the adolescent's role in society.

It is obvious that the institution described is very close to the pattern of life exhibited by hippies. The most striking parallel is with the hippie communities that exist on a few farms or in other rural areas, but other forms of hippie life show most of the same elements. The coincidence, I suggest, is no coincidence at all, but rather the evolution of a social institution to meet a pressing psychological need.

Such a claim obviously requires some validation or test. It implies that certain adolescents would find the hippie culture far more necessary than others: those not involved in any activities with collective goals; those with the affluence not to have had to work; those from families with few shared activities and goals; those whose principal immediate aims are academic, but with only mediocre success in these goals; and those who are not part of stable, close, small sets of long-time friends.

Again, it is problematic whether these implications of the hypothesis and further ones in the same direction will come to be confirmed. Research results on hippies are consistent with the above predictions, although there has not been sufficient systematic research to provide conclusive tests.

It is important to recognize that the evolution of such an institution as "hippie-ism" to satisfy certain pressing psychological needs does not imply that the institution is the only one that might have evolved. Other institutions with some of the same characteristics but taking a very different form could have grown up instead. Some in fact have done so. The widespread phenomenon of "going steady" among adolescents fulfills some of the same functions described above. Also, some relatively minor change in the structural conditions confronting adolescents could generate other responses. For example, if the institutions in which adolescents found themselves, the schools, had provided collective goals rather than wholly individualistic ones, then the psychological need would have been less strong. Or if some other goal accepted by all were imposed from without, such as rigid military conscription in a war that is better justified than the Vietnam war, then those most likely to turn to hippie life should be the ones who find the military experience most rewarding.

Implications of Adolescent Culture for Adult Culture

The "cultural-derivation" model of explanation of the adolescent culture explains this culture as derivative from the adult culture. But it may very well be the case that something like the reverse is true. If some of the aspects of the adolescent culture are a consequence of structural conditions emerging for adolescents, and if some of those structural conditions are coming to characterize the lives of adults as well, then the adolescent culture may provide a preview of new developments in adult culture.

I suggest that this is the case, that we may gain some hints of emerging characteristics of adult culture by a careful study of the structural conditions that spawn certain aspects of adolescent culture.

One of the most important of these changing structural conditions is the increasingly individualistic character of social interaction. As I indicated above, the nuclear family is coming to constitute a less and less adequate psychological home for adolescents. It is less clearly the case, but arguably so, that the nuclear family is similarly coming to be less a psychological home for its two principal members, husband and wife. What was once a diffuse relationship covering a whole range of functions for husband and wife appears to be moving toward greater functional specificity. Social activities have come to be linked more to occupation; the increase of women in the labor force removes some of the wife's interests from the home; the span of time during which a child uses the parental home as his central institution is decreasing—and all these factors narrow the functions of the family for the husband and wife. Outside the family, the increase in individualism is more pronounced. For adults as for adolescents, affluence allows people to reduce the exchange of services that generates social bonds, and mobility allows an increase in the segmental relationships around which modern society is organized.

The consequence of this individualization of society is likely to become for adults much like it is for adolescents: the strong need for common shared goals; for the psychological security of close, pervasive relations with others. It may be useful, then, to conjecture what type of social organization might grow up to satisfy these functions.

The kind of social organization that most fully performs these functions is a close, strong community that pre-empts all an individual's existence. Examples of such communal groups in modern society are the Amish, the Shakers, the Bruderhof, and other communal religious groups. All these communities are focused around religion and in many respects appear to be remnants of bodies formed in earlier times when conditions were more difficult and the benefits of community were more pronounced. However, there are other recently developed groups that have some of these characteristics, and are certainly spawned by conditions of the present. Examples are Synanon, other similar close communities that have developed for similar reasons, and a few rural hippie communities. Other forms of organization that have recently developed with some of the same functions of breaking down barriers between individual selves are therapy groups, sensitivity-training sessions, and similar activities that have developed very recently.

One may conjecture that new forms of social organization are developing for adults, which will have some of the characteristics of these communal groups that stand out in contrast to modern social organization. The ongoing communities, of the form of the Bruderhof, have very special characteristics. They limit sharply their interaction with the outside society, reducing it to near zero, except in some cases for economic transactions. They impose intense discipline upon their members and, as in the Middle Ages, reduce the strength and importance of the individual self, supplanting it by the community.

In reducing the importance of the self and breaking boundaries between individual selves, these communities produce both benefits and losses for the individuals who inhabit them. The severe constraints they impose limit individual freedom, and the breaking of barriers between individuals reduces individual privacy. In short, they are inimical to the concept of the individual. Since action inheres in the individual, most individuals escape such enclaves when they have the opportunity to do so. (Similar reasons very likely account in part for the migration of the young from small towns and villages to urban centers.)

But such communal enclaves offer benefits to their members as well, or else they would become wholly depopulated. In the past, these benefits have been for most people less than the losses, and they have consistently chosen the role-based mode of organization in preference to small close communities. However, a re-examination of the benefits is in order, because of the few cases of newly arisen communal enclaves and because such enclaves might constitute a social invention appropriate for modern society.

The benefits appear to lie principally in two elements: (1) the shift of authority and responsibility from the individual self to the community; and (2) the reinstitution of the whole person rather than the segmental role as the entity that (together with the community as a collectivity of persons rather than roles) enters into relationships.[1] To deal with the former first: this shift

---

[1] As some perceptive studies have shown, in such communal enclaves, the principal relation is not between persons but between the person and the community. Personal relations that differentially lower barriers between selves, creating special relationships within the community, are harmful to the community as an entity, and in most such communities are ruthlessly ferreted out and destroyed.

of authority and responsibility has many consequences, two of which are the loss of freedom and privacy discussed earlier; but others are more desired. One of the most important of these is a psychological extension of self, which, gaining a resonance from that of others, eradicates social isolation and the psychological terror it induces. The individual is never alone and never suffers the psychological trauma of isolation. His joys are collective joys, and the social resonance provided by the identical experience in others raises them to a peak of exhilaration. His sorrows, if individual ones such as physical disability, are diffused throughout the community and thus dampened as an individual loss and, if collective ones, are, although collectively intensified, collectively borne.[2] Another consequence of the shift of authority and responsibility to the community is the psychological consequence of the freedom from responsibility. One shifts the whole burden of decision to the community and is bound by it. In giving up freedom of action, one can be carefree; he rediscovers the pleasures and irresponsibilities of a child.

The second element, the destruction of segmental role relations and their replacement by relations in which the whole person enters, also appears to fill a psychological need for integration. The lowering of barriers between self and others necessarily entails this whole-person relation, just as the organization of society around roles necessarily precludes it.

It appears, then, possible (whether likely or not is more difficult to say) that the communal enclave as an organizational form will increase greatly in modern society. As the organizational complexity of society and the psychological strength necessary to survive it increase, it may well be that two kinds of environments will come to be available to individuals: communal enclaves, into which they can voluntarily commit themselves, and the larger society as an organization of roles, constituting the interstices between these

closed communities. In such organization, the nation (or whatever entity supersedes it) would necessarily grant the community a larger area of authority over its members, relinquishing much of its collective cover of civil rights for those who chose to enter the community. (For example, it would not take cognizance of special marital patterns, as the United States did with the Mormons, nor impose educational requirements, as it has done with the Amish and others; it would relinquish sanction over illegal personal activities within the community, such as drug use; and it would relinquish the right to use force within the community.) The limitations imposed would be wholly on external relations of the community, including communication for purposes of recruiting, requirements for self-support, and the like.

Such a reversal of the general secular movement toward individual rights and civil liberties may be regarded by some as morally repugnant; but given the increasing difficulty that many persons find in creating a satisfying life in the larger society, many may be content to give up all civil rights and liberties, reserving only the right to choose whether to enter and remain in such a communal enclave in return for the psychological benefits it provides.

One can, then, imagine a society consisting of autonomous individuals outside such communities and involved in the complex organizational structure of modern life, and the communities, constituting protective environments for those who choose to relinquish individual autonomy and the stress it entails.

In this way, then, it could well be that the future organization of society will have certain of the aspects of the current social organization of adolescents, in particular, certain elements of the hippie movement. This is not to say that the hippie movement is itself viable; studies of intentional communities have shown the extreme and intense discipline exerted by the community on its members, a discipline almost wholly missing among hippie groups. Such discipline appears to be necessary to hold the community together and to submerge individuality for the common good. Thus, it is unlikely that the hippie movement itself will develop into a viable element of social organization; but it serves as an indicator

---

[2] These and other phenomena in communal enclaves are shown in a remarkable study of a religious community, the Bruderhof, by Benjamin Zablocki, "Christians Because They Believe," Ph.D. dissertation, Johns Hopkins University, 1967.

of social-psychological needs and as an indicator of a possible unit of social organization that can fulfill some of the currently unfilled functions.

It may well be that a similar correspondence exists for other attributes of adolescent cultures. That is, it may be that for modern societies the structural conditions that characterize adolescence will come to define the conditions under which other age groups live as well. When and if this comes to be true, we can expect to see more of the elements of current "adolescent culture" carried over into the culture of adult age groups.

The Function of
Male Initiation Ceremonies at Puberty

John W. M. Whiting   Richard Kluckhohn

Albert Anthony

Our society gives little formal recognition of the physiological and social changes a boy undergoes at puberty. He may be teased a little when his voice changes or when he shaves for the first time. Changes in his social status from childhood to adulthood are marked by a number of minor events rather than by any single dramatic ceremonial observance. Graduation from grammar school and subsequently from high school are steps to adulthood, but neither can be considered as a *rite de passage*. Nor may the accomplishment of having obtained a driver's license, which for many boys is the most important indication of having grown up, be classed as one. Legally the twenty-first birthday is the time at which a boy becomes a man; but, except for a somewhat more elaborate birthday party this occasion is not ceremonially marked and, therefore, cannot be thought of as a *rite de passage*. Neither physiologically, socially, nor legally is there a clear demarcation between boyhood and manhood in our society.

Such a gradual transition from boyhood to manhood is by no means universal. Among the Thonga, a tribe in South Africa, every boy must go through a very elaborate ceremony in order to become a man.[1] When a boy is somewhere between ten and 16 years of age, he is sent by his parents to a "circumcision school" which is held every four or five years. Here in company with his age-mates he undergoes severe hazing by the adult males of the society. The initiation begins when each boy runs the gauntlet between two rows of men who beat him with clubs. At the end of this experience he is stripped of his clothes and his hair is cut. He is next met by a man covered with lion manes and is seated upon a stone facing this "lion man." Someone then strikes him from behind and when he turns his head to see who has struck him, his foreskin is seized and in two movements cut off by the "lion man." Afterwards he is secluded for three months

[1] The following account is taken from Henri A. Junod, *The Life of a South African Tribe* (London: Macmillan & Co., Ltd., 1927), pp. 74–95.

From *Readings in Social Psychology,* third edition, edited by Eleanor E. Maccoby, Theodore M. Newcomb and Eugene L. Hartley, pp. 359–370. Copyright 1947, 1952, © 1958 by Holt, Rinehart and Winston, Inc. Reprinted by permission of Holt, Rinehart and Winston, Inc.

357

in the "yards of mysteries," where he can be seen only by the initiated. It is especially taboo for a woman to approach these boys during their seclusion, and if a woman should glance at the leaves with which the circumcised covers his wound and which form his only clothing, she must be killed.

During the course of his initiation, the boy undergoes six major trials: beatings, exposure to cold, thirst, eating of unsavory foods, punishment, and the threat of death. On the slightest pretext he may be severely beaten by one of the newly initiated men who is assigned to the task by the older men of the tribe. He sleeps without covering and suffers bitterly from the winter cold. He is forbidden to drink a drop of water during the whole three months. Meals are often made nauseating by the half-digested grass from the stomach of an antelope which is poured over his food. If he is caught breaking any important rule governing the ceremony, he is severely punished. For example, in one of these punishments, sticks are placed between the fingers of the offender, then a strong man closes his hand around that of the novice practically crushing his fingers. He is frightened into submission by being told that in former times boys who had tried to escape or who revealed the secrets to women or to the uninitiated were hanged and their bodies burnt to ashes.

Although the Thonga are extreme in the severity of this sort of initiation, many other societies have rites which have one or more of the main features of the Thonga ceremony. Of a sample of 55 societies [2] chosen for this study, 18 have one or more of the four salient features of the Thonga ceremony, e.g., painful hazing by adult males, genital operations, seclusion from women, and tests of endurance and manliness, the remaining 37 societies either have no ceremony at all or one which does not have any of the above features.[3]

[2] The method of sample selection is discussed below.

[3] Seven of these societies have a minor ceremony which generally takes place during adolescence. In these societies the boy's change in status is announced by investing him with some symbol of manhood such as the donning of long pants which played such a role in our society in former years. Specifically these are tatooing—Maori and Ontong Javanese; tooth filing—Alorese, Balinese and Lakher; donning the "sacred thread"—Hindu (Khalapur Radjput). The

Hypotheses

It is the purpose of this paper to develop a set of hypotheses concerning the function of male initiation rites which accounts for the presence of these rites in some societies and the absence of them in others. The theory that we have chosen to test has been suggested by previous explanations for the rites, particularly those of psychoanalytic origin.[4] These explanations were modified to fit the problem of this research in two respects. First, certain of the concepts and hypotheses were restated or redefined so as to be coherent with the growing general behavioral theory of personality development,[5] and second, they were restated in such a way as to be amenable to cross-cultural test, i.e., cultural indices were specified for each variable.

We assume that boys tend to be initiated at puberty in those societies in which they are particularly hostile toward their fathers and dependent upon their mothers. The hazing of the candidates, as well as the genital operations, suggests that one function of the rites is to prevent open and violent revolt against parental authority at a time when physical maturity would make such revolt dangerous and socially disruptive. Isolation from women and tests of manliness suggest that another function of the rites is to break an excessively strong dependence upon the mother and to ensure identification with adult males and acceptance of the male role.

Kwakiutl fall in a similar category. Their ceremony consists of a potlach given for the boy by his father. The ceremonies in these societies are so different in sociopsychological import from those to be described below that they will be classed hereafter with those societies which lack puberty ceremonies.

[4] See, e.g., Sigmund Freud, *Moses and Monotheism* (New York: Alfred A. Knopf, Inc., 1939); Bruno Bettelheim, *Symbolic Wounds* (Glencoe, Ill.: Free Press, 1954); Margaret Mead, *Male and Female* (New York: William Morrow & Co., Inc., 1949).

[5] See, e.g., J. W. M. Whiting and Irwin L. Child, *Child Training and Personality* (New Haven: Yale University Press, 1953); Robert R. Sears, Eleanor E. Maccoby, and Harry Levin, *Patterns of Child Rearing* (Evanston, Ill.: Row, Peterson & Co., 1957); and John Dollard and Neal E. Miller, *Personality and Psychotherapy* (New York: McGraw-Hill Book Co., 1950).

It is to be noted here that the educational and disciplinary functions of the initiation are not limited in time to the actual period of initiation. The boy knows all during childhood and latency about the initiation which he will face at puberty. While he is overtly not supposed to know any of the secrets of the rite, he actually knows almost everything that will happen to him. He is both afraid of what he knows will happen and also envious of the kudos and added status which his older friends have acquired through having successfully gone through this rite. Thus, through the boy's whole life the initiation ceremony serves as a conditioner of his behavior and his attitudes towards male authority, while at the same time emphasizing the advantages of becoming a member of the male group through initiation.

We assume that a long and exclusive relationship between mother and son provides the conditions which should lead to an exceptionally strong dependence upon the mother. Also, we assume that if the father terminates this relationship and replaces his son, there should be strong envy and hostility engendered in the boy which, held in check during childhood, may dangerously manifest itself with the onset of puberty, unless measures are taken to prevent it.

As we indicated above, the hypothesis is derived from psychoanalytic theory. However, it should be noted that there are some modifications which may be important. First, no assumption is being made that the envy is exclusively sexual in character. We are making the more general assumption that if the mother for a prolonged period devotes herself to the satisfaction of all the child's needs—including hunger, warmth, safety, freedom from pain, as well as sex—he will become strongly dependent upon her. In accordance with this we believe rivalry may be based upon a competition for the fulfillment of any of these needs. Second, we do not propose, as most psychoanalysts do, that Oedipal rivalry is a universal, but rather we claim it is a variable which may be strong or weak depending upon specific relationships between father, mother, and son. Thus, we assume father-son rivalry may range from a value of zero to such high intensities that the whole society may be required to adjust to it.

An illustration of cultural conditions which should intensify the dependency of a boy on his mother and rivalry with his father is found in the following case.

Kwoma Dependency. The Kwoma,[6] a tribe living about 200 miles up the Sepik River in New Guinea, have initiation rites similar to those of the Thonga. Examination of the differences in the relationship of a mother to her infant during the first years of his life reveals some strong contrasts between the Kwoma and our own society. While in our society an infant sleeps in his own crib and the mother shares her bed with the father, the Kwoma infant sleeps cuddled in his mother's arms until he is old enough to be weaned, which is generally when he is two or three years old. The father, in the meantime, sleeps apart on his own bark slab bed. Furthermore during this period, the Kwoma mother abstains from sexual intercourse with her husband in order to avoid having to care for two dependent children at the same time. Since the Kwoma are polygynous and discreet extramarital philandering is permitted, this taboo is not too hard on the husband. In addition, it is possible that the mother obtains some substitute sexual gratification from nursing and caring for her infant.[7] If this be the case, it is not unlikely that she should show more warmth and affection toward her infant than if she were obtaining sexual gratification from her husband. Whether or not the custom can be attributed to this sex taboo, the Kwoma mother, while her co-wife does the housework, not only sleeps with her infant all night but holds it in her lap all day without apparent frustration. Such a close relationship between a mother and child in our society would seem not only unbearably difficult to the mother, but also somewhat improper.

---

[6] For a description of the Kwoma child-rearing reported here see J. W. M. Whiting, *Becoming a Kwoma* (New Haven: Yale University Press, 1941), pp. 24–64.

[7] This is, of course, difficult to determine and is a presumption based upon the following factors: (1) Kwoma informants reported that mothers had no desire for sexual intercourse as long as they were nursing the infant and (2) clinical evidence from women in our own society suggests that nursing is sexually gratifying to some women at least. See Therese Benedek, "Mother-child, the Primary Psychomatic Unit," *Am. J. Ortho-Psychiatry*, 1949, XIX; Helene Deutsch, *The Psychology of Women* (New York: Grune & Stratton, Inc., 1944–45), Vols. I and II; Sears, Maccoby, and Levin, *op. cit.*

When the Kwoma child is weaned, a number of drastic things happen all at once. He is suddenly moved from his mother's bed to one of his own. His father resumes sexual relations with his mother. Although the couple wait until their children are asleep, the intercourse takes place in the same room. Thus, the child may truly become aware of his replacement. He is now told that he can no longer have his mother's milk because some supernatural being needs it. This is vividly communicated to him by his mother when she puts a slug on her breasts and daubs the blood-colored sap of the breadfruit tree over her nipples. Finally he is no longer permitted to sit on his mother's lap. She resumes her work and goes to the garden to weed or to the swamp to gather sago flour leaving him behind for the first time in his life. That these events are traumatic to the child is not surprising. He varies between sadness and anger, weeping and violent temper tantrums.

It is our hypothesis that it is this series of events that makes it necessary, when the boy reaches adolescence, for the society to have an initiation rite of the type we have already described. It is necessary to put a final stop to (1) his wish to return to his mother's arms and lap, (2) to prevent an open revolt against his father who has displaced him from his mother's bed, and (3) to ensure identification with the adult males of the society. In other words, Kwoma infancy so magnifies the conditions which should produce Oedipus rivalry that the special cultural adjustment of ceremonial hazing, isolation from women, and symbolic castration, etc., must be made to resolve it.

If our analysis of the psychodynamics in Kwoma society is correct, societies with initiation rites should have similar child-rearing practices, whereas societies lacking the rite should also lack the exclusive mother-son sleeping arrangements and *post-partum* sexual taboo of the Kwoma.

Testing the Hypothesis

To test this hypothesis a sample of 56 societies were selected. First, the ethnographic material on more than 150 societies was checked to determine whether or not there was an adequate description of our variables, e.g., sleeping arrangements, *post-partum* sex taboo, and initiation rites at puberty. Only half of the societies reviewed fulfilled these conditions. Although we had initially endeavored to select our cases so as to have maximum distribution throughout the world, we found that some areas were represented by several societies, while others were not represented by any. To correct for any bias that might result from this sample, we made a further search of the ethnographic literature in order to fill in the gaps, and we thereby added several societies from areas previously not represented. Finally, to maximize diversity and to minimize duplication through selection of closely related societies, whenever there were two or more societies from any one culture area which had the same values on all our variables, we chose only one of them. Using these criteria, our final sample consisted of 56 societies representing 45 of the 60 culture areas designated by Murdock.

The societies comprising our final sample range in size and type from small, simple, tribal groups to segments of large, complex civilizations such as the United States or Japan. In the latter case, our information has been drawn from ethnographic reports on a single delineated community.

When this sample had finally been chosen, the material relevant to our variables was first abstracted, and then judgments were made for each society as to the nature of the transition from boyhood to manhood, the sleeping arrangements, and the duration of the *post-partum* sex taboo. To prevent contamination, the judgments on each variable were made at different times and the name of the society disguised by a code. All judgments were made by at least two persons and in every case where there was a disagreement (less than 15 percent of the cases for any given variable), the data were checked by one of the authors, whose judgment was accepted as final. Our findings with respect to initiation rites have been tabulated in Table 1.

We discovered that only five societies out of the total number had sleeping arrangements similar to our own, that is, where the father and mother share a bed and the baby sleeps alone. In only three societies did the mother, the father, and the baby each have his or her own bed. In the remaining 48, the baby slept with his mother

TABLE 1

THE RELATIONSHIP BETWEEN EXCLUSIVE MOTHER-SON SLEEPING ARRANGEMENTS
AND A *Post-partum* SEX TABOO * AND THE OCCURRENCE
OF INITIATION CEREMONIES AT PUBERTY

Customs in infancy		Customs at adolescent initiation ceremonies		
Exclusive mother-son sleeping arrangements	*Post-partum* sex taboo	Absent	Present	
Long	Long		Azande	hgs †
			Camayura	hs
			Chagga	hgs
			Cheyenne	ht
			Chiricahua	ht
			Dahomeans	hgs
			Fijians	gs
			Jivaro	ht
		Ganda	Kwoma	hgs
		Khalapur (Rajput)	Lesu	gs
		Nyakyusa	Nuer	hs
		Tepoztlan	Samoans	g
		Trobrianders	Thonga	hgs
		Yapese	Tiv	hgs
	Short	Ashanti		
		Malaita	Cagaba	ht
		Siriono		
Short	Long	Araucanians	Kwakiutl	s
		Pilaga	Ojibwa	t
		Pondo	Ooldea	hgs
		Tallensi		
	Short	Alorese	Hopi	hs
		Balinese	Timbira	hst
		Druz		
		Egyptians (Silwa)		
		Eskimos (Copper)		
		French		
		Igorot (Bontoc)		
		Japanese (Suye Mura)		
		Koryak (Maritime)		
		Lakher		
		Lamba		
		Lapps		
		Lepcha		
		Maori		
		Mixtecans		
		Navaho		
		Ontong Javanese		
		Papago		
		Serbs		
		Tanala (Menabe)		
		Trukese		
		United States (Homestead)		
		Yagua		

* Both of a year or more duration.
† The letters following the tribal designations in the right-hand column indicate the nature of the ceremony—*h* = painful hazing, *g* = genital operations, *s* = seclusion from women, and *t* = tests of manliness.

until he was at least a year old and generally until he was weaned. In 24 of the latter, however, the father also shared the bed, the baby generally sleeping between the mother and father. The remaining 24 societies had sleeping arrangements like the Kwoma in which the mother and child sleep in one bed and the father in another. Often the father's bed was not even in the same house. He either slept in a men's club house or in the hut of one of his other wives leaving mother and infant not only alone in the same bed but alone in the sleeping room.

Similarly, the societies of our sample were split on the rules regulating the resumption of sexual intercourse following parturition. Twenty-nine, like our own, have a brief taboo of a few weeks to permit the mother to recover from her delivery. In the remaining 27, the mother did not resume sexual intercourse for at least nine months after the birth of her child, and in one instance, the Cheyenne, the ideal period adhered to was reported as ten years. The duration of the taboo generally corresponded to the nursing period and in many cases was reinforced by the belief that sexual intercourse curdles or sours the mother's milk, thus making it harmful for the infant. In other societies, like the Kwoma, the taboo is explicitly for the purpose of ensuring a desired interval between children where adequate means of contraception are lacking. In these societies the taboo is terminated when the infant reaches some maturational stage, e.g., "until the child can crawl," "until the child can walk," or "until he can take care of himself." For the 27 societies that have this taboo, more than a few weeks long, the average duration is slightly more than two years.

Results at the Cultural Level

Our hypothesis may now be restated in cultural terms as follows: *Societies which have sleeping arrangements in which the mother and baby share the same bed for at least a year to the exclusion of the father and societies which have a taboo restricting mother's sexual behavior for at least a year after childbirth will be more likely to have a ceremony of transition from boyhood to manhood than those societies where*

these conditions do not occur (or occur for briefer periods). For the purposes of this hypothesis, transition ceremonies include only those ceremonies characterized by at least one of the following events: painful hazing of the initiates, isolation from females, tests of manliness, and genital operations.

The test of this hypothesis is presented in Table 1. It will be observed from this table that of the 20 societies where both antecedent variables are present, 14 have initiation ceremonies and only six do not. Where both antecedent variables are absent only two of the 25 societies have the ceremonies. Thus, over 80 percent of the 45 pure cases correspond with the prediction.[8] Though our hypothesis was not designed for predicting the mixed cases, that is, where only one of the antecedent variables is present, it seems that they tended not to have the transition ceremonies.

Although the eight cases which are exceptional to our theory, the six in the upper left-hand column and the two in the lower right-hand column may be simply misclassified through error of measurement, re-examination uncovers some other unanticipated factor which may account for their placement.[9] This analysis turns out to be enlightening.

Reviewing, first the six cases in the upper left-hand column, that is, the societies which have both exclusive mother-son sleeping arrangements and a *post-partum* sex taboo but no initiation, we found that four of them (Khalapur, Trobrianders, Nyakusa, and Yapese) have an adjustment at adolescence which may serve as a psychological substitute for the initiation ceremony. The boys at this time leave the parental home and move to a men's house or a boys' village where they live

[8] Even though we made every effort to ensure at least a reasonable degree of independence for our cases, there are many instances of known historical connections among them. A statistical test of significance is therefore difficult to interpret. If the cases were independent, the probabilities are less than one in one thousand that this relationship could be obtained by chance ($x^2 > 18$).

[9] This procedure was suggested by G. G. Homans and D. M. Schneider, *Marriage, Authority, and Final Causes; A Study of Unilateral Cross-Cousin Marriage* (Glencoe, Ill.: Free Press, 1955). It was used most effectively in their cross-cultural study of authority patterns and cross-cousin marriage.

until they are married. Malinowski [10] observed this type of adjustment amongst the Trobrianders in 1927. He wrote:

> But the most important change, and the one which interests us most is the partial break-up of the family at the time when the adolescent boys and girls cease to be permanent inmates of the parental home . . . a special institution . . . special houses inhabited by groups of adolescent boys and girls. A boy as he reaches puberty will join such a house. . . . Thus the parent home is drained completely of its adolescent males, though until the boy's marriage he will always come back for food, and will also continue to work for his household to some extent. . . .[11]
>
> At this stage, however, when the adolescent has to learn his duties, to be instructed in traditions and to study his magic, his arts and crafts, his interest in his mother's brother, who is his teacher and tutor, is greatest and their relations are at their best.[12]

This account suggests that this change of residence serves the same functions that we have posited for initiation ceremonies, for example, by establishing male authority, breaking the bond with the mother, and ensuring acceptance of the male role. It is important for our hypothesis, also, that there are only two other societies in our sample where such a change of residence occurs. One of these is the Malaita which has one but not both of our antecedent variables; the other is the Ashanti where the boy may move to the village of his mother's brother at or before puberty, but this is not mandatory and only half the boys do so. Thus, if we were to revise our hypothesis such that a change of residence was considered to be equivalent to initiation, the four societies mentioned should be moved over to the right-hand column and the exceptional cases would be reduced from eight to four.

Some comment should be made on the two remaining cases in the upper left-hand column. The Ganda are reported to have an interesting

method of child rearing which may or may not be relevant to our theory. For the first three years of his life, a Ganda child sleeps exclusively with his mother and she is subject to a sexual taboo. At this point the boy is reported to be weaned and transferred to the household of his father's brother by whom he is brought up from then on. It might be assumed that this event would obviate the need for later ceremonial initiation into manhood. Since several other societies that do have initiation also have a change of residence at weaning, however, this simple explanation cannot be accepted and the Ganda must remain an unexplained exception. Finally Lewis [13] reports for the Tepoztlan that there was some disagreement among his informants as to the length of the taboo and exclusive sleeping arrangements. Since again there were other equally equivocal cases, we shall have to accept the verdict of our judges and let this case also remain an exception.

A reconsideration of the two exceptions in the lower right-hand column, the Hopi and the Timbira, which have the type of initiation into manhood required by our theory but have neither exclusive sleeping arrangements nor a prolonged *post-partum* sex taboo, also turns out to be fruitful. In neither of these societies does the father have authority over the children.[14] This is vested in the mother's brother who lives in another household.[15] That these societies should have an initiation rite, again, does not seem to contradict our general theory, even though it does contradict our specific hypothesis. From clinical studies in our own society it is clear that even with the lack of exclusive sleeping arrangements and a minimal *post-partum* sex taboo, an appreciable degree of dependence upon the mother and rivalry with the father is generated. The cases here suggest that, although these motives are not strong enough to require ceremonial initiation into manhood if the father is present in the household and has authority over the child, this may be required if he lacks such authority.

[10] B. Malinowski, *Sex and Repression in Savage Society* (New York: Harcourt, Brace & Co., 1927).

[11] *Ibid.*, p. 67.

[12] *Ibid.*, p. 69.

[13] O. Lewis, *Life in a Mexican Village: Tepoztlan Restudied* (Urbana: University of Illinois Press, 1951).

[14] A consideration of the influence of authority patterns was suggested by the work of Homans and Schneider, *op. cit.*

[15] This is also true of the Trobrianders discussed above, but of no other society in our sample about which we have information on authority patterns.

But what of the cases which have but one of the antecedent variables? Taking into account the societies with exclusive sleeping arrangements but no *post-partum* sex taboo, our theory predicts that these conditions should produce dependency and rivalry. However, since the mother is receiving sexual satisfaction from her husband, she has less need to obtain substitute gratification from nurturing her infant, so that the dependency she produces in her child would be less intense and the need for initiation should be attenuated. Three of the four cases with exclusive sleeping arrangements but no taboo appear to fulfill these conditions. As we have reported above, the Ashanti and the Malaita practice a change of residence which, it could be argued, is somewhat less drastic than initiation. In any case this is permissive and not required for the Ashanti. When the Cagaba boy reaches adolescence, he is given instruction in sexual intercourse by a priest and then sent to practice these instructions with a widow who lives with him temporarily in a specially built small hut. The boy is not allowed to leave this hut until he succeeds in having sexual intercourse with her. This trial is reported to be terrifying to the boy and it is often several days before he does succeed. This type of initiation, however, does not seem to compare with other societies which like the Thonga have a full-fledged ceremony. The Siriono, on the other hand, do not have any ceremonial recognition of the shift from boyhood to manhood and they must be regarded as an exception to our theory.

The final group of cases to consider are those that have a long *post-partum* sex taboo but not exclusive mother-son sleeping arrangements. For these, our theory would also predict an attenuated need for initiation ceremonies. Although the mothers of this group are presumed to gain substitute sexual gratification from being especially nurturant and loving toward their infants, they have less opportunity to do so than with those of societies where there are also exclusive sleeping arrangements.

As in the previous group of societies the ceremonies are, except for the Ooldea which will be discussed below, mild. The Kwakiutl have a ceremony which consists of a potlatch given by the father for the son. There the boys undergo no hazing or genital operations but are secluded and

expected to perform a dance. For the Ojibwa, the boy is expected to obtain a guardian spirit in a vision before he reaches maturity. Thus, generally when he is 11 or 12 years old, he goes alone into the forest where he stays often for several days without food, water, and generally without sleep until he either has a vision or returns home to recuperate before trying again. Again neither hazing or genital operations are involved.

The Ooldea, a tribe situated in southwestern Australia do, however, have a full-fledged initiation rite with hazing, isolation, and a very painful genital operation. This apparently runs counter to our assumption that the rites should be mild if only one determinant is present.

Radcliffe-Brown, however, reports that in many Australian tribes

> . . . the discipline of very young children is left to the mother and the other women of the horde. A father does not punish and may not even scold his infant children, but if they misbehave he will scold the mother and perhaps give her a blow with a stick. He regards the mother as responsible for misbehavior by very young children. When they are a little older, the father undertakes the education of the boys but leaves the education of the girls to the mother and the women of the horde. But the father behaves affectionately and is very little of a disciplinarian. Discipline for a boy begins when he approaches puberty and is exercised by the men of the horde. The big change comes with the initiation ceremonies when, in some tribes, the father, by a ceremonial (symbolic) action, hands over his son to the men who will carry out the initiation rites. During the intiation period of several years the boy is subjected to rigid and frequently painful discipline by men other than his father.[16]

If the Ooldea be one of those Australian tribes described above, they fall, along with the Trobrianders, Hopi, and Timbira, into the class of societies where the function of initiation is to make up for the lack of discipline exercised by a father over the boy during childhood.

[16] Cited from a letter by A. R. Radcliffe-Brown to these authors in Homans and Schneider, *op. cit.*, p. 41.

A study of those societies without exclusive sleeping arrangements and with a long *post-partum* sex taboo which do not have the rites is interesting. In the first place both the Pondo and the Araucanians are reported to have had initiation ceremonies in the recent past, indicating that they are perhaps near the threshold of needing them. The Tallensi also are interesting. An observer notes that the Tallensi should have invented the Oedipus-conflict theory since they are quite open and conscious of the strong rivalry and hostility between father and son, a conflict which remains strong and dangerous, guarded only by ritualized forms of etiquette, until the father dies and the son takes his place. Furthermore, family fissions are reported to occur frequently and the oldest son often leaves the family to establish a new lineage of his own.

Thus, the presence of a *post-partum* sex taboo alone seems to produce tension, which these societies commonly seek to resolve through initiation ceremonies. Societies in this group which do not have ceremonies either had them recently or show evidence of unresolved tension.

Summary

The cross-cultural evidence indicates that:

1. A close relationship is established between mother and son during infancy as a consequence of either (a) their sleeping together for at least a year to the exclusion of the father or (b) the mother being prohibited from sexual intercourse for at least a year after the birth of her child or (c) both of these together having measurable consequences which are manifested in cultural adjustments at adolescence.

2. The cultural adjustments to the presence of the above factors are made when the boy approaches or reaches sexual maturity. These adjustments are either (a) a ceremony of initiation into manhood involving at least one and generally several of the following factors: painful hazing by the adult males of the society, tests of endurance and manliness, seclusion from women, and genital operations, or (b) a change of residence which involves separation of the boy from his mother and sisters and may also include some formal means for establishing male authority such

as receiving instructions from and being required to be respectful to the mother's brother or the members of the men's house.

3. If both the factors specified in (1) are present, the consequences at adolescence tend to be more elaborate and severe than if one is present.

4. The cultural adjustments specified in (2) also occur in societies where the father does not have the right to discipline his son, whether or not the conditions specified in (1) are present.

The evidence for these statements is summarized in Table 2.

The Sociopsychological Implications

So much for the manifest results at the cultural level. But what is the most reasonable sociopsychological interpretation of these relationships? What are the psychodynamics involved? We are not concerned with the bizarre rites of the Thonga or the peculiar life of a Kwoma infant, for their own sakes, but rather in discovering some general truths about human nature. We, therefore, wish to state what we believe to be the underlying processes that are involved. These are processes that we have not directly observed and which must be accepted or rejected on the grounds of their plausibility or, more important, on the basis of further research implied by our theory.

We believe that six sociopsychological assumptions are supported by our findings:

1. The more exclusive the relationship between a son and his mother during the first years of his life, the greater will be his emotional dependence upon her.

2. The more intensely a mother nurtures (loves) an infant during the early years of his life, the more emotionally dependent he will be upon her.

3. The greater the emotional dependence of a child upon a mother, the more hostile and envious he will be toward anyone whom he perceives as replacing him in her affection.[17]

---

[17] If, however, the mother herself is perceived by the child as the one responsible for terminating the early intense relationship, this should lead the boy to both envy her and identify with her. This should produce conflict with respect to his sex role identity, which initiation rites would serve to resolve.

TABLE 2

THE RELATIONSHIP OF INFANCY FACTORS TO CULTURAL ADJUSTMENTS
AT ADOLESCENCE

Customs in infancy and childhood			*Cultural adjustment at adolescence*		
Authority of father over son	Exclusive mother-son sleeping arrangement	Post-partum sex taboo	None	Change of residence	Initiation ceremony
Present	Long	Long	2	3	14
		Short	1	2	1
	Short	Long	4	0	2
		Short	23	0	0
Absent			0	1	3

4. If a child develops a strong emotional dependence upon his mother during infancy, and hostility toward and envy of his father in early childhood at the time of weaning and the onset of independence training, these feelings (although latent during childhood) will manifest themselves when he reaches physiological maturity in (a) open rivalry with his father and (b) incestuous approaches to his mother, unless measures are taken to prevent such manifestations.

5. Painful hazing, enforced isolation from women, trials of endurance or manliness, genital operations, and change of residence are effective means for preventing the dangerous manifestation of rivalry and incest.

6. Even a moderate or weak amount of emotional dependence upon the mother and rivalry with the father will be dangerous at adolescence if the father has no right to (or does not in fact) exercise authority over his son during childhood.

If these sociopsychological hypotheses are true, they have some interesting implications for individual differences in our own society.[18] It has long been known that there is an association between certain types of juvenile delinquency and broken homes.[19] We would predict that the probability of a boy becoming delinquent in such instances would be highest where the separation of the mother and father occurred during the early infancy of the boy and where she remarried when he was two or three years old.

We would further predict that insofar as there has been an increase in juvenile delinquency in our society, it probably has been accompanied by an increase in the exclusiveness of mother-child relationships and/or a decrease in the authority of the father. It is not unreasonable that industrialization and urbanization have done just this, but, of course, this matter should be investigated before such an interpretation is accepted.

Finally, if further research shows that juvenile delinquency in our society is in part a function of the early childhood factors that have been described in this paper, then it can be countered either by decreasing the exclusiveness of the early mother-child relationship, increasing the authority of the father during childhood, or instituting a formal means of coping with adolescent boys

[18] In a study of infant training William Sewell reports that "the children who slept with their mothers during infancy made significantly poorer showings on the self-adjustment, personal freedom, and family relations components of the California Test of Personality and suffered more sleep disturbances than did those who slept alone." W. H. Sewell, "Infant Training and the Personality of the Child," *Am. J. Sociol.,* 1953, LVIII, 157.

[19] Cf. for example, E. Glueck and S. Glueck, *Unravelling Juvenile Delinquency* (New York: Commonwealth Fund, 1950); W. W. Waltenberg and J. J. Balistrieri, "Gang Membership and Juvenile Misconduct," *Am. Sociol. Rev.,* December 1950, XV, 744–752.

functionally equivalent to those described in this paper. Change of residence would seem more compatible with the values of our society than an initiation ceremony. The Civilian Conservation Corps camps of the 1930's were an experiment which should provide useful data in this regard. The present institution of selective service would perhaps serve this purpose were the boys to be drafted at an earlier age and exposed to the authority of responsible adult males.

Name Index

Numbers in italics indicate the page on which the full reference is found. Where references are listed numerically rather than alphabetically, reference numbers are shown in parentheses.

Aberle, D. F., 125, *131*
Abraham, K., 94, *111*
Adkins, M. M., 231, *232*
Ainsworth, M. D. S., 69, 70, *78*, 94, 108, 110, *111*, 195, 197, *202*
Anderson, E. P., 69, *78*
Angermeier, W. F., 49, *53*
Archer, W. K., 303, *312*
Arling, G. L., 132, *141*
Atkinson, J. W., (8) 261, *265*
Avedon, E., 231, *231*

Baer, D. M., 42, *42*
Baker, C. T., (10) 259, (11) 260, (1, 10, 11) 261, (11) 265, *265*
Baker, R. W., (1) 32, *35*
Baldwin, J. M., 277, *289*
Baltes, P., 47, *55*
Ban, P., 69, 74, *78*
Bandura, A., *53*, 319, *321*
Barron, D. H., (2) 26, *35*
Bartlett, F. C., 82, *89*
Bayley, N., (3) 29, *35*, 51, 53, 67, *67*, (2, 3) 259, *265*, 331, *335*
Bee, H. L., 339, *348*
Bell, R. Q., 47, 48, *53, 55*
Bell, S. M., 69, 70, *78*
Beller, E. K., 329, 331, *335*
Bellugi, U., 166, 167, 172, *173*
Bennett, G. K., 51, *53*
Bennett, H. L., 49, *55*
Bentler, P., 188, *192*
Bereiter, C., 267, 270, *273*, 341, *348*
Berlyne, D., 195, *202*

Berman, P., 231, *231*
Bernstein, B., 267, *273*, 339, 344, *348*
Bertalanffy, L., (4) 30, *35*
Bever, T., 345, *349*
Bhavnani, R., 50, *53*
Bijou, S. W., 42, *42*, 320, *321*
Biller, H. B., 49, *55*
Bilous, B., 49, *55*
Birch, H. G., 343, *348*
Blank, M., 266, 269, 272, *273*, 340, *348*
Blomquist, A. J., 134, *140*
Bloom, B. S., 340, *348*
Bloom, L., 166, 168, 169, 171, *172*
Bobrow, M., 47, 48, *55*
Boelkins, R. C., 132, *140*
Bongiovanni, A. M., 46, *53*
Bradway, Katherine, (4) 259, *265*
Braine, M. D. S., 166, 167, 169, 170, *173*
Brandt, E. M., 47, *56*
Bridger, W. H., 266, 269, 272, *273*
Brindley, C., 48, 49, *53*
Brison, D. W., 191, *192*
Brody, Sylvia, 94, *111*
Bronson, G. W., 48, *53*
Brooks, V., (5) 233, *238*
Brown, R., 166, 167, *172, 173*
Bruell, J., (5) 25, *35*
Bruner, J. S., 250, 254, 257, 316, *321*, 344, *348*
Brunswik, E., 341, 346, *348*
Buehler, K., (4) 233, 234, *238*
Buffery, A. W. H., 48, 52, *53, 54*
Burchinal, L. G., 124, *131*
Burg, A., 47, *53*

369

Subject Index

Accommodation, 81–82, 86, 218, 249
  definition of, 81
Achievement
  developmental transformations of, 113–123
  increase in, 27
  need, 17, 82, 85, 259, 260, 261, 262, 263–265
Adaptation, 82–83, 86
Adolescence
  intellectual changes in, 203–209
Adolescent culture, 350–356
Adjustment mechanisms, 177, 179–181
Adrenogenital syndrome, 46
Affiliation
  and conformity, 112–113
  and differential parent treatment, 119–121
  and parent-child interaction, 116–119
  and parent-infant interaction, 114–116
Age differences
  in dramatic improvisation, 229–230
  in play, 293–294
Age psychology, 38
Aggression, 13–16, 261, 262, 263–265, 329–335
  in macaques, 304
Aggressiveness
  in isolate-reared monkeys, 132, 133
  sex differences in, 48–49, 125, 128–130
Aliment, definition of, 82
Anal training, 12–16
Animism Scale, 183, 185
Aphasia, 148, 149
Aptitude, 207–208
  diversification of, 207–208
  and specialization, 208–209
Assimilation, 81–82, 86, 218, 249
  definition of, 81
Attachment
  development of, 57, 58, 60

Attachment (*continued*)
  and fear of strangers, 69–77
  formation of, 60–61, 66–67
  mother-infant, 94
Attachment function, 60–61
  definition of, 60
Autonomy, 12–16, 329–335

Bayley Scales of Infant Development, 196, 197, 198
  Mental Development Index of, 196, 197, 198, 199
  Psychomotor Development Index of, 196
Berkeley Growth Study, 48, 51

Catell Infant Scale, 65
Causality, psychological, 177–186
Change, personality, 315–321
Character, social, 290–302
Child psychology, definition of, 37
Child rearing
  achievement need in, 17
  aggression in, 13–16
  anal training in, 12–16
  Anglo-American tradition of, 5
  autonomy in, 12–16
  cross-cultural study of, 5
  dependency in, 12–16
  extended family and, 15
  guilt reactions in, 16–17
  Kwoma, 359–360
  nuclear family and, 15–16
  oral training in, 5, 12–16
  permissiveness in, 13
  repression in, 13–16
  sexual training in, 12–16
Classification, modes of, 234
Cognition, 176–209
  comparative psychology of, 346–347